Views From the Edge

Essays in Honor of Richard W. Bulliet

Views From the Edge

Essays in Honor of Richard W. Bulliet

Neguin Yavari
Lawrence G. Potter
Jean-Marc Ran Oppenheim

Editors

Columbia University Press
for
The Middle East Institute, Columbia University

New York

COLUMBIA UNIVERSITY PRESS
Publishers Since 1893
New York
Chichester, West Sussex

Library of Congress Cataloging-in-Publication Data

Views from the edge : essays in honor of Richard W. Bulliet / Neguin Yavari, Lawrence G. Potter, Jean-Marc Ran Oppenheim—editors.
p. cm.
Includes bibliographical references and index.
ISBN 0-231-13472-X (cloth : alk. paper)
1. Islamic countries—Civilization. 2. Islamic countries—History. 3. Islamic countries—Historiography. I. Bulliet, Richard W. II. Yavari, Neguin. III. Potter, Lawrence G. IV. Oppenheim, Jean-Marc Ran.

DS35.4.A2V54 2004
909'.09767—dc22

2204052785

∞

Columbia University Press books are printed on permanent and durable acid-free paper.
Printed in the United States of America
c 10 9 8 7 6 5 4 3 2 1

Contents

Preface

This book represents the devotion and scholarship of generations of students of Richard W. Bulliet. It honors the contributions he has made as a historian and the respect he has inspired as an outstanding teacher. But this book is not so much a tribute to the stamina of a many-sided talent as an affectionate celebration of a unique mixture of generosity, insatiable curiosity, stoicism, and humor.

From the hardy band of 10 Harvard freshmen who in 1970 took the course that later resulted in his imaginative and prize-winning book, *The Camel and the Wheel* (1975), to the 180 students who attended his class on "America and the Muslim World" at Columbia in the fall of 2003, Bulliet's students have found in him a master teacher. He began teaching at Columbia in the fall of 1976, and for nearly three decades Richard Bulliet has had a profound effect on the lives of generations of students, listening to them, giving them the courage to follow their own hunches and ideas and not to be intimidated or mesmerized by the latest voguish -isms. Perhaps because the university was Columbia, and the location New York, the students who turned up at his classes and knocked at the door of his office have always tended to be a motley crew from different educational backgrounds and with different expectations. As the years progressed and as his office metamorphosed into an arena for spontaneous debates and unscheduled seminars, a palpable sense of community grew among us as students: a sense of *ʿassabiya* manifesting itself in a shared spirit of inquiry. We became gradually aware of the importance of history and its perennial questions in the context of issues in our own daily life and in our own attempts at making sense of the world around us.

In the process of preparing this work for publication, we met and corresponded with many old friends and fellow students, some of whom are now working outside academia. The most striking common trait that emerged from these encounters and reminiscences was a shared love of history as a discipline and an urge to ask questions and attempt to interpret events past and present with as much lucidity and intellectual honesty as one can. This is largely due to Professor Bulliet's presence and perhaps his single most valuable contribution as a teacher in the humanities. The editors realize that the exigencies of publishing have forced them to choose a small sample from the many voices that could have been included here. We are, however, most grateful to those colleagues and former students of Professor Bulliet who helped so generously towards the production of this volume, to Columbia University Press—and to Anne Routon in particular—for their unstinting assistance and advice regarding the publication, and to Fred Donner for his admirably succinct introduction. A special debt of gratitude is owed to Reeva S. Simon, who not only was first to remember that a volume honoring Richard W. Bulliet was due, but has provided also critical support in every stage of its preparation. Our final thanks and sympathy are reserved for the dedicatee of this book: having spent so many seemingly interminable hours diligently reading our papers and assiduously commenting on their warped logic and weird grammar, he is now presented with an echo chamber of familiar voices elaborating on tunes familiar from the past.

Doing It:
Reflections on Richard W. Bulliet's Scholarship on Islamic and Middle Eastern Studies[1]

Fred M. Donner

Richard W. Bulliet has produced a significant body of solid scholarship that is wide-ranging, innovative, frequently challenges received scholarly wisdom, and often involves meticulously constructed arguments. These features alone suffice to make reading his work a stimulating intellectual adventure. But his works stand out especially for two other reasons: their *conceptual clarity* and their *stylistic clarity.* One always knows exactly what Bulliet means and what his point is—a quality that is, unfortunately, not common enough in academic writing. Not for him the vague final (or opening, or middle) paragraph that offers only ambiguous theses or conclusions, or that leads the reader into an impressionistic fog of suggestions, hints, and high-flown but insubstantial rhetoric. Nor does Bulliet afflict his readers with old commonplaces obscured in murky jargon and fitted into trendy new theories, the intellectual equivalent of aging streetwalkers masquerading in heavy makeup and hip styles—much less appealing on careful examination than when they first meet the eye. On the contrary, one is often gratified—sometimes almost startled—by the clarity, even bluntness, with which Bulliet states his theses and his conclusions, and by the real novelty of what he has to say. And a clearly-stated thesis requires vigorous and frank discussion of its strengths and possible weaknesses, all of which Bulliet invariably provides with gusto. Moreover, even though one may not entirely agree with what Bulliet has said, one also knows that it will not be easy to advance an alternative explanation, given the thoroughness of his work.

This clarity of conception and style comes perhaps in part from Bulliet's thorough training as a historian. (It would be unfair in this context to neglect entirely the formative impact of Bulliet's parents and of his early schooling in Rockford, Illinois; these, too, must have been important in shaping the way Bulliet approaches things, but not knowing the details of these I will pass over them henceforth.) He is one of the few scholars of the Middle East and Islam who is, both by training and by output, primarily an historian. As many have noted over the years—indeed, as Bulliet himself observed in his essay on "Orientalism and Medieval Islamic Studies"—the majority of Western scholars who have dealt with the Middle East and Islam over the past century and a half were not trained as historians. The early generations were almost all trained as philologists; this was probably inevitable, because the first order of business for Orientalists in those days had to be to master the textual traditions (in Arabic, Persian, Ottoman Turkish, etc.) so as to gain some understanding of Islamic civilization from its own products, and to edit and publish key texts in their original languages so others could continue to learn. Because many of these early Orientalists acquired truly stupendous language skills, often in numerous languages, however, they had insufficient time to learn proper historical methodology—even though they did sometimes write about history. One might add that so much purely linguistic training, like any kind of training, shapes the mind in specific ways, and that may make one less receptive to thinking in the manner of an historian, less adept at formulating truly historical (as opposed to philological or literary) questions. The result, Bulliet notes, was that the historical work of early Orientalists, notwithstanding its philological and sometimes literary excellence, was often "remarkably naive in terms of historiographical method" ("Orientalism and Medieval Islamic Studies," p. 98).

Although Bulliet spent his own time in the linguistic trenches, and has competence in Arabic and Persian to prove it, he consistently views the issues that interest him with an historian's eye. His higher historical training took place mostly in the 1960s at Harvard, leading to a B.A. (1962) in History and a Ph.D. (1967) in History and Middle Eastern Studies. This was a time when the passion for "alternative" approaches to history (meaning approaches that looked beyond the arena of rulers and political events) was just reaching the relatively stagnant backwaters of Islamic and Middle Eastern history, even though they had been pursued in more mainstream historical fields for a couple of decades by that time, and it may be that this atmosphere helped shape Bulliet's approach to history. Bulliet focuses overwhelmingly on such things as social history, institutional history, and the history of technology rather than on political history, and he often attempts to utilize categories of evidence that earlier political historians would not have thought (or deigned?) to consult. Not only has Bulliet published in the prestigious French historical journal *Annales: Economies, Societes, Civilisations* (twice, in fact); his work in many ways typifies what he himself, in his article "*Annales* and Archaeology," identifies as a hallmark of the *annalistes:* their willingness try out new sources and approaches, and their experimentation with alternatives to the traditional way of doing history. (pp. 132–33.)

The most obvious category of "new" sources of which Bulliet has pioneered the use is, of course, the sometimes voluminous *tabaqat* books—biographical dictionaries of *'ulama'* (religious scholars) of various localities—which abounded in the medieval Islamic tradition. These works had been picked at for years by Western scholars for the incidental information they provided about various individuals, but most modern scholars found themselves frustrated by the limited and often stereotypical nature of the biographical entries these works contained. Bulliet, however, devised ways to wring more information from these works by approaching them not entry by entry, but as a whole, and by subjecting specific categories of information in the entries, as an aggregate, to various kinds of statistical manipulation. In *The Patricians of Nishapur* (1972) he extracted from them information on factionalism and its social roots; in *Conversion to Islam in the Medieval Period* (1987) he drew on naming patterns to develop theories about conversion rates in various localities for which we have biographical dictionaries; in "The Age Structure of Medieval Islamic Education" he returns to these sources to reconstruct the rhythms of teaching and learning in medieval Islamic societies and how they fit with the life-cycle of people in the educated elite generally. A few others have pursued studies based on a prosopographical analysis of biographical works, but none has been as resourceful as Bulliet in discovering new ways to exploit these old sources.

Many of Bulliet's publications not only utilize new sources, but also advance provocative hypotheses that seem, at least on first hearing, to some extent conjectural. His first major work, *The Patricians of Nishapur,* for example, because it was based on prosopographical analysis of the city's elites rather than on "harder" evidence such as personal letters or official documents (which—except for some coins—do not survive from Nishapur), left at least one reviewer wondering whether it told us who the elites of Nishapur "really" were; we did not, in other words, gain much of an idea of what the individual members of the elite were like, or even what values motivated them, beyond a presumed chauvinism focused on their families and their legal school. His *Conversion to Islam in the Medieval Period,* once again based on prosopographical analysis of biographical dictionaries, raised even more questions because of its method. In this case, Bulliet's effort to establish conversion rates for different provinces of the medieval Islamic world depended upon a number of assumptions, any one of which could be seen as problematic. For example: How accurately does the change from non-Islamic to Islamic names in a person's lineage correlate with the date of his family's actual conversion to Islam? If we make a different assumption than Bulliet does about the average age between generations—which, as everyone knows, varies dramatically from case to case—would it not drastically change his conclusions on conversion rates? Bulliet generates his basic conversion curve from evidence about the province—Iran—that has the fullest supply of biographical dictionaries; but can that curve really be extrapolated to other provinces, for which evidence is much more meager, by correlating certain points on the curve with certain categories of political events (e.g., popular upheavals), as Bulliet proposes?

These and other objections have sometimes been raised against these works. Yet, one must admit that Bulliet's ingenuity in manipulating the sources at least offers us the hope of gaining a general idea about developments for which we otherwise have almost no evidence at all. Moreover, Bulliet defends his hypotheses and the tactical decisions he makes in elaborating them effectively enough in the works themselves that one quickly becomes convinced, while reading them, that he may be on the right track and deserves to be heard out. And in the end, the fact that no plausible counterhypotheses to the conclusions reached in *Patricians* and *Conversion* have been generated, even decades after their publication, has meant that these conclusions have come to be widely accepted as fundamental historical truths, or (in the case of *Conversion)* as the best-informed guess we are likely to get, and therefore the only plausible starting-point for further research.

Bulliet's *The Camel and the Wheel* (1975) does not rely on prosopographical analysis, but its main argument—that camel-borne transport largely replaced wheel-borne transport in the Islamic lands—is based on a wide array of different kinds of evidence and has elicited only occasional criticism; moreover, such objections as are forthcoming are usually limited to a particular setting (e.g., early Islamic Egypt, where the use of donkeys and carts seems to have survived) and hardly affect the broad view Bulliet has drawn. It is not surprising, therefore, that the conclusions reached in *The Camel and the Wheel* have been widely accepted, and the book acclaimed as one of the most important contributions of the twentieth century to the history of transportation. Similarly, Bulliet's most recent major work on the medieval Islamic world, *Islam: The View from the Edge* (1993), despite its novelty, seems to have established its thesis. In it he weaves together various categories of evidence to argue that what we usually identify as "classical Islam" actually began as a regional variant of Islamic practice and thought that first arose in northeastern Iran, and spread westward during the eleventh and subsequent centuries largely because of the political upheavals to which Iran was subjected during the Seljuk and Mongol eras.

As noted above, Bulliet has concerned himself mainly with what can be called, broadly, social history. It can be argued that all history, including social history, is really political history—not in the old-fashioned sense that history deals or should deal only with the rise and fall of political elites, but in the broader sense that whatever the historian studies, even aspects of a society that at first may seem unrelated to politics, will upon closer examination be revealed to be in some way reflective of, or associated with, features of that society's power structure. That is, they form part of what we can call the social foundations of power—the intricate web of relations and understandings (personal, economic, cultural, aesthetic) that sustain social hierarchies over time, sometimes over centuries. Most historians, I think, recognize this at least intuitively: a study of changing styles of shoelaces in twentieth-century America, for example, would seem marginal, if not totally irrelevant, unless it could relate those changes to the emergence of new movements or groups in American society and the eclipse of old ones, or to new understandings of what was important and to new ways of doing things.

But, as with most things, it is much easier to understand something in principle, and even easier to pronounce upon it, as I have just done in the preceding paragraph, than it is actually to do it. Bulliet's publications offer a number of outstanding instances of a historian doing the hard work of connecting changes in diverse aspects of the social web with developments in that society's political superstructure. Perhaps the best example is found in Bulliet's article on "Pottery Styles and Social Status in Medieval Khurasan," where he makes a serious effort to link two of the three main ceramic wares of Nishapur between the eighth and eleventh centuries with the urban factionalism that plagued Nishapur, especially between the tenth and twelfth centuries. Bulliet builds on his hypothesis that this factionalism is at least in part a reflection of tensions between relatively early converts to Islam and later converts. In earlier work (especially his *Patricians of Nishapur),* Bulliet had theorized that the early converts became in the Islamic era a kind of Nishapuri elite. The later converts, on the other hand, represented formerly influential Persian families who had initially resisted the new faith (and the new power structure that went with it); but, now that they had belatedly become Muslims, they wanted to reclaim their former positions of high status. Bulliet makes the case that these two groups favored different types of pottery—the "early Islamic elite" favoring a black-on-white ware usually decorated with bold Arabic calligraphy, while the later converts favored a polychrome ware that was often decorated with traditional Persian motifs of the Sasanian era. This correlates well with the early elite's claim to high status on the basis of their superior knowledge of the Islamic texts—which were in Arabic—and the more recent converts' preference for their native Persian, which by the tenth century was beginning to be used to write Islamic texts. It also correlates, Bulliet shows, with the distribution of these two wares in the archaeological ruins of Nishapur: the black-on-white ware is most common in those parts of the site that were occupied in the earlier Islamic centuries. The polychrome ware, on the other hand, was uncovered mainly in those parts of the site that underwent urbanization as the newer converts from rural areas came to Nishapur in the ninth-eleventh centuries, just when, in Bulliet's view, the more recent converts were challenging the old elite for influence and status in the city.

Another hallmark of Bulliet's work is the holistic quality of his historical vision. He displays an unusual talent for seeing how different categories of historical phenomena are related to one another, and for synthesizing them into a larger and more meaningful whole. Particularly striking is his ability to see how an apparent detail may open up a larger and more significant issue for exploration. For example, his observation of the atrophy of the road system in Islamic Spain, and the return of roads to al-Andalus following the region's conquest by the Christian kingdoms of the north, seems to have sparked the central insights enshrined in *The Camel and the Wheel,* which in turn led him to generate a number of subordinate hypotheses, such as those on the history of animal harnessing. We might see his exploitation of the apparently arcane information in *tabaqat* works, discussed above, as another example of this gift for seeing the significance of the apparently insignificant. In "Naw Bahar and the Survival of Iranian Buddhism," he builds a plausible (if still largely hypothetical) reconstruction of the presence of pre-Islamic Buddhism in Iran, and the significance of that for early Islamic history, partly on the basis of the quirky distribution of towns named Naw Bahar, which he explains by drawing on a variety of hitherto hardly-used evidence in otherwise well-known textual sources. "Medieval Arabic Tarsh: A Forgotten Chapter in the History of Printing" uses what could be a narrow description of some unusual medieval documents as a springboard to jump into a wide-ranging rumination on technology in the medieval Islamic lands. "The Shaykh al-Islam and the Evolution of Islamic Society" takes as its starting-point the apparently anomalous use of the term *shaykh al-islam* in various late medieval or early modern Islamic states, and traces the origins and meaning of the term in a way that links it to major developments in the history of Islamic education and statecraft. "Pottery styles and social status in medieval Khurasan," already discussed above, can also be seen as an example of Bulliet's knack for linking apparently obdurate kinds of evidence (in this case pottery styles) to broader historical developments. "Botr et Baranis" weaves together philology, the history of harnessing and agricultural technology, numismatic and art-historical evidence, and evidence of clothing styles, to address an old question in an ingenious new and very productive way. A similarly wide-ranging essay in historical synthesis is "Local Politics in Eastern Iran under the Ghaznavids and Seljuks," which draws on textual, numismatic, and other evidence to make its case.

Although the bulk of Bulliet's work has focused on the medieval Islamic Middle East, he also has made significant contributions to our understanding of the modern Middle East as well. The clarity of vision noted above serves him unusually well in this work; it helps him to see recent events as part of long-term historical trends and to extrapolate the changes they may introduce, without being constrained by the attachment to familiar present conditions that marks so much writing on contemporary affairs. His essays "Day After Tomorrow. The Future of Islamic Movements" (1997) and "Twenty Years of Islamic Politics" (1999) are particularly worth reading in this respect: both are beautifully drawn sketches of important movements and anticipations of likely future developments, and in some respects seem, in this post-September 11 world, almost prescient. To stray from strict scholarship for a moment, it is worth noting that Bulliet's capacities as prognosticator were already evident in his non-fiction work *The Tomb of the Twelfth Imam.* This book, published in the year of the Iranian revolution (1979) but of course conceived and written before that date, anticipated in fictional form the rise to power in Iran of a figure resembling Imam Ruhollah Khomeini.

Many of the historical themes that Bulliet has dealt with in his scholarship on the Near East are sweeping ones, not limited to medieval Khurasan or Iran, where his scholarly odyssey began. These include, as we have seen, such issues as the history of transportation and of technology more generally, the history and sociology of conversion to Islam, and the long-term development of Islamic educational institutions and their relationship to structures of state authority. But Bulliet's holistic outlook has also drawn him into even broader issues, some of which must be considered of virtually universal historical significance. An early example is his essay, "An Answer for Hichem Djaït—Or Possibly a Question," (1976), which provides a brief sketch of his breathtakingly broad vision of the overall development of Islamic history in five phases, enriched by trenchant comparisons with the historical evolution of medieval Europe. In other words, Bulliet strives in this essay to situate the whole of Islamic history in the context of broader currents of Eurasian history. The same commitment to world history is evident in his more recent contributions to the writing of world history, including the textbook *The Earth and Its Peoples* (1997), the essay on "Themes, Conjunctures, and Comparisons" in a volume devoted to the teaching of world history (1997), and *The Columbia History of the Twentieth Century* (1998), to which he contributed two synthetic essays on "High Culture" and "Popular Culture", as well as editing (and therefore establishing the overall structure of) the volume.

In numerous essays, moreover, Bulliet wades into major historical debates that go far beyond the limits of the Islamic world. His Introduction to the volume (which he edited) entitled *Under Siege: Islam and Democracy* (1994) attempts to slay, or at least wound, the dragon of that kind of pernicious cultural essentialism found in such interpretations as Samuel Huntington's "Clash of Civilizations" thesis. Similarly, his article on "The Individual in Islamic Society" attempts to debunk widely-held misconceptions about this issue, partly by comparing actual conditions in Islamic societies with those in other parts of the world. In "Determinism and Pre-Industrial Technology" (1994) he tackles Robert Heilbroner's theories, which dismiss all pre-capitalist societies as "inconsequential" and privilege economic analysis as the only meaningful form of explanation; this, Bulliet argues, is just another attempt by Western thinkers to deflect attention from the inequitable power relationships between the West and the non-West, particularly in the colonial period, and the way they affected the development of different parts of the world, by positing a set of deterministic laws based in capitalism. Building on his finding in *The Camel and the Wheel,* he effectively shows that technological change is profoundly affected not only by factors of economic advantage, but also by cultural choices. Even Bulliet's essay on the state of the field, "Orientalism and Medieval Islamic Studies" (1994), with all its penetrating observations on what Islamicists do, does not limit itself to the Islamic world, but sees these studies in the context of studying the broader medieval world.

Finally, readers of Bulliet's scholarship (particularly his articles) are regularly treated not only to conceptual and stylistic clarity, but also to occasional delightful turns of phrase that make his scholarship more engaging and memorable. The following quote from his article "*Annales* and Archaeology" in a volume of essays by various authors on this theme provides a wonderful example of all of these characteristics—no-nonsense clarity, directness, and a sense of fun. Distilling the essence of the articles in the volume, Bulliet concludes that they bear the following implications for archaeologists' attempts to utilize the methods of the *Annalistes:*

"First, the authors of the papers do not understand the *Annales* School in the same way. Consequently, they apply significantly different insights deriving from their differing understandings.

Second, the *Annales* School itself does not have sufficient coherence and self-understanding to make appropriating ideas from it an easy or straightforward task.

Third, there is ultimately nothing in the *Annales* School that can take archaeologists much farther intellectually than they have already gone.

And finally, like the fabled bumblebee that defied the predictions of the aeronautical engineer that its wing area would be insufficient to bear it aloft, this effort at interdisciplinary cross-fertilization flies, and buzzes, and makes honey." (pp. 131–32)

In addition to the straightforward original scholarship already discussed, I want briefly to take note of two other arenas in which Richard Bulliet has made signal contributions to the fields of Islamic and Middle Eastern studies. One can be summed up under the rubric of "Professional Service." This includes not only such obvious contributions as his service on the boards of directors of various institutions of the field (Middle East Studies Association, Society for Iranian Studies, American Institute for Iranian Studies) and his service on advisory panels of various kinds for different organizations (Social Science Research Council, College Board), but also his significant work as editor of reference works useful either to scholars in the field of Islamic and Middle Eastern studies, or to students and others who wish to learn more about it. Here, in addition to the *Encyclopedia of the Modern Middle East* (1996), of which he was co-editor and *The Columbia History of the Twentieth Century* (1998), which he edited, we should take special note of his entry on "Islamic World to 1500" in *The American Historical Association's Guide to Historical Literature,* 3rd edition (1995), which offers a select, judiciously annotated bibliography for this vast topic. His numerous book reviews (almost a hundred to date) have, over the years, also been a valuable guide to scholars wishing to get an advance view of the significance, cogency, and usefulness of a colleague's work.

The second arena in which Bulliet has made signal contributions that help advance the field of Islamic and Middle Eastern studies we can call, broadly, "outreach"—that is, pieces written for non-specialist readers in a variety of venues. The importance of such work, which helps get a new generation of people interested in our field and helps keep the general public informed of the realities in the Islamic world and of the importance of continued scholarly efforts to understand it, can hardly be overstated: the vitality of our field depends, in large measure, on the support of a sympathetic and at least somewhat knowledgeable public. Bulliet has been a model citizen in this respect because of his many articles for popular audiences (some on medieval topics, some on modern or current events), including a number of "op-ed" pieces. It is worth noting that his effectiveness in this arena depends on the same qualities we have noted above in his scholarship: clarity of conception, clarity of expression, and at times a certain light touch in making his points, so that the reader remains engaged.

It is time to sum up. Richard Bulliet's scholarly work qualifies him as one of the small handful of scholars of whom it can truly be said that they changed the contours of the field of Islamic and Middle Eastern history during the last forty years. Others (though perhaps not many) have published more words than he, and many have published a greater number of sharply-defined technical studies—"Beitrage/Contributions to the Study of . . ." (followed all too often by an ill-defined, or undefined, larger theme). But very few scholars have had his ability to see things—and to force the rest of us, too, to see things—in a broader context, whether it is the pottery or coins of Nishapur in the broader context of social and political developments in that city, or Islamic history in the broader context of world history. He has continually challenged old ideas and suggested superior ways of looking at things, and our fields are much the richer for it. Perhaps his rare effectiveness as an historian is rooted in a kind of neo-positivistic outlook (I hope he doesn't take umbrage at this suggestion)—not, of course, the old Rankean positivism, the limitations of which he understands as well as any of us, but a basic, common-sense conviction that, after all, the historian *can* say meaningful things about the past, despite inescapable limitations in our sources and despite epistemological doubts. Bulliet, as anyone who knows his work is aware, is quite interested in theory, but he sees it always as the means to an end, not as the end in itself. In this respect he has, it seems to me, been swimming against the prevailing current of much historical practice in recent years, resisting that obsessive devotion to theory that all too often has induced a kind of paralysis, or reluctance to judge, in the historian. Bulliet himself, in his article "Annales and archaeology," typified this era aptly as "decades when many historians have grown more accustomed to talking about the writing of history than actually doing it." (p. 134) We should all be most grateful that, unlike so many others, Bulliet has just gone ahead and done it.

Endnotes

1. The author is grateful to Matthew S. Gordon for reading a draft of this Introduction and making helpful suggestions for improvement.

Richard W. Bulliet: Personal Observations

Leila Fawaz

The first time Richard Bulliet ever heard a foreign language spoken was when he arrived in Cambridge, Massachusetts, as a freshman at Harvard College. The only son of the two children of Mildred (a physicist and a professor) and Jack (an engineer and an inventor), Dick grew up in "an older neighborhood with stately elms, patricians, and an exclusive country club."[1] Yet, his early years in the secure and predictable hometown of Rockford, Illinois, also began to prepare him for a life of curiosity about other cultures and openness to various points of views, since he was well served by his high school education and a supportive family. His roots in Illinois were deep and important to him; he and his wife Lucy stayed in touch with his childhood friends throughout an active career that took him around the United States, Europe, Africa, and Asia. Served by an excellent memory and an affectionate and humorous disposition, he found ways to keep family, friends, and later former students into a life mostly spent in upper Manhattan. Despite his competitive nature, particularly during the early part of his career when, like other promising scholars, he was seeking permanent employment, and despite being a little gauche around more senior scholars whom he could not cater to, he remained comfortable throughout his life with students who loved him wherever he taught—first at Harvard, then Berkeley and Columbia. He reads constantly and has a large book collection that, like his office, was always open to students who borrowed or took what they wanted when they wanted; in fact, for years his office was large enough to be the gathering room of the graduate students. Dick's love for his students is the one constant in a professional life that spanned a whole range of intellectual interests. These include the patricians of medieval Iran, Muslim traditional education, conversion to Islam and the emergence of a Muslim society, numismatics, technology and transport, including by camels and donkeys, Islamic activism, and world history. He uses his elegant and readable prose to reach high school students through collaboration on world history textbooks, as well as lovers of mystery books through his novels. He reads everything, and has a keen instinct for quality. He can tell a very fine thesis or manuscript when he reads one, and in this way and others, he has played an active role in helping to build up the collection of publications at Columbia University Press and has helped develop a wide range of projects. His curiosity is boundless and sometimes comes at a price: in his camel writing phase, I recall him lecturing passionately on camels to sometimes slightly puzzled listeners. But his curiosity is also irresistible, and I also recall that the students who listened to him discuss the role of camels in the history of transportation and technology could not help being drawn to the topic by his enthusiasm and imagination; they loved the topic and contributed to it.

Dick Bulliet fits no traditional mould. In some ways, he is at his best when his work is, to use a sentence from one of his books, "at the edge" of scholarship, looking at important topics of social history from unusual angles, with bold, creative strokes that compare or connect subjects that, until he did, might have gone unnoticed. He writes beautifully. His sense of humor is most apparent in his fictional writing where the plots are clever, imaginative, slightly unusual (one of his novels is entitled *Kicked to Death by a Camel*), but often relevant (*The Gulf Scenario*). His most important contribution remains his extraordinary imagination at the service of history, and his dedication to students who, years after they graduate, recognize his devotion and intellectual stimulation as is evident from this volume in his honor.

Endnotes

1. I am grateful to Tony Adamany, life-long friend of Dick Bulliet, for sharing with me some of his memories of their years in Rockford where they grew up.

Richard W. Bulliet: Bibliography

1968 "City Histories in Medieval Iran," *Iranian Studies* I, pp. 104–109.

1969 "A Mu‘tazilite Coin of Mahmud of Ghazna," *American Numismatic Society Museum Notes* XV, pp. 119–29.

"Le chameau et la roue au Moyen-Orient," *Annales: Économies, Sociétés, Civilisations*, pp. 1092–1103; English version published in *Social Historians in Contemporary France: Essays from Annales*, editors of Annales, Harper and Row, 1972.

Book Reviews: Francesco Gabrieli, "Muhammad and the Conquests of Islam," *Speculum*.

1970 "A Quantitative Approach to Medieval Muslim Biographical Dictionaries," *Journal of the Economic and Social History of the Orient* XIII, pp. 195–211. Arabic translation "Tariqa kamiyya li-dirasat mu‘ajim at-tarajim al-islamiyya fi al-‘usur al-wusta," Scientific Session 12, Islamic University of Medina, Saudi Arabia, 1404(1990).

1971 *Book Reviews*: A. H. Hourani and S. M. Stern, eds., "The Islamic City: A Colloquium," *Speculum*.

M. A. Shaban, "The Abbasid Revolution," *The Middle East Journal*.

1972 *The Patricians of Nishapur: A Study in Medieval Islamic Social History*, Harvard University Press.

"The Shaikh al-Islam and the Evolution of Islamic Society," *Studia Islamica* XXXV, pp. 53-67.

Book Reviews: Hassanein Rabie, "The Financial System of Egypt A.H. 564–741/A.D. 1169–1341," *The Economic History Review*.

1973 *Kicked to Death by a Camel, A Harper Novel of Suspense*, Harper and Row, (under pen-name Clarence J.-L. Jackson; nominated for Edgar Award in the category Best First Mystery).

"The Political-Religious History of Nishapur in the Eleventh Century," in D. S. Richards, ed., *Islamic Civilization 950–1150*, Oxford: Bruno Cassirer, pp. 71–91; Russian translation of entire book.

"Why They Lost the Wheel," *Aramco World* XXIV, pp. 22–25.

Book Reviews: Andrew S. Ehrenkreutz, "Saladin," *The Middle East Journal.*

1974 "Numismatic Evidence for the Relationship between Tughril Beg and Chaghri Beg," in *Near Eastern Numismatics, Iconography, Epigraphy and History: Studies in Honor of George C. Miles*, ed. D. K. Kouymjian, Beirut, pp. 289–96.

Book Reviews: John Masson Smith, Jr., "The History of the Sarbadar Dynasty, 1336–1381 A.D. and its Sources" (place of publication forgotten)

1975 *The Camel and the Wheel*, Harvard University Press, 1975; Morningside Edition with new preface, Columbia University Press, 1990.

1976 "Naw Bahar and the Survival of Iranian Buddhism," *Iran* XIV, pp. 140–45.

"Medieval Nishapur: A Topographic and Demographic Reconstruction," *Studia Iranica* V, pp. 67–89; partial Persian translation by Ali Anvari, "Bazshenasi va jamʿiyatshenasi-ye Nishapur-e qurun-i vostaʾi," *Ayandeh* VIII/8 (1341) 512–20.

"Debate: An Answer for Hichem Djaït—or Possibly a Question," *Diogenes* XCV, pp. 93–102.

Book Reviews: S. D. Goitein, "A Mediterranean Society: The Jewish Communities of the Arab World as Portrayed in the Documents of the Cairo Geniza," vol. 2, "The Community," *International Journal of Middle East Studies.*

S. D. Goitein, "Letters of Medieval Jewish Traders Translated from the Arabic with Introductions and Notes," *International Journal of Middle East Studies.*

Abraham L. Udovitch, "Partnership and Profit in Medieval Islam," *International Journal of Middle East Studies.*

Richard N. Frye, ed., "The Cambridge History of Iran," vol. 4, "The Period from the Arab Invasion to the Saljuqs," *Middle East Studies Association Bulletin.*

Andre Miquel, "La géographie humaine du monde musulman jusqu'au milieu du 11e siecle," vol. 1,

"Géographie et géographie humaine dans la litterature arabe des origines à 1050," vol. 2, "Géographie arabe et representation du monde: la terre et l'étranger," *Speculum.*

1978 "First Names and Political Change in Modern Turkey," *International Journal of Middle East Studies* IX, pp. 489–95.

"Local Politics in Eastern Iran under the Ghaznavids and Seljuks," *Iranian Studies* special issue entitled *State and Society in Iran* XI, pp. 35–56.

Book Reviews: Michael W. Dols, "The Black Death in the Middle East," *Speculum.*

Marshall G.S. Hodgson, "The Venture of Islam," *Journal of the American Oriental Society.*

E. Ashtor, "A Social and Economic History of the Near East in the Middle Ages," *Speculum.*

M. A. Shaban, "Islamic History: A New Intrepretation, vol. 2, A.D. 750–1055," *International Journal of Middle East Studies.*

1979 *Conversion to Islam in the Medieval Period: An Essay in Quantitative History*, Harvard University Press. Persian translation, Tehran: Nashr-e Tarikh-e Iran, 1987.

The Tomb of the Twelfth Imam, A Novel, Harper and Row.

"Conversion to Islam and the Emergence of a Muslim Society in Iran," in N. Levtzion, ed., *Conversion to Islam: A Comparative Study of Islamization*, New York: Holmes and Meier, pp. 30–51.

"Can Iran Attain Stability Under Religious Rule?" *Newsday* (Dec. 12), p. 63.

Book Reviews: Eskandar Beg Monshi, "History of Shah ʿAbbas the Great," translated by Roger M. Savory, *Iranian Studies.*

1980 "Sedentarization of Nomads in the Seventh Century: The Arabs in Basra and Kufa," in P. C. Salzman, ed., *When Nomads Settle*, New York: Bergin, pp. 35–47.

"Camels," *GEO* II (April 1980), pp. 34–54; reprinted as "Let's Hear it for the Camel!" in Elizabeth Cowan, ed., *Reading for Writing*, Glenview: Scott, Foresman, 1983, pp. 97–101.

Book Reviews: Peter Gran, "Islamic Roots of Capitalism: Egypt, 1760–1840," *Africana Journal*.

1981 "Botr et Baranès: hypotheses sur l'histoire des Berbères," *Annales: Économies, Sociétés, Civilisations* (Jan.–Feb. 1981), pp. 104–116; response to critique by G. Fiaccadori (Mar.–Apr. 1983), pp. 475–76.

"Middle East Studies: The Bloom is Off the Rose," *Humanities* II/4 (August 1981), p. 3.

Book Reviews: Jacob Lassner, "The Shaping of ʿAbbasid Rule," *Speculum*.

M. M. Ahsan, "Social Life Under the Abbasids," *Middle East Journal and Arab Studies Quarterly*.

Maxime Rodinson, "La fascination de l'Islam," *Arab Studies Quarterly*.

Roger Savory, "Iran Under the Safavids," *Arab Studies Quarterly*.

Hilde Gauthier-Pilters and Anne Innis Dagg, "The Camel: Its Evolution, Behavior, and Relationship to Man," *Middle East Journal*.

1982 *Book Reviews*: Arnold H. Green, "The Tunisian Ulama 1873–1915," *Journal of the American Oriental Society*.

Andrew C. Hess, "The Forgotten Frontier: A History of the Sixteenth Century Ibero-African Frontier," *Journal of the American Oriental Society*.

Marilyn Robinson Waldman, "Toward a Theory of Historical Narrative: A Case Study in Perso-Islamicate Historiography," *International Journal of Middle East Studies*.

Elizabeth Monroe, "Britain's Moment in the Middle East 1914–71," new and revised edition, *Political Science Quarterly*.

Kathryn Tidrick, "Heart-Beguiling Araby," *The South Atlantic Quarterly*.

Michael E. Bonine and Nikki R. Keddie, eds., "Modern Iran: The Dialectics of Continuity and Change," *Middle East Studies Association Bulletin*.

Patricia Crone, "Slaves on Horses: The Evolution of the Islamic Polity," *Middle East Studies Association Bulletin*.

1983 "The Age Structure of Medieval Islamic Education," *Studia Islamia* 57, pp. 105–117.

"Time, Perceptions and Conflict Resolution," in S. Tahir-Kheli and S. Ayubi, eds., *The Iran-Iraq War: Old Conflicts, New Weapons* New York: Praeger, pp. 65–81.

"How the Camel Got its Saddle," *Natural History* XCII/7 (July 1983), pp. 52–59.

Book Reviews: Bernard Lewis, "The Muslim Discovery of Europe," *American Historical Review*.

Simha Sabari, "Mouvements populaires a Bagdad a l'époque ʿabbaside IXe–XIe siecles," *Speculum*.

A. K. S. Lambton, "Theory and Practice in Medieval Persian Government," *Iranian Studies*.

1984 *The Gulf Scenario, A Novel*, St. Martin's Press.

Host/Narrator and Script Consultant for *The Middle East*, 14 half-hour films produced and written by Denise Boiteau and David Stansfield for TVOntario, Toronto, Canada, 1984.

Book Reviews: Daniel Pipes, "In the Path of God: Islam and Political Power," *Middle East Journal*.

1985 *Book Reviews*: Andrew M. Watson, "Agricultural Innovation in the Early Islamic World: The Diffusion of Crops and Farming Techniques, 700–1100," *Middle East Studies Association Bulletin*.

Joel L. Kraemer and Ilai Alon, eds., "Religion and Government in the World of Islam," *Middle East Studies Association Bulletin*.

Yusuf Khass Hajib, "Wisdom of Royal Glory (Kutadgu Bilig): A Turko-Islamic Mirror for Princes," tr. Robert Dankoff, *Speculum*.

Eliyahu Ashtor, "Levant Trade in the Later Middle Ages," *Canadian Journal of History*.

Shaul Bakhash, "The Reign of the Ayatollahs: Iran and the Islamic Revolution," *Political Science Quarterly*.

A. A. Duri, "The Rise of Historical Writing Among the Arabs," tr. Lawrence I. Conrad, *Middle East Journal*.

Wadad al-Qadi, ed., "Studia Arabica et Islamica: Festschrift for Ihsan ʿAbbas on his Sixtieth Birthday," *al-Abhath*, pp. 43–8.

1986 "Angling for the Spoils of Peace: Sudden U.S. Interest Unsettles All the Iran-Iraq War Watchers," (op-ed) *Los Angeles Times* Nov. 7, II/5.

"Islam: Arabian Nights in a New Day," *National Catholic Reporter* Nov. 28, 9.

Book Reviews: Stuart Piggott, "The Earliest Wheeled Transport: From the Atlantic Coast to the Caspian Sea," *Technology and Culture*.

Ehsan Yar-Shater, ed., "The History of al-Tabari (Ta'rikh al-rusul wa'l-muluk)," vol. XXVII "The ʿAbbasid Revolution," tr. John Alden Williams; vol. XXXV "The Crisis of the ʿAbbasid Caliphate," tr. George Saliba; vol. XXXVIII "The Return of the Caliphate to Baghdad," tr. Franz Rosenthal, *Middle East Journal*.

1987 "Printing in the Medieval Islamic Underworld," *Columbia Library Columns* 36/3, pp. 13–20.

"Medieval Arabic *Tarsh* : A Forgotten Chapter in the History of Printing," *Journal of the American Oriental Society*, 107/3, pp. 427–38.

"Gulf Conflict a Bomb without a Detonator," (op-ed) *Boston Globe*, Oct. 20. Same article under different title in *Los Angeles Times* on same date.

Book Reviews: Juan R.I. Cole and Nikki Keddie, "Shi'ism and Social Protest," *Political Science Quarterly*.

Patricia Crone, "Meccan Trade and the Rise of Islam," *International Journal of Islamic and Arabic Studies*.

G. R. Hawting, "The First Dynasty of Islam: The Umayyad Caliphate AD 661–750," *Middle East Journal*.

Adid Dawisha, "Arab Radicalism," *Journal of Palestine Studies*.

Said Amir Arjomand, "The Shadow of God and the Hidden Imam," *Journal of the American Oriental Society*.

1988 *Book Reviews*: Peter Jackson and Laurence Lockhart, eds., "The Cambridge History of Iran," Volume 6, "The Timurid and Safavid Periods," *American Historical Review*.

Habib Jaouiche, "The Histories of Nishapur by ʿAbdalgafir al-Farisi (Siyaq Ta'rih Naisabur). Register der Personen- und Ortsnamen," *Journal of the American Oriental Society*.

Ahmad Y. al-Hassan and Donard R. Hill, "Islamic Technology," *Technology Review*.

1989 *Book Reviews*: David Pryce-Jones, "The Closed Circle: An Interpretation of the Arabs," *Journal of Palestine Studies*.

Gary Leiser, tr. and ed., "A History of the Seljuks: Ibrahim Kafesoglu's Interpretation and the Resulting Controversy," *Middle East Studies Association Bulletin*.

Jacob Lassner, "Islamic Revolution and Historical Memory," *American Historical Review*.

1990 "Process and Status in Conversion and Continuity" and "Conversion Stories in Early Islam," in Michael Gervers and Ramzi Jibran Bikhazi, eds., *Conversion and Continuity: Indigenous Christian Communities in Islamic Lands Eighth to Eighteenth Centuries* Papers in Mediaeval Studies 9, Toronto: Pontifical Institute of Mediaeval Studies, pp. 1–12, 123–33.

Book Reviews: Ira M. Lapidus, "A History of Muslim Societies," *The American Historical Review*.

C.E. Bosworth, Charles Issawi, Roger Savory, and A.L. Udovitch, eds., "The Islamic World from Classical to Modern Times: Essays in Honor of Bernard Lewis," *Middle East Studies Association Bulletin*.

Majid Khadduri, "The Gulf War," *The American Historical Review*.

1991 *The Sufi Fiddle, A Novel*, St. Martin's Press.

"The Heavy Burden We'll Shoulder," *The Arizona Republic*, Jan. 20; reprinted in *Manchester Guardian*

"A Government to Replace One-Man Rule," *Newsday*, Feb. 10.

"Was it Worth All this Agony?" *The Arizona Republic*, April 14.

"Scholarship in the Public Interest: Notes from a Soundbite," *Gannett Center Journal*, Spring-Summer 1991, pp. 65–70.

"Roots of Present Resurgence of Islam in Middle East," *Kayhan International*, August 29, p. 6. Text of prepared testimony before the Middle East Subcommittee of the Senate Foreign Relations Committee on April 22, 1991.

Verbatim testimony published in "Hearings before the Subcommittee on Near Eastern and South Asian Affairs of the Committee on Foreign Relations, United States Senate, 102d Congress, 1st Session, April 22, 1991.

Book Reviews: Janet L. Abu-Lughod, "Before European Hegemony: The World System A.D. 1250–1350," *American Historical Review*.

Mahmood Ibrahim, "Merchant Capital and Islam," *International Journal of Islamic and Arabic Studies.*

1992 *Crisis in the Middle East,* supplementary high school current events book, Grolier, Inc.

"Pottery Styles and Social Status in Medieval Khurasan," and "*Annales* and Archaeology," in A. Bernard Knapp, ed., *Archaeology,* Annales, *and Ethnohistory,* Cambridge: Cambridge University Press, pp. 75–82, 131–34.

Book Reviews: Abd al-Ghafir al-Farisi, "Al-halqa al-ula min ta'rikh Naisabur: al-muntakhab min al-Siyaq," ed. Muhammad Kazim al-Mahmudi, *Middle East Medievalists Newsletter.*

Ehsan Yarshater, ed., "Encyclopaedia Iranica," vol. 3, *International Journal of Middle East Studies.*

1993 *Islam: The View from the Edge,* Columbia University Press.

"The Israeli-PLO Accord: The Future of the Islamic Movement," *Foreign Affairs,* 72/5.

"Aggression in Historical Perspective," Farhang Rajaee, ed., *The Iran-Iraq War,* Gainesville: University Press of Florida.

Book Reviews: Mark J. Gasiorowski, "U.S. Foreign Policy and the Shah: Building a Client State in Iran," *Political Science Quarterly.*

Rachel Arié, "Études sur la civilisation de l'Espagne musulmane," *Journal of Islamic Studies.*

John L. Esposito, "The Islamic Threat: Myth or Reality?," *Journal of Palestine Studies.*

Jacqueline Sublet, "Le Voile du nom," *Journal of the American Oriental Society.*

1994 *Under Siege: Islam and Democracy,* editor, The Middle East Institute, Columbia University, Occasional Papers 1.

"Determinism and Pre-Industrial Technology," in Merritt Roe Smith and Leo Marx, *Does Technology Drive History? The Dilemma of Technological Determinism,* Cambridge, Mass.: MIT Press, pp. 201–15.

"Orientalism and Medieval Islamic Studies," in John Van Engen, ed., *The Past and Future of Medieval Studies,* Notre Dame: University of Notre Dame Press, pp. 94-104.

"Of Encyclopedias and the End of a World," *Biblion. The Bulletin of The New York Public Library*, 3/1 (Fall 1994), pp. 49–58.

"New Deal with Islamism," interview in *Al-Ahram Weekly*, 24–30 Nov., 1994, p. 16.

Book Reviews: Christian Décobert, "Le mendiant et le combattant. L'institution de l'Islam," *Journal of the Economic and Social History of the Orient.*

Salma Khadra Jayyusi, "The Heritage of Muslim Spain," *Journal of Islamic Studies.*

John R. Bowen, "Muslims Through Discourse: Religion and Ritual in Gayo Society," *Journal of Islamic Studies.*

Susan Sherwin-White & Amélie Kuhrt, "From Samarkhand to Sardis: A New Approach to the Seleucid Empire," *International Journal of Middle East Studies.*

1995 "Islamic World to 1500," in Mary Beth Norton and Pamela Gerardi, eds., *The American Historical Association's Guide to Historical Literature*, 3d ed., New York: Oxford University Press, vol. 1, pp. 498–526.

"Comment on Iriye paper 'The G-3 World' and the Third World," in The Japan Foundation for Global Partnership, *The End of the Century: The Future in the Past*, Tokyo: Kodansha International, pp. 379–82.

"The Revolution Within the Islamic Revolution," *New York Newsday*, "Currents" section, February 26.

Book Reviews: Michael Field, "Inside the Arab World," *New York Times Book Review* (3/5).

Richard Eaton, "The Rise of Islam and the Bengal Frontier," *American Historical Review.*

Barnett R. Rubin, "The Fragmentation of Afghanistan: State Formation and Collapse in the International System," *Newsletter. Southern Asia Institute*, Columbia University.

Ann Zwicker Kerr, "Come with Me from Lebanon: An American Family Odyssey," *culturefront.*

Paul Salem, "Bitter Legacy: Ideology and Politics in the Arab World," *culturefront.*

Peter Christensen, "The Decline of Iranshahr: Irrigation and Environments in the History of the Middle East, 500 B.C. to A.D. 1500," *International Journal of Middle East Studies.*

1996 *The Encyclopedia of the Modern Middle East*, co-editor, New York: Macmillan Publishing Company.

"The Individual in Islamic Society," in Irene Bloom et. al, eds., *Religious Diversity and Human* Rights, New York: Columbia University Press, pp. 175–91.

Book Reviews: Cemal Kafadar, "Between Two Worlds: The Construction of the Ottoman State," *The Journal of Interdisciplinary History.*

Maya Shatzmiller, "Labour in the Medieval Islamic World," *Journal of Social History.*

1997 *The Earth and Its Peoples: A Global History*, co-author, Boston: Houghton Mifflin; second edition 2000; third edition 2004.

"Themes, Conjunctures, and Comparisons," in Heidi Roupp, ed., *Teaching World History: A Resource Book*, Armonk, NY: M. E. Sharpe, pp. 94–109.

"Day After Tomorrow: The Future of Islamic Movements," *Harvard International Review* XIX/2 (Spring 1997), pp. 34–37, 66–67.

Book Reviews: Robert J. Allison, "The Crescent Obscured: The United States and the Muslim World, 1776–1815," *The Journal of Interdisciplinary History.*

1998 *The Columbia History of the Twentieth Century*, editor, New York: Columbia University Press, (translations into Chinese, Polish, and Croatian).

Book Reviews: Xinru Liu, "Silk and Religion: An Exploration of Material Life and the Thought of People, A.D. 600–1200," *American Historical Review.*

1999 "Twenty Years of Islamic Politics," *The Middle East Journal*, 53/2 (Spring 1999), pp. 189–200.

Book Reviews: Heinz Halm, "The Empire of the Mahdi: The Rise of the Fatimids," *The Historian.*

Paul Shepard, "Coming Home to the Pleistocene," *Worldviews.*

2000 "Economic Systems and Technologies" and "Communication and Transport" in M. E. Bakhit, et al. Eds., *History of Humanity: Scientific and Cultural*

Development. Volume IV, *From the Seventh to the Sixteenth Century*, Paris and London: UNESCO and Routledge, pp. 71–83, 84–95.

"Democratic Islamists," *Middle East Insight*, Nov.-Dec. 2000, p. 41.

Internet essays for Fathom:

"Human-Animal Relations in the Era of Postdomesticity" (video interview) <www.fathom.com/story/story.jhtml?story_id=35184>

"Religious Conversion and the Spread of Innovation" <www.fathom.com/story/story.jhtml?story_id=2199>

"Ruminations: Of Encyclopedias and the End of a World" (www.fathom.com/story/story.jhtml?story_id=60803)

"Apocalypse Wow!" <www.fathom.com/story/story.jhtml?story_id=12 2092>

Book Reviews: Bernard Lewis, "The Middle East: A Brief History of the Last 2,000 Years," *International Journal of Middle East Studies*.

Fred M. Donner, "Narratives of Islamic Origins: The Beginnings of Islamic Historical Writing," *Middle East Studies Association Bulletin*.

Efraim Karsh and Inari Karsh, "Empires of the Sand: The Struggle for Mastery in the Middle East, 1789-1923," *The Middle East Journal*.

2001 "A Recruiting Tape of Osama bin Laden: Excerpts and Analyses," Columbia International Affairs On-line <www.ciaonet.org>

"Theorizing Islam," Social Science Research Council <www.ssrc.org/september11>, <October>

"Understanding Religious Violence" (video panel participant) <www.fathom.com/story/story.jhtml?story_id=122403>

Book Reviews: R. Stephen Humphreys, "Between Memory and Desire: The Middle East in a Troubled Age," *The International History Review*.

Fred Halliday, "Nation and Religion in the Middle East," *Middle East Studies Association Bulletin*.

2002 "Islam's Crisis of Authority," *Wilson Quarterly*, (Winter, 2002), pp. 11–19.

"Communication, Transportation, and Exploration," in *World Eras*, vol. 2, *Rise and Spread of Islam 622–1500*, ed. Susan L. Douglass, Detroit: Gale, pp. 138–60.

Book Reviews: Maya Shatzmiller, "The Berbers and the Islamic State: The Marinid Experience in Pre-Protectorate Morocco," *The International History Review*.

Janina Safran, "The Second Umayyad Caliphate: The Articulation of Caliphal Legitimacy in al-Andalus," *Journal of Interdisciplinary History*.

Suliman Bashear, "Arabs and Others in Early Islam," *Der Islam*.

2003 "Islamic Culture, Role of Media in," *Encyclopedia of International Media and Communications* (np: Elsevier Science, 2003), vol. 2, pp. 611–20.

"Westoxication and Its Antidotes," Fu'ad Jabali and Jamhari, eds., *Islam in Indonesia: Islamic Studies and Social Transformation* (Montreal: Indonesia-Canada Islamic Higher Education Project, 2002), pp. 15–23.

Book Reviews: Paul M. Cobb, "White Banners: Contention in 'Abbasid Syria, 750–880," *American Historical Review*.

Nesta Ramazani, "The Dance of the Rose and the Nightingale," *Dance Research Journal.*

Jonathan M. Bloom, "Paper before Print: The History and Impact of Paper in the Islamic World," *Technology and Culture*.

2004 *The Case for Islamo-Christian Civilization,* Columbia University Press.

"Women and the Urban Religious Elite in the Pre-Mongol Period," Guitty Nashat and Lois Beck, eds., *Women in Iran from the Rise of Islam to 1800,* University of Illinois Press.

About the Contributors

Ina Baghdiantz-McCabe holds the Darkjian Jafarian Chair of Armenian History at Tufts University. She is author of *The Shah's Silk for Europe's Silver: The Eurasian Silk Trade of the Julfan Armenians in Safavid Iran and India, 1590–1750* (Philadelphia: 1999); co-author of *Slaves of the Shah: New Elites of Seventeenth Century Safavid Isfahan* (London: 2004); and editor of *Du bon usage du thé et des épices en Asie, Réponses à Monsieur Cabart de Villarmont by Jean Chardin* (Paris: 2002).

Alexander Bligh completed his research under the supervision of Richard Bulliet at Columbia University where he received his Ph.D. in 1981. Bligh is currently senior lecturer and chair of the Political Science and Middle Eastern Studies departments at the Academic College of Judea and Samaria. He has served as an advisor to the prime minister of Israel on Arab affairs, and has published extensively on Palestinian, Jordanian and Saudi topics. Among his publications are, *From Prince to King: Succession to the Throne in Modern Saudi Arabia* (New York: 1981), *The Political Legacy of King Hussein* (Sussex: 2002), and a forthcoming volume on "Democracy and Democratization in the Arab World."

Stuart Borsch is assistant professor of Islamic/Middle Eastern history at Assumption College. His publications include, "Nile Floods and Irrigation," in *Mamluk Studies Review* (2000); and he is currently preparing a monograph based on his dissertation, "The Black Death in Egypt and England: A Comparative Economic Analysis," Columbia University, History Department, 2002; as well as several papers on the social and agronomic history of the Middle East. Before embarking on a university career, Borsch served as an officer in the US Navy.

Jamsheed Kairshasp Choksy is professor of Central Eurasian studies and history, and adjunct professor of religious studies at Indiana University. His A.B. was in Middle Eastern Languages and Cultures from Columbia University in 1985. His Ph.D. was in the History and Religions of the Near East and Inner Asia from Harvard University in 1991. He was elected a Junior Fellow in the Harvard Society of Fellows from 1988–1991. He was a member and NEH fellow at the Institute for Advanced Study in Princeton from 1993–1994. Choksy was awarded a Guggenheim Fellowship in 1996–1997. He held an Andrew W. Mellon Fellowship at the Center for Advanced Study in the Behavioral Sciences, Stanford, during 2001–2002. He is the author of three books: *Evil, Good, and Gender: Facets of the Feminine in Zoroastrian Religious History* (New York: 2002); *Conflict and Cooperation: Zoroastrian Subalterns and Muslim Elites in Medieval Iranian Society* (New York: 1997) with a New Persian (Farsi) translation as *Setiz va Sazesh: Zartoshtiyan-e maqlub va mosalmanan-e qaleb dar jameʿ-ye Iran-e nakhostin-i sadeha-ye Islami* (Tehran: 2002); and *Purity and Pollution in Zoroastrianism: Triumph over Evil* (Austin: 1988).

Fred M. Donner is professor of Near Eastern history in the Oriental Institute and the Department of Near Eastern Languages and Civilizations at the University of Chicago. He studied Near Eastern history and languages at Princeton University (from which he received his Ph.D. in 1975), and Friedrich-Alexander Universität in Erlangen, Germany. His research has focused mainly on early Islamic history. Special interests have been the role of pastoral nomads in Near Eastern societies, the spread of the Arabic language, the beginnings of historical writing in the Islamic community, the character of the early Believers' movement, and the development of the early Islamic state. His main publications are *The Early Islamic Conquests* (Princeton: 1981) and *Narratives of Islamic Origins* (Princeton: Darwin Press, 1998). He taught in the History Department at Yale University before moving to Chicago in 1982.

Tayeb El-Hibri is associate professor of Middle Eastern studies at the University of Massachusetts, Amherst. He has authored *Reinterpreting Islamic Historiography: Harun al-Rashid and the Narrative of the ʿAbbasid Caliphate* (Cambridge: 1999); and several articles on the early ʿAbbasid caliphate. He is currently working on a biography of the Rashidun caliphs.

Matthew Gordon is associate professor of Middle East history at Miami University. His publications include *The Breaking of a Thousand Swords* (Albany: 2001); and a primer on *Islam* (Oxford: 2002). Gordon is currently at work on a monograph-length project on elite courtesans of the early ʿAbbasid period.

Mahmoud Haddad is chair of the Department of History at the University of Balamand in northern Lebanon. He earned his Ph.D. from the Department at History at Columbia University in 1989. He joined that department as assistant professor in 1990, and was promoted to associate professor in 1997. In 2000, he moved to Lebanon. His publications include, "Umar b. al-Khattab and the Meccan Aristocracy," in *Chronos: Revue d'Histoire de l'Université de Balamand* (2002); "Ghihab al-halif . . ." (The Absence of an International Ally: The Central Predicament of Arab Foreign Relations in the Twentieth Century," forthcoming in *Annals of the Faculty of Arts and Social Sciences*, University of Balamand (2001); "The Impact of Foreign Missionaries on the Muslim Community in Geographical Syria in the Nineteenth and Early Twentieth Century," in *Altruism and Imperialism: Western Cultural and Religious Missions in the Middle East,* edited by Reeva Spector Simon and Eleanor H. Tejirian (New York: 2003); "Beirut: The Commercial and Political Rivalries Among Syrian Seaports in the Late Nineteenth and Early Twentieth Century," in *The Syrian Land: Processes of Integration and Fragmentation,* ed. Thomas Philipp and Birgit Schabler (Stuttgart: 1998); "Arab Religious Nationalism in the Era of Colonialism: Rereading Rashid Rida's Ideas on the Caliphate," in *Journal of the American Oriental Society* (1997); and "Iraq before World War I: A Case of anti-European Arab Ottomanism," in *The Origins of Arab Nationalism,* ed. Rashid Khalidi et. al., (New York: 1991). He is now working on a book about Arab religious and secular nationalist trends in the nineteenth and twentieth centuries.

John W. Limbert has been a Foreign Service Officer for 30 years, serving as U.S. Ambassador to Mauritania 2000–03. He is now president of the American Foreign Service Association. His overseas experience includes tours in Algeria, Djibouti, Iran, Saudi Arabia, and the United Arab Emirates. Limbert holds a Ph.D. in history and Middle Eastern studies from Harvard University. Before joining the Foreign Service, he taught in Iran, both as a Peace Corps volunteer (1964–66) and as an instructor in English and history at Shiraz University (1969–72). From 1981–84 he taught political science at the U.S. Naval Academy, and in 1991–92 he was a senior fellow at Harvard University's Center for International Affairs. He has written numerous articles on Middle Eastern subjects and has authored *Iran: at War with History* (Boulder: 1987).

Karen Pinto is currently an assistant professor in the Civilization Sequence Program at the American University of Beirut. Serendipity permitted her to marry an affection for maps with Islamic history. She completed her dissertation on "Ways of Seeing.3: Scenarios of the World in the Medieval Islamic

Cartographic Imagination" in 2002. Appearing shortly are "Surat Bahr al-Rum: Aspects of the Mediterranean in Medieval Islamic Maps," presented at the 18th International Conference on the History of Cartography and to be published by the National Hellenic Research Foundation of Athens; as well as, "Passion and Conflict: Medieval Islamic Views of the West" (forthcoming *Imago Mundi*). Islamic maps have brought her good luck and much financial support from Columbia University, the Mrs. Giles Whiting Foundation, Friends of J. B. Harley, Mellon Foundation, American Research Institute in Turkey, Social Science Research Council, and Social Science and Humanities Research Council of Canada.

Lawrence G. Potter is adjunct associate professor of international affairs at Columbia University. Since 1994 he has also been deputy director of Gulf/2000, a major research and documentation project on the Persian Gulf states based at Columbia. A graduate of Tufts College, he received an M.A. in Middle Eastern studies from the School of Oriental and African Studies, University of London, and a Ph.D. in history (1992) from Columbia University. From 1984 to 1992 he was senior editor at the Foreign Policy Association, a national, nonpartisan organization devoted to world affairs education for the general public. He co-edited (with Gary Sick) *The Persian Gulf at the Millennium* (New York: 1997), *Security in the Persian Gulf: Origins, Obstacles, and the Search for Consensus* (New York: 2002), and *Iran, Iraq, and the Legacy of War* (New York: 2004), and published "The Persian Gulf in Transition" in the Foreign Policy Association's *Headline Series* (January 1998).

Jean-Marc Ran Oppenheim was Richard Bulliet's first doctoral student at Columbia. In Fall 1976, Bulliet's first semester at Columbia, he was one of two students to register for Bulliet's course on Arab history and historiography. He is currently a visiting associate professor of history at Marymount College of Fordham University and has published articles and book chapters on imperialism in the Middle East, the Jews of modern Egypt and the Sudan, the political economy of Western Europe, and sports. He was the project editor of the *Encyclopedia of the Modern Middle East* (New York, 1996). In the early 1970s, he was a nationally ranked horseman in Three-Day Eventing and on the U.S. equestrian team short list. From 1971 to 1986, he trained with one of the last equestrian classicists, the late Henri L.M. van Schaik.

Parvaneh Pourshariati is assistant professor of Islamic studies in the Departments of Near Eastern Languages and Cultures, and History, at the Ohio State University. She received her doctorate from Columbia University's History

Department in 1995. Pourshariati's current research focuses on the popular literature and cultures of the Turco-Iranian world in the late medieval and early modern period as they reflect the "sub-cultures" operating in these societies. For her past and present research she has been partially supported by American Institute for Iranian Studies, the Shaykh Hamad Fellowship in Islamic Numismatics, Social Science Research Council, Association of American University Women, Centre National de Recherche Scientifique in Paris, and most recently, the Department of Women's Studies' Coca Cola Critical Difference for Women Research Grant for Faculty at OSU. She is currently working on the completion of a manuscript on the late Sasanid and early Islamic history of Iran. Her other projects include an edited volume on the popular literature of the Iranian world and a sequel to this work. Her work has appeared in *Studia Iranica* and *Journal of Iranian Studies.*

Sofia Saadeh is currently advisor to the Lebanese deputy prime minister, Issam Fares. She received her Ph.D. from Harvard University under the supervision of Richard Bulliet in 1974. She has taught at the Lebanese American University, the American University of Beirut, and the Lebanese University, where she was promoted to full professor in 1988. She has authored the following monographs: *Ugarit* [in Arabic] (Beirut: 1988); *The Position of Chief Judge in Baghdad, 1000–1300* [in Arabic] (Beirut: 1990); *The Social Structure of Lebanon* (Beirut: 1993); and, *Antun Saadeh and Democracy in Geographic Syria* (London: 2000). Her most recent article is "Les consequences du sectarisme sur l'espace public de Beyrouth," *Cahiers de la Villa Gillet* (2001).

Ariel Salzmann is assistant professor in the Department of History at Queen's University in Ontario. Richard Bulliet supervised her thesis, "Measures of Empire: Tax Farmers and the Ottoman Ancien Régime (1695–1807)," (1995). Her research focuses on early modern political economy, state formation in the Ottoman Empire, and cross-cultural relations in the Mediterranean. She is the author of articles, a short book, *Vita ed Avventure di un Rinnegato nel Mediterraneo del Seicento* (The Life and Times of a Renegade in the seventeenth century Mediterranean), (Venice: 1992); and the forthcoming monograph, *Tocqueville in the Ottoman Empire* (Leiden: 2003).

Reeva S. Simon served as associate director of the Middle East Institute from 1993–2003. She is the author of *Iraq Between the Two World Wars: the Militarist Origins of Tyranny* (New York: 2004), an updated edition of her dissertation (published in 1986) prepared under the supervision of Richard Bulliet and *The Middle East in Crime Fiction* (New York: 1989). Works she has co-edited include *The Origins of Arab Nationalism* (New York: 1991)*; Encyclopedia of the Modern Middle East (New York: 1996); Altruism and Imperialism: Western Cultural and Religious Missions in the Middle East* (New York: 2002)*; The Jews of the Middle East and North Africa in Modern Times* (2003)*;* and *The Creation of Iraq 1914–1921* (New York: 2004).

Denise A. Spellberg is associate professor of history and Middle Eastern studies at the University of Texas at Austin. She is the author of *Politics, Gender, and the Islamic Past: The Legacy of ʿAʾisha bint Abi Bakr* (New York: 1994) and has published in *The Encyclopedia of Women and World Religions*, *The Encyclopaedia of the Qurʾan*, and *The International Journal of Middle East Studies.*

Elizabeth Thompson is associate professor of history at the University of Virginia. She is author of *Colonial Citizens: Republican Rights, Paternal Privilege, and Gender in French Syria and Lebanon* (New York: 2000). Based on a dissertation written under Richard Bulliet in the early 1990s, the book won the American Historical Association's Joan Kelly Memorial Prize.

Uli Schamiloglu is professor in the Department of Languages and Cultures of Asia at the University of Wisconsin-Madison and chair of the Central Asian Studies Program. He received a B.A. in Middle East languages and cultures from Columbia College in 1979 and the Ph.D. in history from Columbia University in 1986. His teaching and research interests include Turkic languages, philology, and linguistics; the social, economic, and cultural history of medieval Eurasia; and the modern intellectual history of the Muslim Turkic peoples. His monograph, entitled "Golden Horde: Economy, Society, and Civilization in Western Eurasia, thirteenth-fourteenth centuries" will be published soon. He is currently working on an introduction to Turkic historical and comparative linguistics, as well as on a project on Turkic and Tatar thought in the liberal age.

Neguin Yavari teaches Islamic studies at Columbia University's Religion Department. She completed her dissertation under the supervision of Richard Bulliet in 1992. Yavari's recent article on "The Conversion Stories of Shaykh Abu Ishaq al-Kazaruni," in *Christianizing Peoples and Converting Individuals*, ed. Guyda Armstrong and Ian N. Wood, was published by the Medieval Institute at Leeds (Turnhout: 2000). She is currently preparing a manuscript on "Nizam al-Mulk Remembered: A Study in Historical Representation" for publication.

1965

Near Sabzevar, Iran 1971

Conference, Hofstra University, 1985

Royal Palace, Kota Bharu, Sultanate of Kelantan, Malaysia 1989

With Lucy and Mark Bulliet, Columbia University 2002

Views From the Edge

Essays in Honor of Richard W. Bulliet

Trading Diaspora, State Building and the Idea of National Interest

Ina Baghdiantz-McCabe

This is a brief comparative study of several trading groups in the seventeenth century and of their participation in state-building in their host societies as "trade diaspora." The word state is used here in its sixteenth century meaning of a political body subject to common government and law.[1] It is generally held that the three European East India Companies served national interest, contributed financially to state building, and followed the mercantilist policies dictated by their home states from their inception. It is also assumed that classical trade disapora such as the Armenians or the Jews remained outsiders to polity with only commercial profit in mind. The question of any form of national interest remains moot for them and is never addressed, nor is their link to their host society assumed to be anything more than the payments made for a right to conduct commerce as cross-cultural brokers.

Defining trading groups remains an interesting problem, although definitions and categorization can often mislead. Most views of the Early Modern period are distorted by the habit of studying history within the framework of modern nation-states. Indeed even such a category as the concept of trade diaspora can cause a serious misreading of the past. Contained within the concept of trade diaspora, there is the idea that these groups remain outside the structures of the host country, alien and perhaps even at times hostile or in competition to the host country's economic and national interests. The examples discussed below contradict this view. It has universally been assumed, save in one article by Sanjay Subrahmanyam on the Iranians in exile and in my book on the Julfan Armenians, that trade diaspora do not participate in the political life of their host county or in state-building in Asia. In addition a brief discussion of the structure of the three East India Companies, (the Dutch, the English and the French) in the same period illustrates why one can argue that there is less difference than has been established between groups traditionally called trade diaspora and what we erroneously perceive as "national" East India Companies serving the home society's interests abroad; as indeed they did in later centuries. Did these companies serve national interest in Early Modern times? Did they contribute to state building in the seventeenth century? Can they be perceived as national companies from their inception as they have been?

In the Early Modern period what was the role of the newly exiled Armenians in Iran, who were the Iranians in India, or for that matter the Europeans in India? To better cope with these complexities, trade historians have come up with the notion of "trade settlement" or "trade diaspora." The term appears applicable to many groups. It could equally apply to the East India Company factors, such as the English in India and the Dutch in Southeast Asia. Yet, the term trade diaspora has been only exceptionally used for European factors. Therefore the question arises as to why the usage has been reserved by most scholars, with a few exceptions, for other trading groups and not for European factors. The term "trade diaspora" was first coined in 1971 by Abner Cohen to refer to "a nation of socially interdependent, but spatially dispersed communities." Even as he defined it, he was criticized for his usage of the word diaspora instead of the more neutral term network. He argues that the usage of the term stands

> "A diaspora of this kind is distinct as a type of social grouping in its culture and structure. Its members are culturally distinct from both their society of origin and from the society among which they live. Its organization combines stability of structure but allows a high degree of mobility of personnel . . . It has an informal political organization of its own. . . . It tends to be autonomous in its judicial organization. . . . Its members form a moral community."[2]

The Europeans unless they settled and went through a form of "nativization" could not, one supposes, be seen as a group distinct from their society of origin. In the past ten years, much has been written about the usage, the meaning and the implications of the concept of diaspora.[3] The criticism against Abner Cohen was that the term was a historically specific one.[4] The notion of Diaspora, first used and coined in the classical world has acquired great importance in the late twentieth century.[5] The intensity of international migration and the phenomenon of globalization, the imminent demise of the nation-state have been crucial to the creation of the current debate about diaspora. The arguments are also fueled by the ensuing interest in different theoretical approaches to nationalism and post-colonial studies. Looking at the future of globalization some scholars are revisiting the past, going beyond the paradigm of the nation-state, trying to date its origins, and even including the weight of human imagination in a field once constrained to archival research. Scholarship on diaspora trading networks, would have been entirely marginal and perceived as irrelevant in mainstream academic debates, be it ten years ago. The present and especially the future can now point to the problem of considering the nation as "natural" to historical discourse. As contemporary problems point the way beyond the nation-state, they demonstrate the need to change this parameter. Paradoxically it is visions of the future beyond the nation-state, that are now encouraging a revisiting of the past. The nation-state, once the ubiquitous model for historical thought has masked many elements, perhaps not least is the participation of outsiders or foreigners in state formation during Early Modern times. This is even reflected in very valuable studies that hoped to transcend the "national" category.

Philip Curtin, in a world-wide study of cross-cultural trade, argues for a clear dichotomy between host societies and outside trading groups: "The traders were specialists in a single kind of economic enterprise, whereas the host society was a whole society, with many occupations, class stratification and political divisions between the rulers and the ruled." Curtin, who first started the debate, makes clear with other passages that he sees trade Diaspora as exempt from political participation in their host societies.[6] He uses the term trade network and trade diaspora interchangeably and argues that these groups were only cross-cultural brokers helping to encourage trade between the host society and their own. He is also a pioneer in the second problem discussed here. In his discussion of trade networks in 1984 he is a pioneer for including European militarized diaspora within the same category as the Armenians, the Banians, and the Fukein Chinese.[7]

The term Diaspora first found in the Greek translation of the Bible, was once exclusively reserved for the Jews. It implied a forcible scattering as it is described in Deuteronomy (28:25). As Robin Cohen argues that the Old Testament also carried the message that "scattering to other land" constituted punishment, for breaking with tradition.[8] Soon it was applied to two more groups, the three classical Diaspora being the Jewish, the Armenian and the Greek. Today the term is used for nearly thirty different groups.[9] The Armenians are considered a classical Diaspora.[10] Based on the secondary scholarship available to him, Philip Curtin has argued that the Armenian trading diaspora was a self-contained and self-regulating body, a commercial organization divorced from political participation in state formation.[11]

The fact that the Armenians are perceived as a classical diaspora has played a significant role in enforcing this view. Even the best critic of this binary model conceived by Curtin, Sanjay Subrahmanyam still follows this pattern for the Armenians. He too has to rely on the usual secondary sources which see the Julfan Armenian as a foreign trade diaspora, autonomous under Persian rule, protected but not politically integrated or active. Subrahmanyam still concluded in his innovative study on the contribution of the Iranian merchant elite to the early state formation in Golconda, the Deccan and Thailand that: "that this does not mean either that the 'Iranian model' can be used as paradigmatic, or that it is one that does away entirely with the concept of diaspora community. Clearly the functioning of the Armenian community—significantly also the one chosen by Curtin to illustrate his theory—does correspond far more closely to the self regulated body, largely divorced from the world of politics . . ."[12] Nevertheless, despite his hesitation to include the Armenians, a diaspora community, in the model he finds for the Iranians, Subrahmanyam is the first to notice that an Asian trade diaspora, specifically the Iranians, participated in state-building.

My work has been on the Julfan Armenians in the silk trade in the seventeenth and eighteenth centuries.[13] New Julfa Armenians, mainly based in a suburb of the Persian capital of Isfahan, formed trading settlements, which spanned the globe from Narva, Sweden to Shanghai, China. They had been deported to the new capital of Isfahan by the Safavid monarch, Shah Abbas, in 1604. I have argued that the Julfan Armenians in Iran made both economic and political contributions to the governments of their host society and were part of its administration, as members of the Royal Household. They were in competition with the English East India Company and the VOC, who gained a minimal share in the trade. Their unusual success in Iran has been explained by platitudes and prejudices such as their Christianity, their hard work, and even by their avarice. My recent research on the Julfan Armenians has uncovered their clear participation in Safavid Iran's political economy. Their integration into the Safavid Household despite their Christianity, made them the financial wing of the Royal Household. Studying them contributes to a better understanding of the yet relatively unstudied Safavid Royal Household system. From the mid-sixteenth century on increasingly this was becoming a household of administrators who were converted Caucasian royal slaves.[14] It was never suspected that there could be a link between the Christian merchants, perceived as foreign by scholars, and the converted administrators. These royal merchants controlled the Iranian silk trade for half a century, although prior to their arrival in Iran, they already were the most renown silk traders on Ottoman markets.[15]

Vladimir Minorsky was the first to portray the New Julfan as an elite, a foreign bourgeoisie, autonomous and protected by the Safavids (1501–1722).[16] Although their economic role in Iran was clearly of tremendous import by all accounts, no official political links to the Safavid power structure were evident before the reading of three neglected Safavid edicts. These edicts, translated and published for the first time in, *The Shah's Silk for Europe's Silver*, demonstrate the direct participation of the Julfan elite in the Safavid political administration and their elevated political rank—one on par with their economic power. The New Julfan leader, Khwāja Nazar, was the *shāh's* banker and ran the Armenian organization of the silk trade. The leading families of New Julfa were in fact one of the pillars on which the organization of the Safavid Royal Household (*khāssa-yi sharifa*) rested. Their financial contribution was essential in more ways than one to shaping the history of Iran in the first half of the seventeenth century. The Royal Household relied heavily on the deportees of the Caucasus, some of them were even converted Julfan Armenians.[17] The mechanism of this political role is explored in *The Shah's Silk*,[18] where one of the major arguments is the contribution of this trade diaspora to Iran's centralization and state-building in the first half of the seventeenth century. They contributed both as administrators themselves and as financiers. It is interesting to note that at this time many prominent Iranian merchants were leaving Iran to emigrate to India, a land that was then viewed as a land of opportunity.[19] In Safavid Iran, wealthy landowners were also merchants, the successful curbing of their feudal power by the Safavids was a factor in their leaving with their surplus capital for other shores. The Safavid monarch's monopolization of the silk trade in 1619 and his integration of the Armenian merchants within the court was probably also a major reason why opportunities declined for local merchants in Iran. The revenues of silk were centrally collected under the responsibility of the head of the Julfan community, much of it went to the salaries of the army. At first the army was provided by the amirs, or feudal lords, and the Safavids were dependent on them The Caucasian administrator of the royal household, were paid salaries through a centralized mint system, much of the cash was brought in by the silk trade. There is direct financing of the administration by the Julfans and a communality of interest with the Caucasian administration that dominated the court and made it powerful for near half a century.[20]

Another recent study on the political economy of Iran in the seventeenth century, still argues, that the Armenians were a commercial bourgeoisie based upon Vladimir Minorsky, Edmund Herzig and others. The fallacious notion that there are no Safavid sources on economy persits in this argument.[21] Only Safavid edicts demonstrate their participation in polity.[22] Foreign company factors were not privy to a country's political mechanisms. There is, however, another major factor at work in disguising the Armenian political role in Iran:

that is, as demonstrated before, the general views held about trade diaspora. K. N. Chaudhuri postulates that the "trade diasporas," or settlements of a nation in diaspora, necessarily have a different outlook from merchants belonging to a nation, the assumption being that only the latter serve national interests.

This immediately begs the question: how do the Armenians in India and Iran fit into this schema? How did they differ from the European factors in India? Did the East India Companies serve national interest in the seventeenth century? Merchants and traders in this period conducted business through closely knit groups, irrespective of their location. In the groups considered, Jewish and Armenian merchants alone had no proper homeland to which they eventually hoped to return. Were the behavior and outlook of these particular members of a nation in diaspora likely to be very different from those traveling merchants with solid connections at home? According to Chaudhuri, the Armenians living in Kashgar, Delhi, and Hugli in the seventeenth century could point to their own suburb in Isfahan, the little town of Julfa on the far side of Zayandah-Rud. Was it a national home?

New Julfa, in Iran, was a second home, far from their original town of Julfa, which was burned to the ground. The creation of an entirely new calendar used in their world-wide silk trading network and dating from their settlement in Iran seems to indicate that they saw this new settlement as a new beginning. The titles held by their provost indicate that they saw themselves as a kingdom within a kingdom.[23]

When the Armenians settled elsewhere, did they serve the interests of their host provinces such as Gujarat, Bengal, or the Netherlands, Russia, or especially the interests of Safavid Iran? It seems clear that up to 1646, they served the Safavid and the organization under their provost over anything else. This changed, as they lost their status and privilege in Iran. They also, much later, contributed to the state-building efforts of Peter the Great, albeit in a smaller scale and as outsiders close to court circles. They received peerage, land and nobility in Russia, but they were never an entire wing of the court. Did they only serve the state building efforts of the Safavids, or those of Peter the Great? Or did they manifest "national" interests of their own, despite the absence of a homeland? Could it be that the merchants' sole aim, beyond simple survival, was the expedient pursuit of lucre, that they had no underlying political goals?

Trading Networks and National Interest

What then of national interest for the stateless Armenians? What were their goals beyond profit? Unlike many Early Modern trading networks which relied solely on the family as the unit of association, the New Julfans were organized in a much wider network under twenty two directors, four main families and one provost. Their municipal government was also their commercial association, and New Julfa was a unique Armenian city state, one with an autonomous jurisdiction under Safavid rule. All trials were sent to New Julfa even when started elsewhere, debts and other problems were centrally judged by the directors in reunions. Losses were absorbed in the way a joint company handled them although we have no indication that there was joint stock, nevertheless the central gathering of the profits of the trade is certain and clear in Safavid documents. Its provost was responsible for centrally gathering the gold and silver proceeds of the silk trade and depositing them into the *khassa* or royal household, we have clear documentation for this for two reigns. Surplus capital necessary to state formation was amassed by the Julfans for Iran. An administrative manual proves that the silver imported by the Armenians, once deposited in the royal household, served to pay the salaries of a new group of administrators, themselves deportees from the Caucasus.[24]

These administrators, the *ghulams* or slaves of the shah could attain very high ranks, even that of Grand Vizier, many of them were Muslim Armenians. The Julfans who remained Christian merchants were outsiders who didn't remain outside the political administration, they were in allegiance with the administrators of the court who were also of Caucasian origin. Both of them were formally attached to the *khassa* or royal household. The provost of New Julfa was so important that in 1629 at the enthronement of Shah Safi he was the second called in to congratulate him.[25] This role probably lasted until at least 1646, when a different balance of power might have diminished their role at court, but we have no clear indication as to when it ceased.

After losing their role in the administration of the Royal Household, the Armenians of New Julfa who already had a centralized system of commerce, formed their own company, and its capital and organization can be compared advantageously to that of the European companies. It has not been believed that Asian merchants, no matter how great their accumulated wealth, were capable of establishing a worldwide organization. The argument of wealth does not suffice when confronting orientalist scholarship, which argues for a lack of "rational organization" among the Asian merchants: "The peddler might have well possessed the habit of thinking rationally. But he had no possibility of making a rational calculation of his costs in a modern sense so long as the protection costs and the risk remained unpredictable and the market non-transparent."[26] The orientalist view contrasts them with the Europeans, who corresponded with a company's home base every few weeks, coupled with the argument that transport insurance and customs costs on the European side were predictable, presumably through an amalgamation of data which led to a transparency of the market. Given the difficulty that the Companies had establishing themselves in India and in Persia, it is arguable whether they had accurate knowledge of the market, as the author supposes. It is wrongly assumed that the Asian merchants only knew of the prices as they reached the markets, and that they had no planning or organization with which to analyze the market. There is clear proof to the contrary.[27]

There certainly was a "comprehensive and coordinated" organization for the Armenians; its headquarters were in New Julfa, a suburb of the capital of Safavid Iran. It had jurisdiction on other Julfans settled across the world from Paris to Tibet. As we have seen, the Armenians have a very important role in the economic and political history of Safavid Iran. Their integration was conscious policy by a dynasty that strove for absolutist power over many feudal strongholds. Nevertheless, as the economic agents of Safavid royal power in the first half of the seventeenth century, the Armenians, merchants and silk growers or simply taxable Christians, cannot be disassociated from the political economy and history of Safavid power in Iran. That they served Iran's interest is now established by documents, that they served their own national interest as they served Iran's is equally certain.

The trading organization of the New Julfans was so elaborate that, allied with the administrative role of the church, it served as an infrastructure for the diffusion and preservation of a common cultural identity, through the financing of scriptoria and presses and the diffusion of books in Armenian to remotest churches and diaspora. This form of support and diffusion was a role played by early states.[28] As such the trading network served Armenian interests well, be they financial, administrative, political and cultural. I have studied their financial support of the first Armenian printing presses elsewhere, but it remains one of the most important stages in forming a cultural canon that would later serve a national discourse.[29] The books were financed by merchant money and carried and diffused through their merchant network. This merchant network was instrumental in rebuilding the main churches of historic Armenia, and in financing the church.

It can be argued that their wealth and Safavid protection saved the Apostolic Church of Edjmiadzin from conversion to Catholicism. Therefore there is no question that while they served the state building aims of monarchs such as Peter the Great or the Safavids they also looked after their own ethno-national interests, interests that were well beyond immediate financial gain. The political autonomy they obtained in diaspora both in Lvov, Poland and New Julfa in Iran was due to their commercial skill. Their contribution as bankers to the king of Poland, or even to the Venetian Doge, gave them the autonomous jurisdiction common to trading diaspora as defined by Abner Cohen. The political aspects of this autonomy are very important. Nowhere, however, were they directly integrated in the administration of an early state as they were in Iran. Nowhere did they achieve the same wealth or success. In Venice and Poland the network was not entirely the Julfan one, although there were serious crossovers and links, both of these diaspora converted to Catholicism.

The question of serving national interests, is not a simple one for the Early Modern period—even when referring to the European Companies as serving nation-states. Traditional views contrast the Europeans, seen as peoples with homelands, to the Jews and Armenians in Diaspora. Yet Bruce Masters, quite exceptionally, classifies the English Levant company with trade diaspora: "The Armenians, the Sephardi Jews, and Syrian Christians, Catholics and otherwise, all represent trading diaspora in the sense of the term suggested by Curtin. To them might be added the English Levant Company factors, who supply an illustrative example of the metamorphosis of a trading diaspora, supported by the bonds of religion or ethnicity, to one built on starkly profit motives, the forerunner of the multinational corporation as it were."[30] He does not see it as serving national interest, or national interest as a bond in the Levant Company, rather profit is the binding element. He does not commit the usual error of seeing the companies as national ones serving the state. As for defining trade diaspora, we have already disagreed over Curtin's model for the Armenians of Julfa, who are, in the main, the ones discussed by Bruce Masters in Aleppo although he identifies other groups of Armenians trading there.

While the trade of the Sephardi Jews expelled in 1492 from Spain deserves further study, such as in the Ottoman Empire, some new light is being shed on specific communities of these Sephardi Jews, such as the very important one of Amsterdam. New studies contradict Curtin's model and Master's views on the Jews. A large group of the Jews exiled from Spain first settled in Portugal as New Christians after 1492. In the seventeenth century as the inquisition threatened even New Christians, they left for Holland. In Amsterdam, where, thanks to Protestantism, there was religious freedom from the inquisition, they slowly but surely returned to practicing Judaism. A masterful study of the Portuguese Jews of Amsterdam in this crucial century of state formation in the States General sheds light on their many endeavors. While this new study dismisses over-amplification of their commercial role, such as Braudel quoting a generalization that "it was only in imitation of the Jews who had taken refuge among them, and who had set up counting houses everywhere, that the Dutch began to set up their own and send their ships all over the Mediterranean."[31] It uncovers the many layers of their participation in Dutch society, many of which are political and go well beyond the purely commercial.

Some contributions are very important, such as the overwhelming contribution of the Portuguese Jews in the colonial settling of Brazil for the Dutch West India Company,[32] the introduction of sugar growing and the entire sugar production of Surinam, where they were the main settlers for the Dutch. There also was the quasi-monopolization of the import, manufacturing and distribution of chocolate, a new product, which like sugar, did not fall under established guild rules.[33] Perhaps even more strikingly, there is the direct the financing of William of Orange's conquest of England, as well as of his Irish wars. In this war for the throne of England, they played an active and direct political role as purveyors of food and equipment to the army. The Jewish firm Machado & Pereyra, which held investments from many prominent Portuguese Jews, was entirely responsible for horses and provisions to the Dutch army. The provisioning of William's Irish campaign against James, the Catholic contender to the throne of England, according to one source required at least twenty-eight bakers, 700–800 horses, and 300–400 wagons.[34]

Just as in Iran, where the Armenians and the Safavids had common interests against the Spanish, Portuguese and French Catholics, the Portuguese Jews found common interests with the Protestant Dutch against the Catholic powers of Europe. Both groups had their own ethno-national interests in common with the new states forming in Iran and the States General, both of which gave them religious freedom and a chance for participation. As the Jews helped the Dutch in their state-building, they rebuilt an identity that they had to hide for two centuries as New Christians. Much has been made of this community as the first community of Modern Jews, who nicknamed Amsterdam "Mokum" (from the Hebrew word for place) and made the Amsterdam-Jerusalem analogy.[35] Finding a second home, religious freedom, and prosperity are common parallels with the Armenians of New Julfa.

Among the Amsterdam Jews was also a prominent banking family, as important as the family of Nazar, head of the Julfans was in Iran. Although, unlike the Julfan Armenians, ten percent of Amsterdam's bankers were Jewish, the Suasso stand alone in their unparalleled wealth. Later, their house became the residence of the Queen of the Netherlands. Franciso Lopes Suasso lent the astronomical sum of 1.5 million Gulden to William of Orange in 1689 as he ascended the throne of England. Recently published figures of Portuguese Jewish trade shows a participation quite disproportionate with their number.[36] Even within the West India Company where their physical representation was no larger than 5 percent among the main investors, but their investment were very large; sufficiently large for them to have political clout. At their request the Dutch West India Company reprimanded Peter Stuyvesant, the governor of the New Netherlands for his anti-Jewish measures.[37]

In studying the Sephardi networks, as for the Armenians, kinship and religion are taken into account by scholars to explain network solidarity. For the European Companies would solidarity be a national one? The evident link between long-distance trade and the creation of surplus capital and state formation need not be stressed here. France, England, and the Dutch Republic were at different stages of state formation. The Dutch had just won their independence at the end of the sixteenth century. In their case, the commercial success of the Dutch East India Company and other trading groups and the formation of the Dutch Republic were parallel processes. Economic and political power in the Dutch Republic were in the same hands, and the City Council of Amsterdam was also entirely a group of merchants. The Dutch Republic, with its Calvinism and overt capitalism, seems the perfect example in support of Max Weber's thesis of the link between Protestantism and capitalism. Yet, as Sephardi Jewish participation clearly demonstrates, even in the most homogenous of European companies, there was no ethnic or religious uniformity to argue for such a thesis. Bruce Masters in including the English Levant Company in the category of diaspora traders, defines it as an ancestor of the multinational corporations, having only profit as an aim for solidarity. He may well have been the first not to be misled by the national names of these Companies. A brief discussion of three East India Companies, in the same period illustrates why one can argue that there is less difference than has been established between groups traditionally called trading diaspora and the "national" West and East India Companies who had a home society.

The three main European groups in question—the French, English, and Dutch, each had very different histories. The European Companies had in each case a different relationship with their governments. Oftentimes, their interests could even be at odds with the state. A striking instance is the assistance that the English East India Company provided the Persians in capturing Hormuz away from the Portuguese in 1622. At the very time they were fighting the Portuguese, the English Crown was hoping for a rapprochement with Lisbon and the Spanish Crown. The English Company's directors safeguarded their independence from the court, and from national interest. In contrast to the VOC and the Dutch West India Company which was run by the same group as ran the city council of Amsterdam, the English East India Company often acted as a state within a state. The aims and interests factors abroad were different from that of the Crown's. This form of conflict of interest has often been brought up for its significance for the issue of colonization by both the French and the English.

As for the contribution of the companies to early modern state building: although France and England both proclaimed to be mercantilist, they were avid to amass bullion from foreign trade for the state, to finance it in its new seventeenth-century incarnation as war machine. How much of this foreign company trade benefited state-building is the object of debate.[38] So pervasive was the practice of factors trading for their own interest, that the English East India Company had to formally allow it beginning in 1660. This clause is what permitted the great fortunes of Elihu Yale and Lord Bryce. European adventurers who had broken their ties with their initial national companies were common in India; they hired themselves out, and worked for rival companies or armies. Many of them also worked in the troops of local potentates. It seems they created a very poor image of the Europeans and were much disdained by the locals.[39] The great role played by some Frenchmen in the local armies and courts of some potentates would deserve further study.

The French East India Company, formed in 1664, had Louis XIV as a major investor and was under Colbert's direction. It was far more of a royal company, although many of its directors were not French. In France, most capital was generated by regional merchant organizations, and the failure of the French East India Company masks the success of other French merchants in Asia. The failing French East India Company was bailed out by the association of the merchants of St. Malo, a regional group which for a while became the new French East India Company. The other successful group in France were the merchants of Marseilles. They had actively resisted joining Colbert's royal Company, fearing that this centralization would destroy their commercial success. Indeed, French factors abroad had their hands tied as they did not have the independent authority of the English factor. Thus, the idea of national company with national interests in the French case is misleading, unless one merges royal and national interests. There is a difference in all three cases between the interests of the East India companies and their respective governments, although the Dutch come the closest to some unity of political and commercial purpose.

In the end, the perception that these commercial companies were "national" companies, which served the interest of nation states, is fallacious. All these fallacies arise from a nineteenth century writing of history as national histories. In the Early Modern period this nineteenth century model does not hold. Furthermore, the interests of participating individuals over and against those of the Company complicates the equation. Many of the men at the service of the European companies were out for their own fortune, some of them even working for rival companies to the detriment of their national companies. One well-known example is the Dutch man François Caron, of the reformed religion, born in Brussels. He was one of the first directors of the French East India Company, after years of work in the Dutch East India Company.[40] Hired by the French specifically for his knowledge and experience, he was naturalized French and given a patent by Louis XIV in 1665.[41] Next to him the other director was an Armenian, Marcara, a New Julfan was also naturalized French, which implied conversion to Catholicism for both directors. Colbert had recruited them from the two most successful groups in Asia in order to compete with the English and the Dutch.[42] In no way can one even invoke the idea of national interest in this early period. Things change considerably, however, in the middle of the eighteenth century, as for a number of highly debated reasons, the balance of power shifts in favor of Western dominance over Asia.[43]

Endnotes

1. Joseph R. Straye, *On the Medieval Origins of the Modern State,* Princeton, 1970.

2. Abner Cohen, "Cultural Strategies in the Organization of Trading Diaspora," in *L'Evolution du Commerce en Afrique de L'Ouest,* Claude Mesailloux, (ed.) Oxford, 1971, pp. 266–81.

3. Some of the best articles on the subject have been gathered in a hefty tome edited by Robin Cohen and Steven Vertovec. The volume has the advantage of gathering articles written in English on both sides of the Atlantic: *Migration Diasporas and Transnationalism,* The International Library of Studies on Migration, 9, Cheltenham, UK, 1999. Will be subsequently referred to as *MDT.* It contains many articles from the main scholarly journal devoted to the subject: *Diaspora a Journal of Transnational Studies,* Khachig Tölöyan, editor. The journal explores many theoretical approaches to the subject and is multidisciplinary. Its contents clearly demonstrate that the term Diaspora is now applied to near thirty groups.

4. Abner Cohen adds a footnote making it clear that he was criticized during the conference of 1969, published in 1971 see footnote 2 on p. 267.

5. Robin Cohen, in *MDT,* p. 267.

6. Philip Curtin, *Cross Cultural Trade in World History,* Cambridge, Cambridge University Press, 1984. Quotation from p. 5.

7. For a general discussion of the financing of monarchs and states by minorities see Anthony Reid "Entrepreneurial Minorities Nationalism and the State." in *Essential*

Outsiders: Chinese and Jews in the Modern Transformation of Southeast Asia and central Europe. Edited by Daniel Chirot and Anthony Reid. University of Washington Press, 1997, pp. 333–75.

8. Robin Cohen, *MDT,* p. 267.

9. See *DMT* and *Diaspora.*

10. The debate as to when the Armenians start being entirely in diaspora without a homeland has no place here, but the artificial date traditionally used by Armenian historiography has been the fall of the Crusading Kingdom of Cilicia in 1375. This small and fleeting kingdom, away from the lands of historic Armenia, was certainly not home to most of the Armenians. Another favorite date is 1071 the Seljuk invasion of historic Armenia, but the same holds true for this date as many Armenians already lived out of historic Armenia even by this date, for example many had left for Rome, Constantinople, and Egypt well before that.

11. Philip Curtin, Chapter 9, pp. 179–207.

12. Sanjay Subrahmanyam, "Iranians abroad: Intra Asian Elite Migration and Early Modern State Formation," *The Journal of Asian Studies,* Volume LI no. 2, 1992, pp. 340–363. Quotation from p. 359.

13. Ina Baghdiantz Mccabe, *The Shah's Silk for Europe's Silver: The Eurasian Silk trade of the Julfan Armenians in Safavid Iran and India (1590–1750).* University of Pennsylvania (Series in Armenian Texts and Studies), Scholar's Press, 1999.

14. Kathryn Babayan, "The waning of the Qizilbash: The spiritual and the temporal in seventeenth century Iran," unpublished dissertation, Princeton University, 1993.

15. Bruce Masters, "Merchant Diasporas and Trading 'Nation'," chapter three in *The Origins of Western Economic Dominance in the Middle East,* New York University Press: New York, 1988.

16. Vladmir Minorsky. *Tadhkirat al-Mulūk, a Manual of Safavid Administration,* Gibb Memorial Series, vol. 16, London, 1943.

17. Annex in Ina Baghdiantz McCabe (1999) and Chapter five.

18. Ina Baghdiantz McCabe (1999) Several Safavid edicts in the Appendix of the book are translated for the first time through the help of my colleague Kathryn Babayan of the University of Michigan.

19. See Sanjay Subrahmanyam (1992).

20. See Baghdiantz McCabe (1999) for a demonstration of this mutual dependence. Also explored in the forthcoming: *Slaves of the Shah; New Elites of Isfahan.* , Sussan Babaie, Kathryn Babayan, Ina Baghdiantz McCabe, Massumeh Farhad, I. B. Tauris, London, 2002.

21. Rudolph Matthee, *The Politics of Trade in Safavid Iran: Silk for Silver, 1600-1730* (Cambridge Studies in Islamic Civilization), Cambridge, 2000. R. Matthee despite his pertinent arguments against Eurocentric views and orientalist methods uses a good amount VOC documents and overlooks the Safavid documents related to Armenian trade and for the Armenians relies on the conclusions of Edmund Herzig "The Armenian Merchants of New Julfa, Isfahan: A study in Pre-modern Asian trade."

Ph.D. dissertation Oxford University, 1991, who had not yet the occasion to examine the pertinent Safavid edicts that spell out the Armenian participation in government. The book also proclaims its Weberian views, school which proclaims a difference between "pariah" traders and those capable of rational organization. The Armenians are viewed as court merchants and it is argued that it would be fallacious to even begin to compare them to the European companies.

22. These documents were published for the first time in the Annex of Baghdiantz McCabe, Ina *The Shah's Silk for Europe's Silver.* They were in the archives of All Saviour's at New Julfa, as they were difficult for me to translate alone, they were translated with the collaboration of Kathryn Babayan, and some of the translations are hers alone.

23. Baghdiantz McCabe (1999), see document in Annexe A, pp. 366–67.

24. See chapter 5 in Baghdiantz McCabe (1999) and annexes. Also explored in chapter 2 of the forthcoming: *Slaves of the Shah: New Elites of Isfahan*, Sussan Babaie, Kathryn Babayan, Ina Baghdiantz McCabe, Massumeh Farhad published by Tauris, London, 2002.

25. This extraordinary privilege of the provost of Julfa is told in a Dutch letter dated February 3, 1630, and is cited in foornote 12 in Matthee (2000), p. 121.

26. Niels Steensgaard, *Carracks, Caravans and Companies: The Structural Crisis in the European-Asian Trade of the Early Seventeenth Century* (Copenhagen, 1973), reprinted as *The Asian Trade Revolution of the Seventeenth Century: The East India Companies and the Decline of the Caravan Trade* (Chicago, 1973), p. 58. Quoted below was an accepted definition of Armenian trade:

> "A peddling trade: buying and selling in small quantities on continuous travels from market to market. But if Hovhannes's journal and the indirect evidence does not deceive us, a peddling trade that makes use of very sophisticated organizational forms such as commenda, bottomry, partnership and combined credit transfers by means of bills of exchange [*sic*] Nevertheless the ordinary entrepreneur operates on the peddlar level, and there is nothing in the sources to indicate the existence of comprehensive coordinated organizations—of an Armenian, Turkish or Persian version of Fugger, Cranfield or Tripp."

27. Steensgaard (1973) a, p. 30.

28. See Chapters 2 and 3 in Benedict Anderson, *Imagined Communities*, London, 1983.

29. "Merchant Capital and Knowledge: the Financing of Early Armenian Printing Presses by the Eurasian Silk Trade" in *Treasures in Heaven. Armenian Art Religion and Society.* Pierpont Morgan Library, New York, 1998. pp. 58–73.

30. Bruce Masters, p. 104.

31. Daniel M. Swetschinski, *The Reluctant Cosmopolitans: the Portuguese Jews of Seventeenth Century Amsterdam, London, 2000,* p. 108.

32. Ibid., pp. 114–17.

33. Swetschinski, pp. 126–29.

34. Ibid., p. 139.

35. See the song with the verse "Amsterdam she [is] Jerusalem!" in Swetschinski, p. 2.

36. For 1634 Vlessing finds that they controlled 4% to 8% of the entire trade that year and 10–20% of the Amsterdam trade excluding the companies. Quoted in Swetschinski, p. 113

37. Ibid., p. 117.

38. James Tracy, (ed.) *The Political Economy of Merchant Empires: State Power World Trade in 1350–1750,* Cambridge, 1991.

39. Philippe Le Tréguilly, Monique Morazé, *L'Inde et la France: Deux siècles d'histoire commune XVII iéme–XVIII ième siècles,* (Paris, CNRS, 1995), pp. 53–64.

40. François Caron is the author of a travel account in Dutch of which there is an English translation, unfortunately it contains little about the author which is typical of the style of the travel accounts of the time. It was compiled for the use of the Dutch East India Company for use in the Far East. See next note.

41. *A True description of the Mighty Kingdoms of Japan and Siam by François Caron and Joos Schouten* (London, 1663; reprint, London, 1935), xv.

42. On this see Ina Baghdiantz McCabe, chapter 10.

43. See Bruce Masters and also several relevant articles in James Tracey, 1991.

Palestinian and Jordanian Views of the Balfour Declaration

Alexander Bligh

If the Israeli-Palestinian conflict were to be analyzed in terms of three major contributory factors, it would focus on the following elements—all relating to former Mandatory Palestine: sovereignty, demography (or the denial of Jewish immigration to Palestine), and territory. Reflecting this line of thought, the root of the conflict is the right (or, denial of the right) of the Jewish people to establish a sovereign Jewish state in former Mandatory Palestine; the rejection of any Jewish presence, or establishment of a foothold through the purchase or reclamation of land in the region within a political and diplomatic context; and, finally, the issue of Jewish immigration to Palestine as part of the Arab repudiation of any significant Jewish presence in the land. The first international instrument to address these three issues was the Balfour Declaration. Most of the Arab world views the document as flawed, problematic, and, in fact, "worthy" of being discarded retroactively. The two main Arab players—the PLO and Jordan—each has its own individual reading of the document.

Even though the "national home" referred to in the Declaration was a far cry from an independent Jewish state, from the Arab perspective it became the source of the diplomatic struggle for Palestine. Many writers, academic and otherwise, still debate the true meaning of the document and the circumstances surrounding its publication on November 2, 1917.[1] However, in comparison to the overall Arab interpretation of this instrument, very little effort has been directed at trying to distinguish between different Arab points of view. This approach, which is the topic of this paper, is most relevant when studying the historical roots of the current political and diplomatic positions of the major Arab players in the Israeli-Palestinian conflict.

Throughout the years, it was obvious every November 2 how the document was interpreted in Israeli-administered territories. Even during relatively peaceful times, teenagers and youth would gather in public places and stone

Israeli passers-by. In a sense, the Israeli understanding mirrored the Arab view: while the latter were expressing their anger, the former were celebrating the first step on the road to the creation of a Jewish state. The bone of contention was the way both sides regarded the Declaration as a cornerstone in the building of a sovereign Jewish presence in Palestine. In spite of this shared view, both sides label the document differently, indicating their contrasting interpretations. From an Israeli and Western diplomatic historical point of view, it is referred to as the Balfour Declaration, i.e., the document constituted a strong statement of support for Jewish aspirations in Palestine, but did not in any way promise the Zionist movement the right to establish an independent state, as different from a "national home." Prior to the publication of President Wilson's 14 Points in early 1918, the term "national home" was in no way synonymous with an independent state. From the Arab perspective, the document is seen in a totally different light. The Arabic term used is "the Balfour *wa'd*,": translation—the Balfour Promise. The chasm between the two is obvious: typically, a declaration refers to a unilateral move, sometimes without any intention of implementing its contents. A promise, on the other hand, involves commitment. This conflicting terminology is above and beyond the common Arab reading of the "secret agreements" of World War One as a collection of contradictory British promises regarding the future of the entire Middle East, and especially Palestine, namely: the Declaration was issued by a body which had no moral authority to have an impact on the future of Palestine. Thus, the Declaration is viewed as the act of a foreign and illegitimate power in Palestine, which had transferred rights it did not possess to another illegitimate player, the Zionist movement.

However, the Arab perspective should not be regarded as a commonly held, unanimous view. Palestinians and Jordan do not attach the same significance to the Declaration. In spite of the continued use of the term *wa'd* both of the Arab parties in former Mandatory Palestine differ with regard to the centrality of the document in establishing present rights and claims over Palestine. The PLO, in its infancy, regarded it as an evil perpetrated on the Palestinian people. Jordan, which attached importance to the Hussein-McMahon correspondence, presented the British rejection of its implementation as the foundation of the injustice inflicted on the entire Arab cause.[2] Within the context of the Jordanian-held view, the issue of Palestine is only one aspect of a larger picture.

In its early stages on the international arena, the PLO needed to establish historical legitimacy for its activities—at the outset, diplomatic and political. Launching an all out frontal attack on the Hashemite Kingdom of Jordan, which at that time controlled the West Bank, would have been tantamount to public and political suicide. However, the presentation of the Balfour Declaration as the source of the trouble in Palestine was obviously acceptable to most Arabs. Consequently, during its first years, PLO spokesmen repeatedly referred to the Declaration and its illegitimacy. On the other hand, during his 46 years on the throne, King Hussein, the great grandson of sharif Hussein b. ʿAli, who provided the Arab party to the Hussein-McMahon correspondence in the context of the "secret agreements," preferred to evade the subject unless forced otherwise by political necessity.[3] This explains the PLO's frequent references to the document, and Hussein's infrequent ones, which nonetheless reveal the Hashemites' interpretation.

A comparison of both sides' public expressions reveals a substantial two-prong split: first, the significance of the Declaration regarding the development of the Arab-Israeli conflict; second, the entire issue of British legality in granting this promise. It must be remembered that whatever the British Government's original intention was in 1917, this document went on to serve as one of the legal sources for the British Mandate over Palestine and issues relating to its interpretation were used in delivering the 1922 White Paper leading, in effect, to the establishment of the Hashemite Kingdom.[4]

Throughout the years enough evidence has been accumulated to assess the significance of the Balfour instrument from the PLO's standpoint. As early as June 1964 the Palestinian National Council approved the first version of the Palestine National Charter,[5] which included Article 18: "The Balfour Declaration, the Mandate System and everything based on the two are considered fraudulent. Jewish claims of historical and spiritual ties to Palestine are not substantiated in history and have no basis for statehood. As a divine religion, Judaism is not a nationality with an independent existence. Furthermore, the Jews are not one single, autonomous people: they are citizens of the various countries to which they belong." This text, stating the centrality of the Balfour Declaration to the Palestinian cause, was further modified at the Fourth Palestinian National Council, which met in Cairo, July 10–17, 1968 and adopted a new version. The new text alludes to the Declaration directly in Article 20 and indirectly in Article 6.[6] Article 20 states: "The Balfour Declaration and the Mandate Instrument, and all their consequences, are hereby declared null and void. The claim of historical or spiritual links between the Jews and Palestine is neither in conformity with historical fact nor does it satisfy the requirements for statehood. Judaism is a revealed religion; it is not a separate nationality, nor are the Jews a single people with a separate identity; they are citizens of their respective countries." In Article 6, it is written: "Jews who were normally resident in Palestine up to the beginning of the Zionist invasion are Palestinians." The resolutions of this Palestine National Council provide the official explanation of the term "the beginning of the Zionist invasion," i.e., "the aggression against the Palestinian nation and its land began with the Zionist invasion of Palestine in 1917. It then follows that elimination of all remnants of the Zionist invasion calls for their removal from the source, and not only since the June 1967 war."

Central as they may be, the number of references to the Declaration has declined throughout the years. Why? With the increased legitimacy of the PLO and its recognition by Arab countries, the non-aligned camp, Europeans and finally the US and Israel in the Oslo accords, the need to emphasize the historical injustice perpetrated on the Palestinians gradually dissipated as ongoing international acceptance of the Palestinian cause helped to rectify the wrongs of the Balfour Declaration. Thus, there was no reference to the Balfour "promise" in a document bearing such significance as the Palestinian Declaration of Independence, which was approved by the Palestine National Council at its Nineteenth Session in Algiers on November 15, 1988.[7]

In retrospect, the Balfour Declaration should be studied for its historical merits and not as a platform for current political activity. In this light, three main lines of reference to the Declaration emerge. First, it served as part of the international legitimacy for the Mandatory Charter over Palestine, the annulment of the Declaration affects documents stemming from it in one way or another. Accordingly, if it had no validity whatsoever, then the Mandatory Charter was equally meaningless. Consequently, several articles should be considered null and void. Article 2, for example, states: "The Mandatory shall be responsible for placing the country under such political, administrative and economic conditions as will secure the establishment of the Jewish national home, as laid down in the preamble, and the development of self-governing institutions, and also for safeguarding the civil and religious rights of all the inhabitants of Palestine, irrespective of race and religion." It is written in Article 5, "The Mandatory shall be responsible for seeing to it that no Palestine territory shall be ceded, or leased to, or in any way placed under the control of the Government of any foreign power."

In denying the Mandatory power any historical or legal rights, these articles allude to the real villains apart from the British: the Zionist movement, clearly the main benefactor of this instrument, and the would-be Hashemite Kingdom which was to receive parts of Palestine. This was contrary not only to the basic Arab understanding that there was no legal basis for issuing the Declaration but that the British violated their own illegal commitment embodied in

Article 5 by dividing Palestine and handing over parts to the Hashemites within British-Hashemite dealings during the war. This line of reasoning is a jigsaw of illegality concerning the handing over of Palestine to the Zionists and the Hashemites: its rationale is the Balfour Declaration. Even though the national emblems used by the Palestinians usually do not include the East Bank of the Jordan River, namely: the present day Hashemite Kingdom, the 1970–71 civil war in Jordan represented a PLO interest in taking over this territory. The resistance to the Balfour Declaration and its later interpretations as presented in the 1922 White Paper and the Mandatory Charter provide the formal validation of the same policy claiming the East Bank.

Second, in the view of the PLO, the Balfour Declaration was the first international document to grant a degree of international recognition to Jewish political rights in Palestine. Thus, the beginning of the Palestinian-Zionist struggle over Palestine dates back to 1917 since at that time a foreign body, Great Britain, granted rights it did not possess to another foreign body, the Zionist movement at the expense of the indigenous Arab inhabitants of Palestine. In this sense, it marked the beginning of the diplomatic cleavage between the Arab and Jewish sides. Therefore, denying the British the right to issue the declaration is only the first step in rejecting all other international instruments, which have ignored Palestinian rights and have served to underscore Zionist control over major international powers.

Third, beyond the perception of the 1917 declaration as the start of the diplomatic conflict, the year 1917 is also noted as the launch of the "Zionist invasion" of Palestine. This is due to the fact that the Declaration was addressed to the Jewish community at large and led to a confrontation between world Jewry and the Arabs of Palestine. Simply stated, in addition to all of its other shortcomings, the Declaration serves indirectly as a license to Jews to immigrate to Palestine. Without immigration, no Jewish entity would ever have existed in Palestine. This explains why the Declaration has been perceived as international confirmation of the illegal Jewish presence in Palestine. Furthermore, without the Declaration, Jewish immigration would not have received the international recognition it has enjoyed throughout the years.

This analysis clarifies the PLO view of the Balfour Declaration as the source of the diplomatic, and later—military—conflict between the Zionist movement and the Arabs of Palestine. However, the Jordanian historical reading of the conflict does not concur. The Hashemite Kingdom's most authoritative spokesman, the late King Hussein, did not share the PLO's view of the Balfour Declaration as central to the conflict over Palestine. Although he defined his relationship with Israel until 1994 as one of conflict, Hussein distinguished between two eras of confrontation before 1948 and after that. The first—the clash with Zionist objectives in Palestine has been the longest, in comparison with all Arab players: the Hashemite struggle against Zionism[8] dates back to the Great Arab Revolt in 1916. This predates the Palestinians' view of 1917 as the start of the struggle. Regarding illegal promises made to the Jews, the Hashemites' understanding is that the conflict began with Britain's broken commitments to the sharif Hussein b. Ali in the Hussein-McMahon correspondence of 1915–16. The difference, however, is not only chronological, but also conceptual. Palestinians repudiate all promises made to any Arab/Palestinian party. For the Jordanians, the last binding document regarding Palestine was the correspondence—making the Balfour Declaration a detour on a road already taken. The difference in terms of Arab political legitimacy is also clear: from the Jordanian standpoint, the existence of Jordan is no more than small compensation for the broken promises of World War One, whereas for Palestinians, neither the Hashemite Kingdom nor Israel can claim legitimacy based on any document dating back to World War One.

Still another Palestinian-Jordanian discrepancy is the start of the conflict. For the former, it began with the 1917 Declaration; for the latter, it began only in 1948, making the Declaration almost meaningless. What's the reason for this gap? The Palestinian stance is very clear: for them, the conflict with the Zionist movement is generations-old, with the PLO assuming responsibility for its continuance, thus overruling the diplomatic basis for the existence of the state in former Mandatory Palestine. The Jordanian vantage point is far more complex: the late King Hussein tried to define the conflict with Israel in territorial terms and ignore the issue of legitimacy—as the formal basis for Jordan and Israel is basically similar. He therefore referred to the correspondence, but downplayed the importance of the Declaration. For Hussein, the correspondence had a territorial dimension, whereas the Declaration was no more than a diplomatic instrument. This explains why the United Nations General Assembly Resolution 181 of November 29, 1947 ("The Partition Resolution") was the first diplomatic document that Jordan regarded as the basis for settlement in former Mandatory Palestine. The resolution referred only to the territory west of the Jordan River, omitting the area that had become the territory of the Hashemites. In adhering to this approach, Hussein labeled all pre-1947 documents as having no relevance to questions of rights and legitimacy in former Mandatory Palestine. However, the PLO's success in directing attention to the rights of the Palestinians presented Hussein with a formidable challenge before 1974, when he claimed some degree of representation of the Palestinians. While speaking of the correspondence, he would often mention that the Great Arab Revolt, the outcome of the correspondence, was intended to guarantee the rights of the Palestinians. The Declaration and its exploitation by the PLO as a diplomatic tool against Hussein posed a problem for the King who was concerned about his own page in the book of world history. The problem was not a simple one: on the one hand, it theoretically raised the question of his dynasty's legitimacy, and, on the other, it rendered him unable to criticize the British for their role in World War One, in light of their assistance to the Hashemite Kingdom in later years. This dilemma was in direct contradiction to the position of the PLO. The organization regarded itself as a member of the non-aligned camp—free from any pro-British or pro-Western considerations and regarding the Declaration as an imperialistic tool used by the enemies of the indigenous people of the area.

When the Declaration is read through the eyes of the PLO and Jordan, a major discrepancy becomes clear: in emphatically rejecting the Declaration and the agreements in its wake, for the PLO the only way for justice to be done in the Middle East is to start anew—to put all issues relating to Israel on the table: sovereignty, land and immigration. For Jordan, which neither rejects nor adopts the Declaration, the formal conflict over Palestine between independent entities only began as late as 1948. Anything prior to that date merely represented or symbolized Zionist objectives in Palestine along with subsequent British reaction, having no more significance or substance than that.

Endnotes

1. See for example: Geoffrey Wheatcroft, "[Op-ed:] Israel's Uneasy State," *New York Times*; New York; Sep 14, 1997; "Letters to the Editor: A Search in History For Arabs' Enmity," *Wall Street Journal*; New York, N.Y.; March 14, 2001; "Letters to the Editor: Palestinian Statehood: It Is Time," *Wall Street Journal*; New York, N.Y.; May 14, 1999.

2. Hussein's interview, *The Independent*, London, February 7, 1991.

3. *al-Majmu'ah al-Kamilah li-Khutab Jalalat al-Malik al-Husayn bin Talal al-mu'azzam* (in Arabic) [the full collection of HM King Husayn b. Talal's speeches], [Amman: 1985?], vol. 3. 357; Amman Home Service in Arabic, September 15, 1971, *FBIS*, September 16, 1971, *BBC*, September 17, 1971; *Time*, January 23, 1978; *al-Anbaa* Kuwait, September 6, 1988; Press conference, May 30, 1989, Amman Domestic Service in Arabic, May 30, 1989, *FBIS*, June 1, 1989.

4. League of nations. Mandate for Palestine. London, 1922; The Avalon Project at the Yale Law School, http://www.yale.edu/lawweb/avalon/avalon.htm.

5. Munazammat al–Tahrir al-filastiniyah, *al-Mithaq al-Qawmi al-Filastini*. [Bayrut], 1964.

6. English translation—Leila S. Kadi, B*asic Political Documents of the Armed Resistance Movement*, Beirut: PLO research center (1969), 131–142; Second version of the English translation—Zuhair Diab (ed.) *International Documents on Palestine*. 1968, Beirut: The Institute for Palestine Studies (1971), 393–5.

7. http://www.palestinegd.fi/stat.html

8. PRO/FCO17/830/1/NEJ26/1/April 23, 1969, Hussein's Speech before the Royal Institute of International Relations, London; September 15, 1971; *BBC*, May 16, 1978; *al-Hawadith*, April 13, 1979; *US News and World Report*, March 15, 1982; *L'Espresso*, May 23, 1982; Amman Home Service in Arabic, January 10, 1983 speech, *FBIS*, January 11, 1983; Amman Home Service in Arabic, November 21, 1983, *BBC*, November 23, 1983; Same speech: *FBIS*, November 22, 1983; *al-Ra'i, al-Dustur*, separation speech, August 1, 1988.

Standards of Living in East and West: England and Egypt Before and After the Black Death

Stuart J. Borsch

Historians of Western Europe have long been familiar with the argument that the Black Death brought about a redistribution of income down the social scale.[1] Nowhere has this outcome been more clearly demonstrated than in England, where a relative abundance of archival sources has allowed for a closer scrutiny of the 150 years following the Black Death.[2] Over thirty years ago, Miskimin, Lopez, and Udovitch published a collaborative article entitled "England to Egypt, 1350–1500: Long Term Trends and Long Distance Trade."[3] Among other things, this article explored the comparative impact of depopulation on different sectors of the economies of England, Italy, and Egypt. As part of his study of Egypt, Udovitch observed that wages increased in the lower stratum of urban society after the plagues. At the same time, he noted that the prices of agrarian goods declined. His arguments suggested that Egypt's urban survivors, like those of England, enjoyed an enhanced purchasing power in terms of agricultural produce. Udovitch's conclusions were based entirely on the pioneering work of Eliyahu Ashtor, who, for a long time, was the one-man machine for the economic history of the Middle East. Ashtor argued forcefully that prices and wages in Egypt had followed the generalized pattern of Western Europe.[4] Ashtor's analysis of prices was fairly comprehensive for the fourteenth century, but relatively sparse for the fifteenth century (given the availability of source material).[5] Ashtor's study of wages was compiled fifty years ago and never updated with new material. His analysis of the data for wages contains some conspicuous errors.[6]

In this article, I will use new material that I have gathered from the Ministry of Religious Endowments in Cairo. The archives of the Ministry contain foundation deeds (*waqfiyyat*) for a variety of different establishments: ranging from mosques, "universities" (*madrasas*), and hospitals to small elementary schools for the Qur'an (*kuttabs*) and public fountains. The waqfiyyat vary in nature from purely charitable donations (*khayri waqf*) to "donations" whose revenues went to the family of the donor, reverting to purely charitable purposes only upon the death of all of the descendants of the family (*ahli waqf*).[7] These archives contain both prices and wages that serve as a vital supplement to the existing material noted in the chronicles of the fourteenth and fifteenth century.[8] In the case of wages, they are a vital source of data. Chronicles give only scant anecdotal references to workers' incomes, and compiling of these references is made problematic by the vastly different categories of employment that do not hold up well for comparison.[9]

New data from the archives, coupled with some of Ashtor's reliable statistics and Boaz Shoshan's compiled price tables for the fifteenth century, presents us with an entirely different picture for Egypt.[10] Urban wages, far from increasing, plunged dramatically after the epidemics. Agrarian prices, rather than decreasing, rose significantly. Egypt's lower-stratum urban survivors, far from enjoying an enhanced standard of living, were confronted with dramatically reduced purchasing power in the wake of catastrophic plague deaths.[11]

The chain of events that led to the disparities in income was both complicated and protracted. Just a few of the main features will be outlined here. The driving force lay primarily in the agrarian sectors of the two economies. England and Egypt had roughly equivalent levels of population before the onset of the Black Death, and suffered equally devastating losses of population from the epidemics.[12] The two countries experienced a severe urban and rural labor shortage in the wake of the epidemics.[13] The ruling elite in both regions attempted to contain the demands of scarce labor by holding wages down and keeping rents stable.[14]

England's aristocracy, via the Statutes of Labor and other measures, tried to restrict rural mobility and oppose the demands of scarce labor.[15] However, landlords were strongly connected to their hereditary and localized estates.[16] Individual concern over revenue prevailed over employer unity in the labor market.[17] Like a weak cartel, cheaters emerged in the system, offering lower rents and higher wages. The cheaters eventually predominated and competition for labor became the norm in the fifteenth century.[18] The manorial system in England, already on the decline, collapsed. In order to bolster their revenues, landlords were forced to direct their efforts toward reinvestment of their incomes, diversified cropping for the market, and convertible husbandry, rather than relying on surplus extraction from rural labor.[19] Villeins in turn benefited from simpler rental contracts, typically copyhold leases.[20] Peasants were thus able to make more rational decisions concerning their rural leases, decisions that also led them to diversify production, intensify convertible husbandry, and reinvest profits into their landholdings.[21] The surplus of land facilitated this process, as it allowed farmers with small plots of land to increase their holdings, utilize more draft animals for traction and manure for fertilizer, and increase fallow time. Formerly marginalized landless workers were able to acquire leases and enter the agrarian marketplace.[22] All of these changes led to efficiency gains in the agricultural sector, which in turn led to higher per-capita output and greater disposable incomes.[23] A positive feedback loop rippled through England's economy. Augmented demand resulting from the increase in disposable incomes allowed other landless workers to produce for the market via rural industry.[24] Although some peasants fled the countryside at various times following the Black Death, the general trend was for peasants to stay on the land, reducing the pressure on workers in the urban marketplace.[25] Laborers, both urban and rural, benefited from these changes, reflected in lower agricultural prices and higher wages, which translated into dramatically enhanced purchasing power.[26]

In Egypt, the ruling elite succeeded where England's had failed. The system of urban-centered absentee landlordism, scattered estates, and short-term prebends, translated into a lack of long-term interest in individual estates. The lack of individual long-term concern over estate revenue allowed the decentralized factions of landholders to present a united front in the face of scarce labor.[27] In the wake of depopulation, this system proved disastrously vulnerable and Egypt's elite scored a dramatically Pyrrhic victory. The tragic consequences affected not only the lower stratum of society, but also the economy of Egypt as a whole. Landlords were able to hold official rents (*kharaj*) at a stable level.[28] Furthermore, in the majority of cases the holders of prebends (*muqtʿis*) were able to raise rents by relying on webs of irregular extractions similar to those that had prevailed in England before the Black Death.[29] The economic distress caused by these extractions (*mudafat* and *diyafa* in Arabic, *consuetudines non taxatas* in Latin) combined with the chaos that resulted from a destabilized currency, induced peasants to flee from their holdings.[30] Facing harsh conditions in the countryside, many resorted to urban flight, where they replenished the ranks of otherwise scarce urban labor.[31] As rural flight and deteriorating rural conditions made the situation in the countryside worse, Egypt faced a negative feedback loop that induced more and more peasants to flee to Cairo and other cities.[32] Over time, prices for staple foods increased, while the pressure of incoming peasants on urban areas, in the context of a decaying agrarian economy, forced wages down. Per-capita income dropped; purchasing power for wage earners declined precipitously.[33]

The graph that follows balances a set of prices for wheat from 1300 to 1350 with a matching set from 1440 to 1490. The same matching time periods

Price of 1 Liter of Wheat in Grams of Silver

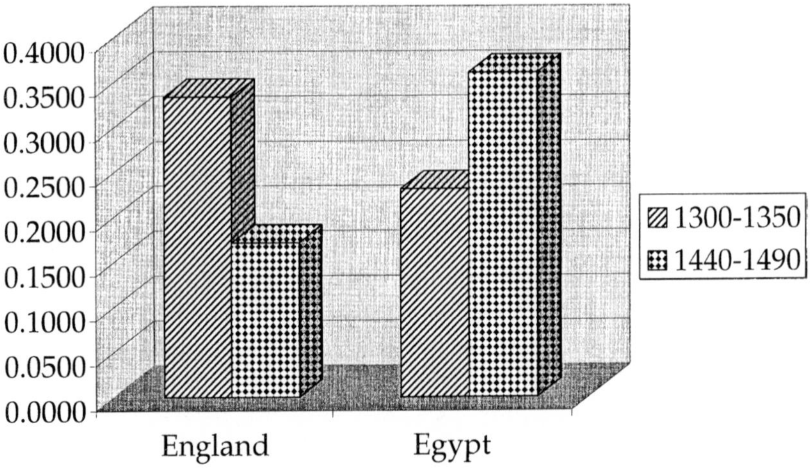

are used for wages. The principle objective is to demonstrate the long-term effects of depopulation. Two periods of equal length bear the most consistent possible measure for a comparison and fifty years serves an optimal fit for these two fixed spans of time.[34]

While it is more difficult to harmonize two data sets of wages for the same periods (1300–1350 and 1440–1490) a few roughly equivalent categories will serve to provide a general picture. The contrast is striking. Wages in England rose significantly.[35] Wages in Egypt declined precipitously.[36] The most telling index for the purposes of comparison is the purchasing power of wages in terms of an agrarian commodity. Wheat is used here, but other staple food crops would yield even more dramatically contrasting results.

The Black Death had vast repercussion on all of the societies it touched. Beyond Western Europe, the socioeconomic effects remain poorly understood. The disparity in prices, wages, and purchasing power shown here vividly demonstrates how depopulation from the Black Death worked in contrasting ways. A comparison between Egypt and England is particularly instructive, as the economies moved in opposite directions in almost every sphere of activity. Many areas of the Old World, equally affected by the Black Death remain untouched by economic historians. Further research, particularly comparative research with the heavily trammeled area of Western Europe, promises rich empirical rewards for scholars attempting to understand this event that was "a random occurrence in history and almost unique."[37]

Wages in Egypt (1300-1350. 1440-1490)

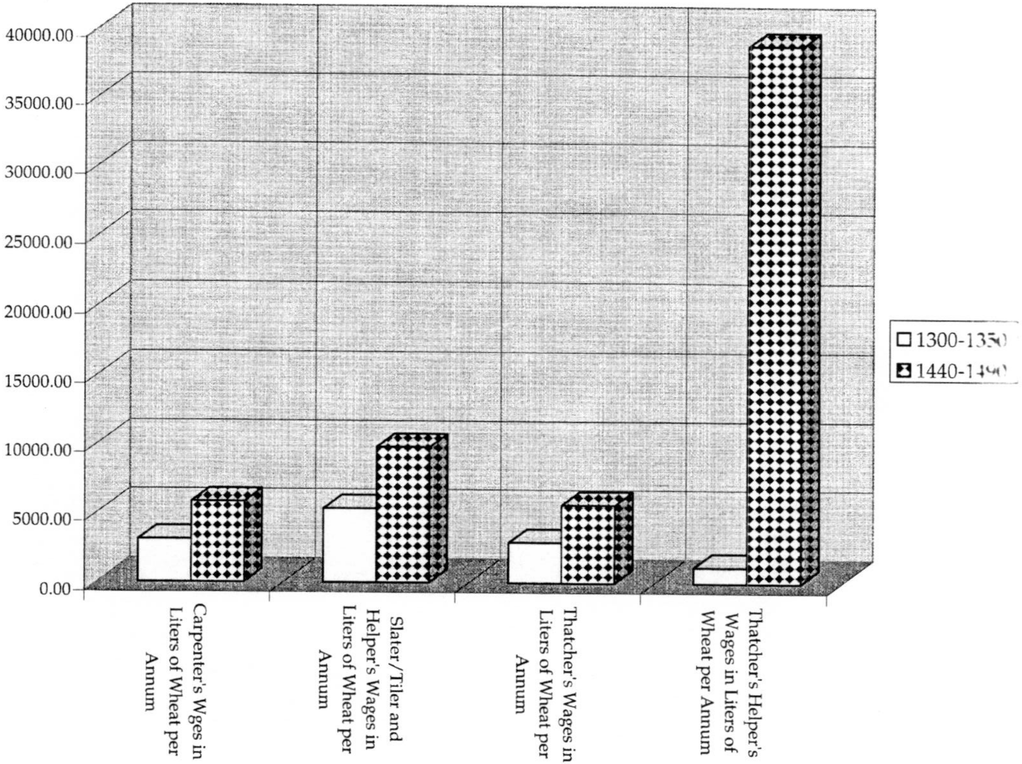

Wages in England (1300–1350. 1400–1490)

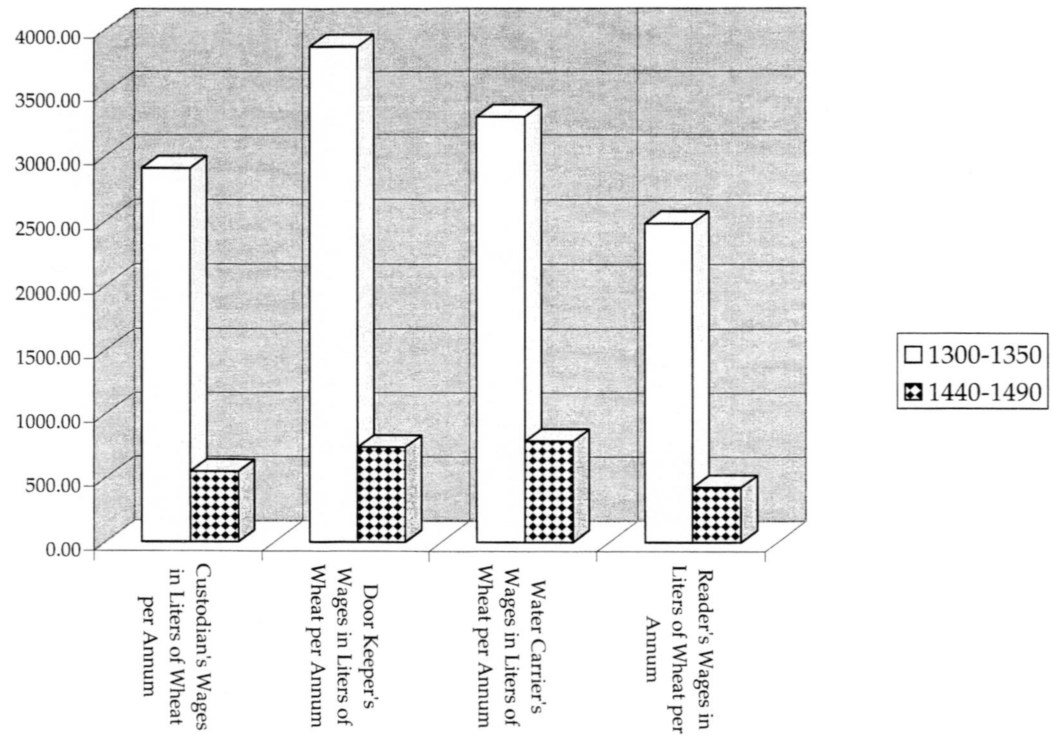

Average of 4 Wages in Liters of Wheat per Annum for England

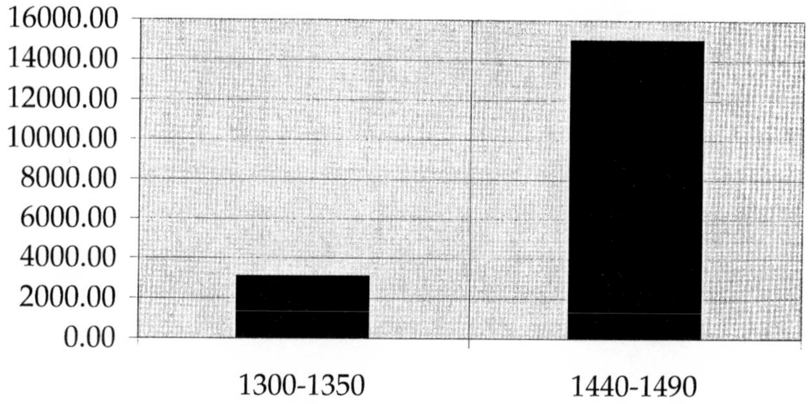

Average of 4 Wages in Liters of Wheat per Annum for Egypt

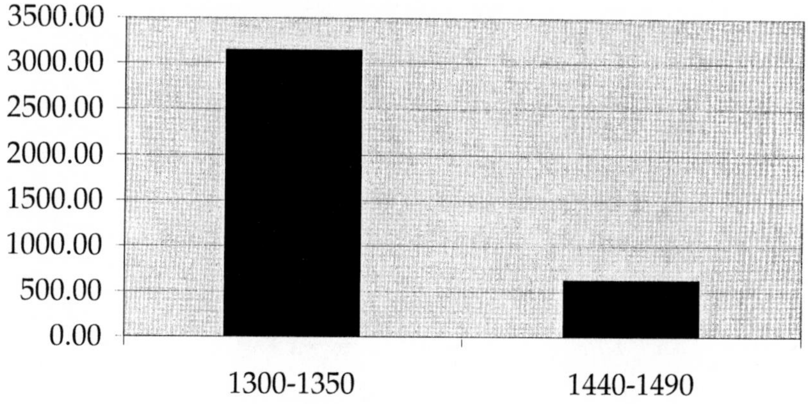

Year C.E.	Season	Price of Wheat in Dirhams Nuqra per Ardabb	Price of Wheat in Dinars Mithqal per Ardabb	Price of Wheat in Grams Silver per Ardabb	Price of 1 Liter of Wheat in Grams of Silver	Price of Wheat in Grams of Gold per Ardabb	Price of 1 Liter of Wheat in Grams of Gold
1300	*	17	1	33.66	0.2	4.25	0.03
1300	*	14	0.82	27.72	0.17	3.49	0.02
1300	Jan	14.5	0.73	28.71	0.17	3.08	0.02
1300	Fall	20	1	39.6	0.24	4.25	0.03
1300	Spring	27	1.35	53.46	0.32	5.74	0.03
1300	Summer	20	1	39.6	0.24	4.25	0.03
1300	Fall	20	1	39.6	0.24	4.25	0.03
1300	Fall	15	0.75	29.7	0.18	3.19	0.02
1303	Fall	40	2	79.2	0.48	8.5	0.05
1303	Fall	25	1.25	49.5	0.3	5.31	0.03
1306	*	20	0.5	39.6	0.24	2.13	0.01
1306	*	40	0.5	79.2	0.48	2.13	0.01
1307	Fall	50	2.5	99	0.6	10.63	0.06
1309	Fall	50	2.5	99	0.6	10.63	0.06
1317	*	2	0.1	3.96	0.02	0.43	0
1324	Jan	10	0.25	19.8	0.12	1.06	0.01
1324	Jan	17	0.43	33.66	0.2	1.81	0.01
1326	*	5.5	0.28	10.89	0.07	1.17	0.01
1328	Jan	13	0.65	25.74	0.16	2.76	0.02
1328	Jan	17	0.85	33.66	0.2	3.61	0.02
1336	Feb	15	0.75	29.7	0.18	3.19	0.02
1336	Feb	50	2.5	99	0.6	10.63	0.06
1336	Dec	40	2	79.2	0.48	8.5	0.05
1337	Winter	9	0.45	17.82	0.11	1.91	0.01
1338	Spring	20	1	39.6	0.24	4.25	0.03
1341	May-Jun	15	0.75	29.7	0.18	3.19	0.02
1341	May-Jun	30	1.5	59.4	0.36	6.38	0.04
1342	Jan	6	0.55	11.88	0.07	2.32	0.01
1343	Fall	10	0.5	19.8	0.12	2.13	0.01
1343	Fall	20	1	39.6	0.24	4.25	0.03
1346	May	55	2.75	108.91	0.66	11.69	0.07
1346	June	30	1.5	59.4	0.36	6.38	0.04
1346	Sep	35	1.75	69.3	0.42	7.44	0.05
1346	Sep	55	2.75	108.91	0.66	11.69	0.07
Raw Average		24.32	1.15	48.16	0.29	4.9	0.03
Average with 1 Standard Deviation		19.3	0.9	38.21	**0.23**	3.82	**0.02**

Year C.E.	Season	Price of Wheat in Dirhams Nuqra per Ardabb	Price of Wheat in Dinars Mithqal per Ardabb	Price of Wheat in Grams of Silver per Ardabb	Price of 1 Liter of Wheat in Grams of Silver	Price of Wheat in Grams of Gold per Ardabb	Price of 1 Liter of Wheat in Grams of Gold
1440	January	300	1.05	35.17	0.21	3.68	0.02
1440	February	330	1.16	38.69	0.23	4.05	0.02
1440	March	225	0.79	26.38	0.16	2.76	0.02
1444	April-May	200	0.7	23.45	0.14	2.46	0.01
1449	June-July	300	1.05	35.17	0.21	3.68	0.02
1449	July-Aug	290	1.02	34	0.21	3.56	0.02
1449	Aug-Sep	400	1.4	46.89	0.28	4.91	0.03
1449	October	600	2.11	70.34	0.43	7.37	0.04
1450	Feb-Mar	800	2.81	93.79	0.57	9.82	0.06
1450	Jun-Jul	500	1.75	58.62	0.36	6.14	0.04
1450	Aug-Sep	650	2.28	76.2	0.46	7.98	0.05
1451	April	900	3.16	105.51	0.64	11.05	0.07
1451	Aug	900	3.16	105.51	0.64	11.05	0.07
1451	Sep	900	3.16	105.51	0.64	11.05	0.07
1452	Jan-Feb	800	2.5	83.53	0.51	8.75	0.05
1452	Apr-May	400	1.25	41.77	0.25	4.38	0.03
1352	Nov-Dec	320	1	33.41	0.2	3.5	0.02
1456	Feb	270	0.84	28.19	0.17	2.95	0.02
1456	Aug	260	0.81	27.15	0.16	2.84	0.02
1456	Dec	470	1.12	37.39	0.23	3.92	0.02
1459	Nov	300	0.71	23.87	0.14	2.5	0.02
1462	July	270	0.85	28.5	0.17	2.99	0.02
1462	July	450	1.42	47.51	0.29	4.98	0.03
1462	August	350	1.11	36.95	0.22	3.87	0.02
1464	Mar-Apr	360	1.14	38	0.23	3.98	0.02
1465	June	350	1	33.41	0.2	3.5	0.02
1466	Jan	420	1.2	40.1	0.24	4.2	0.03
1466	Feb	600	1.71	57.28	0.35	6	0.04
1466	March	540	1.54	51.55	0.31	5.4	0.03
1466	April	1000	2.86	95.46	0.58	10	0.06
1466	May	350	1	33.41	0.2	3.5	0.02
1468	Jan	500	1.43	47.73	0.29	5	0.03
1468	May	600	1.7	56.8	0.34	5.95	0.04
1468	Jun-Jul	700	2	66.83	0.41	7	0.04
1468	August	750	2.14	71.5	0.43	7.49	0.05
1468	Sep	900	2.57	85.87	0.52	9	0.05
1468	Oct	400	1.14	38.09	0.23	3.99	0.02
1468	Oct	900	2.57	85.87	0.52	9	0.05
1468	Nov	900	2.57	85.87	0.52	9	0.05
1468	Dec	900	2.57	85.87	0.52	9	0.05
1469	Mar	600	1.7	56.8	0.34	5.95	0.04
1469	April	600	1.71	57.28	0.35	6	0.04
1469	Jun-Jul	1000	2.86	95.46	0.58	10	0.06
1469	Aug-Sep	1350	3.86	128.88	0.78	13.5	0.08
1470	July	850	2.28	76.18	0.46	7.98	0.05
1472	Apr-May	350	1	33.41	0.2	3.5	0.02
1484	Aug-Sep	400	1	33.41	0.2	3.5	0.02
1486	Oct	1000	2.5	83.53	0.51	8.75	0.05
1486	Nov	1100	2.75	91.88	0.56	9.63	0.06
1487	Aug-Sep	1200	3	100.24	0.61	10.5	0.06
Average with 1 Standard Deviation		596.1	1.78	59.48	**0.36**	6.23	**0.04**

Wheat Prices in England (1300–1350, 1440–1490)

Year C.E.	Price of Wheat in Shillings per Quarter	Price of Wheat in Pence per Liter	Price of 1 Liter of Wheat in Grams of Silver	Price of 1 Liter of Wheat in Grams of Gold
1300-10	5.37	0.22	0.3	0.02
1310-20	7.94	0.33	0.44	0.03
1320-30	6.9	0.29	0.38	0.03
1330-40	5.24	0.22	0.29	0.02
1340-47	4.88	0.2	0.27	0.02
Average	6.07	0.25	0.33	0.03
1440-50	4.93	0.2	0.15	0.01
1450-60	5.63	0.23	0.17	0.02
1460-70	5.6	0.23	0.17	0.02
1470-80	5.76	0.24	0.17	0.02
1480-90	6.85	0.28	0.2	0.02
Average	5.75	0.24	0.17	0.02
Percent Change	5%	5%	49%	39%

Wages in England (Carpenter and Slater/Tiler, 1300–1350, 1440–1490)

England Year C.E.	Carpenter's Wages in Pence per Day	Carpenter's Wages in Pence per Annum	Carpenter's Wages in Grams of Silver per Annum	Carpenter's Wages in Grams of Gold per Annum	Slater /Tiler and Helper's Wages in Pence per Day	Slater /Tiler and Helper's Wages in Pence per Annum	Slater /Tiler and Helper's Wages in Grams of Silver per Annum	Slater/Tiler and Helper's Wages in Grams of Gold per Annum
1300-10	2.89	722.5	962.37	74.03	5.17	1292.5	1721.61	132.43
1310-20	3.1	775	1032.3	79.41	5.82	1455	1938.06	149.08
1320-30	3.12	780	1038.96	79.92	5.04	1260	1678.32	129.1
1330-40	3.2	800	1065.6	81.97	5.38	1345	1791.54	137.81
1340-47	3.03	757.5	1008.99	77.61	5.22	1305	1738.26	133.71
Average	3.068	767	1021.64	78.59	5.33	1331.5	1773.56	136.43
1440-50	5.17	1292.5	932.54	84.78	8.23	2057.5	1484.49	134.95
1450-60	5.45	1362.5	983.04	89.37	9.63	2407.5	1737.01	157.91
1460-70	5.42	1355	977.63	88.88	9.75	2437.5	1758.66	159.88
1470-80	5.83	1457.5	1051.59	95.6	9.82	2455	1771.28	161.03
1480-90	5.71	1427.5	1029.94	93.63	9.17	2292.5	1654.04	150.37
Average	5.516	1379	994.95	90.45	9.32	2330	1681.1	152.83
Percent Increase	80%	80%	-3%	15%	75%	75%	-5%	12%

Wages in England (Thatcher and Thatcher's Helper, 1300–1350, 1440–1490)

England Year C.E.	Thatcher's Wages in Pence per Day	Thatcher's Wages in Pence per Annum	Thatcher's Wages in Grams of Silver per Annum	Thatcher's Wages in Grams of Gold per Annum	Thatcher's Helper's Wages in Pence per Day	Thatcher's Helper's Wages in Pence per Annum	Thatcher's Helper's Wages in Grams of Silver per Annum	Thatcher's Helper's Wages in Grams of Gold per Annum
1300-10	2.5	625	832.5	64.04	1	250	333	25.62
1310-20	3	750	999	76.85	1.25	312.5	416.25	32.02
1320-30	3	750	999	76.85	1	250	333	25.62
1330-40	3	750	999	76.85	1.25	312.5	416.25	32.02
1340-47	3	750	999	76.85	1.25	312.5	416.25	32.02
Average	2.9	725	965.7	74.28	1.15	287.5	382.95	29.46
1440-50	5.25	1312.5	946.97	86.09	4	1000	721.5	65.59
1450-60	5.5	1375	992.06	90.19	3.25	812.5	586.22	53.29
1460-70	4.75	1187.5	856.78	77.89	3.75	937.5	676.41	61.49
1470-80	5.25	1312.5	946.97	86.09	3.75	937.5	676.41	61.49
1480-90	6	1500	1082.25	98.39	3.75	937.5	676.41	61.49
Avg	5.35	1337.5	965.01	87.73	3.7	925	667.39	60.67
Percent Increase	84%	84%	0%	18%	222%	222%	74%	106%

Wages in Egypt (Custodian and Door Keeper, 1300–1350, 1440–1490)

Egypt Year C.E.	Custodian's Wages in Dinars per Annum	Custodian's Wages in Grams of Silver per Annum	Custodian's Wages in Grams of Gold per Annum	Year C.E.	Door Keeper's Wages in Dinars per Annum	Door Keeper's Wages in Grams of Silver per Annum	Door Keeper's Wages in Grams of Gold per Annum
1303	17.4	692.49	73.95	1303	12	477.58	51
1303	15	596.97	63.75	1303	18	716.36	76.5
1331	15	596.97	63.75	1325	36	1432.73	153
				1325	18	716.36	76.5
Avg	15.8	628.81	67.15	Avg	21	835.76	89.25
1461	1.43	47.73	4.93				
1464	3.79	126.68	13.08	1464	3.79	126.68	13.08
1466	10.29	343.67	35.49	1466	10.29	343.67	35.49
1474	8.57	286.39	29.57	1474	10.29	343.67	35.49
Avg	6.02	201.12	20.77	Avg	8.12	271.34	28.02
Percent Decrease	-62%	-68%	-69%		-61%	-68%	-69%

Wages in Egypt (Water Carrier and Reader, 1300–1350, 1440–1490)

Egypt Year C.E.	Water Carrier's Wages in Dinars per Annum	Water Carrier's Wages in Grams Silver per Annum	Water Carrier's Wages in Grams Gold per Annum	Year C.E.	Reader's Wages in Dinars per Annum	Reader's Wages in Grams of Silver per Annum	Reader's Wages in Grams of Gold per Annum
1303	18	716.36	76.5	1303	12	477.58	51
				1331	15	596.97	63.75
Avg	18	716.36	76.5	Avg	13.5	537.27	57.38
1464	7.58	253.36	26.16	1444	4.21	140.68	14.53
1464	3.79	126.68	13.08	1461	1.43	47.73	4.93
1474	14.57	486.87	50.27	1464	1.9	63.34	6.54
				1464	0.95	31.67	3.27
				1466	10.29	343.67	35.49
				1474	9.43	315.03	32.53
AVG	8.65	288.97	29.84	Avg	4.7	157.02	16.21
Percent Decrease	-52%	-60%	-61%		-65%	-71%	-72%

Endnotes

1. For a recent summary of these issues, see Christopher Dyer, "Rural Europe," in *The New Cambridge Medieval History*, ed. Christopher Allmand vol. VII c.1415–c.1500 (Cambridge, 1998), pp. 106–20.

2. John Hatcher and Mark Bailey, *Modelling the Middle Ages: The History and Theory of England's Economic Development* (Oxford and New York, 2001), p. 176.

3. Abraham Udovitch, Robert Lopez, and Harry Miskimin, "England to Egypt, 1350–1500: Long Term Trends and Long Distance Trade." in *Studies in the Economic History of the Middle East*, ed. Michael Cook (London, 1970), pp. 93–128.

4. Eliyahu Ashtor, "Prix et salaires a l'epoque mamlouke: Une étude sur l'état economique de l'Egypte et de la Syrie à la fin du Moyen Age," Revue des études islamiques 17 (1949): 372–81; idem, *A Social and Economic History of the Near East in the Middle Ages* (Berkeley and Los Angeles, 1976).

5. Ashtor, *Histoire des prix et des salaries dans l'Orient médiéval* (Paris, 1969), pp. 284–5.

6 To mention just one example, Ashtor compared fourteenth century unskilled labor with skilled artisans from the fifteenth century. He then used this comparison as part of his argument that wages had increased in the wake of the plagues. See Ashtor, "Prix," pp. 372–81.

7. Muhammad Muhammad Amin, *Al-Awqaf wa'l-Hayat al-Ijtima'iyya fi Misr* (Cairo, 1980), pp. 72-93, 108. See also Muhammad 'Afifii, *al-Awqaf wa'l-Hayat al-Iqtisadiyya fi Misr fi'l-'Asr al-'Uthmani* (Cairo, 1991), pp. 86–94, 139–40.

8. Carl Petry, "A Geniza for Mamluk Studies? Charitable Trust (Waqf) Documents as a Source for Economic and Social History," *Mamluk Studies Review* II (1998): 51–60. For Petry's use of these documents in reconstructing late Mamluk history, see idem, *Twilight of Majesty: The Reigns of the Mamluk Sultans al-Ashraf Qaytbay and Qansuh al-Ghawri in Egypt* (Seattle, 1993); idem, *Protectors or Praetorians? The Last Mamluk Sultans and Egypt's Waning as a Great Power* (Albany, 1994).

9. On the general utility of the chronicles, archives, and other sources for Mamluk history, see Donald Little, "The Use of Documents for the Study of Mamluk history," *Mamluk Studies Review* I (1997): 1–13.

10. Boaz Shoshan, "Money Supply and Grain Prices in Fifteenth Century Egypt," *Economic History Review*, 2nd series, 36 (1983): 47–67; Ashtor, *Histoire des prix et des salaires*.

11. For the waqfiyyat sources and data, see below.

12. For a discussion of historians' estimates of mortality in England, see Rosemary Horrox, *The Black Death* (Manchester and New York, 1994), pp. 229–236. For Egypt, see Michael Dols, *The Black Death in the Middle East* (Princeton, 1977), pp. 172–200.

13. For England, see E. B. Fryde, *Peasants and Landlords in Later Medieval England c.1380–1525* (New York, 1996), pp. 3–6; Rodney Hilton, *The English Peasantry in the Later Middle Ages* (Oxford, 1975), pp. 58-9; Horrox, *The Black Death*, pp. 240, 242. For Egypt, see Ahmad ibn 'Ali al-Qalqashandi, *Subh al-a'sha' fi-sina'at al-insha'*, ed. Muhammad Husayn al-Din (Beirut, 1987) (hereafter *Subh*), 3:516; Ibn Hajar al-'Asqalani, *'Inba' al-ghumr bi-anba' al-'umr,* ed. Hassan Habashi (Cairo, 1969–1972) (hereafter *'Inba' al-ghumr*), 5:137, 6:16-18; 'Abd al-Rahmaan Ibn Abi Bakr al-Suyuti, *Husn al-Muhadara fi Akhbar Misr wa'l-Qahira*, ed. Khalil al-Mansur (Beirut, 1997) (hereafter *Husn*), 2:259. Taqi al-Din Ahmad Ibn 'Ali al-Maqrizi, *Kitab al-suluk li ma'arifat duwul al-muluk*, ed. Sa'id 'Abd al-Fattah 'Ashur (Cairo: 1957–1973) (hereafter *Suluk*), 2:777–86, 832–33, 4:19–20, 43, 349.

14. See the following two paragraphs for details and sources.

15. Luders et. al. (ed.), *Statutes of the Realm 1101–1713*, 11 vols. (London, 1819–1828), as quoted in Horrox, *The Black Death*, pp. 287–9, 312–16.

16. John Hatcher, "English Serfdom and Villeinage: Towards a Reassessment," in *Landlords, Peasants, and Politics in Medieval England*, ed. T. H. Aston (Cambridge, 1987), pp. 255–61; David Stone, "Productivity of Hired and Customary Labour: Evidence from Wisbech Barton in the Fourteenth Century," *Economic History Review*, p. 641; Christopher Dyer, *Standards of Living in the Later Middle Ages: Social Change in England c. 1200–1520* (Cambridge, 1989), pp. 137–38; Tim North, "Legerwite in the Thirteenth and Fourteenth Centuries," *Past and Present* 111 (May, 1986): 3–16. See also Rodney Hilton's Introduction to *Landlords, Peasants, and Politics in Medieval England*, ed. T. H. Aston (Cambridge, 1987).

17. E. B. Fryde, *Peasants and Landlords*, p.3; R. H. Britnell, *The Commercialization of English Society 1000–1500* (Cambridge 1993), pp. 219–21.

18. Rodney Hilton, *The English Peasantry in the Later Middle Ages* (Oxford, 1975), pp. 38, 57; Hatcher, "English Serfdom," pp. 281–83; Britnell, *Commercialization*, p. 200.

19. Mavis Mate, "The East Sussex Land Market and Agrarian Class Structure in the Late Middle Ages," *Past and Present* 139 (1993): 57–60; B. H. Slicher Van Bath, *The Agrarian History of Western Europe* (London, 1963), p.14; Harry Miskimin, *The Economy of Early Renaissance Europe 1300-1460* (Cambridge, 1981), pp. 35, 55; Hilton, *English Peasantry*, p. 45; Dyer, *Living Standards*, pp. 68, 80, 94, 100, 143–45, 156, 202.

20. Hilton, *The Decline of Serfdom in Medieval England* (London and Bassingstoke, 1983), pp. 47–51; Fryde, *Peasants and Landlords*, p. 161; Hatcher, "English Serfdom," p. 282.

21. Mavis Mate, "The East Sussex Land Market," pp. 48, 60, 65; N. J. Mayhew, "Population, money supply, and the velocity of circulation in England, 1300–1700," *Economic History Review* XLVIII (1995): 249; Hatcher and Bailey, *Modelling*, p. 183; Britnell, *Commercialization*, pp. 211ff.

22. Hilton, *English Peasantry*, pp. 13, 40, 52, 82; Dyer, *Living Standards*, p. 185.

23. John Langdon, "Lordship and Peasant Consumerism in the Milling Industry of Early Fourteenth-Century England," *Past and Present* 145 (1994): 3, 4, 7, 1; Mate, "East Sussex Land Market," pp. 48, 60, 65; Dyer, *Living Standards*, pp. 149–50; Mayhew, "Population," p. 249; Stone, "Productivity," pp. 652–3; Britnell, *Commercialization*, pp. 202, 220; Steven Epstein, "Cities, Regions, and the Late Medieval Crisis: Sicily and Tuscany Compared," *Past and Present* 130 (1991): 5–8; Hilton, "Feudalism and the Origins of Capitalism," in Hilton, *Class Conflict and the Crisis of Feudalism* (London, 1985), pp. 291–94.

24. Pamela Nightingale, "Capitalists, Crafts and Constitutional Change in Late Fourteenth-Century London," *Past & Present* 124 (1989): 4, 9, 45; Dyer, *Living Standards*, p. 210: Peter Kriedte, *Peasants, Landlords, and Merchant Capitalists: Europe and the World Economy, 1500–1800* (Cambridge, 1983), pp. 6–7, 13, 29 100; Miskimin, *The Economy of Early Renaissance Europe*, p. 98. Hilton, *English Peasantry*, pp. 37–8, remarks that, "However we interpret urban developments during this period, not even the strictest stagnationist denies the growth of the craft industry in the countryside."

25. Although there was no direct link between the two, rise of rural industry in the 15th century was accompanied by de-urbanization in many areas. See Hilton's collection of essays cited above, *Class Conflict and the Crisis of Feudalism*, see pp. 47, 255–57, 265, 277.

26. For the graphs and data, see below.

27. See my forthcoming study, "The Socioeconomic Dimensions of the Mamluk Landholding System"; For a terse but superlative summation of the general system, see Robert Irwin, *The Middle East in the Middle Ages* (London and Sydney, 1986), p. 152.

28. Jennifer Thayer, "Land Politics and Power Networks in Mamluk Egypt," Ph.D. Dissertation, New York University, 1993, 134; *Suluk*, 4:28, 345.

29. These were *mudafat*, *diyafa*, and numerous other extractions under the direction of local "guards": *mutadarrikin*. See Ibrahim 'Ali Tarkhan, *al-Nizam al-Iqta'i fi'l-Sharq al-Awsat fi'l-'Usur al-Wusta* (Cairo, 1968) (thereafter Tarkhan), p. 482; Khalil bin Shahin al-Zahiri, *Kitab zubda kashf al-mamalik wa bayyan at-turuq wa'l-masalik*, ed. Paul Ravaisse (Paris, 1894), pp. 107, 130; Petry, "A Paradox of Patronage during the later Mamluk Period," *Muslim World* 73 (1983): 182–207; *Suluk*, 2:832–3, 4:226.

30. For a description of the currency instability see, Ibn Taghri-Birdi, *Hawadith al-duhur fi mada al-Ayyam wa'l-shuhur*, ed. William Popper (Berkeley, 1930–1931), 2:237, 3:503–10; *Subh*, 3:510–12, 515; *Suluk,* 4:3, 131, 165, 205, 226, 306, 436, 441, 549, 630, 794, 943, 1090–92.

31. Michael Dols, *The Black Death in the Middle East*, pp. 163–65; William Tucker, "Natural Disasters and the Peasantry in Mamluk Egypt," *Journal of the Economic and Social History of the Orient* 24 (1981): 215–244; *Khitat,* 4:332–35, 343–44.

32. To give just one example from the sources, in 818/1415, during a time of civil disorder and drought, peasants fled from the Delta to Cairo seeking grain, see *Suluk,* 4:332. See Sa'id 'Abd al-Fattah 'Ashur, *al-Mujtama' al-Misri fi 'Asr Salatin al-Mamalik* (Cairo, 1993), pp. 45–46; Shoshan, "Grain Riots and the 'Moral Economy' in Cairo: 1350–1517," *Journal of Interdisciplinary History*, 10 (1980): 462–7; Ira Lapidus, "The Grain Economy of Mamluk Egypt," *Journal of the Economic and Social History of the Orient*, 12 (1969): 8, 11–14.

33. For the graphs and data, see below.

34. The year 1300 is the best possible starting date, as price data for Egypt is much scarcer before the start of the fourteenth century. Moreover, commencing Egypt's price series in 1300 allows us to take into account improvements in the agricultural sector carried out by the early Mamluk regime. During the second half of the thirteenth century, and into the first half of the fourteenth century, the rulers of Egypt were able to increase the amount of arable land by as much as fifty percent. See Tsugitaka Sato, *State and Rural Society in Medieval Islam* (Leiden, 1997), p. 229; Taqi ad-Din Ahmad Ibn 'Ali al-Maqrizi, *Kitab al-mawa'iz wa'l-i'tibar bi-dhikr al-khitat wa-l'athar* (Cairo: 1853–1854), 1:171; *Suluk*, 2:111–13; Tarkhan, pp. 75–76; *Subh*, 13:117. The success of the early Mamluk regime in stimulating agrarian development had a significant impact on prices and is as crucial to an accurate interpretation of the economic trajectory of Egypt from 1300 to 1500 as is the catastrophic failure of the later regime to maintain agricultural productivity after the demographic collapse. It demonstrates how the Black Death played a crucial role in undermining Egypt's economic system. The year 1440 is an appropriate starting point for the second fifty-year series. As it was some ninety years after the initial plague hit both countries, it allows for economic events triggered by demographic collapse to play themselves out. Both countries were close to reaching the nadir of population by 1440, with the worst plague in Egypt (after the Black Death itself) occurring in the year 1429–30. By 1440, enough time had passed

for the reactionary efforts of English landlords (as expressed in Statute of Labourers) to fade into oblivion. In Egypt, by 1440, the effects of the landholding system under demographic strain had taken much of their toll on the agrarian economy. The year 1440 is also an optimal starting point for Egypt if reliable comparative indicators of prices in precious metals are to be found. Before 1440, Egypt had been subject to wild fluctuations in the value of its copper currency. After 1440, the value of copper currency, as expressed in the "dirham min al-fulus" (its money of account) had become relatively stable. Equally, if not more important, by 1440, silver had once again (as in the period 1300–1350) become a currency of frequent, if not comprehensive, usage. Before 1440, silver had been so scarce that, in the early part of the century, it was effectively absent from the Egyptian economy. By starting at 1440, we can use silver as a comparative index. If the starting point for the second data set were placed before 1440, only gold would be available for a precious metal comparison. Although gold will be used here to back up silver for comparison, it is a more tenuous measure of value for 1300–1350, as it was neither minted nor widespread in England during the early fourteenth century. Copper currency would not be an effective index for comparison. Despite its prominence in fifteenth century Egypt, copper currency was merely a tertiary and petty coinage in Egypt from 1300–1350 (after gold and silver). While England was able to adhere the use of silver throughout the period under investigation, copper currency never rose to any prominence in the medieval English economy, and the scarcity of gold coin in England in the early fourteenth century makes the use of silver as a comparative measure all the more important). For Egypt, the price data has been subject to one standard deviation. Only the price of wheat is used here, as the other two regularly reported staple crops (barley and broad beans) follow the trend of wheat prices quite closely. For the 1300–1350 price series, see al-ʿAyni, *ʿIqd al-juman fi tarikh ahl al-zaman*, ed. Muhammad Muhammad Amin (Cairo, 1987 to 1992), IV: 72; *Suluk*, I: 898, 908, 949 II: 17, 39, 55, 278, 300, 394, 398, 401, 424, 437, 456, 522, 592, 719; Ashtor, *Histoire des prix et des salaires*, pp. 284-5. For the 1440-1490 price series, see Shoshan, "Money Supply and Grain Prices," pp. 65–67. The values for silver are based on a *dirham nuqra* of 2/3 silver weighing 2.97 grams and a *nisf fidda* (half a dirham) of 1.5 grams of 90% purity silver (exchanged for gold *Ashrafi dinars* at a rate of 25 to 1. The values for gold are based on a *dinar mithqal* of pure gold weighing 4.25 grams and a dinar Ashrafi of pure gold weighing 3.45 grams. The *ardabb* used here is equal to 165 liters of grain. The 165 liter *ardabb* is larger than that employed by most historians of the Mamluk period. The majority of scholars have used an *ardabb* of 70 kg, equaling roughly 92 liters for wheat. After careful investigation, I have determined that the smaller *ardabb* (which is cited in the sources as the "*ardabb Misri*" and is based on the "*qadah saghir*") yields an impossibly small amount of wheat when market prices are evaluated. For example, if the smaller *ardabb* of 70 kg of wheat is compared with market prices for flour, the resulting calculation yields the absurd result that flour is cheaper than wheat. It is conceivable that there could have been an *ardabb* of wheat equaling approximately 90 kg (119 liters of wheat). This would mean that the *ardabb* of wheat and the *ardabb* of flour were equal in weight. However, an examination of price ratios reveals that, with minimal weight losses upon conversion from wheat to flour added in, flour would still be (in many specific cases cited) more expensive than wheat by weight. Based up an examination of the price ratios, charges for cleaning and milling wheat, and the weight loss incurred in cleaning and milling wheat, the most accurate measure seems to be that calculated by William Popper. Popper's *ardabb* of 275 pounds (125 kg and 165 liters for wheat) fits within all of these parameters. For the source of these calculations see William Popper, *Egypt and Syria under the Circassian Sultans 1382-1468 A.D.: Systematic Notes to Ibn Taghri Birdi's Chronicles of Egypt* (Berkeley and Los Angeles, 1955, 1957), v. 2, pp. 100–104. For grain price ratios, see *Suluk*, 3:818, 1133–4, 4:712, 718, 780, 794, 799, 964. See also Adel Allouche's comparative prices, *Mamluk Economics: A Study and Translation of Al-Maqrizi's Ighathah* (Salt Lake City, 1994), pp. 99–103, 110–11 and William Popper's price ratios in *Systematic Notes*, v. 2, p. 103. For the varying weight and volume of the *ardabb*, see al-Qalqashandi's discussion in *Subh*, 3:511–2. For the prices charged for cleaning wheat, milling wheat, and the weight loss involved, see Taqi al-Din Ahmad Ibn ʿAli al-Maqrizi, *Ighathat al-Ummah bi-Kashf al-Ghummah*, ed. Saʿid ʿAbd al-Fattah ʿAshur (Cairo, 1990), pp. 126–7. Note also that the customary rents in use in 1844 (listed in *ardabbs*) are in close proximity to the *ardabb* rent listed by Mamluk chroniclers. The proximity of these rents in *ardabbs* would seem highly suspicious if the *ardabb* had grown from some 92 liters to 198 liters. A smaller change in volume (e.g. 165 liters to 198 liters) seems much more likely. For the 1844 rents, see Helen Rivlin, *The Agricultural Policy of Muhammad Ali in Egypt* (Cambridge, Mass., 1961), p. 262.

The prices for wheat in England for both periods are from David Farmer, "Chapter 5: Prices and Wages, 1350–1500," in *The Agrarian History of England and Wales*, vol. III: 1348–1500, ed. Edward Miller (Cambridge, 1991), p. 444. The values for gold and silver are from Peter Spufford, *Handbook of Medieval Exchange* (London, 1986), pp. lix, lxi. The prices of barley and peas (rough equivalents to Egypt's regularly reported barley and broad beans), not shown here, fell more precipitously than did the price of wheat. England's wheat "price resilience" in the face of a relative decrease in demand and rise in supply of grain crops was probably due to the greater elasticity of its demand curve. When living standards for the majority of population improved in the fifteenth century, wheat—which had once been a luxury in the early fourteenth century (e.g. during the great famine of 1315–1317)—was more highly prized than other crops that had served as substitutes during difficult times. When wheat became a more readily available staple crop in the fifteenth century, relative demand for it remained higher. See, for example, Dyer's comment on conditions during the early fourteenth century famine: Dyer, *Living Standards*, p. 268.

35. For wages in England for carpenters and slaters/tilers, see David Farmer, "Chapter 5: Prices and Wages, 1350–1500," p. 471. For the wages of the thatchers and

thatcher's mates, see Christopher Dyer, *Living Standards*, p. 215. The values for gold and silver are from Spufford, *Handbook*, pp. lix, lxi. Christopher Dyer has kindly provided me with the basis for converting the daily wages into annual wages based on the following subtractions: 52 Sundays, 40–50 saints days, as well as a few days for illness and bad weather. The approximation used here is therefore 250 working days per year.

36. For Egyptian wages see, for the custodian: Ashtor, "Prix," p. 77 for 1303; Endowment Deed Number 532 (Cairo, *Wizarat al-Awqaf*: Ministry of Religious Endowments) (hereafter *Waqfiya Raqam # W.A.*) for 1331; *Waqfiya Raqam 759 W.A* for 1461; *Waqfiya Raqam 809 W.A* for 1464; Ashtor, "Prix," p.81 for 1466; Ashtor, "Prix," for 1474. For the wages of the door keeper see Ashtor, "Prix," for 1303; 25 *Mahfaza 4* (Endowment deed at the Egyptian National Archives) for 1325; *Waqfiya Raqam 738 W.A* for 1464; Ashtor, "Prix," p. 81 for 1466; *Waqfiya Raqam 886 W.A.* for 1474. For the wages of the water-carrier, see Ashtor, "Prix," p. 77 for 1303; *Waqfiya Raqam 809 W.A.* for 1464; Ashtor, "Prix," pp. 81-2 for 1474. For the wages of the reader see Ashtor, "Prix," p. 77 for 1303; *Waqfiya Raqam 532 W.A.* for 1331; *Waqfiya Raqam 749 W.A.* for 1444; *Waqfiya Raqam 759 W.A.* for 1461; *Waqfiya Raqam 809 W.A.* for 1464; Ashtor, "Prix," p. 81 for 1466; Ashtor, "Prix," pp. 81–2 for 1474. The values for silver are based on a dirham nuqra of 2/3 silver weighing 2.97 grams and a nisf fidda (half a dirham) of 1.5 grams of 90% purity silver (exchanged for gold Ashrafi dinars at a rate of 25 to 1). The values for gold are based on a dinar mithqal of pure gold weighing 4.25 grams and a dinar Ashrafi of pure gold weighing 3.45 grams. The wages given in the waqfiyat are given on a monthly basis and have been converted to annual wages.

37. K. N. Chaudhuri, *Asia before Europe: Economy and Civilization of the Indian Ocean from the rise of Islam to 1750* (Cambridge, 1990), p. 100.

Ancient Iranian Ideas in a Modern Context: Aspects of Royal Legitimacy under Muhammad Riza Shah Pahlavi

Jamsheed K. Choksy

Kingly rank in Iranian society occupied the pinnacle of the social hierarchy. The ruler usually possessed supreme status, great authority, and vast wealth. In theory, each king rested claims to rule on assumed divine sanction. Every other prerequisite for rule, such as royal descent and tradition, also ostensibly received its warrant from god. In practice, monarchs often depended on charisma, personal and family allegiances, alliances with noble families, and loyalty of retainers in order to exercise authority. In Iran, this tradition of rule gradually produced a royal ideology of sacral kingship. Political precedents and propaganda arose to first legitimize, then spread, various rulers' claims to power and authority. In 1925 a military officer named Riza Khan ascended the throne of Iran, took the traditional title of king (New Persian: *shāh*) which in Iranian usage dates back at least to the Achaemenian empire (ca. 550–331 B.C.), and founded the Pahlavi dynasty. In 1941, after the abdication of Riza Khan, or Riza Shah Pahlavi as he was officially known, his son Muhammad Riza was proclaimed king of Iran by the parliament (New Persian: *majlis*). Muhammad Riza Shah Pahlavi ruled from 1941, with one very brief interruption in August 1953, until he was forced into exile by the Islamic Revolution of 1979. In this article, I examine claims of kingship and royal legitimacy promoted by Muhammad Riza Shah Pahlavi and his royal court during nearly four decades in power. I probe how aspects of the past were repossessed and reconfigured in attempts to provide validation, affirmation, and aggrandizement for imperial concepts and actions. I then examine how the royal ideology, created from aspects of the past, was disseminated through multimedia, state institutions, education, social reorganization, and westernization. I also discuss reasons for the failure of the ideology of royal legitimacy to prevent that monarch's ouster.[1]

Historical Background

A detailed exposition of the notion of kingship in Iran is beyond the scope of this inquiry. However, the application of older religiopolitical beliefs in contemporary settings during Muhammad Riza Shah Pahlavi's reign makes a brief survey of the nature of ancient and medieval Iranian kingship essential.

Concepts of kingship in Iran and their relation to organized religion originated from a convergence of ancient Indo-Iranian ideas of leadership with Mesopotamian practices of sovereignty. This melding began under the Medes (ca. 625–550 B.C.) and Achaemenians, then was influenced by Hellenistic ideas of authority under the Seleucids (312–129 B.C.) and early Parthians or Arsacids (238 B.C.–A.D. 224). In the final period of ancient Iranian history, the Sasanians (A.D. 224–651) ensured that the political interdependence of the state and the Zoroastrian religious hierarchy resulted in the full-fledged development of both a royal ideology and a practice of sacral kingship. The basic tenets of this royal ideology can be summarized as follows: Sovereignty over Iran was believed to be restricted to a single family in each period, and national history was perceived as the eras of those ruling families. The chosen family, and especially each king, was thought to be endowed with royal glory (Avestan: x^{v}*arənah*, Old Persian: *farnah*, Pahlavi: *xwarrah*, New Persian: *farr*) and wisdom (Avestan: *xratu*, Old Persian: *xraθu*, Pahlavi: *xrad*, New Persian: *khirad*) by god. This royal glory was believed to mark the monarch as supreme among the people. The king was presented as the omnipotent and all-protecting representative of god on earth, wielding absolute authority granted by Ahura Mazda or god, through the state religion which was Zoroastrianism. His, occasionally her (for example, the Sasanian female rulers Boran and Azarmigdukht in the early seventh century A.D.), function was believed to involve maintenance of the religiously-sanctioned social structure, thus ensuring that law and order prevailed. In that respect, the ruler was expected to serve as the guide of the Iranian people. Each king was required to fulfill a role as supreme protector and enforcer of divine law by defending the sovereignty of Iran, by ensuring submission of the subjects to royal will and intellect, and by maintaining the affluence and well-being of his or her subjects. Since a divinely-appointed ruler was expected to improve the kingdom, especially by bringing peace and prosperity to all its residents, the material opulence of Iran came to be regarded as a sign that authority was vested in a legitimate ruler. Dedication and service to such a ruler were held to be essential components for the exercise of rule. Thus, loyalty to monarchs was emphasized in both imperial proclamations and religious doctrines. However, just as the ideology of sacral kingship provided legitimacy for the rule of just kings, safeguards also evolved to protect the state, religion, and people from monarchs who abused their authority. Any ruler whose actions generated calamity, strife, poverty, and suffering among the subjects or threatened the supremacy of the state religion and its religious hierarchy was considered an evil monarch who had lost royal glory and divine legitimacy. Both in Iranian mythology and in popular belief, calamities and strife have constantly been associated with sovereigns whose authority supposedly did not originate from god and was therefore considered non-sacral. As a result, it became a religious duty to depose such monarchs. This aspect of the doctrine of sacral kingship granted, to the Zoroastrian clergy and nobles, doctrinal sanction and ideological justification for ousting rulers—although political influence, military might, or palace intrigue was usually needed to accomplish such a task.[2]

After the Arab conquest of Iran in the seventh century A.D., and the gradual spread of Islam there over the next six hundred years, both the institution of kingship and its associated tenet of royal legitimacy persisted. Even a *mihna* or confrontation between members of the Islamic religio-scholarly class (Arabic: *ʿulamāʾ*, New Persian: *mullāyān*) and the secular political authorities from the early to the middle of the ninth century could not abate the influence of sacral kingship. Eventually Abu ʿl-Qasim Firdawsi (d. ca. A.D. 1020) codified the legends and royal history of ancient Iranian monarchs in his monumental *Shāh-nāma*, "Book of Kings"—which would become the country's national epic grounded on the concept of sacral kingship and the importance of religiously-sanctioned rulers. The role of monarchs and the legitimacy of kingship were further disseminated through wisdom (Pahlavi: *handarz*, New Persian: *andarz*) literature such as the vizier Nizam al-Mulk's (d. A.D. 1092) *Siyāsat-nāma*, "Book of Government," where it was written that god (named Allah since by this time the majority of urban Iranians followed Islam, rather than Zoroastrianism and its deity Ahura Mazda) raises one person to the rank of ruler in each era and entrusts that individual with all worldly affairs. Thus, the Iranian ideology of kingship and its exploitation by rulers persisted under the Ghaznavids (A.D. 961–1040) and Seljuks (A.D. 1037–1157).[3] Royal families even contrived genealogies in order to assert descent from ancient Iranian, Zoroastrian, dynasties. For example, the Samanids claimed descent from the Sasanian monarch Wahram V (ruled A.D. 421–439) and the Ghaznavids traced their lineage to the last Sasanian king of kings Yazdagird III (ruled A.D. 632–651). Even those Muslim Turkish rulers, who called themselves *sultāns*, thus found the ancient ideology of sacral kingship valuable when governing Iranian subjects. Likewise during the Safavid period (A.D. 1501–1722) the power of each king was based on claims that he possessed the royal glory or *farr*, that he was the shadow of god upon the earth (New Persian: *zīll Allāh fīʾ-arz*), that he served as the representative of the *mahdī* or twelfth Shiʿite imam, and that he functioned as the spiritual director (New Persian: *murshid-i kāmil*) of the Safaviyya order. Furthermore, official Safavid genealogy spread the ruling family's fanciful claim of descent from Ali b. Abu Talib (d. A.D. 661), the fourth caliph and first Shiʿite imam.[4]

From this overview it should be clear that both ancient Zoroastrian kings and medieval to premodern Muslim monarchs utilized epic history, religious tenets, folk beliefs, and charisma associated with kingship to legitimize their claims to the Iranian throne. Furthermore, after the disintegration of the Abbasid caliphate, indigenous Muslim dynasties, freed from the oversight of central Islamic religious authorities, also could incorporate descent from the prophet Muhammad (d. A.D. 632) into their claims, producing a synthesis of Zoroastrian and Islamic prerogatives for rule. However, although Iran had been ruled by monarchs since prior even to the Median period, there had been no ruler of a single state that unified the entire region from the end of the caliphate until the emergence of the Safavid state. In addition, the ideological heritage and charisma of kingship, although persistent throughout Iranian history, had been modified by each succeeding dynasty to fulfill the specific requirements of various ruling families. More importantly, this ideological continuity contrasts with the fact that there had been very little real dynastic continuity. Indeed, many institutions of the monarchy had to be reconstituted by Riza Khan after he became king. As a result, to a limited extent Riza Shah and to a much greater extent his son Muhammad Riza sought to revive, modify, and reinforce the notion and praxis of sacral kingship in order to provide first legitimacy and later justification for their rule over a twentieth century nation-state which was open via multimedia channels to western democratic, Middle Eastern nationalistic, and Islamic fundamentalist ideas.[5]

Claims of Legitimacy

Dissemination of the Pahlavi dynasty's claims to political legitimacy began with a recodification of national history during the early years of Riza Shah's reign. Iran's ancient heritage came to be glorified, the medieval period of Arab rule was decried as a period of barbarism (officially referred to as *vahshigarī-yi ʿarab* in New Persian), and attempts were made to purge the New Persian or Farsi language of Arabic and Turkish words much as medieval Persian poets like Firdawsi had tried to do. The name adopted for the new dynasty itself served to conjure a connection with the Middle Persian language of the Sasanian empire and thus with Iran's Zoroastrian, pre-Islamic, heritage. However, realizing the influence of Islam upon his subjects, that monarch attempted to depict himself not merely as an ideal Zoroastrian ruler along ancient lines but also as a religious Muslim king who, in the words of his son and successor, "often used to visit Imam Riza's holy shrine at Mashhad." Thus, Muhammad Riza would note his father had been named Riza "from Imam Riza, a descendant of our saint Ali, who is respected and revered in my family, so much so that all my brothers are named after Riza, with other names added to distinguish them." An official institution was established, the Association for Fostering and Guiding Public Thought (New Persian: *Kānūn-i parvarīsh va hidāyat-i afkar-i ʿamma*) to oversee resurgent notions of ancient Iranian kingship.[6] The state apparatus in place by 1941, a concerted and carefully planned royal ideology of kingship could be disseminated during the reign of Muhammad Riza Shah Pahlavi by the monarch himself, the ruling family, the imperial court, and the state bureaucracy. This ideology encompassed the king's titulary, a personality cult surrounding him, claims of descent and dynastic continuity from ancient times, and a depiction of the Pahlavi regime as bringers of welfare and prosperity through an extension of endeavors begun by appropriate previous rulers—much as the Sasanian family had attempted to depict themselves during Late Antiquity. The recreation of this national tradition was aided by western historians, and Iranian journalists, and intellectuals—many of whom stressed the importance of kingship as a historically-based institution vital for Iran's national progress.[7]

Muhammad Riza Shah Pahlavi professed, through his titulary, to be the light of the Aryans (New Persian: *Āryamihr*), king of kings (New Persian: *shāhān-shāh*) of Iran, and the shadow of god upon the earth (New Persian: *zīll Allāh fī ʾl-arz*). The appellation *Āryamihr*, which has no precedent in Iranian history, was probably formulated because it linked the monarch to both the Aryan ancestry of the Iranians and the Indo-Iranian (later a Zoroastrian) deity Mithra, originally a divinity of contracts, whose name eventually also came to signify the sun. Certainly, this appellation implied the notion of a covenant between the Iranian people and their monarch who was to oversee public welfare on behalf of god. Since Mithra (Pahlavi and New Persian: Mihr) had come to be associated with the sun, the designation implied that the king was also the light of the Iranians. The title *shāhān-shāh* (Old Persian: *xšāyaθiya xšāyaθiyānām*) had been assimilated by the earliest Iranians from their ancient Near Eastern neighbors—the Assyrians and Urartians—during the first millennium B.C. It had been used by the Medes, Achaemenians, Parthians, Sasanians, Samanids (A.D.

892–1005), Buyids (A.D. 934–1055), and numerous other dynasties—some Zoroastrian and others Islamic (both Sunni and Shiʿite). It was by far the best known and most durable royal protocol in Iranian history. Its adoption by the Pahlavis was thus not surprising, especially as it served to equate Riza Shah and Muhammad Riza Shah Pahlavi to the royal heroes of Iranian history and epic. The epithet *zīll Allāh fī ʾl-arz,* also used by the Safavids, proclaimed the Pahlavi dynasty's view that its members were the chosen representatives of god in the world—albeit in a Muslim context but one which paralleled claims by the Mazda-worshipping Sasanians, on coins and rock inscriptions, to be of "the character of the divinities" (Pahlavi: *čihr az yazadān*).[8]

In addition to claims via titulary, Muhammad Riza Shah Pahlavi and his royal court attempted to present the ruling family and himself as true heirs to Iran's ancient Zoroastrian and medieval Islamic heritage. Most officially authorized biographies, press releases, and government communiqués depicted the king as a titular descendent of the kings of ancient Iran. Directly linking his royal lineage to Cyrus II the great (ruled 550–530 B.C.), the last Pahlavi shah of Iran even stated, "the continuity of our monarchy has remained essentially unbroken." He is recorded as having added: "The story of my life does not begin either with me or with my great father, Riza Shah Pahlavi. My family comes from the ancient and famous Caspian province of Mazandaran, one of the original homelands of the old Aryan tribes. These Aryans gave Iran some of the finest and most famous kings and warriors known to history, from Jamshed to Faridun, Gushtasp to Kavus, Rustom to Sohrab. . . . It was from a traditionally military family belonging to the hardy Bavand clan from the upper Mazandaran region of Savadkuh, which was part of the original homelands of the ancient Aryan races, that my father Riza Shah was happy and proud to trace his ancestry."[9] This legendary, traditionally Zoroastrian, regnal and heroic lineage was supplemented by assertions that Muhammad Riza was blessed with Islamic visions of the Shiʿite imam Ali: "Shortly after my father's coronation, I found myself in bed with typhoid. The worst was feared, until one night, in a dream, I saw Ali. In my child's mind I knew that it was Ali, the first of our Imams. In his right hand he held the double-bladed sword with which he is always depicted, and in the other, a bowl containing a liquid from which he ordered me to drink. I obeyed. The next day my fever left me and I quickly recovered." This miraculous salvation echoed that of Zoroastrian monarchs such as Ardashir I (ruled A.D. 224–240), founder of the Sasanian dynasty, whose own claim of deliverance from harm was recorded in the *Kārnāmag ī Ardashīr Pāpakān*. Another such supernatural rescue, according to Muhammad Riza Shah Pahlavi took place: "A little later, during the summer, on my way to Emamzadeh-Daoud, a place of pilgrimage in the mountains, I fell from my horse on to rocks and passed out. I was taken for dead but I had not so much as a scratch. In falling I had a vision of one of our saints, Abbas, who cradled me as I fell." To supplement Ali and Abbas, the last shah even vowed that he had beheld the twelfth imam (i.e., the Shiʿite savior or *mahdī* whose messianic image echoes both that of the Zoroastrian Saoshyant and the Christian Jesus) near the Shimran royal palace: "It was Imam, the descendant of the Prophet who, according to our faith, must reappear on Earth to save the world." Since he supposedly had been saved from death by Ali and Abbas, then blessed with a vision of the twelfth imam Muhammad al-Mahdi, Muhammad Riza Shah Pahlavi felt he could claim "it was my destiny to become a king."[10]

Beyond the extensive royal titulary, declarations of descent from ancient Iranian heroes and kings, and professed rescues by Shiʿite imams which echoed Sasanian models, Muhammad Riza Shah Pahlavi would also be portrayed as an archetypal ruler of old, empowered by god to rule Iran. The shah described himself as the leader of many peoples who united peacefully under his authority: "We have always had differences of race, color, creed and economic and political situation and conviction; but under the monarchy the divergences have been sublimated into one larger whole symbolized in the person of the Shah." In this claim, the shah echoed aspirations of the Achaemenians, Parthians, and Sasanians. What is possibly the most forceful ancient Iranian depiction of this imperial notion of monarchy uniting the people in common cause can be found at the site of Naqsh-i Rustam where, above the fifth century B.C. tomb of Darius I (ruled 522–486 B.C.), a bas-relief depicts two rows of representatives from various communities within the Achaemenian empire holding up a throne-like platform upon which the king of kings prays before a Zoroastrian fire altar and a winged figure probably representing Ahura Mazda or perhaps *farnah*.[11] Like kings of those earlier regimes, Muhammad Riza asserted that as a youth he had mastered all the skills which—according to popular belief and legend—distinguished a ruler from the subjects: equestrian expertise, marksmanship, academic learning, and statesmanship. In many ways, those skills hark back to the prerequisites for nobles listed in a sixth century Middle Persian text supposedly recounting king Khusro I's (ruled A.D. 531–579) conversations with a Sasanian palace page boy. Such pursuits were, according to Pahlavi royal ideology, supplemented by devotion to god, who allegedly guided and protected the monarch—again harking back to images such as the bas-relief at Naqsh-i Rustam showing Darius I in prayer before a fire altar. Indeed, like most previous Iranian rulers—both Zoroastrian and Muslim—Muhammad Riza Shah

Pahlavi attributed his success to the will of god: "I was reared in a family which . . . believed in God. Since my childhood, I have faced many crises, storms and stresses, but every time I have come out victoriously. This has strengthened my faith in God from day to day." Again, the example of Darius I cannot be ignored, with words on the late sixth century B.C. (ca. 519 B.C.) Old Persian inscription at Behistun reading: "Ahura Mazda granted me the kingdom. Ahura Mazda assisted me in gaining control of the kingdom. I rule by the will of Ahura Mazda." Because enforcement of justice was a requirement of such a divinely-appointed ruler, Muhammad Riza Shah Pahlavi also equated himself to both Darius I and Khusro I, the popular models of just kings in Iranian history. Thus, his laws were referred to as Pahlavi Justice—mimicking the past.[12]

Following yet another well-established model, Muhammad Riza Shah Pahlavi (like his father before him) proclaimed the king had brought peace, stability, and welfare to the land of Iran after turbulence and suffering caused by a preceding dynasty—the Qajars (A.D. 1779–1921). Here an echo of the past was present for the Sasanian kings had made similar claims in relation to the preceding regime of the Parthians. Muhammad Riza Shah Pahlavi also portrayed his family as liberators and unifiers of Iran, just as Ardashir I had done. Moreover, according to imperial claims, kingship was bestowed upon Riza Shah by members of both the *majlis* and the *ʿulamāʾ*. Thus, the secular and religious leaders of the country were presented to the people as legitimizers of Pahlavi rule. Again an echo of Sasanian, Zoroastrian, ideology is heard as recorded in the *Letter of Tōsar*: "religion and state were born from one womb, joined together, never to be separated." Likewise, it was even alleged in official writings that Muhammad Riza had been restored to power by a popular uprising of the common people (rather than a British and American-sponsored covert operation) against Dr. Muhammad Musaddiq in 1953. Memories of the past were evoked here too, for defeat of the non-Sasanian usurper Wahram VI (Bahram Chobin, ruled A.D. 590–591), who was of Parthian descent, was attributed in part within the *Shāh-nāma* to the populace supposedly regarding Khusro II (ruled A.D. 590, 591–628) as their legitimate monarch.[13]

Propagation of Legitimacy

Unlike his ancient predecessors whose means of disseminating royal ideology were restricted to the use of imperial decrees, rock inscriptions, bas-reliefs, coins, seals, clerical sermons, and administrative ordinances, the last Pahlavi shah of Iran was able to mobilize the much wider range of technological resources available in the twentieth century. Because legitimate monarchs have always been required to ensure the welfare and prosperity of the Iranian people, Muhammad Riza Shah Pahlavi's primary means of state propaganda were actions, reforms, and projects instituted by imperial decree. The Pahlavi dynasty sought to depict itself as the savior of the nation from both foreign invaders and internal dissidents—so it was suggested that without Riza Shah and his son Muhammad Riza the nation would have disintegrated, causing much hardship to its inhabitants. According to government statements: "Iran's economy, owing to external and internal crises, was a complete wreck," and the two shahs brought about much needed reform. Wealth, land, and water resources were, to some extent, redistributed to segments of the economically underprivileged social classes, setting the stage for Muhammad Riza to depict himself as a bestower of bountifulness and the creator of a "Great Civilization" (New Persian: *tamaddun-i buzurg*). Imperial claims during the Achaemenian empire, especially under Darius I, cannot be overlooked in this context. The image of the ruler as a bringer of bountifulness was, likewise, disseminated by portraying this Pahlavi shah as one who granted his people "the five necessaries of life: food, clothing, housing, medical care, and education."[14]

Societal development was, according to Pahlavi royal ideology, to be achieved through a "White Revolution" which was heralded as the "Revolution of the Shah and His people." The White Revolution eventually consisted of seventeen points, outlining reforms which were intended to encompass all aspects of Iran's economy, environment, and polity. These reforms, said to be "directly related to existing local institutions and traditions," were communicated throughout the country as evidence of the monarch's beneficence and devotion to his subjects. Indeed, publications of the Royal Ministry of Information compared the shah's White Revolution to those of Darius I. The principles of this White Revolution were even etched on a rock inscription "in the tradition of the ancient Persian kings." In government publications, each reform was introduced using a historical account that defended the shah's ordinance. For example, conservation of forests was justified not through ecological arguments, but by reference to a claim that: "The national religion of the Persian Empire until the coming of Islam was firmly based on agriculture. The desert was seen as a work of Evil; God was manifest in the crops, in the fruit and nut-bearing trees, in the abundance of game, in the multiplying herds of cattle and sheep." Thus, in conserving Iran's forests, Muhammad Riza Shah Pahlavi was portrayed as obeying the will of god—most particularly the Zoroastrian creator deity Ahura Mazda. Likewise, the shah was depicted in popular stories as banishing the "three evil sisters . . . Poverty, Ignorance, and Disease"—aspects regularly connected to evil in the medieval Zoroastrian written tradition—through agrarian, educational, and medical reforms administered by ministries of his government. The shah's irrigation projects were also equated to those of Darius I in official and private communications.[15] Justice, another requirement of divinely-ordained rule, was in theory administered through "Houses of Justice," regulated by the Ministry of Justice, and supposedly established along lines of the Achaemenian "King's Law" and the Sasanian legal codes—renamed "Pahlavi Justice" by the royal court and bureaucracy as already mentioned. Despite concerns expressed by dissidents about the fair application of law in Iran, especially during the final years of his reign, Muhammad Riza Shah Pahlavi would proudly write that "I will always bear in mind those expressions of gratitude of my humble compatriots to whom justice was finally and freely dispensed thanks to our law courts."[16]

Education, yet another aspect of social development that was incorporated into the White Revolution, was controlled by the state, much like it had once been in Achaemenian and Parthian sponsored schools and in the *hērbedestāns* or Zoroastrian seminaries under the Sasanians. European languages, especially French and English, were emphasized as means of enhancing secular learning, industrial progress, and social change. A committee of educators was appointed by Riza Shah Pahlavi in 1938 to oversee the production of textbooks that, in part, spread adoration of the ruler. In 1955, the Royal Organization for Social Services (New Persian: *Sāzmān-i shāhan-shāhī-yi khadamāt-i ijtimāʿī*), led by Muhammad Riza Shah's sister Ashraf Pahlavi and with financial assistance from the Iran-U.S. Mutual Fund, began publishing similar textbooks aimed at primary school students. Iranian history was presented, through coursework, as fundamentally linked to the institution of kingship and to the role of rulers in furthering affairs of state. Patriotic songs, based on the poetry of the *Shāhnāma*, were sung periodically in primary and secondary schools. In those ways, education was utilized as a vehicle for spreading the regime's ideology to people in cities and villages. On another front, the emancipation of women—a feature of the White Revolution widely praised by the educated classes in Iran and in the West—fulfilled the necessary function of incorporating middle class Iranian women into the labor force as educators, physicians, secretaries, translators, and social workers. Since they had been trained in schools which followed curricula established by the king's Ministry of Education, many of those women were well-versed in the official dictum and worked both actively and tacitly to popularize it among other women.[17]

The mass media came to be skillfully employed by the king and his appointees, ensuring dissemination of the royal prerogative to rule. Muhammad Riza Shah Pahlavi used his official autobiography, which was published in several languages in addition to New Persian, to claim that he was king through divine choice and therefore was protected by god—again, it is important to recall both the *Cyropaedia* and Darius I's biographical trilingual inscription. Similar statements were widespread in government bulletins and leaflets. In a booklet entitled the *Philosophy of Iran's Revolution*, the Resurgence Party (New Persian: *Hizb-i rastākhīz-i īrān*) which was founded in 1975 by the king, claimed that Muhammad Riza Shah Pahlavi had resolved all of Iran's societal tensions. It went on to assert: "The king of kings of Irȧn is not just the political leader of Iran. He is also in the first instance teacher and spiritual leader, an individual who not only builds his nation roads, bridges, dams, and irrigation canals, but also guides the spirits, thoughts, and hearts of his subjects." Interviews with local and foreign journalists were usually permitted if it was believed that an image of this shah as a visionary leader would be forthcoming. Indeed, between 1953 and 1973, the foreign press usually presented this king as a progressive ruler whose problems in modernizing his underdeveloped country arose from a handful of religious fanatics and communists.[18] Inside Iran, the royal administration exercised control over the mass media. Persons who sought to publish articles, periodicals, or books were required technically to be at least thirty years of age, have a good reputation, and not possess a criminal record. Furthermore, statements deemed derogatory of the royal family were censored whenever possible. The national and international press was invited to many public ceremonies presided over by the last Pahlavi shah—so newspapers, radio, and television transmitted scenes of the king of kings inaugurating irrigation projects, housing schemes, health centers, and schools, being joyfully greeted by bureaucrats, industrial workers, and peasants, and triumphantly reviewing the military. Perhaps the most grandiose example of such media events was the celebration of the two thousand five hundredth anniversary of Iranian kingship in October 1971. On that occasion foreign and Iranian dignitaries, scholars, and reporters attended a celebration at Persepolis—the imperial capital of the Achaemenians built by Darius I and his son Xerxes (ruled 486–465 B.C.)—partially designed to reinforce the shah's claim to be the successor to Iran's earlier rulers. The celebrations at Persepolis also were aimed at focusing national attention away from a received religious identity—Islam—toward an indigenous imperial one—Iranian kingship. Such celebrations of reconstructed historical events to aggrandize contemporary notions, of course, were by no means unusual to Iran. Additionally, queen (New Persian: *shāhbānū*) Farah also was integrated into the cult of the past, often serving as the shah's representative at media events.[19]

All these details make it clear that Muhammad Riza Shah, his family, and state bureaucrats spread an ideology which sought to legitimize the Pahlavi dynasty as wielders of kingship bestowed by god. This royal ideology, based largely upon Iran's older Zoroastrian faith and ancient heritage of kingship, and to a much lesser extent on Islamic beliefs and praxes, was supported by a modern imperial court and was spread using the modern technology available to the government bureaucracies. Indeed, the dramatic growth of ministries during Muhammad Riza Shah Pahlavi's reign enabled the state to influence the lives and beliefs of a wide spectrum of Iranian society. Through the manipulation of traditions and symbols, attempts were made to convince the population of the vital role of monarchs in modern Iranian society. So successful was this endeavor believed to be, that the last shah declared: "In Iran there is magic in the notion of a king. . . . Our kingship is really an imperial principle, not imperialistic in the foreign expansionist sense, but in the sense of rule and communication between the Shah and the people—the notion of rule which is *Shāhānshāhī*." Hence, to the four pillars of the Pahlavi state already identified by other scholars, namely the bureaucracy, military, court patronage, and a one-party system, a fifth can be added: the royal ideology of sacral kingship.[20]

Failure of Royal Ideology

Between January 1978 and January 1979, however, those five pillars of state crumbled in a revolution that forced the second Pahlavi king of kings into exile and produced the Islamic Republic of Iran. The factors fueling that societal revolution were numerous and complex. Issues as diverse as economic decline, perfidiousness by government officials, and political oppression of dissidents united the array of diverse groups that came to constitute the opposition to Muhammad Riza Shah. Such factors cannot be dealt with in this article. Failure of the royal ideology of kingship to maintain the legitimacy of the shah's position during that crisis is not surprising. No ideology, not even one molded from centuries-old socioreligious traditions, can survive without a monarch enjoying the support of a majority of the population and without him successfully enforcing the claim to power upon his subjects. While not attempting to simplify or overlook the multifarious socioeconomic aspects that fueled the revolution, the preceding analysis indicates that creation and propagation of an imperial system not based firmly upon Islamic ideals gradually produced an attitudinal gulf between the royal regime, with its often westernized supporters, and the majority of a Muslim populace—eventually contributing to the ouster of the Pahlavi dynasty. Essentially, endeavors by the Pahlavi dynasty to inculcate its legitimacy largely upon ancient Iranian ideological bases—while paying lesser attention to Muslim standards of righteousness—as part of a move away from Islamic themes toward imperial symbols, failed to take root at a populist level.

Previous Muslim dynasties had partially co-opted and partially convinced the Shiʿite clerics into recognizing secular authority and propagating claims of royal legitimacy. This was true also of the Pahlavi regime up to 1963. Until then, Muhammad Riza's rule seems to have been supported by many among the Shiʿite establishment including the marjaʿ-i taqlid Ayatullah Husayn Burujirdi (d. 1962). Thereafter, however, the increasing disassociation between the imperial symbols displayed by the ruling family and its government vis-à-vis the Muslim values of the clerics resulted in a slow deterioration of relations between state and religion. So, for instance, many of Ayatullah Burujirdi's students would later serve in the Revolutionary Islamic Government. It appears that Riza Shah's and especially Muhammad Riza Shah's affinity for ancient Iranian images was influenced by notions of Iran's past glory lying in pre-Islamic times and potential future success occurring in post-Islamic settings. Thus, many tenets of the Pahlavi's ideology with its claims of imperial legitimacy came to be based on Iran's early, albeit Zoroastrian, heritage. To the many examples discussed previously, yet another can be added: In March 1975, a calendar reform equated A.D. 1976 to the year 2535 of a Shahanshahi era—replacing the existing solar Hijri or Shamsi calendar. That new Shahanshahi era was based, supposedly, on the accession of Cyrus II to power in Fars during 559 B.C., thus linking the Pahlavi regime chronologically to the Achaemenians. The Shiʿite religious elite, in particular, was repelled by actions such as that one, which they felt glorified the imperial and pre-Islamic past of Iran at the expense of the Muslim one connecting them to their faith. As a direct consequence, in February 1978, Ayatullah Ruhullah Khumaini (d. A.D. 1989) publicly raised the question: "(How) could someone believe in Islam and agree with abolishing the Islamic calendar in favor of the calendar of the unbelievers?" Khumaini's remarks were clearly directed at a growing number of Iranian Muslims who were becoming convinced that Muhammad Riza Shah Pahlavi and his imperial regime saw little of value in Iran's Muslim heritage or beliefs. So, the importance of Islam as a source of political authority was seriously underestimated by the government, despite occasional lip service to it. The growth of Islamic resistance to the monarchy was to some extent a reaction against the Pahlavi regime's acceptance and manipulation of an ancient, Zoroastrian, past in preference to a medieval or modern Islamic one—actions which were construed as anti-Islamic and portrayed as evidence that the regime was disconnected from the Muslim masses. As a result, members of the *ʿulamāʾ* eventually asserted that, in a Muslim country, the secular government should be grounded on the *Qurʾān* and on the *sunna* or customs of the prophet Muhammad. Although both the shah and his religious opponents acknowledged that government should be based upon law, those Muslims believed that this law was that of Allah, not of a king, another divinity such as Ahura Mazda, or western democracies. Consequently, suggestions were made by prominent Muslim clerics that since the shah's authority was not based on the tenets of Islam it had to be illegitimate.[21]

Yet another factor aided the uprising against Muhammad Riza Shah Pahlavi. The royal ideology of kingship itself encompassed a belief that strife, calamity, suffering, and suppression were signs indicating legitimate rule could not be or was no longer vested in the presiding monarch. This belief, historically part of Zoroastrian Iran's dynastic legacy, as mentioned previously, had been utilized on many previous occasions to depose rulers. Essentially, the past provided guidance and lessons both beneficial and detrimental to the monarchy. As Muhammad Riza Shah Pahlavi's regime grew progressively more autocratic, its leader came to be perceived as a ruler who had forsaken his subjects' welfare. Khumaini, among others, urged the king to "desist in this policy and acts like this . . . and . . . to listen to the *ʿulamāʾ* of Islam. They desire the welfare of the nation, the welfare of the country." The king of kings was also decried as the "slavish servant of the foreigners" who had surrendered Iran's national sovereignty to the western nations through economic and social concessions as weak leaders of the Safavid and Qajar regimes had done in earlier times. Muhammad Riza's regime was particularly vulnerable on this issue since the English and the Russians had been influential in bringing him to power in 1941 and the Americans had played an important role in restoring him to the throne in 1953.[22] Thus the past also could be assimilated and manipulated within a Muslim context by the *ʿulamāʾ* to present Muhammad Riza Shah Pahlavi, his government, and his supporters as unworthy of authority—just as the magi or Zoroastrian priests had done in earlier times against other kings.

When loss of general welfare, alleged disregard for Islam, and alienation of Muslim clerics combined with an awareness that Muhammad Riza Shah Pahlavi may have failed to fulfill his duty to the Iranian people, the king lost his prerogative to rule—just as the ancient ideology of sacral kingship stipulated he should. With the loss of that prerogative and the legitimacy it provided, the institution of monarchy was open to deposition, the second Pahlavi king of kings would be forced into exile, his regime's many achievements were swept aside by Islamic fundamentalism, secular ordinances governing non-Muslim religious minorities such as Zoroastrians came to be replaced by Islamic rules, and ancient Iranian monarchist ideas gave way to Muslim theocratic values. In many ways, Zoroastrian aspects of the ideology of sacral kingship pertaining to just rule had been assimilated into Shiʿite Islam and were eventually recast tacitly by the ayatullahs to support their own claims that, because kingship had not succeeded in being completely fair, just, and productive, the state should be administered by sectarian authorities—a late twentieth century Muslim reinterpretation of the Sasanian era's Zoroastrian notion that "religion and state were born from one womb, joined together, never to be separated," which has come to have major sociopolitical consequences for Iran.[23]

Endnotes

1. On the assimilation of the present into the present see, in general, D. Lowenthal, *The Past is a Foreign Country* (Cambridge, 1985), pp. 4, 7, 13, 25–26, 40–41, 412.

2. J. K. Choksy, "Sacral Kingship in Sasanian Iran," *Bulletin of the Asia Institute*, new series, vol. 2 (1988), pp. 35–48, with further references.

3. J. K. Choksy, *Conflict and Cooperation: Zoroastrian Subalterns and Muslim Elites in Medieval Iranian Society* (New York, 1997), pp. 106–109; Nizam al-Mulk, *Siyāsat-nāma*, ed. H. Darke, Persian Texts Series 8 (Tehran, 1962), p. 13., Translated as *Sitīz va Sāzish* (Tehran, 2002), pp. 131-35.

4. See further R. N. Frye, "The Charisma of Kingship in Ancient Iran," *Iranica Antiqua*, 6, 1 (1964) p. 50; C. E. Bosworth, "The Early Ghaznavids," in *The Cambridge History of Iran*, vol. 4, ed. R. N. Frye (Cambridge, 1975), p. 165; and R. Savory, *Iran Under the Safavids* (Cambridge, 1980), pp. 2–3.

5. See also Frye, "Charisma," pp. 51–52; and F. Halliday, *Iran: Dictatorship and Development* (London, 1979), p. 29.

6. Halliday, *Iran*, pp. 59, 61; and D. N. Wilber, *Iran: Past and Present*, 9th ed. (Princeton, 1981), p. 213. Citations of Muhammad Riza Shah Pahlavi from R. K. Karanjia, *The Mind of a Monarch* (London, 1977), p. 42.

7. See the collection of articles in G. Lenczowski, *Iran under the Pahlavis* (Stanford, 1978), for instance, and also L. Blanch, *Farah: Shahbanou of Iran, Queen of Persia* (London, 1978), pp. 16–17. On Iranian scholars consult K. Aghaie, "Islam and Nationalist

Historiography: Competing Historical Narratives of the Iranian Nation in the Pahlavi Period, "*Studies in Contemporary Islam* 2, 2 (2000), pp. 24–25, 26–30, 40–44. B. Lewis, *History: Remembered, Recovered, Invented* (Princeton, 1975), pp. 7–10, 12, 39–41, provides insightful general comments on the role of scholarship in reconstructing pasts that are used for political purposes. One record of the Sasanians' attempts to present themselves as reconstructors of Iranian society is found in the *Letter of Tōsar (Tansar)*, trans. M. Boyce (Rome, 1968), pp. 29–33, 36, 39–40. Perhaps originally composed during the reign of Ardashir I in the third century A.D., that text was revised during the reign of Khusro I in the sixth century, with additions by Muslim transmitters as late as the thirteenth century.

8. Compare Blanch, *Farah*, p. 14. On the name and functions of Mithra see details in I. Gershevitch, *The Avestan Hymn to Mithra* (Cambridge, 1967), pp. 26–44.

9. Recorded by Blanch, *Farah*, p. 17; and by Karanjia, *Mind*, pp. 23, 30–31, citing an interview with Muhammad Riza Shah Pahlavi. The regime's claims to be the heirs to an Achaemenian legacy is also discussed in G. R. G. Hambly, "The Pahlavi Autocracy: Muhammad Riza Shah, 1941–1979," in *The Cambridge History of Iran*, vol. 7, ed. P. Avery and others (Cambridge, 1991), pp. 284–85.

10. Muhammad Riza Shah Pahlavi, *The Shah's Story* (London, 1980), p. 37. See also Karanjia, *Mind*, pp. 96–97. For the account of Ardashir I's rescue from harm see *Kār-nāmag ī Ardashīr Pā pakān*, ed. E. K. Antia (Bombay, 1900), chap. 14:9–26, pp. 43–46 (Pahlavi text section). The Shah's biography was issued in New Persian, English, and French to target large, diverse audiences. In many aspects, its contents paralleled the interview-based book published earlier by Karanjia.

11. Karanjia, *Mind*, p. 23, citing an interview with Muhammad Riza Shah Pahlavi. E. F. Schmidt, *Persepolis: The Royal Tombs and Other Monuments*, vol. 3 (Chicago, 1970), pp. 80–86, with pls. 19, 22A, 25, 28–30.

12. Karanjia, *Mind*, pp. 44–49, 96. *Khusrō ud rēdag*, ed. J. M. Unvalla (Paris, 1921), ll. 8–16, pp. 13–16. See also Iranian Ministry of Information, *12 Points for Progress*, (Tehran, 1968), p. 41. For the Achaemenian model see *The Bisitun Inscriptions of Darius the Great: Old Persian Text*, Corpus Inscriptionum Iranicarum, pt. 1, vol. 1, text 1, ed. R. Schmitt (London, 1991), ll. 24–26, p. 28. Legal maxims ascribed to Khusro I's regime are found in *The Pahlavi Texts*, ed. J. M. Jamasp-Asana (Bombay, 1913), pp. 55–57.

13. Pahlavi, *Shah's Story*, pp. 31–33, 56–57. See also Wilber, *Iran*, p. 148. Perhaps the most famous passage on Sasanian attempts to restore order and tradition is one relating to the codification of the *Avesta*, on which see *Dēnkard*, ed. D. M. Madan (Bombay, 1911), pp. 412–415. On Ardashir's political exploits and other issues see *Letter of Tōsar (Tansar)*, pp. 33–34, 65; and *Kār-nāmag ī Ardashīr Pāpakān*, chap. 8:1–13, pp. 23–40 (Pahlavi text section). For a personal account of the American role in the restoration of the last Pahlavi shah to power see K. Roosevelt, *Countercoup: The Struggle for the Control of Iran* (New York, 1979).

14. Karanjia, *Mind*, pp. 61, 73, 87, 91–92, 146, 149–50, 160–61; and as Muhammad Riza Shah Pahlavi himself wrote both in *Shah's Story*, pp. 75–84, and *Ba sū-yi Tamaddun-i Buzurg* (Tehran, 1978).

15. Citations from *12 Points*, pp. 1–3, 12, 35–36, 42. See further Lenczowski, *Iran*, p. 477, for the aims of the White Revolution. On indigenous opposition to the White Revolution see Hambly, "The Pahlavi Autocracy: Muhammad Riza Shah," pp. 279–87. Zoroastrian examples from the Pahlavi or Middle Persian literature can be found in *Bundahišn*, ed. T. D. Anklesaria (Bombay, 1908), p. 55; and *Zand ī Wahman Yašt*, ed. B. T. Anklesaria (Bombay, 1957), chap. 4:21, 25, 45, 64, pp. 23, 24, 30, 36–37.

16. Pahlavi, *Shah's Story*, p. 97.

17. See further D. Menashri, "Education xvii. Higher Education," in *Encyclopaedia Iranica*, vol. 8, ed. E. Yarshater (Costa Mesa, 1998), p. 218; Halliday, *Iran*, p. 59; and A. Birashk, "Education xvi. School Texts," in *Encyclopaedia Iranica*, vol. 8, p. 215. On the coupling of western-style education with Iranian royalist patriotism consult A. Birashk, "Education x. Middle and Secondary Schools," in *Encyclopaedia Iranica*, vol. 8, p. 203; and Halliday, *Iran*, p. 60. Also see *Iran Girls College Bulletin 1967–68* (Tehran, n.d.), pp. 1–22, for the programs of study available and the purpose of that education. On access of women to secular, state-supervised, education at that time refer to "Education xxvi. Women's Education in the Pahlavi Period and After," in *Encyclopaedia Iranica*, vol. 8, pp. 235–36.

18. Citation from Resurgence Party, *Philosophy of Iran's Revolution* (Tehran, 1976). See further Muhammad Riza Shah Pahlavi, *Mission for My Country* (New York, 1960), p. 54; and his *The White Revolution* (Tehran, 1967), p. 16. Also consult N. R. Keddie, *Roots of Revolution: An Interpretative History of Modern Iran* (New Haven, 1981), p. 143; and P. C. Radji, *In The Service of the Peacock Throne* (London, 1983), p. 260.

19. Wilber, *Iran*, p. 214. On the cross-cultural significance of celebrations such as those at Persepolis, Masada in Israel, and Istanbul in Turkey, consult Lewis, *History*, pp. 3–7, 101. Among the many examples that can be cited where queen Farah played prominent roles were the annual Festival of Arts in Shiraz, the restoration of historic buildings in Isfahan, and pilgrimages to the shrine of Imam Riza at Mashhad. See Blanch, *Farah*, pp. 84–85, 107–109, for more information.

20. Citation from Lenczowski, *Iran*, p. 456, n. 27. In specific consult E. Abrahamian, *Iran Between Two Revolutions* (Princeton, 1982), pp. 438–39. In general see Lewis, *History*, p. 90. For additional details on the four pillars of state refer to Abrahamian, *Iran*, pp. 439–40.

21. Excerpts from lectures delivered by Ayatullah Ruhullah Khumaini, reproduced among a selection of Khumaini's important speeches and writings compiled by H. Algar, trans., *Islam and Revolution: Writings and Declarations of Imam Khomeini* (Berkeley, 1981), pp. 55–57, 222. See also Halliday, *Iran*, pp. 60–61. For an overview of

Shiʿism's important role in modern Iranian society including resistance to the Pahlavi regime consult R. P. Mottahedeh, *The Mantle of the Prophet: Religion and Politics in Iran* (New York, 1985). Alienation of the *ʿulamāʾ* has been examined by S. Akhavi, *Religion and Politics in Contemporary Iran: Clergy-State Relations in the Pahlavi Period* (Albany, 1980). The Iranian Islamic calendar was reinstated only in August 1978, as part of an unsuccessful attempt to stem rising anti-monarchist sentiments.

22. Consult Choksy, "Sacral Kingship," pp. 49–50, for details and references specific to ancient Iranian society. In general also see Lowenthal, *The Past is a Foreign Country*, p. 46. For example, blame was attributed by Ayatullah Khumaini to the shah for street violence in 1978. The assertion was made in a declaration dated August 12, 1978 issued by Khumaini at Najaf. See the text in Algar, *Islam*, pp. 231–32. The citations from speeches delivered by Ayatullah Khumaini on June 3, 1963, at the Faiziya Madrasa in Qum and on February 27, 1988, at Najaf can be found in Algar, *Islam*, pp. 178–79, 228.

23. Richard W. Bulliet's academic interests span ancient, medieval, and modern Iran. It is, therefore, a great pleasure to present this article on continuity and change in Iranian society and politics to that erudite scholar.

A Note on Biblical Narrative and ʿAbbāsid History

Tayeb El-Hibri

Whether by coincidence or design (through emulation, self-representation or projection by narrators), the history of the ʿAbbāsid family has ended up bearing some striking resemblances to that of Old Testament figures. The image given in the Islamic sources of the elders of the ʿAbbāsid family, starting with al-ʿAbbās b. ʿAbd al-Muṭṭalib, then his son, ʿAbdallāh, as the rightful successors to the Prophet Muhammad's legacy, the holders of the keys of esoteric knowledge to Islam (*ta'wīl*), and the ones entitled to pass on the inheritance of religious (and eventually political) authority through designation (*waṣiyya*) closely resembles the images of the Hebrew patriarchs, especially Isaac, Jacob and Joseph.[1] Many intangible factors, spanning the latter's wisdom sayings, drama of interaction, moods and gestures can remind one of some features of Abbasid behavior which can be extended to the ʿAlids as well. With his copious output of *ḥadīth, akhbār*, and *tafsīr* lore ʿAbdallāh b. ʿAbbās occupies a special role as the hinge between biblical and Islamic traditions as he is referred to as "*ḥabr al-ʿArab*."[2] The term "*ḥabr*" itself, generally explained as "*kāhin*,"[3] must have evoked in origin a similarity of role to that of the Jewish sages.

After the victory of the ʿAbbāsid *daʿwa* and establishment of the ʿAbbāsid caliphate, the frame of biblical reference in Ṭabarī shifts from the homey, erudite environment of the patriarchs to that of the kings of Israel. Saul, the energetic but unlucky first king of Israel, does not figure much as a model for the ʿAbbāsids. The reasons for this have much to do with his failure. Saul's loss of divine favor, his thoroughbred genealogy, and tragic push to leadership by followers rather than his own desire are all factors that make him resemble the ʿAlid martyrs, especially ʿAlī b. Abī Tālib. David, however, along with Solomon, give the ʿAbbāsids a rich cache to draw on. The checkered background of these two men, their recognition of their own faults, and their pursuit of the world with fully human impulses, not to mention their victories, very often resemble the profile of more than one ʿAbbāsid caliph, particularly Hārūn al-Rashīd and al-Maʾmūn.[4] The ʿAbbāsid caliphs especially reveled in the Qurʾānic verse that declared, "David, behold, We have appointed thee as viceroy in the earth; therefore judge between men justly, and follow not caprice, lest it lead thee astray from the way of God (*yā Dāwūd innā jaʿalnāka khalīfatan fiʾl-arḍ fa-uḥkum bayna al-nāsi biʾl-ḥaqq*),"[5] which they used to stress their divine right to rule and, one can add, extend a hegemony over the Hāshemite family. The caliph al-Mahdī used this verse as a lightning rod in the public proclamation in A.H. 160/A.D. 776 when he decreed that henceforth the progeny of Ziyād b. Abīhi, the famous Umayyad governor and alleged half-brother of Muʿāwiya, were no longer to be considered as part of the Umayyad (Sufyānid) family and their rights were to be forfeited, since adulterous ties are not considered religiously legal ties.[6]

Al-Mahdī is a caliph about whom historians know very little, save some embellished anecdotes about his carefree life or about the odd dispute with a minister or governor. Still, this caliph's career is especially important because he was groomed by al-Manṣūr to absorb messianic expectations of the time with his unique title, and was tutored by Muḥammad b. Isḥāq whose *Sīra* of the Prophet was once prefaced by a now lost book that covers stories of the biblical prophets.[7] As Gordon Newby has argued in his reassembling of this lost work known as "*Kitāb al-Mubtadaʾ*," both al-Mahdī and Ibn Isḥāq lived at a time when extensive traffic in Jewish stories (*akhbār*) was still permissible in the 8th century Islamic community in Iraq, and before the later consolidation of orthodoxy threw out much of the biblical stories as legend (*isrāʾīliyyāt, qaṣaṣ*) and confined ḥadīth to legal and ritualistic matters.[8] As also evidenced by Newby's approach, Ṭabarī's *Taʾrīkh* and *Tafsīr* works are the places to look if one seeks to reconstruct "*Kitāb al-Mubtadaʾ*." In this exploratory note, I would like to go a step further and argue for a close tie between this work and the ʿAbbāsid narratives.

Fragments of biblical resemblance are woven throughout the fabric of ʿAbbāsid representation. After the victory at the battle of al-Zāb, the caliph al-Saffāḥ recites the Qurʾānic verse, which describes the battle between David and Goliath after crossing a river. The relevant verse reads: "And when Saul went forth with the hosts he said, 'God will try you with a river'. . ." (*wa lammā faṣala ṭāluta biʾl-jund*).[9] The escape of the last Umayyad caliph Marwān b. Muḥammad to Egypt is used to identify him with Pharaoh (*shabīhihi firʿawn*).[10] The saga of conflict between al-Amīn and al-Maʾmūn includes features of the Saul-David conflict, as one between two men of different births (one of high, another of humble origins), but also the conflict between David and Absalom. The execution of al-Amīn, as widely attested to in the sources, is shown to have given al-Maʾmūn considerable grief and turned him in later life against the commander Ṭāhir b. al-Ḥusayn, very much as Ṭabarī describes David's grief over his son and turning against the commander who killed Absalom. Disobeying David's order not to kill Absalom, the commander charged with the mission, Ṭabarī tells us, disobeyed the orders: "After [David] repented to God, the people heeded his rule again. He [i.e., David] achieved victory over his son, and sent after him a commander whom he advised not to murder him and find the means to arrest him (*wa taqaddama ilayhi an yatawaqqā ḥatfahu wa yatalaṭṭaf li-asrihi*)." "The commander," however, Ṭabarī adds, "pursued him (i.e., Absalom) and killed him in violation of David's order." (*wa laḥiqahu al-qāʾid mukhālifan li-amri Dāwūd*).[11] After the murder, Ṭabarī describes David as greatly grieved and having turned against the commander who did this deed. (*fa-ḥazina ʿalayhi ḥuznan shadīdan wa tanakkara liʾl-qāʾid*)."[12]

These resemblances, gaining their repetition from partially similar circumstances, make the boundaries between history and artful construction fuzzy. But if these connections to biblical narrative are recognizable because the broader Islamic religious narrative accepted their frames of reference, whether to Saul, David, or Solomon, other influences of biblical legend are not as discernible anymore. The Islamic reshaping of the Jewish concept of prophethood meant that a number of personalities, such as Samuel, Nathan, and ʿAsaf b. Barkhiyya, had to be eliminated or toned down considerably. This reality of redaction is important to reckon with because there is reason to believe that a considerable part of the profiles of the early ʿAbbāsid vizirs (even after the holder of this office stopped being a Hāshemite *dāʿī* (propagandist) for revolution, as in the case of Abū Salama al-Khallāl or Khālid b. Barmak) stems from inspiration by the portraits of excised biblical prophets, most notably Nathan and Samuel.

The research of many ʿAbbāsid scholars on the vizierate, based largely on anecdotal evidence from historical and belles lettres works, has often reflected frustration with the inconsistent modes of descriptions of these vizirs. The sources yield little by way of a coherent picture of the origins of the office, the functions it commanded, or who among a diverse set of close associates of the caliph in the first half of the 8th-century can even be properly termed "vizir."[13] I have pointed elsewhere to the fact that many references which surround the vizierate picture in the works of Ṭabarī and Jahshiyārī describe a situation that is not political or systemic but moral, religious, and allusive.[14]

The men who advised the early ʿAbbāsid caliphs are inconsistently described both in terms of political function and proximity to the caliphs. While one can sometimes accept descriptions of Abū Ayyūb al-Muryānī and Abū ʿUbaydallāh Muʿāwiya b. Yasār as vizirs (in the bureaucratic sense of the term), the situation becomes more murky with figures like Yaʿqūb b. Dāwūd b. Ṭahmān, reportedly an ʿAlid ally (former *kātib* of the brother of al-Nafs al-Zakiyya, Ibrāhīm b. ʿAbdallāh),[15] who is described as "wazīr" but spends his time giving religious advice on the prohibition of singing and wine-drinking and the primacy of prayer, more than giving political opinions.[16] His clashes with al-Mahdī over the need for a puritanical life are well known. In the end, the caliph imprisoned this advisor on charges of ʿAlid sympathy, an almost cliche charge against ministers (especially the *mawālī* among them) throughout this period.

The problem of ministerial definition gets further complicated in the case of Yaḥyā al-Barmakī who floats in and out of ʿAbbāsid service from the time of al-Manṣūr down to that of Hārūn al-Rashīd. Yaḥyā al-Barmakī was undoubtedly a man of many functions by the time he reached the peak of his power in the reign of al-Rashīd. However, again as I showed before, Yaḥyā's image in the sources is unique. He is represented as a wise man who is pious and discourages the caliph from trifling away in life, but nowhere does Yaḥyā show a substantial role in crafting strategy or advising on governmental policy (except for a few remarks related to Khurasan, a location well-known as a playing field for many topoi of Islamic history).[17] Not coincidently, Barmakid piety gets linked in early ʿAbbāsid officialdom with suspicions of ʿAlid sympathy, which is ultimately counted as a possible motive behind the caliph's turn against this family of ministers. The charge of pro-ʿAlid sympathy on the part of many ʿAbbāsid ministers (or possibly continued role of "*daʿwa*" on behalf of the caliph) can serve the reader as a sign that the office had more of a religious than political function. Yaḥyā al-Barmakī, being the heir to a well known Buddhist spiritual dynasty in Balkh, appears to have functioned in that cosmopolitan constituency of the early ʿAbbāsid caliphs in Iraq as a kind of syncretic seer in the ʿAbbāsid court.

The difficulty in defining the real tasks of the ʿAbbāsid court advisors and the relation between caliphs and ministers may ultimately be unresolvable as a historical issue from the sources. However, when viewed as contrived representations, the images of the ʿAbbāsid vizirs, especially of someone like Yaḥyā al-Barmakī, can benefit from some analogy with biblical legends, especially with the personalities of Samuel, Nathan, and ʿAsaf b. Barkhiyya. The hegemonic role of Yaḥyā over the caliph al-Rashīd, possessing the freedom to enter upon him at any hour of the day or night, something that the caliph eventually complained about to his court physician, Jibrīl b. Bakhtīshūʿ, reminds one of the freedom of access ʿAsaf b. Barkhiyya wielded in Solomon's court.[18] And when upon hearing that his son Jaʿfar was killed and that the Barmakid household got destroyed, Yaḥyā declares, "and so shall his son (i.e., Hārūn's) be killed and his house destroyed,"[19] Yaḥyā's premonition echoes the curse placed by Nathan on the house of David for his adultery with Bathsheba and causing the death of Uriah: "Now therefore the sword shall never depart from your house."[20]

Simply put, stories about the caliphs and their vizirs ring much like the sections of "*qiṣaṣ al-anbiyāʾ*" preserved in Ṭabarī's work and other sources. The challenge to unraveling the similarity and interdependence between ʿAbbāsid and biblical accounts, however, lies in the fact that important personages on the ʿAbbāsid side are rarely, if ever, limited in comparison to one biblical figure (or even to an unaltered, sometimes Islamized version of the biblical frame of reference). Hārūn al-Rashīd's image may bear the most similarity to Solomon, with the images of power and wealth that surround both courts, but it is an Islamized Solomon that the caliph sometimes compares with, not the biblical one, a king who is fond of carrying out *ghazw* and conquest for the faith which is not attested to in the biblical version. But even this analogy gets modified, whether by Hārūn's own desire or representation from others, to make him look like David in some acts. Hārūn's famous routine of alternating every year between carrying out a campaign of conquest and making pilgrimage to Mecca is similar to the characteristic assigned to David of devoting himself to fasting every alternate day.

Hārūn al-Rashīd may have adapted his routine to the perceived memory of David's piety, but, in another instance, narrators may have invented an account that bore little resemblance to reality and much to biblical legend. This time, the ʿAbbāsid story ties in not with David or Solomon but very vaguely with Saul, and the archetypal Barmakid victim bears connections to Samuel. In the biblical story that describes how Samuel prayed to God that Saul be preserved until his own (i.e., Samuel's) time of death arrives, we see a vignette that is not unlike the apprehension shared by Hārūn al-Rashīd and al-Faḍl b. Yaḥyā al-Barmakī that their deaths are closely timed in fortune such that when one of them dies, the other soon follows. As al-Faḍl declared in his prison in Raqqa about Hārūn al-Rashīd: "His death and mine will closely follow one another."[21] And, just as defeat descended on Saul in his war with the Philistines after Samuel died, Khurasan began to unravel in the face of al-Rashīd after the Barmakids died.

More specifically, a reader can note that the story about Hārūn's premonitions of death shows a variation on the story of Saul's encounter with the ghost of Samuel.[22] In the ʿAbbāsid case, the caliph has a dream of a hand stretching out with a fist full of red soil and a voice saying that this is the land where he would die (in Tus). In this context, one recalls the story of Saul summoning the ghost of Samuel at the intercession of a witch, and hears Samuel tell him of where to find redemption: to go out and fight till death in battle against the Philistines. Hārūn's campaign in Khurasan did not present the caliph with the threat that he would be killed in battle, but he did die in his army camp during that fateful campaign which in essence led to a future civil war and the undoing of the empire. Thus, while neither just a temporal leader, nor an infallible prophet in the Islamic sense of the term, the ʿAbbāsid caliph's figure frequently resembled in various stories the biblical king (with shades from other ancient figures) who encounters tribulation but is able through dreams, inner awakening, and premonitions of the future to discover closure and redemption for his errors.

Endnotes

1. U. Rubin has provided an important comparison of the Shiʿī concept of *waṣiyya* and similar ancient Jewish principles. However, the discussion of these connections continues to center on a religious rather than a historical frame, and continues to ignore the ʿAbbāsids and center on the ʿAlids. U. Rubin, "Prophets and Progenitors in the Early Shīʿa Tradition," *Jerusalem Studies in Arabic and Islam*, 1 (1979), 41–65. J. Lassner has provided important conceptual comments on the similarity in techniques of biblical and Islamic narratives, but a more detailed and specific catalogue of analogies between the two fields is still needed. J. Lassner, *Islamic Revolution and Historical Memory*, American Oriental Society Series 66 (New Haven, 1986), pp. 14, 30–33, 63.

2. Ṭabarī, *Taʾrīkh al-Rusul waʾl-Mulūk*, ed. M. J. de Goeje et al., 3 series (Leiden, 1879–1901) I, 461.

3. Ṭabarī, *Taʾrīkh*, I, 462.

4. One can hypothesize further that narrators may have well compared the rivalry between the ʿAlids and the ʿAbbāsids for God's favor in terms analogous to the rivalry between the house of Saul and the house of David.

5. Qurʾan, 38:26. A. J. Arberry, *The Koran Interpreted*, (London, 1955) v. 2, p. 160.

6. Ṭabarī, *Taʾrīkh*, III, 481.

7. G. Newby, *The Making of the Last Prophet* (University of South Carolina Press: Columbia, 1989), pp. 7, 161.

8. G. Newby, *The Making of the Last Prophet*, pp. 10–12.

9. Qurʾan, 2:249. Tabari, *b,* III, 41.

10. Ṭabarī, *Taʾrīkh*, III, 50.

11. Ṭabarī, *Taʾrīkh*, I, 571.

12. Ibid.

13. For a representative sampling of these studies, see D. Sourdel, *Le Vizirat abbaside de 749 à 936*, (Damascus, 1959–60); F. Omar, *al-Judhūr al-Taʾrīkhiyya liʾl-Wizāra al-ʿAbbāsiyya* (Baghdad, 1986); R. Kimber, "The Early ʿAbbasid Vizierate," *Journal of Semitic Studies*, 37 (1992), 65–85.

14. Tayeb El-Hibri, *Reinterpreting Islamic Hisoriography, Hārūn al-Rashīd and the Narrative of the ʿAbbāsid Caliphate* (Cambridge University Press, 1999), p. 50.

15. Jahshiyāī, *Kitāb al-Wuzarāʾ waʾl-Kuttāb*, ed. M. al-Saqqā et al., (Cairo, 1938), p. 155.

16. Jahshiyārī, *al-Wuzarāʾ*, p. 160.

17. T. El-Hibri, *Reinterpreting Islamic Historiography*, pp. 36–41.

18. G. Newby, *The Making of the Last Prophet*, p. 168.

19. Ṭabarī, *Taʾrīkh*, III, 683. Jahshiyārī, *al-Wuzarāʾ*, p. 254.

20. 2 Samuel 12:10.

21. Ṭabarī, *Taʾrīkh*, III, 733.

22. L. Ginzberg, *Legends of the Jews*, p. 70.

Historical Patterns of Higher Education for Women in Morocco since Independence

Patricia C. Gloster-Coates

Preface

The purpose of my research was to ascertain the reasons that women of Morocco are more progressive in their education and professions than their counterparts in North West Africa, the neighboring countries of Algeria, Tunisia, Libya, and Mauretania. I traveled to Morocco during June and July of 1998 and 1999 to study the historical context and the educational structure in higher education for women of the Kingdom of Morocco. To focus my research, I decided to use the pre-colonial and colonial educational models as a means of introducing the educational strategies practiced by the Ministry of Higher Education to train women for full participation in the modern international, global economy.

I was fortunate to acquire research materials from solid primary sources in Morocco as I conducted my survey of women's education in Morocco. First of all, I had to secure permission through the American consulate and the United States Information Service at Rabat, Morocco to use the archives at Sidi Muhammad V University at Agdal and the archives at the Secretariat of the Ministry of Higher Education at Hassan, both in Rabat. I was able to acquire information that is not easily available in the United States to study a very fascinating subject, the women's movement in Morocco with a special focus on the post-independence era. Moroccan women in the feminist movement have accelerated the increasing emphasis of expanding higher education for women.

Introduction

From the writings of a very articulate scholar, Dr. Rahma Bourqia, professor at Muhammadiyyah University and Sidi Muhammad V University, it is apparent that there is emerging in Morocco an articulate women's movement that is distinctly Moroccan. The fact that her work was published in Morocco indicates the outstanding status Moroccan women scholars have gained in spite of the strong political trends Islamic fundamentalism exerts in nearby Algeria, Libya, and Egypt. The foundation of solid women's representation in government, the professions, and teaching was developed during the early years of French colonialism and brought to special prominence by Sidi Muhammad V, the sultan of Morocco from 1927 until 1961, because he placed a high priority on the expansion of educational opportunities for youth, but especially for women. The following essay will discuss the historical causes of the progressive women's movement in Morocco from 1956 until 1999.

The Historical Setting

Around 1900, Egyptian legal scholar and judge, Qasim Amin, wrote an article entitled "The Slavery of Women" to admonish the legal community about the social detriments of confining Egyptian women to a regulated, constricted status which rendered them totally sheltered and totally helpless. In the rural areas of Egypt, women did not have as much access to education as did their urban counterparts. Amin remarked that rural women were seen outside the home only twice in their lifetimes: on the way home from the hospital at birth and on the way out of the home to the cemetery at death. In 1908, the Maghriban publication, *Lissan al-Maghrib* (Arabic, "Voices of the Mahgrib") lamented the terrible position in which women found themselves when they sought employment. They were confined to work as seasonal workers, domestic workers, weed pickers and harvesters. Rahma Bourqia reports the same historical circumstances in her work *Feminist Studies* where she decries the former rural traditional method for the communal announcement declaring the sex of a newborn child: three ululates for the boy as opposed to one or none for the girl. Hence, before the arrival of French colonialism, progressive, humane North Africans decried the lowly estate of women.[1]

In 1912, under the Treaty of Fez, the French colonial administration established the Protectorate of Morocco and named Mulay Sultan Yusuf as head of the Alawite monarchy. Marshal Louis-Hubert Gonzalve—Lyautey became Resident General after he participated in the French campaign to pacify Morocco in 1911–1912. Due to previous experience with capable mentors in the French colonies of Indo-China and Madagascar, he instituted indirect rule in Morocco. Ruling through the traditional, indigenous rulers of a new colony worked as a rule with the British colonial government in India. It became standard practice in British sub-Saharan Africa. For Lyautey to depart from traditional French colonial policy that removed traditional leaders and replaced them with French military or bureaucratic personnel disconcerted his superiors in the colonial office. It is no surprise to discover that he felt great sympathy with the management policies of Frederick Lugard, Governor-General of amalgamated Nigeria. Lugard became famous as the author of *The Dual Mandate in British Tropical Africa* written during the 1920's. It became the textbook for the British policy of indirect rule in Africa. Lyautey set about to construct a modern, efficient bureaucracy in Morocco that would win co-operation and respect from the people and the monarchy.

The colonial administration in Morocco set out to expand higher education for men and women. Lyautey took the initiative to assemble a group of advisors who would create a new educational ministry for the purpose of modernizing the skills of the Moroccan elite. He believed that the French colonial government would function effectively if an articulate, European-trained elite could eventually run the protectorate as representatives of French civilization. Applying the doctrine of indirect rule that claims to respect the religious and social customs of the indigenous people of the colony, he supervised the creation of an educational ministry that oversaw religious and secular training.[2]

The new Ministry of Education was responsible to the Resident-General. He worked with his deputy who was directly responsible to him and worked closely with him. The next important official in the hierarchy was the Secretary-General of the Protectorate who supervised the General Department of Public Instruction, Fine Arts and Antiquities. There were two other departments that reported directly to the Resident-General: The Department of Indigenous Affairs and of Informational Services and the Department of Sharifian Affairs that co-operated with Muslim religious educational institutions.[3] In the new arrangement, it was significant that Lyautey brought religious educators into the colonial educational system without interfering with their religious responsibilities.

The new educational system tried to educate Moroccans on all class levels and of both genders. The children of notables and Moroccan officials who occupied elite positions were sent to schools specializing in government and the professions. Otherwise, children were sent to what we would call vocational schools in the American system. The children of the majority of Moroccans were enrolled in the artisan or craftsmanship schools. In a sense, they were preparing students for industrial or agricultural apprenticeships. There were special schools for girls that taught them the traditional needlecrafts and handicrafts for women like complex, decorative embroidery and the weaving of fabric into carpets. The colonial administration included girls in their new models of education, not as a *cause célèbre* but as part of the general cultural anthropological approach. It was recognized that the Moroccan educational system should approximate the French educational system of its time.[4]

In the chapter on Morocco from the book, *Teaching Methods in the Arab Maghrib*, Muhammad Abd al-Jabriy mentions that the Moroccans were compelled to follow the French educational approach in the early years of the Protectorate. However, it was obvious to the Moroccan educators that French colonial administrators would have difficulty imposing their educational goals. A compromise was worked out so that some latitude was allowed for Muslim educators to continue with their traditional practices of Muslim education.

Lyautey's departure in 1925 ended the colonial philosophy of indirect rule. However the educational system he established set the tone for westernization through modern education. The cooperative relationship Lyautey had striven for brought about new expectations for the university students who despised the abridgement of their rights under the new colonial administration. In 1926, Ahmad Balafrej formed the Moroccan League. Muhammad Allal al-Fassi, the leader of the student discussion group called "The Mint Tea Group" which merged with the Moroccan League almost a year later. The term "Mint Tea" connotes the reflective conversations students developed while they rested from their studies with the strong, sweet, minty tea beverage especially enjoyed in Morocco. It implies for the westerner that Moroccans did not adopt the custom of enjoying wine with their meals. The "Mint Tea Group" and the Moroccan League eventually developed into *Istiqlāl* or Independence Party that was formed in 1943.

At the same time in 1927, a new king came to the monarchy in the person of Sidi Muhammad V, and he became a catalyst for change in the establishment of Moroccan independence. He was cut in the mold of the formerly defiant Mulays such as Abdul Rahman who aided the Algerians under the marabout Abdul Qadir during their first war with the French and criticized the Spanish for their aggression on Moroccan properties near Tetouan and Ceuta. Much to the surprise of the colonial administration, Muhammad V aligned himself with the officers of the *Istiqlāl* party and carried out policies that approximated their reform agenda. In the course of the reforms he would make, education of women was one of his top priorities.

The Depression and the years of the Second World War placed the quest for independence on hold in all of the Maghriban colonies, Morocco, Algeria, and Tunisia. The *Dahir* (Arabic, "Promulgation") of 1930 was enacted by the French colonial administration to distinguish between Berbers and Arabs in Morocco, allowing Berbers to live under separate customary laws. Even though the promulgation was a concession to Berber concerns of ethnic identity, the Muslim community as a whole felt that it was divisive. The *Istiqlāl* party and Sidi Muhammad V were not able to close ranks among Muslims due to the interruption caused by military campaigns leading to the French entry into World War Two. Under the circumstances, enhanced education for women received very low priority.

During World War Two, Morocco served as a site for French resistance against Nazism. When the Vichy administration took over Paris, General Charles de Gaulle moved to North Africa and conducted some of his Resistance efforts from Morocco as well as Algeria. The colonial administration was compelled to rely upon the good graces of the Moroccan people. Ayandele reports that 300,000 Moroccan troops served the French armies during the war.[5] Among the Allied forces were American troops. In 1943, President Franklin Delano Roosevelt visited Morocco to encourage the Allies and the Resistance movement. Oral tradition says the Moroccan king reminded the President that Morocco was the first non-western country and the third international country to recognize American independence back in 1776. Sidi Muhammad is said to have appealed to the Americans to assist the Moroccans in gaining their independence. In any case, the United States did show some sympathy for Moroccan demands for independence after the war. The result was a close political alliance between the United States and Morocco that lasts until this very day.

During the 1950s, Morocco stepped up her quest for independence. Sidi Muhammad V and the *Istiqlāl* party were galvanized by the French losses during the Indo-China (Viet Nam) War and the onset of the Algerian War in 1954. They were determined to gain their independence in as short a time as possible. It was obvious that the French government in Paris under the Fourth Republic placed low priority on the independence movement in their protectorate Morocco at that time.

In addition, the French colonial administration tried to neutralize the work of Sidi Muhammad V by enhancing the status of his opponents, General Alphonse Juin, the Resident General from 1947 until 1952 and Thalmi al-Glaoui, the Pasha of Marrakesh and the Kittaniyyah brotherhood, led by Abd al-Hai al-Kittani. The Moroccan people would not agree to accept the bait of a new colonially approved set of leaders. They supported the king and the *Istiqlāl* party's demands to create a new transitional independent, democratic government. The failure of the French strategy to derail Sidi Muhammad V's plans for independence compelled them to send the king to Corsica for exile lasting two years, from 1953 until 1955. The French found the Morocco people impossible to please during the years of Sidi Muhammad's exile. The *Istiqlāl* party led the campaign to restore their king. They were successful in their attempts, because the French colonial administration restored Sidi Muhammad V as king and granted Morocco her independence in 1956.

In the post independence period, from 1956 until 1962, Sidi Muhammad V enacted a number of reforms that enhanced the growth of higher education in Morocco. First of all, he changed the capital from Tangier to Rabat. At Rabat, he established a premier university that was named after him. Secondly, he increased the number of secondary schools that were available to women. To make the point very clear, he even took his daughters to all of the official ceremonies. To demonstrate that education of women was to be taken seriously, he attended the opening ceremonies of girls' schools. He set a brilliant example also for men by insisting that his son, Hassan II, who later became king of Morocco in 1962, attend and graduate from law school in France. Feminist scholars praise Sidi Muhammad V for the sterling example he set in furthering the cause of increased enrollment of Moroccan women in higher education.[6]

Educational Policies in Morocco since Independence

According to Rahma Bourqia, one of the leading feminist scholars in Morocco, modern higher education started in 1957 with two hundred plus students attending Sidi Muhammad V University, which was modeled on the French system of higher education. The university system underwent dramatic expansion during the late 1960s under the aegis of King Hassan II, when six new universities were built. The statistics reflect the change. In the academic year 1964–1965, five thousand students attended universities. However, in 1990, 198,000 students were participating in higher education. The preferential curriculum was that which encouraged entry into the professions.[7]

There are economic factors, which controlled the expansion and contraction in the years listed above, 1964 to 1990. First, Morocco was a prosperous economy. Twenty one million acres of land was available for cultivation. Morocco placed so much marginal land under new irrigation, that she even sent irrigation and agricultural specialists to Algeria during the 1960s to advise farmers. Morocco had a strong infrastructure from colonial times based on railroad transportation that has been recently modernized into a very efficient network. Morocco possesses one of the world's largest deposits of phosphates. In fact, two-thirds of the world's phosphates are produced by Morocco, enabling her to invest more funds in higher education. Morocco also exports citrus fruits and vegetables to world markets. She is world renowned for the excellent textiles she produces which one may see in abundance at the markets of Sale, near Rabat. Marrakech is the seat of leather items like shoes and handbags that are exported the world over.

In the 1970s, another extrinsic factor was introduced which would hinder economic development. After Spain withdrew from Rio de Oro, the Polisario independence movement claimed possession of the land known as the Western Sahara or the Sahrawi Democratic Republic. The United Nations conducted a plebiscite among the people who said they favored independence. Algeria and Mauretania claimed the land was theirs. It, too, was rich in phosphates that made the Western Sahara a potentially lucrative addition to Morocco. The Moroccans argued that the Western Sahara had been taken from them by Spain during colonialism and the land should be annexed to Morocco. The culmination of argument came when King Hassan II led his nation southward to take part in the "Green March of 1975" to reclaim the land for Morocco.

On the economic front, Morocco was very dependent on the export of raw materials to earn foreign currency. During the 1970s, the world price for phosphates reached its lowest level in many years.[8] The subsequent decline in revenue fuelled discontent over rising unemployment exacerbated by an increase in the birth rate. Furthermore the proportion of youth competing for services soared upward with the increase in the birth rate throughout the 1970s, which compelled many young men and not a few women to seek employment in France. In the 1980s, half the population of Morocco was under 20 years old. The millions of French francs that immigrant Moroccans in the current European Community nations sent to relatives at home contributed a significant amount of foreign exchange to the Moroccan government.[9]

The educational policies of the late 1960s persisted until the late 1990s. Recent surveys conducted by Dr. Rahma Bourqia and her colleagues have yielded interesting results. It appears that Morocco is doing fine work in training her youth to enter the professions. The number of male students matriculating in college is 54.6 percent, while the number of female students is 45.4 percent. Students are distressed that they have prepared for the professions but have much difficulty finding work even if they graduate from Muhammad V University, the mother of universities that produced 26.5 percent of all graduates in the early 1990s.[10] In 1990–1991, the total population of Morocco was estimated to be 10,000,000 people, of which 1,094,000 were unemployed. Unemployment differs among urban and rural dwellers. In the cities, 20.6 percent were unemployed. In the rural areas, 5.6 percent of the population was unemployed. Unless the government takes drastic action, unemployment will continue to rise, because the growth rate of the active female population in the year 2000 is expected to be 3.8 percent among women and three per cent among men. The number of women who enter the employment market is expected to continue growing rapidly.[11]

The Ministry of Higher Education became alarmed at the central government's trend toward cutting grants to education during the early 1970s, for the new policies discouraged expansion of education for all Moroccans. Trouble had been anticipated in 1967 when the Ministry carried out major reforms in the structuring of the curriculum. Then in 1975, another major reform took place in the licensing of the B.A. (Bachelor of Arts) program. The third round of reforms took place in 1997 for the purpose of intensifying and broadening the disciplines in the higher education programs. In the context of reforming the educational system, the World Bank conducted a study of higher education in Morocco and issued a confidential report dated 22 November 1985 entitled *Royaume du Maroc, Programme de Reforme du Secteur Educatif, Rapport d'Evaluation du Programme*. It was issued by the Division Education et Development des Resources Humaines Region Europe, Moyen-Orient et Afrique du Nord. The report studied the unemployment rate among university graduates and discussed the lopsided numbers of vocational education graduates versus university graduates from professional schools.

It was noted in the World Bank Report summary that the government had to find employment for the university graduates and create openings for the majority of Moroccans to enter artisanal work, industrial work, and agricultural sectors where there was a shortage of manpower for potential work that needed to be done to make the economy develop rapidly.[12] In the late 1990s, fifty percent of the population was employed in the agricultural sector. According to World Bank projections back in 1985, if the agricultural sector were to continue to expand, new educational programs would have to be developed on a vocational level as well as a university level.

The Changing Role of Women in Morocco Today

Rahma Bourqia and her colleagues have compiled a book of feminist studies, which accounts for the work women in North Africa and nearby countries are doing at the present time. The book was compiled from a conference at the Faculty of Arts and Letters at Muhammad V University in Rabat in the year April 1994. The theme of the conference was "Women of the Mediterranean from tradition to modernity."

To introduce the writings of the authors of ÉTUDES FÉMININES, *Notes méthodologiques, 1997*, Professor Bourqia describes the development of the women's movement in North Africa. The authors carry forth studies of women in Algeria and Morocco in particular. They also examine the feminist idioms of the hearth and public spaces in North Africa. The book offers a new look at the developing feminist movement in North Africa and points out the differences between western European feminism and North African feminism. The ethnological and gender studies on which the women professors have embarked bring new and stimulating perspectives to conventional western models of feminism.

The editor, Professor Bourqia, tries to bring the North African feminist scene out of its artificial isolation from the feminist movement in southern Europe. She believes that they should exchange ideas and intellectual traditions, even though there is no doubt that the northern Mediterranean countries are more advanced in institutional and theoretical matters than the North African, southern Mediterranean countries. In the northern countries, the intellectual women from elite backgrounds have dominated the feminist movement. Their research takes place within the university structure, whereas in North Africa, feminist intellectuals hesitate to bring their research to the male-dominated university where segregation between the sexes has existed for centuries. What the two cultures have in common is the code of honor among men in Algeria, Greece, Italy, Egypt, and Morocco. The dowry practices are the same; the importance of virginity and certain matrimonial strategies remain the same. The image of women in Mediterranean mythology is very similar. The discipline of anthropology is a good medium of comparison. In many ways, it was the one of the most mentioned tools of analysis. Dr. Bourqia admits that women's studies in North Africa are a new discipline in the developing stage. It is interesting that many of the recent reports about women in the Maghrib have discussed their role in development.[13]

Dr. Bourqia ponders the reasons why the subservient role of women has persisted in Morocco. Upon examining the state of mind called *sbar* (Arabic, "patience and endurance"), she explains the reasons women consent to tolerate male domination, while in the private domain women rely on their essential position in culinary duties and child rearing as a means of asserting retaliation and resistance.[14] The cultural assumption is that women dominate the private domain while men dominate the public domain.

Professor Bourqia examines all phases of the women's movement, from language or definitions, to rituals in marriage where the groom is received as and called a Mulay that is one of the official titles of the sultan or king of

Morocco. She mentions in her analysis that Islamic law spells out the division of labor, code of behavior, and rights of the bride. It is part of the given, the assumptions as to how duties should be done, and what the appropriate role is that gives continuity in a changing society. She also employs the French philosophical tool of analysis termed "deconstruction" to unravel many of the myths of gender. Even though the social sciences on both sides of the Mediterranean have a patriarchal gender bias, one should not discard the gender category, but include it in the research of the social science disciplines like anthropology. The colonial anthropologists studied every phase of social life in Morocco. In doing so, they described the roles and lifestyles of women. Unwittingly, they left a legacy of important research that is useful to women now. It should not be discarded just because its orientation was patriarchal.

Professor Dalila Morsly of the University of Algeria produced an arresting study of the effect of nationalistic violence on women's studies during the current civil strife that she calls the *Islamo-Baahthist* political controversy in Algeria. It is commendable that she summoned the courage to state her concerns amidst the atmosphere of indoctrination and retaliation which has pervaded Algeria since 1991 when war broke out between the Islamic fundamentalist group, Front for Islamic Salvation (FIS) and the official government of Algeria whose controlling political party is the Front for National Liberation (FLN). The FLN holds the position that they are secular Muslims. They do not attempt to impose the *Shari'ah*, the fundamental Islamic legal code, on a pluralistic society, whereas the Front for Islamic Salvation believes that Islamic principles cannot be separated from the secular, mundane daily world in which every person functions. Many intellectuals who have opposed the FIS have had to depart from Algeria, but Professor Morsly is trying to work in the context of the new government set up by Premier Boutaflika of the FLN who has recently won key truces among the opposing Algerian combatants. Her position calls for the enhancement of women's organizations and women's rights including the abolition of the Algerian Family Code. Professor Morsley uses language and linguistics as a tool for comparing behavior patterns and gender studies of men and women. How can one trace and measure violence without mentioning the extreme violence that is being leveled against women in Algeria. In the warfare, women have been subjected to unspeakable and unimaginable brutality. Women have to resort to absolute non-violence if they wish to treat the subject of violence intellectually. They have to use the means of literary productions, scientific research, artistic endeavors and craftsmanship to put their points across.

Professor Morsly describes the technique of rolling the French "r" in French words as a means of distinguishing between the behavior of men and women.

Among educated Algerian women, the "r" is elided and not emphasized. They imitate the French in France as they speak in a flowing manner. The men roll the "r" fiercely as was done in previous decades. It mimics the street culture and shows brusque masculinity which was formerly typical of male colonial behavior. The persistence of the custom shows a persistence of former definitions of strong manhood. By measuring language patterns, Professor Morsly believes that one can trace changes in the interaction between men and women.[15]

Women have not always held subservient positions in modern Algeria. It is ironic that Algerian women were sent back to their veils by the FLN after the Algerian War of 1954 to 1962. Frantz Fanon, the psychiatrist from Martinique, who became an apologist and propagandist for the FLN, praised the role of Algerian women in his book *A Dying Colonialism* published in 1959 shortly after his death. Fanon demonstrated the change that women of the veil underwent in reaction to the terrorism leveled by the right wing Special Army Organization (OAS) as they tried to stop the guerrilla warfare waged by the Front for National Liberation. Working as spies for the FLN, women hid armaments under their veils, wandered into populated centers, and unleashed bombs toward unsuspecting French *colons*. Often the missions women were sent to carry out became suicide missions. Fanon commended them for the crucial role they played in the success of guerrilla warfare during the celebrated Battle of Algiers. Nevertheless, when the end of the war came, brokered by General Charles de Gaulle, the FLN sent women back to their hearths still in their veils. They were not rewarded with key political positions in the new independence government. It was back to business as usual.

The use of the veil appears in the research of Aïsha Belarbi, Faculty of the School of Education, Rabat. She analyzes the dichotomies of life to see if they adequately describe the role of women in Morocco. Using ethno-anthropology, she looks at the use of space by each sex. Private versus public; inside versus outside; interior versus exterior; sexual versus social; profane versus religious; desire versus restraint; consumption versus production; submission versus power; feminine versus masculine space. The oppositions are not really deliberate she argues, but cultural. Instead, the dichotomies reflect separation rather than opposition.

Professor Belarbi's analysis defines the private, feminine space as Hestian after the Greek goddess who concerned herself with domestic matters. Her counterpart was Hermes, the Greek god who defined himself through philosophy, politics, and intellectual constructs. More and more women are desirous of leaving the security of the private space where they prepare the cuisine, rear children, and manage the household. Muslim law gives women the right to manage their own property. Secular law, however, interferes. The Moroccan Personal Statute Code gives husbands additional supervision over their wives and children that go beyond Muslim law. In effect, men become dominant in the public and private sphere, because the woman has to look after their children, treat her husband's family with respect and deference, seek her husband's permission to go outside, avoid polygamous relations and avoid seeking divorce.

Belarbi implies that the dichotomies are artificial, because women find a way to invade the public space while maintaining their own private space. The veil is a symbol of the integration of the public and the private. When a woman wears her veil outside of the home, she is taking her private space with her. As she conducts her business outside the home, her veil warns the onlooker, I am secluding myself from your glance and your domain.

The question of public and private spaces is changing for men and women, because the international context of the hearth and public domain are changing. For an immigrant from Morocco who migrates to France or other European Community nation-states, his private space may be seen as his country of origin, while his public space becomes France or Europe. Globalization has compelled migrating persons to re-define who they are, thus it is dangerous to limit analysis to artificial dichotomies.[16]

The above-mentioned feminist professors Dr. Bourqia, Dr. Belarbi, and Dr. Morsly are three of eight outstanding writers who are defining the women's movement in the Maghrib. Due to the demands of concision, all of the professors' works in ÉTUDES FÉMININES were not summarized. However, it is noteworthy to mention the names of those who were not discussed in my essay. They are: Dr. Margaritha Birriel, Dr. Fatima Hajjarabi, Dr. Nicky LeFeuvre, Dr. Fouzia Benzakour, and Dr. Theofano Papazissi. We look forward to reviewing their work in the near future.

Conclusion

As we noted at the beginning of the essay, the very fact that the female professors conducted a forum at Muhammad V University for the study of women in North Africa indicates the advanced position women hold in Morocco. They have charted the development of the feminist movement in North Africa showing clearly that Muslim women will take notice of the accomplishments of the feminist movement in the northern Mediterranean and subsequently northern Europe as a result of the composition of new member states in the

European Community. The feminist movement in North Africa, however, has different goals from that of the Europeans of the Mediterranean.

Moroccan women do not wish to cast aside their traditions, whether they are Greek myths, Muslim law, French colonial policy or secular legal codes. They do want to extract from the past whatever has produced stability and order in the family, but they want to do away with overly masculine attributes of the Family Code in Algeria and Morocco that inhibit women from contributing to the economic and social development of their countries.

Just as the statistics mentioned above stress the hardship of higher unemployment among women college graduates than of men, women are having difficulty reinforcing recognition of their newly earned economic status. As population pressure rises, so does competition for professional and skilled jobs in the public sector. Acute unemployment and poverty has forced educated women to undertake work that they ordinarily considered traditional and part of the gloomy past of the subservient role of women.

There is some evidence today that the feminist movement has moved one step backward as it has propelled women two steps forward in the field of women's rights. Late in July 2000, the British Broadcasting Corporation aired a program on television on Channel 50, WNJN, Montclair, New Jersey, about rural women migrating to the large cities of Morocco, especially Casablanca. The European informants said that poor, rural women are encouraged to find domestic work in the cities to help their families. They are defenseless as they seek a social life in an urban setting. Often, Moroccan men who had migrated to France, adopted French social mores, and recently returned to Morocco approach them. The newly modernized immigrants returning home wish to establish the same kind of friendships with young women as they did in France, where the immigrants themselves formerly underwent great culture shock. When the young Moroccan women in Casablanca find themselves unmarried and pregnant, they cannot share their problems with their rural families. A Swiss missionary society has started homes for newborn children coming out of these circumstances. It is the obligation of the feminist movement to find, protect, and nurture rural, uneducated women caught up in nontraditional circumstances.

As Rahma Bourqia emphasized in the above-mentioned discussions, Muslim women have a different set of problems from European women. Therefore, the feminist movement in North Africa has to address different issues. Literacy among women is a key issue in a tradition where women were once segregated from men in educational institutions. They were taught to memorize just enough

Arabic to understand their practices of worship. Today, in Morocco, women make up almost half of the students and they are not secluded from men in the classroom. Morocco has led the way in promoting education among women since the days of Sidi Muhammad V and that trend persists until the present.[17]

As a result of gaining a good education, many women in Morocco have attained honorable work in the public spaces. A visitor traveling to Morocco sees women working as officials in banks, universities, private and public businesses. Their numbers in these positions are obviously growing, although they are far outnumbered by men. Usually, women still function in the context of the traditional family manners that stress the presence of husbands and children in close proximity to the woman. Morocco remains one of those countries whose culture has the traditional family as its basis of social life.

Women in Morocco have the advantage of living in a culture that can defend its record on human rights. When Amnesty International attacked the Moroccan government for its position on the Western Sahara issue, the Morocco government stated in late June 1999 that they have amassed a long list of human rights accomplishments. They have always helped their Maghriban neighbors when foreign invaders came to their shores by giving aid, comfort, and shelter. The Moroccans protected the Jewish community from the Vichy regime during World War II. They have served as a refuge for fellow Muslims who are fleeing political persecution in North Africa and the Middle East. They have been at the crossroads of culture between Spain, sub-Saharan Africa, and all points east of the Maghrib and have welcomed persons who are refugees from all of these places. Persons from sub-Saharan French speaking nations that are currently undergoing economic upheaval are finding refuge in Morocco. In the context of treating strangers with respect, it is not surprising the women are accorded the same quality of mercy. As for the Western Sahara issue, it remains to be resolved humanely to the satisfaction of all parties.

The feminist movement and the trend to improve the status of women will proceed in Morocco along the lines of their customs and traditions. Feminism in North Africa may never be like feminism in Europe and America, because the problems are different and ways of solving the problems are different. However, it is significant that Moroccan women acknowledge their place in the economic globalization that is overtaking the world. They seek to learn what feminist scholars around the world are doing to improve the status of women, and they hope that western women scholars will seek to learn what Moroccan women have accomplished in overcoming some very knotty problems that impede women's progress.

Acknowledgements:

I wish to thank my husband Barry Frank Coates for the translations of the French titles cited below and for suggestions based on his experience in development work in Africa and the Middle East.

Endnotes

1. Qasim Amin, "Slavery of Women" from the books *Tahrir al-Mar'ah and al-Mar'ah al-Jadidah* included in the anthology, Farhat J. Ziadeh, editor, *A Reader in Modern Literary Arabic* (Seattle and London: University of Washington Press, 1964), p. 34 ff.; Rahma Bourqia, *Études Féminines* (Rabat: Kingdom of Morocco, Université Mohammad V, 1997), p. 21; Reiner Biegel, editor *Education et Formation Professionelle des Femmes dans le Monde Arabe et en Europe*, Fatima Zohra Zryouil, "Working Women in Morocco: Prospects, Changes, Obstacles "(Tunis: Konrad Adenauer Foundation, 1996), p. 65.

2. Alan Scham, *Lyautey in Morocco* (Berkeley: University of California Press, 1970), p. 145.

3. Ibid, pp. 145–48. Note: "Sharifian" was used during the days of Lyautey's administration to refer to the Sharifian Empire of Morocco.

4. Rahma Bourqia, editor, "Les Femmes: Un Objet de Recherche" *ÉTUDES FÉMININES* (Rabat: Muhammad V Université, Faculty of Letters, 1997), pp. 23–24; Scham, pp. 150–51.

5. E. A. Ayandele, *The Making of Modern Africa* (New York: The Longman Group, 1986, volume 2), pp. 147–48.

6. Fatima Zohra Zryouil, p. 65.

7. Rahma Bourqia, Mokhtar al-Harras, Driss Bensaid *Jeunesse Estudiantine Marocaine* (Rabat: Muhammad V Université, 1995), pp. 9–11.

8. F. Jeffress Ramsay, *Global Studies: Africa* (Guilford, Conn.: Dushkin, 1993), p. 16.

9. *The Encyclopedia Britannica*, Macropedia (London and Chicago), volume 24, 1998, pp. 984, 987.

10. Bourqia, *Jeunesse*, pp. 14, 15, 16.

11. Fatima Johra Zryouil, p. 65.

12. Additional reference material for the World Bank Report on educational reforms in Morocco. It is referenced under *Rapport* No. 5923-MOR, 22 November 1985, 74 pages with annexes.

13. Bourqia, Études Féminines, pp. 11–13; please note also the World Bank Report on the participation of women in development: Royaume Du Maroc, *Etude Economique et Sectorielle Reinforcement de la Participation des Femmes du Development*, 3 May 1995.

14. Bourqia, Ibid., p. 18.

15. Bourqia, Ibid., article by Dalila Morsly, "Réflexions sur la construction d'un objet d'études," pp. 83–90. Note also Frantz Fanon's book, *Dying Colonialism* (New York: Pathfinder Press, 1959), Chapter on Women during the Algerian War.

16. Bourqia, Ibid., article by Aicha Belarbi, "Réflexions préliminaires sur une approche féminste: De la dichotomi *espace public/espace privé*," pp. 73–82.

17. al-Jābriy, Muhammad ʿAbd, al-Taʿlimu fi al-Maghribīal-ʿArabī (Rabat, Morocco: Muhammad V University, 1989), Volume 17 of the Muhammad V University Series, pages 17 ff. The volume is a fine reference for teachings methods in the Maghrib that is, Tunisia, Algeria, and Morocco from colonialism through independence.

ʿArib al-Maʾmuniya: A Third/Ninth Century ʿAbbasid Courtesan[1]

Matthew S. Gordon

Of the elite courtesans of the early ʿAbbasid period, ʿArib al-Maʾmuniya was perhaps the most prominent.[2] Nearly all that is known of her life is contained in an extended set of *akhbar* ("reports") contained in the *Aghani* of Abu al-Faraj al-Isfahani (d. 356/967).[3] An account of her life, drawn from these reports, is the principal goal of the following comments. A secondary concern is to relate aspects of her biography to such patterns of early ʿAbbasid social history as slavery, concubinage, elite patronage and the public performance of music and poetry. This constitutes an exercise in social history with a body of largely "literary" material as evidence: the conversations, chance encounters and other episodes of ʿArib's life that are recounted in the sources are not treated here as the record of actual events. Rather, the attempt is to investigate this material for what it suggests of the life of an individual of ʿArib's standing. The idea, in other words, is that it offers a reasonable reflection of *patterns* of conduct on the part of women of her time and station.[4]

ʿArib's Dates and Legal Standing

The information provided by al-Isfahani indicates that ʿArib led a long life: she is reported to have died at the age of ninety-six. Her birth-date is given as 181 A.H. (797–798 C.E.) which means that she died in 277 A.H. (890–891 C.E.).[5] Ibn al-Jawzi appears to agree on the length of her life but either he or a copyist moved both dates back fifty years and so has her dates as 131–227 A.H. This certainly seems wrong.[6] Al-Safadi has her die in the 230s A.H., and this might also be explained as a copyist's slip.[7] It should be pointed out that the only supporting evidence is internal: a small number of reports place ʿArib in the caliphate of al-Muʿtamid (r. 256–279 A.H./870–892 C.E.).[8] If true, she was among a number of significant persons of the early Islamic period to have lived to advanced old age. Longevity in the early Islamic Near East is a topic to which modern scholarship has devoted relatively little attention.[9]

A denizen of both Baghdad and Samarra, ʿArib was—or so it was held—the child of Fatima, a young handmaiden employed in the Barmakid household, and Jaʿfar ibn Yahya al-Barmaki, a leading member of that same household. ʿArib's birth indicates that her mother, herself perhaps an orphan, was Jaʿfar's concubine, no doubt one of a group of such women in his possession.[10] The Barmakids, an Iranian family of Buddhist origins, dominated the second/eighth century ʿAbbasid administration until their sudden destruction in 187 A.H. (802–803 C.E.) at the hands of Harun al-Rashid (r. 170–193 A.H./786–809 C.E.).[11] As a key member of the family, Jaʿfar played the part of both power broker and devoted patron of the arts.[12] Several short *akhbar* associate him with ʿArib, including one in which a narrator finds her famous eloquence unsurprising given that she was Jaʿfar's daughter.[13] These reports seem, perhaps, to force the point of her noble origins, but if indeed al-Isfahani's intent, he keeps it ambiguous. His older contemporary, Abu Bakr Muhammad ibn Yahya al-Suli (d. 335/947), provides a brief report in which ʿArib herself asserts that she was Jaʿfar's daughter and goes on to describe the circumstances of her birth.[14] The passage may have been the source of Ibn al-Saʿi's more skeptical phrasing: "Abu Bakr al-Suli said: "Arib used to claim that she was the daughter of Jaʿfar ibn Yahya.""[15] Fictional though the claim may be,[16] it is certainly the case that relations between young slave women and males of elite ʿAbbasid society were commonplace. In this sense, the reports seem unremarkable.

The question of ʿArib's parentage also goes to the question of her legal standing. ʿArib's *tarjama* evinces contemporary interest in the fortunes of elite slaves. While the Aghani provides no direct indication that Fatima was enslaved, the widespread practice of using slaves as domestic help suggests that she was. Al-Suli quotes ʿArib as saying that Jaʿfar ibn Yahya had purchased her mother towards the end of his life.[17] According to the legal standards of the time, therefore, ʿArib should have been considered free at birth since the children of slave women and free Muslim men were to be granted the standing of their fathers.[18] The information on hand, however, indicates that it was only due to her emancipation by al-Muʿtasim (r. 218–227 A.H./833–842 C.E.)—that is, at a much later point in her life—that she gained free legal status.[19] In all likelihood, of course, the matter of her standing was of little import to her male handlers. The market, and long-standing convention, encouraged traffic in talented and attractive young people, even in such cases where the law might have objected.[20]

Like many of her peers, then, ʿArib was a slave and so her early career turned on the fact that she could be bought and sold. "Objectified," she was both woman and commodity,[21] and therefore could boast, early on, little social standing. In this Near Eastern urban environment, she also would be relatively free to venture—to display herself, so to speak—in the public sphere. Her first sale is said to have taken place immediately upon the disgrace of the Barmakids. Al-Isfahani cites conflicting accounts, however. One report, provided by Ibn al-Muʿtazz, the well-known poet and ʿAbbasid family member, recounts that when the Barmakids fell, ʿArib, but a young girl, was stolen (and, the implication is, subsequently sold).[22] A longer report occurs next, but it is unclear if its placement is to be understood as a sign of preference on al-Isfahani's part. Citing "a man I trust, on the authority of Ahmad ibn ʿAbd Allah ibn Ismaʿil al-Marakibi," al-Isfahani indicates that upon the death of her mother, Jaʿfar ibn Yahya placed the young girl in the care of a Christian nursemaid. Upon the fall of Jaʿfar's family, she sold ʿArib to a certain Sinbis (?) al-Nakhkhas ("the Slave-trader") who, in turn, sold her to ʿAbd Allah ibn Ismaʿil al-Marakibi (father of the above-mentioned Ahmad). The latter is identified as having been responsible for Harun al-Rashid's ships (*marakib*). Information on the position is difficult to locate in the early Arabic sources.[23] The text goes on to say that al-Marakibi, who is referred to as "her master" (*mawlaha*),[24] provided ʿArib with at least an initial education, this during a sojourn in Basra. The text specifies language arts, poetry and singing.[25] He may have proceeded to Basra with her training specifically in mind although the text is unclear.[26]

These, then, are the first occasions in which ʿArib was sold. Again, if her example is any indication, influential persons could turn a blind eye to the law with regard to treatment of slaves. A further reference to al-Marakibi's ownership of ʿArib suggests such a pattern. It recounts efforts by her *mawla* to reclaim possession of ʿArib following the death of al-Amin (r. 193–198/809–813). The latter had arranged to purchase the young singer but had not yet closed the deal at the time of his assassination. When ordered by al-Maʾmun to appear before a judge who demands to see proof of his ownership, al-Marakibi returns to the caliph to complain that the request was without precedent and that it was unlikely that any owner of slaves possessed such proof.[27]

Two reports, both unique to the *Aghani*, have ʿArib herself address the issue of her legal standing. Both passages concern moments of crisis in her early life. The first moment occurred while she was still in Basra in al-Marakibi's possession. Enamored of a young Khurasani officer, and a frequent visitor to her master's house, one Hatim ibn ʿAdi, she steals away to his home (this after employing a crude ladder that she had fashioned of oud strings). She is finally discovered by al-Marakibi who drags her home and beats her viciously. She responds by screaming, "O you, why would you kill me? I am not bound to you (in any manner)! I am a free woman (but, if you view me) as a slave, then sell me (on the spot)!"[28] The second episode is similar to the first. Following the discovery of a new illicit relationship on her part, her lover, a certain Muhammad ibn Hamid, is arrested and sentenced. In an attempt to forestall his flogging, she bursts out: "I am ʿArib, and if I am a slave, then sell me."[29] On their face, in other words, the reports present ʿArib as clearly aware of her rights and dilemma alike. They also have her clearly unembarrassed to voice her protest aloud.

The text is interested as well in the context in which ʿArib is acquired by the various prominent male actors. As described above, al-Marakibi agrees to sell her to al-Amin and, upon the latter's untimely demise, devotes considerable effort to gain her back. The passages report that al-Amin was so moved by the skill of her performance that he ordered the prominent official, al-Fadl ibn al-Rabiʿ, to open negotiations of purchase with her owner. In a separate episode, al-Amin's brother and successor, al-Maʾmun, following a similar set of negotiations, pays an exorbitant sum to purchase ʿArib. Al-Isfahani provides an account in which a hapless finance official attempts in vain to explain away the huge sum offered for the young entertainer (as well as the sum given to Ishaq ibn Ibrahim al-Mawsili, the famous musician, for having brought ʿArib to the caliph's notice). Al-Maʾmun is said to have found the ruse hilarious.[30] Finally, upon al-Maʾmun's death, ʿArib, who was part of his estate, is acquired by al-Muʿtasim (for the same sum paid for her by al-Maʾmun, one hundred thousand dirhams) and, as noted previously, it is from him that she finally wins her freedom. The text appears to indicate that ʿArib was the only one of al-Maʾmun's slaves to be sold in this manner.[31]

The training that ʿArib received, initially on al-Marakibi's initiative, provides an additional means by which to consider women of her standing as articles of commerce. Training the young women in the relevant arts was to increase their value and this was probably al-Marakibi's initial motivation (he apparently came to regret his efforts, however: it is said that forty days after selling ʿArib to al-Maʾmun, al-Marakibi died of heartbreak after referring to her as "my life").[32] ʿAbbasid society provided a ready market for properly trained slave girls. For those who acquired the girls, the matter was, in part, one of deriving pleasure from their skills and abilities, and, in part, of displaying the young and often expensive entertainers to their guests. The *qayna* (pl. *qiyan*, "singing girl") or, the broader term, *jariya* (pl. *jawari*, "slave girl"), became, no less than coveted material possessions, a symbol of prestige and wealth and, thus, the stuff of social standing.

No less indicative is the practice of distributing slave girls as gifts, a widely used means in the period of awarding peers and followers or, as in the manner of lands and positions, to secure loyalty from the military and bureaucracy. Al-Muʿtasim is reported to have distributed slave women to his Turkish guardsmen immediately upon the foundation of Samarra around 221/836.[33] Three other examples from the later Samarra period concern Ahmad ibn Tulun, founder of the short-lived Tulunid dynasty of Egypt.[34] Al-Mustaʿin (r. 248–252 A.H./862–866 C.E.), a later Samarran caliph with whom Ibn Tulun had close relations, presented him with Miyas, the mother of Khumarawayh, Ibn Tulun's son and successor.[35] There is also the woman given by al-Mutawakkil to Yarjukh, another of Samarra's Turkish officers; the latter's daughter would later marry Ibn Tulun.[36] The third example concerns Ibn Tulun in his capacity as governor of Egypt: Ibn al-Daya reports that he was told by Naʾt, herself a slave concubine,[37] that, when presented with a group of recently acquired young women, Ibn Tulun declined even to see them. When pressured, he agreed to have a quick look and, upon doing so, ordered that each of the women be assigned to one of his own *ghilman* (this much to Naʾt's dismay).[38] According to the anecdote, Ibn Tulun is said to have encouraged the young men to bear offspring with their new slaves.[39] This may be nothing more than an attempt to represent Ibn Tulun as a latter-day al-Muʿtasim or, simply, as a properly moral public figure. The point is that these episodes suggest a perpetuation of conduct by elite society from the imperial center to the provinces. The practice was not visited upon ʿArib, but this may have been simply a matter of accident.

ʿArib's professional life

The sources, as a rule, make much of ʿArib's great physical beauty and her singular performance skills. Her fame, in other words, rested on a compelling mix of sexual appeal and artistic ability.

All indications are that ʿArib's sexual encounters were many and memorable and, on this score, al-Isfahani's text is hardly shy.[40] ʿArib herself is quoted as saying that she had sex with eight of the ʿAbbasid caliphs,[41] while an earlier passage reports that the first of them, al-Amin, took her virginity shortly before his assassination.[42] Perhaps as a reminder that sexual favors were often a professional requirement and, thus, in most cases, lacked intimacy of the kind she apparently enjoyed with Ibn al-Mudabbir (see below), she adds that only one of the caliphs, al-Muʿtazz, gave her any real pleasure and this only because he reminded her of another lover (Abu ʿIsa ibn al-Rashid, also a member of the ruling family).[43] In yet another report, she surprises an interlocutor by guessing what it was that he claims to have long wanted to ask her (but until that moment was too embarrassed to do so): her only two essential "conditions," she says, were a lasting erection (*ayr sulb*) and sweet breath (*nakha tayyiba*).[44] It is true that her *tarjama* relies on the "evidence" of largely male observers who might be expected to traffic in such images, this, in good part, to please a contemporary appetite for such material. It is, nonetheless, reasonable to assume that liaisons between ʿArib and influential male patrons took place on a frequent basis. Success in her line of work, after all, demanded that she make herself available, at the very least, to their gaze.[45]

ʿArib's prominent inclusion in the *Aghani*, however, certainly has more to do with her standing as a singer, composer and performer. It is clear that she was among the artists most in demand in the *majalis* of the third/ninth century caliphs. A useful measure in this regard is simply the number of times in which she appears in contemporary texts.[46] Musical performance was her bread and butter—she is described with oud in hand in numerous stories throughout the *Aghani*—but Abu al-Faraj's *tarjama* of her begins with a warm appreciation of her range of skills.

> ʿArib was a singer of great skill and a poetess of rarefied taste (*shaʿira saliha al-shʿir*). She was a fine calligrapher, an engaging conversationalist and [a woman] of supreme comeliness, beauty and grace; she cut a striking figure and played the oud with brilliance. She displayed excellence in performance, in [her] knowledge of modes and strings, and in the narration of poems and stories. None of her peers could hold a candle to her.[47]

Reference is also made to her mastery of such appropriate skills as chess and backgammon.[48] Singing, however, was her signature skill: her voice, diction and style are the subject of glowing remarks by musicians and other denizens of the ʿAbbasid court. One anecdote records a conversation between Rayyiq and Khishf al-Wadihiya, two of ʿArib's contemporaries, in which, following some disagreement, they rank ʿArib among the very best singers of their age.[49] A second, compelling anecdote speaks of her extraordinary performance at the funeral of Abu ʿIsa ibn al-Rashid, a former lover: the power of her song moves those in attendance, al-Maʾmun among them, to weep, as much, one is told, by her performance as by the grief of the occasion.[50]

According to several of al-Isfahani's sources, an effort was made, apparently shortly after ʿArib's death, to collect and catalogue her songs. A certain Yahya ibn ʿAli reported to Ibn al-Muʿtazz that al-Muʿtamid had ordered him to collect all of the songs that she had composed. "So from her I took her notebooks and folders of loose sheets (*dafatiraha wa-suhufaha*) in which she had gradually assembled her songs and wrote back to him that there were 1000 songs [therein]."[51] Ibn Khurdadhbeh (d. 300/911?), the historian and geographer, is the source of a brief reference in which ʿArib provides the same number,[52] while a third passage records that the singer Qarid (Muhammad ibn Ibrahim al-Jarrahi) collected her songs from Ibn al-Muʿtazz, Abu al-ʿUbays ibn Hamdun, and, directly, from Bidʾa. In this case, they numbered 1125.[53] In his brief entry on ʿArib, Jalal al-Din al-Suyuti (d. 911/1505) refers to a formal collection (*diwan mufrad*) containing her songs but does not indicate whether or not he actually saw such a book.[54]

Given her prominence, it seems hardly surprising that ʿArib earned the envy of her peers. The extent of her repertoire was one target subject: Abu ʿAbd Allah al-Hishami, a bitter rival, on hearing the claim that she had composed a thousand songs, replied that each of her songs was but a variation on a single composition.[55] His comment was mean-hearted and probably wrong. It is true, however, that the task of reconstructing ʿArib's songbook is probably impossible. Even were we to possess all of the songs attributed to her—our best source, al-Isfahani, provides only select lines or passages from a small number of her songs and a short list of titles of other compositions[56]—we would need to grapple with the problem that it was common for musicians and poets to collaborate closely in the composition of new material. No less common a practice was for performers to elaborate upon, or rephrase, parts of songs that had been taught to them. Perhaps the most prudent approach is to treat the references to the size of her songbook as simply a measure of her productivity.[57]

ʿArib eventually donned the hat of teacher and mentor to a younger generation of performers. In many reports, she is shown surrounded by her own singing girls. In the anecdote in which ʿArib claims to have slept with the eight caliphs, she is described as seated in a place of honor as her girls perform. During the *majlis*, she demands to know what two other persons in the room are saying about her, and, when they hesitate to let on, she threatens to release her girls from their duties.[58] Another story describes her quick visit to the home of a patron, this while on the way to the *majlis* of a second client, all the while accompanied by her singing girls (among whom are Bid'a and Tuhfa, her best known protégés). The host of the first gathering pleads with her to remain so she excuses herself from the original event with a clever and elusive note. Ibn al-Mudabbir, her lover, and a guest at the second *majlis*, returns the note with an equally clever reply and so convinces 'Arib to reverse herself once again. She prepares to leave for her original destination but takes with her only some of her singing girls, leaving the rest behind as consolation.[59]

Comments on her singing girls invariably refer to the fine quality of their performance. References to formal instruction on her part are few but one assumes that she led sessions in which she passed on to her students the songs, poems and bon mots that she herself had acquired. One important reference is provided by al-Tanukhi: 'Arib instructs Bid'a and Tuhfa to "to arrange a certain string in a particular style, to strike with a particular finger and to do various things until she had readied them to perform [at which point] she bade them sing the verses in a particular key, and put so and so in such and such a place."[60]

'Arib's part in intense rivalries with other leading performers speaks to her role in contemporary cultural life as well.[61] Al-Isfahani's evidence suggests that her greatest rival was Shariya. Of slave origins, like 'Arib, Shariya is said to have been purchased and trained by Ibrahim ibn al-Mahdi, an 'Abbasid family member, and a poet and singer in his own right.[62] The sketch of Shariya's life in the *Aghani* states early on that because of her training, she was seen by some to surpass 'Arib since al-Marakibi ('Arib's first master) could never even pretend to have Ibn al-Mahdi's background and education.[63] The contest between the two great singers reached the point, al-Isfahani tells us, that their contemporaries were obliged to make their allegiances clear: one either belonged to 'Arib's "camp"[64] or to that of Shariya,[65] and the members of each were never to attend the *majalis* of the other.[66] Betraying his own leanings, in all likelihood, al-Isfahani provides at least two reports on the rift between the two singers and their respective groups of partisans, and, in both encounters, 'Arib triumphs after humiliating her challenger.

The setting of the longer of the two accounts is a large, formal *majlis* in the home of the 'Abbasid prince Abu 'Isa ibn al-Mutawakkil.[67] 'Arib and Shariya are in attendance as are groups of their respective protégés and partisans. Following the customary session of wine drinking, the performance commences with members of each set of singers taking turns ('Arib and Shariya watch silently). The contest is finally decided in favor of Shariya on the basis of a song performed by a certain 'Irfan. 'Arib, calmly, asks her rival about the origins of the song's melody (*lahn*). When Shariya claims it as her own, 'Arib pauses then asks their host to summon the young singer ʿAthʿath who, on her urging, recalls that the tune in question was actually composed by Zubayr ibn Dahman al-Ashqar, a second/eighth century singer and music teacher who had served in both the Umayyad and ʿAbbasid courts.[68] Having thus exposed her rival as a fraud, ʿArib proudly turns to her girls and orders them to continue singing.[69] Her phrasing is significant: "take the way of truth and steer us clear of falsehood—sing in the ancient way!"[70]

Hers is an important reminder, that inasmuch as her rivalry with Shariya assumed a personal dimension—given the intensity of the cultural scene in which they played such a valued part, how could it not?—it also reflected a deeper struggle over the direction and meaning of contemporary music-making and, thus, cultural production. Throughout the *Aghani*, al-Isfahani makes clear that a significant cultural rift of the mid-third/ninth century was that between partisans of the "Ancient," on the one hand, the "Modern," on the other. In the one group were poets, singers and musicians who adhered closely to established styles of composition and performance, and a repertoire rooted in the past; in the second group were those given to innovation, that is, in part, various forms of alteration of the classical themes, melodies and images.[71] Al-Isfahani is keen, throughout the *Aghani*, to communicate this point. His sympathy for the "old school" may explain, in part, his interest in ʿArib, herself a champion of the "Ancient."[72] To Ishaq ibn Ibrahim al-Mawsili, a leader of the "old school," the issue was simply one of ignorance, confusion and poor training: Ibrahim ibn al-Mahdi, a leading "innovator" among the singers of the third/ninth century court, failed to master or even grasp the lessons of the classical tradition.[73] ʿArib, closely associated as she was with al-Mawsili—the two co-authored songs together and performed frequently in the same *majalis*—led this same charge, in effect, against Shariya.

ʿArib's Network

One question that remains a bit obscure is why ʿArib is known as "al-Maʾmuniya" when, in fact, she was owned by, and appears to have had close relations with, among others, al-Amin and al-Muʿtasim. Al-Isfahani does not appear to use the *nisba* at all. Of the sources consulted for the present article, the earliest to do so appears to be the seventh/thirteenth century Ibn al-Saʾi. While he cites al-Suli, it does not appear that the latter author used the *nisba* either.[74] It may be, in other words, that later authors understood her relationship with al-Maʾmun as standing apart from that which she formed with other members of the imperial house. It does seem, in any case, that it was precisely during the reign of al-Ma'mun that 'Arib assumed a position of prominence, and many of the best *akhbar* from the sources situate her in al-Ma'mun's court.

As one would expect of a prominent cultural figure, 'Arib bolstered her standing as a performer and composer with an intricate web of contacts spread throughout the imperial court, bureaucracy and military. In fact, al-Isfahani's account of ʿArib's life can be read as an annotated list of the relationships in which the singer found herself at various points in her life, whether by accident or as the fruit of her own efforts.

These relationships, as suggested earlier, included those with women, notably her own *jawari*. Two of her protégés, Tuhfa and Bidʾa, went on to become prominent performers in their own right. The relative scarcity of biographical information on the two women suggests, however, that they never achieved the standing of their patron.[75] All three performers belonged to an elite society of women that featured its own structures of hierarchy, authority, patronage and status. The reports in which ʿArib presides over sessions in which her girls perform make the presence of these structures clear. Hierarchy and authority were expressed in both vertical and horizontal relationships between women of the court; patronage and prestige were the prizes most cherished in this intense milieu of contests and rivalry. ʿArib's victory over Shariya had only partly to do, in other words, with artistic worth.

As for ʿArib's male consorts, these were usually individuals of influence and wealth, including, again, ruling members of the ʿAbbasid dynasty, both in Baghdad and Samarra.[76] The *Aghani* comments mostly on four rulers and their ties to ʿArib: al-Amin,[77] al-Maʾmun,[78] al-Muʿtasim,[79] and al-Wathiq.[80] Of her relationships in general, the sources give pride of place to another four individuals: Ibrahim ibn al-Mudabbir; some of whose letters to ʿArib are preserved in the *Aghani*;[81] Hatim ibn ʿAdi, a Khurasani officer and purported friend of al-Marakibi;[82] Muhammad ibn Hamid al-Khaqani, another Khurasani officer;[83] and Abu ʿIsa ibn al-Rashid, at whose funeral ʿArib performed with such grace.[84] At least two reports add that, at a certain point, al-Maʾmun ordered her to be married to Muhammad ibn Hamid. One report says he did so after learning that she had given birth to a daughter by Ibn Hamid,[85] while a second report, cited earlier, adds that al-Muʿtasim later forced Ibn Hamid to divorce her.[86]

In lieu of a full discussion of these relationships, a final anecdote will be provided (in summary). Cited earlier, it is preserved in the *Nishwar al-muhadara* of al-Tanukhi. Intricate, as longer *akhbar* tend to be, it suggests the likely dimensions assumed by her relationships with well-placed male companions.

The setting for the anecdote is Samarra. Ibn al-Mudabbir, by now a retired official of the ʿAbbasid court, is summoned by a servant to the small quay that adjoins his property; he has been paid a surprise visit by ʿArib, his former lover. Like him, she is elderly and infirm. As he approaches her small boat, she greets him, saying, in well-practiced fashion, that she had longed for his company. Flattered, he invites her in and, so, accompanied by servants and a retinue of her singing girls, ʿArib is borne by litter into his house. Following a long meal and wine, Ibn al-Mudabbir wonders if she could put to music a set of his verse. She protests that she has given up singing but, giving in, has him teach the verse to Bidʾa and Tuhfa.[87] Moved by their performance, and ʿArib's presence after so long an absence, Ibn al-Mudabbir orders that the two singers be given expensive gifts; these are chosen from the jewelry of his own household. The visit nearly at an end, ʿArib suddenly asks a favor: one of his freedwomen had purchased an estate that she (ʿArib) wished to possess. Could he press the woman to sell it to her? Realizing, with chagrin, that therein lay the reason for her visit, he satisfies her request with alacrity. Following ʿArib's departure, he calculates that between jewelry and land, her visit had cost him a fair sum.[88]

If simply a compelling story, aspects of it ring true. It highlights, for example, ʿArib's gift for language. Among the compliments bestowed upon her in the *Aghani* is that she was unsurpassed in "the skill of her discourse and in the speed of her retorts."[89] Put somewhat differently, language—in its sung and spoken forms alike—was critical to her ability to negotiate the culture of the imperial court.[90] The story also indicates that ʿArib drew handsome benefit from her years as a courtesan and performer. Contemporary sources are rife with accounts of lavish sums showered upon poets, musicians and others of their ilk. Functioning as patronage, such material rewards must have resulted in considerable wealth for those few to whom it was directed on a regular basis. The anecdote suggests that ʿArib was among that small number. The indication that she retired from public performance as an individual of considerable means simply underscores much of what al-Isfahani wishes us to know: ʿArib's patrons—the caliphs, bureaucrats, soldiers and artists—paid tribute, in both word and deed, to the remarkable skills of the individual performing before them.

Endnotes

1. These comments were first presented to the Middle East Studies Association meeting in Washington, D.C. in November 1999. I wish to thank Michael Cooperson,

Patricia Crone, Nasser Rabbat and Everett Rowson for their comments on earlier drafts. I have drawn on much of the same material for my entry on ʿArib in M. Cooperson and S. Toorawa, eds., *Arabic Literary Culture, c. 500-925* (in preparation).

2. See the brief comments by Farmer, *Arabian Music* ("ʿUraib"), pp. 132–33; Pellat, EI2, s.v. "Kayna," 820; and G. Sawa, *Music Performance*, pp. 178–79. Several sources argue for "ʿUrayb" rather than "ʿArib." The example of al-Dhahabi is noted by the editor of Ibn al-Saʿi, *Nisaʾ al-khulafaʾ*, p. 55, n. 2: lines from the Aghani where the rhyme of "raqib/ʿArib" serves as a counterexample. Also see al-Safadi, *Wafi*, 19:553 who cites the *Aghani* (= 22:182) for verse by Ibn al-Mudabbir (on his role in ʿArib's life, see below). Both versions of the names occur in the edition of the *Aghani* used here.

3. Al-Isfahani's tarjama of ʿArib occurs in Aghani, 21:61–103. The tarjama of Ibrahim ibn al-Mudabbir, Aghani, 22:160–188, contains valuable additional information. ʿArib appears, usually in passing, in other anecdotes scattered throughout the rest of the *Aghani*. A few exceptional anecdotes aside, the information provided by al-Shabushti, al-Suli and other writers relies upon al-Isfahani.

4. For an apt description of the form of ʿArib's tarjama in the Aghani, see Kilpatrick, "Modernity," pp. 251–52 (item 'e').

5. *Aghani*, 21:68.

6. *Muntazam*, 11:126.

7. *Wafi*, 19:553. The Arabic "eighty" and "thirty" are easily confused.

8. *Aghani*, 21:63, 89, and see al-Shabushti, *Diyarat*, p. 64 (ʿArib disgusted with the wretched quality of verse sent to her by this caliph), p. 65. These are among the few passages about ʿArib that appear outside the *Aghani*.

9. An interesting example is that of Bugha the Elder, a prominent Turkish commander and ʿArib's contemporary, said to have died at age ninety. See al-Suli, *Awraq* (St. Petersburg), p. 457; al-Masʿudi, *Muruj*, 7:360-61; Ibn Taghribirdi, *Nujum*, 2:392. Al-Masʿudi has Bugha ask the Prophet Muhammad to intercede on his behalf with God so to extend the span of his life. Bulliet, "Age structure," contains valuable comments on age as a variable in early Islamic education.

10. *Aghani*, 21:68. Ibn al-Jawzi, 11:126, apparently read, from the *Aghani*, *qayyima* ("handmaiden") as *yatima* ("orphan").

11. On the family's history, see *EI2*, s.v. "al-Baramika" [W. Barthold and D. Sourdel] and Bulliet, "Naw Bahar." On their fall, al-Tabari's account, *Taʾrikh*, 3:667–688 (= C. E. Bosworth, *Equilibrium*, pp. 201–29 and notes) is invaluable.

12. Barthold and Sourdel, *EI2*, s.v. "al-Baramika." Jaʿfar's constant presence in the *Aghani* makes the point as well.

13. *Aghani*, 21:69.

14. *Ashʿar awlad al-khulafaʾ*, p. 91.

15. *Nisaʾ al-khulafaʾ*, p. 57. Ibn al-Saʿi adds, however, that ʿArib was born to Jaʿfar ibn Yahya "from a woman of noble [*sharifa* = ʿAbbasid?] birth." This is very nearly the opposite of what al-Suli says of ʿArib's mother (see below) and it is difficult to see how the passage could be read to assign her prominent standing.

16. Al-Safadi, 19:553, comments on the reports of her birth and parentage with "God alone knows," but it is unclear if Ja'far's paternity or the entire account of the earlier sources is in question. Bencheikh, "Les Musiciens," p. 145, relies only on the ambiguous information in the Aghani in asserting that 'Arib "prétendait être fille de Ga'far."

17. *Ash'ar awlad al-khulafa'*, p. 91.

18. See Marmon, "Concubinage, Islamic," p. 528 and Brunschvig, *EI2* s.v. 'Abd.

19. *Aghani*, 21:76–77.

20. Seemingly illustrative of this same point is the episode in which al-Mu'tasim distributes slave women to his Turkish slave recruits upon the foundation of Samarra (ca. 221/836). Among his instructions, according to the unique report in al-Ya'qubi, *Buldan*, 258–59, was that the soldiers were not to divorce the women, an apparent contravention of the law, certainly, in any case, Qur'anic injunction.

21. See Ahmed, *Women and Gender*, p. 86 and al-Jahiz/Beeston, *Singing-girls*, p. 24.

22. *Aghani*, 21:68. Ibn al-Mu'tazz cites an unnamed source and Isma'il ibn al-Husayn, the uncle of al-Mu'tasim.

23. It may instead mean the head of the royal stables (although the usual plural for mounts is *marakib*). See Keller, *Kitab Baghdad*, p. 150.

24. Ibn Tayfur, *Kitab Baghdad*, p. 177, identifies him in the same fashion.

25. *Aghani*, 21:70.

26. Pellat, EI2, s.v.,"Kayna," 820, suggests that Basra was the site of a music school in the early 'Abbasid period but his wording is ambiguous. To date, I have been unable to find evidence of a formal school of this kind.

27. *Aghani*, 21:76.

28 *Aghani*, 21:72: *Wa hiya tasih ya hadha taqtuluni! Ana lastu asbir 'alayka ana imra'a hurra in kuntu mamluka fa-bi'ni.*

29. *Aghani*, 21:76. The episode concerns al-Marakibi's attempt, during al-Ma'mun's caliphate, to reclaim her since the intended buyer, al-Amin, was now dead.

30. *Aghani*, 21:77-78. Al-Ma'mun is said to have paid huge sums as well to acquire Turkish slave soldiers. See al-Nuwayri, *Nihayat al-'arab*, 22:239 and Bosworth/al-Maqrizi, 'Book of Contention and Strife', p. 101.

31. *Aghani*, 21:77.

32. *Aghani*, 21:77.

33. Al-Ya'qubi, *Buldan*, pp. 258–59.

34. See Gordon, *EI2*, s.v. "Tulunids."

35. Ibn Sa'id, *Mughrib*, p. 75 and al-Balawi, *Sirat Ahmad ibn Tulun*, p. 39.

36. Al-Balawi, pp. 45–46.

37. She is identified as an *umm walad*.

38. "Protégé" may be the best translation here for *ghulam* (pl. *ghilman*).

39. Ibn Sa'id, pp. 93–94. When pressed by Na't to explain himself, Ibn Tulun replies that his enjoyment in "such matters" had vanished and that he now only found pleasure in the concerns of state and faith. One wonders if he had met 'Arib.

40. On the use of explicit material in the *Aghani*, see Berque, *Musiques*, p. 10.

41. *Aghani*, 21:84.

42. *Aghani*, 21:75–76.

43. *Aghani*, 21:84. If the indication is that she slept with the caliphs when each was in office, then, on the basis of the dates provided by al-Isfahani, she would have been between fifty-one and fifty-four years of age at the time of her encounter with al-Muʻtazz.

44. *Aghani*, 21:84–85.

45. Ibn Tayfur, pp. 150–51, has al-Maʼmun refer to her as a whore (*zaniya*).

46. Of the number of passages in the *Aghani* that refer to ʻArib only in passing, most portray her performing in a given *majlis*.

47. *Aghani*, 21:61. Also see the translation by S. Sawa, "Role of Women, 94," of the same passage.

48. *Aghani*, 21:62

49. *Aghani*, 4:120–21.

50. *Aghani*, 10:232–33.

51. *Aghani*, 21:63. The passage is ambiguous as to whether the action was carried out following her death.

52. Ibid.

53. Ibid.

54. *Mustazraf*, p. 36. Perhaps simply a restatement of information collected from the Aghani.

55. *Aghani*, 21:64.

56. See, for example, *Aghani*, 21:67, 95–96.

57. *Aghani*, 21:64-66: an extended rebuttal to al-Hishami by Ibn al-Muʻtazz.

58. *Aghani*, 21:84.

59. *Aghani*, 21:91–92.

60. *Nishwar*, 1:271–72. The translation is a slightly modified version of that of Margoliouth, *Table-talk of a Mesopotamian Judge*, p. 145.

61. On the place of rivalries and contests in this milieu, see H. Kilpatrick, "Profiles of Poets," pp. 112–13.

62. See Sourdel, *EI2*, s.v. "Ibrahim b. al-Mahdi."

63. *Aghani*, 16:5–6.

64. The text uses the term *hizb*.

65. *Aghani*, 14:210.

66. See, for example, *Aghani*, 16:17.

67. *Aghani*, 14:210–11.

68. See Farmer, 123–24.

69. See the useful summary of the anecdote by G. Sawa, pp. 178–79.

70. *Aghani*, 14:211: lit. "sing the ancient song" (*ghannu al-ghinaʼa al-qadima*).

71. On various aspects of this topic, see Badawi, "ʻAbbasid poetry," pp. 154–56; Bencheikh, pp. 119–22, 125–26; G. Sawa, 186–92; Stetkevych, Abu Tammam, pp. 38–48, 91–99. Kilpatrick, "Profiles of Poets," pp. 122–24, provides a useful translation

of material on Ibn al-Muʿtazz from the Aghani that reflects the tensions between the "Ancient" and the "Modern."

72. See, for example, the *khabar* shared by al-Isfahani, *Aghani*, 21:62–63 and Ibn Tayfur, p. 179. Al-Nuwayri, 5:96, provides a shorter version of the same report.

73. This is a key theme of Bencheikh's article. He notes, p. 125, note 8, that al-Isfahani was a supporter of the "Ancient" school.

74. As suggested in note 15, Ibn al-Saʾi, p. 7, quotes al-Suli, *Ashʿar awlad al-khulafaʾ*, p. 91, incorrectly.

75. Bidʾa does merit brief entries in the sources: see al-Isfahani, al-Imaʾ, p. 201, n. 149.

76. The sources offer apparently no comment on what effect al-Muʿtasim's transfer of the imperial seat to Samarra had upon ʿArib's career. If the transfer probably lessened Baghdad's standing as a socio-cultural nexus, Tahirid patronage in the city allowed it to retain its rank as the premier urban center of the empire.

77. *Aghani*, 21:72–73.

78. *Aghani*, 21:76–78 (among other material).

79. *Aghani*, 21:77, 88.

80. *Aghani*, 21:87–88.

81. See note 3. Kilpatrick, "Modernity," p. 245, translates one of ʿArib's letters to him.

82. *Aghani*, 21:70–72, 77.

83. *Aghani*, 21:76, 83, 93–94, 99. Also see Ibn Tayfur, pp. 150–51 (= Keller, p. 126).

84. *Aghani*, 10:232–33.

85. *Aghani*, 21:78. The sources appear to provide no further information on her daughter.

86. Ibn Tayfur, pp. 150–51. The *Aghani*, 21:82, also refers to ʿArib's secret marriage with one Salih al-Mundhari (the text refers to him as *khadim*, so was he then a eunuch?).

87. Again, both women appear in the *Aghani* as well-known singers in their own right.

88. *Nishwar al-muhadara*, 1:270–73 (= D.S. Margoliouth, trans., pp. 144–46).

89. *Aghani*, 21:62: wa-la ahsan khitaban wa-la asraʿ jawaban.

90. In addition to reports cited earlier, see *Aghani*, 21:74, 85, 92, among other episodes, where her quickness and wit are in evidence.

The Ideas of Amir Shakib Arslan: Before and After the Collapse of the Ottoman Empire

Mahmoud Haddad

In one of his works,[1] Albert Hourani described the modern Islamic revivalist movement that came into being under the impact of West in the nineteenth century as having three types of advocates: those who would concentrate on unifying and directing "the political efforts by the Islamic peoples in defense of the Islamic world against Western penetration" and who were associated with Jamal al-Din al-Afghani (1839–1897) and his Pan-Islamism; those who would emphasize "the necessity for a reconsideration and re-statement of Islamic doctrine and for a revision of Islamic jurisprudence" and were associated with Shaykh Muhammad Abduh (1848–1905) and sometimes called the "Islamic Modernist Movement"; and those who would "see the necessity not simply for political action but for a revival in the religious life of Islam" and were associated with the Wahhabi movement.[2] Hourani tells us that these are "ideal types"; "any particular Arab thinker will probably be found to hold not one of the theories in its pure form, but a distinctive blend of several."[3] Indeed, Shaykh Rashid Rida (1865–1935) was described by Hourani himself as a "religious reformer"[4] during his early career and as a supporter of fundamentalist Wahhabism in the later part of his life.[5] Moreover, Rida tried to combine the political activist character of al-Afghani and the religious reformer character of Abduh. Malcolm Kerr maintained that Rida "elaborated a doctrine of Islamic law and politics much more systematic and specific than anything Abduh had attempted."[6] Yet, unlike Abduh, who withdrew from direct political action after 1888 and took a conciliatory attitude toward the British occupation of Egypt,[7] Rida pursued a different method after Abduh's death in 1905 and more particularly he embraced political activism to promote Muslim and Arab emancipation from foreign powers, just before, during, and after World War I.

The aim of this study is not to investigate Rida's career, but rather the career of another figure who is usually associated with him: Amir Shakib Arslan

(1869–1946), one of the modern Arab Muslim thinkers whose activities and ideas before World War I were least studied. William Cleveland work on him concentrated on his Post-World War I years although he had one chapter on Arslan's formation.[8] Arslan was a member of a notable Mount Lebanese Druze family. He was known to have professed Sunni Islam,[9] without denouncing Druzism, arguing that Druzism is an Islamic sect sharing many common traits with Sunnism.[10] He practiced, for example, the cardinal obligations of Islam (like fasting, praying, and pilgrimage) that are generally ignored by the Druze.[11] Albert Hourani had drawn the following picture of the relationship between him and Rida:

> The element of Arab national feeling is strong in Rashid Rida's writings, and stronger still in those of his friend Shakib Arslan. When they talk of the problems of Islam they are thinking first of all about Arab Islam, and regard other Muslims, in Arslan's own phrase, as 'the pupils of the Arabs.' But the contradiction is apparent only: they believed that, because of the special place of the Arabs in the *umma*, Arab nationalism could be reconciled with Islamic unity in a way impossible for any other—even more, that a revival of the *umma* needed a revival of the Arabs. Islamic thought could not flourish unless the Arabic tongue flourished: it was the language in which Islam could be properly studied and expounded, and therefore it was the duty of any Muslim who could do so to learn Arabic.[12]

Although Hourani makes a note of the quarrel between Rida and Arslan at a point when the former favored and the latter denounced an Arab-British alliance against the Turks to secure independence during World War I,[13] he did not address himself to a systematic study of the intellectual and political relationship between the two men during that period. A preliminary attempt at such an endeavor would necessitate dividing Arslan's career into two distinct phases: the first phase terminates at the end of World War I while the second phase ends with his death in 1946.

Arslan's career was linked before the end of World War I to the Ottoman administration in Mount Lebanon and Syria. In 1902 he served as the governor (*qa'immaqam*) of the Shuf district in Mount Lebanon for a very short period,[14] and was reappointed to the same post again in 1908 which he held until 1910.[15] Unlike Rida,[16] he was not critical of Sultan Abdul Hamid II before 1908 when the "Young Turk" officers forced the sultan to revive the constitution of 1876. However, after the 1908 coup, he allied himself with the "Committee of Union and Progress" (C.U.P.) and was elected deputy of Hawran, a predominantly Syrian Druze district outside Mount Lebanon, in the Ottoman Parliament.[17] A few months earlier Arslan had joined an Arab party formed in Damascus under the name of *Hizb al-islah al-haqiqi* (The Real Reform Party). Its objectives were to back the Ottoman government "in its struggle against external dangers without troubling it with internal disputes."[18] In fact, this party was supposed to counterbalance another Arab party, *Hizb al-lamarkaziyya al-idariyya al-ʿuthmani* (The Ottoman Administrative Decentralization Party). This latter association was founded in Cairo in early 1913 and, interestingly enough, Rashid Rida had been one of its original leaders.[19] It sought reform through autonomy and decentralization for the Arab provinces at a time when the C.U.P. seemed intent on radical centralization and Turkification. Thus Arslan and Rida belonged, for all practical purposes, to two opposing political camps at that juncture.

After his election to the Ottoman Parliament, Arslan published a book, *Ila al-ʿarab: bayan lil-umma al-ʿarabiyya ʿan hizb al-lamarkaziyya* (To the Arabs: A Declaration to the Arab Nation on the Decentralization Party)[20] attacking the Arab reform movement on virtually every issue for which it stood. It was a reply to the book of minutes of the "First Arab Congress" held in Paris in 1913 entitled *Bayan lil-umma al-ʿarabiyya min hizb al-lamarkaziyya al-idariyya al-ʿuthmani* (A Declaration to the Arabs from the Ottoman Administrative Decentralization Party) edited by the president of the congress, Abd al-Hamid al-Zahrawi.[21] In Arslan's opinion, the Arab national or rather racial bond (*al-ʿasabiyya al-jinsiyya*) had been lost in the wider religious Islamic bond (*al-ʿasabiyya al-diniyya*) during the days of Prophet Muhammad. As a result of this transcendent ideal, early Muslim Arabs were able to triumph against the Persians and Byzantines.[22] He argued that the insistence on the racial bond would lead to a regressive up welling of the ideas of the pre-Islamic period (*Jahiliyya*).[23] Rida would have endorsed this position since the final object of his own political thought—according to Hourani—was the re-establishment of a truly Islamic state[24] and he "disapproved of all attempts to create in the Muslim world states based on solidarity other than religion."[25] However, where Rida and Arslan diverged was on the question of how to achieve this goal. Rida gave priority to the Arabic language and culture and defending Syria against the then well-known French colonial designs to control it. When the policies of Turkification intensified he overcame his earlier hesitations[26] and went as far as allying himself with one "Christian European power (Britain)" to defend Syria against another "Christian European power (France)" and to defend Arab culture against the Muslim Ottoman state.[27] As early as 1900 he was expressing views such as:

> To be filled with passion for the history of the Arab, to strive to revive their glory, is the same as working for Islamic union, which in the past was achieved only through the Arabs and which will not be regained in this century except through them.
>
> The basis of this union is Islam itself, and Islam is nothing but the book of the Omnipotent and the *Sunnah* of His prophet.
>
> Both are in Arabic; no one can understand Islam if he does not understand them both correctly, and no one can understand them correctly if he does not understand their noble language.[28]

Before the emergence of nationalism in the Ottoman Empire, no severe conflict existed between the advocates of Turkish or Arabic languages since the first was the language of government while the second was the language of religion and *Shari'a* (Islamic Law).[29]

Arslan's sympathies could not have been on the side of Turkification,[30] yet he chose to gloss over the problem of the role of Arabic in the Islamic polity, at that stage at least. On the question of the looming European colonization of more Arab Ottoman provinces, especially Syria, Rida and Arslan were in tactical disagreement. The latter gave utmost priority to defending the center of Islamic political and military power—that is, the government of Istanbul. He emphasized "the dangers of divisiveness and the importance to the Arabs of the protective shelter of the Ottoman state."[31] Rida, on his part, felt that the Ottoman protective shelter was no more in place, especially after Istanbul failed to rescue Tripolitania from Italian occupation in 1911. In an encounter between Arslan and Abd al-Hamid al-Zahrawi, one of the aforementioned leaders of the Ottoman decentralization party in Egypt a short while before WWI, the former defended the Ottoman state and called for every Arab to stand by it in case war erupts. Al-Zahrawi answered back in a question form, "and where is the [Ottoman] state? It has already disappeared."[32] According to this line of thinking, the Ottoman Empire was already lost after a series of defeats in Tripolitania and the Balkans from 1911 to 1913. Arab self-reliance and Ottoman decentralization were the policies most needed. But Rida could have agreed with Arslan who saw the crisis of Ottoman decline as a confrontation between Islam and Christianity. To him every conquest for "Christian" Europe was a defeat for Islam. He even considered the concept of racial nationalism as a European weapon in the struggle stating:

> After Europe had fought the sublime [Ottoman] state in all kinds of wars it comes now to fight it in a new war that would revive the racial bond

> (*al-jami'a al-jinsiyya*) among the Islamic people. It does so in order that the Muslim bonds would disintegrate and there would be no room left for the affinity of the Chinese Muslim to the Indian, or the Turkish to the Arab.[33]

Arslan's drive to defend the Ottoman Empire led him to describe it as "the oldest dynasty in this era which defended Islam for six hundred years, fighting the European Christian states on one front and the Safavid Persian state on the other."[34] The Ottoman state should be sacred to the Arabs, he maintained, since it upheld the religion which they first gave to the world.[35] In fact, "the origin of this state is Arab, its power is for the Arabs and for those whose religion became the Arab religion."[36] Furthermore, "the Turks are the pupils of the Arabs in Islam."[37]

Looking back at Hourani's ideal types of Muslim revivalists, it is evident that in the first phase of his life Arslan had very little in common with Rida, especially on the intellectual plane. He only rarely expressed an opinion about Islamic modernism or the revival of the religious life of Islam. In terms of Rida's and Arslan's policies, however, there is more to be said. Both sought a unified Islamic Ottoman polity in which the Arabs and Turks would participate. However, where Rida stressed the centrality of Arabic culture and local Arab and Syrian military power, Arslan insisted on the centrality of the political and military power of Istanbul. In short, circumstances and personal preferences led each to emphasize one element and play down the other. In addition, Arslan's emphasis on fighting Western influence contained elements of al-Afghani's Pan-Islamism, but with Ottomanist overtones.[38]

World War I brought important political changes to the region. Britain and France now ruled the Arab East under what was called the Mandate system. The new situation caused Rida and Arslan to forget their previous animosity and join hands in resisting the European powers. Early in World War I, Rida was ready to cooperate with England if it helps the Arabs to secure their independence, but apparently he concluded, during the course of the war, that London was not serious in carrying out its promise for Arab independence.[39] Arslan's anti-European attitudes were already well known. In 1921 Rida and Arslan were leading members of the general Syrian-Palestinian Congress.[40] The Congress sought to coordinate the activities of the Syrian and Palestinian nationalists and voiced demands for Syrian unity and independence.[41] Rida was elected vice-president of the executive Committee of the Congress and Arslan was the leading member of the Congress delegation stationed at the League of Nations in Geneva.[42] Moreover, both were members of one of two factions within the Congress itself: the faction that stressed the Islamic character of

Arab nationalism.[43] Both Arslan and Rida continued after the collapse of the Ottoman state to see common grounds between Turkey and the Arab lands: both nations were Muslim and both were struggling to protect their territories against European designs.[44] Yet, Arslan and Rida forgot whatever hopes they could have had for an Arab-Turkish *rapprochement* in 1924 when Istanbul abolished the Caliphate and later in 1928 dropped the article that stated that "Islam is the religion of the Turkish Republic" and adopted the Latin instead of the Arabic script.[45]

One scholar suggested that the two men had "discovered a profound intellectual compatibility."[46] While this is generally correct, we should point out that unlike Rida, Arslan kept away from tackling the subjects of Islamic doctrine and jurisprudence. Even when he addressed certain religious issues bearing on political matters his views were neither consistent nor always compatible with those of Rida. In 1922, Rida published his book *Al-khilāfa aw al-imāma al-'uzma* (The Caliphate or the Grand Imamate). Here Rida attacked Ibn Khaldun's theory that stressed natural *'asabiyya* (blood bond) as the basis of every state. According to Rida, early Islamic history proved that such *'asabiyya* was subordinated to the religion of Islam.[47] Moreover, while accepting the Ottoman Caliphate as a "Caliphate of necessity,"[48] Rida held that one of the characteristics of the ideal Caliph is his belonging to the tribe of the Prophet, Quraysh. The *rationale* behind this condition was the widely quoted *hadith* that says: "The Imamate is in Quraysh."[49] In 1936, barely a year after Rida's death, Arslan edited a new edition of the *Muqaddima* or study of history of the great Arab historian/sociologist of the fourteenth/fifteenth century, Ibn Khaldun.[50] In the preface, in which he expressed his highest praise for Ibn Khaldun's work, Arslan mentioned nothing about whether its main thesis was compatible with the orthodox Muslim outlook or not.[51] This is quite in line with his pre WWI thinking since he himself had emphasized not the racial, but the religious *'asabiyya* to discredit the Arab nationalists in 1913. More revealingly, he took issue with those who maintained that the Imamate should be of Qurayshite origin and claimed that the *hadith* in question actually says: "the Imamate is in Quraysh as long as it upholds religion." In a manner that clearly aimed to justify his pre-World War I positions, Arslan went on to argue that this meant that a non-Qurayshite Caliphate is permissible when it is more capable:

> If there were non-Qurayshites more powerful to hold the Caliphate, more zealous, and more capable to preserve the frontiers of Islam in the face of foreigners than the Qurayshites, then should the Caliphate be confined to a weak Qurayshite . . . ?[52]

If it is correct to say, after Henry Laoust, that Rashid Rida was "more an Arab Muslim than a Muslim Arab,"[53] Hourani's description of Arslan's as being concerned with Arab Islam more than even Rida does not stand scrutiny. To prove his point Hourani quotes from a work written by Arslan in 1930,[54] to the effect that the Muslims are the "pupils of the Arabs." This evidence is not convincing as Arslan was at that particular point emphasizing the role of Islam in remodeling the Arabs and not the prominent role of the Arabs within Islam:

> The cause of the advancement of the Muslims were, briefly those originating in Islam, which made its advent in the Arabian Peninsula. Its birth gathered together and consolidate the scattered races and tribes of Arabia, brought them out of barabarism into civilization. Not till the advent of Islam did they [the Arabs] gain complete independence. Not till the advent of Prophet Muhammad were they known among the foreign nations or considered as a separate race, or counted as one of the conquering nations. It is our duty to study the cause for their awakening, conquests, acquired supremacy and greatness: Is it [the cause, i.e., Islam] still present in the Arabs who have become backward and alongside them their pupils who are the rest of the Muslims have also become backward or did they lose this cause, so that nothing remained of the faith except its title, of Islam except its shadow, or of the Qurʾan except being lulled by its music without following its canons . . . ?[55]

Our doubts notwithstanding, we should keep in mind that Arslan described the Turks as the "pupils of Arabs in Islam" when he was at odds with Rida in 1913.[56] Furthermore, in 1933 Arslan wrote a short piece on "equality in the Islamic *Shariʿa*" emphasizing the egalitarian nature of Islam and its even-handiness toward "Arabs, Persians, Reds, and Blacks." He explicitly criticized those Arabs, Turks and Persians who blame one another and Islam for their sorry state.[57]

In fact, while Rida was involved as a prominent member of the modenist *Salafiyya* movement in the "Arabization of Islam"[58] during the latter part of his life, Arslan was thinking of the "Islamization of the nationalisms"[59] of the Arabs, Turks, and Persians. Of course, these two approaches are neither mutually exclusive nor contradictory; both men were concerned with the Islamic and Arab frameworks of identity.[60] There is, however, a gap between the two approaches. Rida alone reconciled the two frameworks in a coherent doctrine because—in the words of Hourani—he believed that, "because of the place of the Arabs in the *ummah*, Arab nationalism could be reconciled with Islamic unity in a way impossible for any other—even more, that a revival of the *ummah* needed a revival of the Arabs."[61] Arslan, on the other hand, seemed to have kept his Islamic and Arab-Islamic frameworks somewhat separate and refers to them interchangeably.[62]

The foregoing exposition explains why different scholars made dissimilar and seemingly contradictory evaluations of Arslan's endeavors. Majid Khadduri held that "it was more obvious in Arslan's than in Rida's career that the claim of Islamic unity took priority over the claim of Arab unity."[63] Elie Kedourie, for his part, maintained that Arslan was trying to prove "that Islam is the necessary foundation of Arab nationalism."[64] Hazem Zaki Nuseibeh held that Arslan's views "fall somewhere between Afghani's outright Pan-Islamism and Kawakebi's vision of an Islamic revival based upon the Arab race."[65] All these seemingly contradictory descriptions of Arslan's career are correct. Actually, different scholars were looking at different sides of the many-sided work of Arslan.

What is most interesting is that Arslan even appears to have acquiesced to yet a third framework of identity, the framework of "secular nationalism":

> Some people say: why refer to the Qur'an in urging the Muslims to devote themselves to learning; the renaissance should not be religiously oriented but national, as was the case in Europe. We reply that the primary aim should be a renaissance *regardless of whether it is national or religious* provided it leads to an assiduous devotion to learning. . . .[66] (Emphasis added)

Nevertheless, Arslan's "secular nationalism" draws on that model that does not put religion outside social life. He adds, therefore, explaining:

> But we fear that if the renaissance is divested of the message of the Qur'an it may lead to atheism, license, and sensuality, evils which outweigh the expected benefits. There should, therefore, be religious instruction side by side with secular education. Do people in our East think that Europe's renaissance occurred without religious instruction? Did Japan's renaissance occur without religious instruction?
>
> Moreover, when Europeans talk about various national renaissances, they do not mean by national, the earth, the water, and the trees; nor by a nation, a race descended from one common blood. Nation and homeland, according to Europeans, are two concepts denoting factors of geography, history, culture, religion, ethics, and customs, taken in *toto*.[67, 68]

The interchangeable character of Arslan's political thought is reflected even within the framework of his Arab identity. Although he lived in Geneva in the period between the two wars he published a periodical in French *La Nation Arabe*[69] with a friend, Ihsan al-Jabri. Being a prolific writer in Arabic he expressed his views in many newspapers, journals and periodicals,[70] the most important of which was *al-Manar*, the periodical published until 1935 by Rida in Cairo. In addition, he edited and translated into Arabic a number of books on Arab history. In 1924 he went as far as using the term "*shuʿubiyya*" (anti-Arab racial feeling) to attack such writers as Taha Husayn and Salama Musa who were in the habit of belittling the Arabs' contribution to civilization.[71] He was also known to have associated himself with various groups promoting Arab unity. But here also Arslan did not develop a coherent political doctrine or commit himself to a specific line of thinking; thus he appealed—as al-sharabasi had pointed out—for an "Arab federation" at one point, for an "Arab alliance" at another, for an "Arab League" at a third, and yet for "Arab union" at a fourth.[72]

One could easily get lost in Arslan's interchangeable identity frameworks, but there is, after all, a line of consistency which holds true throughout his thought: the solid commitment of a political activist who was, on the whole, trying to rally different groups to achieve one objective: the ousting of European powers from their position of dominance in the Arab and Muslim lands. In this he can be again associated with al-Afghani's Pan-Islamism, or more precisely, with his anti-Western orientation. That is why Arslan may be only partly associated in the second phase of his life with Rida. Since Rida tried to combine the political-activist character of al-Afghani and the religious-reformer character of Abduh, Arslan's character was only compatible with the first aspect of Rida's personality. It is quite telling that when the latter, focusing on the doctrinal fundamentalism of Sunni Islam, attacked the Shiʿa, Arslan asked him not to go too far in such criticism wishing apparently to preserve Muslim solidarity.[73] Similarly, when Rida was perceived in 1922—wrongly in my view[74]—to expect the caliph to have all the necessary Islamic sharʿi obligations, Arslan wrote him a letter emphasizing the opposite practical necessities.[75]

Conclusion

During both phases of his life Arslan's central thesis revolved around Muslim and Arab emancipation from Western alien political control. Though his goal was well defined, he was not consistent in pursuing his strategy. Thus, he thought of Arab nationalism as contradictory to Islamic ideology when its political implications threatened to dismember the Ottoman Empire. On the other hand, he acted in a way to forge an "ideological complementarity"[76] between the two concepts.[77] when this meant mobilizing various Muslim and Arab groups against Western imperialism. While his loyalty to Istanbul, before the end of WWI, admitted one avenue of political approach, his opposition to Britain and France after WWI, validated several at the same time.

Endnotes

1. Albert Hourani, *Syria and Lebanon: A Political Essay* (London: Oxford University Press, 1946).

2. Ibid., pp. 75–76; for a summary of Hourani's description see, Leonard Binder, *The Ideological Revolution in the Middle East* (Chicago: University of Chicago, 1964), p. 26.

3. Hourani, p. 75.

4. Ibid., p. 37.

5. Albert Hourani, *Arabic Thought in the Liberal Age 1798–1939* (London: Oxford University Press, 1962), p. 231.

6. Malcolm Kerr, *Islamic Reform: The Political and Legal Theories of Muhammad Abduh and Rashid Rida* (Berkeley: University of California Press, 1966), p. 153.

7. Walid Kazziha, "The Jaridah-Ummah Group and Egyptian Politics," *Middle Eastern Studies* (October, 1977), p. 373.

8. William L. Cleveland, *Islam Against the West: Shakib Arslan and the Campaign for Islamic Nationalism*, (London: Al-Saqi Books, 1985). The same may be said about a short study written by Martin Kramer, "The Arab Nation of Shakib Arslan," in his *Arab Awakening and Islamic Revival: The Politics of Ideas in the Middle East*, (New Brunswick: Transaction Books, 1996), pp. 103–10.

9. S. V. "Arslan." *Da'irat al-ma'arif*, 1956 edition.

10. Ahmad al-Sharabasi, *Amir al-bayan Shakib Arslan*, 2 vols. (Cairo: Dar al-kitab al-ʿarabi bi Misr, 1963), 1:72.

11. Ibid., 1:74; Philip Hitti, *History of Syria: Including Lebanon and Palestine* (London: MacMillan & Co. Ltd., 1951), p. 585.

12. Hourani, *Arabic Thought,* pp. 299–300.

13. Ibid., pp. 303–304.

14. Shakib Arslan, *Sira dhatiyya* (Beirut: Dar al-taliʿa, 1969), p. 34.

15. Ibid., pp. 39–41.

16. Hourani, *Arabic Thought*, p. 301.

17. Arslan, *Ila al-ʿarab: bayan lil-umma al-ʿarabiyya ʿan Hizb al-lamarkaziyya* (Dar al-saʿada [Istanbul]: Matbaʿat al-ʿadl, 1332 H [1913/1914]), p. i. Arslan's election

was not without controversy. According to one source, Nazim Paha, the governor (*wali*) of Syria, initially refused to accept Arslan's candidacy in Hawran because he was registered in the Shuwifat district of Mount Lebanon. See *Lisan al-hal*, (Beirut) April 6, 1912, p.2.

18. Amin Saʿid, *Al-Thawra al-ʿarabiyya al-kubra*, 2 vols. (Cairo: Matbaʿat al-halabi, 1934), 1:52–53.

19. George Antonius, *The Arab Awakening* (New York: Capricorn Books, 1965), p. 109.

20. See endnote 17 above.

21. *Bayan lil-umma al-ʿarabiyya min hizb al-lamarkaziyya al-idariyya al-ʿuthmani*, edited by Abd al-Hamid al-Zahrawi, (Cairo: al-Matbaʿat al-salafiyya, 1913).

22. Arslan, *Sira*, p. 6.

23. Ibid., p. 8.

24. Hourani, *Arabic Thought*, p. 229.

25. Ibid.

26. Ibid., p. 240.

27. Ibid., p. 303.

28. Cited in Ernest Dawn, *From Ottomanism to Arabism: Essays on the Origins of Arab Nationalism* (Urbana: University of Illinois Press, 1973), p. 137.

29. Albert Hourani, *Minorities in the Arab World* (Oxford: Oxford University Press, 1947), p. 19.

30. Hourani, *Arabic Thought*, pp. 303–04.

31. Cleveland, *Islam Against the West*, p. 23.

32 Shakib Arslan, *Al-Sayyid Rashid Rida aw ikhaʾ arbaʿyna sanah* (Damascus: Matbaʿat Ibn Zaydun, 1937), p. 154.

33. Arslan, p. 35. In this Arslan's stance is similar to that of the anti-nationalistic attitude of the Albanian Muslim patriot poet Mehmet Akif who had the following to say after the Albanian national rising against the central government in Istanbul in 1912:

> Your nationality (Milliyet) was Islam . . . what is this tribalism (Kavmiyet)? Is the Arab better than the Turk, the Laz than the Cherkes or the Kurd, The Persian than the Chinese? In what? Could Islam be broken up into component parts? What is happening? The prophet himself cursed the idea of tribalism! The Turk cannot live without the Arab. Who says he can, is mad. For the Arab, the Turk is his right eye and his right hand.

Cited in Bernard Lewis, *The Middle East and the West* (New York: Harper & Row Publishers, 1964), p. 89.

34. Arslan, *Sira*, p. 11.

35. Ibid., pp. 11–12.

36. Ibid., p. 12.

37. Ibid., p. 26.

38. Al-Afghani held that if the Ottoman Empire had adopted Arabic its people would have had two links instead of one: the link of religion and the link of language. Cf. Hourani, *Arabic Thought*, p. 118. Significantly enough, at one point al-Afghani had the following to say:

> The Turks have neglected a matter of great importance, that is adopting Arabic as the official language of the state. Had the Ottoman state adopted Arabic as the official tongue and sought to Arabize the Turks it would have been in an invulnerable position . . . but it did the opposite for it thought of Turkifying the Arabs. What a debased policy and what poor thinking.

Cited in Muhammad ʿImara, *Al-Islam waʾl ʿuruba waʾl ʿilmaniyya* (Beirut: Dar al-wahda, 1981), p. 33.

39. Hourani, *Arabic Thought,* pp. 303–304. For the full original Arabic text of a message that Rida wrote to the British prime minister then, Lloyd George, see my, "Risalat al-Shaykh Rashid Rida ila Loyd George fi 1919," in *Chronos: Revue d'Histoire de L'Université de Balamand*, (no. 2, 1999), pp. 159–78.

40. Philip Khoury, "Factionalism Among Syrian Nationalists During the French Mandate" *IJMES* (November 1981), p. 442.

41. Ibid., p. 444.

42. Ibid., p. 447.

43. Ibid., p. 449.

44. Ibid., p. 447; Hourani, pp. 241–42.

45. Shakib Arslan (editor), *Hadir al-ʿālām al-islami* written originally in English by Lothrop Stoddard and translated by Ajaj Nuwayhid, 4 vols. (Cairo: Issa al-Babi al-Halabi, 1352 H [1933], vol. 3, pp. 351–52. It is noteworthy that "in the mosques of Baghdad, the Friday *Khutbah* continued until 1924 to call for prayers by the people for the Ottoman Caliph." Cf. Hanna Batatu, *The Old Social Classes and the Revolutionary Movements of Iraq: A Study of Iraq's Old Landed and Commercial Classes and of Its Communists, Baʿthists, and Free Officers* (Princeton: Princeton University Press, 1978), pp. 323–24.

46. Khoury, p. 448.

47. Rashid Rida, *Al-Khilafa aw al-ʾimama al-ʿuzma* (Cairo: Matbaʾat al-manar, 1341 H [1923]), pp. 134–37.

48. Hourani, p. 240.

49. Rida, pp. 18–19.

50. Shakib Arslan (ed.), *Taʾrikh Ibn Khaldun*, 2 vols. & a supplement to vol. 1 (Cairo: muhammad al-mahdi al-hababi, 1355 H [1936]).

51. Ibid., supplement to vol. 1, pp. xix–xxxii.

52. Ibid., pp. 27–28.

53. Cited in Sylvia Haim, *Arab Nationalism: An Anthology* (Los Angeles: University of California Press, 1962), p. 24.

54. Shakib Arslan, *Limadha ta'akhkhara al-Muslimun wa limadha taqadama ghayrahum* (Beirut: Dar maktabat al-hayat, 1965). For information indicating that the work was first published in 1930, see p. 15 of the same book.

55. Ibid., pp. 35-36; this translation is a corrected translation of M. A. Shakoor (tr.), *Our Decline and Its Causes: A Diagnosis of the Symptoms of the Downfall of Muslims* (Lahore: Ashraf Press, 1944), pp. 4–6.

56. See p. 144 above; on the other hand, Rida described the Arabs as the "germs of Islam," see Rida, p. 61.

57. Arslan, *Hadir al-ʿalam al-islami,* vol. 4, p. 157.

58. For a study of this trend see, Israel Gershoni, "Arabization of Islam: The Egyptian Salafiyya and the Rise of Arabism in Pre-Revolutionary Egypt," *Asian and African Studies* (March, 1979), pp. 22–57.

59. Binder, p. 137.

60. Gershoni, p. 36.

61. Hourani, pp. 299-300; see p. 2 above.

62. Here I find myself in agreement with William Cleveland who challenged Ahmad al-Sharabasi's view of Arslan's emphasis on different identity frameworks. Compare, Cleveland, p. 130 and Ahmad al-Sharabasi, *Amir al-bayan Shakib Arslan,* 1963), 2, pp. 667.

63. Majid Khadduri, *Political Trends in the Arab World: The Role of Ideas and Ideals in Politics* (Baltimore: Johns Hopkins Press, 1970), pp. 181–82.

64. Elie Kedourie, *Nationalism in Asia and Africa* (New York: New American Library, 1970), p. 68.

65. Hazem Zaki Nuseibeh, *The Ideas of Arab Nationalism* (Ithaca: Cornell University Press, 1956), p. 94.

66. Arslan, *Limadha*, p. 147.

67. Ibid., pp. 147–48; Arslan held that European secularization was nothing more than an "administrative separation" between state and church. It does not mean that Christianity lost hold in Europe. He, nevertheless, differentiated between secularization and atheism. Writing in 1933 he denoted, after the French writer Charles Maurras (1868–1952), three atheist governments in the world: Bolshevik Russia, Attaturk's Turkey, and the government of Mexico. See Arslan, *Hadir al-ʿalam al-islami*, vol. 3, pp. 357–58.

68. One could speak also of Arslan having a fourth framework of identity, the Eastern framework. His concern with the solidarity of as many "weak" Eastern people irrespective of their religion in face of the "strong" West is expressed in this manner:

> If some . . . don't like to seek an Islamic bond which [according to them] has the flavor of religion and which estranges their modern attitudes, then let them at least change course to seek an Eastern national bond which encompass all the Eastern people from whatever nation they belong to since one of the rules of survival presupposes the unity of the weak in face of the strong. *Thus the Islamic*

> *bond is not the only bond they can cling to.* The Eastern bond can be, if assembled in the right manner in Asia, of a wider parameter; but this bond too presupposes solidarity with all the other Eastern people who belong to different nations and religions. Undoubtedly there is no hope for the independence of the East as long as it is disunited. (Emphasis added)

See, Arslan, *Hadir al-ʿalam al-islami*, vol. 4, p. 160.

It is noteworthy that Rida also called for a similar kind of Muslim/non-Muslim cooperation but he was clearer in tying up this cooperation with the Shariʿa:

> . . . The Muslim youth . . . should set a good example to the inhabitants of his homeland irrespective of their religion and sects, and that he should cooperate with them in every legitimate action to further the independence of the homeland and to raise it up in learning, virtue, strength, and wealth *according to the rules of Islamic Law* which lays down that rights and duties devolve on the nearest relatives and then on those nearest to them. (Emphasis added)

See Rashid Rida, "Islam and the National Idea," in Haim, pp. 76–77.

69. Hourani, *Arabic Thought,* p. 306.

70. Khoury, p. 448.

71. For the text of Arslan's article see Anwar al-Jundi, *Al-Maʿarik al-adabiyya* (Cairo: Matbaʿat al-risala, n.d.), pp. 426–29.

72. Ahmad al-Sharabasi, *Shakib Arslan: Daʾiyat al-ʾuruba waʾl islam* (Cairo: Al-Muʾasasa al-Misriyya al-ʿamma liʾl taʾlif waʾl tarjama waʾl tibaʿa waʾl nashr, [1963]), pp. 119.

73. Shakib Arslan, *Al-Sayyid Rashid Rida*, p. 22, n. 1.

74. On this controversial point see my, "Arab Religious Nationalism in the Era of Colonialism: Rereading Rashid Rida's Ideas on the Caliphate," *The Journal of American Oriental Society,* vol. 117, no. 2 (April 1997), pp. 253–77.

75. Haim, "The Abolition of the Caliphate and its aftermath," in *The Caliphate* by Sir Thomas W. Arnold with a concluding chapter by Sylvia G. Haim (New York: Barnes &Noble, 1966), pp. 229–31.

76. In discussing the views of L. Gardet in his book, *La Cite Musulamane* (Paris, 1954) on the confluence of Arab nationalism and Islam, Leonard Binder suggested Hasan al-Banna's views as a probable source of Gardet's views: "Al-Banna asserted that the Muslim Brethren did not reject any part of an ideology which was good; hence, if nationalism meant freedom from Western influence, it was good; if it meant love of country it was good . . . but if it meant dividing the community, it was evil—and the community for Hasam al-Banna was a community of belief (*ʿAqida*)." Binder, p. 37. Although the present study is not particularly concerned with whether Arslan thought of the community in the same manner as al-Banna did, the quotation remains telling.

77. Malcolm Kerr sees the relationship between Islam and secular Arab nationalism in the following manner:

> [Secular] nationalism has established itself as a vital political force in the Arab world precisely because it has avoided a confrontation with religion. It has left blurred in the popular mind, and even in many educated minds the difference between the Islamic *Umma* (community) and the Arab *Umma* (nation), capitalizing instead on the inextricable historical relations between the two, by virtue of which each is in some sense a vital part of the other.

Malcolm Kerr, "Islam and Arab Socialism," *The Muslim World* (October, 1966), p. 277.

City Administration in Hafez's Shiraz*

John W. Limbert

Administering Shiraz, a town of 60,000 (sometimes unruly) inhabitants, in the fourteenth century meant keeping the population fed, quiet, and paying taxes. But if ruling Shiraz in Hafez's time was a simpler task than it is in ours, it was still a job that required the rulers to establish and preserve a delicate balance between themselves and numerous centers of influence in the city.

Above all, whoever ruled Shiraz needed enough stability to collect taxes and maintain an army. Such stability, however, never came easily because:

1) The city's economy depended on her countryside, and natural disasters such as floods and droughts could wipe out her economic base and bring famine to the city.

2) Uprisings among the tribes of Fars could threaten the security of the towns and make roads unsafe for travel and trade.

3) There were constant threats of rebellions, riots, and factional strife among the population of Shiraz.

4) External enemies—rival Mozaffarids, Chupanids, and Jalayerids—were always looking to take Shiraz by force or plot.[1]

The Ruling Elite

In a famous poem describing Shiraz in the age of Abu Eshaq, Hafez describes the city's power structure. He names five persons who, in different ways, possessed great influence and power in fourteenth-century Shiraz—the ruler, his minister, a sheikh, and two judges:[2]

1) *The ruler:* Shah Sheikh Abu Eshaq Inju

2) *The leader of the Sufis (Sheikh al-Eslam)*: Sheikh Amin al-Din Baliyani Kazeruni (d. 1344), from a famous family of scholars.[3]

3) *The chief judge (Qazi al-Qozat)* of Fars: Qazi Majd al-Din Esmaʿil Fali (1271–1355).

4) *The scholar:* Qazi ʿAzod al-Din Iji (d. 1355), who served Abu Eshaq and who composed a number of works on theology, ethics, and grammar.

5) *Advisor and minister:* Haji Qavam al-Din *Tamghachi* (d. 1352).

The Ruler and His Court

Until Hafez's time, a Shirazi had never ruled Shiraz. Except for one century of Deilamite rule, Shiraz had never had an Iranian ruler. From the Seljuq period there arose in Iran the idea that only persons of Turkish background were destined to rule, a notion supported by events in Shiraz. From the middle of the eleventh century the city's rulers were Seljuq Amirs and Atabeks, Salghurid Atabeks and Khatuns, and Mongol officers.

Although the Inju and Mozaffarid rulers of Shiraz in the fourteenth century were not originally Turkish or Mongol, their families had intermarried with ruling Turkish and Mongol dynasties such as the Jalayerids of Baghdad and the Qarakhitai of Kerman. Through periods of residence at the Mongol court, the rulers had learned its practices. Thus family ties, imitation of Mongol court ceremony, and the presence of Turkish commanders in the Inju and Mozaffarid armed forces all gave a distinct Turkish-Mongol cast to the ruling house.[4]

The prominence of the women of the ruling house was more characteristic of nomadic Turkish and Mongol practice than urban Persian customs. When the women of Shiraz left their homes they completely covered their bodies and faces; however Tashi Khatun, Abu Eshaq's mother, usually went out with her face uncovered, "as is the custom with Turkish women."[5] Among the Salghurids, Tarkan, Abesh, and Korduchin all either ruled Shiraz independently or acted as regent. In 1365 Khan Sultan, the daughter of Amir Keikhosrow b. Mahmud Shah Inju, took command of the defense of Shiraz against Shah Shojaʿ during the absence of her husband (and Shah Shojaʿ's brother) Shah Mahmud. "She took such care for the walls and towers that conquest of the city was impossible. Each day and night she inspected and encouraged the defenders, thus saving the city for Shah Mahmud."[6]

Modern (male) Iranian historians take a dark view of this period, and cite the "harmful influence of women" in the Il-Khanid court as contributing to the "general moral depravity of the age."[7] These historians love to retell the story of how the wife of Sheikh Hasan Kuchek, fearing for herself and her lover, murdered her husband by squeezing his testicles. Sheikh Hasan Kuchek himself had forced his mother to sleep with an impostor posing as his father, Teimur Tash b. Amir Chupan. Abu Sa'id Bahador, the last ruling Il-Khan, was killed by his wife Baghdad Khatun in revenge for his affection for Delshad Khatun, a rival wife, and for his killing of her (Baghdad Khatun's) father (Amir Chupan) and brothers.

The Minister

Although the ruler was the single most powerful figure in Shiraz, he seldom exercised direct control over the day-to-day affairs of the city. He left that task to appointed officials supervised by the *vazir* or minister, whose basic task was collecting taxes for the ruler. This meant supervision of public order and trade through the police (*shahneh*, *darugheh*), tax collectors (*basqaq*), and the regulator of weights and measures in the bazaar (*mohtaseb*).[8]

In spite of his power, the *vazir* did not usually enjoy a secure tenure of office or a long life. Amir Zahir al-Din Ebrahim Sarrab, minister of Abu Eshaq, was killed by a *rend* (street ruffian) hired by his rivals in 1344 after only a few months in office. His rival and successor, Shams al-Din Sa'en Qazi Semnani, was killed in the following year while on an expedition against the Mozaffarids of Kerman.[9] Another minister of Abu Eshaq, Ghiyath al-Din Ali Yazdi, was executed in 1345 following accusations of adultery with Tashi Khatun, the ruler's mother.[10]

The ministers of the Mozaffarids did not fare much better. Shah Shoja had five ministers, most of whom met violent deaths. His first minister, Qavam al-Din Mohammad *Saheb 'Ayyar* was tortured and executed in 1363 after four years in office. The executioners cut his body into pieces and sent them to the various cities of the Mozaffarid realm. Qavam al-Din had been very close to Hafez, who praised him in a number of poems and who commemorated his death as follows:

اعـظم قوام دولت و دین آنکه بر درش   از بهر خاك بوس نـمودی فلك سـجود
با آن جلال و آن عظمت زیر خاك شد   در نصـف ماه ذی قعده از عرصـه وجود
تا کس امـیـد جود نـدارد دگر ز کس   آمـد حـروف سـال وفاتش امـیذ جود

The great Qavam al-Din, the one for whom
Heaven prostrated itself to kiss the dust at his door,
With all of his splendor and magnificence, has fallen to earth

In the middle of Zu'l-qa'deh, he has left this life.
So no longer should one hope for generosity from another.
The year of his death comes from the word امید جود = 764

It could be equally dangerous for a minister to be in the favor of a ruler, since the latter's fall or death usually meant the end of his favored minister. Thus Borhan al-Din Fathollah, who had served Amir Mobarez al-Din Mohammad Mozaffar for fourteen years, lost his life when the ruler's sons deposed and blinded their father in 1358.[11]

Two of the greatest ministers of this era managed long terms of office and natural deaths. One was Khwajeh Qavam al-Din Hasan Tamghachi, the minister of Abu Eshaq, who died in 1353 during the Mozaffarid siege of Shiraz. According to the sources Qavam al-Din was a model vazir: generous, faithful, culture-loving, and religious. Not only did he generously endow schools and other public works, but he was also instrumental in setting up Abu Eshaq's circle of poetry and high living. He may have brought the young Hafez into the group of Inju court poets who enjoyed Abu Eshaq's patronage and sang the praises of the young ruler. Qavam al-Din had his own circle of learned men and poets, of which Hafez was probably a member.[12]

Another minister who enjoyed a long term of office was Khwajeh Jalal al-Din Turanshah, the minister of Shah Shoja' from 1369 until that ruler's death in 1384.[13] Faithful service in adversity earned Khwajeh Jalal al-Din the trust and gratitude of the ruler, who appointed him minister in 1369 after Shah Shoja' had already imprisoned one vazir and had executed his successor.

Unlike the patrician Salghurid ministers, the origins of the ministers of the Inju and Mozaffarid periods are obscure. But whatever his origins, Khwajeh Turanshah, like Qavam al-Din Hasan, was a serious patron of the arts and poetry. He donated a Qoran copied by the calligrapher Yahya b. Jamal Sufi in 745–6/1344–5 to the *Jame' Atiq*.[14] He was also a patron of Hafez, who praised him in many of his odes and lyrics, sometimes by name and sometimes by such titles as *Asef-e-Sani* (the second Asef), *Asef-e-Dowran* (the Asef of the age), and *Khwajeh-ye-Jahan* (nobleman of the world).[15] Khajeh Turanshah died in 1385 six months after the death of Shah Shoja', and Hafez commemorated his death in these verses:

آصف عهد زمان جان جهان تورانشاه   که در این مزرعه جز دانه خیرات نکشت
ناف هفته بدواز ماه صفر کاف و الف   که بگلشان شد و این گلخن پر دود بهشت
آنکه میلش سوی حق بینی وحق گوئی بود   سال تاریخ وفاتش طلب از میل بهشت

Turanshah, the Asef of the age, the spirit of the world,
Who planted nothing but the seeds of charity on this earth,
Rose to paradise and the stove of heaven
In the middle of the week, on the twenty-first of *Safar*.
Whoever desires truth and righteousness,
Seek the year of his death from the words میل بهشت = 787

The Judges (Qazis): The Shirazi Top Drawer

"All hail, great judge."
—W. S. Gilbert

Everyone's teeth are dulled by sour things
Except the qazis', whose are dulled by sweets.
—Sa'di, *Golestan*

In fourteenth-century Shiraz the king and his minister were outsiders. Their first task was ruling a larger kingdom and they were concerned directly only with those matters in Shiraz that could affect the security of their entire realm. Yet Shiraz was vital to the ruler—it represented both a secure capital and a source of revenue to support his court and army. At first glance this attitude of the Injus and Mozaffarids toward Shiraz might not seem especially pro-urban; but in fact their view was a clear change from the Mongol policy of contempt for and deliberate ruin of the cities. During the lifetime of Hafez, Shiraz witnessed a return, albeit on a smaller scale, to the attitudes of the earlier Buyid and Seljuq periods when rulers had actively encouraged urban life and development.[16]

By establishing an urban, as opposed to a nomadic, capital in the late Il-Khanid period, the Mongol rulers began to identify their own interests, at least to some extent, with those of the city. If a city was to reflect a ruler's power it needed suitable public buildings and a cultural life with learned men to teach in its schools and poets to sing the praises of the prince. If it was to pay taxes and provide a secure military base, it had to be run in an orderly fashion with the cooperation of at least some of its influential citizens. Inju and Mozaffarid princes and ministers, both by choice and necessity, left most of the administration of Shiraz to the city's inhabitants. But the city was not independent or autonomous. The ruler's power, when he chose to exercise it, was almost unlimited, and at times he would use his position to intervene directly in city affairs, removing one official and replacing him by another.[17]

From Ra'is to Qazi

In Shiraz the ruler and his minister needed a loyal official with a local power base. In the Buyid period this person had been the *ra'is*, but by the fourteenth century the title *ra'is* in Shiraz denoted only a *kalu*, or neighborhood chief.[18] In Shiraz, during the Buyid period, the family of *Mard-āsā* held this title.[19] After one of the daughters of this family married the chief judge (*Qazi al-Qozat*) of Fars, Qazi Abu Nasr b. Abu Mohammad ʿAbdollah Afzari, the next Afzari, Qazi ʿAbdollah b. Abu Nasr, inherited both the chief judgeship from his father's family and the *riyasat* from his mother's. The author of the *Farsnameh-ye-Ibn Balkhi* adds, "this Abdollah was the ancestor of the present (ca. 1106) *Qazi al-Qozat*, and from that time the chief judgeship and the *riyasat* of Fars has been in this family, both by right of inheritance and by merit."[20]

By the thirteenth century the title *ra'is* had lost its importance in Shiraz and the chief judge, *Qazi al-Qozat*, had become the most important and powerful local official serving under the ruler and his minister.[21] The *Qazi* was the authority on religious law, and as such had jurisdiction over the many activities covered by that law—property, commerce, religious practice, family, inheritance, and some parts of criminal law. Since the law governing the Islamic community was the law of God, the person interpreting and applying it held power in both civil and religious affairs. In addition to the chief judge of Fars there were other, subordinate judges in the city who made up the "judicial branch" of the government.

The chief judge was a key part of the ruling establishment. He was appointed by the ruler, acted in his name, and could theoretically be dismissed at his will. But the chief judge also represented the inhabitants of the city in their dealings with the government. There are numerous examples of the *qazi*'s acting on behalf of the Shirazis as well as on behalf of the ruler. In the thirteenth century Atabek Abu Bakr appointed Majd al-Din Esmaʿil Fali (d. 1268) chief judge with the express purpose of reviewing old land titles and confiscating land his father, Atabek Saʿd b. Zangi, had given out in *eqtaʿ* (feudal tax-farms). This judge's grandson, also named Majd al-Din Esmaʿil, inherited the chief judgeship and was one of Hafez's five nobles of Fars during the reign of Abu Eshaq. It was this Majd al-Din who averted looting and bloodshed in Shiraz by arranging for Amir Pir Hosein Chupani to enter the city peacefully in 1340 after the citizens had previously expelled him and his forces.[22]

Qazi Esmaʿil was also involved in a famous example of a chief judge's defying a ruler on behalf of the Shirazis. In 1310 Sultan Oljaitu, who had embraced Shiʿism, ordered the *khotbeh* in the cities of Iraq and Iran to be read in the name of ʿAli without the names of the first three caliphs. This command met such violent opposition in Baghdad, Esfahan, and Shiraz that the *khatib*, fearing for his life, was unable to obey. Furious at this disobedience, the Sultan ordered the chief judges of the three cities to report to his *ordu* (camp) in Azarbaijan. Qazi Esmaʿil, the chief judge of Fars, reached the Mongol camp first, where the Sultan ordered him thrown before a pack of man-eating dogs. The Qazi's faith, however, resulted in a miracle, and the dogs simply sat quietly at his feet. The Sultan, convinced of Majd al-Din's holiness, gave him valuable gifts and cancelled his pro-Shiʿa order.[23]

The chief judges were very much a part of the economic elite. Holding vast wealth in land, they shared the economic outlook of the Turkish and Mongol military aristocracy.[24] Chief judges made extensive endowments to schools, and Qazi Majd al-Din, following the miraculous escape described above, received a grant of one hundred villages in the region of Jamkan, about sixty miles south of Shiraz in one of the richest agricultural areas in Fars.[25] In addition to the income from their estates, the qazis also received direct stipends from the government. Both Qazi Majd al-Din Esmaʿil and Qazi ʿAzod al-Din Iji received payments of cash, skins, and riding animals from Rashid al-Din, the great Il-Khanid minister.[26]

Although the satirist ʿObeid Zakani called the *qazi* "the one whom everyone curses," and described the qazi's eyes as "bowls that are never filled," the chief judge of Fars enjoyed not only great power and wealth, but also tremendous respect from even the ruler.[27] Rulers and ministers would entrust judges with important state missions, such as Qazi ʿAzod al-Din's unsuccessful peace mission from Abu Eshaq to Amir Mohammad Mozaffar. Qazi Baha al-Din ʿOsman Kuhgiluyehʾi, chief judge under Shah Shojaʿ from 1366 to 1380, acted as mediator between the imprisoned and blinded Amir Mohammad and his sons.[28] The ambassadors of Sultan Abu Saʿid and Shah Sheikh Abu Eshaq would sit before Qazi Majd al-Din holding their ears, a gesture of great honor and respect among the Mongols given only to kings. The nobles of the city would visit Qazi Esmaʿil every morning and evening; the ruler's wife and sister would bring their quarrels over inheritance for him to settle. The Shirazis did not call Majd al-Din simply *Qazi*, but addressed him as *Mowlanaʾ Aʿzam* (supreme master) and gave him this title even in records and marriage licenses.[29]

Table 1 summarizes the information in the sources concerning the chief judges of Fars. There are numerous gaps, especially for the sixth/twelfth century,

Table 1: Chief Judges of Fars

Name	Dates	Remarks	Sources
I. Fazārī (Afzāri) Family			FN, 135-40 SA, 258-60 SN, 151
Qazi Abu Mohammad ʿAbdollah Fazari	4th/10th century	Chief Judge during reign of ʿAzod al-Dowleh Al-e-Buyeh	
Qazi Abu Nasr b. ʿAbdollah Fazari	4th/10th century	At first chief judge in Fars. Later judge in Ghazneh	
Qazi Hasan b. ʿAbdullah Fazari	4th/10th century	Served jointly with his brother Abu Nasr. Later became sole chief judge. Married into Mardāsī family, who were raʾis of Fars.	
Qazi ʿAbdullah b. Abu Hasan Fazari	Early 5th/11th century	Held both chief judgeship and riyasat by inheritance.	
Qazi Abu Taher Mohammad Fazari	d. 492/1098	Founder of Fazariyeh School in Shiraz	
Qazi Abu Mohammad Fazari	Early 6th/12th century	Chief Judge of Fars at time of composition of Farsnameh-ye-Ibn Balkhi	
II. Fālī-Sīrāfī Family			MF, II, 297; III, 82. SA, 420-26, 442-3 SN, 172-4 TV, 96, 120, 148 IB, 195, 198
Saraj al-Din Mokarram Fali	d. 621/1223	Also khatib of the Masjed-e-Now	
Majd al-Din Esmaʿil Fali	d. 666/1268	Appointed by Atabek Abu Bakr to replace Seyyed Ezz al-Din ʿAlavi	
Rokn al-Din Yahya b. Esmaʿil Fali	d. 707/1307	Served jointly as chief judge with Qazi Naser al-Din Beizaʾi.	
Majd al-Din Esmaʿil b. Yahya Fali	670-756/1271-1355	One of Hafez's five great men of Fars under Abu Eshaq Inju	
III. ʿAlavi (Related to Fali-Sirafi)			TV, 96 SA, 292f SN, 202
Seyyed Sharaf al-Din Mohammad b. Eshaq	d. 641/1243	Son of the naqib (chief seyyed) of Shiraz	
Seyyed ʿEzz al-Din Eshaq b. Mohammad	7th/13th century	Dismissed by Atabek Abu Bakr (uncertain: could have been grandfather, named ʿEzz al-Din Ebrahim)	
IV. Beizaʾi			SA, 77, 303. FNN, II, 183-4 TV, 120 SN, 182-83 Br., III, 63
Fakhr al-Din Mohammad b. Sadr al-Din Ali Beizaʾi	7th/13th century		
Emam al-Din ʿOmar b. Mohammad Beizaʾi	d. 675/1276		
Naser al-Din ʿAbdollah b. ʿOmar Beizaʾi	Uncertain. d. ca. 700/1300	Author of Nezam al-Tavarikh and Asrar al-Tanzil (an Arabic commentary on the Qurʾan). After 1279 held the chief judgeship jointly with Qazi Rokn al-Din Fali-Sirafi	
V. Others			SA, 345ff, 361ff K., 81 FNN, I, 59-60 TV, 93 SN, 171
Jamal al-Din Mesri	d. 653/1255	Chief judge under Atabek Abu Bakr b.	
Borhan al-Din Fathollah	756-60/1355-59	Also minister of Amir Mohammad	
Baha al-Din Abu'l-Mohassen ʿOsman b. Ali Kuhgiluyeh	767-82/1366-80	Appointed by Shah Shojaʿ in 767/1366	

ABBREVIATIONS: Br.=E.G Browne, FN=*Farsnameh-ye-Ibn Balkhi,* TV=*Tarikh-e-Vassaf,* SA=*Shadd al-Ezar,* SN=*Shiraznameh,* IB=Ibn Battuta, FNN=*Farsnameh-ye-Naseri,* K=Kotbi, MF=*Mojmal-e-Fasihi* and the chronology and order are not exact. In some cases it is not clear whether a judge was actually the *Qazi al-Qozat* or an important, but subordinate judge. The information in the table does reveal that, until the middle of the fourteenth century, most chief judges of Shiraz were members of three important families originating in different parts of Fars: Fazārī (Afzārī), Beizā'ī, and Fālī-Sīrāfī.[30] The few exceptions to this rule were either outsiders or *'Alavis* (Shirazi seyyeds) who had intermarried with the family of Fali-Sirafi.

Until the capture of Shiraz by the Mozaffarids in 1353, the office of chief judge was virtually hereditary within either the Beiza'i or some branch of the Fali/Afzari family. Amir Mohammad and Shah Shoja', the Mozaffarid rulers of Shiraz, may have appointed outsiders to the post in order to weaken the Fali-Sirafis, who had been closely associated with the Inju rulers.

The Fali-Sirafi family far surpassed other Shirazi families in both wealth and prestige. Its members did not marry into more modest families of scholars and preachers such as Baghnovi, Zarkub, Ruzbehan, and the like.[31] They intermarried only with families at the top of Shirazi society—ministers, other judges, and *naqibs* (chiefs of the Alavis). The death of the Fali-Sirafi patriarch and a change of ruler, however, brought an end to this family's power. It lost the post of chief judge after the death of the second Qazi Majd al-Din Esma'il in 756/1355 and the Mozaffarid conquest,and the family never recovered its influence.

The chief judge and the ruler maintained a delicate balance of power throughout the thirteenth and fourteenth centuries. In the second quarter of the thirteenth century Atabek Abu Bakr, fearing the growing power and wealth of the seyyeds in the city, dismissed his chief judge, Seyyed 'Ezz al-Din Eshaq 'Alavi, the *naqib* of Shiraz. However, the ruler made no radical change in the office, since the new chief judge, although not a seyyed, was a relative of his predecessor.[32] Later in the century, in 1279, Suqunchaq No'in, the Mongol ruler of Shiraz, planned to appoint Naser al-Din Abdullah Beiza'i as chief judge of Fars. The governor gathered the judges, seyyeds, sheikhs, and other city notables to confirm his decision, but he met resistance from a group supporting Rokn al-Din Yahya Fali-Sirafi. Suqunchaq No'in would not act without unanimous support from the urban elite, so he arranged a compromise by which the two men would share the office.[33] Qazi Rokn al-Din, like his son Majd al-Din Esma'il would occasionally get away with resisting the civil authorities. Rokn al-Din bitterly opposed the Jewish governor of Shiraz, Shams al-Dowleh *Malek-e-Yahud*, who cultivated the favor of the religious classes and claimed to be a secret Moslem. This opposition was reported to Sa'd al-Dowleh, the Il-Khan's Jewish minister, who took no action against the Qazi.[34]

Following the death of Qazi Majd al-Din Esma'il in 1355, Amir Mohammad Mozaffar took the unprecedented step of combining the posts of *Qazi al-Qozat* and *Vazir*, appointing his minister Borhan al-Din Fathollah chief judge. There were two reasons for this step: 1) as mentioned above, Amir Mohammad hoped to weaken the influence of the Fali-Sirafi family, which had been closely associated with the rival house of Inju;[15] and 2) as a newcomer to Shiraz and as a ruler determined to enforce strict religious orthodoxy, Amir Mohammad required a chief judge of proven loyalty. Amir Mohammad trusted almost no one, however, and there were very few candidates for the post who possessed both the required learning and loyalty.

The chief judge of Fars occupied a powerful but delicate position between the rulers and the Shirazis. Theoretically the ruler could appoint and dismiss chief judges at will, but he rarely did so. Theoretically, the chief judge could criticize the rulers for violations of religious law (which were frequent during this period) but he rarely did so. The qazi needed the ruler for the power to enforce his legal rulings, and the ruler needed a qazi who commanded (through his personality, learning, and family connections) enough of a following among the Shirazis to make his opinions effective and to ensure the smooth running of the city. If the judge chose his battles carefully, however, he could use his prestige and local support to take independent action against the ruler.

Poets of that era provide evidence of the power and prestige of the chief judge of Fars. They lavish praise as frequently and extravagantly on judges as they do on kings and ministers. Hafez and others would never have wasted verses praising the *qazi al-qozat* if he were not a powerful and wealthy figure capable of furnishing poets with valuable patronage. Hafez composed verses praising the three great chief judges of his age. About Qazi Majd al-Din Esmaʿil Fali he says:

دگر مربی اسلام شیخ مجدالدین   که قاضی به ازو آسمان ندارد یاد

(Another is) Sheikh Majd al-Din, the leader of Islam,
Heaven cannot recall a greater judge than he.

About Borhan al-Din, the judge and minister of Amir Mohammad, he says:

برهان ملك و دین که زدست وزارتش   ایام کان یمین شد و دریا یسار هم
بر یادی رای انور او آسمان بصبح   جان میکند فدا و کواکاب نثار هم

Borhan al-Din, whose ministry put the days of the earth on the right
and those of the sea on the left,

In memory of his wise vision, in the morning sky
the stars give up their very lives.

And on the death of Qazi Baha al-Din ʿOsman, Shah Shojaʿ's chief judge:

بها الحق و الدین طاب مثاوه   امام سنت و شیخ جماعت
بدین دستور تاریخ وفاتش   برون آر از حروف قرب طاعت

Baha al-Din, may he rest in peace,
The Imam of tradition, the *Sheikh* of the community.
Find the date of his death thus
Find the date of his death thus from the words
قرب طاعت = 782/1380

Local Centers of Power

The Seyyeds

In Shiraz no one but the ruler and his minister matched the personal influence of the chief judge, the *Qazi al-Qozat*. As a group, however, the *Seyyeds*, or *ʿAlavis* (descendents of the prophet through his son-in-law ʿAli) of Shiraz, under their leader the *naqib,* formed a large, cohesive, and influential center of power. Among Iranian cities, Shiraz was especially famous for the number and power of its seyyeds. In the fourteenth century fourteen hundred of them, young and old, lived there and received stipends from the government.[36]

The seyyeds of Shiraz were numerous, powerful, respected, wealthy, and well-organized. As early as 982 the *naqib* prayed at the funeral of *Sheikh-e-Kabir*, according to the last wishes of the deceased saint.[37] *Naqibs* were considered noble enough to make marriage alliances with rulers. For example, Seyyed Majd al-Din Mohammad, *naqib* in the late thirteenth century, married the daughter of the ruler of Shiraz, Sheikh Jamal al-Din Tibi *Malek-e-Eslam. Naqibs* and members of their families also served as judges and married into the powerful Fali-Sirafi family.[38]

The seyyeds of Shiraz also controlled a great deal of wealth in the form of endowments. In 1309 Sultan Oljaitu founded a *Dar al-Seyyadeh* (seyyeds' lodge) in Shiraz, and endowed it with an income of 10,000 dinars a year. At that time the *naqib* of Shiraz was ʿEzz al-Din Ahmad (d. 1313), a member of the famous family of Musavi seyyeds. This *naqib* was an extremely wealthy man who endowed a school, freed slaves, and paid off the debts of the poor. His son, Seyyed Taj al-Din Jaʿfar (d. ca. 1354), held such power and prestige that no meeting could begin without him.[39]

Table 2: Naqibs of Shiraz

Name	Dates	Sources
I. Descendents of Naqib Abi Moʿali Jaʿfar b. Zeid Asud.		SN, 201-2 SA, 292-4
ʿEzz al-Din Eshaq	Early 7th/13th century	
Qazi Sharaf al-Din Mohammad b. Eshaq	Died 641/1243	
Qazi ʿEzz al-Din Eshaq b. Mohammad	7th/13th century	
II. Musavi Seyyeds		SN, 205 SA, 170-2
Taj al-Din Jaʿfar b. Ebrahim	614-703/1217-1303	
ʿEzz al-Din Ahmad b. Jaʿfar	Died 713/1313	
Taj al-Din Jaʿfar b. Ahmad	Died ca. 755/1354	
III. Others		
Seyyed Abu Eshaq	Naqib at death of Sheikh al-Kabir, 371/982	SN, 153
Seyyed Nezam al-Din Ahmad	Died 530/1135	SN, 202-3
Seyyed Majd al-Din Mohammad	Died late 7th/13th century	SA, 346-7

ABBREVIATIONS: SA=*Shadd al-Ezar*, SN=*Shiraznameh*.

Their wealth and prestige gave the seyyeds considerable independence from the ruler. One of them, Amir Asil al-Din ʿAlavi (d. 1286), especially well-known for his outspokenness, forced Atabek Abu Bakr to forbid Shiʿa *maʿrakeh* (popular story-telling shows) in Shiraz by threatening to leave the city. Seyyed Qazi Sharaf al-Din Mohammad (d. 1243) was both "rich and feared by rulers."[40] Apparently this seyyed's family was both too rich and too feared for the ruler, and Atabek Abu Bakr dismissed the seyyed's son, Seyyed ʿEzz al-Din Eshaq, from his position as chief judge of Fars and confiscated the wealth of many prominent ʿAlavis.[41]

The sources do not tell us how the naqib was chosen. Like the *qazi al-qozat*, the *naqib* must have obtained his office through a combination of inheritance, royal appointment, and support from within the community of Shirazi seyyeds. Table 2 shows that, until the middle of the 13th century, the office belonged mostly to the descendents of Abu al-Moʿali Jaʿfar b. Hosein b. Zeid b. Hosein b. Zeid Asud.[42] In the thirteenth and fourteenth centuries the office comes into the family of the Musavi Seyyeds. Some *naqibs* were from neither of these families, although intermarriage among the ʿAlavis of Shiraz may have passed the office along the female side.[43]

The seyyeds of Shiraz had not only a *naqib* but also neighborhood leaders who wielded power and influence in the city. In 1353, during the Mozaffarid siege, Abu Eshaq executed the leader of the seyyeds of the *Darb-e Masjed-e-Now* area. This execution alienated many of the Alavis of Shiraz and eased the subsequent Mozaffarid takeover. The son of this executed seyyed, at Amir Mohammad's order, himself executed Shah Sheikh Abu Eshaq in 1357.

Guilds, Neighborhoods, and Street Mobs

In addition to the judges and the seyyeds, whose chiefs presided over the top of Shirazi society, the leaders of the trade guilds and the neighborhood organizations played key roles in running the city. Any ruler making Shiraz his capital needed the support of the leaders (called *kalu*, pl. *kaluviyan*) of these groups, who were responsible for the security and the day-to-day operations of two of the most important institutions in Shiraz—the bazaar and the neighborhood. In times of siege, for example, these *kaluviyan* oversaw defense of the city wall and those city gates adjoining their neighborhoods.[44]

The *kalus* drew much of their power from their control of street mobs and from their ability to turn those mobs for or against a ruler or official. During the fourteenth century the level and frequency of mob violence increased as security deteriorated and the Injus, Chupanis and Mozaffarids battled for control of the city. Both rulers and city aristocrats feared the power of the *kalus* and the mobs, and attempted to control them by a combination of force and favors. Abu Eshaq, for example, forbade the Shirazis from carrying weapons and kept them out of his personal service, preferring Esfahanis for this purpose.[45] At the same time, Kalu Fakhr, who had fought against Yaghi Basti Chupani for Abu Eshaq during the struggles of 1342, became virtual ruler of the Kazerun Gate quarter of the city and one of the most powerful men in Shiraz.[46] Abu Eshaq's relations with the neighborhood chiefs were not always so fortunate. During the fighting of 1342, a certain Kalu Hosein took the side of the Chupanis. Ten years later, during the Mozaffarid siege of Shiraz, Abu Eshaq alienated some of the *kaluviyan* by executing the chief of the Bagh-e-Now district and plotting against the chief of the Murdestan quarter. These actions led the latter to betray the city to the Mozaffarids.

In the streets and bazaars of Shiraz there existed an undercurrent of resistance to almost all rulers, which, although occasionally expressed in violence, more often appeared as a sullen, passive opposition using weapons of mockery and ridicule. For example, a certain Shah ʿAsheq (whose very name parodied Abu Eshaq's title of *Shah Sheikh*) kept a candy store near the door of the

Masjed ʿAtiq. This storekeeper composed poetry in Shirazi dialect and had a reputation in the city as something of a wit. One Friday, after Abu Eshaq had finished his prayers in the Jameʿ ʿAtiq, the ruler came and sat in the shop and told his officers and courtiers, "Today I am Shah ʿAsheq's shopkeeper—come and buy candy from me." Each officer gave rich clothes, weapons, and cash in return for candy until 100,000 dinars worth of goods had been collected. Abu Eshaq, who considered himself a second Hatam Taʾi (the Arab chief legendary for his generosity), then mounted his horse and left the treasure for the shop owner. Shah ʿAsheq, however, trumped the king's generosity by announcing from the roof of his shop, "O people of Shiraz, the king has given me gifts and I will donate them for the king to the people of Shiraz. Come and loot my shop." The Shirazis looted Shah ʿAsheq's store, and when the king found out what had happened, he could only admit that he had been outdone.[47]

Relations between the *bazaaris* and the Mozaffarid rulers were no better. When Amir Mohammad and his escort passed through the bazaars of Shiraz, they found their way blocked by piles of firewood the shopkeepers had deliberately left in the passages. In general the *kalus* of Shiraz favored Shah Shojaʿ over the other members of his family. After Shah Mahmud, with Jalayerid support, had taken Shiraz from his brother in 1364, the Shirazis sent Kalu Hasan on a mission to Shah Shojaʿ in Kerman. There he appealed to Shah Shojaʿ to return to Shiraz and promised him support in return for relief from the exaction of Shah Mahmud's Tabrizi allies.[48] Two years later when Shah Mahmud, fearing the *kalus* of Shiraz would betray him to Shah Shojaʿ abandoned the city to his brother and withdrew to Esfahan.

Below the *kaluviyan,* and presumably controlled by them, were the urban workers and potential members of street mobs. These groups, whom the aristocrats called by the disparaging names of *rendan*, *owbash*, and *shattar*, attained their greatest strength during the reign of Abu Eshaq. The Mozaffarids earned the gratitude of the Shirazi aristocrats by suppressing the street mobs and restoring security.[49]

Although the upper classes called these *pahlavanan* ruffians (*owbash*), ideally they would also work to uphold *javanmardi* (chivalry), offering hospitality to the stranger and protection to the weak in a violent society.[50] For example, in 1339 Tashi Khatun, the mother of Abu Eshaq, appealed to the *javanmardi* of the bazaar workers of Shiraz, and in response a carpenter named Pahlevan Mahmud started a revolt against Amir Pir Hosein Chupani. Although the sources do not mention any specific organizations of the *javanmardan* or *pahlevanan* in Shiraz, Ibn Battuta mentions societies of young, unmarried men in Esfahan who competed in giving festivals as extravagant as possible. But the upper-class bias of the sources and the semi-secret nature of these popular societies have obscured the true character of these organizations in Shiraz.

Sheikhs and Their Families

In addition to *qazis*, *naqibs*, and *kalus*, who wielded power through official or semi-official positions, others, without any official position, also possessed great influence in Shiraz. This latter group drew its authority from the respect of the population or the ruler for an individual's family, learning, wealth, or piety. The Baghnovi family, for example, held no official post in Shiraz, but one family member, Sheikh Haj Rokn al-Din Mansur Baghnovi (d. 1333) was so blunt in his threats and advice to rulers that he received the title *Rastgu* (the truth-speaker).[51] Another Baghnovi, Rokn al-Din's brother Sheikh Zahir al-Din Esmaʿil (d. 1330), led the Shirazis' resistance to Sultan Oljaitu's attempt to impose a Shiʿa form of the *khotbeh* (Friday prayer address) in 1310.[52]

Sheikh, which originally meant "old man," in this period, was the title of leaders of the Sufis and of eminent preachers. The *Sheikh al-Eslam* was the most pious and learned of the sheikhs, and those persons called *Sheikh al-Eslam* in Shiraz were most famous as Sufi leaders and preachers.[53] Judging by Hafez's inclusion of a *Sheikh al-Eslam* among his five great men of Fars, that individual, whatever his function, must have had great, if unofficial, influence over the religious community and the people of Shiraz. The most famous *Sheikh al-Eslams* of Shiraz included: Qotb al-Din Ali al-Makki and his son, Shahab al-Din Ruzbehan, in the 12th century;[54] Sheikh ʿEzz al-Din Mowdud Zarkub (d. 1265), the ancestor of the author of the *Shiraznameh*; Sheikh Amin al-Din Baliyani Kazeruni (d. 1344), one of Hafez's five great men of Fars; and Sheikh Farid al-Din ʿAbd al-Wodud of the Ruzbehan Farid family in the middle of the eighth/fourteenth century.[55]

The strongest social groups in Shiraz and the base of its cultural and social life were the fifteen to twenty aristocratic families that produced the judges, teachers, scholars, and preachers. These figures made fourteenth-century Shiraz the *Dar al-ʿElm* (abode of knowledge) and the *Borj-e owliyaʾ* (tower of saints) of the Islamic world. Joneid Shirazi's *Shadd al-Ezar* (written ca. 791/1389) contains biographies of over three hundred famous persons buried in Shiraz. Although Joneid included a few notices of rulers, ministers, and governors, he wrote mostly of religious figures—saints, scholars, and martyrs.[56]

About a third of those persons noted in *Shadd al-Ezar* belonged to the fifteen or twenty leading families of the city. We have already seen how the chief judgeship of Fars for centuries remained in the related families of Afzari and Fali-Sirafi. Lesser posts such as those of teacher (*modarres*) and preacher (*va'ez*) also usually stayed within a family. Although outsiders with talent or credentials could earn respect in religious scholarship and teaching, local families which had produced eminent scholars who, having earned the support of a ruler or minister, passed on these occupations by heredity.

Table 3 lists the aristocratic families of Shiraz, showing their origins and intermarriages. The information in Table 3 reveals some central features of Shirazi society.

1) Many leading families in the city held landholdings in the hinterlands of Fars. The Baghnovis and Ruzbehans of Fasa, the Falis from the *Garmsirat* near the Persian Gulf, and the three prominent families from the Beiza area originated as provincial landowners who kept their ties with the countryside after migrating to Shiraz. The family of Baliyani-Kazeruni, for example, maintained close links with their place of origin, and the members of this family continued to be buried in Kazerun after attaining eminence in Shiraz.[57]

2) Two aristocratic families, the Zarkubs and the Salehanis, were immigrants from Esfahan, which relative to Shiraz had suffered a decline in the thirteenth and fourteenth centuries.

3) Families of seyyeds occupied a prominent position among the Shiraz aristocrats.

4) Ethnically, some families, such as the prolific and powerful Baghnovis, boasted of Arab origins, although they had been thoroughly Persianized by their long residence in Fasa before coming to Shiraz.

5) Other families, such as the Falis of the garmsir, the Sheikhs of Beiza, and the Ruzbehans of Fasa were either descendents of the old Zoroastrian, Iranian *dehqans* (landed aristocrats) of Fars or were descended from Deilamite immigrants to Fars of the Buyid era.[58]

6) The family of Najib al-Din 'Ali b. Bozghash was just the most famous of the descendents of the Turks who settled in Shiraz during the Seljuq and Mongol periods.

Almost the entire religious establishment of Shiraz—the preachers, the judges, the teachers, the Sufi leaders, and the Sheikh al-Eslam—came from these aristocratic families. Important religious figures in Shiraz who were not members of these families would establish links with the local aristocrats,

Table 3: Patrician Families of Shiraz

Family	Origins	Remarks	Sources
		The Elite	
Afzari (Fazari)	From Afzar, in the garmsir of Fars	Chief judges of Fars since Buyid times. Related to Fali-Sirafi family	FN 135-40 SA 358-60 SN 151
Qazi Beiza'i	Beiza of Fars	Chief judges of Fars in the 7th/13th century	SA 77, 294-5 SN 182 TV 120
Fali-Sirafi	From the region of Fal near the Persian Gulf port of Siraf. Descended from Afzari judges	Chief judges of Fars in the 13th and 14th centuries. Intermarried with families of ministers and naqibs. Buried in Mosalla area north of the city.	SA 420-44 SN 89, 172-4, 192-3, 202 TV 92, 96, 120, 148 MF II, 297, III, 73, 82.
Musavi Seyyeds	Descended from Imam Musa Kazem	Naqibs of Fars in the 13th and 14th centuries	SA 170-74 SN 205
		Local Aristocrats	
Adib-Salehani	Salehan Quarter of Esfahan	Migrated to Shiraz ca. 600/1204	SA 139, 149 SN 168-9
ʿAlavi-Mohammadi	Seyyeds descended from Mohammad Hanafiyeh b. ʿAli b. Abi Taleb	Amir Asil al-Din ʿAlavi (d. 1286) related through daughters and sisters to families of Vaʿez, Arabshah-Hoseini, and Baghnovi	SA 128, 325-30 SN 204-5 MF II, 364
Baghnovi	Originally from Fasa. Descended from Caliph ʿOmar. Settled in Bagh-e-Now area of Shiraz in the 12th century	Intermarried with families of: Kasa'i, Zarkub, ʿAlavi-Mohammadi, Salmani, and Beiza'i. Very large and wealthy family. Preachers the Jameʿ ʿAtiq. Joneid Shirazi, poet and author of Shadd al-Izar, member of this family.	SA 183-89, 190-210, 227-238, 268, 289-92 SN 178-80, 190
Beiza'i (Sheikhs of Beiza)	Descended from *Sheikh al-Shoyukh* Abu al-Hosein Ahmad b. Mohammad Beiza'i (d. ?) known as Ibn Salbeh	Most of family buried in Beiza. Descendant of Sheikh Mohammad was Sufi master of Sheikh Ruzbehan Baqli. Another descendant married Sadr al-Din Mozaffar Baghnovi (13th century).	SA 299-300, 476 ff SN 148-9, 154
Mosalahi-Beiza'i	From Beiza of Fars. Came to Shiraz in the 12th century	At first family members buried in *Dar al-Salm* cemetery. In 13th century, as family gained prestige, buried in the *Jameʿ ʿAtiq* district	SA 140-43, 330-33 SN 163-4
Baliyani-Kazeruni	From Baliyan, a village 6 miles south of Kazerun. Descended from Abu ʿAli Daqqaq Nishapuri, (d. 1015)	Most of family buried in Kazerun. Family of scholars and *Sheikh al-Eslams* of Fars in the 14th century.	SA 61-4, 484-87 SN 186-7, 194 K 35, FNN II, 255 B 150-54
Bozghash	Bozghash was a Turkish merchant who settled in Shiraz in Salghurid times	Family of eminent teachers, including teacher of historian Moʿin al-Din Zarkub	SA 334-41 SN 177, 191 TV 112-113

Table 3: Patrician Families of Shiraz (continued)

Family	Origins	Remarks	Sources
Dashtaki Seyyeds	Descended from Hosein b. ʿAli b. Hosein b. ʿAli b. Abi Taleb	Ancestors of founder of the *Mansuriyeh* School and of the author of *Farsnameh-ye-Naseri*. Intermarried with ʿAlavi-Mohammadis	SA 300-303, 319-24 SN 204 FNN II, 80
asa'i	Unknown	Intermarried with Baghnovis. Founded Robat-e-Kasa'i outside the Kazerun Gate	SA 117-18, 129 SN 184-5
Ruzbehan Baqli	Descendants of Sheikh Ruzbehan Baqli *Shattah-e-Fars* (1127-1209). Of Deilamite origin from Fasa.	Ruzbehan the greatest mystic of Shiraz. Descendents were chief of *Ruzbehaniyeh* dervishes. Intermarried with Zarkubs	SA 238-39, 243-54 SN 129, 159, 162
Ruzbehan Farid	Descendants of Sheikh Ruzbehan Farid (d. 1221)	Family of *mohtasebs* and *Sheikh al-Islams* in the 13th and 14th centuries	SA 352-54, 394-5 SN 180-1
Salmani	Unknown: Descendants of Faqih Sa'en al-Din Hosein (d. 1266)	Intermarried with Baghnovis	SA 176-79 SN 174
Vaʿez	Unknown	Married into ʿAlavi-Mohammadi family. Eminent preachers in the 14th century	SA 128
Zarkub (Zahabi)	From Esfahan. Descendants of Hafez Esmaʿil Qavam al-Sonnat (d. 1140)	Migrated to Shiraz in the 13th century. Family of *Sheikh al-Eslams* and of historian Ahmad Zarkub. Intermarried with Ruzbehan Baqlis	SA 310-19

ABBREVIATIONS: SA = *Shadd al-Ezar;* SN = *Shiraznameh;* TV = *Tarikh-e-Vassaf;* MF = *Mojmal-e-Fasihi;* IB = *Ibn Battuta;* FN = *Farsnameh-ye-Ibn Balkhi;* FNN = *Farsnameh-ye-Naseri;* HM = *Hezar Mazar;* K = *Kotbi;* B = *Bulliet*

usually as students of some and teachers of others. The great families extended their influence by intermarriage, and through teacher-student or Sufi master-disciple relationships. The influence of Sheikh Sadr al-Din Mozaffar Baghnovi, for example, extended not only to his numerous children, grandchildren, and in-laws, but also to his many students. A teacher's possession of an *ejazeh* (diploma) from a Baghnovi conferred on him much of the same prestige that others acquired by marrying into the family.

Some of these aristocrats were more aristocratic than others. Shiraz had two sorts of first families: the elite and local aristocracy. Among the former were the families of Fali-Sirafi, Afzari, Musavi, and Qazi Beiza'i which gave Shiraz chief judges, *naqibs*, and even ministers. Many members of these families were eminent scholars and teachers, but their real power was political, extending beyond the limits of Shiraz and Fars. These elite families almost never intermarried with the local aristocrats.[59] The first group included figures of international stature, while the second, although possessing considerable prestige and wealth, and holding posts in the important schools, mosques, and Sufi orders of the city, were limited in power and influence to Shiraz and Fars.

Despite considerable intermarriage among members of the second tier, the local aristocrats, there were still important distinctions of power and prestige within this group. The most eminent of the local aristocrats were the families of Baghnovi, Sheikhs of Beiza, Dashtaki, and ʿAlavi-Mohammadi, while at the lower end of the aristocratic scale were the families as Zarkub, Vaʿez, Kasaʾi, and Adib Salehani.[60] Members of these "lower aristocratic" families were often preachers and imams in the smaller mosques of the city.[61] They could raise their status by attaching themselves (by marriage or other means) to more prominent families. Politically these lower aristocratic families were closest to the *kalus* and their neighborhood and bazaar organizations, while the higher group had ties both with the *kalus* and with the ruling elite of ministers, governors, and judges.

Conclusion

The sources draw a picture of fourteenth-century Shiraz that is not one of orderly hierarchies, pyramids and webs. Rather it is a picture of overlapping and undefined jurisdictions that changed according to the personalities of the holders of various offices. This is as it should be. It mattered less *what* you were than *who* you (and your relatives) were. At the top of society was the ruler or governor—always an outsider, aloof from Shiraz and its people. Change of ruler or even of dynasty seldom directly affected life in the city. The minister took a closer interest in the city by looking to both physical security (by means of his police force) and economic prosperity in the town and countryside to ensure that his tax collectors could gather enough money revenue to fill the ruler's treasury.

The authority touching the Shirazis was that of the chief judge, the *qazi al-qozat*. Although often from one of the great families of Shiraz, the chief judge had so much political power and wealth in land that his interests would coincide with those of an alien, ruling class. The *naqib*, thanks to the wealth he controlled and the prestige of his office, ranked only slightly below the chief judge. Sometimes the two were the same person or close relatives. Together they sat atop the Shirazi establishment, representing stability in an age of frequent and violent political change.

Ranking below the chief judge and *naqib*, but still with considerable local influence, were the aristocratic Shirazi families of scholars, *Sheikh al-Eslams*, preachers, and Sufi leaders. The *kaluviyan* of the bazaars and neighborhoods lacked the prestige of the aristocrats but often held greater actual power. Further down the social scale were the *pahlavanan* and their secret societies, groups of street ruffians or popular heroes depending on one's point of view.

All of these groups and individuals stood in vague, undefined relationships to each other. Many young aristocrats were students of eminent qazis and *vice-versa*. The *kalus* of Shiraz had links with both the *pahlavans* and with the aristocratic families. The most powerful of the *kalus*, such as Kalu Fakhr of the Kazerun Gate Quarter, had connections even at the ruler's court, where ministers and princes would compete for their favor and support.

The most important feature of this system (or non-system) of city organization is that it did work to preserve Shiraz. Given the political instability of Iran in the fourteenth century, Shiraz's economic survival and cultural flowering were major accomplishments. Occasional breakdowns of order and security never threatened Shiraz's existence as a city. The network of formal and informal ties among the different groups of Shirazis meant that most of the inhabitants, from the *rend* in the tavern to the ascetic in his cell, shared an interest in their city's survival. Add to this common interest an intense local patriotism and pride, and the result was a loose, but strong, social structure in which all could share Hafez's sentiments when he said:

خوشا شیراز و وضع بی مثالش   خداوندا نگهدار از زوالش

Pleasant is Shiraz and its incomparable site.
O Lord, preserve it from decline.

Endnotes

*This chapter is based upon a section of my dissertation, "Shiraz in the Age of Hafez" (Cambridge: Harvard University, Ph.D., 1973).

1. For Shiraz, security did not always mean resisting outside attacks. The city sometimes changed rulers without violence following a deal between rival pretenders or by agreement of influential officials.

2. For the text and translation of this poem, see Browne, E.G., *A Literary History of Persia* III, (Cambridge: University Press, 1920), pp. 275–76.

3. Moʿin al-Din Zarkub, *Shiraznameh* (Tehran: Iran Culture Foundation, 1971), p. 187. Baliyan is a village six miles south of Kazerun. For an account of this family, see Mohammad Qazvini's notes to *Shadd al-Ezar*, pp. 484–7.

4. Tashi Khatun, the mother of Shah Sheikh Abu Eshaq, and Makhdum Shah Khan Qotlogh, the mother of Shah Shoja, were both Turkish. In 1346, when Abu Eshaq paid a visit to the elderly chief judge of Fars, Qazi Majd al-Din Esmaʿil Fali, the ruler sat opposite the judge holding his ears. This action was a sign of great honor, since the Mongol commanders acted thus only in the presence of their sultan. *The Travels of Ibn Battuta* (Cambridge: University Press, 1962), pp. 195, 198.

5. *The Travels of Ibn Battuta*, pp. 194, 199–200.

6. Haj Mirza Hassan Hosseini-Fasaʾi, *Farsnameh-ye Naseri* (Tehran: Sanaʾi, 1925) I, 59.

7. See, for example, A.H. Zarinkub, *Az Kucheh-ye Rendan* (Tehran: Jibi Publishing, 1970), p. 51.

8. In theory ministers of Iranian origin would serve as intermediaries between a Turkish-speaking ruler and his Iranian subjects.

9. H. Q. Sotudeh, *Taʾrikh-e Al-e Mozaffar* (Tehran: University Publications, 1967–68). Vol. I, pp. 80, 84–5. The poet Khaju Kermani dedicated a number of his compositions to Shams al-Din and his son.

10. Jaʿfar b. Mohammad b. Hasan Jaʿfari (edited by Iraj Afshar), *Taʾrikh-e Yazd* (Tehran: Institute for Publishing and Translation, 1968), pp. 118–19; 239. This minister endowed a school in Yazd which Amir Mohammad Mozaffar destroyed out of enmity for Abu Eshaq.

11. Considering Amir Mohammad's character, remaining in his favor for such a long time was no small accomplishment. In addition to his bloodthirstiness, fanaticism, suspicion, and evil temper, he "used curses that made mule-drivers blush."

12. Zarinkub, *Az Kucheh-ye Rendan*, 38. The most important royal court poets, both older than Hafez, were Khaju Kermani and ʿObeid Zakani.

13. The manner of Turanshah's rise to power is itself indicative of the rulers' need for trustworthy advisors. In 1364, after Shah Shojaʿ had surrendered Shiraz to his brother Shah Mahmud and his Jalayerid allies, he withdrew toward Kerman by way of Abarqu. Khajeh Jalal al-Din Turanshah, who was governor in Abarqu, joined Shah Shojaʿ's retinue and provided supplies for his forces. For the next year Khajeh Jalal al-Din accompanied Shah Shojaʿ in his difficult campaigns in Kerman, where he had to rebuild an army to recapture Shiraz from his brother.

14. Sotudeh, *Taʾrikh-e Al-e Mozaffar*, I, p. 160; Qasem Ghani, *Bahs dar Asar va Afkar va Ahval-e Hafez* (Tehran: Zavvar, 1942), Vol. I, pp. 268–9. Twenty-four leaves of this Qurʾan have survived and in 1972 were in the Pars museum in Shiraz.

15. In Islamic tradition, Asef was the name of the minister of King Solomon. Fars in the thirteenth and fourteenth centuries was known as the *Molk-e Soleiman*, or the "Kingdom of Solomon." See A. S. Melikian-Chirvani, "Le Royaume de Salomon." *Le Monde Iranien et l'Islam*, I (1971), pp. 1-41.

16. See Richard Bulliet, *The Patricians of Nishapur* (Cambridge: Harvard University Press, 1972), p. 61.

17. Abu Eshaq's executing a number of Shirazi notables during the siege of 1352–3 is a blatant case of this exercise of royal power. On a higher level, in the 13th century Atabek Abu Bakr dismissed the chief judge of Fars, from the ʿAlavi family, and replaced him with a member of the (related) Fali-Sirafi family. A. M. Ayati, *Tahrir-e Ta'rikh-e-Vassaf* (Tehran: Iran Cultural Foundation, 1970), p. 96.

18. In Nishapur in the 10th-11th centuries the *ra'is* was a very important figure of the civil administration who acted something like a mayor, and the *ra'is* of Nishapur was usually a member of one of the most powerful local families. Bulliet, *The Patricians of Nishapur,* pp. 66–7.

19. Ibn Balkhi (edited by A.N. Behruzi), *Farsnameh-ye Ibn Balkhi* (Shiraz: Publishing Syndicate, 1958), pp. 152–3. I could find no other record of this family, whose name points to an Iranian origin.

20. Ibid., p. 153.

21. There were probably more fundamental reasons than the union of the *Mardāsā* and Afzari families for the fusion of the two offices and the *qazi*'s power eclipsing that of the *ra'is*. Since Shiraz had been the capital of minor dynasties almost continuously since Buyid times, there was little need for a purely civil official such as the *ra'is* to act as an intermediary between the city and a distant capital.

22. *Tahrir-e Ta'rikh-e Vassaf*, p. 96.

23. Ibn Battuta, II, 302–4.

24. Ann K.S. Lambton, *Landlord and Peasant in Persia* (London: Oxford University Press, 1953), pp. 98–9.

25. Ibn Battuta, II, 304–5.

26. Khwajeh Fazlallah Rashid al-Din Tabib (edited by Mohammad Shafiʿi), *Mokatebat-e Rashidi*, (Lahore: Punjab Publishers, 1954), pp. 56ff.

27. ʿObeid Zakani, *Taʿrifat,* from the *Divan* (Tehran: Eqbal, 1967), II, p. 158. In his *Resaleh-ye Delgosha*, ʿObeid gives humorous anecdotes about several well-known judges of Shiraz, which, if not exactly obscene, show a lighter side of their personalities.

28. Mohammad Qazvini, citing the historian Hafez Abru, in notes to Moʿin al-Din Joneid Shirazi, *Shadd al-Ezar* (Tehran: Majles, 1948), p. 362.

29. *The Travels of Ibn Battuta*, pp. 195–98.

30. See map in *Farsnameh-ye Naseri*, II, 17–18. Fāl is the name of a region near the coast of the Persian Gulf behind the port of Sirāf, an area now called *Kalehdar* or *Galehdar* (Ibid., II, 227). Afzār (or Afzar) is another region of the *garmsir* lying southeast of Shiraz between Qir and Khonj on the road to the Gulf (Ibid., II, 179). Beiza is a region of the *sardsir* located a short distance northwest of Shiraz (Ibid., II, 182–3). It is possible that there were in fact two, rather than three, families of judges, since the family of Fali-Sirafi may have been descendents of the Fazari family. The minister of Atabek Saʿd b. Zangi, ʿAmid al-Din Asʿad Afzari must have been part of the family of the Fazari judges. The minister's descendent, Safi al-Din Abu'l-Kheir Masʿud b. Mahmud b. Abu

Fath Fali Sirafi (d. 1279) was related to the first Qazi Majd al-Din Esmaʿil. The son of Safi al-Din, Mowlana Qotb al-Din Fali (d. 1312), composed the famous *Sharh-e Qasideh-ye ʿAmidiyeh* on a work of his ancestor. For more information about this branch of the powerful Fali-Sirafi family see *Shadd al-Ezar*, pp. 430–5, and *Shiraznameh*, p. 202.

31. Perhaps the best indicator of the pre-eminence of the Fali-Sirafis in terms of wealth is the fact that only rarely was someone not a prince, minister, or chief judge able to afford endowing a school.

32. *Tahrir-e Taʾrikh-e Vassaf*, p. 96.

33. Ibid., p. 120. As far as the sources go, this compromise was a unique instance of a jointly-held chief-judgeship. In fact, as Vassaf adds, Rokn al-Din took precedence in spite of the arrangement.

34. Historians may have overemphasized these incidents and exaggerated the power of the qazi out of wishful thinking for an ideal Islamic state, where everyone, including the ruler, would be subject to the qazi's rulings on Islamic law.

35. In 1355 Shah Sheikh Abu Eshaq, though weakened, was still a threat to the Mozaffarids.

36. *The Travels of Ibn Battuta*, p. 204–5. The close association of the ʿAlavis and Shiraz originated in the presence of the tombs of three brothers of Imam Reza in the city. Many of the great seyyeds of Shiraz were buried in the *Jameʿ ʿAtiq* area, near the graves of the saints Amir Ahmad b. Musa and his brother Mahmud.

37. *Shiraznameh*, p. 153.

38. Moʿin al-Din Joneid Shirazi, *Shadd al-Ezar*, pp. 292–3; *Shiraznameh*, p. 202.

39. *Shadd al-Ezar*, p. 171. It is not clear whether Seyyed Taj al-Din inherited his father's position of *naqib*.

40. *Shadd al-Ezar*, p. 325. *Shiraznameh*, p. 202.

41. *Tahrir-e Taʾrikh-e Vassaf*, p. 96.

42. *Shiraznameh*, pp. 201–2. Zeid Asud had married a daughter of ʿAzod al-Dowleh Al-Buyeh. His descendant Abu Moʿali's dates are uncertain, but he probably lived in the early twelfth century.

43. Our information about the family relationships of the seyyeds of Shiraz is incomplete. We know that they married both ʿAlavis and non-ʿAlavis. But the exact relationship between family and the office of *naqib* is still unclear.

44. For the fourteenth century usage of the word *kalu* (variant *kolu*) which has disappeared from modern Persian, see A. A. Dehkhoda, *Loghatnameh-ye Dehkhoda* (Tehran: University Printing and Publishing, 1994). Vol. XI, pp. 16, 313.

45. *The Travels of Ibn Battuta*, p. 199.

46. Shahab al-Din ʿAbdollah Hafez Abru (edited by Khan Baba Bayani) *Zeil-e-Jameʿ al-Tavarikh-e Rashidi* (Tehran: Elmi, 1934), p. 168. Mahmud Kotbi (edited by A. H. Navaʾi), *Taʾrikh-e Al-e Mozaffar* (Tehran: Ibn Sina, 1955), p. 39.

47. From Rashid al-Din's *Jameʿ al-Tavarikh*, cited by Ghani, *Bahs dar Asar va Afkar va Ahval-e Hafez*, pp. 123–4.

48. Fasaʾi, *Farsnameh-ye Naseri*, I, p. 59.

49. Zarrinkub, *Az Kucheh-ye Rendan*, p. 1, calls Shiraz in this period *shahr-e rendan*, or city of the *rends*. The leaders of the street mobs must have been the popular heroes called *pahlevanan* (strong-men, wrestlers) who were often connected with the *zurkhaneh* (athletic societies). In the 14th century the title *pahlavan* was also given to military officers. For example, Shah Shojaʿ's governor of Kerman was called Pahlevan Asad (Kotbi, 86). In recent times mob leaders have been called *chaqu-keshan* (knife-pullers) by their opponents and *pahlavanan* by their supporters.

50. *Javanmardi* resembles the Arabic *futuwwa*, and the *pahlavans* of Shiraz resembled the *akhis* of Anatolia, described in Ibn Battuta, II, 418–21.

51. According to Joneid Shirazi, in *Shadd al-Ezar*, p. 198, local rulers were all terrified of his tongue.

52. *Ibid*, p. 201.

53. Richard Bulliet, in "The Shaikh al-Islam and the Evolution of Islamic Society" *Studia Islamica*, XXXV (1972), pp. 53–67, suggests that the *Sheikh ol-Eslam* was the head of the educational system with the power to certify teachers' credentials. But the sources do not mention the *Sheikh ol-Eslam's* performing such a function in Shiraz. The biographies of the *Sheikh ol-Eslams* of Shiraz emphasize their positions as preachers and as Sufi leaders, while those persons most famous as teachers were usually called *Mowlana*.

54. *Shadd al-Ezar*, p. 124; *Shiraznameh*, pp. 158–9. These sources say that Qotb al-Din was "popularly called *Sheikh ol-Eslam*." He also held the Sufi title *Sheikh ol-Shoyukh*.

55. *Shadd al-Ezar*, p. 353; *Shiraznameh*, p. 181. He preached for sixty years in the *Songhoriyyeh* Mosque, and was *Sheikh ol-Eslam* at the time of the writing of the *Shiraznameh* in 745/1344.

56. In the case of the political leaders, the author writes of their piety and support of religion, not their military deeds.

57. *Shiraznameh*, pp. 168–9.

58. Names such as Ruzbeh, Salbeh, and Nikruz were common Iranian names in Fars. The sheikhs of Beiza, for example, traced their ancestry to a certain Salbeh and Qazi Majd al-Din Esmaʿil Fali (d. 1268) was known as Ibn Nikruz after some distant ancestor. The Baghnovis, who called themselves *Qoreishi* after the Arab tribe of the prophet, had intermarried with the natives of Fars, and the first of the family to come to Shiraz from Fasa in the twelfth century was named Sheikh Zein al-Din Mozaffar b. Ruzbehan.

59. The sources mention only one case of intermarriage between these groups—between Sheikh Najib al-Din ʿAli b. Bozghash (1197–1279) and a daughter of Seyyed Qazi Sharaf al-Din Mohammad, chief judge and son of the *naqib* of Fars (*Shadd al-Ezar*, 335).

60. This distinction between "upper" and "lower" local aristocrats is based chiefly on their differing treatment in the sources and on such details as burial sites (for example, the *Jameʿ ʿAtiq* area was more prestigious for burial than *Dar al-Salam*) and

association with mosques and schools. Preaching in the Masjed *Songhoriyeh* or the *Jame' 'Atiq* implied more prestige than, for example, preaching in the more modest mosque of Haj 'Ali 'Assar.

61. One Imam of a small mosque in the Kazerun Gate area said such long prayers that he had only a very small congregation (*Shadd al-Ezar*, p. 118).

From Artistic Endeavor to Economic Enterprise; Horsemanship from the 18th to the 20th Centuries

Jean-Marc Ran Oppenheim

Horsemanship, primarily the skill of riding a horse, reflects the society in which it is practiced. As such, it projects the cultural values and, to a significant extent, the economic system of its setting.

Historically, horses and their riders have inspired awe in and a sense of admiration from the pedestrian public. This may be due do to man's mastery—woman's occurs much later—over a sizeable animal whose beauty, spirit, and strength has often been extolled in the literature of both Western and other civilizations: Homer called Troy's Hector 'tamer of horses', and the Prophet Muhammad counseled his followers to heed the pedigree of their mares. Riding horses has also carried political connotations. In republican and imperial Rome, the *Equestors* formed a distinct political class, while medieval civilizations in both Europe and the Islamic world restricted the riding of horses to various privileged members of their respective societies. Today, the image of equitation as an activity of the affluent elite is reinforced by commercial marketing strategies. Both historical experience and contemporary perceptions reflect an activity that is exclusionary, hence desirable.

The French and Industrial Revolutions and their consequences radically transformed horsemanship, along with most other aspects of society. The first event ended the most prolific phase of academic, or artistic, equitation and the second relegated the horse to strictly leisure activities, thereby re-creating the need for teachers steeped in equestrian knowledge. One area in which the use of the horse increased in the twentieth century and, especially since the end of World War II, is sports performance equitation. This includes show-riding in its various permutations, hunting, long-distance trekking, and the basic equitation principles upon which those activities are based. Although some of these forms of riding are, in theory, based on principles initially developed in academic equitation, today these principles are honored mostly in the breach.

While much of society adapted to the social, economic, and political changes wrought by the French and Industrial Revolutions within decades, it took nearly a century and a half for the world of horses to undergo fundamental changes. When the changes became palpable, the result was a synthesis of the traditional and the modern. Traditional horsemen perceived modern horsemanship as anathema to the spirit which guided the classical schooling and use of the horse while the modernists viewed the traditionalists as unable or unwilling to accept the dynamics of change and their impact on an activity that had, historically, adapted to change whenever necessary.

Thus the field of horsemanship, like other areas governed by history and conventions, continues to project a vigorous and often contentious debate between these extremes. Current cultural and demographic trends favor the modernists, since the ranks of the now aging classicists are not being replenished. The debate is also enlivened by the significant economic impact of the breeding industry, commercialization, marketing perceptions, and social mobility. It is also affected by globalization.

Surveying a field such as that of horsemanship during a period which produced radical socio-political change as well as industrialization and mechanized transport provides the observer with a perspective on the cultural and economic transformations of an activity once central to human society. Despite these changes, however, the horse remained in extensive use by the military until World War I and even the early stages of World War II, an important factor in contemporary leisure riding. Thus the trajectory of industrialization, globalization, and cyberspace—horse sales are often conducted via the Internet—has had a direct impact on the world of horses and horsemanship.

Although the horse became marginal in the agricultural context of such developments, it continues to have a significant cultural and socio-economic impact in our own days. Witness the raging animal-rights debate over fox-hunting in Britain, the populist excitement of a Thoroughbred triple crown series in the U.S., and the plethora of equestrian vacation opportunities from Montana to Mongolia. Modern horsemanship is also an activity in which women figure prominently. The methods and goals of schooling and riding horses have adapted to this transformed environment much to the chagrin of the classicists.

The Classical Period

The idea of horsemanship as an art form evolved gradually from the fifteenth century onwards. Earlier, the use of the riding horse in the West was strictly practical and reinforced mainly its military applications. It was the advent of gunpowder which obviated the need for heavy armor by knights mounted on heavy horses. Those military horses of medieval Europe had resembled today's draft animals, with their slow, inelegant movements. Horsemen of Asia and Islam had used lighter breeds, but neither society developed the artistic principles of schooling horses that gained currency in the West and formed the basis of European classical horsemanship. Once the knight no longer needed armor and a heavy-type horse to carry him, lighter breeds were introduced, primarily through crossbreeding with Barb or Arab stallions, and their use in battle evolved from the clumsy charge to more sophisticated maneuvers, thus necessitating focused schooling. As in many creative and applied fields, the Renaissance had a significant impact on horsemanship too. The study of the schooling of horses began in earnest in riding academies, initially in Italy and then in France. From there it migrated to Spain, England, Austria, and some of the German princely states. Its trajectory paralleled that of fencing, court dancing, and other elements of aristocratic etiquette, all of which were addressed in Baldassare Castiglione's *Book of the Courtier,* published in 1528.

It was in seventeenth- and eighteenth-century France that equitation reached its artistic peak. Horsemanship, like most other art forms, benefited from the largesse of the French monarchy. French mercantilism indirectly contributed to this effort because of its emphasis on state subsidies and controls of relevant economic and, occasionally, artistic activities. Thanks to royal patronage, Versailles, with its riding masters recognized throughout Europe, became the center of this activity. Thus, Louis XIV's policy of keeping his nobility at court concentrated the social group most affected by this equestrian activity. Nonetheless, privately-owned riding academies were also established in Paris and in the country's major provincial cities. Although logic would indicate that riding horses is best practiced in a rural outdoor setting, classical horsemanship as an art form evolved primarily in urban centers where noblemen—there is no indication of noblewomen except occasionally in the hunt field—could avail themselves of the services of instructors whose reputations acquired the kind of recognition usually equated with musical composers and other artists. Like those activities, horsemanship progressed in the venues where wealthy and aristocratic patrons subsidized the teachers and practitioners of the art.

The development of artistic horsemanship always practiced indoors under the guidance of masters led to a dichotomy in the way riding was perceived and two main schools that developed. In French these two distinct disciplines are known as *équitation de manège* [school riding] performed in a covered arena, and *équitation de campagne* [cross-country riding].

Equitation de manège was perceived as the essence of classical, or artistic, equitation incorporating movements that, originally, may have been devised to school the post-medieval war horse. Now it aimed to produce a rider in an elegant position guiding his horse through a series of dance-like movements which gave the impression that the horse was a partner in the choreography, doing it freely and willingly without constraint. Further, the guiding aids given by the rider were to be discreet, indeed imperceptible to the audience. Stallions were the rule rather than the exception for the *équitation de manège* because their gaits, especially the trot and the canter, were considered far more majestic than those of either geldings or mares. In contrast to their predecessors, the French revolutionized the schooling of the horse by emphasizing a humane approach in training which used the horse's intelligence rather than his fear of punishment in promoting cooperation with the rider.

Equitation de campagne focused on the application of the horse to outdoor riding, primarily war and the hunt. However, many practitioners of this type of riding admitted that the fundamentals of school riding could, and should, be applied to the warhorse and the hunting horse, since its emphasis was obedience to discreet aids as well as a balanced and more comfortable gait, both being desirable qualities in any riding horse.

Equitation, like any discipline undergoing observation, experimentation, and application, also received the attention of practioner-authors. Thus theories of equitation were spawned, debated, rejected or accepted. The first extant manual of horsemanship, including the care of the horse, was written by Xenophon. Roman as well as medieval Muslim authors penned treatises on the subject, though their focus was primarily the use of the horse in battle rather than theories of schooling and riding. The first modern works addressing such issues and focusing on *équitation de manège* were published in the late sixteenth and early seventeenth centuries.

The creation of a classical form of riding and schooling horses and its impact on horsemanship is amply reflected in the equestrian literature of the period. The French monopoly of this discipline, and the ensuing prestige, may be due to the abundant writings of its practioners. In addition to books addressing such perennial issues as breeding, veterinary care, pasture management, stable construction, and other ancillary concerns, the seventeenth and eighteenth centuries witnessed the publication, almost exclusively in French, of works concerned especially with the schooling of the riding horse. The themes of these publications included the techniques used in training or schooling horses. Emphasis was placed on adherence to classical principles as elaborated by the masters whose work spanned the post-Renaissance to the end of the eighteenth century.

These authors had studied the ancient and pre-modern texts, applied their principles to their own endeavors, and expanded on these foundations. It may be said that the spirit of the Scientific Revolution permeated their approach to an ancient activity; moreover, they did not flinch from providing new principles to their disciples and readers. Their paramount concern was the freedom of the horse's gaits, the discretion of the aids, the balance of the rider in the saddle, and especially the avoidance of any coercion whatsoever including the hurried schooling of the animal lest his spirit and his gait be spoiled. Works on the subject continued to appear almost uninterruptedly until 1789 when the end of the French monarchy, the ensuing emigration of the aristocracy, and the wars of the Revolution closed down those centers of equitation.

The Modern Period

The impact of the French Revolution of 1789 on classical horsemanship was seismic. It relegated the stables and riding arenas of Versailles, known as the *Grande Ecurie du Roy*, to the dustbin of history. Most of the teachers and practitioners of classical riding emigrated or abandoned their equestrian endeavors. The demands of a state in the throes of radical socio-political and economic transformation and under siege by counter-revolutionary forces from within and without would not accommodate the values of what was widely seen as an aristocratic activity. Demand was now on horsemanship applied to vastly increased military activity emphasizing cross-country riding rather than elegant indoor equestrian choreography. Both the wars of the Revolution and those of the Napoleonic period placed great demands on France's equine industry. It was forced to meet the vastly increased need for cavalry mounts, instructors, troopers, and field units, in addition to a significantly expanded network of equine husbandry, pasture management, stable construction, and fodder cultivation. While these last-named activities are integral to any agricultural economy, they were especially strained under a society almost continually at war for a quarter of a century.

Under Napoleon, efforts to reopen some of the schools of equitation were privately pursued but they were constantly disrupted by conscription and the military's need for experienced instructors. The state, however, did establish riding schools to train military instructors who were to transmit their skill in the mounted units either while on garrison duty or in the field. Although the First Empire in France reintroduced the idea of nobility—based on primarily on merit and service rather than birth—it did little to promote the peacetime equestrian activities of the aristocracy. To its credit, however, it did introduce an infusion of Arab blood from horses captured in Egypt and Syria, a development that greatly improved French bloodstock.

The post-Waterloo Bourbon Restoration brought back, along with the monarchy and its entourage, classical equitation. The cavalry school at Saumur, established in 1771 to promote a learned approach to *équitation de campagne* and closed by the Revolution, was revived in 1815. Although strictly a military establishment, throughout the nineteenth century and the first half of the twentieth Saumur produced some of the most influential equestrian authors of post-1789 classical equitation. Nonetheless, the military aspects of equitation were not neglected because it is at Saumur that efforts to synthesize the two systems of academic or classical and cross-country riding were first seriously addressed. These efforts would later in the nineteenth century make a major contribution to a renewed and continuous debate among students of classical riding.

The revival of classical equitation in post-Waterloo France was paralleled in central Europe as well. A number of the classical riding masters who emigrated in the wake of the Revolution of 1789 established academies which attracted members the Germanic and Austro-Hungarian aristocracies. This development was not unexpected: one of the great eighteenth century French works on classical equitation, de la Guérinière's *Ecole de cavalerie*, had been translated in 1791 into German and had been adopted as the manual of instruction at the Viennese imperial court thus ensuring the survival of the French classical method initially developed and ultimately perfected at Versailles. These developments notwithstanding, equitation whether of the classical or cross-country variety was still the preserve of the nobility and of the military. However, the forthcoming Industrial Revolution would restructure the social classes of Europe and, in time, have a powerful effect on all forms of equitation.

Despite the revival of classical equitation, the impact of war and revolutionary change was indelible and confirmed the continued emphasis on the practical needs of military horsemanship. Also evident, as much else among the returned *émigrés,* was a fondness for things English including riding styles and activities. This interest had been acquired during exile in Britain and it had been reinforced by Britain's position of power on the continent in the aftermath of Waterloo. The expanding privileged classes, especially in France, took to fox- and other forms of hunting on horseback in greater numbers and more frequency than their pre-Revolutionary ancestors. Since the latter part of the seventeenth century, the English had been actively engaged in foxhunting and they had introduced horseracing. The latter activity was to have a deep influence on two critical areas related to horses: efforts to breed fast horses hence the concept of sharply focused selective husbandry and the ensuing economic ramifications of such efforts. However, the English were not the originators of hunting on horseback. There exists plenty of early and pre-modern pictorial and archival evidence of such activity among the privileged classes in many societies, including Islam and central Asia.

This increase in the use of the horse in hunting ensured an expansion of the *équitation de campagne* favored by the military. With the reactivation of the French cavalry school at Saumur, the military developed an active interest in the synthesis of both types of equitation. Although theirs was a focus whose application was strictly utilitarian—cavalry riding—it evoked an interest from an urban public, albeit restricted, that was increasingly knowledgeable in the issues of horsemanship. The vehicle for this expanded interest was the circus.

During the July Monarchy, a growing industrializing economy, an expanding bourgeoisie, and more leisure opportunities provided the climate for new forms of entertainment. Equestrian circus performances appealed to both the general public and to a growing circle of aficionados. This form of riding, performed exclusively indoors and in a small arena, lent itself to the form of equitation initially perfected at Versailles: elegant and harmonious choreography displayed as synthesis of human skill and equine talent. Accordingly, an intense effort to revive *équitation de manège* occurred, and an increase in the publication of works devoted to it occurs from the mid-nineteenth century onward. These works received attention because circus riding, especially the French variety, was considered a fashionable activity as long as classical principles provided the foundation. Undoubtedly, there were purists who decried this trend but their critiques only served to enliven the debate.

As industrialization added a new and faster rhythm in society, interest in horsemanship for leisure grew proportionately. The second third of the nineteenth century saw the initial introduction of horseshows at regional fairs, commercial events in existence since the Middle Ages. The horseshows featured various activities, but especially novel was jumping over fences in an arena. It was a blend of hunting and military riding that called for skill, courage, timing, and speed, the perfect crowd pleaser. It was also a vehicle for the promotion of breeding stock, training methods, and required equipment. Commercialization and marketing were becoming factors of concern.

By the end of the nineteenth century, showjumping classes moved from rural settings to urban celebrations such as New York's National Horse Show held annually at Madison Square Garden, Toronto's Royal Horse Fair, and London's White City. The capitals of most countries on the continent also held their version of such events. Three results of this development were the focus on elite society, the near-monopoly of the military in a strictly sporting activity increasingly perceived as exclusionary because of its prohibitive cost, and the introduction of national competition since the competitors, especially those in uniform, were members of national teams. The popular press, now able to include illustrations with its text, gave increasing coverage and commentary to these events and their significance, whether social, commercial, or jingoistic.

High society and commercialization were not the only factors in the growth of showjumping. At the end of the nineteenth century Federico Caprilli, an Italian cavalry officer, introduced a new way of sitting in a saddle on a horse going over an obstacle: leaning forward over the horse's mane at the moment of take-off and remaining slightly ahead of the vertical in between fences. This was in contrast to the traditional form which called for an upright military position on the flat and slightly behind the vertical over fences. Like all innovations, this revolutionary development sparked much debate but ultimately was universally accepted because it allowed for higher fences and greater speed due to less rider interference with the horse's movements.

The popular appeal of equestrian contests led their inclusion in the modern Olympics beginning in 1912 at Stockholm. Because the military were the only participants initially, the Olympic equestrian events reflected the use of the riding horse by the military and continue to do so today. In addition to showjumping, the Olympic discipline include dressage, the modern version of Versailles' *équitation de manège,* and the Three-Day Event—initially called the Military Trials—combining dressage and showjumping and including going some distance cross-country and jumping forbidding natural obstacles. The military predominance in international events and its monopoly of the equestrian Olympics continued through the interwar years.

World War I was a watershed for the military use of horses. Except for the Middle East theater, the use of cavalry tactics en masse gave way first to trenches, then to the tank and the airplane. Nonetheless, both sides used cavalry in a number of ways: as reconnaissance troops, to harass retreating units, to act as screens for troop movements, to haul artillery, ambulances, field kitchens, supplies, etc. When the British introduced the battle tank in 1916, there were over 1 million cavalry, or riding, horses alone in use on all fronts. The number of draught horses used to haul everything from guns to rations by all the armies in the field has never been calculated accurately. The military technology used in this war, however, created an environment far more lethal to the horses than had been seen in any previous war. Used as beasts of burden by all the fighting armies, horses were casualties of explosive shells, land mines, and gas attacks. Indeed, the British and the Germans had designed an equine gas mask, known as a 'horsepirator', though its application was not very successful and tragi-comical since the horse perceived it as a feed bag: the horse tore it apart looking for the nonexistent oats.

World War II was the last equestrian hurrah. Despite its overwhelming industrial character, its *blitzkrieg* synthesis of air and land units, its aircraft carriers battle groups, and its nuclear conclusion, all the combatants, including the U.S., used equine units in a variety of functions. Foremost, however, was the use of the horse as a beast of burden: the number of horses used on the Eastern front alone exceeded two million. Lesser figures apply to other theaters of operation. Because of their traditions, their social prestige, their interwar competitive achievements, their agricultural economies, and the relative slowness of military mechanization, most cavalry units of central European armies participated in the fighting as mounted infantry, using the horse for easy mobility. After the war, many of the surviving cavalry officers became the equestrian link between the traditional but evolving societies of pre-1939 Europe and the post-1945 world of baby-boomers and mass consumption.

The military domination of equestrian sports until the post-World War II period was due to a number of factors. Except for purposes of transportation and agriculture, the horse was perceived as an instrument for war. Hunting on horseback was traditionally the preserve of the aristocracy or military class. When the modern European nation-state was constructed in the seventeenth century, it provided horses for its cavalry in contrast to the pre-modern practice of feudal levies. Late nineteenth century popular sporting equestrian events were, indeed, a modification of military riding. Moreover, producing horses capable of competing successfully at the international level is prohibitively expensive, traditionally undertaken by the state and its organs such as a ministry of war or agriculture. In an age of both increasing nationalism and widespread media coverage beginning with the modern Olympics, modern equestrian competitions, like all sports contests, reflected national images. Lastly, shipping horses safely across long distance is a logistically-complicated and costly enterprise. Therefore, it was paramount that competitors be equipped with the best mounts, training, and equipment.

Even the relevant literature reflected a military dominance. Books on horsemanship published in the first decades of the twentieth century emphasized the principles of military equitation applied to the training and schooling of the sports horse. They reflected their authors' military background and usually encouraged the incorporation of time-tested principles combining *équitation de manège* and *équitation de campagne.* Most of these authors were either active or reserve officers; they had access to equestrian military training facilities; if they held active rank, their mounts were provided by their government; if they held reserve rank, their horses were either privately-purchased or assigned by their units. They also had access to top-ranked military instructors whose own training and experience reflected classical principles and traditional methods.

The Post-World-War-II Period

The military's domination of sports riding began to decline in the years immediately following World War II. Except for ceremonial duties, most Western countries and those of central Europe eliminated their mounted units. They had become a luxurious anachronism. Ironically, newly independent former colonies, both in the Middle East and South Asia, formed cavalry units replete with the supporting logistics: equitation schools for training, husbandry programs, and veterinary services. Like their European predecessors, members of such units came from the privileged classes and rode mostly for sports, especially polo and showjumping; the legacy of cultural imperialism was manifest in deep and in diverse ways, sometimes with success. The Egyptian army produced a showjumping team that won the bronze medal at the 1960 Rome Olympiad at a time when Nasser was nationalizing most privately-held Egyptian assets and launching his economic policy of socialism. Ironically, it was via the Egyptian military equestrian program that Israel inserted in Cairo an intelligence agent masquerading as a former German cavalry officer. The Iraqi army still had a showjumping team trained by an Egyptian brigadier on the eve of the Iran-Iraq war. Latin America, too, was the destination of a number of former German military horsemen. The Chilean cavalry was structured and trained along German lines while the Mexican Army team set a number of showjumping world records in the late 1940s. Quite a few former central European military horsemen, especially Hungarians, landed in the U.S.

The imperial legacy notwithstanding, sports riding in the West was becoming increasingly civilianized. It was at the 1948 London Olympiad that male civilian riders initially competed in the equestrian events; it was also at this time that women riders first made their appearance on the international competitive circuit. Women finally entered the equestrian Olympic arena in 1952; now, they nearly dominate in numbers and achievements both the international circuit and the Olympics.

The demilitarization of sports riding in the West created a glut of former cavalry officers eager to teach their techniques to a civilian public equally eager to acquire their knowledge.

Quite a few of these former officers penned their theories in books and a variety of publications dedicated to horsemanship. Their focus, as in pre-war days, was on military training techniques aimed at sports riding and based on traditional methods. While such methods were essentially uniform, there were differences occasioned by the breeds used and the cultural temperament of the riders. Moreover, a socio-economic shift was taking place in society and it would manifest itself in horsemanship in general and in sports riding in particular.

The 1950s and 1960s were a period of unprecedented affluence for the West's middle classes. Access to leisure activities hitherto limited to the elites became the rule rather than the exception. With this transformation came a pivotal factor: commercialization. The advent of suburban lifestyles in North America and parts of Western Europe as well as an increasing closer connection between rural and urban areas via faster modes of transportation and pervasive media fostered an increased interest in horse sports. Especially affected were groups that could afford the not insignificant expenses involved in horse-keeping.

This newly found affluence provided an introduction into the formerly closed circles of horsemanship which included sports riding, foxhunting, and polo. A number of conduits facilitated this access. Pony clubs, established during the interwar period, were especially designed to educate youngsters to proper horse keeping and instill a love for horse and equine sports. Foxhunting clubs emphasized focus on the prey but social dynamics among the hunt members equaled those found during golf rounds among corporate executives. While hunting on horseback had been a perennial activity of Europe's and north America's landed gentry since the seventeenth century, only after World War II did it bestow acceptance to the middle classes on a significant scale. Polo, too, was transformed from a preserve of officers to one of the extremely affluent. Its image of exclusivity has made the game a favored venue for high-end corporate marketing seeking to convey images of wealth, power, and social prestige.

It is in showjumping, however, that the most radical transformation occurred. Unlike foxhunting and especially polo, activities which still require significant expenditures, and hence have relatively small numbers of adherents, showjumping has become the preferred equestrian activity of the middle classes. This is due to the proximity of riding schools that have sprouted in every community of both Europe and North America. Most of these establishments conduct extensive training programs for all levels of age, skill, talent, and income. They facilitate entry into every level of competition by leasing or even loaning horses to their students. In Western Europe, when the social contract between government and citizen guaranteed wages, benefits, and pensions, even some workers' unions became involved in showjumping by sponsoring riding clubs whose goal was easy financial access to an activity formerly dominated by the social and military elites. Nearly every weekend of the year, there are numerous horseshows taking place in most geographic region the Western world. Some of these events are local affairs for amateurs and small professionals aimed at producing enjoyment and challenge to all participants. Others are extensive and huge productions often funded by multinational corporations which donate prize money, often in the tens of thousand of dollars, to the winners many of whom are large-scale professionals.

Breeding and schooling are two other areas that have been deeply affected by the transformation of horsemanship since the end of World War II. As in every historical context, equine husbandry today reflects the priorities of the market in which horses are used. The horses used in leisure and sports riding have diverse origins. Since royal and state breeding programs as well as military riders no longer exist, such horses now come from a single source: the private market. This is usually in the form of breeders who produce horses for a specific market: showjumping, dressage, pony club, endurance riding, etc. Another, albeit indirect, source of such horses is the racetrack. Bred privately, far more often than not Thoroughbreds and Standardbreds usually finish their short racing careers as leisure and sports mounts. The cost of such mounts, whether especially bred or retired from the racetrack, can span from hundreds to hundreds of thousands of dollars; very occasionally, an exceptional showjumper can fetch one million or more. Such a price reflects pedigree, training and success in the show ring and, if a stallion, potential for breeding.

The market for sports horses has also affected the methods used for their schooling or training. Since the near-extinction of an entire generation of former military horsemen, professional riders, both men and women, now produce the schooled horses and riders that make up the competitive equestrian world. Unlike their military predecessors whose training was nearly uniform, based on classical principles, and steeped in tradition, the new breed of teachers and trainers reflect the conditions in which their own training was conducted.

In some European countries, for example France, Germany, and the U.K, established equestrian societies provide uniform and monitored standards that must be met by institutions which train new teachers. In other countries, including the U.S., there are no national standards, only enterprising individuals who set up training centers for young professionals, charge tuition, and issue a certificate upon completion of the training course.

Whether in the first or second context, the methods used by these riding professionals to produce schooled horses and riders fall far short of the mark established by their military predecessors. Indeed, one of the major criteria of their technique is the speed with which the finished equine or human product can be produced. Lacking the financial support of a military institution, faced with the pressures of the private market, and the competition for clients among professionals, trainers now focus on achieving a finished horse in the shortest time possible: one to two years compared to the four to six years under the traditional and classical methods formerly used by the military. However, producing a finished student may, depending on the talent of both student and teacher, take years. If the student loses perseverance and patience, he or she goes to another instructor in search of success. This is sometime achieved if the student can afford to purchase an experienced showjumping horse that can successfully complete a competition round in spite of his rider.

Despite the rhythm of modernity, or perhaps because of it, occasionally a longing for the classical methods and traditions of riding dictates a return to the historical past. On March 2, 2003, an article in *The New York Times* indicated that the seventeenth-century stables at Versailles, known as the *Grande Ecurie du Roy* and closed since the French Revolution, was reopened as the Academy of Equestrian Arts. In addition to refining their advanced riding techiques, the selected students would also study music, drawing, dance, and fencing. The enterprise was placed "under the guidance of Bartabas, founder and director of the Zingaro Theater, which promotes horsemanship as a contemporary art form through musical accompaniment," in other words, a circus. The article also provided an email address for readers interested in further information.

Despite the reopening of the Versailles stables, horsemanship has not come full circle. It is, however, adapting to the constantly changing conditions in which it is practiced. As in previous periods in history, the use of the horse has altered to reflect contemporary cultural mores and economic priorities. While purists may decry the demise of classical and academic equitation, and sports enthusiasts may long for the guiding experience of traditionally-formed military horsemen, at least the horse is no longer cannon fodder in warfare though he may be an unwitting participant in the upward social mobility of his rider. The latter, realizing the extent of his or her investment, assuredly provides him with the care due a valuable asset.

Capturing Imagination: The Buja and Medieval Islamic Mappa Mundi[1]

Karen C. Pinto

"What constitutes a text is not the presence of linguistic elements but the act of construction so that maps, as constructions employing a conventional sign system, become texts."[2]

—*J. B. Harley, "Deconstructing the Map"*

Every medieval Islamic cartograph of the world contains a curious anomaly. Consistently located on the eastern flank of Africa is a double-territorial ethnonym for an obscure East African tribe: the Buja (marked on Figure 1 with a red circle).[3] Mention of them in medieval Middle Eastern historiography is rare and, at best, superficial, yet no Islamic mappa mundi from the 11th to the 19th century leaves them out. Not only are the Buja privileged with a permanent berth on the Islamic world map, they are also the only place on the map signified with a double territorial marking. The question that I raise in this paper is, quite simply, who were the Buja? Why are they so absent in Islamic historiography, yet so present on the mappa mundi? The answer emerges from a series of droll and puzzling references that hint at the oddest reasons for the emphasis; reasons which, in turn, cause us to question our notions of how and why places make it on to maps. The query reveals surprising answers that can be relegated to the Husserlian domain of "retentions," "reproductions," and "protentions."

> *Retentions* being the perspective view that we have of past phases of an experience from the vantage of a 'now' moment which slips forwards, and in relation to which past phases of our experience of the present are pushed inexorably back. *Reproduction* of some recollected event, by contrast, involves the temporary abandonment of the current 'now' as the focal point around which retentional perspectives cohere, in favour of a

> fantasied 'now' in the past which we take up in order to replay events mentally. Retentions, unlike reproductions, are all part of current consciousness of the present, but they are subject to distortion or diminuation as they are pushed back towards the fringes of our current awareness of our surroundings. . . . Retentions can thus be construed as the background of out-of-date beliefs against which more up-to-date beliefs are projected, and significant trends and changes are calibrated. As beliefs become more seriously out of date, they diminish in salience and are lost to view. We thus perceive the present not as a knife-edge 'now' but as a temporally extended field within which trends emerge out of the patterns we discern in the successive updatings of perceptual beliefs relating to the proximate past, the most proximate past, and the next, and so on. This trend is projected into the future in the form of *protentions*, i.e. anticipations of the pattern of updating of current perceptual beliefs which will be necessitated in the proximate future, the next most proximate future, and the next, in a manner symmetric with the past, but in inverse temporal order.[4]

Out of this questioning of medieval Islamic maps, it is the temporal imagination that emerges as the dominant architect of cartographic space. It presents itself as an imagination that is triggered as much by the extreme alterity of *otherness* as it is by the subtle reflection of *self*.

The study of history through maps warrants, among other things, a close analysis of place from the point of view of time and space. Maps, as graphics of territory—whether real or imagined—require the collapsing of space from a three-dimensional infinite expanse to the flat, constrained surface of a two-dimensional sheet with finite, constrained boundaries.[5]

> Not only is it easy to lie with maps, it's essential. To portray meaningful relationships of a complex, three-dimensional world on a flat sheet of paper or a video screen, a map must distort reality. As a scale model, the map must use symbols that almost always are proportionally much bigger or thicker than the features they represent. To avoid hiding critical information in a fog of detail, the map must offer a selective, incomplete view of reality. There's no escape from the cartographic paradox: to present a useful and truthful picture, an accurate map must tell white lies.[6]

The limitations of space require that the map be ordered and this, in turn, requires that it be distorted. Since the cartograph is a product of a specific

Figure 1: “World Map,” Istanbul, Sülemaniye Camii, Aya Sofya 2971a, fol. 3a (878/1473)[7]

time, in a particular milieu, the distortion of space is necessarily culturally located. It is in the selections, the distortions, and the omissions that the key to culturally proscribed biases of structure and imagination lie. In this way the constraints of space turn paradoxically into a window overlooking a set of cultural constructs—situated just as much in time as in space. Space is informed (if not determined) by time:[8] one without the other would result in a map consisting of no more than a dot.[9]

I seek in this article to extract time—or, rather, the cultural fabric of time—from space by analyzing one site in the ossified matrix of places that overlays every medieval Islamic mappa mundi. Nowhere are the constructs of time more apparent than in the case of world maps, where space is at the highest premium. The ambitious scope of a world map means even less can be included and the cartographer, whether medieval or modern, situated in a global whirl of events (composed of reproductions and retentions, as Husserl suggests),[10] is faced with the task of choosing that which is most important to his/her mind.[11] These choices are necessarily temporally based. It is aspects of this necessary cartographic process of choice that I seek to explore in this article through a close analysis of one place.

Why The Buja?

Try this: Pick up any book on medieval Islamic history and scan the index for "Buja" or other variant spellings of the word: "Beja," Bedja," "Bujah," sometimes even transcribed as "Baja."[12] In at least nine out of ten secondary sources, the name will not occur. If the work moves out of the orbit of the central Umayyad and Abbasid lands to a discussion of the Muslim presence in Africa, it will likely include an extensive exposé on North Africa: namely the Maghrib, Ifriqiyya (Roman Africa),[13] the Berbers, al-Andalus (Muslim Spain), and the early conquests, as well as mention of the main ruling dynasties, along with foci on the Hilali invasions,[14] the slave and gold trade, etc.[15] If the discussion moves beyond North Africa to West Africa, one may also find mention of the gold producing centers of Ghana, Kanem, Takrur,[16] as well as Mali, Timbuktu,[17] etc. Although it is acknowledged that "in the eastern Sudan a mass Islamic society was established at a relatively early date," little has been done to expand understanding of this region in the early Islamic period.[18] When our history books discuss East Africa, the focus tends to be on the two key Christian kingdoms in the region: Bilad al-Habasha (i.e. Abyssinia) [highlighted on the map in Fig. 1],[19] and the kingdom of Nubia [highlighted on Fig. 1]. The lands of the Zanj or its people the "Zanjis" [highlighted on Fig. 1] are also always marked on the Muslim maps and frequently mentioned in the secondary sources. The Zanj appear to have gained an early berth for themselves in the medieval Islamic imagination as a consequence of their famous revolt in southern Iraq contra the Abbasids.[20]

But the Buja are rarely, if ever, mentioned. Ira Lapidus' all-encompassing book on *A History of Islamic Societies* affords an excellent example.[21] He casts a wide net in this voluminous source book for Islamic history, ranging from medieval to modern, from the central lands to the periphery. He discusses Africa at length, including an extensive discussion of West Africa, and the

Muslim connections. Yet, when it comes to East Africa, although he acknowledges the region's importance for the early Muslims, the details are sparse. It isn't until we get to the early modern period and the Funj empire (located south of Ethiopia, around the area of the Blue Nile) of the sixteenth-eighteenth century that details of the Muslim presence in the area increase. For the period prior, Lapidus adopts the standard pattern that dwells on Abyssinia, Nubia, and the Zanj. All he has to say about the lands in between is that:

> The Arabs occupied Egypt as far as Aswan in 641, but it was many centuries before Arab and Muslim peoples penetrated Nubia and the Sudanic belt to the south. The first Arab influx occurred in the ninth century, when Egyptians swarmed south to the newly discovered Allaqi gold fields between the Nile and the Red Sea. In the twelfth and thirteenth centuries Arab bedouin migrations increased the Muslim presence. Arabs married into local families and through matrilineal succession their children inherited the local chieftainships.[22]

Lapidus is unquestionably referring to the Buja, yet he does not even mention them by name.

In works devoted to Africa or Islam in Africa the situation improves a little. The Buja are at least mentioned, but again the details remain sparse, and, more often than not, tangential to the main subject at hand. For instance, in *Race and Slavery in the Middle East* and *Race and Color in Islam*, Bernard Lewis' reference to the Buja is meager and incidental to the Zanj.[23]

Exceptionally, Jay Spaulding in his article on "Precolonial Islam in the Eastern Sudan," devotes almost a page to the subject of the Buja and their Nubian neighbors noting their sporadic contact with the early Muslim colonizers in Egypt.[24] Spaulding's generous one page is a mere blip on the historical radar. In a recent book devoted exclusively to *The Course of Islam in Africa,* Mervyn Hiskett, in spite of extensive chapters devoted to "The Nilotic Sudan," "Ethiopia and the Horn," and "East and South Africa," mentions the Buja in only one brief phrase: "South of ʿAlwa lay vast expanses of savannah and riverain country roamed over by stateless, Hamitic-speaking, nomadic cattle grazers known as the Beja."[25] Yusuf Fadl Hasan's 1966 article on "The Penetration of Islam in the Eastern Sudan," is still the only extensive account of early Muslim settlement in East Africa.[26]

Yet, in spite of their stark under-representation in the mainstream of modern Islamic and African historiography, there is not a single example of an Islamic mappa mundi to be found without the words "al-Buja" (the Buja) marked prominently astride the upper reaches of the Nile between al-Habasha (Abyssinia) and the "Bilad al-Nuba" (Land/Territory of Nubia). Striking is the fact that these rarely heard of Buja are even accorded an additional strip of land between the Red Sea and the Nile, which is referred to on many of the maps as the "Mafaza al-Buja" (i.e. "the deserts of the Buja").[27] In this double marking alone the Buja stand out as conspicuously distinguished from every other territorial marking on the Islamic world map.[28] See, for instance, the close-up of the region from a fifteenth century Timurid world map. [29] (See Fig. 2)

This holds true even when the basic shape of the world map is significantly altered. (See Fig. 3) Even on a highly stylized 19th century Mughal rendition, the illustrator allocated space to the Buja.

While the specific location of their name on the map may fluctuate within the prescribed area one thing is certain—over an eight-century corpus of world maps, their presence is rarely negated. All of this suggests that they were an important component of the medieval Islamic conception of the world and that their place on the world map was never questioned, not even in the seventeenth century Iranian copies, nor the nineteenth century Indian ones.[30]

The question is why? Why would a place so infrequently mentioned in the historiography and, therefore (one would presume) seemingly insignificant historically, receive such a prominent, permanent berth on the Muslim world maps? Why would the Buja receive deliberate attention in deference to other better known locals in Islamic history, such as Ifriqiyya, which surprisingly is not marked on any medieval Islamic map?

Who Were the Buja?

The Muslim geographers consistently locate them textually, as well as graphically, somewhere between the Red Sea and the Nile.[31] Others tell us that the Buja occupied the triangle between Abyssinia, Nubia, and Egypt.[32] Some writers present itinerant descriptions. Ibn Hawqal, for instance, instructs the readers to find the Buja thus:

> Starting from Qulzum, in the occidental part of the [Red] sea, we touch an arid desert where nothing grows and one meets nothing but the islands mentioned previously. In the middle of the spread of this desert live the Buja, who have tents made of hair. Their skin is much darker than the

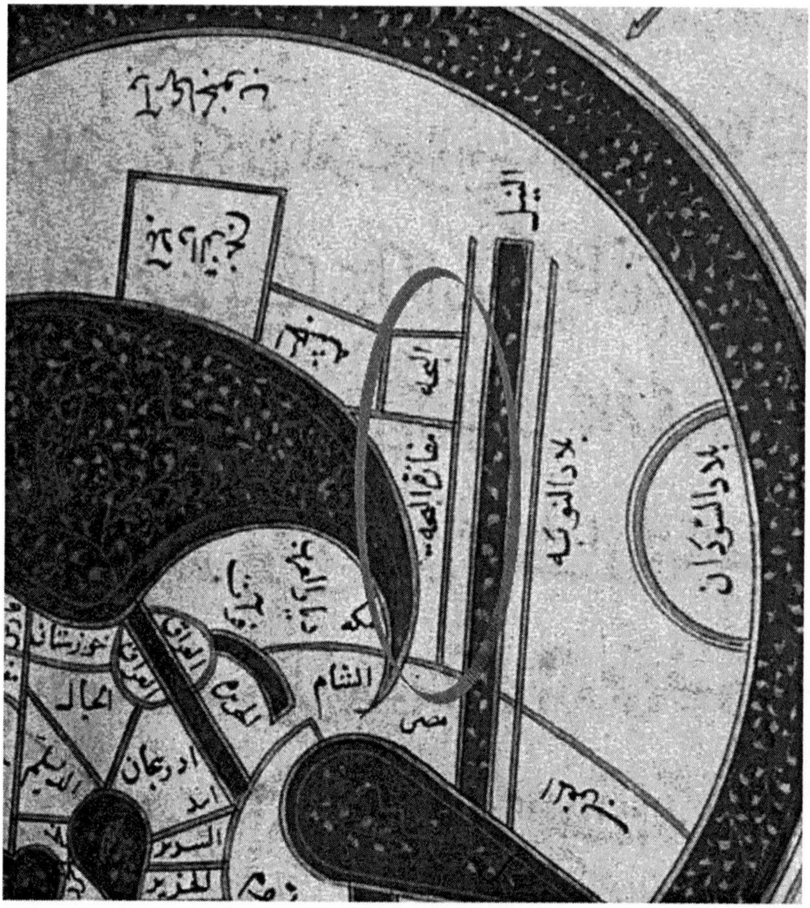

Figure 2: Close-up of "World Map," Istanbul, TKS Ahmet III [A] 2830, fol. 5a.

> Abyssinians, who resemble the Arabs. They have neither villages, nor cities, nor cultivated fields, and subsist from what is brought from the cities of Abyssinia, Egypt, and Nubia.[33]

André Miquel identifies two arms of Buja tribes. One in a west to east direction from the coast, along which lay the caravan route from Qus to Qift, which lead eventually to the mines of Wadi ʿAllaqi and from there on to the port of Aydhab. In this arm he also includes the traffic from Yemen and the Hijaz. Miquel identifies the other arm as going in a south to north direction

Figure 3: London, British Library, MS. Or. 23542: al-Jayhani, World map, fol. 59a

along the hollow of Baraka: beginning in the plateau of Eritrea, moving towards Aswan and Egypt.[34] As the recent map of Buja territories in 2000 shows,[35] they are still to be found today in approximately the same area that the Muslim maps mark them: off the Red sea, south of Egypt, east of Nubia, north of Ethiopia. (See Fig. 4)

Perhaps continuous Buja occupation of the deserts of the western littoral of the Red Sea is why even in the nineteenth century the copyists of the maps did not question the place's presence. Can we presume from this that knowledge of the Buja was never lost?

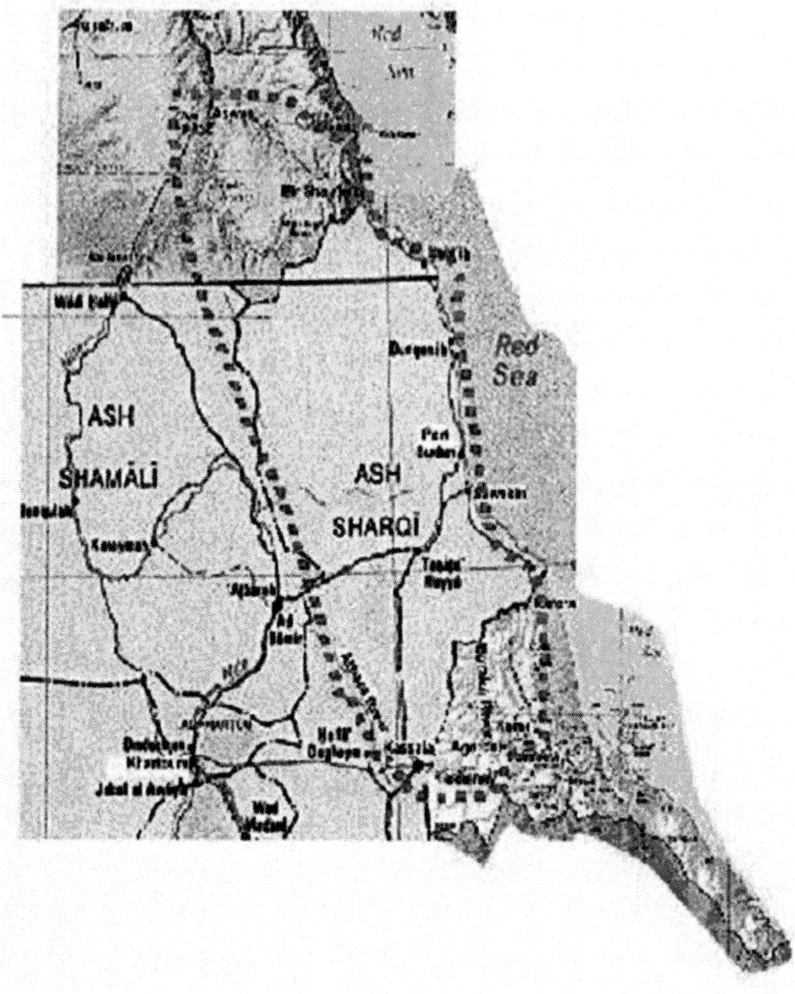

Figure 4: Modern Map Showing the Location of the Buja

One thing that the contemporary map confirms is that, at least, in terms of location, the Muslim cartographers placed the Buja accurately on their world maps demonstrating an active knowledge of the location of Buja tribes and their territories. The mere fact of their existence or even their accurate location does not, however, explain the prominent and consistent presence of the Buja on the Muslim world maps. To understand the reason for the Muslim cartographers' selection we have to turn to their texts and the possible answers contained within. The earliest mention of Muslim-Buja contact occurs in the context of the earliest Arab campaigns in southern Egypt, following the disastrous encounter with the Nubians (31 A.H./651–652 C.E.), in which the penetration of the Arab forces was decisively stalled.[36] On the rebound from Nubian humiliation, ʿAbd Allah b. Saʿd encountered some Buja tribes, but at that point, it seems, in comparison to the mighty Nubians and their famous gold mines, Saʿd regarded the Buja as politically insignificant.[37] It was not long before the Muslims discovered that they had a more easily exploitable treasure trove sitting above the First Cataract of the Nile. At first Buja lands were invaded to bring the upper Egyptian border under control as well as to exact tribute from the chiefs.[38] During the reign of the Umayyad Caliph Hisham (r. 105 A.H./724 C.E. and 125 A.H./743 C.E.), ʿUbayd Allah b. al-Habhab negotiated one of the earliest treaties with the Buja.[39] Forays into Buja territory enabled the Muslims to rediscover the ancient mines of gold at Wadi ʿAllaqi and emeralds at Qift.[40] Precisely when this occurred is not clear and not given by the sources. What is clear is that by the ninth century a major rush for gold and precious stones was under way in Buja territory.[41]

> In their territory, [which lies] between Abyssinia, Egypt, and Nubia, there are emerald and gold mines. These mines extend from around Aswan—at a distance of approximately ten stages in the territory of Egypt—up to the sea, near a fortress named Aydhab. It is here that the tribe of Rabiʿa are grouped—at a point name ʿAllaqi, in the middle of the sands and flat ground, with a few hills scattered between this area and Aswan. The products of the mines are directed towards Egypt. They are mines of pure gold without any silver, which are under the control of the Rabiʿa, who are the sole proprietors.[42]

Simultaneously (or perhaps preceding), the Buja tribes came to be viewed as a ripe source of slaves, especially for the work of mining.[43] What is clear is that by the early ninth century the Buja were getting restive, probably due to the impositions on their land and people.[44] Thereon, at regular intervals, the Buja tribes began to break the treaties, revolt at the mines, and raid southern Egypt—going as far as Fustat. It seems that the Arab tribes of southern Arabia, who had come over in droves to take over, manage, and collect revenues on the mines, were the primary catalyst for Buja irritation.[45] One sympathetic Muslim observer, for instance, notes that:

> The Buja who live in this desert are not bad people, nor are they robbers. It is the Muslims and others who kidnap their children and take them to the towns of Islam, where they sell them.[46]

Could the discovery of gold and emerald mines in Buja territory, along with the fact that they were viewed as a good source of slaves, and the frequent occurrence of their troublesome raids, have secured for them a permanent berth on the Muslim world maps? Perhaps. But there were other places (such as Ghana and Kanem in West Africa) renowned for their gold mines and slaves that did not make it onto the Muslim world maps.[47] And, certainly, troublesome tribes were abundant in the Muslim lands and peripheries. Thus, I still ask: *why the Buja?*

Why the Buja, when the Muslim scholars writing about them do not seem to have respected them at all? Saʿid al-Andalusi, for instance, writing in the thirteenth century, does not mince his words:

> The only peoples that reject these humane institutions and live outside these rational laws [i.e. royal decrees and divine laws] are a few of the inhabitants of the deserts and the wilderness such as the beggars of Bajah [*sic.* Buja], the savages of Ghana, the misers of the Zinj [*sic.* Zanj], and those resembling them.[48]

Four centuries earlier, al-Istakhri said something similar when he opened his treatise on the *Roads and Kingdoms of the World* (*Kitab al-Masalik wa al-Mamalik*) by asserting that he will not discuss the Buja and other such uncouth, irreligious people:

> We have not mentioned the land of the Sudan in the west, nor the Buja, nor the Zanj, nor other peoples with the same characteristics, because the orderly government of kingdoms is based upon religious beliefs, good manners, law and order, and the organization of settled life directed by sound policy (*intizam al-mamalik wa al-diyanat wa aadab wa hukum wa taqwim al-ʿimarat wa al-siyasa al-mutaqima*). These people lack all these qualities and have no share in them. Their kingdoms, therefore, do not deserve to be dealt with separately as we have dealt with other kingdoms. Some of the Sudan, who live nearer to these well known kingdoms, do resort to religious beliefs and practices and law, approaching in this respect the people of these kingdoms. Such is the case with the Nuba and the Habasha, because they are Christians, following the religious tenets

> of the Rum. Prior to the rise of Islam they were in neighbourly contact with the Byzantine Empire, because the land of the Nuba borders on Egypt, and the Habasha live on the Sea of al-Qulzum (Red Sea).[49]

Al-Istakhri even goes on to mention the mines of Buja territory, yet he conveniently forgets to mention the Buja.

> Between the country of the Habasha and the land of Egypt is a desert in which they are gold mines, and the Habasha are linked to Egypt and Syria by way of the Red Sea.[50]

An odd set of statements, given that barely fifteen pages later in his text, in the section on the Bahr Fars (the Persian Gulf/Indian Ocean), al-Istakhri includes an extensive passage on the Buja, their mines, their characteristics and way of life.[51]

> If you go from Qulzum, the western end of this sea [i.e. the Red Sea], extending from it to the empty wasteland there is nothing until you arrive at the desert of the Buja. The Buja are a people of curly hair, much darker than the Habasha [Abyssinians] who are similar to the Arabs. They do not have villages nor cities nor grain except what comes to them from the cities of Abyssinia, Yemen, Egypt and Nubia. Their borders stretch from between Abyssina to Nubia and Egypt, reaching as far as the mines of gold. Going from these mines in the vicinity of Aswan, Egypt, until a fortress on the sea called ʿAydab, it is approximately 20 *marahil*.[52] And the place where the people from these mines gather is called al-ʿAllaqi, and it is sandy land, flat without mountains, and the money of these mines is sent to the land of Egypt. And they are mines of gold not silver. And the Buja are a nation of idol worshippers and what comprises this. Then one arrives at the land of the Abyssinians who are Christian and who are closer in skin colour to the Arabs, [i.e.] between black and white. . . .[53]

Ten pages later, al-Istakhri mentions the Buja again. This time he describes the approach to Buja lands from Aswan instead of the Red Sea.

> And as for the mines of gold they are fifteen days away from Aswan. The mines are not in the land of Egypt, rather in the land of the Buja and they extend until ʿAydhab. And it is said that ʿAydhab is not of the land of the Buja, but that it is one of the cities of Abyssina. The land of

> the mines is flat without mountains, rather sandy and dusty. And the place in which the people collect is called al-ʿAllaqi. And the Buja have no villages nor any prosperity nor any richness, rather they are nomads, and they have nobles [among them]. It is said that among the nobles there are none more lowly than theirs. Both their slaves and their nobles, and everything else in their land, reach as far as Egypt.[54]

The same pattern recurs in Ibn Hawqal's *Kitab Surat al-ʿArd.* He begins his discussion of the Buja employing exactly the same words as al-Istakhri (quoted at the outset of this discussion).[55] Then twenty-five pages later, in the section on the Persian Gulf/ Indian Ocean, Ibn Hawqal inserts one of the most extensive descriptions of the Buja to be found anywhere, comprising seven long pages of a detailed discussion of their lands, the tribal divisions, and the uprisings. In a significant departure from the norm, Ibn Hawqal devotes more detail to the Buja, than he does to discussing Abyssinia or the lands of the Zanj. Albeit a more balanced appraisal, his discussion is still peppered with disdainful statements:

> The Buja are the people of this land. They worship idols and other objects that they consider venerable. . . . They are nomads who breed sheep . . . and their numbers escape all estimates. . . . In the incline of Baraka, live the [Buja] tribes known as Bazin and Bariya—people who fight with bows, poisoned arrows, and lances, but without shields. The Bariya are known for extracting their incisors and for clipping their ears. They live in the mountains and the valleys where they tend to livestock and cultivate the soil.[56]

The tenth century Palestinian scholar, Mutahhar b. Tahir al-Maqdisi in his *Kitab al-Badʾ wa al-Taʾrikh* (Book of the Creation and the History), echoes a similar sentiment when he deprecatingly notes that the Buja are so uncouth that:

> there is no marriage among them; the child does not know his father, and they eat people—but God knows best.[57]

Is it possible then that it is was not the mines nor the potential for slaves that put the Buja on the Muslim world maps, rather the perception that they were some sort of *extreme other*? Could the fact that they were perceived as a group of people with such strange mannerisms and a way of life so contrary to that which the Muslims knew that their extreme alterity captured the Muslim imagination and propelled them right onto the world maps? Are they a signifier on the maps of people who don't have any laws or religion — "pays sans foi ni loi" as André Miquel puts it?[58] Certainly this is what the curious passage in al-Ya'qubi's *Kitab al-Buldan* (Book of Countries) would seem to intimate:

> The Buja live in tents of hides, pluck their beards, and remove the nipples from the breasts of the boys so that their breasts do not resemble the breasts of women (*yanza'una falaka thadai al-ghilman li-ʿalla yushbihu thadaihim thadai al-nisa'*). They eat grubs and similar things. They ride camels and fight in combat on them just like they fight on horseback, and throw javelins without ever missing.[59]

André Miquel concurs with this interpretation but goes on to add a most interesting spin of his own:

> D'un côté, des hommes qui mutilent leurs enfants et suivent un système résolument matriarcal, de l'autre un peuple accroché, tant qu'il le peut, au nomadisme et au désert; un peuple qui "suit l'herbe" et transhume de la mer aux vallés intérieures; un peuple, enfin, qui, pas plus que l'Arabie ne vivrait sans le chameau, véhicule de la guerre et de la course, sacrifice toujours prêt pour l'hôte qu'une folle prodigalité se doit d'honorer.[60]

The Buja are, in other words, not just an extreme manifestation of *other,* they are also a paradoxical manifestation of *self.* Or, rather, one of the many "selves" that make up the Muslim psyche: the *"primordial," "nomadic," "desert-based"* one whence Islam sprang. As Miquel intuitively points out, between the two coasts of the Red Sea one can perceive a kind of latent fraternity, in which Arabia finds reflections of itself. "La description du pays bedja fait voisiner ce qui, pour une mentalité arabo-musulmane, constitue autant de traits aberrants, avec d'autres où l'Arabie se retrouve."[61] Or, as Ibn al-Faqih put it, "A piece of Yemen [on African soil]."[62]

But the maps were not produced in southern Arabia by the Rabiʿa nor the Mudar. Rather they are products of the political and intellectual centers of the Muslim world, where the perceived affinities or extreme alterities between the Rabiʿa and the Buja would not have had a significant effect on the prevailing conception of the world. Thus, I believe we must look farther to find an answer for the Buja presence on the world maps.

Capturing the Imagination

In all of this there is one curious phenomenon: All extensive references to the Buja detailing their strange ways, their mores, their mines, their enslavement, and their raids, occur in treatises from the late ninth century onwards. Al-Istakhri wrote in the early tenth century; Ibn Hawqal and al-Maqdisi in the late tenth; Saʿid al-Andalusi in the mid-thirteenth. The earliest extensive description of the Buja comes from al-Yaʿqubi's *Kitab al-Buldan*, composed in 276 A.H./889–890 C.E. The only other major account comes from the late-ninth/early-tenth century historian al-Tabari who reports events involving the Buja in the year 236 A.H./ 850 C.E.[63]

Prior to the mid-ninth century, references to the Buja are extremely rare, if not totally absent. One of these rare examples comes from Ibn Khurdadhbeh's *Kitab al-Masalik* composed in 232 A.H./ 846 C.E. It is a brief, formulaic phrase referring to the bi-lateral trade agreement (*baqt*) treaty made with the Nubians following the stalemate of 31 A.H./ 665–2 C.E. It only mentions the Buja tangentially:[64]

> In uppermost Egypt[65] are the Nubians, the Buja, and the Abyssinians and ʿUthman b. ʿAffan had reached a settlement with the Nubians for four hundred heads per year.[66]

The fact that there is no detail on the Buja in Muslim sources prior to the mid-ninth century, suggests that they captured the imagination of the Muslim geographers and scholars belatedly. This is surprising since (as I demonstrated in the previous section) active exploitation of the gold mines in Buja territory had begun as early as the mid-eighth century. Why would it take so long for the Buja to make it into the mainstream of Muslim thought?

My theory is that the Buja were not known for their mines in the Muslim centers of power and learning prior to the mid-ninth century. The exploitation of the Buja mines was, at least until the ninth century, a localized, regional phenomenon not well-known beyond the immediate orbit of contact between the Arab tribes of southern Arabia and upper Egypt.

If I am right in reading initial contact with and knowledge of the Buja as a localized phenomenon, then there is no reason why the Buja would make news in the center—where most of the arm-chair scholars and geographers were based—until something dramatic happened. It is to the drama that I believe propelled the Buja into the news, the chronicles, the geographies, and the maps that I turn now.

In the first quarter of the ninth century, there were a spate of Buja uprisings and raids into Egypt and other Muslim towns, reaching all the way to Fustat. These raids became so serious and frequent that they eventually came to the attention of the center, specifically the ʿAbbasid caliph al-Mutawakkil (r. 232–47 A.H./ 847–61 C.E.), who was forced to step in and take action to redress the situation. Tabari reports that:

> He [i.e. al-Mutawakkil] sought advice concerning the circumstances of the Buja. He was informed: They were a nomadic people, tenders of camels and livestock. Getting to their territory was difficult, and it was inaccessible to troops, for it consisted of desert and steppe. It was a month's journey from the land of Islam to the territory of the Bujah, through wasteland, mountains, and barren country, lacking water, vegetation, refuge, or a fortified position. Any government representative who entered Bujah territory would have to be supplied with provisions for his entire stay until he returned to the land of Islam. If the extent of his stay was greater than estimated, he and all his comrades would perish. And the Bujah would simply overcome them without hostilities. Their land did not remit to the central government land tax or any other tax.[67]

It is the series of events related to official caliphal intervention in East Africa along with a dramatic visit by the Buja chief to Samarra that, I believe, catapulted the obscure Buja into the imagination of the Muslim minds at the center. The events triggered a flash of acknowledgement that left an indelible stamp in the form of dramatic narratives, fantastic descriptions and, ultimately, a nomination on the world maps.

Both the geographer Ibn Hawqal and the historian Tabari, describe, with mostly minor, but some major variations, the same series of dramatic events: The start of the Buja uprisings and raids, the Muslim response, and the trip of the Buja chief, ʿAli Baba, to the ʿAbbasid capital, Samarra, to meet with the caliph.[68] The major difference between the two accounts is that Tabari presents a terse view from the center of caliphal power, whereas Ibn Hawqal provides an extremely detailed, localized account of the Buja uprisings, specific reasons for each one of them, and the various Muslim attempts to suppress them. Tabari, for instance, only says that: "From the time of al-Mutawakkil's reign the Buja refrained from delivering [their] tax for several consecutive years" and that the head of the Postal and Intelligence Service, Yaʿqub b. Ibrahim al-Badhghisi, wrote to the caliph to tell him that the Buja had broken the treaty between them and the Muslims and that:

> They [i.e. the Buja] advanced from their territory to the mines of gold and precious stones that were on the border between Egypt and the territory of the Buja. The Buja killed a number of Muslims employed in the mines for mining the gold and precious stones, and took captive a number of the Muslim children and women. The Buja claimed that the mines belonged to them and were in their territory, and that they would not permit the Muslims to enter them.[69]

Ibn Hawqal, on the other hand, provides an elaborate account of the stories behind the early uprisings. It seems the trouble began when in 204 A.H./ 819 C.E., a group of Buja abandoned the Muslim chief of Qift, Ibrahim Qifti, and some of his companions, on their way to pilgrimage, in the desert, leaving them to die of thirst. Ibn Hawqal suggests that the rationale for this was because some of the Buja feared that Qifti knew their lands too well: "We definitely must put to death this Muslim who knows our country so well, our camping spots, our watering holes. We cannot trust him."[70] Word of the deliberate abandonment of Qifti and his followers got back to the other Arabs in Qift and when the Buja chief, Muha, made a trip to town to buy supplies, with thirty notables, the locals enticed them down to one of the churches and massacred the party. The situation kept escalating. According to Ibn Hawqal, in 204 A.H./ 819 C.E., the Buja tribes retaliated by marching on the city of Qift, taking seven hundred prisoners, and massacring many, which, in turn, forced the remaining inhabitants to flee to Fustat. There the petitioners had to wait seven years before their pleas were heard because the local officials were too busy with other matters. In the end, their cause was taken up by a wealthy private citizen, Hakam Nabighi of the Qais tribe, who in 212 A.H./ 827 C.E. executed raids on Buja territory, taking prisoners. He succeeded in freeing the city of Qift from the Buja stranglehold. None of this quieted the Buja for long. Twenty years later in 232 A.H./ 847 C.E., the Buja attacked and occupied Onbu, a city in Upper Egypt.[71] This would have coincided with the Abbasid caliph al-Mutawakkil's ascension to power and it is possible that that is when he was first informed about the troublesome Buja. Tabari does not specify. All he notes is that al-Mutawakkil—who was involved in a power struggle with local Turkish leaders at home[72]—did not respond immediately, hoping that somehow the troubles with the Buja would die down. At this point, Ibn Hawqal presents a variation. He says that the influx of the Rabiʿa and Mudar tribes to the area had increased dramatically following the invasion of Muhammad b. Yusuf Okhaidir Hasani into Yemen, resulting in the mass emigration of local inhabitants to Egypt and Buja territory. This inevitably brought more clashes between the southern Arabian tribes and the Buja resulting in a series of flare-ups. Ibn Hawqal says that one flare-up resulted in some Buja insulting the Prophet and that when this reached the ears of al-Mutawakkil, he finally reacted:

> A brawl flared up between one of their men and one of the Buja, during which the Buja insulted the Prophet (Peace be Upon Him). Al-Mutawakkil was informed and he sent to the site a descendent of Abu Musa Ash'ari, called Muhammad Qummi, who was then jailed for homicide. The caliph provided him [Qummi] with the men and arms that he asked for and promised him his freedom.[73]

According to Tabari, al-Mutawakkil refrained from responding at first, but as the situation worsened, and Buja attacks against the Muslims intensified "to the point that the inhabitants of Upper Egypt feared for their lives and for their children," he appointed Muhammad b. 'Abdallah—known as al-Qummi (who Ibn Hawqal claims was in prison for a homicide)—to take care of the troublesome Buja.[74]

From this point onwards, both texts begin to dovetail. Both concur on Qummi's successful rout of the Buja and provide parallel accounts of the confrontation. Apparently Qummi was seriously outnumbered by the Buja and running short of supplies by the time he reached the heart of Buja territory. He had collected about three thousand men, while the Buja were two hundred thousand men strong with eighty thousand dromedary.[75] When the two armies first met, the Muslims panicked. Qummi urged them to stay and fight for their honor: "There is no escape. Fight for your life and honor and you will be victorious."[76] Then under the cover of night, Qummi, undaunted by being outnumbered, devised a plan to thwart the Buja.[77] According to Ibn Hawqal, he surrounded his camp with a network of horses and drums and prepared a series of cloth banners with gilded writing, which he fixed to the top of some of the spears. At day break he proclaimed: "Behold! Soldiers of the Buja, here are missives for you from the Emir of the believers."[78] The banners distracted the Buja who had formed in groups for battle. Curious, some of them broke ranks to take a closer look at the banners. When this happened, Qummi ordered the camels upon which his banner-men were sitting to rise and indicated that the drums be sounded. Suddenly the Buja found themselves in the middle of a sea of banners with drums pounding. This caused a pandemonium and scattered the Buja forces in disorder. Qummi capitalized on this and routed the Buja army decisively. Many of them were massacred. Others, including the Buja chief, 'Ali Baba, were taken prisoner.[79]

Tabari provides a similar yet varying account. He indicates that at first the Buja chief was just harassing Qummi's army, exhausting them, waiting for their supplies to run out. ʿAli Baba only launched an all out attack when he heard that a ship of fresh supplies had arrived from Baghdad. Like Ibn Hawqal, Tabari also notes the use of noise to cause confusion among the Buja ranks during the battle, but he refers to the use of bells not drums and banners:

> Seeing this [i.e. the arrival of the ships with supplies], ʿAli Baba, the Bujah chief, went on to do battle with the Muslims, rallying troops against them. The two sides clashed and fought violently. The camels upon which the Bujah fought were unseasoned and tended to be frightened and alarmed by everything. Noticing this, al-Qummi rounded up all the camel and horse bells in his camp. He then attacked the Bujah, stampeded their camels with the clanging of bells. Their alarm was considerable. It drove them over mountains and valleys, totally splintering the Bujah forces. Al-Qummi and his men pursued and seized them, dead or alive, until night overtook him. This took place at the beginning of 241 (855–58). Al-Qummi then returned to his camp and could not count the dead they were so many.[80]

Both accounts do concur that the Buja were routed and that ʿAli Baba was taken prisoner, forced to pay the overdue tax, and dragged off to Iraq for an audience with the Caliph al-Mutawakkil. It is to Tabari's dramatic account of this visit and its long-term effects on the imagination of the people (scholars, chroniclers, etc.) located close to the center of power that I turn now.

> ʿAli Baba appointed his son Laʾis as deputy over his kingdom. Al-Qummi departed with ʿAli Baba for the gate of al-Mutawakkil, and arrived there at the end of 241 (855–56). He attired this ʿAli Baba with a silk brocade-lined robe and a black turban covering his camel with a brocade saddle and brocade horse cloths. At the Public Gate, along with a group of the Bujah, were stationed about seventy pages, upon saddled camels, carrying their lances, on whose tips were the heads of their warriors who had been killed by al-Qummi. . . . Some(one) of [the respondents] reported seeing ʿAli Baba with a stone idol in the shape of a young boy to which he prostrated himself.[81]

Stepping back from the texts, for a moment, to imagine the cities of Iraq, especially Basra, Kufa, Baghdad, and Samarra, the new Abbasid capital, of the mid-ninth century, through which ʿAli Baba and his retinue likely marched.

Imagine the throngs of people in the markets and the streets, all rather conservatively dressed. Then imagine in the middle of this the sudden appearance of a bizarre procession wending its way from the port of Basra, perhaps through Baghdad, towards Samarra, and eventually the central zone of the palace with the Buja chief, ʿAli Baba, elaborately dressed in brocade robes and finery followed by his retinue of Buja tribesmen with next to nothing on and, if we are to take al-Yaʿqubi's description at face value, with their nipples cut out, followed by seventy of Qummi's men with the severed heads of Buja victims at the end of their spears. Can one not imagine what a dramatic impact this apparition must have had on the psyche of the people milling around, watching in wonder, no doubt, mouths agape. All this amidst the flurry of stories that must have begun to float around thanks to Qummi's soldiers about the amazing gold and emerald mines to be found in their lands, as well as details about their habits and living conditions. The Buja must have captivated attention and been the subject of many a lively discussion, long after they had come and gone. Or, perhaps, as Ibn Hawqal suggests, they never really left. His rendition of the same story, places the date of the visit of the Buja king to the Abbasid capital at a slightly earlier date (238 A.H./852 C.E.), and incorporates an intriguing caveat. According to Ibn Hawqal, it was not only the chief of the Buja who was dragged off to Samarra but the Nubian king as well,[82] where they were chastised and humiliated for their unruly behavior by being sold as slaves for paltry sums.[83]

> Then, as a result of this imprudence, they [the Buja] all perished—trode on by their camels. For them it was death or captivity. Ali Baba was taken prisoner: placed on a hill, after he swore not to move from there unless the hill disintegrated. After his capture, Qummi took him [Ali Baba] and his booty to Aswan. There he sold everything for fifty thousand ounces of gold. [Next] he sent an ultimatum to Yurki, the king of Nubia, who came to submit himself. He [Qummi] took all his men to Baghdad in the year 238 and presented the two princes to the caliph. There they were put up for auction. The king of the Buja was sold for seven dinars and the king of Nubia for nine. They imposed on each one of them as punishment a daily labor equivalent to the sum of their sale. Qummi returned to Aswan after having secured their agreement on this point.[84]

If Ibn Hawqal's version of the outcome is not hyperbole, and the Buja chief and his followers stayed on in Iraq as slaves, then the center would have had the Buja in view for much longer than just the period of the procession. We may also have an explanation for why the Buja revolted again so soon after Qummi's departure as well as a significant fictional connection between the Buja chief and one of the most famous characters in the *One Thousand and One Nights:* Poverty stricken ʿAli Baba, the famous deceiver of the forty thieves.[85]

The latter is pure speculation and would require further investigation of the relationship between the two ʿAli Baba's—real and fictional—to determine if there is indeed a connection between the two characters.[86] If I am right to make this connection, then we would have a powerful example of the effect that the Buja had on the medieval Islamic imagination such that, via ʿAli Baba, they also found a permanent berth in the fiction of the period. Be this the case or not, what we can conclude from the visit to the ʿAbbasid center of power, was that it catapulted the Buja into the imagination of the populace and the scholars producing the geographies and, eventually, right smack onto the mappa mundi.

Ricocheting in a Husserlian way, the story speaks volumes of the long-term effects of extraordinary people and events on the imagination, such that retentions and reproductions proliferate in the cultural products. Particularly striking is the way in which accounts of the same event vary within the span of a century: from Tabari, writing in the late ninth/ early tenth century to Ibn Hawqal writing in the late tenth. In the late ninth century the Buja were being discovered by the center for the first time in a dramatic way. By the late tenth-century, they had moved from being different and *other* to being of the *self.* So that with Ibn Hawqal we get intimate local accounts of the events in the area leading up to the visit to the ʿAbbasid capital. We also get a sense that these were not just "wild people" *out there somewhere,* rather that they were closely linked to the Arabian mainland through the ebb and flow of immigrants. The way in which the details of the story of Qummi's battle vary presents another way in which retentions morph from the origin, influenced by reproductions from the present "now" moment. In Tabari's account Qummi used bells to scare the unseasoned camels of the Buja, whereas Ibn Hawqal reports that elaborate embroidered banners and drums were employed to achieve the same effect. Why would bells change to embroidered banners and drums over the span of a century of narration?

Similarly, the maps and the way in which the nomination of the Buja varies on them can be viewed through a Husserlian lens. Fluctuations in spatial allocations are the product of time warps and resonances (retentions and reproductions) that can be viewed and understood through a spatio-temporal lens. On the surface the medieval Islamic world map matrix appears to be frozen in time, but close examination of the mutations of one site, reveal that history in fact resonates here.

Conclusion

> Nommer relève d'un véritable "exorcisme," qui introduit la mémoire, le savoir, un repère stable, îlot de sécurité dans l'océan de l'indiférencié car innommé. La nomination est un mode d'appropriation symbolique qui donne une mémoire aux terres vierges, un quadrillage qui dépossède l'espace de son altérité et en fait un objet de discours, assujetti aux contraintes de la référence linguistique, qui veut qu'à chaque lieu identifié corresponde un nom.[87]

The act of "naming," of cordoning off and assigning space, is, as Christian Jacob aptly puts it, an essential act of exorcising the ghost of the unknown, of making virgin lands conquerable, by providing a memory and a link in the middle of an ocean of unknown territory. Nowhere is this more appropriate than in the case of Africa, which looms large and menacing on the Islamic horizon. More often than not the large empty space of the most southerly regions stands in stark contrast to the sparse scattering of identified places. Within this sea of the unknown, indeed upon its periphery, the Buja reign supreme—not only as manifestations of that "strange" *other* world out there in the wild yonder, but also, paradoxically, as a manifestation of *self.* For, if nothing else, the Buja are in eastern Africa, at the height of the medieval period, one of the final frontiers of Islam: a strange and quixotic final frontier where pagan rituals mix with Islamic practices. It is here and not in Egypt that the true mixing of boundaries between Islam, Christianity, and paganism is to be found battling it out on the periphery of the unknown. As we know, Islam eventually wins out. Conversion accelerates and moves through the region past Nubia and down to the Horn of Africa. But the stepping stone for East Africa was the Buja lands and we need to re-remember this in the history books.

The examination of the Buja site on the Islamic world maps reveals the surprising conclusion that what finds its way onto a map is not only the politically significant. Nor is it only about exorcising the ghost of empty, unknown space. It is also very much about what captures the imagination.

> What is involved, therefore, is a production—the production of a space. Not merely a space of ideas, an ideal space, but a social and a mental

> space. An emergence. A decrypting of the space that went before. Thought and philosophy came to the surface, rose from the depths, but life was decrypted as a result, and society as a whole, along with space. If one were of a mind to distinguish, after the fashion of textual analysis, between a genotype and a phenotype of space, it would be from this 'emergence' that the 'genospatial' would have to be derived.[88]

The "constraints" of space thus turn paradoxically into "production;" a production of space that is, on the one hand, *self* and, on the other hand, *other*. In between, the "real" and the "abstract," the "thoroughly historical" and the "imaginary," the "empirical" and the "absurd" dance confusingly in front of our eyes.

Endnotes

1. This article is dedicated to the greatest advisor in the world with much appreciation for his many years of perseverance and patient training. Would that every graduate student could be blessed with an advisor like ours. This article is an excerpt from my doctoral dissertation, "Ways of Seeing.3: Scenarios of the World in the Medieval Islamic Cartographic Imagination," Columbia University, 2001. I would like to thank Richard Bulliet, Cornell Fleischer, Mokhtar Ghambou, Matthew Gordon, Andrew Gow, Jean-Marc Oppenheim, Adele B. Pinto, Dwight Reynolds, and Houra and Neguin Yavari for their expertise and assistance. Original work on the doctoral dissertation was made possible by generous grants from Columbia University, the Social Science Research Council, the Giles Whiting Foundation, and the Friends of J. B. Harley. I would also like to acknowledge the on-going postdoctoral support from the Social Science and Humanities Research Council of Canada and the Dept. of History and Classics at the University of Alberta, Edmonton.

2. J. B. Harley, "Deconstructing the Map," in *Writing Worlds: Discourse, Text and Metaphor in the Representation of Landscape,* Trevor Barnes and James S. Duncan, eds., (London: Routledge, 1992), p. 238.

3. Even the use of an ethnonym as opposed to the customary toponym is unusual for medieval Islamic maps.

4. E. Husserl, *The Phenomenology of Internal Time Consciousness,* (Bloomington: Midland Books, 1966), cited in Alfred Gell, *The Anthropology of Time,* (Oxford: Berg, 1996), pp. 223–5.

5. Globes, of course, present a paradox for mapping. They appear to be three-dimensional and yet they too fall into the constraints of two-dimensional space. They are not flat but they are constrained by surface area. In order to avoid this dilemma one would have to create a 1:1 map of the world—i.e. an exact replica of the world, in

shape, as well as size. And, we already know from Borges about the fate of such idealistic maps, when he says in his novela, "Of exactitude in science": "... In that Empire, the craft of Cartography attained such Perfection that the Map of a Single province covered the space of an entire City, and the Map of the Empire itself an entire Province. In the course of Time, these Extensive maps were found somehow wanting, and so the College of Cartographers evolved a Map of the Empire that was of the same Scale as the Empire and that coincided with it point for point. Less attentive to the Study of Cartography, succeeding Generations came to judge a map of such Magnitude cumbersome, and, not without Irreverence, they abandoned it to the Rigours of sun and Rain. In the western Deserts, tattered fragments of the Map are still to be found, Sheltering an occasional Beast or Beggar; in the whole Nation, no other relic is left of the Discipline of Geography." Jorge Luis Borges, *A universal history of infamy,* English trans. N. T. di Giovanni, (Harmondsworth: Penguin Books, 1975), p. 131.

6. Mark Monmonier, *How to Lie with Maps,* (Chicago: University of Chicago Press, 1991), p. 1.

7. Photo my own.

8. As W. J. T. Mitchell puts it in "Spatial Form in Literature," in *The Language of Images,* ed. Mitchell, (Chicago: The University of Chicago Press, 1980), p. 274: "The fact is that spatial form is the perceptual basis of our notion of time, that we literally cannot "tell time" without the mediation of space. All our temporal language is contaminated with spatial imagery: we speak of "long" and "short" times, of "intervals" (literally, "space between"), of "before" and "after"—all implicit metaphors which depend on a mental picture of time as a continuum."

9. For proof of this point see Denis Wood, *The Power of Maps,* (New York: The Guilford Press, 1992), p. 130.

10. "Reproductions" being action-replays of past experiences of events carried out from the standpoint of a remembered or fantasied reconstructed "now" in the past; "Retentions" being the perspectival view of past phases of experience from the vantage of the 'now' moment which slips forward. Gell, *op. cit.,* pp. 223–4.

11. A discussion (September, 2000) on the online history of cartography discussion group, *maphist*, revealed that women in the production end of the history of cartography are virtually unknown. Members scrambled to dig up two names and even those women cannot be linked to the original construction of known maps. To the best of my knowledge, no women are named as active contributors in Islamic geographic or cartographic sources.

12. Heinz Halm suggests the word is an Arabicized rendition of the Berber "Vaga." Halm also mentions a region called "Baja/Beja" in northern Tunisia. But this region is quite different from the one in East Africa that is the subject of this chapter. What the relationship between the two identical names is, is still not clear. See, Heinz Halm, *The Empire of the Mahdi: The Rise of the Fatimids,* English trans. Michael Bonner, (Leiden: E. J. Brill, 1996), p. 99.

13. Incorporating Tunisia and eastern Algeria.

14. The Hilali and Sulaym tribes are ignominiously credited with devastating and "bedouinizing" vast areas of Central North Africa from the mid-eleventh century onwards.

15. Gerald Endress, *An Introduction to Islam,* (New York: Columbia University Press, 1988), for instance, mentions neither West nor East Africa.

16. Takrur was important for its export of gold and slaves to North Africa, as well as for its commitment to Islamic Jihad.

17. Timbuktu (located in present day Mali) was an important center throughout the late medieval and early modern period for Muslim scholarship and learning.

18. Ira M. Lapidus, *A History of Islamic Societies,* (Cambridge: Cambridge University Press, 1988), p. 524.

19. Abyssinia clearly captured and dominated the Muslim imagination as the ultimate frontier of Africa. Nobody knew what lay beyond the lands of Abyssinia. Hence it is often cited as extending all the way to the Encircling Ocean in the west and, sometimes, even as far as the Maghrib. For more detail on the mythical extension of the mysterious and impenetrable Abyssinia in the Muslim imagination, see, André Miquel, *La géographie humaine du monde musulman jusqu'au milieu du 11e siècle,* (Paris: Mouton & Co., 1967–1988), Vol. 2, pp. 132–3.

20. The Zanj rebelled in 868–83 C. E. in the swamps south of Basra. The black slaves set up their own enclave, which lasted for twenty years until the Abbasids were finally able to suppress the rebels.

21. Lapidus, *op. cit.,* pp. 524–40.

22. Ibid., p. 524.

23. Bernard Lewis, *Race and Slavery in the Middle East,* (Oxford: Oxford University Press, 1990), p. 48, p. 52.; Bernard Lewis, *Race and Color in Islam,* (New York: Harper and Row, Publishers, 1970, 1971). As far as I can tell the texts of these two books are virtually identical!

24. But even this is limited to little more than a page. See, Jay Spaulding, "Precolonial Islam in the Eastern Sudan," *The History of Islam in Africa,* eds. Nehemia Levitzion and Randall L. Pouwels, (Athens, Ohio: Ohio University Press, 2000), pp. 117–18.

25. Mervyn Hiskett, *The Course of Islam in Africa,* (Edinburgh: Edinburgh University Press, 1994), p. 67.

26. Yusuf Fadl Hasan, "The Penetration of Islam in the Eastern Sudan," in *Islam in Tropical Africa,* ed. I. M. Lewis, (Bloomington: Indiana University Press, 1966, 1980), pp. 112–23.

27. On the Persian maps these deserts are referred to as "Biyaban." Some maps abbreviate the entry to just "al-Mafaza" or "Biyaban."

28. Some al-Idrisi maps contain three markings. See, Konrad Miller, *Mappae Arabicae,* Vol. 3, Part 2, (Stuttgart: Selbstverlag des Herausgebers, 1926–27), Section V.

29. For a full version of this map please refer to Karen Pinto, "Ways of Seeing. 3" *op. cit.*, Chapter 1, Fig. 12.

30. In Fig. 3 the area is named in Persian "Zamin Biyaban-e Buja" (Land of the Buja Desert).

31. See, for instance, Abu'l Fida, *Taqwim al-Buldan*, French trans. and edition J. T. Reinaud and Baron MacGluckin de Slane, *Géographie d'Aboulféda*, (Paris, 1840), Vol. 2, p. 157.

32. See, for instance, al-Mas'udi, *Tanbih*, *Kitab al-Tanbih (Le Livre de l'avertissement et de la revision)*, French trans. B. Carra de Vaux, (Paris: À l'Imprimerie Nationale, 1896), Vol. 1, p. 226; Ibn al-Wardi, *Kharidat al-ʿAjaʾib*, Arabic ed., (Cairo: np., 1863), p. 65.

33. Ibn Hawqal, *Kitab Surat al-ʿArd, (Configuration de la Terre)*, French trans. by J. H. Kramers and G. Wiet, (Beirut: Commision Internationale pour la Traduction des Chefs-d'Oeuvre, 1964), p. 48.

34. Miquel, op. cit., Vol. 2, p. 163.

35. Today there are about 2,000,000 Buja spread out between Egypt, Sudan, and Eritrea.

The map is taken from a contemporary evangelist web site, "The Beja Project" of the Oakland Baptist Church (Virginia), who are on an urgent mission to convert the tribes! The Joshua Project 2000 reports a similar "2000 Jesus Mission" in the region.

36. Although Hasan suggests that Muslim contacts date from even earlier. He mentions that the first Caliph Abu Bakr (632-4 C.E.) banished a group of Arabs to the region of Aydhab in Buja country. Unfortunately Hasan does not cite a source for this. See, Hasan, *op. cit.*, p. 116.

37. P. M. Holt, "Bedja," *Encyclopedia of Islam*, 2nd Edition (*EI2*), p. 1157. Ibn Hawqal presents a different version of this event, noting that ʿAbdallah went on from the Nubian defeat to conquer the city of Aswan in the year 31 A.H./652 C.E. In the process of this conquest, Ibn Hawqal tells us that ʿAbdallah also "subdued the Buja and other lords." Ibn Hawqal also gives the name of the commander of Arab forces as ʿAbdallah b. Abi Sarh. See, Ibn Hawqal, *Kitab Surat Al-ʿArd, (Opus geographicum.)* ed. Michael Jan de Goeje. *BGA*, Vol. 2. (Leiden: E. J. Brill, 1873; reedited J. H. Kramers, 1938; reprinted 1967), p. 48.

38. Ibn Hawqal's version is quite different. Instead of exacting tribute, he says that the Buja were actively converted to Islam by force and outwardly adopted certain obligations. However, this would not have permitted the Rabiʿa tribes to subjugate the Buja and use them as slaves in the mines, because conversion to Islam would have automatically meant that they could not be enslaved. So, perhaps Ibn Hawqal was conflating a later phenomenon present during his time with the earlier Muslim forays in the region. Ibn Hawqal, op. cit., p. 48.

39. Holt, op.cit., p. 1157.

40. The mines in the Buja deserts are mentioned by most of the geographers: See, for instance, al-Istakhri, *Kitab al-Masalik wa al-Mamalik (Viae renorum description ditionismoslemicae.)* ed. Michael Jan de Goeje. *BGA*, Vol. 1. (Leiden: E. J. Brill, 1870;

reprinted 1927, 1967; ed. Muhammad Jabir ʿAbd al-ʿAl al-Hini. Arabic ed. Cairo: Wazarat al-Thaqafa, 1961), pp. 31–32; al-Masʿudi, *Muruj al-Dahab, (Les prairies d'or)*, French trans. and ed. C. Barbier de Meynard and J. Pavet Courteille (Paris: A l'Imprimerie Impériale, 1861–77), p. 331, p. 334, p. 336; Ibn Hawqal, op. cit., Vol. 1, pp. 48–9; and Ibn al-Wardi, op. cit., p. 65.

41. See, for instance, al-Yaʿqubi's, *Kitab al-Buldan*. ed. Michael Jan de Goeje, *Bibliotheca geographorum arabicorum,* Vol. 7, (Leiden: E. J. Brill, 1892; reprinted, 1967), p. 336–7, discussion of active trade in the region. Key for pegging a ninth century date to full-blown mine exploitation activity is the occurrence of the Buja uprisings, which begin around the first quarter of the 9th century. From this one would have to presume that the penetration and take over of the mines in Buja territory by the Rabiʿa tribes from the Arabian mainland, must have begun sometime in the late eighth century even though exact dates of the incursion are not mentioned in the texts. S. Hillelson and C. E. Bosworth, in their joint work on the second part of the entry on "Nubia" in *EI2,* p. 90, say that by the 10th century the Rabiʿa had gained control of the mines at al-ʿAllaqi and had imposed their rule on the Buja with whom they had allied themselves through marriage. Hasan notes that proof for extensive Muslim contact lies in the fact that two Arabic treaties were translated in their language, Bujawi. See, Hasan, op. cit., p. 117.

42. Ibn Hawqal, op. cit., p. 48.

43. Spaulding, op. cit., p. 118; Miquel, op. cit., Vol. 2, pp. 163–4. The geographers cited above in footnote 44 also mention the use of Buja slaves for mining.

44. See, for example, Ibn Hawqal, op. cit., p. 48; Also, Miquel, op. cit., Vol. 2, p. 161–2.

45. The Buja raids and uprisings and refusal to comply with the requirements for tribute imposed upon them are cited in numerous sources. See, for instance, Arkell, *A History of the Sudan: From the Earliest Times to 1821,* (London: Athlone Press, 1966), p. 188; Spaulding, op. cit., p. 118; Holt, op. cit., p. 1158; and Miquel, op. cit., Vol. 2, p. 163; as well as Ibn Hawqal, op. cit., pp. 48–53.

46. Spaulding, op. cit., p. 118. Spaulding does not cite his source. He just notes that the comment was made by an Iranian in the eleventh century.

47. There is one notable exception to this: Ghana, Kanem, Kuga, Awdaghost, and a whole host of unidentifiable territories in western Africa are marked on the earliest extant world map of 479 A.H./1086 C.E. However, it is the al-Istakhri model without the detail in west Africa that predominates in the later copies, while the details of the Ibn Hawqal map is all but forgotten with the exception of one Mamluk manuscript of an al-Istakhri manuscript and some confused elements that creep into the so-called Ibn al-Wardi maps. Sijilmasa, however, is never located on the world maps; it does, however, figure in the regional maps of the Maghrib. The Maghrib maps only show the coast of North Africa and Muslim Spain. They cut off short of the Buja territory. The gold mines of Nubia, on the other hand, are never indicated on any map.

48. Sa'id al-Andalusi, *Science in the Medieval World: "Book of the Categories of Nations,"* English trans. and ed. by Sema'an I. Salem and Alok Kumar, (Austin: University of Texas Press, 1991), p. 8. Bernard Lewis presents an alternate and much more severe reading of this passage: "The only people who diverge from this human order and depart from this rational association are some dwellers in the steppes and inhabitants of the deserts and wilderness, such as the rabble of Bujja, the savages of Ghana, the scum of Zanj, and their like." See, Bernard Lewis, *Race and Slavery in the Middle East,* op. cit., p. 48.

49. Al-Istakhri, op. cit., p. 16. Translation based on the rendition in *Corpus of early Arabic sources for West African history,* English trans. by N. Levtzion and J. F. P. Hopkins, (Cambridge: Cambridge University Press, 1981), p. 40.

50. Ibid.

51. Al-Istakhri, op. cit., pp. 31–2. Translation my own. Ibn Hawqal begins his description of the Buja similarly. See earlier citation.

52. A measurement of distance.

53. Al-Istakhri, op. cit., pp. 31–2.

54. Ibid., p. 42. I thank Richard Bulliet for his assistance with the last sentence of this translation and the confusing use of "najab" and "asir."

55. An example of how the geographers often copied verbatim from each other.

56. Ibn Hawqal, op. cit., pp. 48–53.

57. Al-Maqdisi, *Kitab al-Bad' wa al-Ta'rikh,* French trans. and ed. by C. Huart, (Paris, 1899–1919), Vol. 4, pp. 69–70. This passage is cited by both Miquel, op. cit., Vol. 2, p. 161; and Lewis, op. cit., p. 52.

58. Miquel, op. cit., p. 161.

59. Al-Ya'qubi, op. cit., p. 336. Translation courtesy of Paul Cobb who is preparing an English translation of al-Ya'qubi's geography. Thanks also to Matthew Gordon for bringing Paul Cobb's on-going work on this text to my attention. The big question here is what exactly does "falak" mean? Normally it has a sense of "round" as in "as round as a celestial sphere," which is also called *falak.* It is also used to describe the ideal female breasts, round like orbs. But no Arabic dictionary records a meaning of "nipple." Yet it is the only meaning that seems to fit in the context, since the removal of the "roundness" of the male breast makes no sense. If this reading is accurate it is likely the first recorded mention of the removal of male nipples! Presently, the Buja are not known for this practice but, it seems, some Buja tribes in modern Sudan, are still known for removing their front teeth so that they do not resemble asses. Ancient Greek writers used to refer to them as the *Colobi,* meaning the "Mutilated People," because the women practiced infibulation and the men had the habit of removing their right testicle.

60. Miquel, op. cit., Vol. 2, p. 164.

61. Ibid.

62. Ibn al-Faqih al-Hamadani, *Kitab al-Buldan*, Arabic ed. M. J. de Goeje, (Leiden: E. J. Brill, 1906), p. 252.

63. Al-Tabari, *Ta'rikh al-rusul wa al-muluk, The History of al-Tabari*, Trans. series ed. by Ehsan Yar-Shater, (Albany: State University of New York Press, on-going), Vol. XXXIV, *Incipient Decline*, English trans. and annotation by Joel L. Kraemer, p. 142.

64. The phrase also occurs in precisely this formula in other texts. See, for instance, Ibn al-Faqih al-Hamadani, op. cit., p. 76.

65. Some versions of this manuscript say in the "uppermost Nile area of Egypt."

66. The text does not specify "heads" of what. Cattle, sheep, camels, or men?

67. Al-Tabari, *Ta'rikh al-rusul wa al-muluk, The History of al-Tabari*, op. cit., Vol. XXXIV, p. 142.

68. Although the sources don't specify one must presume that it is Samarra because this is where the caliph Al-Mutawakkil was based.

69. Tabari, op. cit., pp. 141–42.

70. Ibn Hawqal, op. cit, p. 49.

71. These stories are discussed at length by Ibn Hawqal, op. cit., pp. 49–52.

72. For more detail on al-Mutawakkil and his troubles with the Turks, see, Matthew S. Gordon, *The Breaking of A Thousand Swords: A History of the Turkish Military of Samarra (A.H. 200–275/815–889 C.E.)*, (Albany: State University of New York Press, 2001).

73. Ibn Hawqal, op. cit., p. 51.

74. Tabari, op. cit., p. 142.

75. The absurdly large numbers cited by Ibn Hawqal reflect the fantasy that he was projecting onto this event. See, Ibn Hawqal, op. cit., p. 51.

76. Ibn Hawqal, op. cit., p. 51.

77. Both Tabari and Ibn Hawqal report this, except their descriptions of the plan vary.

78. Ibn Hawqal, op. cit., p. 51.

79. Ibid., pp. 51–2.

80. Al-Tabari, op. cit., p. 144.

81. Ibid.

82. The latter certainly does seem to be a bit of hyperbole.

83. In Tabari's version of the story, after the audience with the caliph, ʿAli Baba accompanied by al-Qummi, returned to East Africa. Ibn Hawqal mentions the return of al-Qummi to the region but not ʿAli Baba.

84. Ibn Hawqal, *Configuration de la Terre,* op. cit., p. 52.

85. There is a great deal of dispute over the authenticity of *Alf Layla wa Layla (1001 Nights).* Only the first 271 lesser known stories are confirmed by extant fragments. The remainder are considered later innovations, possibly by the original French translator Antoine Galland (1646–1715). He played such an important part in composing and popularizing the tales that some call him the "real author." Not only did Galland freely embellish his translation, one of the four Arabic manuscripts he used is no longer extant and it is theorized that he may have employed a second set of manuscripts that is no longer extant. Many erudite Orientalists have worked to identify the "true" *Nights,*

including Duncan Black Macdonald and, more recently, Muhsin Mahdi. It is Mahdi who proposed in his new edition that only the first 271 tales can be considered authentic based on a thirteenth century Syrian manuscript. Robert Irwin, however, disagrees. He suggests that, "the *Nights* are really more like the New Testament, where one cannot assume a single manuscript source, nor can one posit an original fixed cannon. Stories may have been added and dropped in each generation. Mahdi's stemma suggests that there were very few thirteenth-century manuscripts of the *Nights;* for, in the end, the stemma narrows down to one single manuscript source. The references in the Geniza and in al-Maqrizi's topography of Cairo suggest, however, that the work was quite well known in the eleventh and twelfth centuries. Is it conceivable, then, that only one thirteenth-century manuscript served as the basis of all subsequent copies?" Robert Irwin, *The Arabian Nights: A Companion,* (London: Penguin Press, 1994), pp. 59–60. For in-depth details on the irresolvable dispute, see idem., pp. 1–62.

86. Why is the chief of the Buja named ʿAli Baba? It sounds like an unlikely name for a pagan African chief.

87. Christian Jacob, *L'empire des cartes: Approche théorique de la cartographie à travers l'histoire,* (Paris: Albin Michel, 1992), p. 267.

88. Henri Lefèbvre, *The Production of Space*, tr. by Donald Nicholson-Smith, (Oxford: Blackwell Publishers, 1992), p. 260.

Herat Under The Karts: Social And Political Forces*

Lawrence G. Potter

In order to gain a greater understanding of the social and political forces at work in post-Mongol Iran, this study focuses on the Karts, a small dynasty that flourished in the province of Khorasan from 1245 to 1389. The Karts, ruling from the city of Herat, helped preserve Persian culture and Islamic traditions at a time that the Mongol dynasty of the Īl-Khāns dominated the Iranian world. The Karts were among a number of contemporary dynasties, including the Muzaffarids in Fars, Iraq-e ʿAjam and Kerman (1314–93), the Jalayirids in Iraq, Kurdistan and Azerbaijan (1336–1432) and the Sarbedārs at Sabzevār (1336–81). The founders of the Kart, Muzaffarid and Jalayirid dynasties (the latter alone of Mongol extraction) all governed cities or regions on behalf of the Īl-Khāns but upon their demise lost no time in declaring their independence. This was one of Iran's greatest ages of regionalism and a crucial period of transition for political and religious institutions. Afterwards, with the establishment of the Ottoman and Safavid Empires, a period of greater political and religious rigidity set in.

Herat played an important role in a border zone where Iranian, Turcic and Indian cultures converged. The Karts were closely connected to the Ghurids, a dynasty originating in central Afghanistan that, at their height in the twelfth century, ruled over Khorasan, present-day Afghanistan and northern India. The Karts presided over the city's revival after the Mongols destroyed it and they laid the foundations for the florescence that followed under the Timurids. The French historian Jean Aubin has remarked on the "unjustly neglected history of Herat, an island of native power and Islamic culture in an eastern Iran where nomadism did not manage to overwhelm the old agrarian civilization."[1] This essay seeks to elucidate some of this neglected history.

The constitution of society in medieval Iran is a subject that so far has received little attention, at least in comparison to the Mamluk regions.[2] Although developed originally by Hourani for another time and place, the idea of a "politics of notables" appears to be a particularly helpful concept for understanding Herat.[3] Such a political system is characterized by ties of personal dependence, with society dominated by urban notables (including ulama, amirs, and secular figures) who possess access to authority and are leaders in their own right of the groups they represent. Such leaders perform a key role as intermediaries between the state and its constituent groups.

Richard Bulliet, in his seminal *Patricians of Nishapur*, discerned a social group he termed "patricians," that existed in pre-Mongol Nishapur in eastern Iran. Patricians were a wealthy, hereditary urban aristocracy, led by the ulama, who combined high social rank with local identity and loyalty that held the real power. Bulliet proposes the "type locality" of the patriciate to be Khorasan and Transoxiana, areas with a heritage of weak imperial rule. [4] Building partly on Bulliet's ideas, Shoshan suggests that "the 'politics of notables' could be one historical 'model' for describing the status of provincial towns in Islamic politics throughout the larger period of their history."[5] He believes that it was after the coming of the Turks that this system was particularly effective,[6] and furthermore that the towns with the highest autonomy were those situated on the periphery of Islamic empires—such as those in Khorasan.[7]

The existence of a "politics of notables" in pre-Mongol Khorasan and Transoxiana has more recently been explored by Jürgen Paul.[8] Paul studied the role of the local notables (admittedly a vague terminology, but including figures referred to as *aʿyān, mashāhīr and bozorgān*), for whom the Mongol invasion was only a temporary setback.[9] Paul believes that the invasion shows that the notables felt their first loyalty to their communities rather than to the city as a whole, which facilitated the Mongol conquest.[10] This echoes the situation in pre-Mongol Nishapur, where factional fighting ultimately left the city open to conquest by Turkish tribesmen. The continuity of notable families that Bulliet discerned in Nishapur has been confirmed by Paul, who found that the notables of Herat were able to "maintain a certain measure of control over local affairs throughout the Samanid, Ghaznavid and Saljuq periods (fourth/tenth to the sixth/twelfth century, approximately)."[11] In another part of Iran, Gronke found a considerable degree of continuity in notable families in Ardabil from the pre-Mongol until the Safavid period.[12] Can we apply this concept of a "politics of notables" to Kartid Herat?

***

In the Mongol and Timurid historical narratives, the focus of the author is often on the ruler, political conflicts and warfare. The important social groups, such as the Sufis, the ulama, the amirs, the *aʿyān* (notables) and the *ashrāf* (nobles), tend to get ignored. About others, such as the peasants and ʿayyārān (often robbers, bandits, sometimes with futuwwa associations),[13] there is precious little information indeed. This is true for the major sources for the Kart dynasty, including the historians Seifi, Ḥāfeẓ-e Abrū and Khwāndamīr.[14] Yet it is clear that the leaders of such groups cooperated with each other to ensure the continuity of social and economic relations even in times of political upheaval. Who these people were and how they related to each other are questions difficult to answer, yet important for the understanding of medieval Persian society. To examine the role of the different social groups at the time of the Karts, it is necessary to consider some of the major players—the king, the amirs, the ulama and the peasants—at a time of great social fluidity. We may then consider the larger issue that cut across the entire society—that of Turk versus Tājīk and how well a bicultural society worked.

We might begin by observing how contemporaries perceived the social hierarchy. Sample enumerations of the different social classes given in writings from widely separated intervals (1314, 1381 and the 1460s, respectively) can help here. In a *yarlīgh* appointing the qāẕī of Herat for example, the people enjoined to obey him are the imams (*aʾemmeh*), the descendants of the Prophet *(sādāt)*, the gnostics *(maʿāref)*, the men of place/administrators *(ashāb-e manāṣeb)* and the peasants *(raʿāyā)*.[15] After Malek Pīr ʿAlī Kart surrendered to Timur in 1381, the sādāt, shaikhs, imams, *ashrāf* (nobility) and *akāber* (dignitaries) came to tender their submission also.[16] A more detailed list of the social groups is given in the farmān of Abū Saʿīd confirming in power the *motavallī* (administrator) of the Jām shrine. It includes the sādāt, *qoẕāt* (judges), *darūgheh* (sheriff), shaikhs, *mowlās*, *ashrāf* (nobles), *ahāli* (citizens), *ʿuṣūl* (high-born), *aʿyān* (notables), *ʿommāl* (functionaries), *mobāsherān* (supervisors), *moqīmān* (residents) and *motavattanān* (citizens).[17]

What is interesting about the ranked lists given above is the absence of the category amir. The amirs, it seems, were a separate case from the other groups (which were made up of Tājīks) and not answerable to them.

The Role Of The King

At the head of society—at least in theory—stood the king. Only he was allowed to display the royal insignia which set him apart from others. Regalia commonly given by a supreme to a subordinate ruler—such as from the Mongols to the Karts—included royal edicts *(yarlīgh)*, robes of honor *(khelʿat)*,[18] standards *(ʿalam)* and drums *(ṭabl)*. Thus Shams al-Dīn, the first Kart malek, received from his suzerain, the Mongol Great Khan Möngke, a special *khelʿat*, three golden *paizeh* or badge(s) of authority,[19] bejeweled belts and golden clothing *(jāmeh-ye zarbaft)* and yarlīgh.[20] After assisting the Īl-Khān Abaqa triumph over an opponent, Shams al-Dīn was given presents *(tashrīfāt)*, drum(s), and banner(s).[21] Upon the accession of Malek Moʿezz al-Dīn Kart in 1332, Abū Saʿīd sent him a robe and a yarlīgh.[22] When Pīr ʿAlī Kart, the last of the line, submitted to Tīmūr, the conqueror gave him a crown (*kolāh*) and belt,[23] and when Pīr ʿAlī's son, Amir Ghūrī, surrendered, Tīmūr gave him a robe.[24]

The only Kart ruler to have the temerity to declare independence, following the collapse of the Īl-Khānate, was Moʿezz al-Dīn, the longest reigning Kart ruler (1332–70). In explaining his action to Sultan Moḥammad b. Tughluq, the ruler in Delhi, and seeking his approval, Moʿezz al-Dīn claimed that in the beginning of 750 (i.e. spring 1349) chaos had come to Khorāsān, corrupt people had become dominant, and he was the only one strong enough to restore proper rule and respect for religion.[25] Key symbols of sovereignty that marked Moʿezz al-Dīn as an independent ruler were the royal parasol *(chatr)*[26] and the *nowbat*[27] or flourishes of the trumpet five times a day. After declaring his independence, Moʿezz al-Dīn enjoyed the prerogatives of royalty: "They would carry a royal parasol above his head in the manner of *sultans*. And they made five nowbat for him."[28]

The king, then, was set apart symbolically from the society he governed. What was his role in society at that time? For the Buyid period, Mottahedeh has emphasized the king as someone outside the other social categories who maintained social order and prevented any one partisan interest from gaining dominance over others: "this role of arbiter, distant from the society for which it arbitrated, known to live largely for its own interest and not for any particular interest in society, was the role of the king."[29] Such a conception of kingship seems also to apply at the time of the Karts.

A common Persian attitude toward kingship was expressed by the Saljūq vazir, Neẓām al-Molk, in the pre-Mongol period:

> The most important thing which a king needs is sound faith, because kingship and religion are like two brothers; whenever disturbance breaks out in the country religion suffers too; heretics and evil-doers appear; and whenever religious affairs are in disorder, there is confusion in the country; evil-doers gain power and render the king impotent and despondent.[30]

Such views were still prevalent at the time of the Karts. Thus Ḥāfeẓ Abrū regarded support for religion as the basis of a sovereign's political legitimacy, provided he had the ability to manage his kingdom.[31] Ḥāfeẓ Abrū wrote of

Malek Moʿezz al-Dīn that he changed his ways and ruled his country according to the Sharīʿa.[32] Ibn Baṭṭūṭa attests to this. He says of the city of Herat, "its inhabitants are men of rectitude, abstention from unlawful pleasures, and sincerity in religion."[33] And in his deathbed advice to his son and successor, Pīr ʿAlī, Moʿezz al-Dīn said,

> . . . absolutely do not transgress religious law [*Sharʿ*] and be assiduous in observing the commands and prohibitions of religion, for in our family it has been established that whoever commits acts of sin, and is eager to do prohibited things, has fortune turn its back on him, and misfortune befalls him.[34]

Of course, like other medieval Persian historians Ḥāfeẓ Abrū was probably more concerned with constructing a meaningful narrative than in recording the "facts" of history.[35] His work was meant to legitimate the rule of the Kart maleks and demonstrate that, as long as they discharged their Islamic duties, they deserved to rule. Ḥāfeẓ Abrū is always very circumspect in his criticism of the Karts, blaming their failures on others.[36] This reluctance to criticize the king, however, gives way to open disapproval of Pīr ʿAlī, the last Kart malek.

The Need For Order

For Ḥāfeẓ Abrū, perhaps the key attribute of rulership was the ability to maintain order. As Lambton remarks, he lived in troubled times and was particularly concerned with the need for security.[37] The young Moʿezz al-Dīn had acceded to the throne in the wake of the murder of his predecessor and older brother, Ḥāfeẓ. His major achievement was to restore order in Herat, regain control over the army and unify the amirs and the nobles.[38] This augured well for the Kart state, which prospered until the Chaghatāy invasion two decades later.

The actions of Moʿezz al-Dīn are contrasted with those of his son, PīrʿAlī. The latter's moral turpitude—he is criticized for excessive drinking and preferring to play with his pigeons instead of administering the kingdom—was a direct cause of the downfall of the dynasty: "In this time things fell out of order, and complete weakness and disorder spread to the pillars of the state, and his advice failed to correct it."[39]

نه شاه و نه سالار لشکر بود   که نازک تن و ناز پرور بود
ترا افسر و گنج و فرمان دهی   حرامست اگر سر ببالین نهی

He is neither king nor head of the army
As he is delicate of body and pampered
Crown, treasure and leadership
Is forbidden to you if you put your head on the pillow.

The worst horrors were yet to come. Ḥāfez Abrū cannot conceal his dismay at the disorder that broke out after the city rebelled against Tīmūr's occupying army.

> The city of Herat was left like a house without a master and a ship without a captain . . . the genies of revolt [*fetneh*] broke out of the bottle of their imprisonment . . . chaos found its way among the people. The countries became [filled with] horror [and] the rabble [*arāẕel*] became dominant over the scholars [*afāẓel*] and tails took priority over heads."[40]

The king's role, to repeat, was to maintain order and support religion. Should he cease doing either, he forfeited his right to rule. But the king did not operate in a vacuum. What of the people behind the throne, those who participated in the kingdom's governance and to whom the Kart maleks turned in times of trouble? The most prominent, and military powerful, were the amirs.

The Age of the Amirs

Despite the preeminent position of the king, the amirs, or military commanders, were the ones who exercised real power at Herat.[41] This was typical of the situation elsewhere in Iran. During the Īl-Khānid struggles for succession, individual amirs had always promoted their own candidates, but after the death of Öljeitü in 1316, they exercised power directly and established their own dynasties.[42] The best example of this is Amir Chobān, who, with his sons, virtually ran the empire for a decade after the accession of the 12 year old Abū Saʿīd in 1317.[43]

After the death of Abū Saʿīd, the last Īl-Khān, in 736/1335, amirid power increased throughout Iran. As Manz has shown, the amirs at this time had great mobility and easily moved around among different states offering employment.[44] In Khorāsān, the amirs recognized Ṭaghāy-Teimūr,[45] a descendant of Changīz Khan's brother Jochi-Qasar, as Īl-Khān. Malek Moʿezz al-Dīn maintained cordial relations with Ṭaghāy-Teimūr and even married his daughter, Solṭān-Khātūn, but refused to recognize his political supremacy at Herat.[46] Ṭaghāy-Teimūr briefly held Solṭānīyeh, the imperial capital, but his power was essentially restricted to Khorāsān and he was killed by the Sarbedārs in 1353.[47]

At Herat, the amirs took charge in the troubled period following the death of Malek Ghiyās̱ al-Dīn in 1329 and, in rapid succession, placed three of his sons on the throne. Although they finally selected Moʿezz al-Dīn as malek, there was no question who was running affairs. Sālār, who was among the great amirs at that time, in reality was in charge of the realm.[48] While the Herati amirs acted to constrain the king's power, they did so in cooperation with other key groups such as the ulama. They were evidently on good terms with the latter, for we know that in the 1330s Sālār supported the *faqīh*, Mowlana Neẓām al-Dīn, to enforce the Sharīʿa in Herat.

Who were these Kart amirs? Were they of Persian or Turco-Mongolian stock? In the account of Ḥāfeẓ Abrū, they are a nebulous bunch, and even at climactic moments such as the victory over the Sarbedārs at Zāveh in 1342[49] and Tīmūr's conquest of Herat in 1381[50] none of them emerge as individuals in the narrative. (Ḥāfeẓ Abrū actually gives more names of the Chaghatāy amirs than the Kart ones!)[51] Some amirs were certainly wealthy; one was buried in the 1360s or 1370s in a tomb at Fūshanj.[52]

After the Chaghatāy defeat of the Kart army in 1351, the Ghurid amirs deposed Malek Moʿezz al-Dīn and placed on the throne his brother Bāqer,[53] whom they no doubt thought they could control. However Bāqer must have been a disappointment, for Moʿezz al-Dīn was able to regain his throne fairly quickly. In the interim the Kart ruler fled to his erstwhile enemy, the Chaghatāy leader Qazaghan, for protection. But Qazaghan, afraid that his own amirs would murder the malek, warned him to flee.[54]

Although the Ghurid and Chaghatāy amirs were kingmakers, the amirs in turn needed a king to legitimate their own roles. As McChesney points out about Central Asia in the 17th century, "without a khān, there was no political unity and the amīrs were at the mercy of each other's ambitions. Without a khān, too, there was no hope of military campaigns or territorial expansion."[55] This seems to hold true at Herat also, considering the disorder that broke out when the malek was absent or the succession was unclear.

The ʿUlama[56]

Clearly the Karts lived in a religious age, with the descendants of the Prophet held in special esteem. This was true regardless of political or religious affiliation, and not only among the Karts. Īl-Khāns such as Ghazan and Öljeitü[57] as well as rebels such as the Sarbedārs[58] all had reverence for the *Ahl al-bait* or family of the Prophet. The era of the Karts was one of religious fluidity and a time when two major Sufi brotherhoods, based at Jam and Chisht, competed for allegiance at Herat.[59] It was not a period of conflict between ʿulama and Sufis; rather the two groups were on good terms with each other. Thus in his description of the leading religious figures of the time, Khwāndamīr treats the biographies of Sufis and the Sunni ulama together, rather than separately.

This fluidity resulted in a web of friendships and ties among religious figures. The powerful Herati ʿālem, Mowlānā Neẓām al-Dīn, influenced the Sufis at both Jām and at Chisht. Zein al-Dīn Tāyebādī, an important disciple of Ahmad-e Jām, was regarded as one of his students,[60] while Abū Aḥmad Chishtī was a close friend. Mowlana Saʿd al-Dīn Masʿūd b. ʿOmar al-Taftāẓānī, one of the eminent scholars of the age, in turn was a believer in Shaikh Zein al-Dīn.[61] Taftāẓānī later influenced another prominent shaikh of Jām, Khwaja Ẓiyāʾ al-Dīn Yūsof.[62]

Although a full-scale prosopographical study of the ʿulama at Herat is desirable, for the time being a few observations may be ventured from scattered references. The power wielded by top religious officials at this time is illustrated in an anecdote about Mowlānā Neẓām al-Dīn,[63] who was the *faqīh* at Herat in the 1330s. He was known as the Pīr of Taslīm (submission) due to the rigor of his views, and he worked hand-in-hand with Sālār and the *khatīb* to foster a climate of religious intolerance.

Moʿezz al-Dīn, a teenager at his accession, was evidently intimidated by Neẓām al-Dīn; as Ḥāfeẓ Abrū puts it, he "endeavored to the farthest ends to honor and respect him and not to transgress his words."[64] Once when Neẓām al-Dīn caught the king drinking wine, he and the khatīb rallied 6,000 citizens at the gates of the palace. Moʿezz al-Dīn was forced to admit them and personally submit to the legal penalty of 80 lashes.[65] Neẓām al-Dīn, however, unwisely got into a quarrel with the Turks (or Mongols) living in the northern province of Bādghīs, which jeopardized the security of Herat. The situation was not resolved until he was martyred by the Turks.[66] After this incident, no other ʿālem exercised such power at Herat. The king sought to assert control over the religious establishment and the influence of the Jām Sufis became predominant.[67]

One issue that arises is who selected the qāẓīs, or judges, of which there appears to be fairly rapid turnover. In the Saljūq period in Nishapur, we know they were chosen by the patricians, or local elite.[68] In Herat in the early 1300s, they were personally selected by the Kart malek. Thus Mowlana Vajīh al-Dīn Nasafī, the *qāẓī al-qoẓẓāt* of Herat at the time of Dāneshmand's attack on the city (706/1306), was chosen by Malek Fakhr al-Dīn Kart.[69]

We also possess a copy of a yarlīgh concerning the appointment of Mowlānā Ṣadr al-Dīn as qāẓī of Herat in 714/1314.[70] It transpires that the shaikhs of Herat wrote a letter complaining to Öljeitü that the existing qazi was devoid of knowledge of the Sharīʿa. Öljeitü, who had decided to release Ghiyāṣ al-Dīn Kart from detention and allow him to return to Herat, agreed to give the qazi-ship to anyone the malek proposed. Ṣadr al-Dīn, who was from the Kart stronghold of Kheisār in central Ghūr and presumably trustworthy, was chosen.

There is evidence that high religious office at Herat was hereditary, as was the case at Shiraz.[71] Mowlānā Qoṭb al-Dīn, the son of the martyred Mowlānā Neẓām al-Dīn, was the head of the imams and ulama of Herat at the time of Tīmūr's invasion. This means that father and son dominated religious life at Herat from the 1330s to the 1380s.[72]

An important issue, if a difficult one to clarify, is the extent of the spread of Shiism.[73] Factional differences were supposedly the reason for warfare between the Karts and the Sarbedārs, although pragmatic considerations seem more important. Assessing the strength of Shiʿism at this time is complicated by the widespread reverence for the *Ahl al-bait* or family of the Prophet on the part of Sunnis.[74]

By the time of Pīr ʿAlī, distinctions between the law schools had lessened. Before setting out to attack the Sarbedārs, he obtained a fatwā justifying this from the scholars of the Neẓāmīyeh.[75] (This is interesting in that the Neẓāmīyehs were all founded as Shāfiʿī institutions,[76] while the Karts were Ḥanafī.) The Karts may have increasingly attempted to incorporate the ulama into the state apparatus. This culminated, by the time of Shāh Rokh, with the monarch himself appointing the ulama at the mosque of his wife, Gowhar Shād.[77]

The Peasants

It is regrettable that the sources are largely silent on the condition of the peasants, the raʿīyat or flock that made up the majority of the population. "The peasant's bitter toil earned him little but contempt and exploitation in his own day, however, and while we are ready enough to accord him at least a modicum of respect (if not to romanticize him beyond recognition), we have had very little to say about him," in the words of historian R. Stephen Humphreys.[78] To which Lambton adds, "the historical literature seldom reveals details about the common people except at times of natural disasters, riots and public disorders, and so what emerges tends to be a distorted picture."[79] If their condition is reflected in the prosperity of the state, we would expect the peasants to be in dire straits during most of the thirteenth century, with gradual improvement during the fourteenth until a high point is reached under the last two Kart maleks.

Under the early Īl-Khāns, the peasants were severely exploited and there was considerable hostility between rulers and subjects. They suffered from a severe tax burden, harsh repression and forced labor, which led to resistance.[80] Some peasants simply ran away, as is evident from Rashīd al-Dīn's instructions to return those who had escaped to their native provinces.[81] The ruinous taxation policy led to revolts, including one in Fūshanj in the 1290s.[82] This contributed to a significant decline in the land's productivity.[83] Things had reached crisis proportions before Ghazan introduced economic reforms around 1300. In a famous speech urging his amirs to lessen their oppression of the peasants, he said,

> I am not protecting the Persian peasantry. If it is expedient, then let me pillage them all—there is no one with more power to do so than I. Let us rob them together. But if you expect to collect provisions and food in the future . . . I will be harsh with you. And you must consider: if you commit extortion against the peasants, take their oxen and seed, and cause their crops to be consumed—what will you do in the future?[84]

The duty of *bīgār*, or supplying unpaid labor (corvée) for agricultural work or the construction of roads, buildings and irrigation works, was required of all landowners in Iran from early Islamic times.[85] The annual number of days of work required varied depending on local tradition, and rulers occasionally granted exemption from such duty.

It is unclear how onerous the corvée was for peasants under the Karts.[86] The prosperity of the later Kart period is undoubtedly partly accounted for by Malek Moʿezz al-Dīn's enlightened attitude toward the peasantry, if his words are to be believed. On his deathbed he summoned the pillars of state (*arkān-e dowlat*) and nobles of the court (*aʿyān-e ḥaẓrat-e khwīsh*) and told them, "it is my desire that the subjects [*raʿāyā*] which are trusts of the Creator should not be subjected to anarchy, and justice might be established in [its] deserving position."[87] This exhortation echoes the concerns of Ghazan, and may reflect notions of what a legitimate ruler should feel for his subjects. Unfortunately for the peasants, the campaigns of Tīmūr were still ahead.

The use of forced labor at Herat, at least by the time of the later Karts, appears to be the exception rather than the rule. The corvée was employed when a city wall was built to defend against the expected attack of Tīmūr. Such was the seriousness of the threat that the Kart malek impressed people "from the countries which were in his possession" to build it, the only such mention of forced labor (*bīgār*) in Ḥāfeẓ Abrū's entire account of the dynasty.[88] Thus it seems that only in the most dire straits was the corvée resorted to.

A Bicultural Society

From around the year 1000 A.D. there was a steady movement of Turcic tribesmen across the Oxus River into Iranian lands. This meant, especially in the period up to around 1500, the rise of a bicultural society, in which military leadership was usually in the hands of the Turks while civil administration and religious affairs were directed by Tājīks, or native Persians.[89] This led the historian Marshall Hodgson to posit a system of social power for the pre-Mongol period that he called the "aʿyān-amīr system." It was one in which power was divided between the aʿyān (the chiefs of the different groups in the city)[90] and the amirs (military commanders). The aʿyān were drawn from the native settled population and the amirs from the Turkic and Mongol invaders. These two groups were mutually supportive and operated with minimal interference from the state.[91] While the amīrs tended to change with each new dynasty, the bureaucracy and religious classes had a strong hereditary tendency and provided continuity.[92] Subtelny refers to the relationship between Turk and Tājīk as one of symbiosis, a relationship of ecological interdependence and mutual benefit deriving from economic ties between nomads and sedentary peoples.[93]

The dichotomy between Turk and Tājīk was starkly evident in the notions of political legitimacy that prevailed in the wake of the Mongol invasion. Legitimacy no longer flowed from the Caliph, but through the descendants of Changīz Khan. This understanding helped to account for the Karts' longevity, for generally they did not contest the suzerainty of the Īl-Khāns. The acceptance of this concept made the declaration of independence by Malek Moʿezz al-Dīn Kart untenable. Even powerful Chaghatāy amirs such as Qazaghan and Tīmūr did not rule in their own names, but in that of a Changizid puppet.

The disdain that Mongol rulers felt for Tājīks such as the Karts was often expressed at times of conflict. When the Chaghatay Amir Yasūr attacked Herat in 719/1319, he was enraged to see Malek Ghiyās̱ al-Dīn display the royal tent his suzerain, Abū Saʿīd, had given him. Yasūr exclaimed, "See how this proud Ghurid has dared to confront and oppose us, who are of the Changizid clan *(oroq)*."[94] And at the time of his attack on Herat in 752/1351, another Chaghatay, Amir Qazaghan, dismissed Moʿezz al-Dīn, saying, "Of what descent is he that he is making pretensions to the sultanate? . . . How can a Tāzīk pretend to be a king *(pādeshāh)*?"[95]

Tīmūr shared these sentiments. As Barthold points out, "he regarded a Tājīk as a man devoid of military valour and not dangerous to his enemies."[96] Before storming Herat, Tīmūr warned the emissaries of the Kart king,

> These lands [*mamālek*] have always belonged to the Mongol kings [*pādeshāhān*], and today if you [choose] war and fighting and insist on rebellion and you take refuge [behind] a fortress and wall, the end result of it will be the destruction of the land and the wasting of possessions and blood.[97]

On the broadest level, therefore, there was consciousness of the difference between Turk and Tājīk. Minorsky wrote, referring to the Safavid period, "Like oil and water, the Turcomans and Persians did not mix freely and the dual character of the population profoundly affected both the military and civil administration of Persia."[98] Yet how significant was this in everyday life? As noted in a recent study of the process of identity formation in medieval India, perhaps categories such as "Turk" and "Tājīk," like "Hindu" and "Muslim," are too bounded and only serve to inhibit our understanding.[99] In the early Īl-Khānid period (1230–89), Aubin has demonstrated that Mongols and Persians could work closely together and that the process of acculturation affected them both.[100] (The founder of the Kart dynasty, Shams al-Dīn, for example, fought hard for the Mongols and evidently gained knowledge of their laws.[101]) Manz found that there was no definite ethnic stratification in post-Mongol Herat; Mongols could serve with or below Persians in the army.[102]

It is instructive to examine the ethnic composition of the Kart army, which, like most armies in this period, we would expect to be dominated by Turks. At Herat, though, this is not so—the majority of the army is clearly of Tājīk stock. In the year 701/1302, for example, the army of Fakhr al-Dīn Kart was composed of forces from Herat, Bākharz, Tūlak and Ghūr, plus the Nīkūdarīs (Negüderis).[103] And at the time of the war with the Sarbedārs in 743/1342, the Kart army was drawn from "Ghūr and Gharjeh and Balūch and Khalaj and Nīkūdar and Sajzī [i.e. from Sajestān or Sīstān], from far and near, Turk and Tājīk."[104] The exceptions to Tājīk forces are the Khalaj Turks, probably mercenaries,[105] and the Nīkūdarīs, renegade Mongol tribesmen that the Karts protected from the Īl-Khāns.[106]

To proceed from the level of ethnic blocs down to that of individuals, the outstanding fact about the Kart amirs is that most of them were of Ghurid origin, like the maleks themselves.[107] Thus during the critical siege of Herat by Dāneshmand (the Īl-Khānid commander), Malek Fakhr al-Dīn Kart entrusted the defense of the city's citadel to his ablest commander, Jāmāl al-Dīn Sām—obviously a Tājīk from his name. When Dāneshmand was lured into an ambush, Sām's nephew, Tāj al-Dīn Yaldūz,[108] struck him first, after which Abū Bakr Sadīd had the honor of beheading him. We know that the Sadīdīs were renowned warriors from Ghūr.[109]

What stands out in the sources consulted is the lack of friction between the two groups, the lack of any mention of Turk and Tājīk forming opposing factions or quarreling to undermine the state. Perhaps this was specific to Herat, located as it was in a cultural border zone; the situation may have been different elsewhere. In Timurid Herat, bilingualism was widespread; many Turks knew Persian if not vice versa.[110] The phrase "Turk and Tājīk" is frequently invoked, but often as a rhetorical device to emphasize people from far and near. Thus when Malek Moʿezz al-Dīn wrote to the Delhi sultan after declaring his independence, he said that "they sent the news all around, near and far, to Turk and Tājīk."[111] And the inscription on the gravestone of a Kart amir boasts, "I conquered Turk and Tājīk."[112] "By the fifteenth century," according to Subtelny, "the phrase 'Turk and Tajik' (türk u tajik) had become standard when referring to the entire population of a realm, both sedentary and nomadic, both Turkic and Iranian."[113]

Marriage alliances

The significance of the difference between Turk and Tājīk was lessened during the late Kart period by the number of marriage alliances taking place between ruling families.[114] Tīmūr, for example, as a matter of policy established matrimonial relations with the dynasties governing Khwārazm, Fārs, Kalāt and Mārdīn,[115] as well as Herat. In this the direction of bride-giving is significant, since bride-giving groups are normally clients of bride-receiving groups. In the Herat context this means that the Mongols were people of lower status providing brides to the higher-status Karts.[116] Here the Karts were an exception, for the Īl-Khānid women were rarely given to local rulers.[117] In the case of the Sufis at Jām the situation is reversed, with the lower-status Karts offering a daughter in marriage to the higher-status saints of Jām. And the Jām Sufis would never intermarry with the Chaghatāy tribesmen.

The two sons of Malek Moʿezz al-Dīn Kart both had mothers of Changizid descent, which perhaps would ensure their legitimacy to rule but diluted the "purity" of their Tājīk stock. The mother of one son, Ghiyās̱ al-Dīn Pīr ʿAlī, was Solṭān-Khātūn, the daughter of Ṭaghāy-Teimūr (the last Changizid ruling in Khorāsān).[118] The mother of the other son, Malek Moḥammad (who became ruler at Sarakhs) was from the Arlāt tribe of the Ūlūs Chaghatāy.[119]

Pīr ʿAlī married a woman from the Jawun-e Qorban, a Turco-Mongolian tribe,[120] and their son was Pīr Moḥammad, who married Sīvinj Qutluq Āghā ("a pearl of a great jewelbox"), the niece of Tīmūr.[121] Pīr Moḥammad, therefore, was three quarters Mongol by blood, and his sons, Zein al-ʿĀbedīn and Maḥmūd, had they not been murdered at the direction of Tīmūr, would presumably have reigned as Kart maleks even though they were seven-eighths Mongol.

At the highest level, then, the distinction between Turk and Tājīk did determine who could and could not aspire to independent rulership. On the lower, everyday level, it had little practical relevance at Herat. Manz found that Tīmūr and his successors actually fostered a dual cultural loyalty in order to legitimize their exercise of power. "To rule required an appeal to both Islamic and Turco-Mongolian traditions, and a balance between them. Rulers moreover were not using these ideologies to appeal to two fully distinct and separate ethnic groups of opposing tendencies, but to accommodate a wide range of attitudes across a mixed population."[122] Under the early Safavids, however, the struggle between the two groups (at least at the top) became so serious that Shāh Ṭahmāsp introduced a new element—Caucasian Christians—of proven loyalty to the crown. They served, finally, to blur the old ethnic distinctions and allow the shah to get the powerful Turcoman *qizilbāsh* amirs under control.[123]

* * *

The era of the Karts was a period of transition for Iran, a time when it was coming to terms with the Mongol conquest and a new bicultural society was being born. It was perhaps paradoxical that the descendants of nomadic conquerors such as Toghrïl, Changīz and Tīmūr should embrace and patronize the urban Persian "high culture," yet the social synthesis that resulted set the stage for powerful, long-lasting states beginning with the Safavids.

In Herat, Turk and Tājīk worked well together and both supported the Kart dynasty. Relations between the different social groups were good, at least compared to other cities, resulting in a minimum of civil strife.[124] It was without question a religious age, and the religious elite—seyyeds, Sufis and ʿulama—were accorded pride of place in the social order. The amirs and urban notables also represented powerful groups which operated easily together in something approximating Hodgson's "aʿyān-amīr" system. These groups could constrain the king's actions and even govern without him,[125] but without a king Herat did not prosper.

Loyalties seem primarily guided by pragmatic considerations. When the chips were down, political necessity overrode allegiance to one's own ethnic group. Thus when they found it in their interest, the powerful Sufi shaikhs at Jām, who were related to and long helped legitimate the Kart dynasty, did not hesitate to welcome the conqueror Timur, who rapidly extinguished the Kart polity.[126] Kart maleks and prominent Īl-Khānid amirs alike sought protection at each other's courts when threatened at home. Moʿezz al-Dīn even was prepared to swear fealty to his enemy, the Chaghatāy Amir Qazaghān, if he would restore his throne.[127]

The basic strength of the Kart dynasty was the *ʿaṣabīya* or solidarity derived from their Ghurid heritage. Thus it seemed to Ibn Baṭṭūṭa that "[the men of Harāt] all belong to a single tribe called the Ghawrīya [i.e. Ghurids]."[128] Authors, Ibn Baṭṭūṭa and Būzjānī, for example, commonly refer to Malek Ghiyās̱ al-Dīn Kart as Ghiyās̱ al-Dīn Ghūrī.[129] This gave the Kart maleks a legitimacy in the eyes of the people that outsiders were forced to acknowledge. That is why the Īl-Khāns, and initially Tīmūr, were prepared to delegate the rule of Herat to the Karts despite the fact that they were not of Changizid descent.

The Kart era was above all one of fluidity, when rigid social distinctions, such as between Sufi and ʿālem and Turk and Tājīk, were becoming less important. The leading political figures—amirs, Sufis and ʿulama—all circulated freely within the Iranian realm and could change political loyalties. Despite this, the Kart dynasty was notable for its longevity and stability, and by reviving Herat set the stage for the Timurid florescence that followed. Perhaps it was Herat's location as a multicultural and bilingual city on the border that accounts for the Karts' unique achievement. The reign of Moʿezz al-Dīn (1332–1370) appears as a watershed during which the social distinctions of the earlier period were breaking down. Religious orthodoxy, as enforced by the powerful faqīh in the 1330s, seems to have given way later in the century to more diverse forms of religious observance. Marriage taboos were breached by the 1330s and 1340s, when the Karts begin intermarrying with the Jām shaikhs and the Chaghatāy tribesmen. The power of the Herati ʿulama declined in relation to the king and the shaikhs of Jām achieved the height of their influence over the Kart polity. The Karts' achievement was that of a minor dynasty at a time of weak or nonexistent central government, but the social synthesis taking place at that time would find fuller expression in the Timurid state to follow.

Endnotes

* This article is based on a chapter in my doctoral dissertation, "The Kart Dynasty of Herat: Religion and Politics in Medieval Iran" (New York: Columbia University, 1992). The Persian transliteration system of the Library of Congress has been used, with a few exceptions. I am grateful to Prof. Beatrice Forbes Manz and Ms. Haideh Sahim for their comments on the revised text.

1. Jean Aubin, "Le Khanat de Čaġatai et le Khorassan (1334–1380)," *Turcica* 8 (1976), p. 20.

2. Much research on urbanism in medieval Islamic cities has been inspired by the work of Lapidus on Mamluk Damascus and Aleppo. Lapidus discerned a model of social organization that emphasized the role of the quarters, fraternal organizations (Sufi brotherhoods, youth clubs and criminal gangs) and the religious community, all held together by the ulama. See Ira M. Lapidus, "Muslim Cities and Islamic Societies," in *Middle Eastern Cities: A Symposium on Ancient, Islamic, and Contemporary Middle Eastern Urbanism,* ed. Ira M. Lapidus (Berkeley: University of California Press, 1969), pp. 47–79.

For Iran, see Ann K.S. Lambton, *Continuity and Change in Medieval Persia: Aspects of Administrative, Economic and Social History, 11th–14th Century,* Columbia Lectures on Iranian Studies 2 (Albany, New York: State University of New York Press for Bibliotheca Persica, 1988), Chapters 7 to 10. Also consult Ahmad Ashraf and Ali Banuazizi, "Classes in Medieval Islamic Persia," in *Encyclopædia Iranica* V (1992), pp. 658–67. For the pre-Mongol period, see Roy P. Mottahedeh, *Loyalty and Leadership in an Early Islamic Society,* Princeton Studies on the Near East (Princeton: Princeton University Press, 1980), and Jürgen Paul, *Herrscher, Gemeinwesen, Vermittler: Ostiran und Transoxanien in vormongolischer Zeit,* Beiruter Texte und Studien, 59 (Beirut/Stuttgart: Franz Steiner Verlag, 1996).

3. Albert Hourani, "Ottoman Reform and the Politics of Notables," in *The Modern Middle East: A Reader,* eds. Albert Hourani, Philip S. Khoury and Mary C. Wilson (Berkeley: University of California Press, 1993), pp. 83–109, esp. pp. 87–91. Here Hourani is concerned with the beginnings of modernization in the Ottoman Empire, from around 1760 to 1860.

4. Richard W. Bulliet, *The Patricians of Nishapur: A Study in Medieval Islamic Social History* (Cambridge: Harvard University Press, 1972), esp. Chapter 2, "The Patriciate," pp. 20–27.

5. Boaz Shoshan, "The 'Politics of Notables' in Medieval Islam," in *Asian and African Studies* 20 (1986), 179–215; quote here is on p.180.

6. Ibid., p. 186.

7. Ibid., p. 213.

8. Paul, *Herrscher, Gemeinwesen, Vermittler.*

9. Jürgen Paul, "L'invasion Mongole comme 'révélateur' de la société iranienne," in *L'Iran face à la domination Mongole,* ed. Denise Aigle (Tehran: Institut Français de Recherche en Iran, 1997), p. 42.

10. Paul, "L'invasion Mongole comme 'révélateur' de la société iranienne," 51.

11 Jürgen Paul, "The Histories of Herat" in *Iranian Studies* vol. 33, nos. 1–2, Special Issue on *Persian Local Histories* (Winter/Spring 2000), p.111.

12. Monika Gronke, *Derwische im Vorhof der Macht: Sozial und Wirtschaftsgeschichte Nordwestirans im 13. und 14. Jahrhundert,* Freiburger Islamstudien XV (Stuttgart: Franz Steiner, 1993).

13. Mohsen Zakeri, "The ʿAyyārān of Khurasan and the Mongol Invasion," in *Proceedings of the Third European Conference of Iranian Studies* [Cambridge, England, September 11–15, 1995], Part 2, *Mediaeval and Modern Persian Studies,* ed. Charles Melville (Wiesbaden: Dr. Ludwig Reichert Verlag, 1999), pp. 269–76. Also, see W. L. Hanaway, Jr., "ʿAyyār in Persian Sources," *Encyclopædia Iranica* III (1989), pp. 161–63.

14. Major primary sources on the Karts include: for the early period, Sayf ibn Muhammad ibn Yaʿqūb al-Harawī, *The Taʾrikh Nama-i-Harat (The History of Harát),* ed. Muḥammad Zubayr al-Ṣiddīqī (Calcutta: Baptist Mission Press, 1944; reprint Tehran: Khayyām, 1352/1973) (Hereafter Seifī, *Tārīkh-e Harāt*); and for the later period, Felix Tauer, ed., *Cinq Opuscules de Ḥāfeẓ Abrū concernant l'histoire de l'Iran au temps de Tamerlan* [Critical partial Persian edition of his *Majmūʿa*], Supplement 5 to the *Archív Orientální* (Prague: L'Académie Tchécoslovaque des Sciences, 1959, hereafter Ḥāfeẓ Abrū/Opuscules). The dynasty is also mentioned in major Timurid histories, such as Ghiyāṣ al-Dīn Khwāndamīr, *Ḥabīb al-siyar fī akhbār-e afrād-e bashar,* ed. Jalāl Homāʾī (Tehran: Khayyām, 1333/1954-55), vol. 3, pp. 367–90. The chapter on the Karts has now been translated by W. M. Thackston, *Khwandamir: Habibu's-Siyar,* Tome Three: *The Reign of the Mongol and the Turk,* Part One: *Genghis Khan-Amir Temür,* Sources of Oriental Languages and Literatures 24, ed. Şinasi Tekin and Gönül Alpay Tekin (Cambridge: Department of Near Eastern Languages and Civilizations, Harvard University, 1994), pp. 213–25. For a Persian secondary source see ʿAbbās Eqbāl, *Tārīkh-e mofaṣṣal-e Īrān: az estīlā-ye moghol tā eʿlān-e mashrūṭīyat* [Complete history of Iran from the Mongol conquest to the announcement of the Constitution], vol. 1, *Tārīkh-e moghol az ḥamleh-ye Changīz tā tashkīl-e dowlat-e Teimūrī* [History of the Mongols from the attack of Changīz until the establishment of the Timurid state], 4th impression (Tehran: Amīr Kabīr, 2536/1977), pp. 366–78.

15. Saifi, *Tarīkh-e Harāt,* 613.

16. Sharaf al-Dīn ʿAlī Yazdī, *Ẓafarnāmeh,* ed. Moḥammad ʿAbbāsī ([Tehran]: Amīr Kabīr, 1336/1957), vol. 1, 236.

17. (Letter) of Sultan Abū Saʿīd Mīrzā concerning the *khāneqāh* of Shaikh al-Islām Khwajeh Raẓī al-Dīn Aḥmad al-Jāmī, composed by ʿAbd al-Ḥayy, in ʿAbd al-Ḥosein Navāʾī, *Asnād va mokātebāt-e tārīkhī-ye Irān,* vol. 1, *Az Teimūr tā Shāh Esmāʿīl,* in series Enteshārāt-e bongāh-e tarjomeh va nashr-e ketāb, no. 145 (Tehran 1341/1962–63), pp. 314–15.

18. On the custom of bestowing *khel'at,* a standard symbol of investiture, see N. A. Stillman, "Khil'a," *EI*[2] vol. 5 (1979): pp. 6–7.

19. On the *paizeh* see 'Ala-ad-Din 'Ata-Malik Juvaini, *Ta'rikh-i-Jahan-Gusha,* trans. John Andrew Boyle as *The History of the World-Conqueror* (Manchester: Manchester University Press, 1958), vol. I, p. 158, footnote 14. *Paizeh* or *paitza* were metal plates issued to officials of different ranks which usually served as diplomatic passports.

20. Saifi, *Tarīkh-e Harāt,* pp. 165, 168, 170–71.

21. Khwāndamīr, *Ḥabīb al-siyar* (Homā'ī) vol. 3, p. 369; (Thackston), p. 213.

22. Ḥāfeẓ Abrū/Opuscules, p. 31.

23. Ibid., p. 65.

24. Ibid., p. 66.

25. Jalāl al-Dīn Yūsof-e Ahl, *Farā 'ed-e Ghiyāṣī* ed. Heshmat Moayyad. Vol. 1, Zabān va adabīyāt-e Fārsī 50, enteshārāt no. 260 (Tehran: Bonyād-e farhang-e Iran, 2536/1977), Document 41, p.183, "Malek Jamāl al-Dīn Ekhtesān as told by Mo'ezz al-Dīn Abū'l Ḥosein Kart to Sultan Moḥammad Tughluq concerning his accession at Herat." I am grateful to Prof. M.R. Izady for help in translation.

26. The parasol has been used as a symbol of sovereignty in Iran since Achaemenid times (Eleanor Sims, "Čatr," *Encyclopædia Iranica* V (1992), 77–79.) In the sultanate of Delhi, the most important symbol of sovereignty was the royal umbrella. (See Ishtiaq Husain Qureshi, *The Administration of the Sultanate of Dehlī,* 5th ed. (New Delhi: Oriental Books Reprint Corporation, 1971), p. 75, fn.2.

27. Bosworth says one of the prerogatives of the Saljuq sultans was the "nauba," which he calls a "salute of military music." (See C. E. Bosworth, "The Political and Dynastic History of the Iranian World (A.D. 1000–1217)," in *Cambridge History of Iran* vol. 5, *The Saljuq and Mongol Periods,* ed. J. A. Boyle (Cambridge: Cambridge University Press, 1968), p. 136.

28. Ḥāfeẓ Abrū/Opuscules, p. 37.

29. Mottahedeh, *Loyalty and Leadership*, p. 175, see esp. pp. 175–90.

30. Niẓām al-Mulk, *The Book of Government or Rules for Kings: The Siyāsat-nāma or Siyar al-Mulūk,* trans. Hubert Darke, in Persian Translation Series of the United Nations Educational, Scientific and Cultural Organization (UNESCO) (London: Routledge and Kegan Paul, 1960), p. 63.

31. A. K. S. Lambton, "Early Timurid Theories of State: Ḥāfiẓ Abrū and Niẓām al-Dīn Šāmī," *Bulletin d'Études Orientales* 30 (1978): 3.

32. Ḥāfeẓ Abrū/Opuscules, p. 31.

33. Ibn Baṭṭūṭa, *The Travels of Ibn Baṭṭūṭa A.D. 1325–1354,* trans. H.A.R. Gibb (Cambridge: Cambridge University Press for the Hakluyt Society, 1971), Vol. 3, p. 574.

34. Ḥāfeẓ Abrū/Opuscules, p. 49.

35. Julie Scott Meisami, *Persian Historiography to the End of the Twelfth Century* (Edinburgh: Edinburgh University Press, 1999), p. 3.

36. For example, he emphasizes that the disastrous policies which led to the rout of the Kart army by the Chaghatāy Mongols in 1351 were decided not by

Moʿezz al-Dīn alone, but in consultation with the amirs of the army and the aʿyān and ashrāf of his kingdom. (Ḥāfeẓ Abrū/Opuscules, p. 40).

37. Lambton, "Early Tīmūrid Theories of State," p. 9.

38. Ḥāfeẓ Abrū/Opuscules, p. 31.

39. Ḥāfeẓ Abrū/Opuscules, p. 62. Meisami points out that the image of the pleasure-loving ruler who would rather drink than administer his kingdom, thus precipitating its downfall, is a recurring theme among medieval Persian historians (Meisami, *Persian Historiography,* p. 298, Note 2).

40. Ḥāfeẓ Abrū/Opuscules, pp. 68–69.

41. The amirs increased in power in Iran starting in the late Saljūq period and under the Khwārazmshāhs, according to Lambton. However, she notes that the amirs tended to use power for their own aggrandizement, and mutual jealousy usually prevented them from working together (Lambton, *Continuity and Change,* p. 243–48). Szuppe concludes that in the struggle between Safavids and Uzbeks in early 16th century Herat, the amirs sought above all to safeguard their own interests. See Maria Szuppe, *Entre Timourides, Uzbeks et Safavides: Questions d'Histoire Politique et Sociale de Hérat Dans la Première Moitié de XVIe Siècle* (Paris: Association Pour l'Avancement des Études Iraniennes, 1992), especially chapter on "Les Fidélités des Élites de Hérat," pp. 143–60.)

42. Lambton, *Continuity and Change,* p. 257.

43. See "The Fall of Amir Chupan and the Decline of the Ilkhanate, 1327–37: A decade of discord in Mongol Iran" by Charles Melville, *Papers on Inner Asia* No. 30 (Bloomington, Indiana: Indiana University Research Institute for Inner Asian Studies, 1999).

44. Beatrice Forbes Manz, "Military Manpower in Late Mongol and Timurid Iran," in Proceedings of the Third Colloquium of the Institut Français d'Études sur l'Asie Centrale, in *Cahiers d'Asie Centrale* (1997), pp. 43–55.

45. Here I follow the vocalization established by John Masson Smith, Jr., *The History of the Sarbadār Dynasty 1336–1381 A.D. and its Sources* (The Hague: Mouton, 1970), pp. 181–82.

46. Ḥāfeẓ Abrū/Opuscules, p. 32.

47. Smith, *History of the Sarbadār Dynasty,* for more details.

48. Ḥāfeẓ Abrū/Opuscules, p. 31. According to Khwāndamīr, Sālār was "among the rank of the great amirs" (*Ḥabīb al-siyar* (Homāʾī) vol. 3, 384; (Thackston), p. 223). Aubin ("Le Khanat de Čaġatai," 21) identifies Sālār as the Malek of Varna, although Ibn Baṭṭūṭa, who met the Malek of Varna, refers to him as the *khaṭīb* of Herat *(Travels,* vol. 3, 577).

49. Ḥāfeẓ Abrū/Opuscules, pp. 32–36.

50. Ibid., p. 63.

51. Ibid., pp. 38–43.

52. Bernard O'Kane, "The Tomb of Muḥammad Ġāzī at Fūšanğ," *Annales Islamologiques* (Cairo) 21 (1985): pp. 113–28. This tomb is a rare example of Kart architecture.

53. Ḥāfeẓ Abrū/Opuscules, pp. 44–45; also Faṣīḥ Khwāfī, *Mojmal al-tavārīkh,* ed. Maḥmūd Farrokh (Mashhad: Ketābforūshī-ye Bāstān, 1339/1960–61), vol. 3, p. 79 (under year 753).

54. Ḥāfeẓ Abrū/Opuscules, p. 45.

55. R. D. McChesney, "The Amirs of Muslim Central Asia in the XVIIth Century," *Journal of the Economic and Social History of the Orient* 26 (1983), p. 38.

56. See Khwāndamīr, *Ḥabīb al-siyar (*Homā'ī) vol. 3, pp. 384–87; (Thackston), pp. 223–24 for an account of the shaikhs and scholars contemporary with Malek Moʿezz al-Dīn. For those contemporary with Tīmūr, see Khwāndamīr, *Ḥabīb al-siyar,* trans. by Wheeler Thackston, in *A Century of Princes: Sources on Timurid History and Art* (Cambridge, Mass.: Aga Khan Program for Islamic Architecture, 1989), pp. 107–14.

57. Lambton, *Continuity and Change,* p. 325.

58. Faṣīḥ, *Mojmal al-tavārīkh,* vol.3, p. 96.

59. Lawrence G. Potter, "Sufis and Sultans in Post-Mongol Iran," in *Iranian Studies* 27 (1994), pp. 77–102.

60. Gūyā Eʿtemādī, "Darbār-e molūk-e Kart" [The court of the Kart kings], *Āryānā* 2 (S̲owr 1323/May 1944) p. 51.

61. Ibid., p. 52.

62. Ibid., p. 50, and Moḥammad Esmaʿīl Gharjestānī, "Dāneshmandān-e moʿāṣer-e dūdmān-e Kart," *Āryānā* 18 no.1 (Dalv 1338/January 1960), p. 51.

63. Ḥāfeẓ Abrū/Opuscules, 31. Here his *nisba* or affiliation is given as Mābarzhnābādī; Khwāndamīr cites his full name as Mowlā Neẓām al-Dīn ʿAbd al-Raḥīm al-Khwāfī (*Ḥabīb al-siyar* (Homāʾī) vol. 3, p. 384; (Thackston), p. 223 (reads as *mowlānā*).

64. Ḥāfeẓ Abrū/Opuscules, p. 31.

65. As reported in Ibn Baṭṭūṭa, *Travels,* vol. 3, pp. 577–78.

66. There are two accounts of this conflict which differ in details but not the end result. See Ibn Baṭṭūṭa, *Travels,* vol. 3, pp. 578–80; also Khwāndamīr, *Ḥabīb al-siyar* (Homāʾī) vol. 3, pp. 384–85; (Thackston), p. 223.

67. Potter, "Sufis and Sultans."

68. Bulliet, *Patricians of Nishapur,* p. 62.

69. Moḥammad Gharjestānī, "Nevīsandegān, dāneshmandān, va ṣūfīyān-e moʿāṣer-e dūdmān-e Kart" ["Authors, scholars, and Sufis contemporaneous with the Karts"], *Āryānā* 17 no. 2 (Jady 1338/ December 1959), p. 28, citing Ḥāfeẓ Abrū, *Z̲eil-e Jāmeʿ al-Tavārīkh.* The people of Herat regarded Vajīh al-Dīn as a traitor and the main instigator of the Īl-Khānid attack.

70. Seifī, *Tārīkh-e Harāt,* pp. 609–14. The date is inferred from preceding and following chapters.

71. John W. Limbert, "Shiraz in the Age of Hafez," (Ph.D. diss., Harvard University, 1973), p. 145.

72. Yazdī, *Ẓafarnāmeh,* vol. 1, p. 237. Tīmūr sent Mowlānā Qoṭb al-Dīn, along with 200 reputable *kadkhodās* from the city and the velāyat, to Shahr-e Sabz.

73. See Monika Gronke, "La Religion Populaire en Iran Mongol," in Aigle, *L'Iran face à la domination Mongole,* pp. 205–30. Also, for a later period, consult "Le problème du sunnisme et du chiisme à Hérat," in Szuppe, *Entre Timourides, Uzbeks et Safavides,* pp. 121–42.

74. McChesney comments on the prevalence of *"ahl al-baytism"* in Iran and Central Asia (R. D. McChesney, *Waqf in Central Asia: Four Hundred Years in the History of a Muslim Shrine, 1480–1889* (Princeton: Princeton University Press, 1991), pp. 33–34 and 268–69).

75. Ḥāfeẓ Abrū/Opuscules, p. 52.

76. The Neẓāmīyeh in Herat was probably built between 459/1067 and 485/1092 by Neẓām al-Molk. It was repaired and reendowed in the late Tīmūrid period by ʿAlī-Shīr Navāʾī (Terry Allen, *A Catalogue of the Toponyms and Monuments of Timurid Herat*, Studies in Islamic Architecture No. 1 (Cambridge, Mass.: Aga Khan Program for Islamic Architecture, 1981), p. 135, no. 477, "Madrasah-i Niẓāmīyah"). I am grateful to Prof. Neguin Yavari for additional detail.

77. Mīr ʿAlī-Shīr Navāʾī, *Majāles al-nafāʾes,* ed. ʿAlī Aṣghar Ḥekmat (Tehran 1322/1945), p. 104, cited in Bernard O'Kane, *Timurid Architecture in Khurasan,* Islamic Art and Architecture vol. 3 (Costa Mesa, Cal.: Mazdā Publishers in Association with Undena Publications, 1987), p. 91.

78. R. Stephen Humphreys, *Islamic History: A Framework for Inquiry,* revised edition (Princeton: Princeton University Press 1991; reprint London: I. B. Tauris, 1999), p. 284.

79. A. K. S. Lambton, "Local Particularism and the Common People in Pre-Modern Iran," in *Durham Middle East Papers* No. 67 (Durham, U.K.: Institute for Middle Eastern and Islamic Studies, University of Durham, December 2001), pp. 4–5.

80. I. P. Petrushevsky, "The Socio-Economic Condition of Iran Under the Īl-Khāns," in *The Cambridge History of Iran* vol. 5, *The Saljuq and Mongol Periods,* ed. J. A. Boyle (Cambridge: Cambridge University Press, 1968), esp. pp. 522–29; V. M. Masson and V. A. Romodin, *Istoriia Afganistana: sdrevneishikh vremen do nachala 16 veka* [History of Afghanistan: From Ancient Times to the Beginning of the 16th Century], vol.1 (Moscow: Nauka Publishers, 1964), pp. 303–05 and 320; Ann K. S. Lambton, *Landlord and Peasant in Persia: A Study of Land Tenure and Land Revenue Administration* (Oxford: Oxford University Press, 1953; reprint 1969), pp. 88–89.

81. A. ʿAli-Zade, "The Agrarian System in Azerbaijan in the XIII–XIV Centuries," in *Akten des vierundzwanzigsten Internationalen Orientalisten-Kongresses* (München, 28 August–4 September 1957), ed. Herbert Franke (Wiesbaden: Deutsche Morgenländische Gesellschaft, 1959), pp. 341–42.

82. Rashīd al-Dīn, *Jāmeʿ al-tavārīkh,* cited in Masson and Romodin, *Istoriia Afganistana*, p. 304.

83. Lambton, *Landlord and Peasant,* p. 99.

84. Rashīd al-Dīn, *Jāmeʿ al-tavārīkh,* ed. A.A. Alizade (Baku, 1957), vol. 3, 478, cited in David Morgan, *The Mongols*, The Peoples of Europe series (Oxford and New

York: Basil Blackwell 1986), p. 167. Slightly different version in Petrushevsky, "Socio-Economic Condition of Iran," p. 494.

85. Yuri Bregel, "Bīgār, Bīgārī," *Encyclopædia Iranica* IV (1990), 249–51; Lambton, *Landlord and Peasant,* pp. 330–36. Bīgārī was still common in parts of Khorāsān in the 1940s. According to Lambton, "it is perhaps in the field of personal servitudes that the survival of medieval customs and even more of a medieval attitude of mind is most striking" (p. 336).

86. In the small Sufi state established at Āmol, Sayyid Fakhr al-Dīn, who became the *ra'īs* of the community in 763/1362, used forced labor *(bīgārī)* to construct his buildings. (Zahīr al-Dīn Mar'ashī, *Tārīkh-e Ṭabarestān va Rūyān va Māzandarān,* in B. Dorn, *Muhammedanische Quellen zur Geschichte des Südlichen Küstenländer des Kaspischen Meeres,* Part 1 (St. Petersberg, 1850), pp. 401–02, cited in Lambton, *Landlord and Peasant,* p. 99 fn. 2.)

87. Ḥāfeẓ Abrū/Opuscules, p. 49.

88. Ibid., p. 60.

89. The Joveinī family of Khorāsān is perhaps the best example of Tājīks who held high office under the Saljūqs, Khwārazmshāhs and Īl-Khāns, often in the capacity of finance minister or *ṣaḥeb-dīvān.* (Boyle, *History of the World-Conqueror,* Translator's Introduction, xv–xvi.)

90. On the *a'yān* see Mottahedeh, *Loyalty and Leadership,* pp. 123–29.

91. Marshall G. S. Hodgson, *The Venture of Islam: Conscience and History in a World Civilization,* vol. 2, *The Expansion of Islam in the Middle Periods* (Chicago: University of Chicago Press, 1974), pp. 91–135.

92. Lambton, *Continuity and Change,* 297ff.

93. Maria Eva Subtelny, "The Symbiosis of Turk and Tajik," in *Central Asia in Historical Perspective,* ed. Beatrice F. Manz (Boulder: Westview Press, 1994), p. 46.

94. Mo'īn al-Dīn Moḥammad Zamchī Esfezārī, *Rowẓāt al-Jannāt fī Owṣāf Madīnat al-Harāt,* Part 1, ed. Sayyed Moḥammad Kāẓem Imām (Tehran: Enteshārāt-e Dāneshgāh-e Tehrān, 1338/1959, p. 485.

95. Ḥāfeẓ Abrū/Opuscules, p. 38. Amir Qazaghan also deprecated the malek's military strategy. The Kart forces, he pointed out, were stationed at the bottom of a hill, where they would have the sun in their eyes and face the dust-laden north wind—all significant drawbacks which contributed to their defeat.

96. V. V. Barthold, *Four Studies on the History of Central Asia,* vol. 2, *Ulugh-Beg,* trans. V. and T. Minorsky (Leiden: E.J. Brill, 1963), p. 24.

97. Ḥāfeẓ Abrū/Opuscules, p. 65.

98. V. Minorsky, trans., *Tadhkirat al-Mulūk: A Manual of Ṣafavid Administration (circa* 1137/1725), Persian Text in Facsimile, E. J. W. Gibb Memorial Series, New Series, XVI (Cambridge, England: E. J. W. Gibb Memorial Trust, 1943; reprint 1980), Appendix 1, p. 188.

99. David Gilmartin and Bruce B. Lawrence, "Introduction," in *Beyond Turk and Hindu: Rethinking Religious Identities in Islamicate South Asia,* ed. Gilmartin and Lawrence (Gainesville: University Press of Florida, 2000), pp. 1–20.

100. Jean Aubin, *Émirs Mongols et Vizirs Persans dans les Remous de l'Acculturation,* Studia Iranica, Cahier 15 (Paris: Association Pour l'Avancement des Études Iraniennes, 1995), especially Chapter 10.

101. On his knowledge of the Yasa and Törä see Khwāndamīr, *Ḥabīb al-siyar* (Homā'ī) 368; (Thackston), p. 213.

102. Manz, "Military Manpower in Late Mongol and Timurid Iran," p. 51.

103. Seifī, *Tārīkh-e Harāt,* p. 444, cited in Russell George Kempiners Jr., "The Struggle for Khurāsān: Aspects of Political, Military and Socio-Economic Interaction in the Early 8th/14th Century" (Ph.D. diss., University of Chicago, 1985), p. 157.

104. Ḥāfeẓ Abrū/Opuscules, p. 32.

105. Manz, *Rise and rule of Tamerlane,* pp. 97 and 193 fn. 59.

106. The Karts borrowed their military tactics from the Mongols. Their armies were decimally organized, such that the entire force was made up into detachments of 10 men *(dahjāt)*. Every 10 detachments were put under the commander of 100, and a commander of 1,000 oversaw every 10 detachments of 100. (Ḥāfeẓ Abrū/Opuscules, p. 34.)

107. Ḥāfeẓ Abrū/Opuscules, p. 43.

108. Esfezārī, *Rowẓāt al-Jannāt,* l, pp. 448–49. The name of this commander is problematical, as the Persian name Yaldūz and the Turkish Yïldïz (which means "star" in Turkish) are both given. The latter orthographic form was probably based on the pronunciation. Seifī once refers to him as Yaldūz and calls him a *pahlavān* (p. 455). On other occasions he gives the form Yïldïz (pp. 427 and 495). Ḥāfeẓ Abrū says he was Sām's nephew ‘Hāfez-i Abrū, *Chronique des Rois Mongols en Iran* [section from his *Zeil-e Jāme' al-Tavārīkh*], vol. 2, trans. K. Bayani (Paris: Librairie d'Amérique et d'Orient, 1936), p. 24.) Khwāndamīr (*Ḥabīb al-siyar* (Homā'ī) p. 374; (Thackston), p. 217) says he was a Ghurid officer. This definitely indicates he was a Tājīk.

109. Ḥāfeẓ Abrū/Opuscules, p. 67.

110. Manz notes that the Chaghatay aristocracy was largely bilingual in Turkish and Persian, even if the nomads continued to speak Turkish ("The Development and Meaning of Chaghatay Identity," in *Muslims in Central Asia: Expressions of Identity and Change,* ed. Jo-Ann Gross (Durham: Duke University Press, 1992, p. 31.) Also Subtelny, "Symbiosis of Turk and Tajik," pp. 49–50.

111. Yūsof-e Ahl, *Farā'ed-e Ghiyāṯī,* vol.1, Document 41, p.184.

112. O'Kane, "Tomb of Muḥammad Ġāzī," p. 125.

113. Subtelny, "Symbiosis of Turk and Tajik," pp. 48–49

114. This is not to say that intermarriage was common at lower levels; for example, Woods found virtually no political or social assimilation between Turk and Tājīk among the Aqquyunlu during the 15th century. See John E. Woods, *The Aqquyunlu: Clan, Confederation, Empire: A Study in 15th/9th Century Turko-Iranian Politics,* Studies in Middle Eastern History, no. 3 (Minneapolis & Chicago: Bibliotheca Islamica, 1976), p. 9.

115. Syed Jamaluddin, "Hereditary Chiefs Under Amir Tīmūr (1370–1405)," *Archív Orientální* 57 (1989), p. 225.

116. Already in the 1290s the third Kart malek, Fakhr al-Dīn, was married off to the niece of Nowrūz, the powerful Īl-Khānid commander. See Khwāndamīr, *Ḥabīb al-siyar* (Homā'ī) p. 371; (Thackston), p. 215; also in *Taḥrīr-e Tā'rīkh-e Vaṣṣāf,* ed. ʿAbd-al-Moḥammad Āyatī (Tehran: Enteshārāt-e bonyād-e farhang-e Īrān, 18/ Manābeʿ-e tā'rīkh va joghrāfīya-ye Īrān, 4, Khordād 1346/May–June 1967), p. 207).

117. Lambton, *Continuity and Change,* p. 287.

118. Ḥāfeẓ Abrū/Opuscules, p. 32.

119. Ibid., p. 49. On the Arlāt see Manz, *Rise and rule,* pp. 155–56.

120. Aubin, "Le Khanat de Čaġatai et le Khorassan," Chart, 58. See further James J. Reid, "The Je'ün-i Qurbān Oirat Clan in the Fourteenth Century," *Journal of Asian History* 18 (1984), pp. 189–200.

121. Ḥāfeẓ Abrū/Opuscules, p. 58.

122. Beatrice Forbes Manz, "Temür and the problem of a conqueror's legacy," in *Journal of the Royal Asiatic Society,* Third series, vol. 8, part 1 (April 1998), p. 36. (See esp. pp. 34–41.)

123. Roger Savory, *Iran Under the Safavids* (Cambridge: Cambridge University Press, 1980), pp. 32–33, 91 and 185.

124. In Shiraz, by contrast, mob violence was not infrequent. See Limbert, "Shiraz in the Age of Hafez," pp. 155–56.

125. A similar situation prevailed in Delhi, where the sultan's power was sharply limited by the nobles and ulama. (See Qureshi, *Administration of the Sultanate of Dehlī,* pp. 51–52).

126. Potter, "Sufis and Sultans," pp. 97–100.

127. Ḥāfeẓ Abrū/Opuscules, p. 45.

128. Ibn Baṭṭūṭa, *Travels,* vol. 3, p. 576.

129. Ibn Baṭṭūṭa, *Travels,* vol. 3, p. 574 and Darvīsh ʿAlī Būzjānī, *Rowẓat al-Rayāḥīn,* ed. Heshmat Moayyad. In Persian Texts series, 29, ed. E. Yarshater (Tehran: Enteshārāt-e bongāh-e tarjomeh va nashr-e ketāb, 1345/1966), p. 105.

Khurāsān and the Crises of Legitimacy: A Comparative Historiographical Approach

Parvaneh Pourshariati

In recent years a number of significant studies have approached the early Islamic history of the Middle East from a source and literary critical perspective.[1] This methodology has been particularly fruitful in studies which have dealt with the conquest period as contained in the *futūḥ* literature.[2] With a few exceptions,[3] however, the early Islamic history of the Iranian East has not been the subject of this type of scrutiny. The early Islamic history of Khurāsān, in particular, has been neglected by this new historiographical trend. We do not need to belabor here the importance of Khurāsān in the early history of the caliphate in general and of Iran and territories further east in particular. Suffice it to say that some of our fundamental notions of the role of the region in early Islamic history might be radically altered through such source and literary critical studies.

The present chapter examines the accounts of three significant junctures in the history of Khurāsān in order to highlight an implicit narrative contained in them. The narratives of the periods of the Arab conquest of the region, the Umayyad-ʿAbbāsid contention for power, and the Caliphate/Imāmate dispute over legitimacy will be compared, where applicable, in selective samples of the three genres of early Islamic, Shīʿite, and Iranian historiography. It will be argued here that the transfer of legitimacy between contending rival powers in these periods of early Islamic history of Khurāsān takes place, unexpectedly, through Ṭūs. Ṭūs is a region with a highly significant role in subsequent Shīʿite and "national" Iranian historical memory, but, otherwise, seemingly obscure during this early Islamic history of Khurāsān. A number of personalities become emblematic in representing issues of legitimacy in particular historiographical narratives. It is through these, and in Ṭūs that the conflicting parties wage their wars in narratives wrought with symbolic meanings that are never articulated explicitly.

The Conquest of Khurāsān through Ṭūs?

The narratives of the conquest of Khurāsān in classical Islamic sources[4] agree upon a set of givens that together form the kernel of traditions handed down to us about this important juncture in the history of the region. There are minor variations in these, but their general theme remains the same. The following sample by Ya'qūbī in *al-Buldān* (composed 278/892) can be considered to incorporate the major historical elements as well as narrational devices found in other accounts:

> The first person to enter Khurāsān was ʿAbdallāh ibn ʿĀmir ibn Kurayz ibn Rabīʿa ibn Ḥabīb ibn ʿAbd al-Shams. In the year 30/651, ʿUthmān ibn ʿAffān wrote to ʿAbdallāh, who was at the time the governor *(wālī)* of Baṣra, as well as to Saʿd ibn ʿĀṣ, his agent in Kūfa. He ordered them to set out for Khurāsān. He told them that whosoever reaches Khurāsān first, he will become the governor of that province. [Now] a letter arrived from the king of Ṭūs to ʿAbdallāh ibn ʿĀmir proposing to him that "I will [help] make you the first to reach Khurāsān if you promise the governorship of Nīshāpūr to me." He [the king of Ṭūs] fulfilled his promise. ʿAbdallāh [then] gave him [the king] a letter which is to this day with his offspring . . .[5]

Most other narratives of the conquest of Khurāsān repeat the kernel of information provided by Yaʿqūbī: that ʿAbdallāh b. ʿĀmir must be credited with the conquest of Khurāsān; that there were other, unsuccessful, expeditions sent to the region; and finally that the successful conquest of the region took place under the rule of the third Caliph, ʿUthmān b. ʿAffān (644–656 A.D.) Besides furnishing us with the names of Arab generals involved in the conquest, these narratives seem to possess very little informational value. There is, however, another set of uncontested information, and a series of subtly contended facts surrounding these, through which the narratives of the conquest become animated. The further undisputed, and for our purposes crucial, piece of information upon which most of the narratives of the conquest agree is the central role played by a personage variously identified as the *kanārang,*[6] *kanār,*[7] or *Kanādbak*, the ruler (*amīr*) of Ṭūs,[8] Kanārī b. ʿĀmir,[9] *marzbān,*[10] king (*malik*) of Ṭūs,[11] and, at times, as the governor of Khurāsān.[12] According to most narratives it is the *kanārang* of Ṭūs who writes a letter to ʿUthmān, or, as some narratives have it, ʿAbdallāh b. ʿĀmir, and invites him to conquer Khurāsān, or, alternatively, promises the Arabs to aid them in their conquest of the region.

The narrative of the *kanārang*'s complicity with the conquerors can be found in most of the classical sources that deal with the conquest of Khurāsān. Among the series of disputed facts surrounding the conquest of Khurāsān,[13] there is the issue of the compensation that the *kanārang* expected to receive in return for collaborating with the conquerors. In some accounts the *kanārang* promises to facilitate the conquest in return for being given the governorship of Khurāsān. In others he merely asks for the governorship of Nishapur. (The conquest of Ṭūs and Nishapur are closely connected in these accounts.) Ya'qūbī's contention that in exchange for fulfilling his promises the ruler of Ṭūs receives a letter—presumably containing his order of governorship over Nishapur—which remains "to this day[14] with his [i.e. the *kanārang*'s] offspring,"[15] is unique in this tradition.

The role of the *kanārang* of Ṭūs, therefore, is central to all of the *futūḥ* narratives of Khurāsān, and is highlighted more than any other pre-Islamic persona in these narratives. The narratives surrounding him serve to introduce the inception of the conquest of Khurāsān and the beginnings of Arab hegemony over the region. While the putative letter written by the *kanārang* to 'Uthmān or 'Abdallāh b. 'Āmir can be considered as a literary topos—no actual letter is reproduced through the traditions—the centrality of the *kanārang*'s function in the narratives of the conquest of Khurāsān cannot be contested.

Through most of the Umayyad period there is a remarkable silence in Islamic chronicles regarding events in Ṭūs, or personalities associated with it. From the hindsight of the information provided through the *futūḥ* literature and in view of the (more or less) substantive narratives that detail the course of events in Khurāsān during the next century, this dearth of information is disquieting, and obstructs the possibility of constructing linear research. What lends credence to the possibility of an alternative, non-narrational, reading of the information at hand, however, is the juncture at which point Ṭūs, and the figures associated with it, reappears in the narrative structures of Islamic chronicles.

'Abbāsid/Umayyad Struggle in Ṭūs

After the lapse of a century Ṭūs becomes the focus of the narratives at the height of the 'Abbāsid revolution. The bare outlines of this story, according to the narratives of Islamic historiography, once all the contentious sets of information are set aside, is this: After the inception of the 'Abbāsid revolution under the "Black Banners," Abū Muslim enters Marv victoriously on 130

A.H./15 January 748. Besides Marv, the revolutionaries also conquer Sarakhs, Nasā and Abīvard. Together with his army, Naṣr b. Sayyār, the octogenarian governor of Khurāsān, retreats to Nishapur. The son of the governor, Tamīm b. Naṣr, together with a large army is positioned in Ṭūs. In order to combat this situation Abū Muslim first bestows the governorship of Ṭūs and Nishapur to Ḥumayd b. Qaḥṭaba, the son of Qaḥṭaba b. Shabīb,[16] the second commander of the ʿAbbasid army. He then sends Ḥumayd b. Qaḥṭaba and his army against Tamīm b. Naṣr to Ṭūs. In the war that subsequently ensues in Ṭūs, Ḥumayd b. Qaḥṭaba defeats and murders Tamīm b. Naṣr and roots out the Umayyad army.

Even in this condensed form, and reduced to its minimum components containing geographical information on the ʿAbbāsid revolution and the names of some of its most central participants, this narrative maintains its informational value. In fact it bears testimony to the contention that geographical and topographical data, along with names, "form the backbone of factual information in historical tradition."[17] In order to get a sense of the sort of acute political crisis that the Umayyad defeat in Ṭūs occasioned, however, it is perhaps apt to quote the narrative of the anonymous *Kitāb al-ʿUyūn wa ʿl-Ḥadāʾiq fī Akhbār-i ʿl-Ḥaqāʾiq* in full:

> . . . Qaḥṭaba then set out for Nīshāpūr in pursuit of Naṣr b. Sayyār. With Qaḥṭaba there were the leading commanders *(wujūhu al-quwwād)* such as Abīʿ Awn and Khālid b. Barmak and Khāzim b. Khuzayma and ʿUthmān b. Nahīk and others like them . . . Qaḥṭaba sets out for al-Sūdhqān [sic. the location is actually Nawqān of Ṭūs, the army base of Tamīm b. Naṣr . . . [Qaḥṭaba then] called them to the Book of God . . . and rule by an acceptable member of the family of the Prophet . . . But they did not consent (*wa da ʿāhum ilā kitāb-i Allāh . . . wa ilā . . . al-Riḍā min āl-i Muḥammad . . . falam yujībūhu*). So he killed them. And Tamīm b. Naṣr was killed in the struggle. And a great many [others] were massacred alongside him. [The rest of his army] was captured, [while others] fled. The Bānī (*al-Bānī*) took refuge in the city (*taḥaṣṣana al-Bānī bi ʿl-madīna*). They entered and killed him and [killed] those that were with him. The rest fled to Naṣr b. Sayyār who was in Nīshāpūr and informed him of the great number [of the ʿAbbāsid army] and of the murder of Tamīm and al-Bānī and those that were with them. Naṣr fled . . .[18]

The narrative of Tamīm b. Naṣr's defeat in Ṭūs and Ḥumayd b. Qaḥṭaba's victory in the region is recounted in as great detail in al-Ṭabarī, Balʿamī, al-Dīnawarī,

Khalīfat b. Khayyāṭ, Al-Maqdisī and other classical Islamic sources.[19] It occupies a central position in the narrative of the ʿAbbāsid rise to power in the anonymous *Akhbār al-ʿAbbās.*[20] In the edited version of the *Akhbār al-ʿAbbās* the narrative of the conquest of Ṭūs takes up four pages, as opposed to half a page for the conquest of Nishapur,[21] and one page for the conquest of Sarakhs, for example. Reminiscent of the actions of the *kanārang*, Khalīfat b. Khayyāt even singles out the Ṭūsīs as inviting the forces of Naṣr to their territory and extending their allegiance to him.[22] In Yaʿqūbī's *Taʾrīkh* the potentially anti-ʿAbbāsid stance of the Ṭūsi's is highlighted in a very interesting narrative where the ʿAbbāsid missionaries are advised to "stay away from Abarshahr and Ṭūs . . ."[23] It is interesting to note here that the assignation of Ṭūs as a problematic region for the cause of the revolutionaries is inserted in Yaʿqūbī's narrative also in the context of the highly contested, putative, transfer of the Imāmat from the Hāshimiyya to the ʿAbbāsids.[24]

Once again, therefore, Ṭūs, together with a number of central personae associated with it, assumes center stage in the narratives of classical Islamic historiography. What strikes the reader after an initial reading, furthermore, is the structural affinities between the two episodes of the conquest and the ʿAbbāsid revolution considered so far. The narratives of both depict transition periods in the early Islamic history of Khurāsān. Both focus on a period of crisis and the transfer of political authority in the region where the issue of the legitimacy of this transfer is a point of contention. In the narrative of the ʿAbbāsid rise to power the crisis of political legitimacy among the nascent political parties of the early Islamic polity is highlighted, exposed and resolved in Ṭūs.[25] Tamīm's defeat in Ṭūs epitomizes the Umayyad defeat in Khurāsān, as Ḥumayd's victory signals the ʿAbbāsid takeover of power in the region. Islamic historiography's treatment of Ṭūs as the central site of the Umayyad-ʿAbbāsid struggle in Khurāsān is highly emblematic. Like the emphasis that the *futūḥ* narratives put on Ṭūs and the figures of the *kanārang* and ʿAbdallāh b. ʿĀmir, it highlights the structural properties of the Islamic historical narratives.

Till Death Do Us Apart: The Caliph and the Imām: Post-Mortem rivalry in Ṭūs

Ḥumayd b. Qaḥṭaba's victory in Ṭūs provides the structural link for the reemergence of the region in the subsequent history of Khurāsān around three quarters of a century later. In 3 Jumādā II 193 (March 24, 809) Hārūn al-Rashīd dies in Ṭūs. Only a decade later, in 203/818, the eighth Shīʿite Imām

Riḍā dies in the same territory. As with the span of close to a century that separated the period of the conquest from that of the ʿAbbāsid revolution, the time span between this latter and the death and burial of Hārūn and Riḍā in Ṭūs is devoid of any substantial narrational content. The only tacit link is contained in the very brief narratives that detail the death of these two important Islamic figures in Ṭūs.

Hārūn and Riḍā's death and burial in Ṭūs is naturally contained in most classical narratives. Al-Ṭabarī provides the following narrative on the death of Hārūn:

> A certain authority has mentioned that, when his [i.e. Hārūn al-Rashīd's] illness became severe, he gave orders for his grave, and it was dug in one spot of the residence where he was lodging, in a place called al-Muthaqqab in the residence of Ḥumayd b. Abī Ghānim al-Ṭāʾī . . . [26]

With slight variations the same information occurs in Balʿamī,[27] al-Maqdisī,[28] al-Dīnawarī,[29] and al-Kūfī.[30] We are told that Hārūn and Riḍā come to be buried in Ṭūs because Ḥumayd b. Qaḥṭaba chooses his residence at Ṭūs. This purported palace of Ḥumayd becomes a "royal" edifice where high-ranking ʿAbbāsid officials take up residence, and forms the only causal explanation provided for the death of these dignitaries of all places in Ṭūs, not say in Nishapur and Marw which "logically" might be considered as more "natural" choices. The "residence in Ṭūs" is also the subject of a long poem inserted by al-Ṭabarī immediately after his narrative on the murder of al-Amīn.[31]

It might be pointed out here that while the narratives of the death of Hārūn and Riḍā in Ṭūs do not exhibit the same sort of structural characteristic which we find in those of the early Islamic conquests and that of the ʿAbbāsid revolution, they, nevertheless, betray similar symbolic traits. Whereas the *futūḥ* narratives of Ṭūs serve to illustrate the transition of political authority in Khurāsān from pre-Islamic Iranian to post-Islamic Arab polities as personified in the figures of the *kanārang* and ʿAbdallāh b. ʿĀmir, and that of the ʿAbbāsid revolution lays out the ʿAbbāsid-Umayyad struggle for legitimacy as embodied in the figures of Tamīm b. Naṣr and Ḥumayd b. Qaḥṭaba, the juxtaposition of Hārūn and Riḍā underlies the tension between the Caliphate and the Imāmat. In fact the issue of legitimacy is most acute here.

If tacit in Islamic historiography, this transfer of legitimacy from the ʿAbbāsids to the Shīʿites in Ṭūs is most clearly illustrated in one of the canons of Shīʿite historiography, the *ʿUyūn al-Akhbār al-Riḍā* of Ibn Bābūya al-Qumī. It should be observed at the outset that the *ʿUyūn* provides a literary genre unto itself. The whole conceptual and ideological underpinning of the work was meant to legitimize twelver Shīʿite history. The source in question, in other words, did not partake in the repertoire of classical Islamic historiography. It therefore provides for us an independent text, "outside the bounds of the ancient historical tradition" through "which we can try to control it . . ."[32]

What underlines the determinative role of Ṭūs in typifying issues of legitimacy in the structure of early Islamic narratives as well as that of Shīʿite historiography is the concurrent focus on one and the same person(s). For clear reasons Ṭūs assumes center stage in the narrative of *ʿUyūn al-Akhbār al-Riḍā*. The protagonist of its hagiography died in its territory. Together with Ṭūs, however—once again—the central figure through whom the Umayyad-ʿAbbāsid struggle is translated into the Caliphate-Imāmat one is the person of Ḥumayd b. Qaḥṭaba. In Ibn Bābūya's *ʿUyūn al-Akhbār* this tension over legitimate political authority is most clearly illustrated in the section titled "On mentioning those of the Prophet's descendants who were murdered in one night by Hārūn al-Rashīd." The narrative recounts the course of events in Ṭūs as told by Ḥumayd b. Qaḥṭaba al-Ṭāʾī al-Ṭūsī.[33]

> He said: 'one night, when Hārūn was in Ṭūs, he sent someone [asking] me to go to . . . him [Hārūn]. When I went to him, I saw [him sitting,] in front of him a burning candle and a green sword. In front of him a servant was standing. He raised his head and said: "What is the nature of your obeisance to the Amīr al-Muʾmenīn? (*keyfa ṭā ʿatuka lī Amīr al-Muʾminīn*). I said: "with my soul, and wealth, I obey." (*bi-lʾnafs waʾl-māl*) He brought his head down and gave me permission to leave . . .

In the narrative this episode is repeated two more times, at which point Hārūn

> . . . laughed and said: "take this sword and do as this servant tells you." The servant gave the sword to me and . . . took me to the door of a house which was shut. I opened the door and saw a well in the middle of the house, and inside the house three [more] houses, the doors of which were closed. So I opened the door of one of the houses. I saw twenty people in the house, some of whom were old, some in their mid-life and some young. All had braided hair. Their heads were not shaven. All were in captivity (*muqayyadūn*). The servant told me: "Amīr al-Muʾmenīn has ordered you to kill these [people]. They are all ʿAlawīs, descendants of ʿAlī and Fātima, and they are in captivity here. Then he brought them out, one by one, and I decapitated them . . . [34]

This episode is likewise repeated three times in the course of which Ḥumayd b. Qaḥṭaba kills a total of 60 of the Prophet's descendents. In the final episode, the last ʿAlid awaiting death at the hands of Ḥumayd warns him: "Woe unto you, for you are a sinner. . . . What excuse are you going to have in front of our ancestor, the Prophet of God, at the Day of Judgment, for you have murdered sixty of his offspring, all of whom were the descendants of ʿAlī and Fātima?" Ḥumayd recounts that it was while trembling that he joined the aged, long-haired ʿAlid, to the rest of his kindred.[35]

Ḥumayd b. Qaḥṭaba's allegiance to the ʿAbbāsids is here spelled out in dramatic form through his compliance to the wishes of Hārūn and his subsequent murder of sixty ʿAlawīs. Now Ḥumayd b. Qaḥṭaba had died in 159/776. Hārūn died more than a quarter of century later in 193/809. That Hārūn is depicted as the culprit for murdering the Shīʿites in Khurāsān—even if the veracity of this information were to be admitted—while he was sojourning in the house of Ḥumayd b. Qaḥṭaba in Ṭūs could potentially have a narrational logic. That Ḥumayd b. Qaḥṭaba was the instrument for effecting the mass murder, taking his orders from Hārūn personally, however, is beyond any logic. The anachronistic juxtaposition of Ḥumayd and Hārūn, in the context of the murder of sixty Alawīs, is here meant to highlight the contention for religio-political legitimacy, as depicted through the actions of an ʿAbbāsid revolutionary figure, between the ʿAbbāsids and the Shīʿītes. In the finale of the narrative there remains an ambivalence towards Ḥumayd's allegiance to the ʿAbbāsids. Ḥumayd recounts these events while weeping. He is depicted as swaying between repentance and resignation to his sin.

Lest there remain any doubt about Ḥumayd's potential Shīʿite sympathies, the *ʿUyūn* clarifies these in a subsequent narrative, this time through his association with ʿAlī b. Mūsā al-Riḍā.

> Muḥammad b. Mūsā . . . said: "I heard from ʿAlī b. Ibrāhīm b. Hāshim who heard from his father, who heard from Yāsir al-Khādim, who said: "when Abūʾl-Ḥasan ʿAlī b. Mūsā al-Riḍā came to (*nazala*) the castle of Ḥumayd b. Qaḥṭaba, he took off his clothes and gave them to Ḥumayd. Ḥumayd took the clothes and gave them to his servant [in order to be washed]. After a while the servant came back holding a letter (*ruqʿa*) which she gave to Ḥumayd and said that she had found it in ʿAlī b. Mūsā al-Riḍā's pocket . . . Ḥumayd said, I said to . . . Riḍā: "Sir . . . the servant has found a letter in your pocket. What is it? . . . Riḍā said: it is an amulet (*ʿawdha*) which I never leave behind. I said: . . . Acquaint me with it [s] contents. He said it is a charm which will protect anyone who

> carries it . . . Calamity will be warded off from him . . . And he will be protected from Satan . . . [36]

In Shīʿite historiography Ḥumayd is clearly used to barter issues of legitimacy between the ʿAbbāsids and the Shīʿites. If Ḥumayd needs to be juxtaposed with Hārūn to cast skepticism on the intentions and motives of the ʿAbbāsid *daʿwa,* he needs to be amicably associated with Riḍā in order to illuminate the course of a revolution gone astray. Here, he is depicted as not only providing hospitality to the eighth "martyred" Imām, but soliciting religious instruction—by gaining knowledge of the contents of an amulet—from him. Riḍā died in Ṭūs in 203/818. Again, no feasible connection between Ḥumayd and Riḍā could have existed in reality.

Yet an echo of this imaginary connection between Ḥumayd and Riḍā has been sustained, elaborated, and transmitted into modern Shīʿite historiography. The author of one of the most authoritative modern sources on the life of al-Riḍā renders this connection in the following narrative:

> I heard from Mr. Faqīh Sabsivārī, the keeper of the holy shrine that the *ḥadīth* have it that when . . . Imām Riḍā reached this territory [i.e. Ṭūs], he sat down in one of the corners of the garden [i.e. the garden of the estate of Ḥumayd] to rest a while. As was his usual habit when he was alone, he brought out a Qur'ān, written in his own hand, and [started] reciting it. Ḥumayd b. Qaḥṭaba came. He saw the Qur'ān and became interested. He asked: "In whose handwriting is this Qur'ān?" Imām Riḍā said: "It is my own writing . . ." Ḥumayd said: "Sell me this Qur'ān." Imām Riḍā said: "I will, in return for the garden that you have." Ḥumayd accepted [the offer] and sold the garden for the price of the Qur'ān and obtained the Qur'ān. That same night Imām Riḍā ordered the trees [of the garden] to be cut. For this reason they call that place *qatʿgāh*. In the morning Ḥumayd came [and said:] "I am not willing to trade. He [Imām Riḍā] said: "If a garden remains, you may take it and return the Qur'ān." When he [Ḥumayd] sent [someone to check], he saw that all its trees have been cut. He agreed and accepted the Qur'ān and the land came under the ownership of the *ḥaḍrat* . . . [37]

The castle and the land of the ʿAbbāsid general, Ḥumayd b. Qaḥṭaba, in Ṭūs becomes the mechanism through which the legitimacy of the transfer of religio-political authority from the ʿAbbāsids to the Shīʿīs is finally decided upon and effected. A Qur'ān is bartered in place of the land, with Ḥumayd as the ultimately unwilling partner in the exchange. The very ethnic identity of Ḥumayd goes through a metamorphosis in this historiography. Ḥumayd b. Qaḥṭaba becomes an Iranian *mawla*, one of whose ancestors had become a captive of the tribe of Banī Ṭayy in Khurāsān at the time of the conquest of the region in the mid-seventh century.[38] But Ḥumayd serves the emblematic function expected of him. From Ḥumayd to Riḍā, through the castle of the former in Ṭūs, legitimacy is transferred from the Caliphate to the Imāmat, even while Ḥumayd retains his ambivalent role in Shīʿite historiography.

Contesting Views of History: The ʿAjam vs. the Arab and Shāhnāma Production in Ṭūs

In the tenth century Ṭūs becomes the most prolific center for the production of the "national" Iranian historiographical literature in the form of the *Shāhnāma*.[39] The possible causal explanations that can account for the systematic production of this genre in Ṭūs, and what connections can possibly exist between the issues considered here and this literary activity is beyond the scope of the present study and has been dealt with elsewhere.[40] For the purposes of the present study we will be concerned with the ways in which two of the most canonical and extant versions of this genre have incorporated in their texts information relevant to the transitional periods under consideration. The two works in question are the "Introduction" to the prose *Shāhnāma*, known as the *Shāhnāma-i Abū Manṣūrī*, composed in Ṭūs (circa 346/957) by Abū Manṣūr al-Muʿamerī,[41] and the *Shāhnāma* of Abolqāsim Ferdowsī.[42]

A number of observations about the nature of information contained in these sources are warranted at the outset. To begin with, while much has been said about the inefficacy of the *Shāhnāma* of Ferdowsī as a source for reconstructing the pre-Islamic history of Iran, it must be borne in mind that this criticism does not pertain to the Sasanid sections of the work, comprising the last quarter of the opus.[43] As we shall see, the narrative of the last years of Sasanid rule, and the flight of Yazdgird III to Khurāsān, in particular, contain a very important core of data which not only adds substantially to our efforts in reconstructing the late Sasanid history and early Arab conquest of the region, but seems to hint to the existence of a "native" Khurāsānid tradition about the aforementioned events.

Closely related to the issue of the historicity of this material is the question of the nature of sources that informed the production of the *Shāhnāma*.[44] It is generally agreed that the *Shāhnāma* partakes in both an oral as well as a textual pre-Islamic Iranian tradition, although some have cast doubt on the strength or even the existence of a textual tradition for the *Shāhnāma*.[45] While the mode of transmission of this pre-Islamic Iranian textual tradition—known as the *Khwādāy-Nāmag*, or the "Book of Kings,"[46]—into the Islamic period has been the subject of debate, its existence can be said to have been established beyond any doubt. Much of what we know of the pre-Islamic history of Iran—transmitted to us not only through the *Shāhnāma*, but also in the corpus of early Islamic historiography, seems to have been grounded in the information contained in this same pre-Islamic Iranian historiographical tradition. In fact the discrepancies in the narratives of various *Islamic* histories about crucial episodes in both the legendary and the "semi-historical" history of pre-Islamic Iran, as well as that between some of these accounts and that contained in the *Shāhnāma* seems to have been caused by the fact that no "original" stemma of the *Khwādāy-Nāmag* seems to have existed in the late Sasanid period. At any rate it is important to underline the fact that the Iranian historiographical tradition under consideration here took shape completely independently of the Islamic historiographical tradition. When in 346/957–8 Abū Manṣūr Muḥammad b. ʿAbd al-Razzāq commissioned Abū Manṣūr Muʿamerī to translate the "Book of Kings" from its original Pahlavi into modern Persian, it was four Zoroastrians who were charged with undertaking the task under the supervision of Muʿamerī. As Nöldeke observes, "only Zoroastrians could have been able to read the Pahlavi books, which had to serve as authority."[47] Ferdowsī seems to have used this prose *Shāhnāma* for composing his *opus*. The question that remains to be answered is the following: How have the transitional junctures under consideration here been depicted in the *Shāhnāma*?

The first narrative under consideration is contained in the last sections of the *Shāhnāma* where the Sasanid history of Iran is given in predominantly "factual" terms. The closing pages of this section depict the course of events in the final days of the last Sasanid king, Yazdgird III (632–651). Briefly and in broad outline the *Shāhnāma* provides us with the following information in this narrative: After his defeat by the Arab armies, Yazdgird III is in a fix. His royal capitals in the west, Ctesiphon and Istakhr, have fallen into enemy hands and the king himself is now in search of a refuge.[48] His chief commander, Farrukhzād, advises him to flee to Ṭabaristān. Yazdgird forgoes Farrukhzād's advice and opts for Khurāsān instead, arguing with Farrukhzād that in Khurāsān he is ensured of the protection of the *marzbāns* of the region who have a reputation for bravery and warfare.[49]

According to Ferdowsī, in his search for help Yazdgird writes two letters to his officials in the East. The first letter, nine couplets in total, is said to have been written to Māhūy, the *marzbān* of Marv.[50] It is curt and descriptive and is preceded by a very slanderous depiction of the Māhūy.[51] The second letter is written to no other than the *kanārang* of Ṭūs. This letter, 83 couplets in total, has an extremely affective tone.[52] It is wrought with apocalyptic fervor depicting the end of the world. In fact, it is one of the only two sections of the *Shāhnāma* in which the pre-Islamic Zoroastrian apocalyptic tradition has obviously been incorporated.[53] Yet, it contains information of great interest.

In this foreboding letter the king requests the help of the *kanārangiyān* of Ṭūs, who in Ferdowsī's rendition—and in contrast to the poet's depiction of Māhūy—assume all the normative conditions of royalty.[54] Here Yazdgird informs the *kanārang* that, after consulting with his advisors and sending reconnaissance dispatches to various parts of his realm, he has decided that small fortresses cannot accommodate his large army and therefore he is heading towards the realm under the control of the *kanārangiyān* in Ṭūs. Ṭūs, he maintains, will protect him both from the Arabs on his trail as well as the Turks. As I have argued elsewhere, there are clear topographic and sound strategic reasons behind this choice. Be this at it may, we next come to a rather detailed description of the actions to be taken until the king's arrival. The letter ends by exalting the *kanārang*'s family and reminding them of their prior exhibitions of loyalty in the dynasty's times of need. The *kanārang* and his family are clearly the focus of the larger part of this narrative. In spite of this, and significantly, however, the *kanārang*'s response to Yazdgird is absent from Ferdowsī's narrative. While we are informed of the circumstances of the ultimate death of the Sasanid king, in his omission of the *kanārang*'s response, Ferdowsī leaves a lacuna in his narrative.

It is through Abū Manṣūr al-Thaʿālibī's *Ghurar* that this gap is filled. Thaʿālibī, who was a contemporary of Ferdowsī, composed his work around 1019 C.E. He is one of the Muslim historians who seem to have used the *Khwādāy Nāmag* and other Sasanid works extensively. His work contains information that closely follows the *Shāhnāma* in "minor details . . . in its account of events [and] even in many rhetorical modes of expression."[55] It has been argued, therefore, that the author's source must have been either the same used by Ferdowsī, or one closely related to it.[56]

Thaʿālibī gives the following account of Yazdgird's correspondence with the *kanārang* of Ṭūs.

> [Yazdgird] went to [Ṭabaristān]. This was in the time of the caliphate of ʿUthmān ibn ʿAffān (may God be pleased with him). In those times ʿAbdallāh ibn ʿĀmir ibn Kurayz and Aḥnaf ibn Qays had invaded the environs of Ṭabaristān. When Yazdgird reached Nīshāpūr he was, on

> the one hand, fearful of the Arabs, and on the other, apprehensive of the Turks. He did not trust the walls (*ḥiṣār*) of Nīshāpūr and its fortification (*dizh*). He had heard (the description) of the strength and sturdiness of the fortifications of Ṭūs. He [therefore] sent someone to acquaint himself with the situation there. The *marzbān* of Ṭūs, *kanārang*, was not pleased with the possibility of his [Yazdgird's] arrival. He [therefore] gave directions to a remote fortress and, together with presents, sent the envoy back. He [asked the messenger to tell Yazdgird that] it [Ṭūs] has a small fortress that did not meet the needs of him and his entourage.[57]

Whether Ferdowsī consciously omitted the *kanārang*'s response from his account, or whether the information was simply not contained in his source, but existed in that of Thaʿālibī, cannot be determined satisfactorily. Whatever the case, Thaʿālibī's account of the *kanārang*'s response furnishes not only a logical response to Yazdgird's demand for refuge, but also sheds light on the different sets of information provided in the *futūḥ* narratives. It is most significant for our purposes that the account of Yazdgird's correspondence with the *kanārang*, found in the *Shāhnāma* and the *Ghurar*, is not found in any of the *futūḥ* narratives, which concentrate on the *kanārang*'s actions vis-à-vis the Arab army and ʿAbdallāh b. Āmir. This contrasting informational emphasis is itself a reflection of the different sources used by the respective historiographies. The information contained in the *futūḥ* narratives belongs to the Arabo-Islamic tradition with all the normative and compositional characteristics that this entailed. The story found in the *Shāhnāma* and *Ghurār* seems to have its source, in part, in a combination of oral and written pre-Islamic Iranian historical tradition. Ferdowsī ends his work with the last days of the Sasanid king, and for obvious reasons stops short of recounting the Arab takeover of the Sasanid polity. That he must have had access to traditions concerning the Arab conquest of Khurāsān seems to be borne out by the information contained in the second Iranian historiographical source under study here, the *Shāhnāma-i Abū Manṣūrī*.

In the "Introduction" to the *Shāhnāma-i Abū Manṣūr*, Muʿamerī, the author of the work, begins by informing us of the circumstances through which the king, or *pādishāh* of Ṭūs, that is Muḥammad b. ʿAbdalrazzāq, had instructed him to compose the prose work of the *Shāhnāma*.[58] In this narrative Muḥammad b. ʿAbdalrazzāq[59]—the patron of the work who played a significant part in the dynastic struggles of the Sāmānid realm during the mid-tenth century—assumes all the paraphernalia of kingship: kingly glory (*farr*), regal ancestry (*nizhadi bozorg*), as well as the accouterments of kingship (*dastgahi tamām az pādishāhi*.) Shortly thereafter Mu'ameri takes the opportunity to trace the lineage of himself as well as Muḥammad b. 'Abdalrazzāq.

Here Mu'ameri traces the ancestry of his patron[60] as well as himself not only to the Sasanids, but more specifically, to the person of the *kanārang* and his family, the *kanārangiyān*. In the narrative that follows immediately afterwards, there is a detailed story relating the circumstances through which Khusrow Parvīz (591–628), the Sasanid king, gave control of Ṭūs and Nishapur to the *kanārang*.[61] Following this comes the narrative on the Arab conquest of Khurāsān and the part played by the *kanārang* in this.

> When ʿUmar ibn al-Khaṭṭāb sent ʿAbdallāh ibn ʿĀmir to call people to the religion of Muḥammad (Peace be upon Him and his Family), *kanārang* sent his son to Nīshāpūr to welcome him; and people were in the old fortress and did not obey. He [ʿAbdallāh ibn ʿĀmir?] asked his [*kanārang*'s son's?] help. He helped so affairs were set in order. Then he [ʿAbdallāh ibn ʿĀmir ?] asked for a loan of a thousand dirhams. Then he [ʿAbdallāh ibn ʿĀmir] asked for hostages (*girowgān*); [*kanārang*] said that he didn't have any. So he [ʿAbdallāh ibn ʿĀmir] asked for Nīshāpūr. He [*kanārang*] gave him Nīshāpūr. When he [ʿAbdallāh ibn ʿĀmir] took the money, he [ʿAbdallāh ibn ʿĀmir] gave it [Nīshāpūr] back. ʿAbdallāh ibn ʿĀmir gave him the war (*ān ḥarb ū rā dād*) and *kanārang* fought him (?). And the story remains that Ṭūs belongs to so and so who holds Nīshāpūr as a hostage.[62]

The Persian text of the "Introduction" which contains this information was edited, based on nine extant manuscripts, by Qazvini. Nevertheless, its language remains extremely unclear and confusing. Due to the constant use of the third person Persian pronoun (ū), it is rarely clear who is undertaking which action. The language of this particular narrative, however, is the same as the rest of the text: one of our first examples of archaic modern Persian prose, devoid of almost any Arabic words. At the same time, the narrative contains the same set of information as that contained in the *futūḥ*, even in its retention of unclear elements in the chronology, the issue of *ṣulḥan/ʿanwatan*, and finally the question of what the *kanārang* received in exchange for his aid to the conquerors. It is hard at this point to determine the purview of the source(s?) of the "Introduction." Some familiarity with the rendition of events as contained in the *futūḥ* narratives seems plausible. As the agenda of the patron of the work, Muḥammad b. ʿAbd al-Razzāq, involved an effort at establishing the historicity of his "family's" claim to Nishapur, it might be even argued that the segments of the *futūḥ* narratives were used in such a way as to substantiate this claim. For our purposes what is of utmost significance in Muʿamerī's narrative is not its rendition of the account of the conquest, but its claim as to the terminus of the rule of the *kanārangiyān* family over the land. Immediately after the narrative of conquest, Muʿamerī provides us with the following information: "Ṭūs always belonged to the *kanārangiyān* until the time of Ḥumayd-i Ṭā'ī who took it away from them. And rule passed to another lineage (*ān mihtarī bi dīgarī dūdhih oftād*) . . ."

One of the outstanding features of this narrative is the way in which it underscores the role of Ḥumayd-Ṭā'ī, without prior contextual reference, and unexpectedly so. "Ṭūs always belonged to the Kanārangiyān until the time of Ḥumayd-Ṭā'ī who took it away from them." In Muʿamerī's narrative Ḥumayd b. Qaḥṭaba is the figure through whom the continuity of the Sasanid line is broken, and the pre-Islamic section of genealogy is transferred to the Islamic, "*ān mihtarī bi dīgarī dūdhih oftād.*" It is important to observe here that the transfer of power from a pre-Islamic polity to an Islamic one in Muʿamerī's narrative does not take place in the period of conquest, but at the inception of ʿAbbāsid rule in Khurāsān. Likewise, as in Islamic historiography's narrative on the ʿAbbāsid-Umayyad struggle in Ṭūs, and like the Shīʿite historiography's focus on the Caliphate-Imāmat strife in the region, so in the Iranian historiography's explication of the pre-Islamic/Islamic contention for power in Ṭūs, the personage of Ḥumayd b. Qaḥṭaba is highlighted as the connecting link for the transfer of legitimacy.

Conclusion

In the narratives of the Islamic, Shīʿite and Iranian historiographies thus far considered issues of legitimacy in Khurāsān are bartered in Ṭūs. Invariably, Ṭūs becomes the matrix through which the crisis of political legitimacy is articulated, played out, and resolved. This emblematic assignation of issues of legitimacy to Ṭūs and the significant political personae connected with it seems to betray an *a priori* and sanctioned connection of the region with legitimate political power in Khurāsān. This connection is never explicitly stated in the narratives that have been considered so far and is conveniently obscured in the general mainstream narratives of Islamic historiography. Elsewhere I have argued that the center of political power in "Inner Khurāsān" during the Sasanid period was in fact the region of Ṭūs, and not as hitherto generally assumed, that of Nishapur. This proposition is an unfamiliar one due to the

Nishapur-centered bias of our Islamic sources, most of which were written at a time when the city had become the provincial economic, political and cultural center of Khurāsān. It is a reflection of the limitations of particular historiographical genres that Ṭūs's prior political centrality, subsumed in the narratives thus far considered, is most forcefully articulated in an account that we have in a geographical treatise, the *Aḥsan al-Taqāsīm* of the tenth century geographer, Shams al-Dīn al-Maqdisī:

> If one says: 'Hasn't Nīshāpūr taken the place of Ṭūs?' It will be said: 'Ṭūs was never a center to be abandoned. If it be said: 'If you deny the abandonment of Ṭūs, [will you also deny that of] Marv, which surely has taken place?' I will say: We have said that with Islam, some cities took the place of others; and Nīshāpūr substituted Marv!'[63]

Al-Maqdisī is hard-pressed to acknowledge the position of Ṭūs as a provincial center prior to Nishapur, and refuses to admit its veracity, all the while informing us of the prevalence of this view among his audience.

The pre-Islamic history of Ṭūs is shrouded in obscurity. There is substantial evidence, however, that the role of Ṭūs as the provincial capital of "Inner Khurāsān" harks back to remote Achaemenid times when the region was the seat of the Empire's satrapy in Khurāsān.[64] There is enough evidence too that points to Ṭūs as one of the pre-eminent religious centers of the region in the Parthian and the Sasanid periods.[65] An investigation into these aspects of the region's pre-Islamic history is beyond the concerns of the present study and has been undertaken elsewhere. Suffice it to say that a view of the region that strives to integrate its pre-Islamic history with the course of its history during the Islamic period will better be able to account for the systematic and rigorous *Shāhnāma* production in the city in the tenth century, as well as the role it assumed as a Shīʿite center in later centuries.

Were we to grant a significant pre-Islamic past to the region the symbolic functions it assumes in postulating issues of legitimacy can be explicated more readily. Later historiographies seem to have appropriated the pre-Islamic past of the city. It seems to be a result of this symbolic historiographical displacement that Islamic historiography appropriates the pre-Islamic political history of Ṭūs and the inception of Islamic history of Khurāsān takes place through this territory. Similarly it seems to be due to this same historiographical mechanism that the person of the *kanārang* of Ṭūs assumes such a symbolically significant role in the narratives of Islamic historiography. Through a direct connection with the *kanārang* of Ṭūs Islamic historiography also seizes the region's pre-Islamic history. It is significant that the *kanārang* maintains his symbolic role even in the Iranian "national" historiographical memory and in his juxtaposition with Yazdgird, the last king of the pre-Islamic Sasanid polity. It is, likewise, due to the same reasons that in the narrative of Islamic historiography the most decisive battle in the Umayyad-ʿAbbasid bid for supremacy in Khurāsān is waged in Ṭūs and the Caliphate-Imāmat contention for power is played out through the region. Ḥumayd assumes center stage in a number of narratives, perhaps most significantly in that of the *Shāhnāma-i Abū Manṣūrī*. Various prominent historical personas thus become the adversaries through whom the contention for legitimate political power is waged in these narratives. The *kanārang*, ʿAbdallāh b. Āmir, Yazdgird, Ṭamīm b. Naṣr, Ḥumayd b. Qaḥṭaba and finally Hārūn and Riḍā, fight a war in the symbolic realms of the narrative that are as poignant as their real life struggles in remote history.

Endnotes

1. Chief among these recent endeavors is that of Albreth Noth in collaboration with Lawrence Conrad, *The Early Arabic Historical Tradition: A Source Critical Study*, translated by Michael Bonner, second edition, Princeton, 1994. Source critical studies of early Islamic history have, of course, a long tradition behind them. For an assessment of the state of the field see Chase F. Robinson, "The Study of Islamic Historiography: A Progress Report," JRAS (1997) , series 3,7, 2, pp. 199–227. Also see, Fred Donner, *Narratives of Islamic Origin: The Beginnings of Islamic Historical Writing*. Princeton, 1998.

2. See, in particular, Lawrence I. Conrad, "The Conquest of Arwād: A Source Critical Study in the Historiography of the Early Medieval Near East," in *The Byzantine and Early Islamic Near East (I): Problems in the Literary Source Material*. Edited by A. Cameron and L. I. Conrad, Princeton, 1992; Ibid, "Al-Azdī's History of the Arab Conquests in Bilād al-Shām: Some Historiographical Considerations," in *Proceedings of the Second Symposium on the History of Bilād al-Shām during the Early Islamic Period up to 40 AH/ 640 AD*. Edited by Muḥammad ʿAdnān al-Bakhīt and Muḥammad ʿAṣfūr, Amman, 1987.

3. Martin Hinds, "The First Arab Conquests in Fārs," *Iran: Journal of the British Institute of Persian Studies*, vol. XXII, 1984, pp. 39–55, reprinted in *Studies in Early Islamic History*, eds. Jere Bacharach, Lawrence I. Conrad and Patricia Crone, with an introduction by G.R. Hawting, Princeton, 1966, pp. 199-231.

4. Aḥmad ibn Yaḥyā al-Balādhurī, *Kitāb Futūḥ al-Buldān*. M. J. de Goeje edited, Leiden, 1866, p. 334; Ibn al-Faqīh al-Hamadānī, *Kitāb al-Buldān*. M. J. de Goeje

edited, Leiden, 1885, p. 307; Aḥmad b. Muḥammad Aʿtham al-Kūfī, *al-Futūḥ*, Beirut, 1986, 8 vols., vol. I, p. 338; Aḥmad ibn Abī Yaʿqūb, *al-Buldān*. Gaston Wiet translated, Cairo, 1937, p. 114; Muḥammad b. Jarīr al-Ṭabarī, *The History of al-Ṭabarī*, vol. XV, *The Crisis of Early Caliphate: The Reign of ʿUthmān*. Translated and annotated by Stephen Humphreys, New York, 1990, p. 91; Abu'l Faḍl al-Balʿamī, *Tā'rīkhnāma-i Ṭabarī*, edited by Muhammad Rowshan, vol. II., Tehran, 1366/1987, p. 589. Abū Manṣūr al-Thaʿālibī, *Ghurar Akhbār Mulūk al-Furs wa Sīyarihim*. N. Zotenberg edited, Paris, 1900, p. 743; Khalīfat b. Khayyāṭ, *Ta'rīkh Khalīfat b. Khayyāṭ*, second edition, Beirut, 1397/1977, pp. 164–65; Shams al-Dīn al-Maqdisī, *Kitāb al-Bad' wa'l-Ta'rīkh*. Edited and translated by C. Huart, Paris, 1899-1919, vol. V, p. 195; Abū ʿAbdallāh Ḥākim al-Nīshāpūrī, *Ta'rīkh Nīshāpūr*. Edited and annotated by M. Shafiʿi Kadkani , Tehran, 1375. Also see Muʿīn al-Dīn Muḥammad Isfazārī, *Rawḍāt al-Jannāt fī Owṣāf Madīnat al-Harāt*. Seyyed Muhammad Kazim Imam edited, Tehran, 1338, vol. I, pp. 248–49.

5. Yaʿqūbī, *al-Buldān*, p. 114.
6. Richard Frye edited, *The Histories of Nishapur*, the Hague, 1965, folio 61.
7. al-Ṭabarī, *Ta'rīkh*, pp. 2156–57.
8. al-Kūfī, *Futūḥ*, tr. Aḥmad b. Muḥammad Mustuwfī al-Ḥirawī, 1300/1800, Tehran, p. 115.
9. Khalīfat b. Khayyāṭ, *Ta'rīkh*, pp. 164–65.
10. Ibn al-Faqīh, *al-Buldān*, p. 307.
11. Yaʿqūbī, *al-Buldān*, p. 114.
12. *The Histories of Nishapur*, folios 60–61.
13. There is the issue of whether or not Ṭūs and Nishapur were finally conquered *sulḥan* or *ʿanwatan*, for which see Khalīfat b. Khayyāṭ, *Ta'rīkh*, pp. 164–65. Al-Ḥākim Nīshāpūrī's *Ta'rīkh-i Nīshāpūr*, Kadkani edited, pp. 202–207. The matter of the chronology of the conquest remains equally unsettled. While the question of chronology cannot be settled with any degree of certainty, the comparative examination of various narratives makes it highly probable that it was, in fact, through two campaigns and not one that Khurāsān was finally conquered. See P. Pourshariati, "Local Histories of Khurāsān and the Pattern of Arab Settlement," *Studia Iranica*, Tome 27:1, 1998, pp. 41–81.
14. Yaʿqūbī composed *al-Buldān* in 278/892. He apparently spent most of his time in the Tahirid (205–261/821–875) court at Khurāsān, presumably at the newly established Tahirid capital at Nishapur. For the implications of this on the nature of Yaʿqūbī's work, see Hugh Kennedy, *The Early ʿAbbāsid Caliphate: A Political History*, London, 1981, p. 216.
15. Yaʿqūbī, *al-Buldān*, p. 114.
16. For a discussion of the role of the Qaḥṭaba family in the initial period of ʿAbbāsid rule see Jacob Lassner, *The Shaping of ʿAbbasid Rule*, Princeton, 1980, p. 105.
17. Stefen Leder, "The Literary Use of *Khabar*: A Basic Form of Historical Writing," in A. Cameron and L. I. Conrad, *The Byzantine and Early Islamic Near East (I):*

Problems in the Literary Source Material, pp. 277–315, here pp. 309–10. Until recently, the geography and topography of the ʿAbbāsid revolution have not been the subject of any serious investigation, and critical studies of the history of Khurāsān in the post-conquest century lacked the sort of investigation of this set of data conducted for other parts of the Islamic lands. In this connection see the author's chapter on "Topography and Geography and the Pattern of Arab Settlement," in "Iranian Tradition in Ṭūs and Arab Presence in Khurāsān," Ph.D. Dissertation, Columbia University, 1995, pp. 110–55. For investigations of topography in the study of early Islamic history of Mesopotamia see in particular Fred McGraw Donner, *The Early Islamic Conquests*, Princeton, 1981, and Michael G. Morony, *Iraq After the Muslim Conquest*, Princeton, 1984.

18. *Kitāb al-ʿUyūn w ʾal-Ḥadāʾiq fī Akhbār-i ʾl-Ḥaqāʾiq*, anon., ed. de Goeje, Leiden, 1869, pp. 191–93.

19. See, among others, al-Ṭabarī, *The History of al-Ṭabarī: The Abbasid Revolution: A.D. 743–750/A.H. 126–132*, vol. XXVII, John Alden Williams translated and annotated, Albany, 1985, 107–108; al-Balʿamī, *Tāʾrīkhnāma-i Ṭabarī*, p. 1016; Anonymous, *Akhbār-al Dowlat al-ʿAbbāsiyya wa fīhī Akhbār-i ʿl-ʿAbbās*, ʿAbdalaziz al-Duri edited, Beirut, 1972, pp. 323–26; Abū Ḥanīfa al-Dīnawarī, *Akhbār al-Ṭiwāl*. Edited by ʿAbd al-Muʾnim ʿAmir & Gamal al-Din al-Shayyal, Cairo, 1960, pp. 362–64; Khalīfat b. Khayyāṭ, *Taʾrīkh*, p. 390; *ʿUyūn wʾal-Ḥadāʾiq*, pp. 191–93; al-Maqdisī, *Kitāb al-Badʾ*, vol. 6, pp. 64–5; Also see Isfazārī, *Rawḍāt al-Jannāt*, vol. I, pp. 185–86.

20. Anonymous, *Akhbār-i Dowlat al-ʿAbbāsiyya*, ibid.

21. Ibid., 327.

22. Khalīfat b. Khayyāṭ, *Taʾrīkh*, p. 390.

23. Yaʿqūbī, *Taʾrīkh*, ed. M. T. Houtsma. Leiden, 1883, vol. II, pp. 356–57.

24 Moshe Sharons argues that Nishapur's lack of support for the ʿAbbāsid movement was caused by the specifically Hāshimiyya sympathies of its inhabitants, which explains the existence of the above tradition. See M. Sharon, *Black Banners from the East: The Establishment of the ʿAbbāsid State—Incubation of a Revolt*, Leiden, 1983. For a refutation of this argument see the author's chapter "Contemporary Historiography: Arab Settlement and the ʿAbbāsid Revolution," in Pourshariati, "Iranian Tradition in Ṭūs and the Arab Presence in Khurāsān," especially pp. 96–110.

25. For the significance of battle scenes in symbolizing issues of legitimacy see M. Waldman, *Toward a Theory of Historical Narrative: A Case Study in Perso-Islamicate Historiography*, Columbus, 1980, p. 12.

26. al-Ṭabarī, *The History of al-Ṭabarī: The War between Brothers*, vol. XXXI, Michael Fishbein translated and annotated, Albany, 1992, pp. 310–12.

27. al-Balʿamī, *Tāʾrīkhnāma-i Ṭabarī*, vol. II, p. 1209.

28. al-Maqdisī, *Kitāb al-Badʾ*, vol. 6., p. 107.

29. al-Dīnawarī, *Akhbār al-Ṭiwāl*, p. 392.

30. Kūfī, *Futūḥ*, vol. IV, pp. 427–28.

31. See al-Ṭabarī, *The History of al-Ṭabarī: The War between Brothers*, p. 225. This juxtaposition of Ṭūs with royal residence is all the more revealing as it is conveyed through political verse. For the "interpretive" and "evaluative" function of poetry in historical texts see Humphreys' comments in *Islamic History: A Framework for Inquiry, Studies in Middle Eastern History*, no. 9, Minneapolis, 1988. p. 85.

32. Humphreys, *Islamic History*. Ibid.

33. As told by ʿUbaydallāh Bazzāz Nīshāpūrī, "an old man . . . [with] business transactions" with Ḥumayd b. Qaḥṭaba.

34. Ibn Bābūya al-Qumī, Muḥammad b. ʿAlī b. Ḥusayn, or Shaykh al-Ṣadūgh, *ʿUyūn al-Akhbār al-Riḍā*, Tehran, 1363, pp. 108–111.

35. Ibid.

36. Ibn Bābūya, *ʿUyūn*, p. 137–38.

37. ʿImad al-Din Husayn-i Isfahani, known as ʿImadzadaʾ, *Zindigānī-i Ḥaḍrat-i Imām ʿAlī b. Mūsā al-Riḍā*, second print, Tehran, 1361/1982, vol. II, pp. 144–45.

38. Imam, Seyyed Muhammad Kazim, *Mashhad-i Ṭus: Yek Faṣl az Tārīkh va Jughrāfiyā-i Tārīkhī-i Khurāsān*, Mashhad, 1348/1929, pp. 111–12.

39. The entire extant genre of the *Shāhnāmas* was produced in this city: Abū Manṣūr Muḥammad b. Aḥmad Daqīqī (d. 976-981), who authored the first poetic rendition of the rise of Zoroaster under Gushtāsp; Abū Manṣūr al-Muʿamerī, the author of the prose version of *Shāhnāma-i Abū Manṣūrī* (composed circa 346/957); and finally Abolqāsim Ferdowsī whose version of the *Shāhnāma* superseded all the rest, were all natives of the city. Other cities participated in the production of Iranian "national" literature. Balkh in particular stands out. But none did so with such a persistence and vigor. None of the *Shāhnāmas* produced in Balkh are presently extant. We are informed of their existence only by references made to them by subsequent authors. For information on the *Shāhnāmas* produced in Balkh see D. Safa, *Ḥamāsa Sarāʾī dar Iran*, Tehran, 1324/1945, p. 93 and Muhammad Qazvini edited, "Muqaddama-i Qadīm-i Shāhnāma," in *Bīst Maqāla-i Qazvīnī*, Abbas Iqbal and Ustad Purdavud general editors, 1363/1984, p. 16.

40. Pourshariati, "Iranian Tradition," chapter VI, "Historical Memory and Ṭūs: Islamic and Iranian Historiography and Deleted Memories."

41. Only the "Introduction" to the *Shāhnāma-i Abū Manṣūrī* is currently extant. For a critical edition of this see, Qazvini, "Muqaddama" pp. 30–90. The "Muqaddama" was subsequently translated by V. Minorsky as "The Older Preface to the *Shāh-Nāma*" in *Iranica: Twenty Articles*, Tehran, 1964, pp. 260–73.

42. See Shahpur Shahbazi, *Ferdowsī: A Critical Biography*, California, 1991.

43. The first three sections of the work on the Pīshdādiyān, Kiyāniyān and Ashkāniyān, can be most properly described as mytho-history putting the value of the source squarely within the debate on the historicity of myth and mythic dimensions of history. Even here, however, as Theodore Nöldeke has observed, it is highly probable that the history of the major feudal families of the Parthian and the Sasanid periods

were inserted in the Kiyāniyān section of the work under the guise of the myth. See Theodore Nöldeke, *The Iranian National Epic of the Shahnameh*, translated by Leonid Bogdanov, Porcupine Press, Philadelphia, 1979. First published by the K. B. Cama Oriental Institute Publication, No. 7, 1930.

44. On the sources of the *Shāhnāma*s see Safa, *Ḥamāsa Sarā'ī*; E. Yarshater, "Iranian National History" in *The Cambridge History of Iran*, vol. 3, *The Seleucid, Parthian and Sasanian Periods*, E. Yarshater edited, Cambridge, 1983, pp. 359–477; Theodore Nöldeke, *Iranian National Epic*, Bozorg Alavi translated, with an introduction by Sa'id Nafisi, No. 25, 1327/1948; Shahpur Shahbazi, "On the X^w^adāy-Nāmag," *Acta Iranica: Papers in Honor of Professor Ehsan Yarshater*, vol. VXI, Leiden, 1990, pp. 208–29.

45. Olga Davidson, *Poet and Hero in the Persian Book of Kings*. Ithaca, 1994. A more nuanced version of this argument is presented by my colleague Dick Davis in "The Problem of Ferdowsi's Sources," *Journal of the American Oriental Society*, vol.116, no.1, Jan-March 1996. pp. 48–57.

46. The *Khwādāy-Nāmag* seems to have been compiled in three stages. The first compilation seems to have been made under the rule of Bahrām V, known as Bahrām-i Gūr (420–438 A.D.) During the rule of Khusrow Anūshīrvān (d. 531–579 A.D.), it seems to have acquired a definitive form with new material being added to it during the reign of Khusrow Parvīz (591–628). A final chapter seems to have been added to this "Book of Kings" "just after the Arab conquest and the death of Yazdgird III."A. Shahpur Shahbazi, "On the X^{w}adāy-Nāmag," p. 214.

47. Nöldeke, *The Iranian National Epic*, Bogdanov, p. 27.

48. Abolqasim Ferdowsī, *Shāhnāma-i Ferdowsī: Matn-i Intiqādī bar Asās-i Chāp-i Moskow*, 9 vols., Tehran, 1373/1994–95, vol. IX, pp. 311–32.

49. Ibid., pp. 332–33.

50. Ibid, p. 338.

51. Ibid, p. 334.

52. Ibid, pp. 339–46.

53. For a very interesting discussion of the nature of this tradition as preserved in the *Shāhnāma*, and some of its variance with the Zoroastrian traditions, as preserved in the Avestan and Middle Persian literature, see Anna Krasnowolska, "Rostam Farroxzād's Prophecy in Dāh-Nāme and the Zoroastrian Apocalyptic Texts," in *Folio Orientalia*, vol. XIX, 1978, pp. 173–84.

54. Ferdowsī, *Shāhnāma*, ibid, pp. 460-61. The *kanārang* of Ṭūs has blood and lineage, land and property, but most importantly kingly glory, that is *farr*, a quality generally bestowed in the Sasanid period only on royalty or those on a par with royalty. Arthur Christensen, *L'Iran Sous Les Sassanides*, 2nd edition, Copenhague, 1944, p. 103. For *far* or *farr* in New Persian, *farrah* in Middle Persian, *xvarena* in Avestan, see Richard N. Frye, *The Golden Age of Persia: The Arabs in the East*, Great Britain, 1975, p. 8.

55. Yarshater, "Iranian National History," p. 362.

56. Ibid.

57. Thaʿālibī, *Ghurar*, p. 743.

58. Qazvini, *Muqaddama*, pp. 31–37.

59. For most of his career Muḥammad b. ʿAbdalrazzāq was the governor of Ṭūs. Yet, he had ambitions not only for the governorship of Nishapur but that of Khurāsān as a whole. The latter he achieved twice, for a period of two years in total, in 349/960, and 350/961 from the Samanids. For an account of the political career of Abū Manṣūr see among others, Abū Saʿīd ʿAbd al-Ḥayy ibn Īaḥḥāk ibn Maḥmūd Gardīzī, *Zayn al-Akhbār*, ed. ʿAbd al-Habibi, Tehran, 1347/1968, pp. 160–63; Abū Bakr Muḥammad b. Jaʿfar al-Narshakhī, *Tārīkh-i Bukhārā*, ed. Muddaris Razavi, Tehran, 1363/1984, pp. 135, 366. For other references to him see Qazvini, *Muqaddama-i Qadīm-i Shāhnāma*, p. 19. Also see Jalal Khaleqi Motlaq, "Yikī Mihtarī Būd Gardanfarāz," in *Majalla-i Dānishkada-i Adabīyāt o ʿUlūm-i Insānī-i Dānishgāh-i Mashhad*, XII, Mashhad, 1356, pp. 197–215 and ibid, "Javan Būd o az Gowhar-i Pahlavān," in *Nāmvāra-i Doktor Maḥmūd Afshār I*, Iraj Afshar and K. Isfahaniyan edited, Tehran, 1364, pp. 332–58.

60. Abū Rayḥān Bīrūnī (*circa* A.D. 1000) singles out ʿAbdalrazzāq's genealogy as an example of forged pedigree. Note, however, that in both instances, our concern here is not with the veracity of the claim, but the claim itself. Al-Bīrūnī, *al-Athār al-Bāqiya*, E. Sachau edited, Leipzig, 1923, p. 38. See also Qazvini's note to the last part of this genealogy, *Muqaddama*, p. 72.

61. Unless otherwise indicated the references here are to Qazvini's edition of *Muqaddama*, pp. 80–87.

62. Ibid. In light of other sources at our disposal, I am here proposing an alternative reading of the above passage to that offered by V. Minorsky in "The Older Preface to the *Shāh-Nāma*," p. 273.

63. Maqdisī, Shams al Dīn, *Aḥsan al-Taqāsīm fī Maʿrifat al-Aqālīm*, edited by M. J. de Goeje, Leiden, 1877, p. 390.

64. Ernest Herzfeld, *Persian Empire: Studies in Geography of the Ancient Near East*, edited by Gerold Walser, Wiesbaden, 1968, pp. 318–19. Also see A. D. H. Bivar, "The Political History of Iran under the Arsacids," *Cambridge History of Iran*, vol. 3 (1), p. 26; Markwart, "A Catalogue of the Provincial Capitals of Eranshahr: Pahlavi Text, Version and Commentary," ed. G. Messina in *Analecta Orientalia Commentationes Scientificae de Rebus Orientis Antiqui: Cura Pontificii Instituti Biblici Editae,* 3, (1931), Rome. V. Minorsky, "Ṭūs," EI, 1st edition, vol. IV, pp. 974–75.

65. Christensen, Arthur, *L'Iran*, pp. 165–67; Herzfeld, *Persian Empire,* p. 319.

Women in the Sectarian Politics of Lebanon

Sofia Saadeh

Although Lebanon prides itself on being the most democratic country among the Arab states, yet, women in neighboring Syria and Jordan have been able to accede to ministerial positions while this development never took place in the history of Lebanon.[1]

My hypothesis is that the division of the country along vertical sectarian lines rather than horizontal class lines has been the major factor in barring women from decision-making positions, despite the aura of democracy prevalent in Lebanon.[2] A constitutional monarchy as is the case of Jordan, can always modify laws to integrate women within the system, and so does dictatorship, but religious laws have proved to be the most resistant to change.

The Impact of Religious Law on the Status of Women

The personal status laws that permeate the life of Lebanese citizens, are none other than the religious laws imposed by the various sects. Each religious sect has acquired a legal status allowing it to be the sole judge and overseer of its community.[3]

Historically, all religious laws were based on the patriarchal system. Consequently, religious laws have consecrated gender inequality as a divine dictum, a natural phenomenon not to be questioned. Differences between male and female have incessantly meant the supremacy of the male and the relegation of the female to subaltern positions. There has been not one single example where women were able to reach an equal status from within the religious order, or religious law. Time and again, the equality of women and their emancipation have been the result of the strengthening of the secular state. A civil constitution may oppress women but its major asset is that it is amenable to change, for it is created by men and follows the rules of rational law that is constantly adjusted to the needs of society. Today, in the Arab world at large, women's emancipation has progressed in inverse proportion to the development of religious movements: the more the latter flourished, the more women were subdued. Lebanon is no exception.

Besides its patriarchal nature, other aspects of the religious laws contribute to the oppression of women. It should be noted that these laws are not bound by the principle of territoriality. This means that the power or powers guiding the lives of the Lebanese are extra-territorial, and may conflict with territorial laws without the ability of the Lebanese government to interfere. Hence, if a sect decides to copy the laws of another country and apply it to its community in Lebanon, the government is unable to stop the religious leaders from so doing. This has led to a weakening of the state on one hand, and an uneven evolution of the status of women among the various communities.[4] Unlike the western experience, it is impossible to look at women in Lebanon as one bloc since they follow 18 different laws.

Consequently, and this is the crux of the matter, any movement created by women demanding their emancipation, would by definition, mean the establishment of a civil code, for it is impossible for women to set common goals while they are being ruled by a wide variety of sectarian laws.

The challenge facing women in Lebanon today is how to accede to positions of power when they are subjugated and ordered to obedience by the religious laws? How can women who are, by law, deprived of their freedom, be allowed to hold enough power that would not only make them independent, but would also place them in such a way that would empower them to decide the fate of others? An even more difficult problem to solve is how can the state be made to interfere and grant equality when its own Constitution, the Taif Accord of 1989, forbids it from doing so?

The mere attempt by the former President of the Republic, Elias Hrawi, to implement an optional civil code, ended into a furious and angry outcry of the religious heads, both Christians and Moslems, with some demanding the resignation of the President of the Republic for having dared to interfere with what they consider their own domain.[5]

I believe that a necessary condition for the advancement of women to positions of power, would be their acceptance as equal citizens, a decision that the successive governments have been unable to implement for fear of the backlash of the religious heads who control society through the personal status laws.[6] Up till now, women in Lebanon need the signature of their husbands to be able to have a passport and travel.[7]

Women's Involvement in Social Institutions

Even within social institutions, women are barred from reaching the upper levels of a hierarchy. This is why a female boss still sounds like an anachronism in Lebanon. Examples are plentiful: 80 percent of the media are women, yet not a single one is present at the top echelon. The same situation is prevalent in the educational system. There are 45,000 female teachers and 13,000 male teachers in both the private and public sectors, yet, we only have two female principals, and both of them are foreigners.[8] Again 37 percent of employees in banks are women, but no women at the managerial level are to be found.[9]

The relegation of women to lower positions does not stem from inequality on the educational level. Quite the contrary, at present, women form the majority of the student body in all universities. The Lebanese State University that harbors 33,000 students, has a 50.19 percent ratio of women. The French University, Saint Joseph, has a 58.9 percent ratio. Balamand University located in the North of Lebanon has a majority of 67 percent, the Catholic Kaslik University, 54.42 percent. The 1992 statistic for the American University of Beirut is of 43.67 percent, and the Lebanese American University had a 48 percent enrollment of women.[10] Furthermore, 49.15 percent of those women were able to graduate.[11]

The discrimination against women does not pertain solely to barring them from reaching a high rank, it touches on the very content the media is propagating. The television stations in Lebanon have daily interviews with politicians and political thinkers, yet no woman was ever interviewed on that basis. The same pattern is repeated in leading newspapers that do not bother to ask the opinion of a professional woman, although many are professors in universities. A striking example was the special edition of the supposedly most open-minded newspaper that dealt with the problem of democracy in Lebanon. That special edition did not include one woman in the interview. Moreover, the men who discussed in detail the problems facing democracy did not mention women at all. They were simply non-existent in the vision of the Lebanese politicians.[12]

Women in Parties

A very powerful social institution is party formation. It is the vehicle through which the public is able to express its choice in politics.

Women started enrolling in parties in the forties and fifties of the twentieth century. However, several factors contributed to their withdrawal from the political scene. The reluctance of women to be involved in politics is due partly to their indoctrination by their parents who portray political activity as not being suitable for a woman who would like eventually to get married and follow her husband's political inclinations. Moreover, the mere mixing with the males within party circles is not condoned by traditional families who fear that this would smear the reputation of their daughters and would consequently, lessen their chances of marrying well.

In addition, the religious war and the triumph of the religious sects in 1989 resulted in a worsening of conditions regarding women's involvement in politics. The religious parties such the Shiite Amal and Hizbullah, the Druze Progressive Socialist, the predominantly Maronite Phalange, and its offshoot the Maronite Lebanese Forces became the most powerful and influential forces during fifteen years of war. Being essentially religious parties, they condemned the involvement of women in public life and preferred to relegate them to the private sphere. If involved at all, the women members, or wives of members, in these parties were given the task of overseeing charity functions, and distributing medical aid. The secular parties did not fare better. The Syrian Social Nationalist Party and the Communist, both secular parties who had a larger number of women members than the religious parties prior to the war, hardly have women members at present.[13] As parties were progressively transformed into militias, women withdrew from them; the main activity of the parties having been restricted to fighting and armament.

However, the main reason for women's staying away from parties is the fact that they are unable to identify with a creed or a course of action where men prevail, and where no attention is paid to women's grievances. Whatever party wins does not change one iota in women's status in Lebanon. No party has espoused in its electoral campaign a change of women's lot. Moreover, women found out that as party members they were not granted equality, and were used as a stepping-stone for men to reach powerful positions. This led to the odd position of these parties demanding the government to follow democratic rules while their leadership ruled supreme as a male oligarchy!

Due to these reasons, young women are not interested in politics and their enrollment in parties does not exceed 4.7 percent.[14]

Women within the Consociational State

In 1943 and upon independence, the two major sects at the time, the Christian Maronite and the Moslem Sunni, decided to run the country on a consociational basis. This came to be known as the National Pact. The latter saw the state as made up solely of Christians and Moslems, and devised schemes for sharing the government between those two major religious groups in accordance with the size of each sect.[15]

Yet, although the National Pact was a verbal agreement, it came to supersede the written Constitution of Lebanon. The latter was a modified copy of the French Constitution and guaranteed an absolute equality between citizens. Moreover, it stipulated the separation of Church and State, and stressed the concept of a republic that derives its authority from the people.

Nonetheless, the verbal National Pact that was supposed to be a temporary arrangement as clarified by article 95 of the Lebanese Constitution, ended by triumphing over the principles of the modern state. This verbal agreement became an integral part of the Constitution of the Third Republic. This new Constitution better known as the Taif Accord, signed by the deputies in 1989, defines explicitly governmental positions along an even division of parliamentary seats between Moslems and Christians.

Thus, secularism became a taboo in Lebanon. No secular movement is allowed to accede to a political position, as it is not recognized in the Constitution. No deputy, male or female, is allowed to run as a candidate for Parliament on the basis of a secular creed. She/he can only run on the basis of their religious creed.

In order to perpetuate this sectarian structure at the state level, it became necessary to keep implementing it within society. Hence, Lebanon preserved the obsolete *millet* system that the Ottoman Empire had decided to discard during its reform movement, the *Tanzimat,* starting in 1839. The *millet* system is none other than the 18 personal status laws that gear the life of the Lebanese population. So far, no civil code is established in the country; the reason is obvious. Any introduction of such a code would mean the secularization of the state. By definition, a civil code cannot differentiate people on the basis of their religious creed. Consequently, the government would be at a loss on how to determine the religious sect of persons desiring to run for Parliament, or wishing to vote! Furthermore, the *millet* system is needed to account for the number of the members of each sect in order for the political representation to be proportionate to the size of each sect. Thus, the *millet* system which was needed during Ottoman times because the Ottoman Empire was Sunni Moslem and could not apply its *shari'a* to non-Moslems, was used by the Lebanese authorities for an altogether different purpose. Mainly, it became the cornerstone upon which the Lebanese political system was established, hence, consociationalism.

In the West, the secular state was established first. The emancipation of women followed as the logical conclusion of the adoption of the equality of citizens before the law. In other words, it was the triumph of the principle of citizenship that led women to acquire rights similar to those of men. In Lebanon, we do not have a modern state. What we have is a Grand Coalition made up of prominent heads of sects. However, besides the three immutably fixed positions of the three major sects: A Maronite President of the Republic, a Sunni Prime Minister, and a Shii Speaker of the House, all other appointments are in a state of flux as to the sects of the incumbents. Most of the politicking is involved in determining which sect will get what governmental positions. Squabbling and fighting did last for two years, in 1992 and 1993, for example, over appointments, as the President of the Republic, Elias Hrawi, and the Prime Minister, Rafik Hariri, and Speaker of the House, Nabih Berri, were each presenting his sectarian list for the administrative appointments to be made.[16]

Under this perspective, women who, to start with, are neither free nor equal due to the restraints of religious laws, are furthermore handicapped at the political level, by the compulsory sectarian representation. Since these same sects are responsible for the oppression of women, it becomes clear why women are unable to get out of this vicious circle. As a voter, and by law, women are appended to their husbands' religious identity. If a woman is originally a Greek Orthodox and gets married to a Catholic, two things change in her civil register: One, her register is automatically moved to the area of her husband's ancestral village even if she objects to such a removal on grounds that she is not living in that village. As a consequence, she loses her political constituency and the support of her primary family. Second, when voting time comes she is not allowed to vote as a Greek Orthodox and is forced to cast her vote as a Catholic. In politics, law requires her to follow the same religious denomination as her husband, although on her identity card she is still a Greek Orthodox! Thus, the political system forces her to remain subject to her spouse, and forbids her from acquiring an independent entity.[17]

A quick look at the history of the Parliament in Lebanon since independence in 1943 points to the fact that the few women who were able to become deputies did not do so on their own; rather, they inherited that position basically from a deceased husband.[18]

From 1943 and till the present day we have had only four women in the Parliament. The first woman to become deputy in 1963 was Mirna al-Bustani. Her father, Emile Bustani, was a very wealthy businessman and a deputy who died accidentally in an airplane crash. The government decided not to have elections in his district and to appoint his daughter for the remainder of his term.

Between 1972 and 1992 no elections took place due to the war. In the meantime, the Constitution had been changed in 1989 from a ratio favoring a slight Christian majority in the Parliament, to an equal representation between Moslems and Christians.[19] The 1992 elections resulted in three women becoming deputies out of 128. These are:

> Nayla Mouawad was appointed in 1991 as deputy to replace her husband. Rene Mouawad had been killed while in office as President of the Republic.
>
> Bahiyya al-Hariri, who was never active in politics, suddenly presented herself as a deputy on the strength of her multi-billionaire brother Rafik al-Hariri who, in the meantime, had become Prime Minister.
>
> Nuhad Sayid was also elected in 1992 to replace her deceased husband.
>
> The same three women were re-elected in 1996. Nonetheless, women who tried on their own, and as independents to run for the parliament, lost so dismally that women in general, refrained from presenting their candidature for fear of humiliation.[20]

However, and as said earlier, no woman was allowed to become minister. To me, the reason is obvious. The Cabinet has always been formed on the basis of the Grand Coalition between the major sects. It becomes understandable under these conditions, that no sect would want to be represented by a woman. A woman at the head of a sect would mean in a traditional setup the lowering of status of that sect vis-à-vis the other sects headed by male ministers.

The same phenomenon took place at the level of the municipalities. In 1998, the government decided to allow municipal elections to take place. These were long overdue since these elections were last carried out in 1963. No women mayors were ever elected to the 390 municipalities that compose Lebanon. Moreover, out of 1300 Council members, only 5 were women in 1995.

During the 1998 municipal elections, thousands of people ran for office. Also, more women presented themselves than was the case with the 1996 parliamentary elections. One main reason is that municipal elections do not entail the same financial expenses. With no parties backing women, it becomes very difficult for women to raise the expenses necessary for campaigning in Lebanon, as the government stipulates no ceiling for spending.[21]

A second reason is that the municipalities being smaller units, family politics play a more influential role, and hence many families whose sons had migrated decided to allow a daughter to run. A third and crucial reason is that the lists made up for the municipal elections are intra-sectarian and not inter-sectarian.

This results in more tolerance into accepting a woman as "being one of us," rather than choosing her to confront other sects.

This last trend was very obvious in the 1998 municipal elections. Going over the lists for the 390 municipalities, I found out that the names of women appeared whenever there were opposing lists vying for the Municipal Council. Thus, if a municipality had two opposing lists, each list saw it fit to include a woman. However, in the municipalities where they tried to apply the rules of consociationalism and entente, women no longer figured in the list.[22] Consequently, in the combined list made up by the National Bloc, the National Congregation party and the Communists, no women were included.[23] Another list made up of the Syrian Social Nationalist Party, the Communist, General Aoun Movement, and the Phalangists in the Mrouj municipality in the Metn region also did not include women. Again a combined list of Aley formed by the Syrian Social Nationalist Party, the Ba'ath, the Socialist Progressive, and the Communist, excluded women. The same goes for the South of Lebanon where a list composed of the Communist party, the Socialist Progressive and Hizbullah had no women candidates. In Sidon, a list calling itself "The Democratic Option" did not feel obliged to include women as part of the democratic process![24]

It is interesting to note that 80 percent of the deputies serving in the 1996 Parliament stated raising kids as the main obstacle facing women who would like to get involved in politics.[25]

To conclude, women in Lebanon face a dilemma. If they aspire to advance to decision-making positions, then women are bound to promote their cause with demands for the establishment of a democratic state and the equality of citizens, not sects. To this end, they would have to confront the heads of sects and religious leaders that bar them from reaching such positions.[26] In other words, women's advancement is intimately connected with the eradication of the sectarian structural system. For as long as the immutable religious laws within society subjugate them, all their efforts would come to naught. Attempts to establish a woman's movement that would cut across the sectarian cleavages have failed to create momentum specifically because the sectarian institutions are all powerful on all levels. The segregation of women along sectarian lines has triumphed because the legal status of women, and hence, their daily existence is irrevocably connected to the laws of the sect. Any move away from the sect turns a woman into an outcaste that is deprived of all rights and privileges.

This is a heavy task indeed. The advancement of women will have to go hand in hand with a shift from a traditional society and the imposition of religious laws, to a modern state and equality of citizens regardless of gender.

Endnotes

1. Layla Sharaf is Minister of Culture in Jordan, while Dr. Najah al-Attar is holding the same position in Syria.

2. Sofia Saadeh, *The Social Structure of Lebanon: Democracy or Servitude?* (Beirut: An-Nahar Editions, 1993).

3. On the legal status of sects see Sofia Saadeh, "*Basic Issues Concerning the Personal Status Laws in Lebanon.*" Paper presented at a conference sponsored by the European Union in Beirut, Lebanon (September 11–13, 1998). The paper will be published soon in a book titled: *Religion: Between Violence And Reconciliation.*

4. An example is the emulation of the Shi'a in Lebanon of the behavioral patterns prescribed by the Islamic Republic of Iran. The Sunnis however, try to follow social regulations set by Saudi Arabia, while the Christians look toward the West in general.

5. For the full text of President Hrawi's proposal for an optional marriage see *An-Nahar* newspaper (December 20, 1998).

6. Claude Lēvi-Strauss, *The Savage Mind* (London: 1966), p. 124.

7. "Each social group will tend to form a system no longer with other social groups, but with particular differentiating properties regarded as hereditary, and these characteristics exclusive to each group will weaken the framework of their solidarity within society."

8. Shaykh Muhammad Mahdi Shamseddine who heads the Higher Shi'i Council asserts that the government has no right to establish civil or secular law, and that both of these domains belong to the religious realm. *The Daily Star* (November 5, 1997).

9. The two women principals in question are an American who heads the American Community School and a French woman who is at the head of the Collège Protestant Français.

10. *Musharakat al-Mar'ah fil-Siyasah* (Beirut: Rene Mouawad Foundation, 1998), p. 27.

11. For statistical information see *An-Nahar* newspaper (October 24, 1997).

12. *Musharakat al-Mar'ah fil-Siyasah,* p. 24.

13. *An-Nahar 'Al-Mulhaq:* (October 11, 1997).

14. While in the 1970's the wives of the politicians were always present at cocktail parties and dinners, this is no longer the case in the 90's where political functions exclude women in a typically Saudi Arabian and Iranian style of life.

15. For recent statistics see *An-Nahar* (February 19, 1997).

16. Sofia Saadeh, *Social Structure of Lebanon,* pp. 57–65.

17. Ibid. p. 106.

18. Women with a college degree confided that they voted in the 1996 parliamentary elections, the way their husbands wanted. The acceptance of women to vote against their own political inclinations denotes their realization that in a traditional society, their worth emanates directly from the worth of their husbands.

19. *The United Nations And The Advancement Of Women, 1945–1996.* (New York: UN Publisher, 1996), p. 164. The percentage of women in the Lebanese parliament is only of 2.3 percent while in Iraq it is of 10.8 percent.

20. The shift into a Lebanese population where the majority is Moslem took place during the religious war when the Christians who were professionals fled the country to the West. Attempts are being made by the government to bring, those professionals and businessmen, back to Lebanon.

21. *Musharakat al-Mar'ah fil-Siyasah,* pp. 45–47.

22. Each prospective candidate has to pay the government the non-refundable sum of 7000 US dollars. Moreover, any candidate who hopes to win will have to put his name in a list. The latter works as a political bloc for the duration of the elections. To be part of the list candidates pay between 100,000 US dollars and one million if not more.

23. For a complete rendering of the municipal elections see *An-Nahar* (Special Edition: May 22–30, 1998).

24. *An-Nahar* (May 21, 1998).

25. *An-Nahar* (Imay 22, 1998).

26. *Al-Barnamij al-Watani li-Da'm Musharakat al-Mar'ah fil-Hayat al-Siyasiyah* (Beirut: Tarkiya Institute, 1998), p. 50.

27. On the objection of all religious leaders to implement either a secular state or a civil society see *The Daily Star* (November 5, 1997).

Notes From Rome: Islam, Italy's Internal Frontier

Ariel Salzmann

There was something new about the "Eternal City," in its Jubilee year. Cleaned and polished for Christianity's second millennium, Rome's pilgrims and tourists perambulated from the Coliseum to the Capella Sistine. They wandered through Renaissance streets, by Baroque fountains and stood in front of the massive public buildings of the *Risorgimento*. Amidst the bustle of Roman life and the spectacular events of the year, they also noticed something changed. Like Italy itself, this most Catholic of cities is becoming a global and pluralistic metropolis. To the large domed synagogue of the ghetto visible from Tiber, there is now an Islamic Center (Centro Islamico Culturale d'Italia) near the gardens of Mount Antenne. Its mosque, built of blonde and travertine stones and imbued with a *sfumatura* of Baroque, both blends and diverges from the city's monumental architecture.

Although the polychromatic facades of the medieval churches of Amalfi, the Murano glass of Venice, and the Fatimid-style paintings of Sicilian palaces all testify to the antiquity of Islam to its shores, Italy's Muslim community, now some 600,000 strong, are mostly recent arrivals. The Moroccans, Albanians, Somalis, Bosnians and Senegalese who arrived as students, refugees, and migrants compose but a fraction of the 10 million Muslims who will shape the new Europe.[1] Their belated arrival derives from Italy's tardy economic "take off" and strong internal migration from its Mezzogiorno. These conditions precluded the type of guest-worker agreements that brought Turks to Germany. Italian colonialism, limited in scope, did not displace the millions of Africans and Asians who now make up the French working class. Instead of a receiving nation, for decades, Italy served as Europe's gatekeeper: it filtered Balkan migrants at its frontier in Friuli and migrants from the Maghreb at its ports in Calabria and Sicily.

The dissolving borders of the nation-state have given Italy, by virtue of geography, its relatively monolithic Catholic culture, and through the presence of the Vatican, a special role in the cultural redefinition of the European Union.[2] Yet the future accommodation of Italian society to its Muslim communities and the possibilities for a constitutional "intesa" with Islam as a religion of state also depends on a candid reassessment of the past. The barriers that new citizens face cannot be attributed to a modern "clash of civilizations" a residue of colonialism or echoes from medieval crusades. Rather, today's stances toward Islam have strong roots in Italy's early modern relationship with the Ottoman Balkans and Middle East, and North Africa. As a religious, social, and political, force this Muslim, but also pluralist, empire presented Catholic states with unprecedented political and social challenges. Inspired by studies on the relationship between conversion and polity pioneered by my professor, Richard Bulliet,[3] this essay considers the institutional reaction of Italian and Catholic societies before a permeable religious frontier.

"Farsi Turco": Early Modern Conversion to Islam

The European common expression for conversion to Islam during the early modern period, "to make oneself a Turk," denotes the singular ethno-political identification of religion with the Ottoman conquests. Throughout the early modern period, the Roman Church would call for unity before the common enemy of Christendom.[4] Popes would stoke discontent among Christian subjects and attempt to shore up existing churches and orders in "Turkey in Europe."[5] Yet lacking the scholarly tools and theological framework to prepare for the encounter with Islam (or for that matter, much of Eastern Christianity), the Roman Church could not accurately gauge the appeal of 'Turcism.'[6] As "rite," not a religion, Islam was considered anathema to both cult and civilization. One who "made himself a Turk" negated faith itself. As a renegade he was an exile, who, having betrayed all, transgressed the starkest social, political and religious frontier.

It is little wonder why Catholicism was so ill prepared for the social impact of Ottomanization on the Mediterranean. As social movement, the Ottoman *gaza* in the Balkans bore little resemblance to the Spanish riconquista. An expanding Ottoman state encompassed the Greek Orthodox populations of the Balkans intact, allowing churches to regain a liturgical and organizational autonomy lost under Latin rule. Forced conversion, most notably, the child levy (*devşirme*) was an instrument for the recruitment and training of a loyal civil service and a standing army. Even the conversion of the people of Trabzon, it could be argued, was less a product of state ideology than of the strategic 'closure' of the Black Sea.[7]

Certainly, Ömer Lütfi Barkan is correct in citing the role of "colonizing dervishes" in creating a religious beachhead in the Balkans.[8] However, the high rate of conversion to Islam in particular regions, such as Albania and Bosnia, owes much to the very weakness of local churches. Elites, too, much like the Sassanian landholders that Richard Bulliet followed in Iran after the Arab conquest must have resigned themselves to the politically dominant faith in order to preserve privilege and property.[9]

Less anticipated than even the rather qualified conversion under Ottoman hegemony, were the waves of Western European Catholics and Protestants who crossed political frontiers to become Muslims during the sixteenth and seventeenth centuries. A pre-modern passport, conversion to Islam secured safe conduct in a new society. Poverty pushed the Croat, Tuscan, Ragusan, Sardinian, Corsican, Maltese, or Sicilian—those 'Turks by profession—toward the frontier while the swelling ranks of the Ottoman military pulled them into service. Italian renegades, Cağaloğlu Yusuf Sinan Pasha, Admiral of the Ottoman fleet between 1591 and 1605, and "Frenk" Ibrahim Pasha, Grand Vizier between 1523 and 1536, as well as the Queen Mother (*valide sultan*) Nurbanu, an illegitimate daughter of Venice, whose son Sultan Murad III ruled between 1574 and 1595,[10] advertised a unique political system which offered incomparable opportunities for social advancement. In stark contrast to Europe the Ottoman elite forgave birth, servile status, and recent conversion.[11]

As Renaissance intellectuals took up the crusade against the Ottoman social system, warning audiences of the evils of a despotism that denied hereditary nobility and private property, Rome launched a theological offensive domestically while continuing to reinforce existing churches and monasteries within the Balkans and Aegean. The primary concern of the Catholic hierarchy during the early sixteenth century remained the "heresies" of Luther and Calvin, and "Judaisizing," the backsliding of recent Jewish converts. Through such orders as Ignatius Loyola's Society of Jesus, the Counter-Reformation took this duel between Western Christianities across the seas through its ambassadors and missionaries. The establishment of an overarching institution for the trial of converts and heretics, the Congregazione della Suprema ed Universale Inquizionale (1542), also sought to rein in many regional tribunals under Spanish or Italian sovereignty. However, lacking a coherent policy toward Islam generally, or a formula for the reconciliation ex-Catholics specifically, the Roman

Inquisition often sanctioned, *post facto*, local decisions, such as the forced baptism of the Mudejars by the Tribunal of Valencia. Nonetheless, the Holy See did attempt to moderate extremes of punishment, from the harsh sentences given renegades by courts under Spanish sovereignty, including the multiple *auto de fé* of renegades in Sicily in 1572, to the lenient and pragmatic penalties handed out by the Holy Office of Venice.[12] Halfway houses, residences for penitence, including the La Pia Casa and the Case dei Catecumeni[13] were also founded in Rome.

Despite the belated development of a uniform position on conversion to Islam, Inquisition tribunals all tried to accommodate involuntary conversion. Individuals who adopted Islam as minors or under threat of death were not held fully responsible for their actions. Slaves and others whose conditions did not permit them to flee, just as those who fled spontaneously from Muslim households and armies, were also considered converts against their will and hence guilty of the lesser charge of "suspicion of apostasy."[14] Yet as the numbers of renegades exiting and re-entering the Church rose during the late sixteenth and early seventeenth centuries,[15] the clergy was forced to refine its understanding of the conversion process.[16] Inquisition tribunals that interrogated renegades searched for the signs of consensual conduct. Learning the "lingua turchesca," knowledge of doctrine and particularly, demonstration of true belief "in the new doctrine" earned the full charge of "apostasy and heresy."[17]

A Fluid Frontier: The Eastern Mediterranean

The destruction of the Ottoman fleet at Lepanto in 1571 carried far more symbolic than military value for contemporary Christians. Celebrated in painting, in a triumphal arch in Palermo, and in the Map Gallery of the Vatican, which set Rome against Italy and the world, this victory also occasioned eschatological prophecies that foretold the immanent collapse of Christianity's greatest foe and prognosticated Catholic rule over Jerusalem. This momentary cooperation among European Catholic states, did not, however, save Latin Cyprus, "the last Christian bastion."[18] The Ottoman military advance in the Aegean, checked by conflicts with Safavid Iran, resumed in earnest during the second half of the seventeenth century. After a long and costly conflict, Venice retreated from Crete in 1669. However, the Ottoman attempt to conquer Vienna forged a rare revival of unity.[19] A Venetian pope managed to secure both naval cooperation from the Republic's doge and land forces from the Polish and Habsburg monarchies for a final crusade. Although the Ottomans would concede Austria one of Europe's first modern borders, the other territorial settlements of Karlowitz (1699) proved more tentative. Thus even the Morea, occupied by Venice under the principle of *uti possidetis,* reverted to Muslim rule within a generation.

So long as the frontier between the Ottoman world and the Catholic Mediterranean remained fluid,[20] because of war and the piracy that often accompanied and followed it, the flow of slaves, captives, and willing migrants between shores, as well as the transfer of loyalties between Islam and Christianity, continued unabated. Given the state of research and the documents at hand, a census of these migrations eludes scholars. Future research on slavery within the Mediterranean, using Ottoman tax registers on slaves, archival sources in Morocco and Egypt, and accounts of auctions in slaving ports like Malta, may eventually enable us to quantify this traffic.[21] Until that time, scholars must realize that the records of the Inquisition trials of "renegades" represent only the tip of an iceberg of populations in flux. Nonetheless the hundreds of cases found in Spanish and Italian archives open a window on the myriad pathways to Muslim lands and the social process of conversion. They also may help us appreciate these conditions and periodicity of the renegades' return.

Precisely because of overriding theological concerns of the tribunals to determine culpability, the reading of these transcripts presents numerous problems of interpretation, particularly with regard to the coercive or consensual aspect of conversion. Bartolomé Bennassar, whose investigation of trials of renegades before the Spanish Inquisition represents the most comprehensive study to date, rightly questions our ability to determine motivations and urges caution in accepting the courts' decisions at face value.[22] It is difficult to resist, however, drawing some tentative conclusions from these scattered statistics.[23] That the overwhelming number of returning converts were captives before the age of 15, does raise the issue of coercion, or, at least, the degree of informed consent. There is, moreover a significant regional variation among individuals convicted of apostasy. Voluntary conversions among Eastern Christians, often captured on land, were exceedingly low, less than five percent of the total. By contrast, the rate among Catholics from the central Mediterranean, whose passage occurred at sea, was far greater: one of out of four Spaniards were deemed willing converts. It was highest among Italians, of whom more than one third, the court determined, "freely" chose to become Muslim.

Considering that many cases involved individuals who had resided as Muslims for many years, indeed, some longer than a decade, the reasons why these individuals re-crossed the border are no less intriguing. Not a few, it seems, sought to escape maltreatment or to regain their liberty after years of bondage.[24] For others, it was a crisis in conscience or a yearning for family and home. Indeed, many of the tales told to the Inquisition remind us of modern migrants whose integration in an adopted culture depended on social, rather than doctrinal, factors. Many converts conceded that it was bonds of affection, such as ties of marriage to Muslim women and responsibilities for children that delayed their return voyage for many decades. In this regard, the rarity of trials of women speaks not only to the lack of equivalent opportunities for escape or the rarity of ransom. Rather, it may owe to the fact that female captives were easily incorporated into Muslim households, with or without conversion, through marriage, domestic labor, or concubinage.[25]

Although Inquisition records bring us no closer to appreciating the actual numbers of Christian converts during the early modern period, exact accounts from Spain and Italy consistently point to a sharp decline in the number of cases of renegadism after the second decade of the seventeenth century.[26] In part, the declining numbers may be explained, as Bennassar suggests, by civil disorder in the Maghreb which discouraged potential migrants.[27] During the last quarter of the century, French campaigns against the deys of Tunis, Tripoli and Algiers, as well as greater restraints on the Maltese, curbed the profitable traffic in Muslim and Christian slaves in the central and western Mediterranean. Similarly, Peter the Great's advances in the Crimea reduced the Ghiray Khans' ability to conduct slave raids into Christian areas of the Black Sea and Eastern Europe. Nonetheless these developments still do not explain the overall decline in the number of trials during the middle decades of the century, a time when warfare, the most powerful catalyst for conversion, escalated.[28]

Among the many economic and social factors that might have influenced individual and collective destinies, the apparent decline in numbers of converts to Islam may also have been the result of new and more aggressive Catholic policies in the Ottoman Empire itself. In addition to waging its theological war against Protestantism, evangelizing its own, and members of Eastern Churches, Rome brought the Inquisition to the Levant, by allowing missionaries, from the early seventeenth century onward, to process cases of renegadism without recourse to authority across the sea.[29] Mid-seventeenth century revisions to the mandate of the Congregation for the Propagation of Faith, founded in 1622, included explicit instructions for the reconciliation of both "infidel and heretic."[30] The new Catholic strategy carefully assessed the geography of missionary activity. It sought to limit the autonomy of orders under the sponsorship of Catholic states, to police the most precarious zones of the frontier, and to coordinate efforts at proselytization among Greek "schismatics," Armenians, Maronites, and new Muslims. Apostolic nuncio, and vicars in the Ottoman east reported to centers in Istanbul, Jerusalem and Alexandria. Rome also reinstated former Catholic Sees in Izmir and Chios.[31]

Despite the Holy See's desire to maintain its missionaries' independence from temporal powers, its new offensive benefited tremendously from improving diplomatic and commercial relations between European states and the Ottoman Empire, as well as from the administrative decentralization of Egypt, Syria, and Cyprus. French tutelage in particular, could not be taken for granted, given that the Bourbon-Ottoman treaty of 1673 brought all Latin Churches and clergy under French protection. Although Louis XIV, the "most Christian king," declined the pope's invitation to join the Holy League (1683–1699), French neutrality bore fruit for Christendom in other ways. Ottoman concessions, particularly those wrested in 1690, furnished the French, and by extension Catholic missionaries with unprecedented privileges in Palestine and access to the Red Sea.[32] By the same token, both Papal and state support for the establishment or new missions, such as the French patronage of the Capuchin order, and the increasing number of Catholic clerics and lay brothers generally, created a cultural medium and a social base for European merchants in Levantine cities, including Damascus. It was this second line of defense around the perimeters of the empire, a firewall of missions, Jesuit, Franciscan, Dominican, Carmelite and others, that with the collaboration of Western merchants, both Catholic and Protestant, helped staunch the flow of religious migrants across an all too open and still inviting Islamicate frontier.

Testing the Frontier: One Story Among Many

From this perspective, Inquisition transcripts aid us in understanding not only the motivations and paths of individual converts to Islam. They also provide a means for retracing the growing networks of the Catholic Church and gauging their efficacy in policing the 'internal frontier' during the second half of the seventeenth century. The case of a certain Franciscan, Fra Alfonso of Malta, whose double conversion between 1689 and 1690, and multiple attempts at absolution, that I present, was a dramatic test of the strength of the Catholic firewall in the Mediterranean.[33] Although not a new phenomenon, the conversion of a cleric posed the question of the religious frontier in its most acute and compromising fashion.[34] The cleric who accepted the "riti de Maometani" delivered a devastating blow to the prestige and authority of the Church, especially in the Middle East and the Aegean where Catholics struggled against rival Orthodox hierarchies.[35] As intellectuals and theologians, a post-Counter-Reformation priest's conversion conferred on what the Church held to be only a "profane rite," a particular legitimacy. Moreover it constituted a cognizant and supremely consensual act.

The story of the future renegade, Alfonso Moscato, began in Malta in mid-century. A stifling culture, his birthplace, La Valletta, was the scene of one of the most violent Inquisitions under Spanish rule. Its economy and society gravitated around the pursuit of holy war.[36] Although a tickle of Maltese natives had begun to infiltrate the ranks of the Knights of St. John, its social hierarchy remained rigid, capped at its summit by the European aristocracy and at its base by Muslim galley slaves.[37] For the son of a doctor, the priesthood was one of the few professional and, certainly intellectual, outlets.[38] Alfonso trained in canon and civil law abroad, in Sicily and later Turin. He was ordained into one of the minor Franciscan orders, that of St. Buonaventura and may have taken his place among the brothers of the well-known Convento di Santa Maria di Ges' de Frati Minori Dell 'Osservanza di San Francesco.

Other than an inordinate curiosity and an aptitude for study, there is little to explain Alfonso's desire to convert to Islam. His attempt to cross the frontier occurred at the conclusion of another period of scholarship in Northern Italy in 1687-1688. In Bologna, a center of cartography and medicine, the reading of travelogues and crusader tales about Egypt might have sparked his curiosity. For some reason he decided to take an alternate route to return home, departing Venice in the spring of 1689 aboard a ship bound to Crete and Alexandria.

The young cleric's arrival in Alexandria did not please the superiors in the Franciscan mission. Rome was encouraged about the progress of its mission there, especially its rapprochements with the Coptic Church and had created a special apostolic prefecture for Egypt two years before.[39] In times of war the Latin clergy's anxieties about the comings and goings of new "Franks" must have been heightened. Resident Catholics worried about the intent and susceptibility of an untutored brother in a permissive setting. Latin missionaries throughout the Ottoman Empire vied for adherents to their sect and over the use of holy sites with the Middle Eastern churches.[40] In contrast to the Spanish Pacific and the Americas, Catholic clerics in Mediterranean served as policemen as much as missionaries: they maintained a constant vigil against infractions and defection. They guarded against multiple or mixed marriages (with other Christian sects) and recourse to the Muslim courts to obtain divorces. They faced a civil authority that often favored the Orthodox churches and conceded demands for state penalties against co-religionist who adopted Catholicism.[41]

The young Maltese's experience certainly justified these concerns. The dejected cleric who wandered in a nearby market, was soon approached by a "Turco." According to his account at trial, this Muslim, presumably a renegade, tried to convince Alfonso of the maliciousness of his co-religionists who were plotting to send him back "to Christendom in chains." Yet it is very likely that the same independent streak and intellectual curiosity that had brought him to Egypt in the first place, also the young man accepted his offer of friendship, hospitality at the house of the Muslim judge ("Cadi"). Alfonso might have hoped to find civil remedies for his dispute with the Catholic mission.[42]

Naturally, Alfonso's Inquisition-account of the evening's events may have been purposefully elusive in order to minimize the number of incriminating details. Nevertheless, he reveals that his exchange with his Muslim hosts was cordial, even jocular. After several hours, he related, the two Muslims proposed that "it was necessary to become a 'Turk' and they gave [me] something to eat and drink." Astutely, he volunteers no information about whether he made a profession of faith. He does admit to having accepted their offer to don Muslim garb, a rather negligible infraction by Inquisition standards.[43] This is the extent of his complicity. After drinking coffee, ("they also gave [me] something, I don't know what, some type of black coffee."[44]), he fell into a deep sleep and the next morning he awoke to find that he had been circumcised.[45]

Word of a cleric's conversion spread quickly throughout the city of Alexandria and soon reached Cairo. Alfonso was summoned by the "Pasha" who wanted to fête his conversion.[46] Although the repentant cleric did not find a haven in Alexandria, he did manage to obtain absolution from the Capuchin mission in Rosetta before departing to Cairo. After spending more than month as the guest, and perhaps, the personal physician, of the Pasha, Alfonso made a choice. Rather than disappearing into the Muslim world as so many before him, he determined to make his way back to the Catholic nest. From Damietta, the friars smuggled the renegade, now an apostate from Islam, off to Cyprus "where he might find the means of passage toward Christianity."

The choice of Cyprus as a type of halfway house for renegades does not seem to have been arbitrary. Before the conquest Cyprus had been home to many Latin monasteries, including those of the Dominicans, Carmelites, Augustinians, Benedictines and Franciscans. The expulsion of the Latin population in the sixteenth century and the conquest of Crete a century later, had reduced it to a minor port of call for merchants. Nonetheless, Catholics, for whom it remained a transit stop toward Jerusalem, struggled to reestablish for themselves a Franciscan convent. The seventeenth century saw new Catholic missions, including a convent at Larnaca founded by Capuchin monks in 1662.[47] In addition to preaching to the Greek, Armenian and Maronite Christians of the island, the Prefect of the "Missions in the Region of Cyprus and Karaman," Batista da Todi, also seemed to specialize in the rehabilitation of wayward Catholics. In a letter from 1650 the Franciscan boasted of his accomplishments to the Holy See. His report listed the names of renegades from Lucca, Palermo, Paris, Marseilles, Tuscany, Vicenzo, Ferrara, Milano, Bressano and Bergamo, all of whom he had dispatched to Christendom ("habiamo imbarcati per christianitá") at Church expense.

With Venetian forces already occupying Athens and investing many of the Morean ports in 1690, the renegade's reception in Cyprus was no warmer than it had been in Alexandria. Anxious to set an example for others, the monks, according to Alfonso, exposed him to the ridicule of both visiting merchants and other clerics. Infuriated by this treatment in Larnaca and still wearing his garment marked by the letter "A" for apostate, he left the convent in anger. He would later claim that his sole purpose was to seek counsel from a superior belonging to his own order of Franciscans. However, Nicosia was also the seat of the government, headed by a rebel janissary, Boyaçioğlu Mehmed Ağa, who had seized control of the island during the unstable interregnum following the overthrow of Sultan Mehmet IV in 1687.

Frustrated and rebuffed by the Franciscan mission in Nicosia as well, he made up his mind to seek other remedies. In a fit of defiance and perhaps blind fury, as he would argue before the Venetian Inquisition, Alfonso burst into the home of the one of the prominent merchants who was entertaining Boyaçioğlu Mehmed Ağa. Before the leaders of the European community and the French representative, the ex-renegade threw himself at the janissary's feet and proclaimed himself to be a Muslim. He offered proof of his claims by revealing his circumcision and by denouncing the European merchants who were hiding two runaway Christian slaves.

What had been a religious scandal within the Church had now escalated into a major diplomatic incident involving all the Western Europeans resident on the island. The French consul who, it should be noted, not only protected the Catholics but also represented the commercial interests of the Netherlands and Great Britain on the island, raised a sum of money from the European merchants resident in Cyprus. Gifts and assurances of their continuing financial support finally persuaded Mehmed Ağa to overlook the matter of the Christian slaves and convinced him of Alphonso's insanity.[48] The French consul personally made arrangements for Alfonso's speedy deportation to Venice.

Over the next four years, the Sant'Uffizio assembled its case against the ex-Franciscan. In addition to the eyewitness accounts brought by the ship's captain, the court solicited and received documentation from merchants and clerics in La Valletta, Alexandria, Cairo, Damietta, Larnaca and Nicosia.

Conclusion: The Renegade's Return

The picaresque tale of Fra Alfonso da Malta, who made his final reconciliation with the Church in 1694, is but one among many events that help retrace the religious frontier on the eve of the modern state system. Long before the fixing of boundaries and the control of passports,[49] European powers and the Catholic Church established a number of checkpoints and border crossings in the form of missions. Inquisition trials served as forerunners of immigration and naturalization services. By late seventeenth century, even the Holy See urged the Venetian tribunal to use its offices to expedite the return, and not the ostracism, of the many Catholic converts to Islam who were the by-products of its own crusade.[50] Given the Catholic Church's increasingly social as well as doctrinal appreciation of conversion, it should not surprise us that the Venetian tribunal, despite the overwhelming evidence presented against him, did not condemn the renegade cleric of the harshest charge. Instead, Alfonso was found guilty of being "suspect," albeit "vehemently," of apostasy and was sentenced to prison and penance.[51]

As a frontier station, Venice should be considered an exceptionally open port of call by the standards of Western Christendom. In a period when no Western European state, including France, permitted the entry of a merchant ship under Ottoman flag, Venice continued to be a crossroads for Islam, Greek Orthodoxy and Latin Christianity. However, we should not mistake Venetian pragmatism for an Ottoman form of pluralism, much less modern tolerance. Until their liberation by Napoleon, Jews continued to build their homes higher for want of space in the ghetto; and the city's famous Fondacco dei Turchi, the famous trade station established for Ottoman sojourners, still confined these suspicious travelers from the East together, locking them in by night.

In the pre-modern period such barriers to transgression were part of Western Europe's urban plan. While many of these obstacles to pluralism have been removed from space, they persist in custom and language. Diet, dress, marriage, belief, and art, even quotidian expressions, such "smoke as a Turk" (fumare come un turco) establish the lines between civilization and incivility, modernity and an alien, backward-looking tradition.[52] As an adjective as well as noun, "turco" continues to denote the foreign, the outsider (forastiere, straniere, oltramarine) the slave and the migrant. Although the traces of a past encounter with the Ottoman Empire continue to inform the modern reception of Muslims throughout the West, they take on particular meaning in Italy, since their function was not only to keep the "Turk" out. Rather it was also to patrol an internal frontier, keeping the Italians, peoples who resided at the heart and yet at the very edge of Christendom, well inside the theological and social fortifications of Europe.

Endnotes

1. Andrea Pacini, UI musulmani in Italia: Dinamiche organizzative e processi di interazione con la societa'e le instituzioni italiane, Silvio Ferrari, *Musulmani in Italia: La condizione giuridica delle comunita islamiche* (Bologna: Il Mulino, 2000), p. 23.

2. On the "intesa" see Stefano Allievi, "The Muslim Community in Italy," in Gerd Nonneman, Tim Niblock, and Bogdan Szajkowski, *Muslim Communities in the New Europe*, (Reading: Ithaca, 1996), pp. 215–327.

3. Richard W. Bulliet, *Conversion to Islam in the Medieval Period: An Essay in Quantitative History* (Cambridge: Harvard University Press, 1979).

4. Dorothy M. Vaughan, *Europe and the Turk: A Pattern of Alliances 1350-1700* (Liverpool: University Press, 1954), pp. 215–36.

5. See Charles Frazee, *Catholics and Sultans. The Church and the Ottoman Empire 1453–1917* (Cambridge: Cambridge University Press, 1983).

6. Lucia Rostagno, *Mi faccio Turco: Esperienze ed immagini dell 'Islam nell 'Italia moderna* (Roma: Istituto per l'Oriente C.A. Nallino, 1983), p. 13.

7. Heath W. Lowry, *Trabzon Şehrinin Islamlasma ve Turklesmesi 1461–1583: Trabzon orneğinde Osmanlı tahrir defterinin Şehirlesme demografik tarihi için kaynak olarak kullanılması* (Bebek, Istanbul: Boğaziçi Universitesi Yayınları, 1981).

8. Ömer Lütfi Barkan, Les fondations pieuses come méthode de peuplement et de colonisation. Les dervisches colonisateurs de l'époque des invasions et les couvents (zaviye) *Vakıflar dergisi* (1942): 59–65.

9. John Fine, *The Late Medieval Balkans: A Critical Survey from the Late Twelfth Century to the Ottoman Conquest* (Ann Arbor: University of Michigan Press, 1987), pp. 485, 589–90, 606, 610.

10. Leslie P. Peirce, *The Imperial Harem, Women and Sovereignty in the Ottoman Empire* (Oxford: Oxford University Press, 1993), pp. 222–26.

11. Rostagno, (*Mi faccio Turco*, 78) emphasizes the peculiar attractiveness of Ottoman Islam.

12. Rostagno, *Mi faccio Turco,* pp. 23, 34–35.

13. Ibid., p. 45.

14. Ibid., pp. 15–18.

15. Bartolomé Bennassar and Lucille Bennassar, "*Les chrétiens d'Allah: l'histoire extraordinaire des renégats, XVIe et XVIIe siècles*" (Paris: Perrin, 1989).

16. For a contrasting perspectives on popular attitudes toward Islam, see Carlo Ginzburg, *The Cheese and the Worms: The Cosmos of a Sixteenth-Century Miller* (New York: Penguin, 1982), pp. 49–51.

17. Rostagno, *Mi faccio Turco*, pp. 15–23.

18. Frazee, *Catholics and Sultans*, p. 111

19. See Rifa'at'Ali Abou-El-Haj ("The Formal Closure of the Ottoman Frontier in Europe," *Journal of the American Oriental Society 89* (1969): 467–75.

20. On the religious formation of frontiers, see *Richard White, The Middle Ground: Indians, Empires, and Republics in the Great Lakes Region, 1650–1815* (Cambridge; New York: Cambridge University Press, 1991).

21. Professor Mehmet Genç points out (oral communication with the author) that Ottoman registers of "*pencik resmi*" (the traditional tax of one slave in five) may help in this regard. See M. Zeki Pakalın, *Osmanlı Tarih Deyimleri ve Terimleri Sözlüğü*. 3 vols. (Istanbul: Milli Eğitim Bakanlğı Yayınları, 1971, 1983.) 2:769.

22. Bartolomé Bennassar, "Conversion ou Reniement? Modalitiés d'un adhesion ambiguë des Chrétiens a L'Islam (XVIe–XVIIe siècles)" *Annales ESC*, (1988) 6:1349–1366. Rare indeed are the cases of conversion like that of Alonso de Luna in Grenada, a learned physician and student of Arabic, whose theological and intellectual conviction earned him a life sentence in prison in 1619. Ebu Soud Efendi, the famous Ottoman Jurist regards 12 years as the age at which conversion was considered a consensual act. M. Ertuğrul Dūzdağ Seyhülislâm Ebussuûd Effendi Fetvalari (Istanbul: Enderun Kitaberi, 1983), p. 90.

23. Bennassar, *Les Chrétiens d'Allah,* pp. 195–201. Among Poles, Hungarian, Valchs, Slavs, Russians Greeks, and Albanians, only 11 of 297 were considered "willing" Muslims. Of 400 Spaniards, the Inquisition found 110 "voluntary" conversion; but among a pool of 351 Italians, 131 were considered "true" apostates.

24. Rostagno, *Mi faccio Turco*, p. 50 n. 80.

25. See Ronald C. Jennings, *Christians and Muslims in Ottoman Cyprus and the Mediterranean World, 1571–1640* (New York: New York University Press, 1993), pp. 137–43. On the structure of late Ottoman families, see Alan Duben and Cem Behar, *Istanbul Households: Marriage, Family and Fertility, 1880–1940* (Cambridge: Cambridge University Press, 1991).

26. Bennassar, *Les Chrétiens d'Allah*, p. 201. Spanish records indicate relatively lengthy sojourns within the *Dar al-Islam*; Rostagna (*Mi faccio Turco*, pp. 39–41) also notes that the Italian courts witness a sharp decline in cases after mid century. Of 358 cases in Naples, only 24 cases were prosecuted after 1621; Pisa, was exceptional: cases doubled from 33 cases between 1611 and 1638 to 67 cases between 1638 and 1700.

27. Bennassar, *Les Chrétiens d'Allah,* p. 209. See also Peter Lamborn Wilson, *Pirate Utopias: Moorish Corsairs and European Renegadoes* (Brooklyn, N.Y.: Autonomedia, 1995).

28. See Osman Aga, fl. 1671–1725. *Prisonnier des infidèles: un soldat ottoman dans l'empire des Habsbourg,* ed. and trans., Frédéric Hitzel, (Paris: Sindbad and Arles: Actes Sud, 1998) and Luigi Ferdinando Marsili, *Ragguaglio della schiavitù* ed. Bruno Basile (Roma: Salerno, 1996).

29. Rostagno, *Mi faccio Turco*, p. 24.

30. Matteo Sanfilippo, "La Congregazione de Propaganda Fide e la dominazione turca sul Mediterraneo centro-orientale nel XVII secolo," in *I Turchi il Mediterraneo e l'Europe,* ed. Giovanna Motta, (Milano: FrancoAngeli. 1998), pp. 205–8.

31. Bernard Heyberger,, *Les Chrétiens du Proche Orient au Temps de la Réforme Catholique (Syrie, Liban, Palestine, XVIIe–XVIIIe siècles)* (Rome: École Françaises, 1994), p. 268.

32. Halil Inalcık, "Imtiyâzât" *EI2*, 3: Jean Berenger, "La politique ottomane de la France dans les années 1680," in *I Turchi, il Mediterraneo e l'Europa*, pp. 269–75.

33. *Archivio di Statudi Venezia Sant 'Ufficio*, busta 126; all quotations Ariel Salzmann, *Vita e avventure di un rinnegato* (Venezia: Centro Internazionale della Grafica, 1992); Heyberger, (*Les Chrétiens du Proche Orient*, p. 322), discusses the very deliberate and reflective conversion of a Capuchin in 1650 in Aleppo.

34. For another account of Alfonso's conversion see Paolo Preto, *Venezia e I Turchi* (Firenze: G.C. Sansoni, 1975).

35. Frazee, *Catholics and Sultans*, 136. See also Salvatore Bono, "Conversioni all'islam e riconciliazioni in Levante nella prima meta del Seicento" in *I Turchi il Mediterraneo e l'Europe,* pp. 325–39.

36. Henry Charles Lea, *The Inquisition in the Spanish Dependencies; Sicily–Naples–Sardinia–Milan–the Canaries–Mexico–Peru–New Granada.* (New York, London: Macmillan & Co., 1908), p. 39.

37. Michel Fontenay,"La place de la course dans l'économie portuaire: L'example de Malte et des Ports Barbaresques," *Annales ESC*, (1988) 6:1321–347.

38. For a more favorable view of Malta's intellectual scene, see Fr. GioFrancesco Abela (1582–1655) *Malta illustrata, ovvero Descrizione di Malta isola del mare Siciliano e Adriatico: con le sue antichitą, ed altre notizie*, Malta: Nella Stamperia del Palazzo di S.A.S., 1772–1780).

39. Frazee, *Catholics and Sultans*, p. 149.

40. André Raymond, *Les commerçants au Caire au XVIIIe siècle* (Damas, Institut Français de Damas, 1973–74) 2 vol., 2:454. Heyberger, *Les Chrétiens du Proche Orient*, pp. 222, 166, 178.

41. Heyberger, *Les Chrétiens du Proche Orient*, 76, 174. The Armenian Church had Catholic converts sentenced to the galleys. Uriel Heyd, *Studies in Old Ottoman Criminal Law*, (Oxford: Oxford University Press, 1973), p. 306.

42. Salzmann, *Vita e Avventure di un Rinnegato.* The "Turk" was reported to have said that muslims would never treat "a stranger in such a fashion" and the judge "would fix everything."

43. Jews were not prosecuted for wearing the clothing of Christians, because, the Venetian Tribunal reasoned, "Time and again we have seen Christian in the Levant call

themselves by Turkish names and live among the Turks for reasons of their own, but without being circumcised or committing those acts by which one accepts the faith of Islam." Cited in Brian S. Pullan, *The Jews of Europe and the Inquisition of Venice, 1550–1670* (Totowa, N.J.: Barnes & Noble, 1983), p. 69.

44. On the benefits of coffee, see Angelo Rambaldi, *Ambrosia Arabica overo Dealla Salutare Bevanda Cafe, dedicato. Signor Gio: Francesco Bergomi* (Bologna: Per il Longhi Stampatore, 1691), p. 23.

45. Consider also James A. Boon, "Circumscribing Circumcision/Uncircumcision: An Essay Amid the History of Difficult Description, in *Implicit Understandings: Observing, Reporting, and Reflecting on the Encounters Between Europeans and Other Peoples in the Early Modern Era*, ed. Stuart B. Schwartz, (Cambridge: Cambridge University Press, 1994), p. 564.

46. Paul Rycault, (*The Present State of the Ottoman Empire,* [London: John Starkey and Henry Brome, 1668], 157) notes that young boys would be paraded on horseback and feted after circumcision as are "those who of riper years become Mohametans."

47. See Charles A. Frazee, *Catholics and Sultans. The Church and the Ottoman Empire 1453–1917* (Cambridge University Press, 1983) Zach N. Tsirpanle, ed., trans., *Anekdota engrapha ek ton Archeion tou Vatikanou (1625–67)* (Levkosia: Kentrou Epistemonikon Evevnon, 1973), p. 152–58, 178.

48. Anna Pouradier Duteil-Loizidou, *Consulat de France à Larnaca (1600–1696)* (Nicosie: Centre de Recherche Scientifique: Source et Étude de L'Histoire de Chypre, 1991), p. 169–70.

49. On European boundaries, see Peter Sahlins, *Boundaries: The Making of France and Spain in the Pyrennees* (Berkeley: University of California Press, 1989), pp. 274–5.

50. Archivio Seqreto Vaticano (Venezia) 139: 457. Rome expressed its concern in 1691, about the "ritorno degli apostate e fugitari alle loro Religione."

51. Venice had bigger fish to fry at this moment of crisis. The former bailo and author of the first work on Turkish literature, Giambattista Dona, was accused of treason (Preto, *Venezia e I turchi*, pp. 106, 345); so too Admiral Mocenigo, for having lifted the blockage of Crete in 1692. L'Abbè Laugier, *Histoire de la Republique de Venise, Depuis sa fondation jusqu'a present* (Paris: Chez le Veuve Duchesne, 1748), 12:183.

52. Preto, *Venezia e i turchi*, pp. 117–19. See also, Salvatore Bono, Schiavi Musulmani nell 'Italia Modrna: Galeotti, vu' Cumpurà, Domestic, (Napoli: Edizioni Scientificks Italiano, 1999).

The Rise of the Ottoman Empire: The Black Death in Medieval Anatolia and its Impact on Turkish Civilization

Uli Schamiloglu

Introduction

The Black Death—the popular name for the infamous epidemic of bubonic plague which spread widely across Asia, Europe, and Africa in the fourteenth century—was only the second of three major waves of bubonic plague in world history: the first major epidemic began in the time of the Byzantine Emperor Justinian (sixth century), the second was the Black Death (fourteenth century on), and the third is the modern plague (nineteenth century on).[1] While the geographic origin and many specific characteristics of these historical epidemics remain controversial (including whether they were all caused by the bacillus *Yersinia pestis*), the effects of the Black Death of the 14th century on human populations in medieval Europe have been treated exhaustively in the historical literature.[2] At the same time, with a few notable exceptions historians have generally ignored the effects of the plague in the time of Justinian and the Black Death in regions of the world other than Europe. I hope that this essay examining the plague in the time of the Emperor Justinian and its impact on early Turkic history, the Black Death in the 14th century and its impact on medieval Turkish civilization, and the Black Death as a major factor in the rise of the Ottoman Empire will be a fitting tribute to Professor Richard W. Bulliet, who has advanced the cause of innovative scholarship on the Islamic world through his own example as scholar and teacher.

The Plague in the Time of Justinian

The consequences of the great outbreak of bubonic plague in 541–42 during the reign of the Byzantine Emperor Justinian (r. 527–65) have not received the

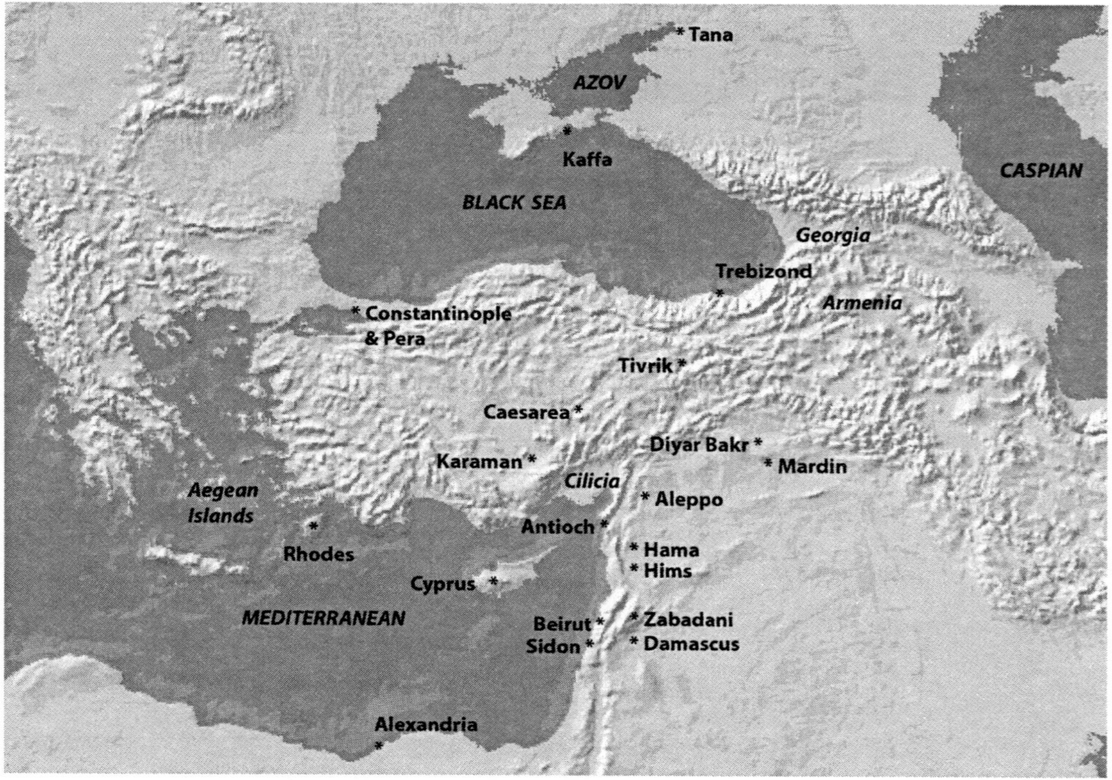

Map 1. Cities in Anatolia and Neighboring Regions Struck by the Black Death (1347–1348)

same level of attention as those of the Black Death of the fourteenth century.[3] It can be argued, however, that this earlier epidemic of bubonic plague was just as significant in world history as the Black Death.

According to the sources the plague in the time of Justinian had a southern origin in Ethiopia, although this claim remains controversial.[4] The classic description of this outbreak—and the first historical description of the symptoms of bubonic plague[5]—is offered by Procopius in his *History* (Book II, xxii–xxiii and xxiv: 8, 12).[6] To briefly summarize the important points in Procopius's account, the plague began among the Egyptians living in Pelusium. One wave then moved on to Alexandria and the rest of Egypt, the other wave moved towards Egypt's border with Palestine. The epidemic did not miss any centers of population and always spread from the coast to the interior. In the second year it reached Byzantium in the spring. Procopius, who was an eyewitness to the epidemic, vividly describes how fever would suddenly overtake victims regardless of whether they were just getting up from sleep or walking about. This would be followed on the same day or not more than several days later by "bubonic swellings" that took place in the groin, armpit, next to the ears, and on the thighs. After this some victims would fall into a coma, while others became delirious and would no longer be able to take care of themselves. In some cases death came immediately, in some cases after many days. Those with hemorrhagic symptoms died immediately.

This disease afflicted Byzantium for four months, and during three of these months the disease was highly virulent. As mortality increased it rose first to 5,000 deaths per day and then later to 10,000 deaths per day. In the beginning households were able to attend to the burial of their own members, but disorder and chaos soon followed. Some households were completely emptied of their inhabitants, for which reason many victims remained unburied for days. The Emperor placed soldiers from the palace under the command of Theodorus to distribute money to see to the burial of all the victims. After they filled up all the tombs in the city of Constantinople, they were then forced to dig trenches to bury the victims. Finally, once they could no longer keep up with the digging and filling of trenches, they mounted the towers of the fortifications in Sycae (modern Galata in Istanbul) and tore off the roofs so they could throw the bodies in. Then, once the towers were filled with bodies, they put the roofs back on. The inhabitants of the city forgot their former differences as they worked together to bury the dead without being able to observe any of the traditional rituals for burying the dead. Finally, Procopius indicates that this epidemic soon afflicted the Persians as well.

According to Evagrius (b. 536?) plague afflicted Antioch two years after its conquest by the Persians and continued to afflict this city for the fifty-two years up to the writing of his *Ecclesiastical History* (Book IV, xxix). No man was left with experience of the disease, which struck some cities so heavily that they were emptied of their inhabitants, while other cities were affected only lightly. It struck during different seasons, and within cities it could devastate one section of a city but leave other parts of the city unaffected. As with Procopius's description, Evagrius's description of the symptoms also documents that this disease was bubonic plague: the presence of the well-known buboes and fever, as well as the sudden death of many of its victims and the dementia that afflicted other victims.[7]

The accounts of Procopius and Evagrius are confirmed or supplemented by information in the accounts of Agathias (d. 582), Theophanes (d. ca. 818), John of Ephesus (d. ca. 585), and other sources. According to a description of the return of plague to Constantinople in 558 by Agathias in his *History* (Book V, x), the plague had never really ended. It afflicted the entire world, and while it moved from one location to another it emptied out certain places of habitation while leaving others alone. Its victims died suddenly, as though afflicted by a severe apoplexy, while others could survive as long as five days.[8] John of Ephesus describes the difficulties presented by the burial of plague victims in 542 echoing the account of Procopius, adding that depopulation was severe enough in the countryside to disrupt the harvesting of crops.[9] He also indicates that in the worst days of the epidemic there were over 16,000 victims per day and that workers stopped counting the dead when they reached 230,000.[10] Surprisingly, Theophanes offers no significant details about bubonic plague during the reign of Justinian except to confirm the outbreak.[11]

Just as with the Black Death, the plague in the time of Justinian exhibited recurring cyclical waves in Byzantium, Europe, southwest Asia, and elsewhere. Evagrius observes that the plague strikes in fifteen year cycles and that he had just experienced the fourth major cycle only two years earlier.[12] According to Biraben, various reports in the sources indicate that Constantinople was struck by waves of bubonic plague in 542, 543, 544, 558, 573, 574, 599, and 608? (sometime between 602–610), 618, 640 (?), 697, 700 (?), 717, and 747.[13] According to Allen there are also reports of plague in the east in other years, including 560–61, 567–68, 583–84, 592, 598–99, sometime during 612–17, 639, 673–74, 687–88, 716–17, and other years until the plague had run its course by the mid-eighth century.[14]

There is a valuable description by Theophanes of plague in Constantinople in 745–46 reminiscent of the accounts for Constantinople two centuries earlier.

This wave of plague apparently began in Sicily and Calabria and spread rapidly through Monobasia (Monemvasia in the Peloponnese), Hellas, and adjoining islands before reaching Constantinople. Theophanes reports of hallucinations that overtook the population. The plague intensified and by the summer it flared up suddenly, as a result of which entire households were shut up. It was impossible to bury the dead, and special animal carts were devised to transport the deceased.[15] The dead filled up all the urban and suburban cemeteries, urban cisterns and ditches, many vineyards, and even the orchards within the old walls. Every household was destroyed by this wave, which is presented by Theophanes as a calamity resulting from "the impious removal of the holy icons by the rulers."[16]

What observations are we to make about the impact of this earlier epidemic which—based on the symptoms described by Procopius and Evagrius— appears to be an earlier wave of bubonic plague and therefore a precursor of the Black Death of the fourteenth century? Certainly the accounts by Procopius and others offer an irrefutable basis for concluding that in the mid-sixth century there was large-scale depopulation in Constantinople and elsewhere in Anatolia. The reports of recurring waves and the account of Theophanes for 745–46 suggest there must have been a continuing long-term decline in the population of Constantinople and other regions as a result of plague. According to Russell, Procopius's account suggests that 300,000 died during the first year it afflicted Constantinople, but he rejects both this figure as well as the even higher estimate by Agathias that 400,000 died in Constantinople in a later epidemic as too high, since he does not believe that the population of Constantinople even reached 300,000 in this period. Seeing a parallel with Egypt in this period, he offers an estimate of 20–25 percent loss in population during the first wave, with a total decline to perhaps 50–60 percent of the pre-plague population during the period 541–700.[17] Russell also suggests that plague had different effects on sedentary and nomadic populations. Conrad offers a similar argument that in the Arab lands depopulation affected sedentary regions more than the nomadic regions.[18]

What were the results of depopulation on such a dramatically large scale? Depopulation is seen as a cause of the crisis in taxation in this period.[19] Russell argues that after recurring waves of bubonic plague Byzantium was only able to field armies that were greatly reduced in size: while the Byzantine army was estimated at 350,000 for the east in the 5th century, by the time of Justinian's death in 565 it was estimated to be only 150,000.[20] We also see a fundamental restructuring of Byzantine administration under the Byzantine emperor Heraclius (r. 610–41) first foreshadowed under the emperor Maurice (r. 582–602). The new *theme* system, first introduced in Anatolia, consisted of military zones into which troops were settled. This system, which replaced the earlier system of provinces (several of which were organized into one *theme*), took advantage of local Byzantine peasants and later imported Slavic populations to serve as soldiers. This effectively relieved the empire of recruiting and paying for the earlier standing army which it replaced.[21] I would argue that the development of the *theme* system should be seen as a response to depopulation in Anatolia. Finally, Vasiliev also sees this period as a "dark age" in Greek letters.[22] Despite substantial evidence in the sources, however, very few accounts of Byzantine history consider the effects of the plague in the time of Justinian.[23] In the case of the most popular accounts in English, Vasiliev mentions the plague in the time of Justinian only in passing[24] while Ostrogorsky does not mention it at all.

It is clear today that the impact of the plague in the time of Justinian and the succeeding waves of bubonic plague in Anatolia, Syria, Egypt, Arabia, Iran, and elsewhere in Asia through the mid-eighth century have only begun to be considered in our understanding of the history of these regions. Not only does the plague in the time of Justinian and its aftermath deserve to be better integrated into the study of the Byzantine and Sasanid Empires, it also deserves to be better integrated into the study of the early Caliphate. To what extent did depopulation in Byzantium, Iran, and other regions pave the way for the rapid early expansion of the Islamic Empire across North Africa as far as southern France in the west and Central Asia in the east by the mid-eighth century? Did recurring waves of bubonic plague weaken the Umayyad Caliphate, as suggested by Dols?[25] With such important questions remaining unconsidered in the standard accounts of Islamic history, more systematic study of these questions for the region as a whole remains a desideratum for future research. It may well be that the rapid expansion of the early Islamic Empire is more properly attributed to depopulation resulting from bubonic plague throughout Africa, Europe, and Asia than to the "sword."

The Plague in the Time of Justinian and its Impact on Early Turkic History

According to a famous notice in the *History* of Theophylactus Simocatta (d. ca. 630–40) on the Western Türk embassy to the Emperor Maurice (598), the Türk are said to boast that they had never seen the occurrence of contagious disease since the earliest times.[26] If accurate, this suggests that the epidemic of bubonic plague in the time of Justinian did not have a Central Asian origin. Since this notice is believed to apply to the Issıq Köl region, it stands in stark contrast to the path of the spread of the Black Death in the fourteenth century, which first afflicted the Issıq Köl region before reaching Crimea and then Constantinople.[27]

Evidence suggesting that the plague in the time of Justinian does not have an East Asian origin is offered by Denis Twitchett, who writes that bubonic plague appears to have been described for the first time in Chinese sources in a work completed only in 610.[28] He offers ample evidence suggesting that plague was well known throughout East Asia during the time of the T'ang dynasty (618–907), with major waves of epidemic disease documented for 636–55 and 682–707. According to Twitchett it is tempting to see the major wave of plague during 636–55 as parallel to the waves of bubonic plague sweeping through the Middle East, although he cautions that there is no evidence in the Chinese sources establishing that any of these epidemics was an outbreak of bubonic plague. I would argue that it is reasonable to assume that these waves of epidemic disease in China were indeed the same epidemic of bubonic plague that was ravaging broad regions in Africa, Europe, and elsewhere in Asia in this period.

If plague did not have a Central or East Asian origin in this period, it must have arrived in China from the Middle East via Central Asia. We know that the plague spread to Iran, from where it could have spread easily to Central Asia. If one considers maps showing the wide distribution of plague in the time of Justinian,[29] one can also easily imagine that the first wave of 542 and/or subsequent waves could have reached other parts of the Black Sea region such as Crimea, which was historically in close maritime contact with Constantinople. In fact, there is important information in the Byzantine sources concerning plague among the Türk. According to Theophylactus Simocatta, some Türk who fell prisoner to Chosroes had been marked on the forehead with the sign of the cross by their mothers upon the advice of Christians in order to escape the effects of a strong plague.[30] Theophanes offers a similar account under the year 588–89:

> The Turks had on their foreheads the symbol of the cross tattooed in black, and when asked by the emperor how they came to have that sign, they said that many years earlier there had been a plague in Turkey and some Christians among them had suggested doing this and from that time their country had been safe.[31]

These two accounts establish that plague had struck Central Asia or perhaps the region north of the Black Sea, the Caucasus, or the Caspian "many years earlier" than 588–89.[32]

I would argue that it is likely that many important events in the Western Eurasian steppe in the era of Justinian have some relationship with recurring waves of plague. The arrival of the Avars (558) coincides with a wave of plague in Anatolia, as does the arrival of the Türk (568).[33] In the post-558–68 period we see the disappearance of many peoples in the North Caucasus, the Black Sea, and the Danubian region. According to Agathias (Book V, xi):

> The Ultizuri and Burugundi were considered powerful and famous up to the time of the Emperor Leo and the Romans who lived in that time. We who live now do not know them and I think we never shall, for they have either perished or have settled in very distant places.[34]

Many Turkic groups also disappear, including various Odur Turkic groups as well the Sabirs, whose territory was in the steppeland north of the Caucasus and who according to one notice could field an army of 100,000 earlier in 515.[35]

Although my remarks concerning the Eurasian steppe in this period are of a tentative nature, I believe that an awareness of the effects of the plague in the time of Justinian can offer new insights into the partition of the Eastern and Western Türk and the complicated and often murky history of the First and Second Türk Empires in the east (552–744).[36] After all, if the plague arrived via Central Asia and resulted in important periods of plague in China, it is not to be excluded that plague also affected the territories of the eastern Türk before 610, during 636–55 and 682–707, or during other years for which the Chinese sources are silent. Clearly in the Western Eurasian steppe this was a time of tremendous upheaval: the out-migration of certain groups of people and the in-migration of others, the disappearance of significant groups of population, the absorption of once powerful tribal groupings into the Western Türk state, and civil war. It is in the aftermath of this confusion that the Khazar state emerges as a distinct state (circa 630–50).[37] This topic requires further study, as does the impact of other serious outbreaks of epidemic disease among the Turkic peoples prior to the Black Death in the fourteenth century.[38]

The Black Death in Anatolia in the Fourteenth Century

The infamous Black Death began its course through Asia and Europe with devastating effects on large parts of China in the 1330s. It then spread throughout Central Asia and the territories of the Golden Horde before reaching the Genoese colony of Kaffa in Crimea.[39] One of the best known sources on the origins of the Black Death in Kaffa is the *Historia de Morbo* by Gabriele de' Mussis,[40] a resident of Piacenza. According to this source, in 1346 countless numbers of Tatars ("Tartars") and Saracens were afflicted with an illness that resulted in sudden death. Large portions of these provinces, kingdoms, towns, and settlements were soon stripped of their inhabitants. The illness spread among the Tatars while they were holding under siege the Genoese colony of Kaffa (modern Feodosiya) in Crimea, which at that time included among its numbers Italian merchants who had fled Tana, a Pisan colony on the mouth of the Don River. Unexpectedly thousands of Tatar soldiers began to die with the sudden swelling of the armpit or groin followed by a fever. The soldiers soon abandoned their seige, they began to place the corpses onto catapults and launch the bodies of their comrades who had fallen victim to the disease into the Genoese fortress of Kaffa. Although the Italians tried to dump as many of the bodies as possible into the Black Sea, the rotting corpses filled the air with a stench and poisoned the water supply.

These symptoms clearly identify this disease as bubonic plague. As we know from countless studies, this epidemic of bubonic plague that would come to be better known as the "Black Death" would soon spread to Egypt and Italy, from where it would spread rapidly thoughout the Middle East and Europe. According to Gabriele de' Mussis, this illness had spread among "the Chinese, Indians, Persians, Medes, Kurds, Armenians, Cilicians, Georgians, Mesopotamians, Nubians, Ethiopians, Turks, Egyptians, Arabs, Saracens and Greeks (for almost all the East has been affected)." The same author also relates further that in the city of "Babylon"[41] 480,000 subjects died in less than three months in 1348, which is known from the Sultan's register because he receives a gold coin to record the name of each deceased.

Unfortunately Gabriele de' Mussis was not an eyewitness to the events he relates, which can serve as a basis for doubting many important details contained in his account. Fortunately there are some corroborating details for Crimea to be found in other sources. According to Ibn al-Wardī, the outbreak arrived in the "land of Özbek" (*bilād Uzbak*) in Racab 747/October–November 1346, where villages and towns were emptied of their inhabitants. There were approximately 1,000 deaths per day in Crimea, and a report from a *qādī* in Crimea estimates the death toll at 85,000.[42]

There are two important accounts in the Byzantine sources which allow us to document in great detail that the Black Death then visited Constantinople with predictable results. According to Gregoras Nicephorus (1295–1359/1360) in his *Roman History* (Chapter 15.1.5), the people were overcome by a severe epidemic which began among the "Scythians" of the Maiotis (the Sea of Azov) and the mouth of the Tanais (the Don River) in the beginning of spring 1347. It raged for a whole year along the coasts of the country, destroying both the city and the countryside as far as Gadeira (Cádiz in Andalusia) and the columns of Hercules. In the second year it spread to the islands of the Aegean, including Rhodes, Cyprus, and other islands, striking men and women, rich and poor, and young and old alike. Countless houses were emptied of their inhabitants in one day or sometimes by chance in two, and there was nothing anybody could do about it. The illness spread uninterrupted not only among human beings, but also among the other living creatures living together in the same house with human beings such as dogs, horses, all kinds of birds, and even the mice living in the walls. The symptoms of this disease and the indicators of impending sudden death were a swelling at the end of the legs and arms and the eruption of blood. Sometimes this illness took away most rapidly those who had just been sitting or walking, including the youngest son of the Emperor, Adronikos, who also died at that time.[43]

According to the much lengthier account of John Cantacuzenus (d. 1383) in his *History* (Book IV, 17), the disease had begun among the "Scythians" of the extreme north and spread to almost every coastal region of the civilized world, killing a large number of inhabitants. According to this source, this disease affected the Pontic region (i.e., coastline of the Black Sea), Thrace, Macedonia, Greece, Italy, all the islands, Egypt, Libya, Judea, and Syria, and nobody was able to resist it. Some died on the same day or hour they exhibited the first symptoms, others were first gripped with a high fever and then lived for another 2–3 days. John Cantacuzenus describes that some would fall into a coma and wake up unable to speak, while others suffering from pneumonic plague would spit up blood. These individuals would also suffer from inflammations and black blisters. After a painful extended description of the horrible symptoms of plague, the author continues that many distributed their belongings to the poor before the disease could afflict them. Both those who were suffering as well as those who survived the plague became more virtuous and moderate in spirit.[44]

While it is true that the language of the accounts of both Procopius in the time of Justinian and John Cantacuzenus in the fourteenth century echoes earlier accounts by Thucydides,[45] I would argue there is no reason to doubt the veracity of their accounts. After all, these descriptions clearly document the symptoms of bubonic plague in Constantinople in a manner that is fully consistent with descriptions of the Black Death for other parts of Africa, Asia, and Europe in this period. Given the existence of two such detailed accounts, ideally there should no question of the impact of the Black Death in Constantinople and the rest of Byzantium. Yet the traditional historiography offers very little discussion of the impact of the Black Death on the city of Constantinople and what was left of the Byzantine Empire in the fourteenth century. In his *History of the Byzantine Empire*, Vasiliev writes that the claims that two-thirds or eight-ninths of the population of Constantinople died seem an exaggeration.[46] Vasiliev's brief description—all of one page in total length—is one of the few traditional surveys of the history of Byzantium that mentions the Black Death. As with the plague in the time of Justinian, Ostrogorsky does not mention the Black Death at all.

It is important to note that these two Byzantine accounts are confirmed and supplemented by Arabic sources. Maqrīzī for one confirms that the plague struck Isṭanbūl.[47] The Andalusian writer Ibn Xātimah, author of a treatise on bubonic plague, writes that the bubonic plague afflicted the Genoese fortess of Kaffa while it was under seige. Afterwards the disease spread to Pera (the colony adjoining Constantinople, modern Pera in Istanbul), then to great Constantinople, the islands of Armenia on the coast of the Mediterranean, Genoa, and France. This work then describes the further spread of the disease to Andalusia, Aragon, Barcelona, Valencia, the kingdom of Castile as far as Seville in the extreme west, and the Mediterranean islands of Sicily, Sardinia, Mallorca (Majorca), and Iviza (Eivissa). It then crossed over to the coast of Africa, from where it spread further to the west.[48]

According to an important treatise on the Black Death, Ibn al-Wardī's *Risālat an-naba' 'an al-waba'*,[49] the plague had struck many countries, including China, India, Sind, the land of Özbek, Transoxiana, the Persians, Crimea, Byzantium (*Rūm*), Cyprus, and the islands. Ibn al-Wardī also indicates that the plague struck Gaza, 'Asqalān, Acre, Jerusalem, the coast towards Sidon and Beirut, Damascus, Mizza, Barza, Ba'labakk, Qārā, Ghasūla, and from Zabadānī north to Ḥimṣ. Among the other places it afflicted we may include Ḥamā, Ma'arrat an-Nu'mān, Sarmīn, Fu'a, Antioch, Shayzar, Ḥārim, 'Azāz, Kalza, Bāb, Tall Bāshir, Dalluk, Ḥāshir, Aleppo, and other towns and cities.[50] Ibn al-Wardī himself died in Aleppo in March 1349 of the same plague whose ravages in Aleppo he had described so well for posterity.[51]

Other sources provide additional details concerning the Black Death in many other regions of Anatolia as well. The Black Death attacked Trebizond in September 1347, while the earliest evidence for the plague in central Anatolia, from the Armenian monastery in Tivrik (modern Divriği), is dated September 10, 1348.[52] According to Maqrīzī (under the year 749/1348–49), when the plague reached Antioch (modern Antakya or Hatay), the people fled to Rūm (Byzantium or in this case Anatolia) and carried the disease to the regions of Qaramān (modern Karaman) and Caesarea (modern Kayseri in Cappadocia).

The plague was also present in Mārdīn and Diyār Bakr (modern Diyarbakır), where Kurds tried to flee from it. Horses returned riderless to Antioch, and there were reports of beasts of burden and cattle dying from the disease in Qaramān and Caesarea. The region around Sīs (the capital of the Armenian kingdom of Cilicia) became empty.[53] Maqrīzī describes similarly calamitous conditions in Cyprus, Rhodes, and elsewhere. As Dols observes, "mortality in the ports was so great that bodies were thrown directly into the sea."[54]

Despite such rich details from Byzantine and Arab sources for the fourteenth century, the Black Death is a phenomenon that is—inexplicably—almost completely absent from the pages of the historiography of the Ottoman Empire. For example, Hammer-Purgstall does not mention the Black Death in the fourteenth century at all.[55] Ernst Werner, one of the few authors to even mention the Black Death in the fourteenth century, included it in the first edition of his work, but wrote it out completely from the later "corrected and expanded" fourth edition![56] More recently, a monumental work devoted to the social and economic history of the Ottoman Empire during the period 1300–1914 does not include a single reference to the Black Death in the fourteenth century, let alone a consideration of its effects on Ottoman population or economy in this period.[57]

Generally we must wait until the fifteenth century for references in the historiography to outbreaks of plague. For example, Hammer-Purgstall makes a few brief remarks about deaths at the Ottoman court in 1431.[58] Babinger writes that in 1455 Sultan Mehmet II, fearing "one of the terrible outbreaks of the plague which so frequently visited Thrace, had left Edirne for the pure air of the Balkan Mountains."[59] Babinger also describes in detail the plague which struck the entire coast of the Hellespont and the Black Sea in 1467 and 1469. This recurrence of the Black Death depopulated Bursa, and there were also 600 deaths per day in Istanbul, turning the city into a "desert." Aware of the situation in Istanbul, Sultan Mehmet and his troops headed for the mountains of northern Bulgaria.[60] This suggests that modern historians of the Ottoman Empire need to rediscover what Sultan Mehmet II knew intuitively.[61]

The Impact of the Black Death on Medieval Turkish Civilization

In the absence of a body of scholarship examining the effects of the Black Death of the fourteenth century on medieval Turkish civilization, I would like to draw upon the lessons I have learned from my study of the Black Death in the Golden Horde.[62] The major phenomena that I have observed for this state include severe depopulation of the urban areas (including the educated urban elite), complete political collapse after 1360 once the rules for succession could no longer be observed in collaboration with the tribal leadership in the "four-bey system," and social and economic disruption. The cities of the state soon fell into ruin. As in Europe, there is evidence of an increase in religiosity as seen from a literary work entitled the *Nehc ül-feradis* (whose Turkic subtitle *Uştmaxlarnıŋ aêuq yolı* may be translated as "The Clear Path to Heaven"), a work produced during a plague year in the Golden Horde (1358).[63] After this work, the new Islamic Turkic literary language that had emerged in the Golden Horde ceased to be used for new works. Nascent Turkic literary languages used for funerary inscriptions came to a sudden end near Issıq Köl (Syriac Turkic) and in Volga Bulğaria (Volga Bulğarian), reflecting depopulation, cultural and technological regression, and perhaps inflation as well. This was followed by six decades of almost no new works being written in Turkic, after which there slowly developed new literary and epigraphical dialects closer to the spoken vernacular.[64] Later a series of smaller xanates replaced the earlier larger Golden Horde, while nomadic groups, who did not suffer as much from the impact of the plague, became relatively populous and powerful enough to begin a steady push to the south to Central Asia.

How much of this is applicable to Turkish civilization in Anatolia in the second half of the fourteenth century and later? This is of course difficult to say. Much of it will not be applicable because the new capital cities of the Golden Horde were the result of a recent process of urbanization resulting from the tremendous wealth from commercial revenues accruing to the formerly nomadic elite of the state. The state had converted officially to Islam only recently and new Islamic Turkic literary languages had just begun to develop on its territory. In contrast, Anatolia was not newly Islamized, Muslim Turkic literary languages had a longer history there, and the existing urban centers were not made possible exclusively through the support of a powerful, newly sedentarizing state elite. Nevertheless I believe that some of these insights can find application in the case of medieval Turkish civilization in Anatolia.

In the sphere of literature, it is difficult to compare the medieval Muslim Turkish literary culture of Anatolia with that of the Golden Horde, which had barely begun to emerge in the 1340s.[65] We do note, however, that the dominant literary languages of Anatolia in the thirteenth-first half of the fourteenth centuries were Arabic and Persian. While there were a few Turkish poets in the first half of the fourteenth century, notably Gülşehri and Aşıkpaşa, it seems there was a prominent shift to Turkish after 1347. As Mansuroğlu observes:[66]

> Turkish literary output in Anatolia increased suddenly in the 14th century, and reached a level incomparably greater than that of the preceding century. As a matter of fact the works surviving from this period are so numerous and varied as to defy any exact reckoning. The existence of specimens of folk literature and simple religious-mystical works side by side by with historical works and books written to appeal to the upper classes demonstrate that the aesthetic needs of every class of the community were satisfied by literary works in both verse and prose. Besides these works, a large proportion of which are anonymous, there grew up a number of writers whose fame has gradually spread across the boundary of their centuries. . . . The principal cause of the abundance of Turkish works was the ignorance of Arabic and Persian shown by the Anatolian feudal lords.

Perhaps we can think of "specimens of folk literature and simple religious-mystical works" or innovative poets of the second half of the fourteenth century such as Kadı Burhaneddin, ʿIzzeddin Ahmed, Fahreddin Yaʿkub, Yusuf Meddah, Şeyhoğlu, and Ahmedi as representing a new trend in vernacular literature comparable to Boccaccio in Italy. This would be comparable to the decline of Latin and the rise of vernacular literatures in Western Europe, a result in part of the decimation of the learned classes as a result of the Black Death.

In the case of an increase in religiosity, Anatolia was far more Islamized than the Golden Horde, for which reason it would be difficult to document increased religiosity. Perhaps we can point to the *Mevlid* of Süleyman Çelebi, composed in Bursa in 1409, as a pious devotional act.[67] Even its Arabic name, *Vesilet ün-necat* ("The Path of Safety"), suggests a work parallel to the *Nehc ül-feradis*. The *Mevlid* in Ahmedi's *İskendername* also dates to this period.[68]

Finally, this new resurgence in literary activity offers an unexpected additional category of evidence, namely the shift in the orthographic system of written Turkish from the norms of Old Anatolian Turkish to the new orthographic norms of Ottoman Turkish.[69] The orthographic system of the Central Asian Islamic Turkic literary dialect had a tremendous influence upon the earliest specimens of Turkish written in Anatolia. Although written in Arabic script, this system generally continued orthographic principles used earlier by Old Uyğur written in the Uyğur script (subsequently adopted by Mongolian and later Manchu). Among the general characteristics of this system we may include a tendency to write all vowels plene; write /ŋ/ as *n* + *k* (*nūn* + *kāf*); write /t/ as *tāʾ* and /s/ as *sīn* in both back- and front-vowel words; write /b, p/ as *b* (*bāʾ*); write /c, ç/ as *c* (*cīm*); write suffixes as separate words; and certain other features. There are also numerous grammatical elements that link the language of thirteenth century Anatolian Turkish with the Central Asian Islamic Turkic literary dialect, and therefore with Old Uyğur. Of course, the Ottoman Turkish which emerges after this period is based on different orthographic principles, including a tendency to not write most vowels plene (following instead the system for short vowels in Arabic); write /ŋ/ as *k (kāf)*; distinguish graphically /t/ in back- and front-vowel words and /s/ in back- and front-vowel words; distinguish /b, p/ and /c, ç/ graphically as in New Persian; and write suffixes as a part of the word where ligatures permit.

These changes indicate that Old Anatolian Turkish was based in large part on a pre-Islamic orthographic system which reflected specialized knowledge on the part of a learned class of scholars. We must assume that as a result of the ravages of the Black Death in the fourteenth century and beyond, the sudden death of large segments of that learned class disrupted the transmission of such specialized knowledge. The new orthographic and grammatical principles that were adopted as innovations were based upon the Arabic and Persian models that were close at hand. Ottoman Turkish as it developed was also closer to the spoken Turkish of Anatolia and Rumeli in the fourteenth to fifteenth centuries. Such a fundamental transformation in an orthographic system also suggests that the impact of the Black Death on medieval Turkish civilization might be even more profound than our meager sources indicate.

The Black Death and The Rise of the Ottoman Empire: Ten Theses

The spectacular rise of the Ottoman state is a fundamental problem that has remained unresolved in the historiography of the Ottoman Empire. The major theories of the twentieth century on the origins of the Ottoman Empire proposed by M. Fuat Köprülü, Paul Wittek, and Rudi Lindner remain required reading for all students of Ottoman history.[70] In framing this problem we may recall the words of the great historian of the Ottoman Empire, Halil İnalcık:[71]

> In the 1350s the Ottoman state was no more than one of many frontier principalities, but events after 1352 so firmly established its superiority over the others that, within thirty years, they had become Ottoman vassals.

The earliest Ottoman state was the principality (*beylik*) founded by Osman (d. 1326) in northwestern Anatolia at the end of the thirteenth century. This principality, the Turkish principality nearest to Constantinople, gained its first major victory in Baphaeon (1301). As a result of this important victory the Ottomans began to attract numerous followers. Under Osman and his successor, his son Orhan, the Ottoman principality led a steady and successful campaign of expansion, but it was not yet a serious rival to Byzantium, now admittedly a much weaker state than it had been centuries earlier and mired in civil war. İnalcık rightly observes that over the course of the second half of the fourteenth century we see a major transformation in the Ottoman state.

I would argue that the most important fact overlooked in all the theories on the rise of the Ottoman Empire and missing perhaps in the entire historiography devoted to the Ottoman Empire is the impact of the Black Death. In response I offer below ten theses on the rise of the Ottoman Empire that consider the impact of this important phenomenon:

1. *The Black Death was a generalized phenomenon in Anatolia beginning in* 1347. Countless cities and regions throughout Anatolia were ravaged by recurring waves of bubonic plague: after arriving from Crimea the plague struck Pera, Constantinople, the coastline of Byzantium, the Aegean islands, the Mediterranean coast, Rhodes, Cyprus, Sīs, Antioch, Aleppo, Trebizond, Tivrik, Mārdīn, Diyār Bakr, Qaramān, Caesarea, and many other cities and regions. The Black Death ravaged not only the territory of Byzantium, but the territories of the Turkish principalities, Greater Armenia, Lesser Armenia (Cilicia), Azerbaycan, and various territories inhabited by Arabs, Kurds, and others. We know from the history of the Black Death elsewhere that mortality from plague varied from town to town, and that individual cities, towns, and even neighborhoods could escape the ravages of plague during specific waves. On the other hand, the sources indicate quite clearly that the Black Death had catastrophic results in many cities and regions in Anatolia. For this reason it would be important to have a better understanding of the course of the Black Death throughout Anatolia in the mid-fourteenth century and throughout the territories of the Ottoman Empire in later centuries.

2. *After the arrival of the Black Death in spring* 1347 *Byzantium fell into crisis, resulting in an invitation to the Ottomans for military cooperation.* In 1352 John Cantacuzenus invited his son-in-law Süleyman, son of Orhan, to cross over to Adrianople (modern Edirne) to assist Byzantium against the armies of the Serbs and Bulgarians. There can be no doubt that there is a direct causal relationship between the latest crisis in Byzantium resulting from the Black Death and the invitation to Süleyman to assist the Byzantine armies. This proved to be a watershed event in Ottoman history, for Süleyman was able to

gain a foothold in Rumeli, the European territories across the Bosphorus from Anatolia. The earthquake of March 1-2, 1354—only the latest in the series of natural disasters befalling the Byzantines—allowed the Ottomans to capture the damaged fortresses at Gallipoli (modern Gelibolu) and elsewhere and to establish permanent control over these territories.

3. *The Turkish principalities that were the rivals of the Ottomans were devastated by the Black Death.* Most of these principalities—Karası, Saruhan, Aydın, Menteşe, Tekke, and Karaman—were located directly on the Aegean or Mediterranean coast. The sources cited above indicate that all coastal areas were struck by bubonic plague, which would have affected Byzantium and all these principalities situated along the coastal regions as well as Cilicia. If we consider the observation by Procopius in the sixth century that plague always spread from the coast to the interior and did not miss any centers of population, there is no need to assume that Germiyan and Hamideli were spared, either. According to İnalcık the two major rivals of the Ottomans in Anatolia in the second half of the fourteenth century were Karaman and Eretna (with its capital in Sivas).[72] We know, however, that both Karaman and Tivrik (only 100 kilometers from Sivas) were struck by plague.

4. *The Ottoman principality suffered less than its rivals because it was largely nomadic.* We do not know whether the urban centers of the Ottoman principality were ever affected by the Black Death or whether they were spared. In either case, the Ottomans were to a large extent nomadic.[73] As noted above, epidemic disease does not spread as easily among nomadic populations, and this has been offered as an explanation of why nomadic populations became relatively stronger in the medieval Arabian Peninsula or following the collapse of the Golden Horde. For this same reason the Ottoman nomadic population could have remained largely unaffected by the plague while Byzantium and the other Turkish principalities suffered from depopulation and instability. As a result the Ottomans would have suddenly gained in relative size and strength.

5. *Ottoman expansion was aided by depopulation in Southeastern Europe.* As we have seen above, the sources for the fifteenth century speak regularly of recurring waves of bubonic plague in the Balkans, which necessarily meant depopulation in these areas as well. This may also have relevance for the development of the *tımar* system and the population transfers known as *sürgün*, both of which may be seen as an administrative response to depopulation parallel to the development of the *theme* system in Byzantium following the plague in the time of Justinian.

6. *The city of Constantinople became depopulated as a result of the Black Death.* The recurring waves of plague in Constantinople and the other coastal regions of Byzantium resulted in a process of depopulation beginning in 1347. This factor ultimately favored Sultan Mehmet II, known in Turkish as *Fatih*, "Conqueror" of Constantinople. By the time of the Ottoman conquest in 1453 the population of Constantinople is estimated to have been only 30,000–50,000, with the army consisting of only about 7,000–9,000 soldiers.[74] This process of depopulation also continued after the Ottoman conquest, as noted above.

7. *There was a decline in indigenous ethnic and religious communities in Anatolia as a result of the Black Death.* I attribute the so-called "decline of Hellenism," the virtual disappearance of the Armenian kingdom of Cilicia in the second half of the fourteenth century,[75] and the decline of Christian communities in Anatolia beginning in this period in large measure to the catastrophic effects of the Black Death.

8. *The Byzantines and Ottomans became serious rivals only after* 1347. There was no Byzantine-Ottoman rivalry of equals before 1347. It is only after the implosion of Byzantium beginning in 1347 and the establishment of a permanent Ottoman presence in Rumeli after 1354 that we see the beginning of a rivalry between two states that may be considered to have been in the same league. Even so, it is significant that it was only after another century of recurring waves of plague in Constantinople that the Ottomans would finally be able to conquer the city.

9. *The increase in religiosity in Anatolia after* 1347 *contributed to the development of a new ideology of religious war against Byzantium.* There was an increase in religiosity in Anatolia following the arrival of the Black Death, which had many important consequences. One of them, I would argue, is that the new (post-1347/1352/1354) rivalry between the Byzantines and the Ottomans came to be interpreted—sooner or later—in terms of a religious ideology of holy war. Therefore it is likely that the ideology of *gaza* or "holy war"—which figures so prominently in theories of the rise of the Ottoman state—is a phenomenon that came into existence only after 1347/1352/1354, that is in the climate of a new Byzantine-Ottoman rivalry and increased religiosity in Anatolia.[76]

10. *The Black Death is not mentioned in the Ottoman sources, even though this historical phenomenon is well documented in other sources.* As far as I am aware the Ottoman chronicles simply do not mention the Black Death in their

accounts of events in the fourteenth century.[77] This is why modern historians of the Ottoman Empire—who naturally base their work on the Ottoman sources—have been misled in their study of the transformation of the Ottoman principality into a major empire. Is it possible that the later chroniclers did not preserve a memory of the Black Death in the mid-fourteenth century, even though waves of bubonic plague were a fact of life in the fifteenth century, too?[78] Is it possible that there was a strict taboo against invoking the name of such a powerful disease lest one unleash its awesome power, as Turkic peoples of Central Asia or Siberia would have believed? Or is it the case that the Ottoman chronicles—almost none of which date from the fourteenth century—are so much a product of later efforts to legitimate the Ottoman dynasty in Islamic religious terms that many inconvenient earlier historical facts (the Black Death, possible dynastic origins emerging from the Golden Horde, etc.) have simply been discarded in favor of later ideologies?[79]

Endnotes

1. For scientific literature on the transmission and genetic composition of bubonic plague see most recently M. J. Keeling, C. A. Gilligan, "Metapopulation Dynamics of Bubonic Plague," *Nature* 407 (19 October 2000), pp. 903–6; Stewart T. Cole, Carmen Buchrieser, "Bacterial Genomics: A Plague o' Both Your Hosts," *Nature* 413 (04 October 2001), pp. 467–470; and J. Parkhill, B. W. Wren, N. R. Thomson, R. W. Titball, M. T. G. Holden, M. B. Prentice, M. Sebaihia, K. D. James, C. Chu et al., "Genome Sequence of *Yersinia pestis*, the Causative Agent of Plague," *Nature* 413 (04 October 2001), pp. 523–27.

2. For surveys of the most important historical literature see J.M.W. Bean, "Plague, Population, and Economic Decline in England in the Later Middle Ages," *Economic History Review* 15 (1963), pp. 423–37; "The Black Death: The Crisis and its Social and Economic Consequences," *The Black Death: The Impact of the Fourteenth Century Plague*, ed. Daniel Williman (Binghamton, New York: Center for Medieval and Early Renaissance Studies, 1982); F.D. Shrewsbury, *A History of the Bubonic Plague in the British Isles* (Cambridge, 1970); Jean-Noël Biraben, *Les hommes et la peste en France et dans les pays européens et méditerranéens*, i–ii, Civilisations et sociétés 35–36 (Paris: Mouton, 1975–1976); *The Black Death*, ed.-trans. Rosemary Horrox, Manchester Medieval Sources Series (Manchester: Manchester University Press, 1994); David Herlihy, ed. Samuel K. Cohn, Jr., *The Black Death and the Transformation of the West* (Cambridge, MA: Harvard University Press, 1997); and most recently Edward A. Eckert, "The Retreat of Plague from Central Europe, 1640–1720: A

Geomedical Approach," *Bulletin of the History of Medicine* 74:1 (2000), pp. 1–28. See also the contribution in this volume by Stuart J. Borsch, whom I would like to thank for sharing bibliographic information from his recent Ph.D. dissertation.

3. See J.C. Russell, "That Earlier Plague," *Demography* 5:1 (1968), pp. 174–84; Michael W. Dols, "Plague in Early Islamic History," *Journal of the American Oriental Society* 94:3 (1974), pp. 371–83; *The Black Death in the Middle East* (Princeton, 1977); Biraben, *Les hommes et la peste*, i, pp. 25–48; Lawrence I. Conrad, "The Plague in the Early Medieval Near East," Ph.D. dissertation (Princeton University, 1981); "The Plague in Bilād al-Shām in Pre-Islamic Times," *Proceedings of the Symposium on Bilād al-Shām during the Byzantine Period*, ed. M. A. Bakhit and M. Asfour (Amman, 1986), ii, pp. 143–63; P. Allen, "The 'Justinianic' Plague," *Byzantion* 49 (1979), pp. 5–20; and additional works (some cited below).

4. On the geographical origins of this plague see the comments of Dols, "Plague in Early Islamic History," p. 373; Allen, "The 'Justinianic' Plague," p. 6; Conrad, "The Plague in the Early Medieval Near East," pp. 92–98; and Evagrius, trans. Michael Whitby, *The Ecclesiastical History of Evagrius Scholasticus*, Translated Texts for Historians 33 (Liverpool: Liverpool University Press, 2000), pp. 229–30 n. 78.

5. Dols, "Plague in Early Islamic History," p. 373.

6. Procopius, trans. H. B. Dewing, *History of the Wars* (London: 1954), i, pp. 451–73, 475, 477. Procopius's account is considered to echo Thucydides's description of an earlier plague, see Allen, "The 'Justinianic' Plague," p. 6.

7. Evagrius, trans. Whitby, *The Ecclesiastical History of Evagrius Scholasticus*, pp. 229–32.

8. Agafiy, trans. M.V. Levçenko, *O tsarstvovanii Yustiniana* (Moscow, 1953), pp. 146–47.

9. Allen, "The 'Justinianic' Plague," p. 12. Information from his *Ecclesiastical History* is preserved in the later work of Michael the Syrian: ed. J.-B. Chabot, *Chronique de Michel le Syrien*, ii (Paris, 1901), pp. 235–40.

10. Allen, "The 'Justinianic' Plague," p. 10.

11. See Theophanes, *The Chronicle of Theophanes Confessor. Byzantine and Near Eastern History, AD* 284-813, trans. Cyril Mango et al. (Oxford: Oxford University Press, 1997), pp. 322 (under the years 541–542), 337 (555–556), 340 (557–558), 345 (560–561), 389, 503 (683–684), 559 (725–726), 569 (732–733), 573, 585–86 (745–746).

12. Evagrius, trans. Whitby, *The Ecclesiastical History of Evagrius Scholasticus*, pp. 229–32.

13. See Biraben, *Les hommes et la peste*, i, pp. 27–32.

14. Allen, "The 'Justinianic' Plague," pp. 13–14. Russell, "That Earlier Plague," p. 179, gives the dates 556–558, 561, 567-568, 573, 577, 586, 618, and 622. For a discussion of the chronology of the epidemics see Conrad, "The Plague in the Early Medieval Near East," pp. 328–52 (including Tables 1-4) and the critical comments on p. 132 and elsewhere.

15. See also Herlihy, *The Black Death and the Transformation of the West*, p. 61, who cites parallel observations by Boccaccio on this same topic.

16. Theophanes, trans. Mango et al., *The Chronicle of Theophanes Confessor*, pp. 585–86.

17. Russell, "That Earlier Plague," p. 180. On the other hand, Dols suggests that we should approach many of Russell's estimates with caution, see Dols, "Plague in Early Islamic History," p. 371 n. 3; and *The Black Death in the Middle East*, p. 16. See also the discussion in Conrad, "The Plague in the Early Medieval Near East," pp. 434–41.

18. Conrad, "The Plague in the Early Medieval Near East," pp. 465–82; and "The Plague in Bilad al-Sham in Pre-Islamic Times." I have made a similar argument for the Golden Horde, see my "Preliminary Remarks on the Role of Disease in the History of the Golden Horde," *Central Asian Survey* 12:4 (1993), pp. 447–57.

19. J. B. Bury, *History of the Later Roman Empire* (New York, 1958), ii, pp. 352, 358; J. L. Teall, "The Barbarians in Justinian's Army," *Speculum* 40 (1965), pp. 294–322; and Russell, "That Earlier Plague," p. 182.

20. Russell, "That Earlier Plague," p. 182.

21. George Ostrogorsky, trans. Joan Hussey, *History of the Byzantine State* (New Brunswick: Rutgers University Press, 1969), pp. 80, 95–100.

22. A. A. Vasiliev, *History of the Byzantine Empire,* 324–1453 (Madison: University of Wisconsin Press, 1958), p. 230; and Russell, "That Earlier Plague," pp. 181–82.

23. See for example the limited descriptions in Bury, *History of the Later Roman Empire*, ii, pp. 62–66; and E. Stein, *Histoire du Bas-Empire* (Paris, 1949–1959), ii, pp. 758–760. See also E. Patlagean, *Pauvreté économique et pauvreté sociale à Byzance, 4e-7e siècles*, Civilisations et sociétés 48 (Paris, 1977), pp. 85–89.

24. Vasiliev, *History of the Byzantine Empire*, p. 162.

25. Dols, "Plague in Early Islamic History," pp. 380–81.

26. See E. Chavannes, "Documents sur les Tou-kiue (Turcs) Occidentaux," *Documents sur les Tou-kiue (Turcs) Occidentaux. Recueillis et comments. Suivi de Notes additionelles* (St. Petersburg, 1900–1903/Paris, n.d.), p. 248; Dols, "Plague in Early Islamic History," p. 373; and Dols, *The Black Death in the Middle East*, p. 16. For translations of this source see: Feofilakt Simokatta, trans. S. P. Kondrat'ev, *Istoriya*, Pamyatniki srednevekovoy istorii narodov Tsentral'noy i Vostoçnoy Evropï (Moscow, 1957), p. 161; and Theophylactus Simocatta, trans. Peter Schreiner, *Geschichte*, Bibliothek der griechischen Literatur. Abteilung Byzantinistik 20 (Stuttgart: A. Hiersemann, 1985), p. 188. See also Theophylactus Simocatta, trans. Michael Whitby and Mary Whitby, *The History of Simocatta: An English Translation With Introduction and Notes* (Oxford: Oxford University Press, 1986).

27. See my "The End of Volga Bulgarian," *Varia Eurasiatica. Festschrift für Professor Andr s Róna-Tas* (Szeged, 1991), pp. 157–63; "Preliminary Remarks on the Role of Disease in the History of the Golden Horde"; "Bolgar tele kaya kitkän?," *Idel* 1994:4, pp. 46–48; and *The Golden Horde: Economy, Society, and Civilization in Western Eurasia, Thirteenth-Fourteenth Centuries* (Madison: Turko-Tatar Press, in press), Chapter 9.

28. Denis Twitchett, "Population and Pestilence in T'ang China," *Studia Sino-Mongolica. Festschrift für Herbert Franke*, ed. Wolfgang Bauer, Münchener ostasiatische Studien 25 (Wiesbaden: Franz Steiner Verlag, 1979), pp. 35–68, especially pp. 42–45.

29. Biraben, *Les hommes et la peste*, i, pp. 34–41.

30. Theophylactus Simocatta, trans. Schreiner, *Geschichte*, pp. 154–55 and n. 739. See also Denis Sinor, "The Establishment and Dissolution of the Türk Empire," *The Cambridge History of Early Inner Asia*, ed. Denis Sinor (Cambridge, 1990), pp. 285–316, especially p. 306. Sinor does not indicate a source, nor does he connect this epidemic with the plague in the time of Justinian.

31. Theophanes, trans. Mango et al., *The Chronicle of Theophanes Confessor*, p. 389 (compare as well the motif of oily crosslets, p. 585).

32. Later Theophanes uses "Turkey" to refer to Khazaria, see for example Theophanes, trans. Mango et al., *The Chronicle of Theophanes Confessor*, p. 567, n. 1 under Masalmas's invasion of "Turkey" (730–731).

33. On this period see P.B. Golden, "The Peoples of the South Russian Steppes," *The Cambridge History of Early Inner Asia,* pp. 256–284; and *An Introduction to the History of the Turkic Peoples. Ethnogenesis and State-Formation in Medieval and Early Modern Eurasia and the Middle East*, Turcologica 9 (Wiesbaden: O. Harrassowitz, 1992), pp. 97–113. Golden does not consider the plague in the time of Justinian or its possible effects.

34. I have cited the translation of this passage in Peter B. Golden, *Khazar Studies. An Historico-Philological Inquiry into the Origins of the Khazars,* i–ii, Bibliotheca Orientalis Hungarica 25 (Budapest, 1980), i, p. 33. See also Agathius, *O tsarstvovanii Iustiniana*, pp. 147–148; and Golden, *An Introduction to the History of the Turkic Peoples*, p. 98.

35. Golden, *Khazar Studies*, i, pp. 33–39. Elsewhere Golden considers this figure "an exaggeration that nonetheless indicates a considerable military presence," see *An Introduction to the History of the Turkic Peoples*, p. 105.

36. On the Türk Empire see Denis Sinor, "The Establishment and Dissolution of the Türk Empire"; and Golden, *An Introduction to the History of the Turkic Peoples*, pp. 127–41.

37. Golden, *Khazar Studies*, i, pp. 39, 50–51.

38. See Dols, *The Black Death in the Middle East*, p. 32, on the plague in Samarqand and Balkh in 448–449/1056–1057 that killed 6,000 people per day in Samarqand and Balkh, which suggests an outbreak of pneumonic plague.

39. See William McNeill, *Plagues and Peoples* (Garden City, NY, 1976); and my "Preliminary Remarks on the Role of Disease in the History of the Golden Horde"; and *The Golden Horde: Economy, Society, and Civilization in Western Eurasia, Thirteenth-Fourteenth Centuries*. See Twitchett, "Population and Pestilence in T'ang China" for doubts concerning the Black Death in China in the fourteenth century.

40. *The Black Death*, ed.-trans. Rosemary Horrox, Manchester Medieval Sources Series (Manchester: Manchester University Press, 1994), pp. 14–26, especially pp. 17–18, 20.

41. This is presumably a reference to Bābalyūn in the vicinity of Cairo, see C.H. Becker, "Bābalyūn," *Encyclopaedia of Islam*, CD-ROM Edition v. 1.0 (Leiden, 1999) [I:844b].

42. Ibn al-Wardī, *Tārīx Ibn al-Wardī* (Najaf, 1969), ii, p. 492. See also my comments in "Preliminary Remarks on the Role of Disease in the History of the Golden Horde," p. 455 n. 29.

43. Gregoras Nicephorus, trans. Jan-Louis van Dieten, *Rhomäische Geschichte*, iii: *Kapitel XI–XVII*, Bibliothek der griechischen Literatur. Abteilung Byzantinistik 24 (Stuttgart, 1988), pp. 175–176; and C.S. Bartsocas, "Two Fourteenth Century Greek Descriptions of the 'Black Death'," *Journal of the History of Medicine and Allied Sciences* 21:4 (1966), pp. 394–400, especially p. 395. My paraphrase is based on the German translation.

44. Timothy S. Miller, "The History of John Cantacuzenus (Book IV): Text, Translation, and Commentary," Ph.D. dissertation (The Catholic University of America, 1975), pp. 185–88; and Bartsocas, "Two Fourteenth Century Greek Descriptions of the 'Black Death'," pp. 395–97.

45. Allen, "The 'Justinianic' Plague," p. 6; and Bartsocas, "Two Fourteenth Century Greek Descriptions of the 'Black Death'," pp. 397–98.

46. Vasiliev, *History of the Byzantine Empire*, pp. 626–27.

47. Maqrīzī, *As-sulūk li-maʿrifat duwal al-mulūk*, ii/3, ed. M.M. Ziada (Cairo, 1958), p. 773.

48. Taha Dinānah, "Die Schrift von Abī Ğaʿfar Aḥmed ibn ʿAlī ibn Moḥammed ibn ʿAlī ibn Ḫātimah aus Almeriah über die Pest," *Archiv für Geschichte der Medizin* 19:1 (1927), pp. 27–81.

49. M. Dols, "Ibn al-Warğī's *Risālah al-nabaʾ ʿan al-wabaʾ*: A Translation of a Major Source for the History of the Black Death in the Middle East," *Near Eastern Numismatics, Iconography, Epigraphy and History. Studies in Honor of George C. Miles*, ed. D. K. Kouymjian (Beirut, 1974), pp. 443–55.

50. Alfred von Kremer, "Über die grossen Seuchen des Orients nach arabischen Quellen," *Sitzungsberichte der Kaiserlichen Akademie der Wissenschaften. Philologisch-historische Klasse* 96:1 (Vienna, 1880), pp. 69–156, especially pp. 136–37; and Dols, *The Black Death in the Middle East*, p. 62.

51. Dols, "Ibn al-Wardī's *Risālah al-nabaʾ ʿan al-wabaʾ*," pp. 445, 451–54.

52. Dols, *The Black Death in the Middle East*, pp. 46, 62–63.

53. Maqrīzī, *As-sulūk li-maʿrifat duwal al-mulūk*, ii/3, pp. 773–74; and Dols, *The Black Death in the Middle East*, pp. 58, 62, 157 n., 174. For a later episode reported for Anatolia in 1429 see Dols, *The Black Death in the Middle East*, p. 205.

54. Maqrīzī, *As-sulūk li-maʿrifat duwal al-mulūk*, ii/3, p. 776; and Dols, *The Black Death in the Middle East*, pp. 58–59.

55. Joseph von Hammer-Purgstall, *Geschichte des osmanischen Reiches*, i (Pest, 1827/Graz, 1963), pp. 138ff.

56. Ernst Werner, *Die Geburt einer Grossmacht—Die Osmanen (1300–1481). Ein Beitrag zur Genesis des türkischen Feudalismus*, Forschungen zur mittelalterlichen

Geschichte 13 (Berlin: Akademie-Verlag, 1966), index: "Pest"; and *Die Geburt einer Grossmacht—Die Osmanen (1300–1481). Ein Beitrag zur Genesis des türkischen Feudalismus*, Forschungen zur mittelalterlichen Geschichte 32 (Weimar: H. Böhlaus Nachfolger, 4th ed., 1985).

57. See *An Economic and Social History of the Ottoman Empire,* 1300–1916, ed. Halil Inalcik and Donald Quataert (New York: Cambridge University Press, 1994), index: "epidemic," "plague" (cf. pp. 231–32, 471 n. 27, 651).

58. Hammer-Purgstall, *Geschichte des osmanischen Reiches*, i, pp. 443–44.

59. Franz Babinger, trans. Ralph Manheim, ed. William C. Hickman, *Mehmed the Conqueror and His Time,* Bollingen Series 96 (Princeton: Princeton University Press, 1978), p. 133.

60. Babinger, *Mehmed the Conqueror and His Time,* pp. 253–54. This is also the earliest episode of plague mentioned in *An Economic and Social History of the Ottoman Empire*, pp. 231–32, citing the fifteenth century historian Kritovoulos. See Kritovoulos, trans. Charles T. Riggs, *History of Mehmed the Conqueror* (Princeton: Princeton University Press, 1954), pp. 219–21.

61. One must wait for the modern period for a monographic treatment of bubonic plague in the Ottoman Empire, see Daniel Panzac, *La peste dans l'empire ottoman,* 1700–1850, Collection Turcica 5 (Leuven: Éditions Peeters, 1980); and trans. Serap Yılmaz, *Osmanlı imparatorluğunda veba (1700–1850)*, Tarih vakfı yayınları 51 (Istanbul, 1997). I was not been able to consult the works of A. Süheyl Ünver for the purposes of this essay (see the citations in Dols and Panzac).

62. See my "Preliminary Remarks on the Role of Disease in the History of the Golden Horde"; and *The Golden Horde: Economy, Society, and Civilization in Western Eurasia, Thirteenth-Fourteenth Centuries*, Chapter 9. Most—but not all—of these phenomena are well known from the literature on the Black Death in Europe and the Middle East (see the literature cited above).

63. See my "The Islamic High Culture of the Golden Horde," *Proceedings of the John D. Soper Commemorative Conference on the Cultural Heritage of Central Asia*, ed. András J. E. Bodrogligeti (in press); "Islamskaya tsivilizatsiya v Zolotoy orde," proceedings of the conference on Islam in the Volga Region (Kazan: Institute of History, in press); and *The Golden Horde: Economy, Society, and Civilization in Western Eurasia, Thirteenth-Fourteenth Centuries*, Chapter 8.

64. See my "The End of Volga Bulgarian"; and "Bolgar tele kaya kitkän?"

65. On Turkish literature in Anatolia in the 13th–14th centuries see in English Alessio Bombaci, trans. Kathleen R.F. Griffin-Burrill, *The Literature of the Turks* (Madison: Turko-Tatar Press, forthcoming), Chapters 15–16.

66. M. Mansuroğlu, "The Rise and Development of Written Turkish in Anatolia," *Oriens* 7 (1954), pp. 250–64, especially p. 261. It will be apparent to readers of this essay that I disagree with Mansuroğlu's explanation in his article of why this shift took place.

67. See Bombaci, *The Literature of the Turks,* Chapter 16.

68. Ahmedi, ed. İsmail Ünver, *İskender-nāme. İnceleme—Tıpkıbasım*, Türk Dil Kurumu Yayınları 504 (Ankara, 1983), p. 14. See the forthcoming edition and study of the historical section of the *İskendername* by Kemal Silay for new evidence regarding the Black Death in Anatolia. I would also like to thank Professor Silay for his comments on this paper.

69. Many of these points are made in Mansuroğlu, "The Rise and Development of Written Turkish in Anatolia," pp. 255–62, while some are my own observations as a Turkologist.

70. M. Fuat Köprülü, *Les origines de l'empire ottoman* (Paris, 1935); trans. Gary Leiser, *The Origins of the Ottoman Empire* (Albany: State University of New York Press, 1992); Paul Wittek, *The Rise of the Ottoman Empire* (London, 1938); and Rudi P. Lindner, *Nomads and Ottomans in Medieval Anatolia*, Uralic and Altaic Series 144 (Bloomington, 1983). It cannot be my task here to review these theories in detail. I refer the reader to the discussion of these and other works in Cemal Kafadar, *Between Two Worlds. The Construction of the Ottoman State* (Berkeley: University of California Press, 1995). For an overview of major scholarship on the history of the Ottoman Empire in this period see most recently the essays in *Osmanlı*, i (Ankara: Yeni Türkiye Yayınları, 1999); and *Türkler*, ix (Ankara: Yeni Türkiye Yayınları, 2002). Many important essays concerning the rise of the Ottoman Empire are translated into Turkish in *Söğüt'ten İstanbul'a. Osmanlı Devleti'nin Kuruluşu üzerine Tartışmalar*, ed. Oktay Özell and Mehmet Öz (Ankara: Fmage Kitabevi, 2000).

71. Halil Inalcik, trans. Norman Itzkowitz—Colin Imber, *The Ottoman Empire. The Classical Age*, 1300–1600 (London: Weidenfeld & Nicolson, 1973), p. 9.

72. Inalcik, *The Ottoman Empire. The Classical Age*, 1300–1600, p. 14.

73. See the discussion in Lindner, *Nomads and Ottomans in Medieval Anatolia.*

74. See the figures in Babinger, *Mehmed the Conqueror and His Time*, pp. 82–83.

75. See V. F. Büchner, "Sīs," *Encyclopaedia of Islam*, CD-ROM Edition v. 1.0 (Leiden, 1999) [IX:678a].

76. I am well aware of the controversial evidence for the use of the terms *gazi* and *gaza* before 1347. See Kafadar, *Between Two Worlds. The Construction of the Ottoman State*, pp. 38, 50–59, 62–90, 109–14, 119–20, and elsewhere.

77. See for example the treatment of this period in Aşıkpaşazade, *Tevarih-i al-ı osman* (Istanbul, A.H. 1332).

78. I am not convinced that this is a plausible or likely explanation.

79. For a discussion of early Ottoman historiography see Kafadar, *Between Two Worlds. The Construction of the Ottoman State*, pp. 90–114 and elsewhere. Kafadar does not, however, give adequate consideration in his work to the historical section in Ahmedi's *İskendername*. See also Heath W. Lowry, *The Nature of the Early Ottoman State* (Albany: State University of New York Press, 2003), a valuable study which appeared after this essay had been submitted for publication.

The Tomb of the Twelfth Imam and Other Tales of Crime

Reeva Spector Simon

The handsome, somewhat disingenuous university professor stumbles upon a plot by some mullahs to overthrow the Shah of Iran, and almost single handedly thwarts the evil machinations of a messianic pretender. Virtually ignored when it first appeared in 1979, re-read today, Richard Bulliet's *The Tomb of the Twelfth Imam* stands as a transitional work in the continuum of twentieth century Anglo-American crime fiction that incorporates Iran as a backdrop. It signals the return of Iran and Iranians as principals in a genre of popular fiction that relies on the exotic, the threat, and Western heroes.

A part of popular culture that began to receive wide readership during the nineteenth century with the detective tales of Edgar Allan Poe and Sir Arthur Conan Doyle, today, the genre includes the detective story, the gothic romance, and the spy novel/thriller, many of whose practitioners cross literary lines to incorporate exotic locales and trendy villains in their work. *The Tomb of the Twelfth Imam* falls into the spy novel/thriller category, as do most of the fifty-three identifiable novels about Iran that have appeared to date. These include two bona fide mysteries—both with Iranian detectives—and one romance.[1] The rest fall under the rubric of thrillers or spy novels.

Less likely to be puzzles where the object of the plot is to solve the crime of murder, spy novels and thrillers rely more on plot and less on character development. Not merely a story, the plot is designed to cut to the cultural quick. It is usually a devious plan for the destruction of the hero, his country—usually Britain or the US, his culture, and in the American tradition—of Western civilization, itself. It necessarily follows that the reader must not identify with the villain. He must support the hero and oppose the evil plans of the villain, which are also projections of attacks on him personally, or why should he bother to read the book? The villain's preparation for implementing the disaster, down to the most minute details, contributes to the suspense and interest that keeps the reader turning the pages.

Despite the disdain of literary critics, who have until recently denigrated or ignored the significance of popular culture, there is a human need for escapist entertainment, be it action movies, spy novels, heroic epics or fairy tales, science fiction, or television. All of these appeal to the emotions and tend to contain, in addition to plots of varying simplicity, the desire to escape from the personal and focus on the global where the reader who identifies with the hero can vicariously overcome cataclysmic adversity.

Characters as well-drawn personalities are less important than what they represent. In this format, they tend to be simplistic, and authors must create heroes and villains that respond with a psychological and cultural resonance to an Anglo-American reading public or one that identifies with the Western mores that are advanced as normative values by the books. In this sense, crime fiction can be described as a type of formulaic literature that perpetuates certain myths, stereotypes, and value projections in the characterization of good and evil and could then, if it were determined that the impact of popular culture were dynamic enough, be used as a vehicle to transmit particular ideas, assumptions, and prejudices. Unlike the British "boys fiction" that supported the imperial ethos of the 19th and early 20th century,[2] however, authors and publishers of contemporary popular fiction more often than not try to anticipate the cultural predilections of the marketplace and take positions that will sell more books.

Generally, the hero embodies only culturally designated positive attributes. He is obviously good, handsome, brave, honorable, chivalrous towards women, defender of country, a striver above the fray, and a winner—all that a popular western hero should be. With the novels of Eric Ambler in the 1930s, we also find the hero as an innocent caught in the web of circumstance much like Professor Asa Groves in *The Tomb of the Twelfth Imam.* He thwarts the conspiracy in spite of himself, rather than as the knight in full armor charging against the dragon. Teachers and Peace Corps volunteers who served there have written some of the best novels about Iran. Standing as correctives of the standard stereotypes, they also impart reliable information about Iranian history and life, caution against ecological dangers of oil spills, impart sympathetic views of the Kurds, and critique American foreign policy.[3]

As the Other, the villain is supposed to represent a negative counterpart to the hero. He is morally weak, sneaky, a coward, often physically ugly or superciliously handsome, a criminal mastermind, and a foreigner. If the villain is not a Westerner, the author can exaggerate differences in ethnicity, dress, speech patterns, and customs or provide him with sociopathic peculiarities in order to create a character that is a direct opposite to the hero. Or, he may be seen to "mimic" the hero—having the educational and cultural accoutrements of the west, but not really being of it, and hence, the object of ridicule or scorn by both his indigenous confrères and the Westerners with whom he so longs to belong. In the early novels about Iran, when either the Shah or his sycophantic SAVAK agents are the villains, sleazy courtiers drawing special characterization appear regularly. Note the officer described in Christopher Landon's *Flag in the City* (1954) where the tribes, "noble savages," are depicted as heroic in contrast to the citified Persians and effeminate banana republic officers: "Shahbahkti," of course, arrived first:

> he was not one to miss a second of anything that was going fine. Greased, scented, and dressed up like a Christmas tree, he was, from the top of his neck-stretching, high-braided collar to the tips of his too pointed lacquered shoes, entirely bogus and repellent. It was a relief to be able to let go of his plump wet hand and turn to escort him round the waiting officers. Two of my captains stared in fascination at the galaxy of medals and orders that danced on his chest. [pp. 16–17]

Despite the caricatures, in this novel about World War II, the real villain is not Iranian, but a German agent called "The Skull." "Islamic" fanatics—initially depicted as "mullahs with scraggly beards," replaced secular Iranians in post-Shah Iran, becoming part of a long tradition of "Islamic fanatic" villains that began to appear in crime fiction as early as 1915.

What is perplexing is that with the popularity of thrillers brought about by the explosion in paperback book publishing in the 1960s and the enormous success of Ian Fleming's James Bond series, there are so few novels using Iran or Iranians for the exotic setting, plots, or villainous characterization. Even as the Middle East increasingly came into the American consciousness after the Arab-Israel War of 1967, with terrorism plots abounding, it took the oil boycotts of the 1970s and the Iranian Revolution at the end of the decade to spark authors' interest in using Iran in their novels. From a sample of more than eight hundred titles covering the entire Middle East that were published from 1911 through 1999,[4] more than five hundred of them appeared after 1970. Of these, only some forty-five were about Iran. In all, we can identify a mere fifty-four novels concerning Iran that appeared from 1942 through 1999. Compare this tally with Egypt where beginning in 1911, we note at least 125 titles and counting.

One can speculate why this is so. For a good part of the twentieth century, neither the British who dominated the genre and the Middle East until the late 1960s, nor Americans whose priority was the Cold War gave much thought to Iran. This general disinterest is reflected in how Iran is depicted in crime fiction of the era. If we examine the plots of novels about Iran, we note that of the twenty novels published before 1979, only three appeared before 1960. One concerned World War I, another looked at the Teheran Conference during World War II, and the third purportedly discussed the Mossadegh regime in the 1950s.[5] Novels written from 1960-1972 placed Iran and the Shah in the context of the Cold War as British and American agents fought to save him from coups by the Soviets and their supporters. Then, for a short period, the Shah became the villain as he attempted to control oil, and the West itself. By the 1980s Iran, under an Islamic regime, emerged as the foil for U.S. agents. In many of the thirty-four novels written after 1979, the plot concerns a direct confrontation between the United States and the Islamic Republic.

The contrast with Egypt is noteworthy. Many of the identifiable plots are concerned with archaeology and Pharaonic Egypt while for Iran, few concern the Shah's preoccupation with pre-Islamic Persia that incorporated the 2500th anniversary of Iranian imperial rule and the celebrations at Persepolis. Eric Pace, journalist for *The New York Times,* uses the ancient Persian capital as a backdrop for his jewel caper *Nightingale* (1979). For Iran, however, unlike Egypt, there is no comparable Egyptomania; the ancient Persians have not drawn the fascination by the West that Egypt has because Persians are "Orientals," not the ancestors of Western civilization. As Persia was never part of the British Empire, British concerns with empire are not relevant in the Iranian context. Egypt under occupation, the Middle East campaigns during World War I and World War II are used for plots even though villains are Europeans. With the Cold War and accession to power of Gamal Abdul Nasser, Egypt is viewed in direct opposition to the West. Sympathetic portrayals return with Anwar Sadat and the view of a secular Egypt combating religious fanaticism.

In fact, Iran does not even appear on the West's radar screen until the Cold War. It was not occupied by the British and was too far removed from India to be a part of the British imperial Great Game. Despite the fact that Russia and Britain carved the country into spheres of interest and the European powers removed Reza Shah from the throne during World War II, the novels appearing before 1960 are gunrunning tales featuring German agents and assassination plots during the two world wars. Unlike other Middle Eastern countries, little changes even with the Cold War, when Iran does appear on the spy novel map. But even here, plots are a true reflection of the West's disinterest in Iran; they are lackadaisical and routine, and Iranians are never depicted out of stereotype. We do not see Westernized Iranians operating and assisting Western agents as Turks do when, for example, James Bond clone Nick Carter is on a mission in Turkey. And Carter, who appears in more than two hundred novels, is not sent to Iran to retrieve microfilm or even to save the Shah who, as both a victim and a negative personality draws authors to plot east of the Levant.[6]

It is rather when Iran becomes personified by the Shah, who, in the context of the Cold War, is used as a diversion for British agents, peripatetic dentists sent on secret missions, or European playboys sent to Iran to protect the ruler from plots by the Soviets, Iranian generals, or even the CIA, that authors set their novels there.[7] In de Villiers's *Versus the CIA*, for example, hero Malko Linge is sent to Teheran to stop a revolution, in which the Shah was to be assassinated and replaced by a CIA puppet. Able to trust only an expatriate Belgian journalist who had a "friend" in Washington and a German airline hostess who had accompanied him on his journey, the Austrian agent working for the United States had to stop the plot before the Russians had time to interfere and before the Shah succumbed to foul play. Other plots have included blackmail: the theft of the Iranian crown jewels and their return in exchange for political power by the communists.[8]

When, in the mid-1970s, the Shah is perceived as threatening to the West—as the megalomaniacial mastermind who contrived to control oil and, through it, the economic destiny of the West—he suddenly emerged as a villain. From that point forward, the Shah, Iran, and the Islamic Republic that followed became a magnet for authors writing of villainy against the West. When Paul Erdman's *The Crash of '79* became a bestseller in 1976, readers suddenly discovered Iran. More than seven months on *The New York Times* bestseller list, the thriller combined a primer on international finance with Iranian villainy—for wasn't the Shah responsible for the long gasoline lines in America during the oil boycott of 1973? U.S. banks, we read, are broke and the stock market is falling, and an American financial wizard is summoned to save America and the West. But, the Shah has the bomb—and with it tries to manipulate control of Persian Gulf oil. In a Four Day War, under the advice of his astrologers and court historian, the Shah makes his move on Saudi Arabia, intending to revive the "Sassanid Empire, an empire that included all the lands bordering on the Persian Gulf on the east, west, and north, and one which had lasted for more than four centuries. It was the reestablishment of the glory of ancient Persia that was the goal of the King of Kings in 1979. For he was fifty-nine, and time was running out." [385] The trouble was that not all of the planes took off: "The King of Kings had won his empire. But now it lay under a cloud of lethal radioactivity; its people were either dead or dying, or fleeing for their lives. And nothing remained of the Shah of Iran. His command bunker—and he—had been vaporized." [423–424]

With the popularity of Erdman's book, other authors capitalized on the Shah's notoriety. In *Red Carpet for the Shah,* the villain attacks the Soviet Union. In other novels, he supervises assassination attempts against himself, drives up the price of silver and bankrupts the West, and contrives a major oil spill that will cause irreparable ecological damage.[9] Other authors took the Shah to task for the Iranian-American abandonment of the Kurds during the 1970s.[10] In these novels and, as he was increasingly seen in Western media during the 1970s, the villainous Shah of Iran is depicted as a megalomaniacal autocrat whose somewhat royal, pristine physiognomy seen on photographs proves to be marred in reality: "The hair, with its deep widow's peak, looked stiff and artificial, like a wig; and the nose was coarse and fleshy, with a slight shine that she had observed increasing during the evening."[11] Even after the Shah fell, authors were unwilling to relinquish SAVAK agents as colorful villains. In Andrew York's *The Combination,* published in 1983, the Shah reverts to victim when he becomes ill and is hospitalized in Egypt.[12]

The Iranian Revolution of 1979 seemed to usher in a new era. Nasser of Egypt was no longer on the scene (1970) and Egypt signed a peace treaty with Israel (1979), which left terrorism as the most visible threat emanating from the region, seemingly with another cast of characters. Islamic fanaticism or Islamism was the danger that once again spilled over into fiction. But, the "Islamic fanatic" plots were hardly new to crime fiction. As far back as World War I, John Buchan's *Greenmantle* (1916) was concerned with the possibility of an Islamic holy war against Britain during World War I. Sax Rohmer's *The Mask of Fu Manchu* (1932) used the theme as did A. J. Quinnell in *The Mahdi* (1982).

What sets these books apart from most of the novels with "Islamic fanatic" villains that appeared during the past two decades is their approach. The British viewed Muslims either as the enemy of Christendom to be conquered politically or economically—or, as noble savages, the biblical residents of the Holy Land.[13] The West had overcome the fear of Islam that was a part of European mythology since the age of the Muslim conquest of Spain and it now looked east to conquer and to dominate. Islam was viewed as an inferior faith or even quaint. What did it say about a people who would be swayed into holy war, wrote Sax Rohmer in 1932, in "response to a mad rumor that El Mokanna, the Masked Prophet [from Khorasan] has come out of his tomb to lead them." This worried the British because "religious revival is overdue among the Moslems, and this business may fill the bill. Superstition is never very far below the surface in even the most cultured Oriental. And these waves of fanaticism are truly incalculable. It's a kind of hypnotism, and we know the creative power of thought"—even for a false prophet.[14] How could an author have the temerity to dedicate his novel to "all believers in Islam; that the simplicity of their faith not blind them to the dangers."[15] It would follow then that submission to faith could be subverted and used to control the otherwise uncontrollable Muslims. In other words, plant a Western mole in "Islam" and manage it.[16]

By the early 1980s it was obvious that "Islam" could not be controlled. The return of Ayatollah Ruhollah Khomeini to Iran, the American hostage crisis, the success of the Islamic revolution, Islamist victories in Afghanistan, and the subsequent emergence of Islamist political parties and regimes throughout the Middle East resuscitated the fear of a direct attack by the irrational East upon the secular, enlightened West. In the 1930s Dennis Wheatley wrote of returning Turkey to the Ottoman-Islamic days before Ataturk[17] and today, the combustible mix of religion and politics has become an even more common theme.

In the Middle East venue, the mullahs replaced the Arab sheikhs and the Shah, who resumed the role of pitiable victim after 1979,[18] when plots about terrorists and economic domination were combined with a dose of religious nationalism.

Initially, plots were replete with explanations of how such a change in Iran could have occurred as authors were at a loss for factual material. Although *The Tomb of the Twelfth Imam* clearly presages the events by describing how the mullah co-opted young Marxist opponents of the Shah, other authors required more complicated conspiracies against the West. There could be an Israeli plot to extirpate a nascent Iranian nuclear capability controlled by an official of the Shah who also has ties to the mullahs who, coincidentally, set the students marching against the military forces in Qom.[19] Americans and British agents are rescued from terrorist mobs, and mercenaries are hired to expedite their exit; oil companies plot to overthrow the Shah and install Khomeini who then turns against his original backers.[20] With the hostage crisis (1979–1980) that, in part, dictated United States foreign policy for the next two decades, Iran was legitimized as a designated foe, and Muslims as "Islamic fanatics" became villains by extension.

Now, not only was the West threatened by control of the oil spigot by the mullahs who also managed to acquire nuclear weapons[21] but "Islamic" conspiracies mirrored the terrorist plots of the 1970s, providing authors with conspiratorial alternatives for the Palestinians who, by the 1990s, were engaged in a peace process with Israel and were slowly being replaced by Islamic "fanatics." These could be Palestinian terrorists who worked for an Islamic regime that controlled them or Lebanese or Shi'ite terrorists who attacked American interests as in a plot to inundate major world cities with anthrax unless Israel is dismantled. In one plot, Palestinian terrorists are controlled by the mullahs of Iran who have "mules" carry the deadly material in perfume bottles past airport authorities.[22] Just as in the generic terrorism plots popular in the 1970s, if authors were at a loss for material, they could have their villains bring on World War III, a nuclear holocaust, Armageddon, and the usual bacterial, chemical, and biological warfare, as well as plant nuclear devices in the United States, kidnap the daughter of the U. S. president, or even plot the assassination of the American leader.[23]

Or, we have the example of the Iranian "enforcer" who harkens back to the medieval Assassins and their leader Hassan-i Sabah in his mountain hideout at Alamut. In this case, "The Anvil," the product of an Iranian father and a British mother whose parents were killed in an Iraqi missile attack during the Iraq-Iran War, is totally devoted to the Ayatollah Khomeini. The modern assassin is sent abroad to kill those who betray the Islamic Republic and before each mission, he goes to the mountain redoubt for inspiration.[24]

When, however, to the surprise of many in the publishing industry, Tom Clancy's *The Hunt for Red October*, published in 1984, became a runaway bestseller, villains had to be upgraded. Lauded by both President Ronald Reagan and Secretary of the Navy John Lehman, Clancy's non-action techno-thriller that reads like a combination chess game and hi-tech manual injected a new element into the spy novel genre that spotlighted American technological capabilities and weapons superiority and revivified the American hero who could once again, in the post-Vietnam era, successfully vanquish the enemy. He could fly a jet or a stealth bomber, command a ship, design a missile, and direct SMART bombs exactly to target without the blood and gore that characterized paperback pulp serials. Consequently, believable adversaries had to be equally technically agile. The villain could no longer be a bumbling terrorist directed by someone else, usually a nasty Westerner.

In the thrillers of today, when Iranians are depicted, they may be terrorists directed by mullahs "with scraggly beards" who have negative attitudes toward women, but the operatives are equal to the American and British heroes in military capability and technological expertise. Whether trained by the Americans or the Russians, Iranians of the Islamic Republic are portrayed in current techno-thrillers as perfectly capable of twenty-first century villainy as they nuke Baghdad, plant nuclear devices in the United States, attempt to steal a stealth bomber, or control the oil supply to the West by controlling computer chip technology.[25]

The combination of Clancy's financial success with the Gulf War victory and the lingering characterization of Saddam Hussein as current designated villain has enabled authors with military hi-tech experience to generate thrillers that star American military technology operated by the American military, former astronauts, and ship commanders.[26] Requiring villainous adversaries for the heroes to shoot at, authors use Iraqis and Iranians, sometimes in interesting combinations. In David Mason's *Shadow over Babylon,* the British wonder who really was behind the assassination of Saddam in an operation that they thought they were controlling; but the reader notes the wink between the Iranian mullahs sitting in the car as they drive away from the meeting.[27] Other authors praise the virtues of officers from the Shah's army who now must avert war with Saudi Arabia and deal with duels between nuclear submarines in the Persian Gulf[28] or pit the Security Minister, a Mr. Akhbar al-Yawm who supports a pro-Western prime minister, against a Minister of Defense who is a religious fanatic.[29]

By the end of the 1990s, Iranian characters mirror an evolving, although begrudging respect by American authors for the Islamic Republic that could use Western technology without absorbing the ideology. There are even Westernized Iranian operatives walking the streets of New York City trying to infiltrate groups of Islamic militants while working for super-secret offices within the Iranian intelligence organization in an attempt to prevent a major terrorist attack.[30] It will be interesting to see where authors take the Iranians from here.

When he wrote *The Tomb of the Twelfth Imam*, Richard Bulliet predicted the emergence of the Islamic Republic. After September 11, Americans have become acutely aware of the significance of Pakistan. Will Pakistani control of the Saudi oil fields be next?[31]

Endnotes

1. Joseph Koenig, *Brides of Blood* (New York: Grove Press, 1993); Salar Abdoh, *The Poet Game* (New York: Picador, 2000); Donald R. Barton, *Once in Aleppo* (New York: Scribner's, 1955).

2. John M. Mackenzie, ed., *Popular Imperialism and the Military, 1850–1950* (Manchester: University of Manchester Press, 1992); Joseph Bristow, *Empire Boys: Adventures in a Man's World* (London: Harper Collins Academic, 1991).

3. William Copland, *Five Hours from Isfahan* (New York: G. Putnam's Sons, 1975); Efrem Sigel, *The Kermanshah Transfer* (New York: Macmillan, 1973); Hammond Innes, *The Black Tide* (Garden City: Doubleday, 1983); James Aldrige, *Mockery in Arms* (London: Joseph, 1974).

4. The sample comes from Reeva Spector Simon, *Terrorists, Fanatics, and Spies: The Middle East in Twentieth Century Thrillers and Detective Novels* (forthcoming).

5. Rex Adams, *Star of Persia* (London: George Harrap and Company, Ltd., 1942); Christopher Landon, *Flag in the City* (New York: Macmillan, 1954); Donald R. Barton, *Once in Aleppo* New York: Scribner's, 1955).

6. These James Bond-type series rarely used Iran even for location. See, for example, Edward Aarons, *Assignment Moon Girl* where Iran is the setting for operations of a Chinese agent.

7. James Leasor, *Passport to Oblivion* (London: Heinemann, 1965). Leasor, a dentist by trade is also a British agent who is sent to Teheran to thwart an assassination plot against the Shah. See also Simon Harvester, *Unsung Road* (London: Jarrolds, 1960).

8. In Peter Somerville-Large's *Couch of Earth* (London: Gollancz, 1975), the British thwart a Communist and Left-wing coup against the Shah; Eric Pace, *Nightingale* (New York: Random House, 1979) concerns a plot to steal crown jewels and return them to the Shah in exchange for power for the communists.

9. Peter Ritner, *Red Carpet for the Shah* (New York: William Morrow, 1975); In Alan Williams, *Shah-Mak [A Bullet for the Shah]* (London: Blond, 1976) the Shah plots an assassination attempt against himself; Benjamin Stein with Herbert Stein, *On the Brink* (1977) concerns a conspiracy by Saudi Arabia and Iran to drive up the price of oil that leads to runaway inflation and prospects of economic disaster in the US and the West.

10. Efrem Sigel, *The Kermanshah Transfer* (1973); James Aldridge, *Mockery in Arms* (1974); Yoram Hamizrahi, *Golden Lion and the Sun* (New York: Dutton, 1982).

11. Williams, *Shah-Mak,* p. 260.

12. Andrew York, *The Combination* (Garden City: Doubleday, 1983).

13. Henri Baudet, Paradise on Earth: Some Thoughts on European Images of Non-European Man (New Haven: Yale University Press, 1965), pp. 1–2.

14. Sax Rohmer, *The Mask of Fu Manchu* (New York: Pyramid Books, 1932), p. 21.

15. A. J. Quinnell, *The Mahdi* (New York: William Morrow, 1982), dedication page.

16. Examples: John Buchan, *Greenmantle* (London: Hodder, 1916); Sax Rohmer, *The Mask of Fu Manchu*; Peter Abrahams, *Tongues of Fire* (New York: M. Evans, 1982); A. J. Quinnell, *The Mahdi* (New York: William Morrow, 1982).

17. Dennis Wheatley, *The Eunuch of Stamboul* (London: Hutchinson, 1935).

18. Andrew York's *The Combination* is a tale of the attempt to steal the crown jewels of Iran while the Shah lay dying in Egypt.

19. Colin MacKinnon, *Finding Hoseyn* (New York: Arbor House, 1986).

20. Examples: Rick Rider, *Dyed for Death* (New York: Belmont-Tower, 1980); Gerald Seymour, *Running Target* (New York: William Morrow, 1989); Barry Chubin, *The Feet of a Snake* (New York: TOR, 1984); Joseph Koenig, *Brides of Blood* (New York: Grove Press, 1993).

21. Timothy Rizzi, *The Phalanx Dragon* (New York: Donald I. Fine, 1994).

22. Gordon Thomas, *Deadly Perfume* (London: Chapman's, 1991).

23. See, for example, John D. Randall, *The Jihad Ultimatum* (Dallas: Saybrook, 1988); Hashian, *Shanidar* (New York: Wynwood Press, 1990); William Christie, *The Warriors of God* (New York: Lyford Books, 1992).

24. Gerald Seymour, *A Line in the Sand* (New York: Simon and Schuster, 1999).

25 Michael Skinner, *First Air* (Presidio, 1991); John D. Randall, *The Jihad Ultimatum* (1988); Timothy Rizzi, *The Phalanx Dragon* (New York: Donald I. Fine, 1994); Dale Brown, *Shadows of Steel* (New York: Putnam, 1996).

26. Timothy Rizzi, *The Phalanx Dragon*; Jack Merek, *Target Stealth* (New York: Warner Books, 1989).

27. David Mason, *Shadow over Babylon* (New York: Dutton, 1993).

28. Sean Flannery, *Kilo Option* (New York: Tom Doherty, 1996).

29. Timothy Rizzi, *The Phalanx Dragon* (New York: Donald I. Fine, 1994).

30. Salar Abdoh, *The Poet Game* (New York: Picador USA, 2000).

31. Richard Bulliet, *The Gulf Scenario* (New York: St. Martin's Press, 1984).

Islam on the Eighteenth-Century Stage: Voltaire's *Mahomet* Crosses the Atlantic

D. A. Spellberg

Before 1500 Europeans crossed the Atlantic in order to circumvent Islamic presence and power in the Mediterranean. Christians went West to find the East and exploit it, but their medieval perceptions of Muslims were not so easily avoided. In the realm of fictive history, in the minds of Christians of varied persuasions, Islam remained symbolically central to an emerging, increasingly mobile form of European polemic about power, faith, and identity. One might say that Atlantic history, as a European construction in space and time thus begins, implicitly, with Islamic hegemony.[1]

Before Europeans ever thought to control the Middle East, they posited a transitional, premodern form of Orientalism that reflected their own self-absorption with the nature of Christian religion and empire. Ultimately, these multiple, culturally distinct vocabularies of religion and empire were first depicted in a Transatlantic trial run before the advent of nineteenth-century European imperialism in the Middle East. It should be recalled that until 1783, even the British colonies that would become the United States were part of an imperial system.[2]

In terms of European historiography, I situate Transatlantic images of Islam and Muslims in North and South America as both variations and extensions of extant medieval assumptions that were reworked over time to suit new challenges. These American categorizations defined new populations with consistent reference to old ones, no matter how inaccurate or strained the conceptual shift. From the perspective of the history of the Middle East and its Muslim majority, this imperial European Atlantic experiment may be perceived as an intermission in the Christian struggle to assert cultural superiority over the Islamic Mediterranean and points East. Aspects of the European depiction of Muslim as Other would reinvigorate the nineteenth-century Christian incursion into the Middle East, but that journey from medieval to modern may best be understood in the intermediary context of Western, Transatlantic expansion and empire with each European imperial player struggling with "new" populations while entrapped within Old World paradigms. This included Islam as a civilizational enemy, both practically and symbolically. It is during this period that we may map European thought enroute and in America from 1742 through 1782. During this period French ideas about Islam provoked new registers of meaning in performance in London, Dublin, New York City, and Baltimore. One play about Islam and its Prophet would dramatize changing Christian religious and political notions when it crossed the Atlantic.

Voltaire's *Fanatisme*, or *Mahomet the Prophet*, was not merely translated, but transformed in the Transatlantic Anglophone world of the eighteenth-century theatre. After being banned by French censors in Paris in 1742, Voltaire's original work underwent changes in form and substance as well as perfomative strategies that resulted in a series of dramatic consequences unintended by the author and most certainly out of his control.

Through the use of prologues, newspaper reviews, and broadsides, the play became freighted with a variety of polemics about faith, empire, and identity. The circulation of the play in both Europe and America dictated the different ideological transformations in which the work might be both framed and received. Immediate and quite distinct political and religious concerns in London, Dublin, New York City, and Baltimore quickly transformed Voltaire's *Mahomet* into a play that might be perceived and received quite differently despite its core, allegedly static, central text about the origins of Islam. Although played to majority Christian audiences in the same British imperial sphere, the meaning of Islam as an enemy faith was never so simply troped as a monolithic Other. Instead Muslims held the mirror up to Christians: their contested interpretations of faith, their conflict over world empire, and their emerging notions of national identity. In the history of the United States, *Mahomet* is most certainly the first play containing informational content about the founding of the Islamic faith to be publicly presented both in the colonial and the fledgling United States.[3] The tragedy in five acts is reflected in the chronological and spatial structure of this essay.

Act I: Paris 1742

Most scholars of Western history and Islamic culture concur that this play was a vehicle for Voltaire's roundabout attack on Christianity.[4] As yet another Western appropriation of the East, Voltaire made a distorted founding history of Islam and its Prophet a vehicle for the critique of all religious zealots and the violence they inevitably produced. Although the original was titled *Le Fanatisme, ou Mahomet Le Profète*, Voltaire never uses the word "Islam," and refers to "Musulman," or Muslim only once.[5] Voltaire had earlier read George Sales' English translation of the Qur'an and would later take a much more positive stance toward Islam in his *Dictionnaire Philosophique*, but his play must be perceived as a series of conscious polemical choices designed to challenge the religious complacency of a French Catholic audience. In this work, faith is merely a tool through which to achieve political power, one of many messages that was not lost on French clerics, who closed *Fanaticism* after three performances at La Comédie Française. As if to complicate matters further, the Ottoman ambassador visiting Paris also lodged a protest against Voltaire's play.[6] A most unlikely holy alliance was formed by the distinctly different objections of the Muslim ambassador together with the Catholic clergy. The politics of faith, both national and international, stopped *Fanaticism* cold. It would not be performed in Paris again until 1751, when the Pope himself acknowledged Voltaire's repeated appeals. Voltaire praised the Pope as the head of the "true religion" and declared Muhammad, the ostensible subject of his banned play, "the founder of a false and barbarous sect."[7] The Church of France had finally to yield to the will of Rome, but Voltaire's religious politics in the matter of fanaticism seemed somewhat muddied in the process.

Act II: London 1744

According to one historian of theatre, it is "one of the little ironies of dramatic history that *Le Fanatisme*, attacked by supporters of the Church in France, should have been introduced to England by two clergymen, James Miller and John Hoadley."[8] Of course, the appeal of Voltaire's work on Islam for these two Anglicans revealed that the very controversy it had aroused in Paris might assure its instant popularity on the London stage. The English usage of Voltaire in this instance provided a vehicle for an attack against France and its faith. Reborn across the channel as *Mahomet the Impostor*, the Anglican vision of Islam became a distinct opportunity to express English intolerance and superiority in the face of the French enemy across the channel.[9]

The plot of this rather different version was still set in Arabia at the time of Prophet Muhammad's attempt to take final control of Mecca and convert all to his monotheist message. It featured hidden identities, patricide, a hint of of incest, and hardly any accurate Islamic history. The English translators quickly excised Voltaire's original incestuous yearning between the young captives Palmira and Zaphna, who do not know until it is almost too late that they are, respectively, sister and brother. In this state of ignorance, both are raised by Mahomet. Zaphna becomes a patricide and is poisoned before he can expose Mahomet as a charlatan. Palmira dies rather than succumb to the muted libidinous interest of this theatrical prophet. Thus, the impostor succeeds at the bloody expense of innocence and virtue making quite a final morbid tableau on stage.

In the *London General Advertiser* of 1744, the censorship of Voltaire's work in Paris was in itself summoned as a tactic to promote increased ticket sales in London:

> The original was by Authority forbid to be played in France on account of the free and noble Sentiments with regard to Bigotry and Enthusiasm, which shine through it; and that Nation [France] found as applicable to itself, as to the bloody propagators of Mahomet's Religion.[10]

Taking the form of a news bulletin, the promotion for the play conflated a European nation, France, with the "propagators of Mahomet's religion." A more explicit simile in the next few lines then defines Catholic Christianity as a form of fanaticism analogous to Islam in which the true Protestant object of persecution is revealed.

> . . . So that it was equally impossible for the poet, by cutting and mangling his play, to lop it to their standard of Orthodox poetry, as it were for their Inquisitors by torturing and burning a poor protestant, to convince him of their Christian love and charity . . . [11]

Voltaire himself may have intended to draw this very predictable parallel between forms of Christianity at the expense of Islam.

The prologue of the play, a polemical and didactic piece, designed to direct the audience's attention, was spoken at the first performance by a certain actor surnamed Harvard. Considering the singularity of the earlier promotion and the heavy-handed theme of the thirty-two verse prologue, it is not unlikely that both works may be attributed to Rev. Hoadly, an Anglican and a radical Whig. His ideology bound ideas of tyranny, empire, and identity closely to Anglican definitions of faith. Thus, the prologue frames Catholic France as a threat to Protestant Britain, conflating it as a fanatic menace to both Voltaire and "true" faith.

On English ground he makes a better stand
And hopes to suffer no hostile Hand
No clergy here usurp the free-born mind,
Ordained to teach, and enslave mankind;
Religion here bids persecution cease,
Without, all order, and within, all Peace;
Religion to be Sacred must be free;
Men will suspect—where bigots keep the key.[12]

Still, somehow Voltaire retains a special, exalted place in England, his literary inclinations and his travels to that land well remembered.

Britons, these numbers to yourselves you owe;
Voltaire hath strength to shoot in Shakespeare's bow;
With English Freedom, English wit he know,
And from the inexhausted Stream profusely drew.

Despite the promotion, the play was not an instant hit.[13] It would need to be rewritten once more, shortened really, in a 1765 version by David Garrick, actor-manager of the Drury Theatre, for it to become a smash. In the interim, it would play the provinces and create a riot in Dublin before returning to greater fame in the metropole.

Act III: Dublin 1754

As part of the British empire, Ireland's theatrical life in the eighteenth century was closely tied to London and, by extension, Paris. Recent studies suggest that Voltaire's plays, in their English versions, represented the majority of French dramas viewed on the Dublin stage.[14] These ties were also supported by exchanges between actors from London and Dublin. *Mahomet* played the Theatre-Royal Smock Alley in Dublin in 1754, but at the second performance a riot ensued between two local Protestant political parties. The audience in the Dublin theatre had no reaction whatsoever to the virulently anti-Catholic prologue of *Mahomet* because they were mostly Protestants for whom such sentiments did not prove offensive.

The politics of the local Irish Protestant elite were complex. Two groups emerged: one, the Government or Courtier Party, staunchly loyal to the Castle, the seat of the British-appointed Lieutenant Governor in Dublin, and the other, an emerging Protestant Country or Patriot group. Both, proud of their British Protestant identity, strove against one another for greater control of the Irish Parliament, with the Patriots attempting to assert their desire for greater local freedoms.

The riot in the Smock-Alley theatre was a carefully orchestrated attempt to assert Patriot party protest against both the Government Party and the behavior of the theatre manager, Thomas Sheridan (d. 1788), who like all those in his position held a royal warrant for his appoinment.[15] Sheridan, father of Richard Brinsley, had weekly dinners at which he demonstrated a marked preference for the Government party. His partisan behavior made him a target for Patriot party enmity, which was thus transferred to his theatre and the performances he staged.

The Patriot party demanded that the following lines be repeated on the first night of *Mahomet's* performance:

> If ye powers divine
> Ye mark the movements of this nether world
> And bring them to Account;
> Crush, crush the vipers,
> Who singl'd out by a community
> To guard their nights, Shall for a grasp of ore
> Or paultry office, Sell them to the foe.[16]

The newspaper, *The Dublin Spy,* immediately interpreted these lines as pro-Patriot in intent after the first performance. Had Miller intended this in his translation? Had Voltaire even thought of Ireland when penning the very different, original French lines? Doubtful. Still, an Irish journalist asserted of the moment:

> A spirit of Freedom enlivens the tragic Scenes of *Mahomet the Impostor,* indeed almost every line carries with it its point. If it had been calculated purely for the Meridian of Ireland, the acumens which run through some of the spirited Speech could not carry a keener edge.[17]

The focus on these ideas in transit from France to London to Dublin as somehow more pertinent to Ireland than elsewhere reveals the importance of examining circulating theatrical ideas in the specific context in which they were performed. Theatrical content was not shaped, in the case of *Mahomet*, by a static text, but even in its English adaptation was subject to very different interpretations by very different audiences. In Dublin, responses to *Mahomet* had absolutely nothing to do with Islam or Catholicism or Protestantism, or pleas for religious tolerance or empire. Instead, the Dublin performance provoked a display of political and personal intolerance. Once abstracted, the play became a facile, potentially universal allegory about tyranny, freedom, and partisanship. The message in its Irish context transcended any definitions of authorial intent, either by Miller or Voltaire, and was readily recalibrated to the political rhetoric of Dublin party politics.

On the second night of the performance, March 2, 1754, Patriot partisans demanded the actor repeat the same speech a second time. The actor hinted that the manager, Sheridan, known to be pro-Government, would not let him obey the audience's partisan Patriot request. When Sheridan failed to address the crowd in person, the mob, some with swords, some with bottles, and some with fire, proceeded to destroy the theatre. By morning all that was left was a burned out shell. Sheridan resigned and returned to London, from whence he wrote "A Vindication of the Conduct of the Late Manager of the Theatre-Royal Humbly Adddres'd to the Publick." This pamphlet was too little, too late, but it did raise interesting questions about the nature of the theatre as an autonomous professional arena for political debate, even strife given the right contextual cues, which in this case included words attributed to Voltaire about Islam.

Act IV: New York 1780

During the American Revolutionary War, *Mahomet the Impostor* was performed by both sides in the conflict, a testament to a shared theatrical heritage, as well as the demonstrated ideological flexibility of this particular play. British military forces, especially officers, often staged amateur theatrical performances during the Revolutionary War. The officer corps were the primary actors for these productions. In New York the troup was dubbed "Clinton's Thespians" after the Commander in Chief of the Colonies. They were quartered and besieged in the year 1780 in New York City. We have evidence of a single performance of *Mahomet*, on November 11, from a Tory newspaper, which also records a new prologue for this entertainment. It should be noted that while colonial rebels ringed New York City, the British were now also fighting the French, who had allied themselves with the Americans two years before. The prologue was spoken by a young officer who, we are told, was dressed as "An Indian Chief."

I am a Chief, native of these Lands,
Proud to obey the British King's Commands,

Charmed with Your Virtue, and Superior Grace,
Knowledge we Seek from your Englighten'd Race;
Though Christian Moral Truths to us are new—
Yet pleas'd with Virtue, we are charm'd with you,[18]

These lines contain, in miniature, an ode to British superiority which must have pleased the British and Tory audience enormously. The native American impersonator manages to inflect his paternalist ventriloquism with just the right mix of racism and imperialism. It was also an indisputable fact of the conflict that Native Americans sided with the British against the Colonists during the Revolutionary War. The rebellious rebels are rebuked, by the Chief in both harsh religious and strongly maternal terms.

Make false apostate Subjects blush to own,
That Indians are more Loyal to the Crown,
Than those the Parent Country bred and bore,
Clasp'd to her Breast, and nourish'd on this Shore.[19]

Yet the global imperial mission still targets England against France the audience is reminded. When this little American uprising is finished, Britain will return to the greater global mission.

Teach false perfidious France and haughty Spain,
That British Sailors will command the Main.[20]

Voltaire's play, with its newly minted British prologue, preached to an audience of partisans that they were entitled to rage against the ingrates who now fought them in North America, rejecting their long protection and many civilizing gifts. Once hostilities had ended, however, the British would still rule the world and continue to defeat the French in the global contest.

Voltaire's play formed the backdrop for this timely propaganda, but it is doubtful that this abuse of his dramatic work had been forseen by its French author in 1742. Voltaire may have had no love for his fanatic French Catholic Church, but there is strong evidence that he supported his country when they declared their support for the colonies against Britain in the Revolutionary War. The hack who penned this New York prologue praising the ultimate international superiority of Britain over France added a new dimension to the play's original title, *Fanaticism*, a somewhat ironic and also unintended consequence of the play's Anglophone fame.

Act V: Baltimore 1782

The performance of *Mahomet* in Baltimore in 1782 was undertaken by a pro-Revolutionary group, the American Company of Comedians, whose purpose was to entertain American and French troops in the wake of the pivotal defeat of British troops at Yorktown in 1781. Finally, Voltaire's work, albeit in English and in North America, would play to an audience of his countrymen. As a venue for the performance of *Mahomet*, Baltimore was ideologically and demographically the antithesis of New York City in 1780, the site of the play's North American debut. Baltimore had never been occupied during the Revolutionary War by British troops. Instead, the support of its citizenry and the control of its single newspaper remained anti-British throughout the conflict. The play, as performed in October 1782, would also reflect the celebratory atmosphere of the Revolutionary War's near triumphal conclusion in 1783.

The theatre manager's life in Baltimore 1782 was not an easy one according to extant sources. The eighteenth-century audience appears to have been somewhat unruly.

> No person will, on any Pretence, be admitted behind the Scenes. Any Gentleman possessed of good Comedies or Farces, and will lend or dispose of them to the managers, greatly oblige them. Whereas several evil-disposed Persons frequent the Theatre for no other Purpose than to create Disturbance, by throwing Apples, Bottles &c. on the Stage—This is to give Notice, that proper Means will be taken to detect such Practices for the Future, and bring the Perpetrators to the most exemplary Punishment.[21]

The single Baltimore newspaper working during this time is full of praise for the 500 French troops that remained stationed in the fall of 1782. They may well have been the most obvious audience at whom the performance of Voltaire's *Mahomet* was intended.[22]

Extant broadsides of the play, which was twice performed in Baltimore, stated that *Mahomet* was "Translated from the French of the celebrated Voltaire by the Rev. Mr. Miller." Thus, the author's play had come full circle, finally finding a venue in English in which decidedly pro-French political sympathies combined with an American and French audience, a literary and patriotic combination. These same broadsheets preserve the income generated by the two performances of the play in Baltimore. For the first performance, the play set a Company low, with only fifty-four pounds generated. The revenues of the second presentation, however, more than doubled the earnings of the work at one hundred and thirteen pounds.[23] These totals were calculated by the managers upon the advertised price per seat of boxes one dollar and the pit one shilling. Warnings were also posted that "Children in Laps will not be admitted."[24]

In an ideal world the historian might uncover a prologue to one of the Baltimore performances of *Mahomet* which would preserve an American tirade against the tyranny of the British enemy and King George III. Although such patriotic prologues do exist from this Baltimore company, they are attached to other plays, one of which is dedicated to "his Excellency General Washington."[25] Spoken by a female actor, the poem is a moving recitation of a wife's lot, mixing ideals of manhood with a parallel typology of patriotism. All key concepts of the period: liberty, freedom, independence are coupled with a feminized domestic view of a gendered nation, one in which women order the married hierarchy.

To be a patient wife, I grant's a curse;
But then, old Maid! O Lud! that's surely worse,
Suppose we marry then, and stand the test—
But hold, what kind of men will suit us best?
A Fool—no, no—there we can't agree———
The Man of Courage is the man for me.
Who fights for glorious Liberty, will find
His empire rooted in the female mind.
'Tis base Slave that stains the name of Man,
Who bleeds for Freedom will extend his plan;
Will keep the generous principle in view,
And with the Ladies Independent too.[26]

The twin themes of female perspective and masculine ideals assert here a predictable patriotic theme in a distinctly different voice. Yet this formulation of political theory, with its harsh words for "slave" and its praise for masculine empire "rooted in the female mind" suggests ideology turned on its head to entertain. Whether male or female, the author of this theatrical entertainment demonstrated that British tyranny would not interrupt a nascent national conversation on the domestic fray.

Mahomet continued to be performed in the United States throughout the rest of the late eighteenth and early nineteenth centuries. In the midst of great national and local debates about freedom of religion in the Constitution, the play would continue to attract audiences in Boston, New York City, and Charleston, South Carolina.[27] Replete with prejudice toward the origins of a faith most Americans hardly knew, *Mahomet* insulted the Prophet and demeaned the origins of a major monotheism, an artifact of European Orientalism that survived the Transatlantic voyage and the Revolution.

Yet there were more truthful representations of Islam to be found in eighteenth and nineteenth century America than were offered in European dramas. The sources for such knowledge were contemporary Muslims of West African origin who had also crossed the Atlantic. Unfortunately, their enslavement severely limited their didactic range and impact. The evidence of a living Islam in America is attested by the preservation of more than one hundred and fifty names of Arabic origin[28] during this early national period of United States history. Many of these Muslim survivors of the Atlantic slave trade left written Arabic testimony to their faith as evidence of a very real rather than theatric Islamic tragedy.[29] The advertisement for the play *Mahomet* in the *Baltimore Advertiser* in 1782 is flanked by the offer of a reward for a runaway slave.[30] Such proximity seems no accident.

Endnotes

1. In August 2000 a longer version of this essay was presented at the International Seminar on the History of the Atlantic World, 1500–1800 at Harvard University, directed by Dr. Bernard Bailyn.

2. A point somehow overlooked by Edward Said, *Culture and Imperialism* (New York: Vintage Books, 1993), who also, as in previous works, deletes the Orientalist and imperialist impact upon the presence of both Americas until the twentieth century.

3. I fondly recall that this play was also first briefly presented in Professor Richard W. Bulliet's graduate seminar in September 1980. Then, I had no notion of an eighteenth-century American connection.

4. Djavad Hadidi, *Voltaire et L'Islam,* (Paris: Publications Orientalistes de France, 1974); Magdy Badir, "Voltaire et L'Islam," in T. Besterman, ed., *Studies on Voltaire and the Eighteenth Century,* pp. 5–226 (Banbury, England: The Voltaire Foundation, 1974); Robert J. Allison, *The Crescent Obscured: The United States and the Muslim World* (New York: Oxford University Press, 1995), pp. 43-7; and Ahmad Gunny, *Images of Islam in Eighteenth Century Writings* (London: Grey Seal,1996), pp.140–1.

5. Francois Marie Arouet de Voltaire, *Mahomet: tragedie*, Bruxelles, 1742. Houghton Library, Harvard University; Francois Marie Arouet de Voltaire, *Le Fanatisme ou Mahomet Le Profète* (Paris: Garnier Frères, 1938).

6. Badir, "Voltaire," p. 94; Fatma Muge Gocek, *East Encounters West: France and the Ottoman Empire in the Eighteenth Century* (New York: Oxford University Press, 1987), p. 80.

7. Voltaire, *Fanatisme,* ed. Garnier, pp. 222–3.

8. Harold Lawton Bruce, "Voltaire on the English Stage," *University of California Publications in Modern Philology* 8 (1918): 57.

9. James Miller, *Mahomet the Impostor. A Tragedy. As it is acted at the Theatre-Royal Drury Lane, by His Majesty's servants.* London: 1744. Humanities Research Center, The University of Texas at Austin.

10. Arthur H. Scouten, ed. *The London Stage 1660–1800: A Calendar of Plays, Part 3: 1729–1747* (Carbondale, Illinois: Southern Illinois University Press, 1961), p. 1104.

11. Ibid.

12. Miller, *Mahomet,* 1744.

13. Ibid.

14. Simon Davies, "Ireland and the French Theatre," in *Ireland and the French Englightenment, 1700–1800*, ed. G. Gargett and G. Sheridan (New York: St. Martin's Press, 1999), p. 200.

15. Allison, *Crescent,* p. 44, who incorrectly dates the Dublin riot to 1744, and states, without support, on p. 43 that, "It is hard to recover the immediate political meaning that provoked this response." Many others have done so, including Simon Davies and Thomas Sheridan himself, "A Vindication of the Conduct of the Late Manager of the Theatre-Royal: Humbly Address'd to the Publick," Dublin, 1754.

16 . Miller, *Mahomet,* 1744.

17. La Tourette Stockwell, *Dublin Theatres and Theatre Customs, 1637–1820* (Kingsport, Indiana: Kingsport Press, 1938), p. 111.

18. *Rivington's Royal Gazette,* November 1, 1780. American Antiquarian Society, Worcester, Massachusetts. For what is perhaps an earlier and too strongly asserted confluence between Muslims and Indians, see Nabil Matar, *Turks, Moors & Englishmen in the Age of Discovery* (New York: Columbia University Press, 1999), pp. 169–181. See also, Jared Brown, *The Theatre in America during the Revolution* (New York: Cambridge University Press, 1995).

19. Ibid.

20. Ibid.

21. MS 2415, "Theatrical Playbill Collection," Maryland Historical Society, Baltimore, Maryland. See also Silverman, Kenneth, (*A Cultural History of the American Revolution* (New York: Crowell Company, 1976), p. 26.

22. Thomas J. Scharf, *The Chronicles of Baltimore,* (Baltimore: Turnbull and Brothers, 1874), pp. 203–205; *The Maryland Journal and the Baltimore Advertiser,* September 3, 1782, which states that "about 500 French Troops remain in and near this Town, under the Command of General La Valette," American Antiquarian Society, Worcester, Massachusetts. See also, Lynn, Haims, "First American Theatre Contracts:

Wall and Lindsay's Maryland Company of Comedians, and the Annapolis, Fell's Point, and Baltimore Theatres, 1781–1783," *Theatre Survey* 17 no. 2 (November 1976): 193.

23. Broadside, October 1, October 15, 1782, New York Historical Society.

24. Ibid.

25. MS 2415, Maryland Historical Society, Baltimore, Maryland. The play is *Gustavas Vasa, the Deliverer of His Country.*

26. Ibid. June 28, 1782.

27. Bruce, *Voltaire*, p. 142; and Waldo Lewis, *The French Drama in America* (Baltimore: Johns Hopkins Press, 1942), p. 128.

28. Sylviane Diouf, *Servants of Allah: African Muslims Enslaved in the Americas* (New York: New York University Press, 1998).

29. Allan D. Austin, *African Muslims in Antebellum America: Transatlantic Stories and Spiritual Struggles* (New York: Routledge, 1997).

30. *The Maryland Journal and Baltimore Advertiser*, September 3, 1782. American Antiquarian Society, Worcester, Massachusetts.

The Gendered Edge of Islam

Elizabeth Thompson

In his book *Islam: The View from the Edge*, Richard Bulliet offers a new, dialectical paradigm for Islamic history.[1] He proposes that Islamic society has been fundamentally shaped by converts and the process of conversion; that is, by Muslims located on the edges of Islamic society far from the caliphal courts in Damascus and Baghdad and from the centers of learning in Medina, Cairo and elsewhere. As this orthodox "center" absorbed waves of converts into Islamic society (the umma), it was itself modified by the encounter with newcomers and marginal peoples. This dialectical process produced, at critical historical periods, the social and religious institutions that have structured life in cities throughout the Islamic world.[2] As I have come to understand it in the classroom and in his book, Bulliet's paradigm represents a broad and radical rereading of Islamic history, which has usually been studied from the perspective of caliphs and scholars seated securely in the orthodox center. My reading also suggests the value of the center-edge paradigm when applied to specific areas of Middle Eastern history.[3]

I will propose here that viewing Islam's historical development as a negotiation between center and edge throws new light on the gender history of the region. With the rise of Islamic institutions in the middle ages, women were constituted as an edge, far from the centers of religious authority. Unlike other edges, however, women were not targets of absorption by the center. In seeming violation of Bulliet's center-edge dialectic, writings of prominent ʿulama suggest that they viewed women as a permanent edge never to be absorbed, a bulwark against the historical pressure to change. Re-viewing medieval women's history through Bulliet's lens, in turn, offers a new perspective on the modern period. It helps to explain why the transformation of gender roles since the nineteenth century has produced such violent reactions from (male) Muslim leaders, evident in interminable debates about the woman question and in the agendas of nationalist and Islamic movements. It also suggests that the most radical Muslim feminists today are not those who reject Islam and embrace secularism, but rather those who study scripture and sharia law. They pose the graver threat to the old center, as they seek to appropriate a measure of religious authority for themselves.

Bulliet's Dialectical Paradigm

Converts played such an important role in the development of Islamic institutions, Bulliet argues, because the fluid nature of authority in Islam did not encourage a hierarchical power structure. In the early Islamic centuries, converts were free to choose as religious leaders whoever provided satisfying answers to their questions. Just as the Prophet did not designate a strict principle of succession to his leadership of the early community, so each generation of Muslims would debate and determine the kind of leadership it deemed appropriate. Converts wielded greater influence on Islamic history at certain conjunctures, such as in Iran in the early medieval period. In Bulliet's parlance, cities like Gorgan and Nishapur became a powerful "edge" in Islam, a place where people crossed into the umma. Geographical and demographic factors made cities in northeastern Iran (Khurasan) important centers of religious practice and learning. By the 900s, their populations swelled with converts from the hinterland. These converts sought guidance in living a pious Muslim life from urban preachers, mystics and legal scholars. Sayings of the Prophet (hadith) were collected and transmitted in the early centuries of Islam primarily to provide answers to converts' questions about how to behave like Muslims. These hadith formed the backbone of Islamic law (shariʿa) as it developed in the eighth and ninth centuries, often in towns far from Arabia like Basra, Kufa, Baghdad and Cairo.

Over time, popular patronage and pious giving in Khurasan came to support a class of experts (ʿulama) whose authority lay in their knowledge of scripture and the law. They routinized their teachings in formal colleges (madrasas) with printed books as their curriculum. Many were welcome to learn, although only a few would eventually be admitted to the ranks of teachers. The institutions that the ʿulama built provided a sense of community and solidarity especially as Khurasan came under the pressures of overpopulation and repeated Turkish invasions after 1000. When invasion and factional strife destroyed Khurasan's cities in the 1100s, Iranian ʿulama would transplant their system of learning to Arab, Turkish and Indian cities. Over the next two centuries, Iranian-style madrasas appeared in Cairo, Damascus, Tunis, Fez and elsewhere. Absorbed into the core Arab lands of Islam, the Iranian edge reconstituted the Islamic center, relocating it from the caliphal courts to shariʿa courts and madrasa law colleges. By 1258, the influence of the caliph in Baghdad had weakened so much that it could not survive the Mongol invasion of that year; thereafter the caliph became a puppet of slave soldiers (Mamluks) in Cairo. Religious authority now lay pre-eminently in the hands of legal scholars, especially jurisprudents (muftis) who issued legal opinions (fatwas) in response to believers' questions.

This legalistic center of Islamic authority has held until the twentieth century, through the sustained operation of the center-edge dialectic. For example, centered Islam ineluctably absorbed the Turks into the mainstream of belief, even though they were viewed by Persian and Arab Muslims as barbarians when they arrived. Descendants of Turkish migrants embraced the legal center of Islam under the Ottoman, Safavid and Mughal empires that rose by the sixteenth century. Suleyman Kanuni (the Lawgiver) epitomized the trend when he strengthened the powers of the chief mufti, the Shaykh al-Islam, who codified and standardized official Hanafi law in the Ottoman Empire.[4] Centered Islam also absorbed other rural peoples, like those belonging to tribes in Arabia and North Africa. These converts in turn modified the center: While the Ottomans bureaucratized the legal system, for example, Arabian tribesmen spread their Wahhabi beliefs far beyond their homeland, and Berber tribal beliefs melded with urban Arab practices to create a distinct style of Islamic kingship in Morocco.[5] Islam's legal center has most recently been challenged by urban Islamist movements that, since the late nineteenth century, have striven to reconcile the demands of piety and modernity; that is, to defend the Islamic lifeworld against American and European influence. They also seek to abolish the division between political and religious authority set nearly 1,000 years ago. In Bulliet's view, these movements seek a more democratic and diffused authority among newly literate Muslims who can now largely read the scriptures for themselves. Although some groups call for a homogeneous form of Islam never before practiced, Bulliet believes they will not succeed. Islamic states like Saudi Arabia and rigid Islamist groups like Algeria's FIS are trying, and failing, to defy the center-edge dialectic that has tolerated divergent religious belief and practice through the centuries.[6] "I believe that the sheer abundance of people actively seeking answers to religious questions, in keeping with the engrained pattern of Islamic history, affords a better augury of the future of the Islamic world than the specific teachings or political policies of religious leaders," he says, noting that the process of change is slow. "Eventually, however, a new Islamic synthesis will be achieved."[7] In other words, the twentieth and twenty-first centuries may represent a historical conjuncture as transformative of Islamic society as the eleventh to thirteeth centuries were. Will the new democratization of Islam include women? Bulliet's paradigm is encouraging, if not ultimately convincing, to scholars and activists concerned with women's place in Islamic societies.

The Historical Construction of Islam's Feminine Edge

Scholars differ on how the coming of Islam affected women's status in the region we now call the Middle East. Most would agree that women's position in the new Islamic society was ambiguous. On the one hand, women exercised a certain degree of religious authority during the early seventh century, when the Prophet Muhammad transmitted his divine message. In the first Muslim city, Medina, they enjoyed the right to sit on councils and to petition and debate with male leaders. The Mothers of the Believers, the Prophet's wives, lived right at the center of the community, next to the first mosque at Medina. After the Prophet died in 632, their status was recognized with state pensions. These wives, and especially his favorite, ʿAisha, became honored and important sources of hadith, reports of the Prophet's words and actions that served as models of Islamic piety. They also appeared to wield some political influence. ʿAisha asserted her voice in the choice of the Prophet's successors by taking to the battlefield against the fourth caliph, ʿAli, in 656. In time, women also became honored spiritual advisors and revered mystics, like the well-known Rabiʿa al-ʿAdawiyya (d. 801). Access to religious authority appears linked to broader improvements in women's status promised by revelations in the Qurʾan, which outlawed female infanticide and guaranteed married women's rights to personal property and to their husbands' support, among other provisions. While the Mothers of the Believers veiled themselves, early Muslims apparently did not adopt universal rules about women's seclusion from men, a practice known in the Middle East long before the coming of Islam.[8] Indeed, prominent scholars have argued that the Qurʾan embraced an egalitarian spirit that promised to raise women's status over ancient Arabian, Persian, or Roman practice.[9]

On the other hand, historical evidence also suggests that scripture and practice subordinated women to men and distanced them from religious power. Some Qurʾanic revelations placed women solidly under the authority of male relatives and granted them lesser rights in divorce and inheritance and as legal witnesses. Successors to the Prophet sought to extend seclusion and veiling to common Muslim women. The second caliph, ʿUmar, tried and failed to ban women from praying in Medina's mosque; he did succeed in segregating women's and men's prayers.[10] And while women at first participated in the public affairs of the Muslim community, later generations banished them from politics by reinterpreting reports about ʿAisha's behavior. ʿAisha was blamed for splitting the Muslim community and fostering political chaos by appearing at the Battle of the Camel in 656. Indeed, while the Qur'an did not specifically forbid women from exercising political rule, hadith circulated in later centuries that forecast misfortune for any society ruled by women.[11]

Attempts to resolve this ambiguity in women's relationship to religious authority lay at the core of later developments in the belief and practice of Islam. From the ninth century, belief and practice came to center on the articulation, teaching, and imposition of sharia law. By the 1000s (A.H.), four distinct legal traditions, or schools, dominated religious learning. Bulliet argues that the emergence of law schools and law colleges was linked intimately to the rise of ulama as a scholarly class chosen by converts to answer their spiritual needs. Missing from Bulliet's story—and missing from most standard histories of Islamic institutions—were women. Certainly, this textual absence reflects a historical absence. In contrast to their earlier importance in religious and communal affairs, women simply did not figure among the elite of politicians and ʿulama in medieval Iranian cities. More striking, women hardly appeared even in minor roles, as students or worshippers or common mystics. Their appearance in biographical dictionaries of religious notables diminished steadily after the fourteenth century. Women's historical and textual exclusion from the center of Islam may not be surprising in a world of nearly universal male domination. But the dramatic change in Muslim women's status does demand explanation. Bulliet's own dialectic of center and edge forming each other suggests that the rise of Islamic law was linked to the emergence of not only a new class structure, but also a new gender order.

Evidence of such a link comes in the writings of medieval ʿulama, which strenuously worked to exclude women from religious authority and institutions. Indeed, we might surmise that ʿulama viewed women as a necessary edge against which the new Islamic center was defined. Women's proper role in Islam was no minor or peripheral issue: ʿUlama directly tied it to the definition of the broader community. The figure of ʿAisha, for example, was used by religious scholars to define the boundaries of the Sunni and Shiʿi communities. According to Denise Spellberg, Shiʿites in the tenth century scorned her as unfaithful to the Prophet and as a traitor to their revered martyr ʿAli. To them, ʿAisha represented the opposing Sunni party led by her father, the first caliph, Abu Bakr. Shiʿites rooted their condemnation of ʿAisha, significantly, in hadith that claimed that women's interference in politics always leads to chaos. Sunni scholars, responding to this Shiʿite attack on Sunni legitimacy, also condemned women's public presence, although they held ʿAisha less to blame for her actions. By the fourteenth century Sunnis rehabilitated ʿAisha's reputation explicitly as a refutation of Shiʿite opinion. Either way, religious scholars in both camps enlisted ʿAisha's legacy to define their communal identity.[12] Most importantly for our purposes, both Sunnis and Shiʿites anchored community identity in the exclusion of women from public affairs and both downplayed ʿAisha's reputation as a religious authority. Other medieval portraits of early Muslim women also de-emphasized their agency in favor of passive ideals of female behavior.[13]

Another urgent case of boundary-keeping concerned sexual identity. Medieval Islamic scholars produced numerous texts on how to determine the true sex of seeming hermaphrodites. The problem of hermaphrodites loomed large because the ʿulama had built Islamic law around the notion of clearly defined sexes, male and female, where each performed distinct roles and where males were granted ultimate power and privilege within the family. There was no room for blurred gender identity in this schema. Only when a hermaphrodite was assigned a gender by ʿulama could she/he bathe, attend prayer, marry, inherit, and participate generally in the affairs of family and community. As Paula Sanders put it, "What was at stake for medieval Muslims in gendering one ungendered body was, by implication, gendering the most important body: the social body."[14] In other words, hermaphrodites threatened the Islamic social order. The possibility that a non-male (misdiagnosed hermaphrodite) might enjoy male privileges provoked much anxiety; conversely, the health of the umma rested on keeping women to their proper (subordinate) place.

ʿUlama did not confine their concerns about gender boundaries to scholarly texts and court documents. They also sought to impose their prescriptions on society. ʿUlama have systematically excluded women from the entire legal edifice of Islam constructed since the ninth century. Women were only rarely admitted as students in madrasas, and never appointed as teachers. Their importance as living links in oral history was undermined with the adoption of textbooks and official collections of hadith. By the Ottoman era, virtually no women were noted as hadith transmitters. No women ever served as judges (qadis) or muftis. Only women fortunate to have educated brothers, fathers, or husbands obtained lessons in their religion. Female mystics still drew some interest, but women's participation in rituals (dhikrs) with men declined.

While some separate women's Sufi (mystical) orders appeared alongside men's orders in the thirteenth and fourteenth centuries, they were often criticized by ʿulama for unorthodox belief and potentially illicit social relations.[15] They too disappeared over time. In sum, while women continued to practice their religion and to study scripture, they did so in an informal milieu that was increasingly distanced from the world of the scholarly men who now monopolized the official interpretation of texts.

Women were edged out of political, as well as religious, authority. In 1249, when a woman inherited rule at the end of the Ayyubid dynasty in Cairo, the caliph in Baghdad warned Egypt's generals that he would not tolerate a female sultan at the heart of Islamdom: "If you have no man to rule over Egypt mayhap we can send you one."[16] The generals quickly convinced the female claimant, Shajarit al-Durr, to marry one of their own, thereby beginning the era of Mamluk rule. Scholars also counseled against women's exercise of lower political offices, like vizier or judge.[17] Two exceptions to women's exclusion from political power both occurred, notably, on geographic edges of the Islamic world that had only slight contact with the Iranian edge. In Yemen, Queen Sayyida Hurra exercised both political and religious leadership during the late eleventh and twelfth centuries. Her rule reflected the influence of the Fatimids, whose support of women's education was rooted in a religious culture that predated the Iranian diaspora.[18] It may be noted that Sayyida Hurra's reign was one of prosperity and religious activism, not the chaos predicted by hadith about ʿAisha. A second female ruler was Radiyya bint Iltutmish, sultan of Delhi from 1236 to 1240, only shortly after the Iranian diaspora might have introduced the madrasa-legal system.[19]

In addition to these few queens, wealthy women often asserted a connection to religious authority through the financing of institutions. In Mamluk Cairo, after 1260, women commonly owned the endowments (waqfs) of madrasas.[20] Elite women also commonly financed pilgrimages to Mecca for themselves and others. Money, however, did not buy admission into the central ranks of the pious. Pilgrimage officials strenuously maintained segregation of the sexes so as not to pollute the rituals. As in education, segregation consequently distanced women from the center of power. As one observer noted about women at Mecca: "Usually, when they are with the men, they are left apart; they look upon the Noble House without being able to go in; they contemplate the Black Stone but do not touch it at all."[21]

The link between women's peripheralization and the "recentering" of Islam, as Bulliet terms it, was perhaps never clearer than when the ʿulama sought to impose gender boundaries on urban populations. Gender was used to absorb the deviant masses into orthodox, centered Islam. The case of Mamluk Cairo is thus far the best documented, thanks to the treatises left by a prominent scholar, Ibn al-Hajj. In the early fourteenth century, Ibn al-Hajj called on ʿulama to teach the urban masses the rightful way of legalistic Islam. He and other ʿulama routinely denounced the religious practices of the poor and rural migrants as harmful innovations and a product of ignorance. In particular, they called on men to keep their women at home and to prevent them from attending public festivals. They also condemned women's important role in popular religious customs, like funeral processions and grave visits. Ibn al-Hajj, according to Huda Lutfi, represented the feminine as the antithesis of the shariʿa order. He wrote:

> The origin of all chaos and corruption in society is one of three things: neglecting the advice of religious scholars on matters regarding proper Muslim behavior; the infiltration of base customs and traditions to the extent that they become the accepted religious practices; and the acceptance of the opinion of those whom the Lawgiver, may God be pleased with him, has regarded as lacking in religion and reason [that is, women].[22]

As ʿulama tried to turn Cairo into a properly Islamic city, they constituted women as the barbaric other to be excluded. Women were a chaotic, irrational force against which the order and reason of the law were arrayed. As the anti-Muslim that defined the Muslim, females defined sacred space by their absence. Mosques were holy sites of worship and madrasas were spaces of sacred learning precisely because they were male spaces. So too, the proper Islamic city should be male; mixing sexes on the streets would pollute it.

Various explanations for why women were edged out of sacred space and religious authority have been advanced. Leila Ahmed has argued that Persian and Byzantine misogyny corrupted the egalitarian spirit of Arab Islam when converts from these "androcentric" cultures engaged in the development of Islamic law in the crucial eighth and nineth centuries.[23] Schimmel likewise notes that Islamic law progressively stiffened standards of male superiority over women in contrast to the alternative traditions of mysticism, which made Sufism a haven of relative equality.[24] Mernissi locates the roots of Islamic misogyny much earlier and within Arab society. The establishment of the Umayyad dynasty in the mid-seventh century, Mernissi argues, erased the egalitarian values of tribal society and the Prophet's social experiment at Medina. Wars of succession and monarchical rule infused Islamic scholarship with hierarchical values, distorting the Prophet's original message.[25]

These models of Islam's corruption by prevailing patriarchal practice in the Middle East seem plausible, but they remain sketchy about exactly how those pre- or non-Islamic values were infused into shariʿa law. Bulliet's paradigm, with its focus on converts and conversion as the motor to the historical development of Islam, helps us to conceptualize the process more clearly and compellingly. Bulliet argues that many hadith, sound and unsound, were transmitted through the generations as answers to non-Arab converts' questions. The transmission was not a one-way process. Answers to converts' questions implicitly engaged with values and practices drawn from outside of Islam, for converts' ideas about religion had been forged in a non-Islamic milieu. This was likely a primary way that non-Islamic gender attitudes entered Islam—for better or worse. Guity Nashat has emphasized the role of converts in constructing the ideal Muslim woman, by observing that none of the compilers of the six canonical hadith collections was of Arab origin.[26] Mernissi notes that the hadith commonly used to bar women from politics ("Those who entrust their affairs to a woman will never know prosperity") was first reported after ʿAisha's appearance at the Battle of the Camel, more than three decades after the Prophet's death. The source was a convert to Islam in Basra named Abu Bakra, who had prospered quickly after his conversion. His vulnerability as a parvenu contributed to the many political reasons he would have had to condemn ʿAisha.[27]

Because it links conversion to the rise of Islamic institutions, Bulliet's paradigm also helps to sort the various and seemingly contradictory influences of converts. Not all converts strengthened patriarchy within Islam. Turkish converts, for example, apparently brought a different set of gender assumptions to Islam: both Shajarit al-Durr of Cairo and Radiyya of Delhi were placed in power by recently converted Turkish soldiers.[28] The historical timing of Turkish conversion, however, limited their impact on recentered Islam. While Abu Bakra's seventh century hadith remained one among many, and perhaps unknown to many Muslims in the first Islamic centuries, its incorporation into official hadith collections by the 10th century gave it a universal power. In contrast, the Turks arrived in the Middle East after 1000; that is, after hadith collections had been standardized and sharia law had been institutionalized. Their promotion of female rulers was therefore destined to be condemned, as the Baghdad caliph condemned Shajarit al-Durr, or relegated to the distant edges of the Islamic world. As we have seen above, descendants of these Turkish converts eventually embraced the Islamic center, including its gender values. The Bektashi Sufi order, which was quite popular in the Ottoman military, eventually ceased to admit women as full members. By 1599 an Ottoman bureaucrat would dare to assert that Turks' standards of piety were higher than Arabs': Mustafa ʿAli traveled that year from Istanbul to Cairo, the former Mamluk capital now a provincial seat. In an account of that trip he scorned Egyptian women for their lewd habits of dress and public display in contrast to the modesty of Turkish women.[29] Onetime frontiersmen now posed as paragons of Islamic gender propriety.

In the Bullietian perspective, those Cairene women were a defiant edge that would not be centered. Women resisted the orthodoxy of seclusion from the medieval era to the modern. Implicit in Ibn al-Hajj's polemics, and in repeated Mamluk orders that women stay indoors, was women's defiance of the norms of centered Islam. Cairene women not only continued to practice their healing ceremonies and grave visits, but also mixed with men at public festivals. They preferred loose clothing that Ibn al-Hajj called bawdy, and even asserted the right to wear turbans. They also apparently cowed husbands who tried to lay down sharia law with threats to withhold sexual favors.[30] Women throughout the Middle East continued to claim their own measure of political and religious authority. At times, women exercised a remarkable degree of political power in India, the Ottoman Empire, and elsewhere, albeit in informal capacities.[31] They remained quite influential in the practice of folk religion and medicine, as Abraham Marcus found in eighteenth century Aleppo.[32] North African women continued to participate actively in Sufi orders into the nineteenth century, and some of them inherited leadership from male kin.[33] And while women were shut out of practicing the law, they vigorously pursued their interests and defended their rights in the courts throughout the Middle East, as revealed in legal documents from the seventeenth through nineteenth centuries.[34] Contrary to common belief, shariʿa courts often upheld women's rights against abusive families and patriarchal local customs.[35]

But, paradoxically, these women had no choice but to remain uncentered. Submission to shariʿa courts and to Ibn al-Hajj's dictates would serve only to distance them from religious education and authority more firmly. This paradox in women's historical experience stands in contrast to the experience of the many men who crossed into recentered Islam from nomadic highlands, poor villages, and non-Islamic lands. Their male descendants could and did attend madrasas and sit as qadis in court. While the social and spiritual frontier between Muslim and non-Muslim men was eternally permeable, women's place on the edge was essentially durable. Women—whether rich or poor, urban or rural, Arab or not—could not hope to cross over into the center. Their biology held them at a distance from the sacred, unless, like hermaphrodites, they could be juridically declared male. Women thus represent a historical conundrum that apparently violates Bulliet's paradigm. According to the Bulietian dialectic, the Islamic center seeks always to absorb what it views as ignorant or heretical edges. In other words, the Islamic center contains the seeds of its own destruction: as it absorbs its edges it is necessarily transformed by those edges. But by refusing to admit women, the Islamic center has for centuries negated the dialectical logic of its self-negation.

The Modern Era: Can the Center Hold?

Thinking of women's marginalization as an anomaly in Bulliet's dialectic permits us to reconceptualize recent gender history in the Middle East. The story of Islam in the nineteenth and twentieth centuries has usually been told in terms of the powerful impact that European economies and ideas exerted on stagnant Middle Eastern societies. New research, however, challenges the idea that the Middle East had stagnated, with evidence of dynamic change in economic markets, political institutions, and social manners through the eighteenth century. Islamic law had not rigidified as previously thought, and Islamic thought inspired fundamental debates like those between the ʿusulis and akhbaris in eighteenth century Iran.[36] Bulliet's paradigm reflects this preference for internal causes of change over external ones. Popular Islamic reform movements that emerged in the twentieth century represent the continuing quest of Muslims for answers to their questions about how to live a pious life. Movements like the Muslim Brotherhood and the revolutionaries in Iran are simply, in Bulliet's view, new edges seeking to reform the center. By the same logic, we might conceptualize the modern Middle Eastern women's movement a reformist edge originating within Islamic society and history. This view challenges criticism of women's reform as external to—and therefore a corruption of—Islam. This view also highlights a contradiction: While male Islamic reformers have often reached compromises of sorts with establishment ʿulama, women's efforts have only provoked backlash: minor reforms to women's legal status made in the mid-twentieth century were rolled back in many countries by century's end. The violence of reactions to women's reform in the past century, however, may suggest that the ʿulama's effort to guard the Islamic center as a male bastion has come under increasing strain.

The modern women's movement in the Middle East arose in the early twentieth century out of women's continued activity in trade and philanthropy. Turkish, Iranian and Arab women formed societies first to support girls' education, and then to promote reforms in women's legal status. They looked to the contemporary Salafi reform movement for inspiration. The Salafi movement embraced the historicity of Islam, viewing the legal edifice built in the Middle Ages as but one possible expression of God's will. As a consequence, Salafi thinkers reasoned, each era must adapt the Prophet's message to its needs. From this general call to renew interpretation (ijtihad), women's leaders specifically called for a revision of medieval interpretations of scripture that concerned divorce, marriage, inheritance and seclusion. While some women's leaders, like Egypt's Huda Shaʿrawi, were overtly secularist and dismissive of Islamic law, others, like Turkey's Halide Edib and Egypt's Malek Hifni Nassef sought reform from within the established religion.[37] Their heirs today study the Qur'an and Islamic law, and often adopt Islamic dress. An international group, Women Living under Muslim Laws, promotes legal education as a primary means of women's emancipation.[38] Viewed through the lens of Bulliet's paradigm, these latter women are far more revolutionary than secularized women are. With their demand for women's greater voice in religious affairs, they seek to scale medieval walls of exclusion and to end women's long exile on the edge of Islamic society.

Bulliet's paradigm not only reveals what seems conservative to be revolutionary, it also explains the reaction to female Islamic reform. From my own research, the case of a Lebanese writer-activist shows that the ʿulama viewed women religious reformers with much greater alarm than secularists.[39] In 1928, Nazira Zayn al-Din, the daughter of an appeals court judge in Beirut, published a 420-page book entitled *Unveiling and Veiling*.[40] The book called not only for the unveiling of women, but the unveiling of Islamic society as a whole through legal reform. Following Salafi ideas, she argued that the jurisdiction of Islamic law should be limited only to those matters explicitly addressed in the Qur'an, thereby limiting the authority of the ʿulama. Second, she argued for ijtihad, reinterpretation of Qur'anic verses in the spirit of Islam's egalitarian values. Correction was needed most in the way medieval scholars had differentiated legal rights according to sex. Specific privileges granted to men in the Qur'an, like their greater share of inheritance, should not be generalized to justify men's universal superiority over women. Similarly, Zayn al-Din argued, the Qur'an's requirement that the Mothers of the Believers veil should not be extended to all women, because the spirit of Islam generally favored freedom. The continued veiling of the Islamic world under medieval law, she concluded, blocked social progress.

Zayn al-Din's book sparked two years of often vicious polemic. While ʿulama had quietly ignored the writings of secularist women, they now published treatises and lectured in mosques, deploring the nerve of a young woman to speak publicly on matters pertaining to religious law. They even cast doubt on her authorship, suggesting that Orientalists hostile to Islam had written the book, and that Zayn al-Din was a traitor to Islam for collaborating with them.[41] Populist preachers and politicians rallied youths to attack women deemed too lightly veiled on the streets. Zayn al-Din became a pariah, shunned by other women activists as a dangerous lightning rod. Syrian and Lebanese women had tentatively and figuratively unveiled by publishing their writings in new women's magazines. Perhaps not coincidentally, those magazines folded by the early 1930s, as women's right to speak in public came under fire. By asserting authority in religious law, Zayn al-Din had sought to unmake the Islamic center by breaking down the walls of gender segregation that had defined the sacred for so long. Zayn al-Din was, in effect, an agent of Bulliet's center-edge dialectic.

In recent decades there have been numerous heirs to Zayn al-Din's crusade, including the Algerian founder of Women Living under Muslim Laws, Marie-Aimée Hélie-Lucas. She promotes educating women about their local Islamic laws precisely so that they will gain greater legal autonomy. When women learn that laws enacted in other countries vary, even though they are supposedly based on the same scripture, Hélie-Lucas argues, they will recognize that the laws are historically and politically contingent. Like Zayn al-Din nearly 75 years ago, Hélie-Lucas and the WLUML seek to strip away accretions upon Islam's original message, and so reduce the jurisdiction of establishment ʿulama over women's status. Like Zayn al-Din, these women reformers are accused of collaborating with that enemy to undermine the values and traditions that bind and define the ʾumma. In response to this opposition, WLUML seeks to allow Muslim women "to speak out freely in the secure space of the Muslim umma" and to expose the political use of religion. Hélie-Lucas hails women theologians who promote a "liberation theology" in Islam, although she allows that publicity may cause violence and even cost them their lives.[42]

The Turkish scholar Nilüfer Göle also sees women reformers as agents of a new Islamic synthesis. In her book *The Forbidden Modern* she argues that women who have retaken the veil in Turkey are defying and potentially overcoming the binary opposition between Islam and modernity that has hamstrung Islamic societies since the start of European imperialism. She argues that politicized Islam offers a new historical paradigm, and that women are the touchstone of a process that promises a real historical and social transformation. That is because "the production of central social values is contingent upon the social position women hold," particularly in the delineation of public and private spaces that lies at the core of Western modernity.[43] By disrupting that line, re-veiled women of the Islamic reform movement can reclaim historical agency for Turkey, which has languished in the imitation of Western civilization since its creation in 1923.[44] Like Zayn al-Din, Göle met a storm of controversy upon publication of her book, but this time from secularists. Her Kemalist critics saw Göle's book as a dangerous concession to Islamists and a step backward toward medieval theocracy. Göle dismissed them as prisoners of the very binary opposition that she critiqued.

Bulliet's dialectical perspective is an optimistic one. Because it sees the absorption of edges as the motor to Islamic history, it foresees the eventual and necessary success of women's efforts to storm the male bastions of legal authority. Many Muslim women today might agree with Bulliet: They believe that the Qur'an decrees equality for men and women, regardless of what legal experts of the orthodox center may say.[45] Many don the veil not to reinforce their segregation and silence, but rather to ease their entrance into public and to raise their voices "to challenge androcentric ideology through Qor'anic passages," as Farzaneh Milani explains about women in Iran.[46]

Not all scholars, however, share Bulliet's dialectical optimism. Leila Ahmed, like Göle and Milani, sees the potential for revolutionary reconceptualization of Islam. She has argued that secularist feminists who have opposed Islamic law are doomed, by their elitism and identification with the West, to failure. But while Islamic feminists might speak with more authenticity, Ahmed worries that they will be simply fall prey to the domination of legalistic Islam all over again. Like Ahmed, Barbara Stowasser argues that many women in Egypt and Jordan today are drawn to Islamisms that deny them religious and political authority because preachers portray feminism as a stalking-horse for imperialism.[47] Here, figures like Zainab al-Ghazali, founder of the women's wing to the Egyptian Muslim Brotherhood, are highly problematic. Revered for her religious authority, her knowledge of sacred text and law, she preaches to women that their primary duty is motherhood. Women's public efforts to promote Islam must come second.[48] Ghazali appears as both an agent of Bulliet's dialectic and a guardian of the center that continues to hold. A second cause for pessimism, Ahmed says, is the collusion of Islamists with authoritarian states like Iran and Pakistan. She and other scholars see these two factors working together to weaken the revolutionary potential of women's Islamic reform: the power of modern states to institutionalize, centralize and reify legal authority combines with the power of male Islamic reform movements in political bargains that assure continued patriarchal control over politics and the family.[49]

Has the institutional power of the modern state disrupted the historical dialectic of Islamic social change? Will the Islamic center forever resist absorption of the female periphery? Bulliet, who sees skepticism about state legitimacy and fluidity of religious authority as enduring traits of Islamic society, would likely respond in the negative. The short-term frictions so apparent today in Afghanistan and elsewhere, he would argue, are simply part of a longer-term and inevitable transformation, ultimately entailing the disappearance of Islam's gendered edge. May his insight be foresight.

Endnotes

1. Richard W. Bulliet, *Islam: The View from the Edge* (New York: Columbia University Press, 1994).

2. Bulliet summarizes the dialectic on p. 195 of *Islam: The View from the Edge.*

3. I am not sure whether my reading reflects Bulliet's intent; however, in the creative spirit of misreading evoked by Harold Bloom in his study of Romantic poetry, I proceed boldly to stake out my own intellectual territory while honoring my mentor. As Bloom wrote: ". . . Strong poets make [poetic] history by misreading one another, so as to clear imaginative space for themselves." Harold Bloom, *The Anxiety of Influence: A Theory of Poetry* (New York: Oxford University Press, 1973) p. 3. I have developed my ideas about Islam's gendered edge through six years of lecturing and through my research on gender and colonialism in the early twentieth century. My lectures began as imitations of Bulliet's, but developed a distinctive voice in response to questions from my students at the University of Virginia. So the question-answer motif of medieval Islamic education has been replicated in the twenty-first century American academy.

4. See Colin Imber, *Ebu's-su'ud: The Islamic Legal Tradition* (Stanford: Stanford University Press, 1997).

5. See Elaine Combs-Schilling, *Sacred Performances: Islam, Sexuality, and Sacrifice* (New York: Columbia University Press, 1989).

6. Bulliet, *Islam: The View from the Edge*, p. 195–207.

7. *Ibid,* pp. 206-207.

8. See Leila Ahmed, *Women and Gender in Islam* (New Haven: Yale University Press, 1992), pp. 11–37, and Guity Nashat and Judith E. Tucker, eds., *Women in the Middle East and North Africa* (Bloomington: Indiana University Press, 1999) p. 5. On the general distinction between Islam and patriarchy, see Deniz Kandiyoti, "Islam and Patriarchy: A Comparative Perspective," in Nikki R. Keddie and Beth Baron, eds., *Women in Middle Eastern History* (New Haven: Yale University Press, 1991) pp. 23–42.

9. Ahmed, *Women and Gender in Islam*, pp. 67, 96–98; Barbara Freyer Stowasser, "Women and Citizenship in the Qur'an," in Amira El Azhary Sonbol, ed., *Women, the Family, and Divorce Laws in Islamic History* (Syracuse: Syracuse University Press, 1996) pp. 23–38. See also Fatima Mernissi, *The Veil and the Male Elite: A Feminist Interpretation of Women's Rights in Islam*, (Reading, MA: Addison Wesley, 1991) and Annemarie Schimmel, *My Soul is a Woman: The Feminine in Islam* (New York: Continuum, 1997).

10. Ahmed, *Women and Gender in Islam*, pp. 60–61.

11. Denise A. Spellberg, "Political Acton and Public Example: ʿAʿisha and the Battle of the Camel," in Keddie and Baron, *Women in Middle Eastern History*, pp. 45–57. See also Spellberg's book, *Politics, Gender and the Islamic Past: The Legacy of ʿAʿisha bint Abi Bakr* (New York: Columbia University Press, 1994).

12. Spellberg, *Politics, Gender, and the Islamic Past*, pp. 2–17, 101–49, 174–78, 191–95.

13. See also David Pinault, "Zaynab Bint ʿAli and the Place of the Women of the Households of the First Imams in Shiʿite Devotional Literature," in Gavin R.G. Hambly, ed., *Women in the Medieval Islamic World* (New York: St. Martin's Press, 1999) pp. 69–98.

14. Paula Sanders, "Gendering the Ungendered Body: Hermaphrodites in Medieval Islamic Law," in Keddie and Baron, *Women in Middle Eastern History*, pp. 74–95.

15. Schimmel, *My Soul is a Woman*, pp. 34–53; Ahmed, *Women and Gender in Islam*, pp. 115–16.

16. Afaf Lutfi Al-Sayyid Marsot, *A Short History of Modern Egypt* (New York: Cambridge University Press, 1985) p. 25.

17. See, for example, excerpts from Mawardi's *Rules of Government*, written in the early eleventh century, in Ruth Roded, ed., *Women in Islam and the Middle East: A Reader* (New York: I. B. Tauris, 1999) pp. 112–14 He, like many Muslim theorists since, relied on the hadith "Those who entrust their affairs to a woman will never know prosperity," discussed in Mernissi's *Veil and the Male Elite*, pp. 1–11, 49–61.

18. Farhad Daftary, "Sayyida Hurra: The Ismaʿili Sulayhid Queen of Yemen," in Hambly, ed., *Women in the Medieval Islamic World*, pp. 117–30.

19. Peter Jackson, "Sultan Radiyya Bint Iltutmish," in Hambly, *Women in the Medieval Islamic World*, pp. 181–97.

20. Jonathan P. Berkey, "Women and Islamic Education in the Mamluk Period," in Keddie and Baron, *Women in Middle Eastern History*, pp. 143–57.

21. Ibn Jubayr as quoted in Marina Tomacheva, "Female Piety and Patronage in the Medieval Hajj," in Hambly, ed., *Women in the Medieval Islamic World*, p. 167.

22. Huda Lutfi, "Manners and Customs of Fourteenth-Century Cairene Women: Female Anarchy versus Male Shariʿ Order in Muslim Prescriptive Treatises," in Keddie and Baron, *Women in Middle Eastern History*, p. 100.

23. Ahmed, *Women and Gender in Islam*, pp. 65–101.

24. Schimmel, *My Soul is a Woman*, pp. 14–15.

25. Mernissi, *The Veil and the Male Elite,* p. 191.

26. Guity Nashat and Judith E. Tucker, *Women in the Middle East and North Africa: Restoring Women to History* (Bloomington: Indiana University Press, 1999) p. 61.

27. Mernissi, *The Veil and the Male Elite*, pp. 49–61. Mernissi also argues that since Abu Bakra had been flogged previously for false testimony he should not have been considered a sound source of hadith by later scholars, p. 60.

28. Jackson, in Hambly, *Women in the Medieval Islamic World*, p. 189.

29. Andreas Tietze, trans. and ed., *Mustafa ʿAli's Description of Cairo of 1599* (Vienna: Verlag der Österreichischen Akademie der Wissenschaften, 1975) pp. 40–43.

30. Lutfi, "Manners and Customs of Fourteenth-Century Cairene Women," p. 118.

31. Leslie P. Peirce, *The Imperial Harem: Women and Sovereignty in the Ottoman Empire* (New York: Oxford University Press, 1993); Richard B. Barnett, "Embattled Begams: Women as Power Brokers in Early Modern India," in Hambly, ed., *Women in the Medieval Islamic World*, pp. 521–36.

32. Abraham Marcus, *The Middle East on the Eve of Modernity: Aleppo in the Eighteenth Century* (Columbia University Press, 1989) pp. 226–27.

33. Julia Clancy-Smith, "The House of Zainab: Female Authority and Saintly Succession in Colonial Algeria," in Keddie and Baron, *Women in Middle Eastern History*, pp. 254–75.

34. See for example Judith E. Tucker's two books, *In the House of the Law: Gender and Islamic Law in Ottoman Syria and Palestine* (Berkeley: University of California Press, 1998) and *Women in Nineteenth Century Egypt* (Cambridge: Cambridge University Press, 1985); see also the various articles collected in Sonbol, ed., *Women, the Family, and Divorce Laws in Islamic History*.

35. Recent works include Tucker's, *In the House of the Law*; Yvonne J. Seng, "Invisible Women: Residents of Early Sixteenth-Century Istanbul," in Hambly, ed., *Women in the Medieval Islamic World,* pp. 241–68; and Fariba Zarinebaf-Shahr, "Women, Law, and Imperial Justice in Ottoman Istanbul in the Late Seventeenth Century," in Sonbol, ed., *Women, the Family and Divorce Laws in Islamic History*, pp. 81–95.

36. Wael B. Hallaq, "Was the Gate of Ijtihad Closed?" *International Journal of Middle East Studies* 16 (1984) 3–41; Nikki R. Keddie, *Roots of Revolution: An Interpretive History of Modern Iran* (New Haven: Yale University Press, 1981) p. 21. On the revisionist view of Ottoman history see Ariel Salzmann, "An Ancien Regime Revisited: Privatization and Political Economy in the Eighteenth-Century Ottoman Empire," *Politics & Society* 21:4 (1993) pp. 393–423 and, more generally, Suraiya Faroqhi, et. al., *An Economic and Social History of the Ottoman Empire: Volume Two 1600–1914* (New York: Cambridge University Press, 1994).

37. On this dichotomy, and the rise of the women's movement, see Ahmed, *Women and Gender in Islam*, pp. 169–207. On Shaʿrawi, see Huda Shaarawi, *Harem Years: The Memoirs of an Egyptian Feminist,* Margot Badran, ed. (New York: The Feminist Press, 1987) and Margot Badran, *Feminists, Islam, and Nation: Gender and the Making*

of Modern Egypt (Princeton: Princeton University Press, 1995). The rise of the women's movement in the Levant is discussed in my *Colonial Citizens: Republican Rights, Paternal Privilege and Gender in French Syria and Lebanon* (New York: Columbia University Press, 2000) pp. 91–100.

38. Marie-Aimée Hélie-Lucas, "The Preferential Symbol for Islamic Identity: Women in Muslim Personal Laws," in Valentine M. Moghadam, ed., *Identity Politics & Women* (Boulder, CO: Westview Press, 1994) pp. 391–407.

39. Thompson, *Colonial Citizens*, pp. 127–40.

40. Nazira Zayn al-Din, *Al-Sufur wa al-hijab* (Beirut: Matabiʿ Quzma, 1928).

41. For Egyptian attacks on Orientalists' and reformers' views of women in Islamic scripture, see Barbara Freyer Stowasser, *Women in the Qurʿan, Traditions, and Interpretation* (New York: Oxford University Press, 1994) pp. 119–32 and Ahmed, *Women and Gender in Islam*, pp. 144–68.

42. Hélie-Lucas, "Preferential Symbol for Islamic Identity," pp. 400–403. See also the group's mission statement, on its website: http://www.wluml.org.

43. Nilüfer Göle, *The Forbidden Modern: Civilization and Veiling* (Ann Arbor: The University of Michigan Press, 1996) p. 131.

44. Göle, *Forbidden Modern*, pp. 11–13, 131–37.

45. Elizabeth Warnock Fernea, *In Search of Islamic Feminism* (New York: Doubleday, 1998) p. 416; Ahmed, *Women and Gender in Islam*, p. 227.

46. Farzaneh Milani, *Veils and Words: The Emerging Voices of Iranian Women Writers* (Syracuse: Syracuse University Press, 1992) p. 233. See also Elizabeth Fernea's 1982 film on the women's Islamic movement in Egypt: *A Veiled Revolution*, and Leila Hessini, "Wearing the Hijab in Contemporary Morocco: Choice and Identity," in Fatma Müge Göcek and Shiva Balaghi, eds., *Reconstructing Gender in the Middle East* (New York: Columbia University Press, 1994) pp. 40–56.

47. Barbara F. Stowasser, "Women's Issues in Modern Islamic Thought," in Judith E. Tucker, ed., *Arab Women: Old Boundaries, New Frontiers* (Bloomington: Indiana University Press, 1992) pp. 20–25.

48. Ahmed, *Women and Gender in Islam*, pp. 197-202; Stowasser, "Women's Issues," p. 25; Valerie J. Hoffman, "An Islamic Activist: Zainab al-Ghazali," in Elizabeth W. Fernea, ed., *Women and the Family in the Middle East* (Austin: University of Texas Press, 1985) pp. 233–54.

49. Ahmed, *Women and Gender in Islam*, pp. 228–34. Other scholars have also argued that the modern state is a critical new variable in the gendered history of Islam. See, for example, Deniz Kandiyoti, "Women, Islam and the State: A Comparative Approach," in Juan Cole, ed., *Comparing Muslim Societies* (Ann Arbor: The University of Michigan Press, 1992) pp. 237–60.

Polysemous Texts and Reductionist Readings: Women and Heresy in the Siyar al-Mulūk*

Neguin Yavari

Niẓām al-Mulk Ḥasan b. ʿAlī b. Isḥāq al-Ṭūsī, vizier of two Saljūq sultans, Ālp Arsalān (r. 455/1063–465/1073) and Malikshāh (r. 465/1073–485/1092), was born in April 408/1018 at Ṭūs. A young boy wearing Sufi dress assassinated him in 485/1092 in Siḥna, a village near Isfahan. Not only did he succeed in retaining his office for a long time, but he also secured the continuation of his policies by installing a number of his relatives in prominent positions. Five of his sons, two of his grandsons and one great-grandson held the office of vizier to one or another of the sultans or *maliks* after him; none achieved his eminence. Perhaps his single most spectacular accomplishment was to remain in office for as long as he did. The ʿAbbāsid caliphate (r. 132/750–656/1258) was but a shadow of its former self. The Shiʿi Fāṭimids (r. 297/909–567/1171) of Egypt rivaled them in caliphal authority, and Turkish sultans from the East overpowered them militarily. The demise in centralized ʿAbbasid rule by the fourth/tenth century and the subsequent array of dynasties sovereign over parts of the Islamic lands was concomitant with the completion of the conversion process in the central Islamic lands. "Conversion to Islam leads almost inevitably, after it has passed its halfway point, to the weakening or dissolution of centralized government; and second, the conversion process in and of itself gives rise to a clash of interests between elements of the population that converts at different periods of time. These political factions that arose at a later point came with a religious coloration."[1] The medieval chronicles abound in stories of sectarian strife, not just between Sunnis and Shiʿis, but also among Ḥanafīs and Shāfiʿīs, the former with Ashʿarīs, and the Ḥanbalīs in Baghdad with the Shiʿis. By the fifth/eleventh century, Nizam al-Mulk's contemporaries and fellow Ashʿaris in various fields of Islamic studies, jurists and theologians, political theorists and *ḥadīth* scholars, sought to modify normative Sunni precepts of legitimate leadership.

Al-Māwardī (d. 450/1058) in his *Aḥkām al-sulṭāniyya wa al-wilāya al-dīniya,* the Imām al-Ḥaramayn al-Juwaynī (d. 478/1085) in his *Ghiyāth al-ʾumam fī iltiyāth al-ẓulam,* and al-Ghazzālī (d. 505/1111) in his *Kitāb al-iqtiṣād fī al-i ʿtiqād* as well as the *Iḥyāʾ ʿulūm al-dīn,* alluded to the legitimacy of the sultans in face of the impotency of the ʿAbbasid caliphs. Juwayni sought solace in the grandeur of Nizam al-Mulk. Mawardi, in his theoretical elaborations on legitimate rulership in Islam, upheld allegiance to the caliph as a necessary condition for the implementation of the *sharīʿa,* but also included a chapter on the exigencies of situations where the caliph is compromised because he is at the mercy of superior military power. Ghazzali argued that while the reigning ʿAbbasid is caliph; de facto government is carried out by sultans, who possess military power. In the words of one of the earliest social historians of medieval Islam, H. A. R. Gibb, "From this passage it is clear that the caliphate, as represented by the Abbasid family, was no longer regarded as conferring authority, but merely legitimating rights acquired by force, provided that the holder of military power, by giving allegiance to the caliph, recognized the supremacy of the Shariʿa."[2] According to Mawardi, once the caliphate is usurped by the caliph's entourage or army generals, "[I]n such cases, his title to the office stands and the validity of his investment is unquestioned. If his custodians, who are in control of affairs, are also in accordance with the rules of the faith and the demands of justice, they may be endorsed and implemented in order to avoid any interception of religious duties that may place the people in jeopardy;" and, elsewhere, "Two changes of policy disqualify him for leadership: lack of justice and physical disability. Lack of justice or probity is classified into submission to desire and suspicious acts. The former has to do with sinfulness, committing forbidden deeds and venturing on violations of decency in pursuit of pleasure. The second has to do with suspected unorthodoxy, which would preempt investiture and continuation in office in the opinion of some scholars, on the ground that mere suspicion is sufficient as in the case of utter disbelief."[3]

I will focus here on Nizam al-Mulk's famous *Siyar al-mulūk,* as an exposition of his thoughts on these and other pressing political and religious concerns of his times. The *Siyar al-muluk* was conceived in 479/1086 at the behest of the Saljuq dynast, Malikshah.[4] The first part of the book was prepared after 481/1088, and the second part probably around 484/1091. Nizam al-Mulk and Malikshah both died in 485/1092, and the succession chaos following their deaths was not resolved until 498/1105. Ghazzali refers to the *Siyar al-muluk* in his *Naṣīḥat al-mulūk* (*Book of Counsel for Kings*). The book therefore, dates from sometime between 498/1105 and 505/1111. Modern scholarship customarily characterizes the work as paradigmatic of the genre of mirrors for princes, consisting of moral advice and a litany of do's and don'ts for the prince. Read as such, the *Siyar al-muluk* appears to be no more than a series of anecdotes repeated in almost all other mirrors of the medieval Islamic period, and hence of little import for deciphering historical information. Oblivious to accurate chronology, repetitious, and faulty in its factual contents, Nizam al-Mulk's string of anecdotes tie together pre-Islamic kings, Aristotelian tidbits, stories about the prophet Muhammad, and episodes from the lives of the earlier caliphs. Not only do we find the same kind of information strewn about in practically all medieval Islamic mirrors, but also similarities and echoes much further afield. Although there is little historical evidence of direct or indirect intellectual and political exchange with medieval England, there are striking typological resemblances between the content of Nizam al-Mulk's *Siyar al-muluk* and Gower's offering to the English dynast Richard II, his *Confessio Amantis*,[5] the first version of which was written in 1380. How do we account for such recurring patterns, and what was the significance of Nizam al-Mulk's mirror in his times? Why was it read and re-read and relished, given its apparent repetitiousness and supposed meager and stale fare? Can it all be explained away by attributing to its medieval readership a lamentable weakness for oft heard banalities and repeated platitudes and a perennial urge for re-structuring the same material?

Several underlying assumptions in earlier studies on Islamic mirrors are significant in this context. One arises from an obsession with constricting classifications. Taxonomies are imposed and the material itself is then trimmed and adapted to fit the scaffolding. Mirrors are considered political tracts, which seek to modify and ameliorate religious precepts of Islam to make them compatible with the exigencies of legitimate secular rulership.[6] It is only recently that Charles-Henri de Fouchécour, in his magnum opus, *Moralia*, has questioned the wisdom of such a sharp segregation.[7] The second point is raised most recently and poignantly by Patricia Crone, in her questioning of the authorship of Ghazzali's *Nasihat al-muluk*, and concerns the inadequacy of anecdotes—the favorite format of narrative in the mirrors—for the provision of the historical data. Ghazzali's mirror is made up of two sections, distinguished not only for their subject matter, hence content, but also narrative form and structure. The second part, less sober than the first, was not, according to Crone, penned by the great *imām:* "First the stylistic contrast is glaring. While the first part of the *Naṣīḥat al-Mulūk* is a well-organized treatise, the second part is a rambling compilation of anecdotes, aphorisms and poetry loosely strung together in no particular order and adding up to no particular point."[8] Thirdly, when mirrors are seen, primarily, as treatises on incipient political theory, the provenance of political thought is then tied to ancient Greece and ancient Iran on the basis of allegories, tales, anecdotes and tidbits attributed to personages from the two oikumenes. Clearly, the incorporation of Greek and Iranian political precepts in the Islamic tradition followed a different trajectory from the inclusion of the Greek material into Western political thought in the late medieval period. The more frequent use of interchangeable anecdotes and the fluidity of the names of the great and the good associated with them either as tellers or doers in the Islamic tradition (Aristotle replacing Buzurgmihr or a Sāsānid monarch exchanging hats with Alexander or vice versa) tended to convey a less delineated and more diffused intellectual and political landscape. With medieval political thought considered as the end product of these two parallel processes, the lack of genuine political doctrines in the Islamic tradition is then attributed to the failure of Islam in accommodating a public and political sphere, with religion subsuming all other intellectual edifices. The three points are interrelated, as we shall see, and share an origin in the story of the itinerant pseudo-Aristotelian *Secretum Secretorum*.[9]

I mentioned earlier that Nizam al-Mulk's *Siyar al-muluk* had an English cousin, the *Confessio Amantis* of Gower. In the seventh book of the *Confessio Amantis*, Gower claims to be repeating in detail the instructions given by Aristotle to Alexander.[10] The king should possess five virtues (truth, liberality, justice, pity, and chastity). While the first four are abundant in medieval Islamic mirrors, the fifth is somewhat more problematic, and will be discussed later. Scholars have identified two major sources of influence on medieval western mirrors, St. Augustine's *City of God*, and the pseudo-Aristotelian *Secretum Secretorum*.[11] The latter is in the form of an epistle from Aristotle to Alexander, while he was in the process of conquering Persia, and was intended as a substitute for the presence of the old tutor and philosopher himself, who had stayed at home on grounds of age. As evident from its title, the text comprised the secret of secrets, a key to statecraft, medicine, deciphering omens and talismans, proper hygiene, and rules of conduct. The pseudo-Aristotelian treatise made its way into the Latin West, purportedly, from an anonymous Arabic original, the *Kitāb Sirr al-asrār*.[12] Mario Grignaschi has spent many long years studying the various Arabic (the oldest extant manuscript dates from the fourth/tenth century), Latin and vulgate versions of the *Secretum Secretorum*. It was a great success in the Latin world, as witnessed by some 200 extant manuscripts, preserved in various libraries and in several European languages. According to Grignaschi, that version of the *Secretum Secretorum* that reached

Europe could not have been anterior to the fifth/eleventh century.[13] It was a reworking of the *Siyāsa al-ʿāmiyya*,[14] a compendium of Greek and Pahlavi treatises translated by a group of scholars working with Sālim Abū al-ʿAlāʾ (d. ?),[15] the famed secretary of Hishām b. ʿAbd al-Malik (r. 105/723-125/743), the Umayyad caliph. In his *Fihrist*, Ibn al-Nadīm (d. 380/990) writes, "Sālim was related to ʿAbd al-Ḥamīd by marriage and was also one of the masters of literary style and eloquence. He made a translation from the 'Epistle of Aristotle to Alexander,' or else it was made for him and he made corrections. There is a collection of about one hundred leaves of his epistle."[16]

Salim and the group of translators and secretaries working with him crafted the *Siyasa al-ʿamiyya* on the basis of Arabic translations of several Hellenistic texts, most notably the pseudo-Callisthenes *Alexander Romance*, as well as Sasanid treatises on ideal kingship, Byzantine mirrors for princes, Aristotle's *Nichomachean Ethics*, and finally, Hermetic texts circulating among the Sabeans of Harran. The Arabic epistolary novel which derived from a Hellenistic original, the third century Egyptian pseudo-Callisthenes mentioned above, was known in the Islamic world as "The Epistles of Aristotle to Alexander," and the *Siyasa al-ʿamiyya* of Salim Abu al-ʿAlaʾ is its main piece.[17] The *Alexander Romance* of pseudo-Callisthenes contains three letters by Alexander himself: an account of his exploits to his mother after the assassination of Darius, the Persian dynast; a second to Aristotle on the marvels of India; and a final one to his mother, describing his visit to the palace of Hercules. The *Siyasa al-ʿamiyya* contains pseudo-Homeric phrases, perhaps with a faint echo of the texts of the *Iliad* and the *Odyssey*. Those pseudo-Homeric phrases, popular in Hellenistic literature, a verse from Hesiod (an accurate rendering of the Greek original), a lost verse from Euripides, and finally a verse from Pindar, demonstrate that Salim had the Greek text, as well as a Pahlavi or Syriac translation, at his disposal.[18] Salim grafted onto the Egyptian romance, proverbs, aphorisms, and themes from Sasanid Iran.[19] The Aristotle of Salim's epistolary novel is not just a philosopher and monotheist, but a magician and alchemist as well. The *Siyasa al-ʿamiyya*, contains sixteen sections: 1) on the encouragement to study philosophy; 2) the offer made to Aristotle to educate Alexander; 3) Aristotle's response; 4) chapter on ethics; 5) Aristotle's advice (testament) to Alexander; 6) felicitations on the conquest of Scythia, this being a province of the West; 7) felicitations on the conquest of Anfisan, a province of Babylonia; 8) detailed book on the art of governance; 9) general account of the queries of Alexander on rulership; 10) the response and felicitation on the conquest of Persia; 11) query to Aristotle on whether the important nobles in Persia should be eliminated; 12) the negative response to this; 13) felicitations on the conquest of the provinces of Khurasan; 14) on the essence of gold in the nature of the world, and on the most beautiful palace of gold seen by Alexander in India; 15) letter of recommendation; 16) choice of funerary rites.[20] The *Siyasa al-ʿamiyya* was a rare book even in the Arab world, for the first definite reference to it occurs in al-Makīn's (d. 672/1273) universal history, "Al-Majmuʿ al-mubārak."[21]

The infusion of Sasanid treatises on ideal kingship unto the Arabic epistolary novel,[22] paved the way for a later incarnation of the *Siyasa al-ʿamiyya* as a veritable mirror for princes, the *Kitāb al-siyāsa*. The anonymous author/compiler of the *Kitab al-siyasa* culled the strictly political instructions for statecraft and typologies of kings and polities from the *Siyasa al-ʿamiyya*. It is the *Kitab al-siyasa*, which is the prototype for both the Arabic and subsequent Latin versions of the *Sirr al-asrar*, and dates to the period between 950 and 975. The *Kitab al-siyasa* is extant only in a manuscript dating to the sixteenth century.[23] Out of the *Kitab al-siyasa* come the two versions of the *Secretum Secretorum* that circulated in Europe by the thirteenth (or perhaps twelfth) century. The Latin text circulated in medieval Europe in two forms, the long and the short, the short form being the older form. The long form dates to the mid-twelfth century. Written/translated by John of Seville, it is extant in some hundred and fifty copies. The short form was made during the first half of the 11th century or the first part of the twelfth century (Grignsaschi)[24] or the first quarter of the tenth century (Manzaloui)[25] and has survived in more than three hundred and fifty manuscripts. The gradual waning in the popularity of the *Kitab al-siyasa*, together with the concomitant increase in the popularity of the *Secretum Secretorum* in the medieval Christian world is attributed by Grignaschi to the overwhelming interest in the occult sciences, astrological history and other non-political sections of the latter in the West. On the ʿAbbasid side, Gutas has documented the official ʿAbbasid espousal of the 'universal empire' ideology of the Sasanids, and as its auxiliary, interest in and state sponsorship of the translation of ancient treatises on astrology, primarily, alchemy and other occult sciences. The movement gained ground in the reign of al-Manṣūr (r. 158/775–169/785), whose building of the city of Baghdad should be seen as part of the same concerted effort.[26] The Arabic *Kitab Sirr al-asrar* claims dissemination by the 940s, and references to it are common in eleventh century Arabic and Persian texts, although these sources never cite the name of the text from which they cull Aristotle's advice to Alexander. An early attestation in advice literature is found in the *Sirāj al-mulūk* of Abū Bakr b. Abū Randaqah al-Ṭurtūshī (d. 520/1126), completed in 516/1122.[27] Ibn-Miskawayh's (d. 421/1030) *al-Ḥikma al-khālida* refers to a will left by Aristotle for Alexander on statecraft: a section on Aristotelian ethics, and the transcript of an exchange between an emissary of Aristotle and Alexander on the secrets of happiness.[28] Manzalaoui traces the appearance and trajectory of the pseudo-Aristotelian corpus in the Islamic world. The *Sirr* claims to have been written in Greek, and translated in two stages, via Syriac, into Arabic. "Even the roughest investigation of provenance," Manzalaoui writes, "must therefore be prepared to cover a period of almost a thousand years, taking in the Roman, Byzantine, and Arab periods, and should be prepared to encounter Greek, Persian, Seleucid, Egyptian and Arab elements. The world-picture of the *Sirr* may be described by using the term 'Hellenistic' in an extended sense. It springs from the middle range of gnomic and sub-philosophical literature, which was written in the Hellenistic world proper, and in the Roman and Byzantine, as well as in the Arab, and, later, the medieval European world—in spite of the obvious and important differences between these periods and cultures. The belief, continuous in this tradition, in "correspondences" between three entities, the individual man, the universe, and the body politic, made it possible to attach both philosophical concepts, and practical rules of, for example, hygiene, to a treatise in the form of a *Fürstenspiegel,* a mirror for princes."[29]

The dating of the *Kitab Sirr al-asrar* remains controversial, some positing an Umayyad and others a later, ʿAbbasid period.[30] For our purposes here, the early provenance of a corpus of apocrypha attributed to Aristotle and found in circulation in multiple versions by the fifth/eleventh century is sufficient. As Fouchécour has demonstrated in his *Moralia*, mirrors for princes, and the pseudo-Aristotelian corpus, form but a part of the larger genre of advice literature, in which he correctly includes the *Shāhnāma* of Firdawsī (d. 410/1019 or 416/1025), the *Haft paykar* of Niẓāmī (d. 605/1208), and the version of the *Kalīla wa dimna* translated by Abū al-Maʿālī Naṣrallāh b. Muḥammad Munshī, completed between 538/1143 and 540/1145 and dedicated to the Ghaznavid Bahrāmshāh, before the sack of Ghazna in 545/1150. The thematic similarities between the *Kalila wa dimna* (a Perso-Arabic avatar of the Indian collection of fables, *Panchatantra*) and the mirrors of the eleventh and twelfth centuries are manifold. The litany of virtues praised in the *Kalila wa dimna* is almost identical to those found in Ghazzali's *Nasihat al-muluk:* the prince should possess *ḥilm* (forbearance and grace), patience, friendship, trust, and intimacy. He should uphold the social hierarchy, and maintain hereditary professions. In the *Kalila wa dimna*, this advice is attributed to Anūshīrvān (r. 531–78).[31] As mentioned above, the legend of the genesis of the *Secretum Secretorum* has it that while Alexander was away campaigning in Persia, he wrote to Aristotle to ask him to join him, as he needed his advice. Aristotle defied the king, parading his advanced age as a pretext for refusing to follow Alexander to the East, and instead wrote him a manual for kingship, a guide to the secrets of statecraft. The genesis of advice then, in the *Secretum Secretorum*, lies both in the defiance shown by Aristotle in refusing to leave Greece and meet the king, as well as in his endeavor to compile a handbook of sayings attributed to old sages, including himself: a safe, traditional, and time-tested concoction. Aristotle has the secrets to kingship, so the king is dependent on Aristotle for proper rule. The trope of traditional advice provides a veil, as we shall see, for the expression of dissent, and innovation.

The question of provenance goes a long way in explaining the contents and the semantic range of Islamic (and Christian) mirrors, and to address the problem of "unconnected anecdotes, ahistorical information, and lack of organization," referred to above. The long form of the *Secretum Secretorum* comprises the following sections: 1) kinds of kings, classified according to their liberality; 2) conduct, which is subdivided into four chapters on proper behavior, defense of astrology, health, and physiognomy; 3) justice; 4) ministry; 5) secretaries; 6) ambassadors; 7) governors; 8) generals; 9) wars; 10) the occult and the pseudo-scientific, which has chapters on theory, stars, talismans, the Philosopher's Stone, *The Emerald Table* (*Tabula Smaragdina*), lapidary, herbal, astronomy and onomancy. The titles of some of the English versions of the *Secretum Secretorum* can be illuminating here, Johannes Hispaniensis called his translation "The Booke of Goode Governance & Guyding of the Body;" Johannes de Caritate, in a manuscript dated to ca. 1484, called his version, "The Purity of Purities;" and John Shirley's translation dating to around 1450 called his translation, "The Governance of Kyngs and of Prynces Called the Secrete of Secretes."[32] Like the *Secretum Secretorum* itself, the Islamic mirrors, and advice literature in general, are ideological prescriptions masquerading as narratives, worldviews spun into texts. Over time and in diverse geographical locations, different authors found different stories to tell the tale of their times, or "translated" different material to convey their message. The interpretation of the past in the medieval Islamic sources is best understood as the imposition of a particular worldview onto a narrative structure, which is then modified to accommodate the specific exigencies of the author and his times. It is true that medieval historical writing resorted to templates for the presentation of their material, but the templates provided a basic form, onto which was crafted the events and issues of various epochs. It is the message, in conjunction with the template that needs to be "deciphered" to decode the meaning of these medieval texts. In his perceptive analysis of the evolution of modern political thought in Europe, Quentin Skinner wrote, "To study the context of any major work of political philosophy is not merely to gain additional information about its aetiology; it is also to equip ourselves with a way of gaining a greater insight into its author's meaning than we can ever hope to achieve simply from reading the text itself 'over and over again'. What we should be doing is to characterize what their authors were doing in writing them. For to understand what questions a writer is addressing, and what he is doing with the concepts available to him, is equivalently to understand some of his basic intentions in writing, and is thus to elicit what exactly he may have meant by what he said—or failed to say. When we attempt in this way to locate a text within its appropriate context, we are not merely providing historical 'background' for our interpretation; we are already engaged in the act of interpretation itself."[33] In attempting to understand the ideologies presented in medieval Islamic advice literature, of which mirrors for princes are but a part, recourse to the *Secretum Secretorum* and medieval Christian mirrors enables us to avoid facile generalizations and superficial contextualization. To announce pre-Islamic and Greek influences on the mere basis of names—which as we have seen, is more symptomatic of the general ethical worldview of the medieval Islamic world—is to ignore the meaning of the texts, the worldview of their authors, and the pressing concerns of their times. It results in a superficial and distorted understanding of the past. A case in point and one that we shall look at in more depth later is the treatment of women in the Islamic mirrors of the fifth/eleventh century. For that, we will turn to the anecdotes on the trope of advice and of women compiled in the *Siyar al-muluk*.

The *Secretum Secretorum* begins with the question of good advice. Whom can the king trust, and whose advice should he reject? The mere seeking of advice compromises his absolute authority, and the advice itself is ambiguous; it can be both beneficial and harmful. How should the king distinguish between good and bad advice? The trope of advice is thus a fecund rhetorical tool used across cultures in the medieval period. To rule well, the king must be ruled. Surely, the historical relationship between so many kings and their counselors, spread over various centuries and cultural formations, could not be borne out of the relatively static and uniform content of the medieval mirrors for princes. As manuals of instruction, would their didactic value not be severely hampered by their apparent neglect of the changing times and varied cultural settings? In addition, the hierarchical model that the manuals seem to support is too simple to describe the actual relations between kings and advisers.[34] The treatise lists people and things not to be trusted, including women, doctors (one should always seek many opinions) and poison. This colorful list culminates in Aristotle's reminiscences about how the secrets he had learned from Indian books had enabled him to save Alexander from a poisonous woman.Aristotle claims here to have saved the king from both chance and his own (weak) will.[35]

The preface of the *Siyar al-muluk* resembles the template provided by the *Secretum Secretorum.* Here, Malikshah, once firmly established in his reign, gathered the elders and sages of his court, and asked them to ponder the meaning of the state, and seek what it is good but not observed by our court, or what is good and hidden from us. The secret of kingship is what he is after. And so he asked several of his trusted courtiers, Nizam al-Mulk, Sharaf al-Mulk and Majd al-Mulk and the likes of them to prepare a tractate. None of the final products pleased the Sultan save the one prepared by the vizier Nizam al-Mulk. The Sultan then declared that the book would be his guide and he ruled the country accordingly. Before he leaves on his fateful trip to Isfahan, the old vizier, with characteristic prescience, gives the text to a secretary, who does not reveal its contents until the dust has settled from the succession crisis following the death of both vizier and sultan. "And now that the Sultan is dead, I am presenting the book to his successor and son, Ghiyāth al-Dunyā wa al-Dīn, Muḥammad b. Malikshāh (r. 498/1105–511/1118). For there is no king or ruler who can escape knowing what is in this book, especially in this day and age where knowledge of affairs of religion and politics are so crucial to efficient and proper administration of the empire. For what is in the book is information on courtly etiquette, rules for audience with the king, well-positioned officials, the military, capital and commerce and the condition of the peasantry and everything that goes on in the empire."[36]

Nizam al-Mulk's death, attributed by some medieval historians to the subversive ploys of the Ismaʿīlīs and to the machinations of the Sultan's wife and her Shiʿi entourage, shocked the Islamic world. What is significant here is that Nizam al-Mulk was murdered after his removal from office, when presumably, he no longer posed a threat to the political intrigues of the Sultan's wife or to the takeover plans of the enemies of the state. The details of the demise of Nizam al-Mulk are related in a series of anecdotes in other historical texts of the medieval period. The histories tell us that Iraqi and according to some, covert Shiʿi (Bāṭinī) officials, had penetrated the Saljuq court. Moreover, the Sultan's favorite wife had also joined their cause. When alone with the dynast, Turkān Khātūn (d. 487/1094) consistently plants the seeds of suspicion in her husband's mind: Who rules this empire, you or Nizam al-Mulk? He has created a dynasty of his own, with his sons and sons-in-law and relatives occupying every important position throughout the empire? The sultan finally fell prey to Turkan's instigations. Why did Turkan dislike Nizam al-Mulk? The familiar trope of succession; Nizam al-Mulk favored Malikshah's first son, whose mother had died. Turkan wished to secure the throne for her own son. Malikshah sent a note to Nizam al-Mulk, querying his nepotism and conduct of state. The messengers who relay the old vizier's response back to the king distort the message. Nizam al-Mulk, they inform Malikshah, had said that, "He who had bestowed the crown on the King, had also given him the turban to administer the state. Should one go the other will follow suit."[37] The trope of divine justice, another familiar feature of mirrors for princes. Malikshah is outraged, and he removes Nizam al-Mulk from the vizierate. A month later, Nizam al-Mulk is murdered by one of the same Batini Shiʿis he had so advised the Sultan against. The Sultan follows Nizam al-Mulk in the journey back to the Maker, he dies 35 days later. Disorder in the state is paralleled by disorder in the religious sphere, a coalition of women and "peoples of bad religion" bring about the downfall of the wise vizier, and as a result, the people of bad religion succeed in permeating every level of Saljuq military and civilian administration. Or is it the disorder of affairs that is made into a story, an anecdote, with a beginning, middle and an end, to endow events with meaning: an orderly cogent account of a time of confusion and disorder?

Nizam al-Mulk's illustration of the disturbing effect of women in the body politic centers on an anecdote from the life of the Prophet's favored wife, ʿĀʾisha (d. 58/678), the daughter of his first successor, Abū Bakr (d. 13/634). A few years after the Prophet's death, in a succession dispute between two groups of his followers, ʿĀʾisha led the forces against ʿAlī b. Abū Ṭālib (d. 40/661) in battle. Known as a *fitna*, this instance of discord within the nascent Islamic community is firmly linked to ʿĀʾisha's historical legacy. Her participation and leadership in the battle is marked in its title, the battle is known as the Day of the Camel, as ʿĀʾisha sat in her litter atop a camel and observed at first hand the progress of war. The battle pitted the proto-Shiʿis, the followers of ʿAli, against the rest of the early Muslim community, who would later evolve into the Sunni creed. It marked the creation of the first permanent split within Muhammad's community, a rift that has defined Muslim politics and theology for the next 1400 years.

Mention of ʿĀʾisha in the *Siyar al-muluk*, is in two contexts. On one occasion, he evokes her name to remark on the irreligiosity of the Shiʿis in their willingness to curse ʿĀʾisha for her role in the Battle of the Camel. In another and longer anecdote, Nizam al-Mulk relates how Muhammad was once sick, and had to find a substitute to lead the communal prayers. ʿĀʾisha favored ʿUmar (the second caliph, d. 23/644), and the Prophet wanted Abū Bakr. She insisted several times, and with his head lying on her breast, he turned around and asked one of the men present to ensure that Abu Bakr was called upon, thus following the adage that the advice given by women should be reversed since the exact opposite of their suggestions is invariably the right choice. In this particular case, the anecdote is interesting on several levels, for here we see ʿĀʾisha advocating against her own father, and Muhammad ignoring her counsel. ʿĀʾisha's subsequent success in determining the course of Muslim politics, when the elders of the Muslim community did in fact—on her instigation as we are told in the sources—decide to oppose the caliphate of ʿAli in the Battle of the Camel, heralded calamity on two fronts. Not only was it an imprudent political choice, creating dissent in the community, but also, it went against the precedent set by Muhammad. On the one hand, Nizam al-Mulk vilifies her role in Muslim history: ʿĀʾisha is the paradigmatic bearer of bad counsel. She advocates confrontation, and fails to see that ultimately, the unity of the *ʾumma* is more important in preserving the glory of Islam than the accession to the throne of one's favored candidate. Like Turkan Khatun, ʿĀʾisha demands complete and immediate victory; she is bellicose, hasty, and uncompromising. On the other hand, he valorizes her memory as the Prophet's beloved who is wrongfully cursed by the Shiʿis. The controversial legacy of ʿĀʾisha is further complicated by her almost universally recognized authority as an important transmitter of the deeds and dicta of the Prophet. Her recollection if not her advice remain trustworthy. Ghazzali's presentation of women as perennial obstacles to proper leadership is that of victims and villains, they are compromised, naturally, in both religion and wits, and at the mercy of men by divine injunction, however evil, treacherous and seductive.[38] Nizam al-Mulk also tells us, on the authority of no less a Muslim hero than ʿUmar, that the words of women resemble their genitals—meant to be concealed. Ghazzali informs us that ʿUmar has said to keep women illiterate, for teaching them to read and write will have an undesirable impact on their character. ʿUmar also is said to have advised against speaking to women of love, "[B]ecause their hearts will be corrupted. For women are like meat left in a desert; God's help is needed to preserve them.[39] The *Nasihat al-muluk* also brings an anecdote about a pre-Islamic Persian king who narrowly escaped punishing an innocent man while under the influence of his wife.[40]

As obedient wives, women are praised; as advisors, they are vilified. In medieval Islamic political discourse, the political persona of women is juxtaposed with that of the viziers, their nemesis: without the advice of the latter the prince cannot rule, and by obeying the advice of the former he will fall. The correspondence between the feminine and the seditious is at least as old as the Bible. Nizam al-Mulk invokes that first instance of disobedience instigated by Eve against God. "The first man who suffered loss and underwent pain and trouble for obeying a woman was Adam who did the bidding of Eve and ate the wheat with the result that he was expelled from paradise, and wept for two hundred years until God had mercy on him and accepted his repentance."[41] The section on women, "On Those Who Wear the Veil," continues with examples of women spurned by the objects of their passion who dupe their uxorious husbands, which resonates with the story of Siyāvash in the *Shahnama*. Sūdāba, the wife of King Kaykāvūs, enamored of his son, accused Siyāvash of adultery; this clearly echoes the story of Joseph in the Qur'an. Siyavash resisted her advances. In a pre-emptive move, Sudaba lied to the King, telling him that Siyavash had designs on her. To prove his innocence, the young prince offered to go through with the ordealof fire. Siyavash was vindicated, but brokenhearted, he left Iran. At the court of Afrāsiyāb, the king of Tūran and Kaykavus' nemesis, Siyavash received great favor, so much so that Afrasiyab was said to have held him more dear than his own children. The king's brother was jealous and conspired to kill him. When news of Siyavash's death reached Iran, Rustam, the legendary Iranian hero, came from Sīstān to the capital. Without permission he entered the King's harem, dragged Sudaba out by the hair, and cut her into pieces with his sword. No man dared to chastise or praise him. A lengthy war ensued when the Iranians set out to Turan to avenge the death of Siyavash. The cause of all this, Nizam al-Mulk tells us, "was Sudaba and her domination over the King Kai Kavus."[42]

Qur'anic as well as biblical, the conflation of the temptress with agency in thwarting the will of God and causing dissent is a bygone conclusion, in the case of Eve as well as Potiphar's wife. Recall here Gower's insistence on chastity and abstinence. We have also seen Muhammad, ʿUmar, Ghazzali, and practically every other luminary in between warn against the influence of women. The depiction of heresy is frequently coupled with travesties of chastity and honor in women. In the section on heretical movements, Nizam al-Mulk raises the accusation of communal wives and the abolition of private property against Mazdak, the false prophet. Another conflation of godliness is with succession, for one who has submitted to the will of God, does not choose a successor, as Muhammad did not. The laws of primogeniture are subverted in the Bible, as God favors, time after time, the younger but the more virtuous son. Turkan Khatun's opposition to the vizier stemmed, of course, from her support for her own son, rather than Msalikshah's first-born, as successor to the throne. Nizam al-Mulk, the righteous vizier, is contrasted in all Saljuq histories with Turkan Khatun, the wife. One is the purveyor of good advice, and the other the source of decline. In thwarting the will of God, through bad advice and meddling in affairs of succession, women in the scriptural traditions are in fact subverting the divine plan for just rule. The presence of women signals the faltering of the rational faculties of men; they are thus in a sense the allegoric extension of man's lower carnal self. It is uxorious men who are denounced. The women are the medium, and the vizier is the narrator.

Against this, Denise Spellberg, in an article on the role of women in Islamic government, has taken Nizam al-Mulk's allusions to 'A'isha as symptomatic of his misogyny. In what brings to mind Skinner's proposition against the provision of historical background as a poor substitute for context, Spellberg interprets Nizam al-Mulk's anti-women stance to be a direct result of his rivalries with Turkan Khatun. "Nizam al-Mulk's chapter on women may be read as a succinct treatise on female inferiority. The vizier's pronouncements were not novel in the Islamic context. . . . Finally, the vizier's anxiety about the influence of women is linked to his own immediate political confrontation with Turkan Khatun."[43] Carole Hillenbrand has taken the anecdotes on the active participation of women in Saljuq politics to testify to the increased power of women in the Saljuq empire, mainly thanks to their nomadic and tribal social organization: "Clearly, then, the Saljuq Turks, although drawn to Islamic modes of government and civilization, did not forget certain aspects of their pre-Islamic nomadic heritage. Seljuq women often plotted, bribed, and murdered. They are portrayed as machinating and conniving, vigorous and effective. In any case they were not to be ignored."[44]

The association of women with treachery, like the template of the succession crisis, is a staple of medieval treatises on ethics, used in numerous medieval western and Islamic mirrors. The topos of women as a disruptive influence is not only scriptural, but also linked again to Alexander and Aristotle. In a perceptive study on the topos of women in the medieval period, Susan Smith traces the trajectory of both literal and artistic representations of the tale of the mounted Aristotle, to elaborate on its subversive potential. Alexander had fallen in love with a beautiful woman and neglected the affairs of the state. Aristotle advises him to refrain from any further contact, so that he may again attend properly to governance. Alexander takes his advice to heart. In the meantime, the woman in question, resenting her fall from the king's favor, seeks to teach Aristotle a lesson. She appears, every day, in suggestive poses, outside the old sage's window. Inevitably, Aristotle falls in love. When confronted with his amorous intentions, the woman postulates one condition, that he allow her to mount him in the garden before she succumbs to him. Aristotle agrees. Alerted to the ensuing event by the woman, Alexander sees for himself his old counselor, mounted by a woman, crawling the palace grounds. When found exposed, Aristotle is said to have confirmed his earlier advice:

"If she has the power to degrade a man of my age, just imagine what she is capable of doing to you."[45] In the Islamic tradition, the tale of the mounted Aristotle is told of Khusraw and his *mobed-e mobedān* (Zoroastrian high priest). The mobed angers Queen Shīrīn by his habitual greeting to Khursraw, which includes the wish that he may "be spared obedience to women." Shirin gives him the slave-girl Miskdāna, who refuses to sleep with him unless he lets her ride him naked. The king and queen watch from a balcony. When the priest realizes this, he tells the king, "What did I tell you about not obeying women?" The king replies, "You are a pathetic old man and so would be whoever took your advice."[46] The use of the topos of women in politics to signal discord and instability is also a common feature of medieval Italian and French chivalric epics. Many a tale is told of Charlemagne's sister or daughter who falls in love with a Saracen and brings demise upon her people.[47]

Almost all studies of medieval Islamic history have taken Nizam al-Mulk's lengthy anecdotes about the evils of Mazdakism, Shiʿism, Batinism and Ismaʿilism to be the formulation of an Islamic orthodoxy that excludes even non-Hanafi and non-Shafiʿi Sunnis. This net is too wide to be credible. I have provided elsewhere examples of Nizam al-Mulk's policies toward the Shiʿi interest groups in the empire. He cooperated with them on different matters, and married one of his daughters to a Shiʿi general. Shiʿi sources as early as the twelfth and the thirteenth centuries, praise his legacy.[48] In present-day Iran, the main Shiʿi country in the Islamic world, Nizam al-Mulk is praised as a national hero. Rather than heresy, Nizam al-Mulk is outlining in his anti-Shiʿi anecdotes, the turbulent and unstable world he is experiencing: the demise of centralized rule, the proliferation of non-caliphal dynasties, economic collapse, and lack of order and stability. A glorious past is reconstructed in the *Siyar al-muluk*, where good religion ruled and women kept to their places, and prosperity ensued. The body politic the old vizier tells us is sickly and diseased. The king needs to heed his advice, to restore justice, and to heal the polity. Good religion is the backbone of the virtuous prince, and good advice is another segment of his worldview. Women and heresy are the rhetorical devices used in the genre to warn of political and social unease. Their presence is a cataclysm for the renewal of purity, for the re-establishment of order and for the restoration of political might. Women negate the non-religious education, which is learnt from a counselor, and heresy nullifies good religious instruction. Herein lies the "meaning" of the overwhelming emphasis in mirrors of all sorts on the necessity of justice. Anushirvan is just, because he listened to the advice of Buzurgmihr, and we know that he was just because he succeeded in saving his throne from the heresy of Mazdak. He tricked Mazdak into revealing the falsity of his claim. The justice of the prince reflects, in the mirrors, the justice of God. Divine justice is an indisputable pillar of salvation history. The dualistic juxtaposition of the counselor and the wife is inevitable in this schema: the vizier triggers the prince's rational faculties, the woman flames his carnal desires; the vizier has long-term interests in mind, while the woman offers only immediate gratification. In shunning women, the prince is, in fact, shunning his own weaknesses and nature. The justice of a prince is the end result of his education, and his education, this according to the *Secretum Secretorum*, and every one of the mirrors we have discussed, reflects the quality of his educator, the counselor. The demise of Nizam al-Mulk, then, is a tale foretold. It is foretold because the just king, again like the biblical template of Solomon, is but a myth. The advice of Nizam al-Mulk is meant to go unheeded. Adam listened to Eve, and the Muslim elders followed 'A'isha into battle. Sudaba dominated Kaykavus, and that brought about the death of his son and a lengthy war between Iran and Turan.

The discourse of politics in the medieval Islamic world then, the normative vocabulary for the expression of threat, political or social, is reflected in the tropes particular to the mirrors for princes. 'Abbasid impotence is refracted through the lens of a mighty Fatimid threat. Both king and caliph are seduced, one by women, the other by heresy. It is the task of the ethical counselor—or as the mirrors have it, the counselor of the good religion—to guide the princes, to keep them alert to travesties of justice, imminent threats, and their own weaknesses. And here one last anecdote from the *Siyar al-muluk* is noteworthy.

> There was in Baghdad a man who was famous for being able to extract anything he desired from the Caliph. When asked about the origins of this extraordinary relationship, he gave the following answer: "Let it be known that I have been the *mū'adhdhin* at this mosque for the past thirty years, and that by vocation I am a tailor. I have never drunk wine, committed adultery or engaged in homosexual acts, nor have I ever sinned. There is also a military commander living on this street. One day after having performed the call to prayers, I was going to my shop, and I saw the commander on the other side of the street, swaying as a drunkard. He was pulling off the veil of a young woman, forcing her to go with him, and she was yelling frantically for help. "O Believers, save me. I am not a prostitute, I am the daughter of so and so, and the wife of so and so, and I live on such and such street. Every one knows that I am pure and righteous. This Turk is abducting me to sin with me. My husband has sworn that he will divorce me if I spend even one night away

from home." She was crying and nobody was intervening, for this officer was so powerful and vicious, he had one thousand men and nobody dared oppose him. I yelled out a few times, to no avail, the Turk took her to his house. I was distressed, and the impiety bothered me. I gather the old men of the quarter and we went to the commander's house. Evoking the religious duty of commanding good and forbidding evil, we yelled out, "Do you think there is no Muslim left in Baghdad? How dare you, right under the Caliph's nose, drag a pious woman to your house to sin with her? Either hand this woman over to us right now, or we shall take our grievance to al-Muʿtaṣim. When the Turk heard us, he ordered his servants to give us a good beating and to break our limbs. Confronted by such violence, we all fled. I performed the nightly prayers and remained pensive for a while. I put on my nightgown and lay down. My sense of justice and valor kept me awake. I was thinking to myself that if the Turk wanted to satisfy his desire, he must have done so already. There is nothing to be done about that. However, her husband has sworn that he will divorce her if she stays out for the night. Her marriage can still be salvaged. I have heard that drunkards pass out when they are drunk. Once they sober up, they cannot tell how many hours have passed into the night. I shall go and say the call to prayers now instead of at dawn. The Turk will wake up, and thinking it is the morning, he shall let her go. She will probably pass by the mosque on her way home. I shall stop her and accompany her to her house, so that I can vouch for her integrity and innocence in front of her husband. I did just that. The Caliph al-Muʿtasim was awake, and got cross at this untimely call to prayer. He sent his guard to arrest the pernicious muʿadhdhin. Meanwhile, I was standing at the entrance of the mosque waiting for the woman to pass by. Muʿtasim's *ḥājib* (chamberlain) asked me whether I knew the sinner who had tried to disorient Muslims by saying the prayers at night. I told him that I was the culprit, and that I would only tell the reason to the Caliph himself . . . When we reached the palace, al-Muʿtasim received me immediately. I told him the whole story about the Turk and the innocent woman. He sent his hajib to go and fetch the Turk and to send the woman to her husband with this message: "Muʿtasim greets you, and seeks to intervene on your wife's behalf to obtain her pardon. She is innocent, and whatever passed on her was against her will. You should respect her more than before." He ordered me to stay in his audience . . . When the Turkish commander

> appeared before him, Muʿtasim said, "What in my policy toward my subjects and toward the religion of Islam have you seen that has propelled you to such actions? Have I manifested laxity in religious matters, or oppression? Am I not the same person who left Baghdad and fought the Byzantines and defeated their Caesar only because they had taken one Muslim boy prisoner? Did I not burn Constantinople, did I not decorate the city with numerous mosques? Today, I have dispersed so much justice throughout this empire that sheep and wolves drink from the same stream! How dare you, in Baghdad itself, in front of my eyes, take a righteous woman and defame her, and when confronted by people following the command of God, beat them up?" He then had him put in a sack and beaten till there was not one bone left intact. Then they threw the sack into the Tigris.[49]

The moral of this anecdote, like others, is multivalent. On the one hand, it is a clarion call for the ʿAbbasid caliph, to set wrongs right, to wrest from the Turks the fate of his subjects. On the other, it is a glorification of the presence of mind of the religious leader, who could not bear to let injustice pass him by. Without the duty-bound muezzin, the "chaste" woman would have never been rescued, if not her honor, at least her marriage. Far from a call for Islamic orthodoxy, the medieval political language of the mirrors reflects a culture that is capable of self-criticism, and of speaking to an ideal whilst at the same time deconstructing some of the main pillars of that ideology. Rather than a testimony to the greatness of the Saljuq sultans, the *Siyar al-muluk's* string of anecdotes and unrelated tidbits of advice bespeak a political reality that is far from ideal, and in subverting the absolute power of the monarch through the trope of advice, by relating anecdote after anecdote of fallen kings and ill-intentioned viziers, it provides a meta-critique of the Saljuq political entity. The double topoi of heresy and women are employed as artifacts of medieval political discourse, rather than prescriptions for religious orthodoxy or locutions for misogyny. The conflation of revolution with an alternative religious claim, like the conflation of sexuality with bad advice, is medieval parlance for political instability, and the vicissitudes of fate. Like illness, which brings about death, women and heresy bring about a decline in fortune. The secret is this: fate prevails, and against fate, there is no good advice. Uncertainties mark every stage of human life, but the end is by contrast, in cold certainty. Like fate, women as symbolic of surrendering to one's nature, in spite of appeals to reason brought about by advice and education, will prevail ultimately. The prescription for invincibility, like that for ideal rulership is in essence flawed. The alchemist thwarts the alchemy of just rule. The prescription contains in it, the seeds of its own reversal. The vizier, the teacher, is murdered.

By comparing mirrors from different traditions and historical periods, what begins to emerge, is precisely the contours of medieval political discourse. Facile identifications, such as pre-Islamic origins, or a monolithic, hegemonic Islam that is the guiding principle of all cultural expression in the medieval period should be brought under serious questioning. The divide between secular and religious, too, needs to be revisited. Are the mirrors religious texts? Do they propound an overwhelmingly Islamic or religious worldview? The medieval political language of the Islamic world, then, is in dialogue with numerous other influences; and more importantly, they are beings in time. The imagery of an unchanging, self-contained, withdrawn and lethargic gigantic empire, smug and complacent, engaged primarily with orthodoxy and religious concerns, strangers to change, reform, in sum, is contradicted by the depictions of religion and politics in those very same medieval sources that have customarily been taken to refract the impermeability and unchanging nature of the Islamic body politic. The multivalent representations of religion, expressed in tropes of justice, orthodoxy or the subordination of women, owe more to rhetorical conventions of advice literature than cultural norms of Islam. Finally, "[This] runs counter to the fundamental concept of Islam as a totalistic religion uniting all aspects of life."[50]

Endnotes

1. Richard W. Bulliet *Conversion to Islam in the Medieval Period* (Cambridge: Harvard University Press, 1979, pp. 128–38.

2. H. A. R. Gibb, *Studies on the Civilization of Islam* (Princeton: Princeton University Press, 1982), pp. 142–43.

3. Al-Māwardī, *The Ordinances of Government*, tr. Wafaa H.Wahba (Reading: Garnet, 1996), pp. 17, 20.

4. The clearest and best preserved manuscript of the *Siyar al-muluk* was copied in 673/1274, and is known as the Nakhjavānī manuscript. See Darke's introduction in, Nizam al-Mulk, *The Book of Government or Rules for Kings*, tr. Hubert Darke. (London: Routledge and Kegan Paul, 1960).

5. On Gower and the influence of the *Secretum Secretorum*, see, Allan H. Gilbert, "Notes on the Influence of the *Secretum Secretorum, Speculum*, 3 (1928), pp. 85–98.

6. I refer here, primarily, to Lambton's often repeated assertion that, "All political theories in Islam start from the assumption that Islamic government existed by virtue

of a divine contract based on the *Sharī ʿa.* None, therefore, asks the question why the state exists. Political science was thus not an independent discipline aspiring to the utmost heights of intellectual speculation, but a department of theology. There was no distinction between state and society, or between Church and state; and no doctrine of the temporal end which alone belonged to and was the prerogative of the Church." A. K. S. Lambton, "Islamic Political Thought," in *The Legacy of Islam,* ed. Joseph Schacht with C. E. Bosworth, 2nd edition (Oxford: Oxford University Press, 1974), pp. 404–24; reference is on p. 404. It should be mentioned that Lambton goes on in that same essay to elaborate on many medieval attempts at addressing historical situations and modifying theories of government accordingly. To the contradiction, she is oblivious. Elsewhere, she refers to Gibb, "Nizām al-Mulk, by re-stating the old Persian tradition of monarchy, with its independent ethical standard based on force and opportunism, perpetuated the inner disharmony which has always proved to be the principal weakness of Islam as a politico-social organism." Lambton, "The Persian Theory of Government," *Studia Islamica,* 5 (1956), pp. 125–48, reference is on p. 136.

7. Fouchécour, *Moralia,* pp. 357-440. It is not surprising that Fouchécour, too, argues against reading the mirrors as treatises on early political thought in Islam.

8. Patricia Crone, "Did al-Ghazālī, Write a Mirror for Princes? On the authorship of *Naṣīḥat al-mulūk,*" *Jerusalem Studies in Arabic and Islam,* 10 (1987), pp. 167–91; reference is on p. 175.

9. I am not presenting in this article, the elaborate textual evidence mustered by Grignaschi and Manzalaoui to prove that the *Sirr al-asrār,* at least in its earlier recensions, was the prototype for advice collections in the Islamic and Christian worlds of the medieval period. A main pillar of the argument, and an interesting one that I pick up in my larger study on Nizam al-Mulk, rests on passages on the occult sciences, magic, and medicine found in the *Secretum Secretorum* and its offspring. Scholastics in the West and ʿulamaʾ in the East censored the text, excluding bits that smacked of necromancy. Other, more secular interlocutors, preserved only the occult and medicinal sections. A case in point is the tenth century *Rasāʾil Ikhwān al-Ṣafāʾ* on the Islamic side, and the Hebrew and Russian translations in the thirteenth and the fourteenth centuries of the *Secretum Secretorum.* Grignaschi argues for instance, that the immense popularity of the *Secretum Secretorum* in the thirteenth, fourteenth and fifteenth centuries rested more on its teachings on magic, astrology, and oneirocriticism than its political instructions. The decline in the fortune of the *Kitab al-siyasa,* progenitor of both the short and long versions of the *Secretum Secretorum,* Grignaschi attributes to its exclusion of all non-political segments of the *Secretum Secretorum.* See, footnote 14, below.

Mention here needs to be made of a more recent study on the *Secretum Secretorum,* which argues against the aversion of medieval scholastics to the occult sections of this text. See, Steven J. Williams, "Roger Bacon and his Edition of the Pseudo-Aristotelian *Secretum Secretorum,*" *Speculum,* 69:1 (1994), pp. 57–73; and, idem, "The Scholarly Career of the Pseudo-Aristotelian *Secretum Secretorum* in the Thirteenth and the Early

Fourteenth Century," unpublished doctoral dissertaion, History Department, Northwestern University, 1991.

10. It is important to note here that the *Secretum Secretorum* is not considered as the sole progenitor of the genre of *fürstenspiegel* in the West. There is an independent tradition of mirrors, dating back, at least, to the *Rules of St. Gregory* and St. Augustine's *City of God*. These treatises are influenced by ecclesiastical thought and training, and are generally in favor of monarchies, much like Ghazzālī's *Naṣīḥat al-mulūk* and Māwardī's *Aḥkām al-sulṭāniyya*. They flourished in the twelfth and the thirteenth centuries, the *Policraticus* of John of Salisbury being one of the oldest ones. See on these mirrors, Lester Kruger Born, "The Perfect Prince: A Study in Thirteenth and Fourteenth-Century Ideals," *Speculum*, III (1928), pp. 470–504. It is the other strand of mirrors, those influenced by the pseudo-Aristotelian model, which are of interest to us here. This model is evident, for instance, in Gower's *Confessio Amantis,* and also in Hoccleve's *Regement of Princes*. Hoccleve's treatise claims to be a translation of the *De Regimine Principum* of Egidio Colonna. Like most instances of medieval translations, the author here is describing his activity as "translation" rather than "creation" to embed his text in the teachings of authoritative figures of the past, rather than being accused of inventing new mores, of *bid'a*. On Hoccleve, see Richard Firth Green, *Poets and Princepleasers: Literature and the English Court in the Late Middle Ages* (Toronto: University of Toronto Press, 1980); chapter 5, "An Adviser to Princes," pp. 135–67; and, Allan H. Gilbert, "Notes on the Influence of the *Secretum Secretorum,*" *Speculum*, III (1928), pp. 84–99.

11. Robert Steele, ed., *Opera hactenus inedita Rogeri Baconi,* vol V, (Oxford: Oxford University Press, 1920); and, *Secretum Secretorum, Nine English Versions*, ed. Mahmoud Manzalaoui (Oxford: The Early English Text Society, 1977).

12.. The Arabic text of the *Sirr al-asrar* was first published by ʿAbd al-Rahman Badawi, *Al-Uṣūl al-yūnāniya lī al-naẓariyāt al-siyāsiya fī al-islām* (Cairo: Maktaba al-Nahḍa al-Miṣriya, 1954), pp. 67–171; there is also a lithograph edition prepared by Sami Salman al-Aʿūr, *Sirr al-asrār: al-siyāsa wa al-firāsa fī tadbīr al-riʾāsa lī al-Arisṭutālīs* (Beirut: Dar al-ʿUlūm al-ʿArabīya, 1995).

13. Among Grignaschi's articles on the *Secretum Secretorum*, "La "Siyāsatu-l-ʿāmiyya" et l'influence iranienne sur la pensée politique islamique," *Acta Iranica*, 6, Deuxième Série, Monumentum H. S. Nyberg, III, (Tehran-Liège: Bibliothèque Pahlavi, 1975), pp. 33–287; Les "Rasāʾil Arisṭutālīsa ilā al-Iskandar" de Sālim Abū al-ʿAlāʾ et l'activité culturelle à l'époque omayyade," *Bulletin des études orientales,* 19 (1965–66), pp. 7–83; "Le roman épistolaire classique conservé dans la version arabe de Sālim b. Abū al-ʿAlāʾ," *Muséon,* 80 (1967), pp. 211–63; "Remarques sur la formation et l'interprétation du *Sirr al-asrār,*" in *Pseudo-Aristotle, The "Secret of Secrets," Sources and Influence*, ed. W. F. Ryan & Charles B. Schmitt, Warburg Institute Surveys, IX (London The Warburg Institute, University of London, 1982), pp. 3–33; and, "*La diffusion du Secretum Secretorum (Sirr al-asrār)* dans l'Europe occidentale," *Archives d'histoire doctrinale et littéraire du Môyen Age*, XLVII (1980), pp. 7–70.

14. Abū al-Ḥasan Muḥammad al-ʿĀmirī (d. 381/992), the celebrated author of the *Kitāb al-saʿāda wa al-isʿād*, draws substantially on the *Siyasa al-ʿamiyya*; see, Abū al-Ḥasan b. Abū al-Durr Muḥammad al-ʿĀmirī al-Nīsābūrī, *Kitāb al-Saʿāda wa al-isʿād fī al-sīra al-insāniyya*, ed. Mujtaba Minovi (Wiesbaden: Franz Steiner Verlag, 1957), p. 75.

15. Not much is known about the life of Sālim. He was a *mawlā* of the sons of ʿAbd al-Malik, the Umayyad caliph (r. 65/685-86/705). On his extant epistles, see, Ihsan ʿAbbas, *ʿAbd al-Ḥamīd b. Yaḥyā al-Kātib wa mā tabqī min rasāʾilihi wa rasāʾil Sālim Abī al-ʿAlāʾ* (Amman: Dar al-Shuruq, 1988), pp. 28–32, 302–23.

16. Ibn al-Nadīm, *The Fihrist of al-Nadīm,* ed. & tr. Bayard Dodge, vol. I (New York: Columbia University Press, 1970), pp. 257–8.

17. Secondary literature on the *Alexander Romance* is abundant, and the classic still remains, George Cary, *The Medieval Alexander* (Cambridge: Cambridge University Press, 1967, 2nd printing), esp. pp. 105–110.

18. Grignashci, "Le roman épistolaire classique," pp. 234-40; Mahmoud Manzalaoui, "The pseudo-Aristotelian *Kitāb Sirr al-Asrār*," *Oriens*, 23-24 (1974), pp. 147–257, reference is on pp. 194–201; and, Dimitri Gutas, *Greek Thought Arabic Culture* (London: Routledge, 1999), pp. 23–5.

19. See, Grignaschi, "La 'Siyāsatu-l-āmiyya' et l'influence iranienne sur la pensée politique islamique," pp. 33–287; and, Fouchécour, *Moralia*, pp. 69–76.

20. For the full text of the *Siyasa al-ʿamiyya*, see, Grignaschi, "La 'Siyāsatu-l-ʿāmiyya' et l'influence iranienne sur la pensée politique islamique," pp. 97–197.

21. I have not seen, nor did I find references to, the Arabic original of this text. According to Claude Cahen, Jirjīs b. al-ʿAmīd al-Makīn, was an Arabic speaking Coptic historian whose *al-Majmūʿ al-mubārak*, generally known as the *History*, covering the period from the creation of the world to the year 658/1260, was one of the very first medieval oriental chronicles to become known in Europe. Biographical information on al-Makīn derives from a manuscript that must have been available to the eighteenth century encyclopaedists. Brockelmann and others have simply repeated what they have found in the early modern European sources. The manuscripts of the *History* have not been classified; and it is unclear how much of his *History* al-Makīn has borrowed from other sources. The chronicle is divided into two major sections: the first concerning pre-Islamic history as far as the eleventh year of Heraclius; the second Islamic history to the year 658/1260. Grignaschi and Manzalaoui have derived their information on al-Makīn's universal history from Budge's English rendition of the Ethiopic translation of the Arabic text of the *History*, contained in a manuscript in the British Museum. See, Claude Cahen, "Al-Makīn b. al-ʿAmīd, Djirdjīs," *EI2*; Ernest A. Wallis Budge, *The Alexander Book in Ethiopia* (London: Oxford University Press, 1933), pp. 214–35; and, Grignaschi, "La diffusion du *Secretum Secretorum*," p. 25; Manzalaoui, "The pseudo-Aristotelian *Kitāb sirr al-asrār*," p. 244.

22. Prime among these is Ibn Miskawayh's (d. 421/1030) *al-Ḥikma al-Khālida*, which was translated (allegedly translated first from Perisan into Arabic) into Persian during the reign of the Mughal dynast, Jahāngīr b. Akbar (r. 1014/1605–1037/1627).

Whilst Ibn Miskawayh claims to have had access to the Pahlavi original of the *Jāvīdān khirad*, it is impossible to extract the original text from the larger treatise. Consequently, the search for a pristine Sasanid ethical code reconstructed from the quotations in *al-Hikma al-khalida* has proved futile. As is the case with the *Kitab sirr al-asrar* itself, influence is established in the form of aphorisms attributed to pre-Islamic Iranian sages and kings, which are historical, if not true. See in particular, the editor's introduction to the Persian translation: Taqī al-Dīn Muḥammad Shūshtarī, *Javīdān khirad*, ed. Behruz Sirvatiyan (Tehran: Institute of Islamic Studies, McGill University, Tehran Branch, 1976). For other examples, see, Grignaschi, "La 'Siyāsatu-l-ʿāmiyya' et l'influence iranienne sur la pensée politique islamique," pp. 33–96.

23. The heterogeneous Turkish composition is the work of Manṣūḥ Nawālī; Grignaschi, "Remarques sur la formation et l'interprétation du *Sirr al-asrār*," p. 6. One of the earliest references to the *Kitab al-siyasa* is in Ibn Juljul al-Andalūsī's (d. after 384/994) *Ṭabaqāt al-ʿaṭibbāʿwa al-ḥukamā*, ed. Fu'ad Sayyid (Cairo: Maṭbaʿa al-ma'had al-ʿilmī al faransī li al-āthār al-sharqiya bi al-Qāhira, 1954), pp. 25–26.

24. Grignaschi, "Remarques," p. 6.

25. Manzalaoui, "The pseudo-Aristotelian *Kitāb sirr al-asrār*," p. 159.

26. Gutas writes, "Apart from administrative handbooks and literary or historical sources, a third set of texts were translated from Pahlavi into Arabic, and this around the time of the ʿAbbāsid revolution (ca. 720–754). These texts, which can be considered as carriers of Zoroastrian Sasanian ideology, were primarily of an astrological nature, dealing specifically with political astrology or astrological history. The translations would appear to be related to the incipient ʿAbbāsid cause *(daʿwa)* and to have played a significant role in the ideological campaigns of those groups aspiring to a return to the Sasanian past. Their influence is most visible during the reign of al-Manṣūr." Dimitri Gutas, *Greek Thought Arabic Culture*, pp. 27–60.

27. Al-Turtushi's text does not contain a direct reference to the Arabic *Sirr al-asrar.* It does refer, repeatedly, to the *Kalīla wa Dimna* (p. 480), and Iranian and Greek sages. In describing the characteristics of the ideal king, al-Turtushi likens him to natural phenomena, such as rain, wind and seasons, the beneficent qualities of which outweigh their adverse ramifications. Manzalaoui posits that these comparisons are taken from the Long Form of the *Sirr al-asrar*; while the text itself attributes them to Arab and *ʿajam* sages. Abū Bakr Muḥammad b. al-Walīd al-Ṭurṭushī, *Sirāj al-Mulūk*, ed. Muhammad Fathi Abu Bakr (Cairo: Al-Dar al-Misriyya al-Lubnaniyya, 1994), I: 202–4; and, Manzalaoui, "The pseudo-Aristotelian *Kitāb sirr al-asrār*," pp. 158–9.

28. Abū ʿAlī Aḥmad b. Muḥammad b. Miskawayh, *Al-Ḥikma al-Khālida,* ed. ʿAbdalrahman Badawi (Cairo: Maktaba al-Nihda al-Misriyya, 1952), pp. 219–25, 267–70, 278–81.

29. Manzalaoui, "The Pseudo-Aristotelian, *Kitāb sirr al-asrār*," p. 160.

30. Latham sides with Grignaschi, see, J. D. Latham, "The Beginnings of Arabic Prose Literature," in *The Cambridge History of Arabic Literature, vol. I, Literature to*

the End of the Umayyad Period, ed. A. F. L. Beeston, et al (Cambridge: Cambridge University Press, 1983), pp. 154–79.

31. Fouchécour, *Moralia*, pp. 414–17.

32. The table of contents of medieval Islamic advice literature bears striking similarity to those of the variegated recensions of the *Secretum Secretorum*. The *Qabūsnāma* of Kaykāvūs b. Qābūs Vushmgīr, written in 457/1065, contains, among other topics, a section on the virtue of seeking knowledge; the advice of Anushirvan; on youth and old age; restraint and the etiquette of dining; the etiquette of drinking wine; rules of hospitality; proper joking and rules of chess (it is Buzurgmihr who is credited in ancient lore with "deciphering" the rules of chess, another Indian import, and designing the game of *nard*, or backgammon) and nard; love; the rites of bathing, resting and sleeping, hunting, polo, warfare, wealth accumulation, trustworthiness, purchasing of slaves, horses, and obtaining of wives; the virtue of friendship; the advisability of seeking religious knowledge and the company of jurists; the organization of commerce, medicine, astrology, poetry, and minstrelsy; the rules of conduct for the king's servants, his scribes, secretaries, and ministers; the rule of kingship; preserving agriculture and maintaining a strict hierarchy of professions; and, finally, the rites of chivalry. See, ʿUnṣūr al-Maʿālī Kaykāvūs b. Iskandar b. Qābūs b. Vushmgīr b. Ziyār, *Qābūsnāma*, ed. Gholam-Hoseyn Yusofi (Tehran: Bungah tarjoma va nashr kitab, 1966). A sample from Nizam al-Mulk's *Siyar al-muluk* would contain the following sections: on the turn of fortune's wheel and in praise of the master of the world; on recognizing the extent of God's grace towards kings; on holding court for the redress of wrongs and practicing justice and virtue; concerning tax-collectors and constant enquiry into the affairs of viziers; concerning assignees of land and enquiry into their treatment of the peasantry; concerning judges, preachers, and censors and the importance of their activities; on enquiry and investigation into matters of religion, religious law and suchlike; concerning intelligence agents; on sending pages; on being careful about messages in drunkenness and sobriety; concerning the steward of the household and the importance of his post; concerning boon companions and intimates of the king and the conduct of their affairs; on having consultation with learned and experienced men; on the provision and use of jeweled weapons; on having troops of various races; concerning the rules and arrangements for drinking parties; on the inadvisability of hastiness in affairs on the part of kings; on showing mercy to creatures of God; on the subject of titles; on giving two appointments to one man; on giving appointments to men of orthodox faith and good birth, and not employing men of perverse sects and evil doctrines, and keeping that latter at a distance; exposing the facts about heretics; on the subject of those who wear the veil; on the revolt of Mazdak; on the emergence of Sinbad the Magian; on dealing with complaints; and on keeping account of the revenue of the provinces. See Nizam al-Mulk, *The Book of Government or Rules for Kings*. The *Nasihat al-muluk* of Ghazzali includes elaborations on: the principles of the creed, which are roots of faith; the branches of the tree of faith; the two springs which water the tree of faith; on qualities

required in kings; on the viziers; on the art of the pen and the functions of secretaries; on magnanimity in kings; aphorisms of the sages; on intelligence and intelligent person; on women and their good and bad points.

33. Quentin Skinner, *The Foundations of Modern Political Thought,* vol. I, The Renaissance (Cambridge: Cambridge University Press, 1978), pp. xiii–xiv.

34. Judith Ferster, *Fictions of Advice: The Literature and Politics of Counsel in Late Medieval England* (Philadelphia: University of Pennsylvania Press, 1996), pp. 1–14.

35. Steele, *Opera hactenus inedita Rogeri Baconi*, p. 191.

36. Nizam al-Mulk, *The Book of Government*, p. 2.

37. Muḥammad b. ʿAlī b. Sulaymān al-Rāwandī, *Raḥat al-ṣudūr wa āyat al-surūr dar tāʾrīkh Āl-i Saljūq*, ed. M. Iqbal (Tehran: Amir Kabir, 1985), p. 134.

38. Ghazālī, *Ghazali's Book of Counsel for Kings,* tr. F. R. C. Bagley (Oxford: Oxford University Press, 1964), pp. 158–73.

39. Ibid., p. 162.

40. Ibid., pp. 171–73.

41. Nizam al-Mulk, *Siyar al-Muluk,* ed. Hubert Darke, Persian edition (Tehran: Bungah Tarjomeh va Nashr Kitab, 1962), chapter 42.

42. Nizam al-Mulk, *The Book of Government*, p. 181.

43. Denise Spellberg, "Nizām al-Mulk's Manipulation of Tradition: ʿAʾisha and the Role of Women in the Islamic Government," *The Muslim World*, 78:2 (1988), pp. 111–17.

44. Carole Hillenbrand, "Seljuq Women," in *The Balance of Truth: Essays in Honour of Professor Geoffrey Lewis*, ed. Çiğdem Balım-Harding & Colin Imber (Istanbul: Isis Press, 2000), pp. 141–63.

45. Susan Smith, *The Power of Women: A Topos in Medieval Art and Literature* (Philadelphia: University Pennsylvania Press, 1995), pp. 67–103.

46. Pseudo-Jāḥiẓ, *Al-Maḥāsin wa al-aḍdād,* ed. Muhammad Amin al-Khaniji (Cairo: Matabʿa al-saʿāda, 1906), pp. 170–71.

47. Julian Vitullo, *The Chivalric Epic in Medieval Italy* (Gainesville: University Press of Florida, 2000), pp. 74–93.

48. Nāṣir al-Dīn Abū al-Rashīd ʿAbd al-Jalīl al-Qazwīnī al-Rāzī, *Baʿḍ al-mathālib al-nawāṣib fī naqḍ "Baʿd faḍāʾiḥ al-rawāfiḍ,"* ed. J. Muhaddith, vol. I (Tehran: Instisharat Anjuman athar milli, 2nd ed., 1980).

49. Nizam al-Mulk, *Siyar al-muluk*, pp. 69–72.

50. Bulliet, *Conversion to Islam in the Medieval Period,* p. 129. Here Bulliet was referring of course, to conclusions drawn from his study on comparative conversion patterns in the Islamic world.